Louis Fischer was b
After a period as a s
volunteer in the Bri
1920. Fischer made
worked in Europe and Asia from 1921 onwards. He
wrote for the *New York Times*, the *Saturday Review* and
for European and Asian publications, reporting on
events in Russia, Spain and India, among other
countries. The author of numerous books, chiefly
on political topics, he was a member of the Institute
of Advanced Study, Princeton and was a member
of the faculty of Princeton University. Louis Fischer
died in 1970.

LOUIS FISCHER

THE LIFE OF
MAHATMA GANDHI

HarperCollins*Publishers*

HarperCollins*Publishers*
77–85 Fulham Palace Road,
Hammersmith, London W6 8JB

This paperback edition 1997
16

Previously published in paperback by Grafton 1982
Reprinted nine times

First published in Great Britain by
Jonathan Cape Ltd 1951

The Author asserts the moral right to
be identified as the author of this work

ISBN 0 00 638887 6

Set in Baskerville

Printed and bound in Great Britain by
Clays Ltd, St Ives plc

Contents

PART THREE

THE BIRTH OF TWO NATIONS

23 MARCH, 1946 – 30 JANUARY, 1948

Illustrations

Gandhi with his wife Kasturbai photographed
after his return from South Africa.
(*Camera Press*)

Gandhi at Buckingham Palace dressed in the
homespun cotton sheet that was his uniform.
(*Camera Press*)

Gandhi leans his hand on the shoulder of
Lady Mountbatten as they enter the Viceregal
Lodge, New Delhi.
(*Popperfoto*)

The 'Father' of India lying in state in New
Delhi following his assassination.
(*Keystone Press*)

To
Markoosha

PART ONE
The End and the Beginning

CHAPTER 1

Death Before Prayers

At 4.30 P.M., Abha brought in the last meal he was ever to eat; it consisted of goat's milk, cooked and raw vegetables, oranges and a concoction of ginger, sour lemons and strained butter with juice of aloe. Sitting on the floor of his room in the rear of Birla House in New Delhi, Gandhi ate and talked with Sardar Vallabhbhai Patel, Deputy Prime Minister of the new government of independent India. Maniben, Patel's daughter and secretary, was also present. The conversation was important. There had been rumours of differences between Patel and Prime Minister Jawaharlal Nehru. This problem, like so many others, had been dropped into the Mahatma's lap.

Abha, alone with Gandhi and the Patels, hesitated to interrupt. But she knew Gandhi's attachment to punctuality. Finally, therefore, she picked up the Mahatma's nickel-plated watch and showed it to him. 'I must tear myself away,' Gandhi remarked, and so saying he rose, went to the adjoining bathroom and then started towards the prayer ground in the large park to the left of the house. Abha, the young wife of Kanu Gandhi, grandson of the Mahatma's cousin, and Manu, the granddaughter of another cousin, accompanied him; he leaned his forearms on their shoulders. 'My walking sticks', he called them.

During the daily two-minute promenade through the long, red-sandstone colonnade that led to the prayer ground, Gandhi relaxed and joked. Now, he mentioned the carrot juice Abha had given him that morning.

'So you are serving me cattle fare,' he said, and laughed.

'Ba used to call it horse fare,' Abha replied. Ba was Gandhi's deceased wife.

'Isn't it grand of me,' Gandhi bantered, 'to relish what no one else wants?'

'Bapu (father),' said Abha, 'your watch must be feeling very neglected. You would not look at it today.'

'Why should I, since you are my timekeepers?' Gandhi retorted.

'But you don't look at the timekeepers,' Manu noted. Gandhi laughed again.

By this time he was walking on the grass near the prayer ground. A congregation of about five hundred had assembled for the regular evening devotions. 'I am late by ten minutes,' Gandhi mused aloud. 'I hate being late. I should be here at the stroke of five.'

He quickly cleared the five low steps up to the level of the prayer ground. It was only a few yards now to the wooden platform on which he sat during services. Most of the people rose; many edged forward; some helped to clear a lane for him; those who were nearest bowed low to his feet. Gandhi removed his arms from the shoulders of Abha and Manu and touched his palms together in the traditional Hindu greeting.

Just then, a man elbowed his way out of the congregation into the lane. He looked as if he wished to prostrate himself in the customary obeisance of the devout. But since they were late, Manu tried to stop him and caught hold of his hand. He pushed her away so that she fell and, planting himself about two feet in front of Gandhi, fired three shots from a small automatic pistol.

As the first bullet struck, Gandhi's foot, which was in motion, descended to the ground, but he remained standing. The second bullet struck; blood began to stain Gandhi's white clothes. His face turned ashen pale. His hands, which had been in the touch-palm position, descended slowly and one arm remained momentarily on Abha's neck.

Gandhi murmured, 'Hey Rama (Oh, God).' A third shot rang out. The limp body settled to the ground. His spectacles dropped to the earth. The leather sandals slipped from his feet.

Abha and Manu lifted Gandhi's head, and tender hands raised him from the ground and carried him into his room in Birla House. The eyes were half closed and he seemed to show signs of life. Sardar Patel, who had just left the Mahatma, was back at Gandhi's side; he felt the pulse and thought he detected a faint beat. Someone searched frantically in a medicine chest for adrenalin but found none.

An alert spectator fetched Dr D. P. Bhargava. He arrived ten minutes after the shooting. 'Nothing on earth could have saved him,' Dr Bhargava reports. 'He had been dead for ten minutes.'

The first bullet entered Gandhi's abdomen three and a half inches to the right of a line down the middle of the body and two and a half inches above the navel and came out through the back. The second penetrated the seventh intercostal space one inch to the right of the middle line and likewise came out at the back. The third shot hit one inch above the right nipple and four inches to the right of the middle line and embedded itself in the lung.

One bullet, Dr Bhargava says, probably passed through the heart and another might have cut a big blood vessel. 'The intestines,' he adds, 'were also injured, as next day I found the abdomen distended.'

The young men and women who had been Gandhi's constant attendants sat near the body and sobbed. Dr Jivraj Mehta arrived and confirmed the death. Presently a murmur went through the group: 'Jawaharlal'. Nehru had rushed from his office. He knelt beside Gandhi, buried his face in the bloody clothes and cried. Then came Devadas, Gandhi's youngest son, and Maulana Abdul Kalam Azad, Minister of Education, followed by many prominent Indians.

Devadas touched his father's skin and gently pressed his arm. The body was still warm. The head still lay in Abha's lap. Gandhi's face wore a peaceful smile. He seemed asleep. 'We kept vigil the whole of that night,' Devadas wrote later. 'So serene was the face and so mellow the halo of divine light that surrounded the body that it seemed almost sacrilegious to grieve . . .'

Diplomats paid formal visits; some wept.

Outside, a vast multitude gathered and asked for one last view of the Mahatma. The body was accordingly placed in an inclined position on the roof of Birla House and a searchlight played upon it. Thousands passed in silence, wrung their hands and wept.

Near midnight the body was lowered into the house. All night mourners sat in the room and, between sobs, recited from the *Bhagavad Gita* and other holy Hindu scriptures.

With the dawn arrived 'the most unbearably poignant moment for all of us', Devadas says. They had to remove the large woollen shawl and the cotton shoulder wrap which the Mahatma was wearing for warmth when he was shot. These pure white clothes showed clots and blotches of blood. As they unfolded the shawl the shell of a cartridge dropped out.

Gandhi now lay before them dressed only in the white loincloth as they and the world had always known him. Most of those present broke down and cried without control. The sight inspired the suggestion that the body be embalmed for at least a few days so that friends, co-workers and relatives who lived at a distance from New Delhi might see it before it was cremated. But Devadas, Pyarelal Nayyar, Gandhi's chief secretary, and others objected. It was against Hindu sentiment, and 'Bapu would never forgive us.' Also, they wished to discourage any move to preserve the Mahatma's earthly remains. It was decided to burn the body the next day.

In the early hours of the morning disciples washed the body according to ancient Hindu rites and placed a garland of handspun cotton strands and a chain of beads around its neck. Roses and rose petals were strewn over the blanket that covered all but the head, arms and chest. 'I asked for the chest to be left bare,' Devadas explains. 'No soldier ever had a finer chest than Bapu's.' A pot of incense burned near the body.

During the morning the body was again placed on the roof for public view.

Ramdas, third son of Gandhi, arrived by air from Nagpur, in the Central Provinces of India, at 11 A.M. The funeral had waited for him. The body was brought down into the house and then carried out to the terrace. A wreath of cotton yarn encircled Gandhi's head; the face looked peaceful yet profoundly sad. The saffron-white-green flag of independent India was draped over the bier.

During the night the chassis of a Dodge 15-hundredweight army weapon-carrier had been replaced by a new superstructure with a raised floor so that all spectators could see the body in the open coffin. Two hundred men of the Indian Army, Navy and Air Force drew the vehicle by four stout ropes. The motor was not used. Non-commissioned officer Naik Ram Chand sat at the steering wheel. Nehru, Patel, several other leaders and several of Gandhi's young associates rode on the carrier.

The cortège, two miles long, left Birla House on Albuquerque Road in New Delhi at 11.45 A.M., and, moving forward inch by inch through dense masses of humanity, reached the Jumna River, five and a half miles away, at 4.20 P.M. A million and a half marched and a further million watched. Branches of New Delhi's splendid shade trees bent under the weight of persons who had climbed upon them to get a better view. The base of the big white monument of King George V, which stands in the middle of a broad pond, was covered with hundreds of Indians who had waded through the water.

Now and then the voices of Hindus, Moslems, Sikhs, Parsis

and Anglo-Indians mingled in loud shouts of '*Mahatma Gandhi ki jai* (Long Live Mahatma Gandhi)'. At intervals the multitude broke into sacred chants. Three Dakota aircraft flew over the procession, dipped in salute and showered countless rose petals.

Four thousand soldiers, a thousand airmen, a thousand policemen and a hundred sailors, in varied and vari-coloured uniforms and head-dress marched before and after the bier. Prominent among them were mounted lancers bearing aloft red and white pennants – the bodyguard of the Governor-General Lord Mountbatten. Armoured cars, police and soldiers were present to maintain order. In charge of the death parade was Major-General Roy Bucher, an Englishman chosen by the Indian government to be the first commander-in-chief of its army.

By the holy waters of the Jumna, a million people had stood and sat from early morning waiting for the cortège to arrive at the cremation grounds. The predominant colour was white, the white of women's saris and men's garments, caps and turbans.

Several hundred feet from the river, at Rajghat, stood a fresh funeral pyre made of stone, brick and earth; it was about two feet high and eight feet square. Long thin sandalwood logs sprinkled with incense had been stacked on it. Gandhi's body was laid on the pyre with the head to the north and the feet to the south. In this position Buddha had met his end.

At 4.45 P.M., Ramdas set fire to his father's funeral pyre. The logs burst into flame. A groan went up from the vast assemblage. Women wailed. With elemental force the crowd surged towards the fire and broke through the military cordon. But in a moment the people seemed to realize what they were doing and dug in their bare toes and prevented an accident.

The logs crackled and seethed and the flames united in a single fire. Now there was silence . . . Gandhi's body was being reduced to cinders and ashes.

The pyre burned for fourteen hours. All the while prayers were sung; the entire text of the *Gita* was read. Twenty-seven hours later, when the last embers had grown cold, priests, officials, friends and relatives held a special service in the guarded wire enclosure around the pyre and collected the ashes and the splinters of bone that had defeated the fire. The ashes were tenderly scooped into a homespun cotton bag. A bullet was found in the ashes. The bones were sprinkled with water from the Jumna and deposited in a copper urn. Ramdas placed a garland of fragrant flowers around the neck of the urn, set it in a wicker basket filled with rose petals and, pressing it to his breast, carried it back to Birla House.

Several personal friends of Gandhi asked for and received pinches of his ashes. One encased a few grains of ash in a gold signet ring. Family and followers decided against gratifying requests for ashes which came from all the six continents. Some Gandhi ashes were sent to Burma, Tibet, Ceylon and Malaya. But most of the remains were immersed in the rivers of India exactly fourteen days after death – as prescribed by Hindu ritual.

Ashes were given to provincial prime ministers or other dignitaries. The provincial capitals shared their portions with lesser urban centres. Everywhere the public display of the ashes drew huge pilgrimages and so did the final ceremonies of immersion in the rivers or, as at Bombay, in the sea.

The chief immersion ceremony took place at Allahabad, in the United Provinces, at the confluence of the sacred Ganges, the Jumna and the Saraswati. A special train of five third-class carriages left New Delhi at 4 A.M. on 11 February; Gandhi had always travelled third. The compartment in the middle of the train containing the urn of ashes and bones was piled almost to the ceiling with flowers and guarded by Abha, Manu, Pyarelal Nayyar, Dr Sushila Nayyar, Prabhavati Narayan and others who had been Gandhi's daily companions. The train stopped at eleven towns *en route*; at each, hundreds of thousands bowed reverently, prayed and laid garlands and wreaths on the carriages.

In Allahabad, on the 12th, the urn was placed under a miniature wooden palanquin and, mounted on a motor truck, it worked its way through a throng of a million and a half people from the city and the surrounding countryside. Women and men in white preceded the truck singing hymns. One musician played on an ancient instrument. The vehicle looked like a portable rose garden; Mrs Naidu, Governor of the United Provinces, Azad, Ramdas and Patel were among those who rode on it. Nehru, fists clenched, chin touching his chest, walked.

Slowly the truck moved to the river bank where the urn was transferred to an American military 'duck' painted white. Other 'ducks' and craft accompanied it downstream. Tens of thousands waded far into the water to be nearer Gandhi's ashes. Cannon on Allahabad fort fired a salute as the urn was turned over and its contents fell into the river. The ashes spread. The little bones flowed quickly towards the sea.

Gandhi's assassination caused dismay and pain throughout India. It was as though the three bullets that entered his body had pierced the flesh of tens of millions. The nation was baffled, stunned and hurt by the sudden news that this man of peace, who loved his enemies and would not have killed an insect, had been shot dead by his own countryman and co-religionist.

Never in modern history has any man been mourned more deeply and more widely.

The news was conveyed to the country by Prime Minister Nehru. He was shaken, shocked and cramped with sorrow. Yet he went to the radio station shortly after the bullets struck and, speaking extemporaneously, driving back tears and choking with emotion, he said:

'The light has gone out of our lives and there is darkness everywhere and I do not quite know what to tell you and how to say it. Our beloved leader, Bapu as we call him, the father of our nation, is no more. Perhaps I am wrong to say that. Nevertheless, we will not see him again as we have seen him these many years. We will not run to him for advice and seek solace from him, and that is a terrible blow not to me only but to millions and millions in this country. And it is difficult to soften the blow by any advice that I or anyone else can give you.

'The light has gone out, I said, and yet I was wrong. For the light that shone in this country was no ordinary light. The light that has illumined this country for these many years will illumine this country for many more years, and a thousand years later that light will still be seen in this country, and the world will see it and it will give solace to innumerable hearts. For that light represented the living truth, and the eternal man was with us with his eternal truth reminding us of the right path, drawing us from error, taking this ancient country to freedom.

'All this has happened. There is so much more to do. There was so much more for him to do. We could never think that he was unnecessary or that he had done his task. But now, particularly, when we are faced with so many difficulties, his not being with us is a blow most terrible to bear.

'A madman has put an end to his life . . .'

On 30 January, 1948, the Friday he died, Mahatma Gandhi was what he had always been: a private citizen without wealth, property, official title, official post, academic distinction, scientific achievement, or artistic gift. Yet men with governments and armies behind them paid homage to the little brown man of seventy-eight in a loincloth. The Indian authorities received 3,441 messages of sympathy, all unsolicited, from foreign countries. For Gandhi was a moral man, and a civilization not richly endowed with morality felt still further impoverished when the assassin's bullets ended his life. 'Mahatma Gandhi was the spokesman for the conscience of all mankind,' said General George C. Marshall, United States Secretary of State.

Pope Pius, the Dalai Lama of Tibet, the Archbishop of Canterbury, the Chief Rabbi of London, the King of England, President Truman, Chiang Kai-shek, the President of France, indeed the political heads of all important countries (except Soviet Russia) and most minor ones publicly expressed their grief at Gandhi's passing.

Léon Blum, the French Socialist, put on paper what millions felt. 'I never saw Gandhi,' Blum wrote. 'I do not know his language. I never set foot in his country and yet I feel the same sorrow as if I had lost someone near and dear. The whole world has been plunged into mourning by the death of this extraordinary man.'

'Gandhi had demonstrated,' Professor Albert Einstein asserted, 'that a powerful human following can be assembled not only through the cunning game of the usual political manoeuvres and trickeries but through the cogent example of a morally superior conduct of life. In our time of utter moral decadence he was the only statesman to stand for a higher human relationship in the political sphere.'

The Security Council of the United Nations paused for its members to pay tribute to the dead man. Philip Noel-Baker, the British representative, praised Gandhi as 'the friend of the poorest and the loneliest and the lost'. Gandhi's 'greatest achievements', he predicted, 'are still to come'. Other members of the Security Council extolled Gandhi's spiritual qualities and lauded his devotion to peace and non-violence. Mr Andrei Gromyko, of the Soviet Union, called Gandhi 'one of the outstanding political leaders of India' whose name 'will always be linked with the struggle of the Indian people for their national liberation which has lasted over such a long period'. Soviet Ukraine delegate Tarasenko also stressed Gandhi's politics.

The UN lowered its flag to half-mast.

Humanity lowered its flag.

The world-wide response to Gandhi's death was in itself an

important fact; it revealed a widespread mood and need. 'There is still some hope for the world which reacted as reverently as it did to the death of Gandhi,' Albert Deutsch declared in the New York newspaper *PM*. 'The shock and sorrow that followed the New Delhi tragedy shows we still respect sainthood even when we cannot fully understand it.'

Gandhi 'made humility and simple truth more powerful than empires', US Senator Arthur H. Vandenburg said. Pearl S. Buck, novelist, described Gandhi's assassination as 'another crucifixion'. Justice Felix Frankfurter called it 'a cruel blow against the forces of good in the world'.

General Douglas MacArthur, supreme Allied military commander in Japan, said: 'In the evolution of civilization, if it is to survive, all men cannot fail eventually to adopt Gandhi's belief that the process of mass application of force to resolve contentious issues is fundamentally not only wrong but contains within itself the germs of self-destruction.' Lord (Admiral) Mountbatten, last British Viceroy in India, expressed the hope that Gandhi's life might 'inspire our troubled world to save itself by following his noble example'. The spectacle of the general and the admiral pinning their faith on the little ascetic would certainly seem to justify the verdict of Sir Hartley Shawcross, British Attorney General, that Gandhi was 'the most remarkable man of the century'.

To the statesman and politicians who eulogized him Gandhi was at least a reminder of their own inadequacies.

A California girl of thirteen wrote in a letter: 'I was really terribly sad to hear about Gandhi's death. I never knew I was that interested in him but I found myself quite unhappy about the great man's death.'

In New York, a twelve-year-old girl had gone into the kitchen for breakfast. The radio was on and it brought the news of the shooting of Gandhi. There, in the kitchen, the girl, the maid and the gardener held a prayer meeting and prayed and wept. Just so, millions in all countries mourned Gandhi's death as a personal loss. They did not quite know why; they did not quite know what he stood for. But he was 'a good man' and good men are rare.

'I know no other man of any time or indeed in recent history,' wrote Sir Stafford Cripps, 'who so forcefully and convincingly demonstrated the power of spirit over material things.' This is what the people sensed when they mourned. All around them, material things had power over spirit. The sudden flash of his death revealed a vast darkness. No one who survived him had tried so hard – and with so much success – to live a life of truth, kindness, self-effacement, humility, service and non-violence throughout a long, difficult struggle against mighty adversaries. He fought passionately and unremittingly against British rule of his country and against the evil in his own countrymen. But he kept his hands clean in the midst of battle. He fought without malice or falsehood or hate.

CHAPTER 2

The Beginnings of an Extraordinary Man

Gandhi belonged to the Vaisya caste. In the old Hindu social scale, the Vaisyas stood third, far below the Brahmans who were the number one caste and the Kshatriyas, or rulers and soldiers, who ranked second. The Vaisyas, in fact, were only a notch above the Sudras, the working class. Originally, they devoted themselves to trade and agriculture.

The Gandhis belonged to the Modh Bania subdivision of their caste. Bania is a synonym in India for a sharp, shrewd businessman. Far back, the Gandhi family were retail grocers; 'Gandhi' means grocer. But the professional barriers between castes began to crumble generations ago, and Gandhi's grandfather Uttamchand served as prime minister to the princeling of Porbandar, a tiny state in the Kathiawar peninsula, western India, about half way between the mouth of the Indus and the city of Bombay. Uttamchand handed the office down to his son Karamchand who passed it to his brother Tulsidas. The job had almost become the family's private property.

Karamchand was the father of Mohandas Karamchand Gandhi, the Mahatma.

The Gandhis apparently got into trouble often. Political intrigues forced grandfather Uttamchand out of the prime ministership of Porbandar and into exile in the nearby little state of Junagadh. There he once saluted the ruling Nawab with his left hand. Asked for an explanation, he said: 'The right hand is already pledged to Porbandar.' Mohandas was proud of such loyalty: 'My grandfather,' he wrote, 'must have been a man of principle.'

Gandhi's father likewise left his position as prime minister

to Rana Saheb Vikmatji, the ruler of Porbandar, and took the
same office in Rajkot, another miniature Kathiawar princi-
pality 120 miles to the north-west. Once, the British Political
Agent spoke disparagingly of Thakor Saheb Bawajiraj,
Rajkot's native ruler. Karamchand sprang to the defence of
his chief. The Agent ordered Karamchand to apologize.
Karamchand refused and was forthwith arrested. But Gandhi's
father stood his ground and was released after several hours.
Subsequently he became prime minister of Wankaner.

In the 1872 census, Porbandar state had a population of
72,077, Rajkot 36,770 and Wankaner 28,750. Their rulers
behaved like petty autocrats to their subjects and quaking
sycophants before the British.

Karamchand Gandhi 'had no education save that of
experience,' his son, Mohandas, wrote; he was likewise
'innocent' of history and geography; 'but he was
incorruptible and had earned a reputation for strict
impartiality in his family as well as outside.' He 'was a lover of
his clan, truthful, brave and generous, but short-tempered.
To a certain extent he might have been even given to carnal
pleasures. For he married for the fourth time when he was
over forty'. The other three wives had died.

Mohandas Karamchand Gandhi was the fourth and last
child of his father's fourth and last marriage. He was born at
Porbandar on 2 October, 1869. That year the Suez Canal was
opened, Thomas A. Edison patented his first invention,
France celebrated the hundredth anniversary of the birth of
Napoleon Bonaparte, and Charles W. Eliot became president
of Harvard University. Karl Marx had just published *Capital*,
Bismarck was about to launch the Franco-Prussian War, and
Victoria ruled over England and India.

Mohandas was born in the dark, right-hand corner of a
room, 11 feet by 19½ feet and 10 feet high, in a three-storey
humble house on the border of the town. The house is still
standing.

The little town of Porbandar, or Porbunder, rises straight out of the Arabian Sea and 'becomes a vision of glory at sunrise and sunset when the slanting rays beat upon it, turning its turrets and pinnacles into gold,' wrote Charles Freer Andrews, a British disciple of the Mahatma. It and Rajkot and Wankaner were quite remote, at the time of Gandhi's youth, from the European and Western influences which had invaded less isolated parts of India. Its landmarks were its temples.

Gandhi's home life was cultured and the family, by Indian standards, was well-to-do. There were books in the house; they dealt chiefly with religion and mythology. Mohandas played tunes on a concertina purchased especially for him. Karamchand wore a gold necklace and a brother of Mohandas had a heavy, solid gold armlet. Karamchand once owned a house in Porbandar, a second in Rajkot and a third in Kutiana. But in his last three years of illness he lived modestly on a pension from the Rajkot prince. He left little property.

Gandhi's elder brother Laxmidas practised law in Rajkot and later became a treasury official in the Porbandar government. He spent money freely and married his daughters with a pomp worthy of petty Indian royalty. He owned two houses in Rajkot. Karsandas, the other brother, served as sub-inspector of police in Porbandar and ultimately of the princeling's harem. His income was small.

Both brothers died while Mohandas K. Gandhi was still alive. A sister, Raliatben, four years his senior, survived him. She remained resident in Rajkot.

Mohania, as the family affectionately called Mohandas, received the special treatment often accorded a youngest child. A nurse named Rambha was engaged for him and he formed an attachment to her which continued into mature life. His warmest affection went to his mother Putlibai. He sometimes feared his father, but he loved his mother and always remembered her 'saintliness' and her 'deeply religious' nature. She never ate a meal without prayer, and attended temple services daily. Long fasts did not dismay her, and arduous vows, voluntarily made, were steadfastly performed. In the annual Chaturmas, a kind of Lent lasting through the four-month rainy season, she habitually lived on a single meal a day and, one year, she observed, in addition, a complete fast on alternate days. Another Chaturmas, she vowed not to eat unless the sun appeared. Mohandas and his sister and brothers would watch for the sun, and when it showed through the clouds they would rush into the house and announce to Putlibai that now she could eat. But her vow required her to see the sun herself and so she would go out of doors and by then the sun was hidden again. 'That does not matter,' she would cheerfully comfort her children. 'God does not want me to eat today.'

As a boy, Mohandas amused himself with rubber balloons and revolving tops. He played tennis and cricket and also 'gilli danda', a game, encountered in so many widely separated countries, which consists in striking a short, sharpened wooden peg with a long stick: 'peggy' or 'pussy' some call it.

Gandhi started school in Porbandar. He encountered more difficulty in mastering the multiplication table than in learning naughty names for the teacher. 'My intellect must have been sluggish and my memory raw,' the adult Mahatma lays charge against the child of six. In Rajkot, whither the family moved a year later, he was again a 'mediocre student,' but punctual. His sister recalls that rather than be late he would eat the food of the previous day if breakfast was not ready. He preferred walking to going to school by carriage. He was timid: 'my books and lessons were my sole companions.' At the end of the school day, he ran home. He could not bear to talk to anybody: 'I was even afraid lest anyone should poke fun at me.' When he grew older, however, he found some congenial mates and played in the streets. He also played by the sea.

In his first year at the Alfred High School in Rajkot, when Mohandas was twelve, a British educational inspector named Mr Giles came to examine the pupils. They were asked to spell five English words. Gandhi mis-spelled 'kettle'. Walking up and down the aisles, the regular teacher saw the mistake and motioned Mohandas to copy from his neighbour's slate. Mohandas refused. Later the teacher chided him for this 'stupidity' which spoiled the record of the class; everybody else had written all the words correctly.

The incident, however, did not diminish Gandhi's respect for his teacher. 'I was by nature blind to the faults of elders . . . I had learned to carry out the orders of elders, not to scan their actions.' But obedience did not include cheating with teacher's permission.

Perhaps the refusal to cheat was a form of self-assertion or rebellion. In any case, compliance at school did not preclude revolt outside it. At the age of twelve, Gandhi began to smoke. And he stole from elders in the house to finance the transgression. His partner in the adventure was a young relative. Sometimes both were penniless; then they made cigarettes from the porous stalks of a wild plant. This interest in botany led to the discovery that the seeds of a jungle weed named dhatura were poisonous. Off they went to the jungle on the successful quest. Tired of life under parental supervision, they joined in a suicide pact. They would die, appropriately, in the temple of God.

Having made their obeisances, Mohandas and his pal sought out a lonely corner for the final act. But perhaps death would be long in coming and meanwhile they might suffer pain. Perhaps it was better to live in slavery. To salvage a vestige of self-respect they each swallowed two or three seeds.

Presently, serious matters claimed the child's attention.

Mohandas K. Gandhi married when he was a high school pupil – aged thirteen. He had been engaged three times, of course without his knowledge. Betrothals were compacts between parents, and the children rarely learned about them. Gandhi happened to hear that two girls to whom he had been engaged – probably as a toddler – had died. 'I have a faint recollection,' he reports, 'that the third betrothal took place in my seventh year,' but he was not informed. He was told six years later, a short time before the wedding. The bride was Kasturbai, the daughter of a Porbandar merchant named Gokuldas Makanji. The marriage lasted sixty-two years.

Writing about the wedding more than forty years later, Gandhi remembered all the details of the ceremony, as well as the trip to Porbandar where it took place. 'And oh! that first night,' he added. 'Two innocent children all unwittingly hurled themselves into the ocean of life.' Kasturbai, too, was thirteen. 'My brother's wife had thoroughly coached me about my behaviour on the first night. I do not know who had coached my wife.' Both were nervous and 'the coaching could not carry me far,' Gandhi wrote. 'But no coaching is really necessary in such matters. The impressions of the former birth are potent enough to make all coaching superfluous.' Presumably, they remembered their experiences in an earlier incarnation.

The newlyweds, Gandhi confesses, were 'married children' and behaved accordingly. He was jealous and 'therefore she could not go anywhere without my permission', for 'I took no time in assuming the authority of a husband.' So when the thirteen-year-old wife wanted to go out to play she had to ask the thirteen-year-old Mohandas; he would often say no. 'The restraint was virtually a sort of imprisonment. And Kasturbai was not the girl to brook any such thing. She made it a point to go out whenever and wherever she liked.' The little husband got 'more and more cross'; sometimes they did not speak to each other for days.

He loved Kasturbai. His 'passion was entirely centred on one woman' and he wanted it reciprocated, but the woman was a child. Sitting in the high school classroom he daydreamed about her. 'I used to keep her awake till late at night with my idle talk.'

'The cruel custom of child marriage,' as Gandhi subsequently castigated it, would have been impossible but for the ancient Indian institution of the joint family: parents and their children and their sons' wives and children, sometimes thirty or more persons altogether, lived under one roof; newly wed adolescents therefore had no worry about a home, furniture, or board. Later, British law, seconding Indian reformers, raised the minimum marriage age. In its time the evil was mitigated by enforced separations for as much as six months in a year when the bride went to live with her parents. The first five years of Gandhi's marriage – from thirteen to eighteen – included only three years of common life.

The 'shackles of lust' tormented Gandhi. They gave him a feeling of guilt. The feeling grew when sex seemed to clash with the keen sense of duty which developed in him at an early age. One instance of such a conflict impressed itself indelibly. When Mohandas was sixteen his father Karamchand became bedridden with a fistula. Gandhi helped his mother and an old servant to tend the patient; he dressed the wound and mixed the medicines and administered them. He also massaged his father's legs every night until the sufferer fell asleep or asked his son to go to bed. 'I loved to do this service,' Gandhi recalls.

Kasturbai had become pregnant at fifteen and she was now in an advanced stage. Nevertheless, 'every night whilst my hands were busy massaging my father's legs,' Gandhi states in his autobiography, 'my mind was hovering about [my wife's] bedroom – and that too at a time when religion, medical science and common sense alike forbade sexual intercourse.'

One evening, between ten and eleven, Gandhi's uncle relieved him at massaging Karamchand. Gandhi went quickly to his wife's bedroom and woke her. A few minutes later the servant knocked at the door and urgently summoned Gandhi. He jumped out of bed, but when he reached the sick room his father was dead. 'If passion had not blinded me,' Gandhi ruminated forty years later, 'I should have been spared the torture of separation from my father during his last moments. I should have been massaging him and he would have died in my arms. But now it was my uncle who had had this privilege.'

The 'shame of my carnal desire at the critical moment of my father's death . . . is a blot I have never been able to efface or forget,' Gandhi wrote when he was near sixty. Moreover, Kasturbai's baby died three days after birth and Mohandas blamed the death on intercourse late in pregnancy. This doubled his sense of guilt.

Kasturbai was illiterate. Her husband had every intention of teaching her, but she disliked studies and he preferred lovemaking. Private tutors also got nowhere with her. Yet Gandhi took the blame upon himself and felt that if his affection 'had been absolutely untainted with lust, she would be a learned lady today.' She never learned to read or write anything but elementary Gujarati, her native language.

Gandhi himself lost a year at high school through getting married. Modestly he assert he 'was not regarded as a dunce.' Every year he brought home a report on study progress and character; it was never bad. He even won some prizes but that, he says, was only because there were few competitors.

When Mohandas merited a teacher's rebuke it pained him and he sometimes cried. Once he was beaten at school. The punishment hurt less than being considered worthy of it: 'I wept piteously.'

Gandhi neglected penmanship and thought it unimportant.

Geometry was taught in English, which was then a new language for him, and he had difficulty in following. But 'when I reached the thirteenth proposition of Euclid the utter simplicity of the subject was suddenly revealed to me. A subject which only required a pure and simple use of one's reasoning powers could not be difficult. Ever since that time geometry has been both easy and interesting for me.' He likewise had trouble with Sanskrit, but after the teacher, Mr Krishnashanker, reminded him that it was the language of Hinduism's sacred scriptures, the future Mahatma persevered and succeeded.

In the upper grades, gymnastics and cricket were compulsory. Gandhi disliked both. He was shy, and he thought physical exercises did not belong in education. But he had read that long walks in the open air were good for the health, and he formed the habit. 'These walks gave me a fairly hardy consititution.'

Mohandas envied the bigger, stronger boys. He was frail compared with his older brother and especially compared with a Moslem friend named Sheik Mehtab who could run great distances with remarkable speed. Sheik Mehtab was spectacular in the long and high jump as well. These exploits dazzled Gandhi.

Gandhi regarded himself as a coward. 'I used to be haunted,' he asserts, 'by the fear of thieves, ghosts and serpents. I did not dare to stir out of doors at night.' He could not sleep without a light in his room; his wife had more courage than he and did not fear serpents or ghosts or darkness. 'I felt ashamed of myself.'

Sheik Mehtab played on this sentiment. He boasted that he could hold live snakes in his hand, feared no burglars and did not believe in ghosts. Whence all this prowess and bravery? He ate meat. Gandhi ate no meat; it was forbidden by his religion.

The boys at school used to recite a poem which went:

Behold the mighty Englishman,
He rules the Indian small,
Because being a meat-eater
He is five cubits tall.

If all Indians ate meat they could expel the British and make India free. Besides, argued Skeik Mehtab, boys who ate meat did not get boils; many of their teachers and some of the most prominent citizens of Rajkot ate meat secretly, and drank wine, too.

Day in, day out, Sheik Mehtab propagandized Mohandas, whose older brother had already succumbed. Finally, Mohandas yielded.

At the appointed hour the tempter and his victim met in a secluded spot on the river bank. Sheik Mehtab brought cooked goat's meat and bread. Gandhi rarely touched baker's bread (the substitute was chappatis, an unleavened dough cushion filled with air) and he had never even seen meat. The family was strictly vegetarian and so, in fact, were almost all the inhabitants of the Gujarat district in Kathiawar. But firm in the resolve to make himself an effective liberator of his country, Gandhi bit into the meat. It was tough as leather. He chewed and chewed and then swallowed. He became sick immediately.

That night he had a nightmare: a live goat was bleating in his stomach. However, 'meat-eating was a duty,' and, in the midst of the terrible dream, therefore, he decided to continue the experiment.

It continued for a whole year. Irregularly throughout that long period he met Sheik Mehtab at secret rendezvous to partake of meat dishes, now tastier than the first, and bread. Where Sheik got the money for these feasts Gandhi never knew.

The sin of consuming and liking meat was made the greater by the sin of lying. In the end he could not stand the dishonesty and, though still convinced that meat-eating was 'essential' for patriotic reasons, he vowed to abjure it until his parents' death enabled him to be a carnivore openly.

By now Gandhi developed an urge to reform Sheik Mehtab. This prolonged the relationship. But the naive and younger Gandhi was no match for the shrewd, moneyed wastrel who offered revolt and adventure. Sheik also knew how to arrange things. Once he led Gandhi to the entrance of a brothel. The institution had been told and paid in advance. Gandhi went in. 'I was almost struck blind and dumb in this den of vice. I sat near the woman on her bed, but I was tongue-tied. She naturally lost patience with me and showed me the door, with abuses and insults.' Providence, he explains, interceded and saved him despite himself.

About that time – Mohandas must have been fifteen – he pilfered a bit of gold from his older brother. This produced a moral crisis. He had gnawing pangs of conscience and resolved never to steal again. But he needed the cleansing effect of a confession: he would tell his father. He made a full, written statement of the crime, asked for due penalty, promised never to steal again and, with emphasis, begged his father not to punish himself for his son's dereliction.

Karamchand sat up in his sick bed to read the letter. Tears filled his eyes and fell to his cheeks. Then he tore up the paper and lay down. Mohandas sat near him and wept.

Gandhi never forgot that silent scene. Sincere repentance and confession induced by love, rather than fear, won him his father's 'sublime forgiveness' and affection.

Lest he give pain to his father, and especially his mother, Mohandas did not tell them that he absented himself from temple. He did not like the 'glitter and pomp' of the Hindu temples. Religion to him meant irksome restrictions like vegetarianism which intensified his youthful protest against society and authority. And he had no 'living faith in God'. Who made the world; who directed it, he asked. Elders could not answer, and the sacred books were so unsatisfactory on such matters that he inclined 'somewhat towards atheism'. He even began to believe that it was quite moral, indeed a duty, to kill serpents and bugs.

Gandhi's anti-religious sentiments quickened his interest in religion and he listened attentively to his father's frequent discussions with Moslem and Parsi friends on the differences between their faiths and Hinduism. He also learned much about the Jain religion. Jain monks often visited the house and went out of their way to accept food from the non-Jain Gandhis.

When Karamchand died in 1885, Mohandas's mother Putlibai took advice on family matters from a Jain monk named Becharji Swami, originally a Hindu of the Modh Bania sub-caste. Jain influence was strong in the Gujarat region. And Jainism prohibits the killing of any living creature, even insects. Jain priests wear white masks over their mouths lest they breathe in, and thus kill, an insect. They are not supposed to walk out at night lest they unwittingly step on a worm.

Gandhi was always a great absorber. Jainism, as well as Buddhism, perceptibly coloured Gandhi's thoughts and shaped his works. Both were attempts to reform the Hindu religion, India's dominant faith; both originated in the sixth century BC in north-eastern India, in what is now the province of Bihar.

The Jain monk, Becharji Swami, helped Gandhi to go to England. After graduating from high school, Gandhi enrolled in Samaldas College, in Bhavnagar, a town on the inland side of the Kathiawar peninsula. But he found the studies difficult and the atmosphere distasteful. A friend of the family suggested that if Mohandas was to succeed his father as prime minister he had better hurry and become a lawyer; the quickest way was to take a three-year course in England. Gandhi was most eager to go. But he was afraid of law; could he pass the examinations? Might it not be preferable to study medicine? He was interested in medicine.

Mohandas's brother objected that their father was opposed to the dissection of dead bodies and intended Mohandas for the bar. A Brahman friend of the family did not take the same dark view of the medical profession; but could a doctor become prime minister?

Mother Putlibai disliked parting with her last-born. 'What will uncle say? He is the head of the family, now that father is no more.' And where will the money come from?

Mohandas had set his heart on England. He developed energy and unwonted courage. He hired a bullock cart for the five-day journey to Porbandar where his uncle lived. To save a day, he left the cart and rode on a camel; it was his first camel ride.

Uncle was not encouraging; European-trained lawyers forsook Indian traditions; cigars were never out of their mouths; they ate everything; they dressed 'as shamelessly as Englishmen'. But he would not stand in the way. If Putlibai agreed, he would, too.

So Mohandas was back where he had started. His mother sent him to uncle and uncle passed him back to mother. Meanwhile, Gandhi tried to get a scholarship from the Porbandar government. The British administrator of the state rebuffed him curtly without even letting him present his case.

Mohandas returned to Rajkot. Pawn his wife's jewels? They were valued at two to three thousand rupees. Finally, his brother promised to supply the funds, but there remained his mother's doubts about young men's morals in England. Here Becharji Swami, the Jain monk, came to the rescue. He administered an oath to Mohandas who then solemnly took three vows: not to touch wine, women and meat. Therewith, Putlibai consented.

Joyfully, in June 1888, Gandhi left for Bombay with his brother, who carried the money. That did not end his tribulations. People said the Arabian Sea was too rough during the summer monsoon season; one ship had sunk in a gale. Departure was delayed. Meanwhile, the Modh Banias of Bombay heard about the projected trip. They convened a meeting of the clan and summoned Mohandas to attend. No Modh Bania had ever been to England, the elders argued; their religion forbade voyages abroad because Hinduism could not be practised there.

Gandhi told them he would go nevertheless. At this, the headman ostracized Mohandas. 'This boy shall be treated as an outcast from today,' the elder declared.

Undaunted, Gandhi bought a steamer ticket, a necktie, a short jacket and enough food, chiefly sweets and fruit, for the three weeks to Southampton. On 4 September, he sailed. He was not yet eighteen. Several months earlier, Kasturbai had borne him a male child and they called it Harilal. Now the voyage to England gave Gandhi 'a long and healthy separation' from his wife.

CHAPTER 3

'M. K. Gandhi, Attorney-at-Law'

Gandhi had himself photographed shortly after he arrived in London in 1888. His hair is thick, black and carefully combed with the parting slightly to the right of centre. The ear is large. The nose is big and pointed. The eyes and lips are the impressive features. The eyes seem to mirror puzzlement, fright, yearning; they seem to be moving and looking for something. The lips are full, sensuous, sensitive, sad and defensive. The face is that of a person who fears coming struggles with himself and the world. Will he conquer his passions, he wonders; can he make good? He has either been injured or is afraid of injury.

In an out-of-doors group picture of the 1890 Vegetarians' Conference at Portsmouth, Gandhi was wearing a white tie, hard white cuffs and a white dress handkerchief in his front pocket. His hair is neatly dressed. He used to spend ten minutes every morning combing and brushing it.

Dr Sachchidananda Sinha, an Indian then a student in London, recalls meeting Gandhi in February 1890, in Piccadilly Circus; Gandhi, he says, 'was wearing at the time a high silk top hat "burnished bright", a stiff and starched collar (known as a Gladstonian), a rather flashy tie displaying all the colours of the rainbow, under which there was a fine striped silk shirt. He wore as his outer clothes a morning coat, a double-breasted waistcoat, and dark striped trousers to match, and not only patent-leather shoes but spats over them. He also carried leather gloves and a silver-mounted stick, but wore no spectacles. His clothes were regarded as the very acme of fashion for young men about town at that time, and were largely in vogue among the Indian youth prosecuting their studies in law at one of the four institutions called the Inns of Court.' There were four Inns of Court: Lincoln's Inn, Gray's Inn, the Middle Temple and the Inner Temple, and the last, where Gandhi had enrolled, was, says Dr Sinha, considered by Indians 'the most aristocratic'.

Gandhi says his 'punctiliousness in dress persisted for years'. His top hat, he writes, was expensive, and he spent ten pounds for an evening dress suit tailored to order in Bond Street. He asked his brother to send him a double watch chain of gold. He abandoned his ready-made cravat and learned to tie one himself. Further 'aping the English gentleman', he invested three pounds in a course of dancing lessons. But 'I could not follow the piano' or 'achieve anything like rhythmic motion'. Adamant and logical, he thought he would develop an ear for music by mastering the violin. He purchased an instrument and found a teacher. He acquired Bell's *Standard Elocutionist* and took elocution lessons. Very soon he abandoned that too.

Playing the gentleman would, Gandhi mistakenly thought, bring him into key with the dominant note in British life. He always needed harmony, and the need helped him to develop delicate antennae of leadership.

Throughout life, Gandhi concentrated on man's day-to-day behaviour. In London, his central concern was the day-to-day behaviour of M. K. Gandhi. His autobiographical reminiscences of London student days deal entirely with his food, clothes, shyness, relations with acquaintances and his religious attitude.

George Santayana, the American philosopher of Spanish descent, visited London as a young man when Gandhi was there. Decades later, in *The Middle Span*, the second volume of his memoirs, he described the visit and commented on the quality of the theatre, the character of Englishmen and the appearance of London houses, parks and streets; there are references to literature and philosophy. Santayana, the artist, attempts to reconstruct a life and an era. Gandhi, the reformer, omits the cultural and historical background and dissects himself for the instruction of others.

Experiences are interaction between self and objective world. But Gandhi's autobiography is called *Experiments in Truth*; an experiment in this sense is induced by the objective world, but it is essentially an operation within and upon oneself. To the end of his days, Gandhi attempted to master and remake himself.

Gandhi always focused attention on the personal. English friends tried to persuade Gandhi to eat meat. One of them read to him from Bentham's *Theory of Utility*. 'These abstruse things are beyond me,' Gandhi pleaded; he would not break the vow he had given his mother

Gandhi's 'capacious stomach' demanded filling, but the family with whom he lived served no more than two or three slices of bread at each meal. Later the two daughters of the household gave him a few extra slices; he could have done with a loaf. 'I practically had to starve.' He found a vegetarian eating house in Farringdon Street, near Fleet Street, not far from the Inner Temple. He invested a shilling in Henry Salt's *A Plea for Vegetarianism* which was being sold at the entrance. Inside, he ate his first hearty meal in England: 'God had come to my aid.'

The Salt treatise made him a vegetarian by choice. In the beginning was the act, and only then the conviction.

Frugal eating led to frugal spending. Even during the brief spree of 'aping the gentleman', Gandhi kept minutely accurate accounts of all outlays for food, clothing, postage, bus fares, newspapers, books, etc. Before going to bed each night he balanced his finances. Now, after an experiment in boarding with a family, he found lodgings about a half an hour's walk from school. He thus saved on fares as well as rent and, to boot, got some exercise. He walked eight to ten miles a day.

The example of poor Indian students in London and the guilty sense of being prodigal with his brother's money impelled Gandhi to economize still further. He abandoned his suite and moved to one room. He cooked his own breakfast of oatmeal porridge and cocoa. For lunch he went to his favourite vegetarian restaurant; dinner consisted of bread and cocoa prepared at home. Food cost him one and threepence a day.

All the while sweets and spices had been coming to him by sea from India. He discontinued this luxury. He began to eat, and enjoy, boiled spinach with no condiments. 'Many such experiments', he remarked, 'taught me that the real seat of taste was not the tongue but the mind,' and Gandhi had commenced that remarkable lifelong task of changing his mind.

Under the influence of food reformers Gandhi varied his menu, giving up starches for a period, or living on bread and fruit, and again on cheese, milk and eggs for weeks at a time. He had become a member of the executive committee of the Vegetarian Society of England. An expert convinced him that eggs were not meat; the consumption of eggs injured no living creatures. After a while, however, Gandhi thought better of it. His mother, he reasoned, regarded eggs as meat, and since she had received his vow, her definition was binding. He gave up eggs; he gave up dishes, cakes and puddings made with eggs, even when they were served at the vegetarian restaurant. This was an additional privation, but satisfaction in observing the vow produced 'an inward relish distinctly more healthy, delicate and permanent' than food.

Gandhi had reduced his weekly budget to fifteen shillings. He learned to prepare English dishes. Carrot soup was a speciality. Sometimes he invited Narayan Hemchandra to partake of a meal in his room. Narayan was a young Indian who had just arrived from home after having earned a reputation as a writer. 'His dress was queer,' Gandhi reports.

Gandhi's English was still far from perfect but Narayan's was worse, and Mohandas began giving him lessons. Once Narayan arrived at Gandhi's home clothed in a shirt and a loincloth. When the landlady opened the door she ran back in fright to tell Gandhi that 'a madcap' wanted to see him. 'I was shocked' at Narayan's clothes, Gandhi wrote.

Narayan planned to learn French and visit France, to learn German and visit Germany, and to travel to America. He did go to France and translated French books. Gandhi revised several of the translations. Narayan also visited America, where he was arrested for indecent exposure.

Stirred by Narayan Hemchandra, Gandhi crossed the Channel in 1890 to see the great Paris Exhibition. 'I had heard of a vegetarian restaurant in Paris. So I engaged a room there and stayed seven days,' Gandhi recalls. 'I managed everything very economically . . . I remember nothing of the Exhibition except its magnitude and variety. I have a fair recollection of the Eiffel Tower as I ascended it twice or thrice. There was a restaurant on the first platform, and just for the satisfaction of being able to say that I had my lunch at a great height, I threw away seven shillings on it.'

Count Leo Tolstoy had called the Eiffel Tower a monument to man's folly. Gandhi read this disparaging remark and concurred. 'The Tower', Gandhi felt, 'was a good demonstration of the fact that we are all children attracted by trinkets'; neither beauty nor art recommended it, only its size and novelty. However, Gandhi did enjoy the grandeur and peace of the ancient churches of Paris, notably Notre-Dame with its elaborate interior decorations and sculptures. After the noisy, frivolous streets and boulevards, Gandhi found dignity and reverence in the houses of God. French people kneeling before a statue of the Virgin were 'not worshipping mere marble' but rather 'the divinity of which it is symbolic'.

Gandhi made no comment on British churches. In England, he played bridge, wore his 'visiting suit' on occasions and evening dress for festivities, and took an active organizational part in several vegetarian societies. But he could not make the most informal remarks, and had to write out his views and ask others to read them. 'Even when I paid a social call the presence of half a dozen or more people would strike me dumb.'

The purpose for which Gandhi came to England receives only a few lines in his reminiscences, far fewer than his dietetic adventures. He was admitted as a student at the Inner Temple on 6 November, 1888, and matriculated at London University, in June 1890. He learned French and Latin, physics and Common and Roman law. He read Roman law in Latin and bought many books. He improved his English. He had no difficulty in passing the final examinations. Called to the bar on 10 June, 1891, he enrolled in the High Court on 11 June, and sailed for India on 12 June. He had no wish to spend a single extra day in England.

Gandhi does not seem to have been happy in England. It was a necessary interim period: he had to be there to get professional status. His chief English contacts were a group of aged, crusading vegetarians 'who', he later declared, 'had the habit of talking of nothing but food and nothing but disease.' He neither received nor gave warmth.

Gandhi did not yet feel at home in English. Later, as a Mahatma, he constantly stressed the importance of studying and speaking in one's native tongue; otherwise one lost much mental effort bridging the gulf of language. British life was very foreign to him.

At first, Gandhi had thought he could become an 'Englishman'. Hence the fervour with which he seized the instruments of conversion: clothes, dancing, elocution lessons, etc. Then he realized how high the barrier was. He understood he would remain Indian. Therefore he became more Indian.

Gandhi's two years and eight months in England came at a

formative phase in his life and must have shaped his personality. But their influence was probably less than normal. For Gandhi was not the student type; he did not learn essential things by studying. He was the doer, and he grew and gained knowledge through action. Books, people and conditions affected him. But the real Gandhi, the Gandhi of history, did not emerge, did not even hint of his existence in the years of schooling and study. Perhaps it is unfair to expect too much of the frail provincial Indian transplanted to metropolitan London at the green age of eighteen. Yet the contrast between the mediocre, unimpressive, handicapped, floundering M. K. Gandhi, barrister-at-law, who left England in 1891, and the Mahatma leader of millions is so great as to suggest that until public service tapped his enormous reserves of intuition, will power, energy and self-confidence, his true personality lay dormant. To be sure, he fed it unconsciously; his loyalty to the vow of no meat, no wine, no women, was a youthful exercise in will and devotion which later flowered into a way of life. But only when it was touched by the magic wand of action in South Africa did the personality of Gandhi burgeon. In *Young India* of 4 September, 1924, he said his college days were before the time 'when . . . I began life.'

Gandhi advanced to greatness by doing. The *Gita*, Hinduism's holy scripture, therefore became Gandhi's gospel, for it glorifies action.

CHAPTER 4

Gandhi and the Gita

At one time Gandhi lived in the Bayswater district of London. There he organized a neighbourhood vegetarian club and became its secretary. Dr Josiah Oldfield, bearded editor of *The Vegetarian*, was elected president, and Sir Edwin Arnold vice-president. Sir Edwin had translated the *Gita* from Sanskrit into English and published it under the title of *The Song Celestial* in 1885, just a few years before Gandhi met him.

Gandhi first read the *Gita* in Sir Edwin Arnold's translation while he was a second-year law student in London. He admits it was shameful not to have read it until the age of twenty, for the *Gita* is as sacred to Hinduism as the *Koran* is to Islam, the Old Testament to Judaism, and the New Testament to Christianity.

Subsequently, however, Gandhi read the original Sanskrit of the *Gita* and many translations. In fact, he himself translated the *Gita* from Sanskrit, which he did not know very well, into Gujarati and annotated it with comments. His Gujarati translation was in turn translated into English by Mahadev Desai.

Gita or song is short for *Bhagavad Gita*, the song of God, the song of Heaven. Gandhi ascribed great virtues to it. 'When doubts haunt me, when disappointments stare me in the face, and I see not one ray of light on the horizon,' Gandhi wrote in the 6 August, 1925, issue of *Young India* magazine, 'I turn to the *Bhagavad Gita*, and find a verse to comfort me; and I immediately begin to smile in the midst of overwhelming sorrow. My life has been full of external tragedies and if they have not left any visible or invisible effect on me, I owe it to the teaching of the *Bhagavad Gita*.' Mahadev Desai declared that 'every moment of [Gandhi's] life is a conscious effort to live the message of the *Gita*.'

The *Bhagavad Gita* is an exquisite poem of seven hundred stanzas. Most stanzas consist of two lines; a few run to four, six, or eight lines. The entire book is divided into eighteen discourses or chapters; each, according to an appended colophon, deals with a specific branch of the science of yoga. The *Gita* is thus a book on the science and practice of yoga.

The *Bhagavad Gita* is part of a much bigger book, the *Mahabharata*, the greatest Indian epic and the world's longest poem, seven times as long as the *Iliad* and *Odyssey* combined. The *Mahabharata* sings of men and wars in the distant past, ten centuries before Christ. Like European classics, it describes battles in which gods mix with humans until it is impossible to know who was historical, who mythological. It contains fables, philosophical dissertations, theological discussions; and it contains the *Gita*, its brightest gem.

The *Bhagavad Gita* was written by one person. Scholars agree that it came into existence between the fifth and second centuries BC. It is a conversation between Krishna and Arjuna. Krishna, the hero of the *Bhagavad Gita*, and of the *Mahabharata* as well, is worshipped in India as God; many Hindu homes and most Hindu temples have statues or other likenesses of Lord Krishna. In the story of Krishna's life, legend competes with hazy prehistoric fact. He was apparently the son of a king's sister. Lest a rival for the throne arise, the king had been killing all newborn royal children. But God incarnated himself in the womb of the king's sister, and Krishna, having thus been born without the intervention of man, was secretly transferred by divine hand to the family of a lowly herdsman in place of its own infant daughter. As a child Krishna miraculously defeated all the nether world's efforts to destroy him. Later he tended the cows with other youngsters. Once during a flood he lifted up a mountain with his little finger and held it so for seven days and nights that the people might save themselves and their animals. Not suspecting his divinity, all the village maidens loved him and he danced with them. Grown to young manhood, Krishna killed his tyrant uncle and won renown throughout the land. After many adventures, Krishna retired into a forest where a hunter, mistaking him for a deer, shot an arrow into his heel. As the huntsman drew near he recognized Krishna and was stricken with grief, but Krishna smiled, blessed him and died.

Krishna is Lord Krishna. 'The representation of an individual as identical with the Universal Self is familiar to Hindu thought,' writes Sir Sarvepali Radhakrishnan, a Hindu philosopher and Oxford professor who also translated the *Gita*. 'Krishna,' he says, 'is the human embodiment of Vishnu,' the Supreme God.

The opening couplets of the *Gita* find Krishna on the battlefield as the unarmed charioteer of Arjuna, chief warrior of a contending faction. Opposite are Arjuna's royal cousins arrayed for the fratricidal fray. Arjuna says:

As I look upon these kinsmen, O Krishna, assembled here
eager to fight, my limbs fail, my mouth is parched, a tremor
shakes my frame and my hair stands on end.
Gandiva slips from my hand, my skin is on fire,
I cannot keep my feet, and my mind reels.

Gandiva is Arjuna's bow.

I have unhappy forebodings, O Keshava,
and I see no good in slaying kinsmen in battle.
I seek not victory, nor sovereign power, nor earthly joys,
What good are sovereign power, worldly pleasures, and
even life to us, O Govinda?

Keshava and Govinda are among the many names of Lord Krishna.

Rather than murder members of his own family, Arjuna would let them kill him: 'Happier far would it be for me if

Dhritarashtra's sons, weapons in hand, should strike me down on the battlefield, unresisting and unarmed.'

With a firm 'I will not fight,' Arjuna now stands speechless awaiting Krishna's reply. The Lord remonstrated:

> Thou mournest for them whom thou shouldst not mourn,
> and utterest vain words of wisdom. The wise mourn neither
> for the living nor for the dead.
> For never was I not, nor thou nor these kings; nor will
> any of us cease to be hereafter.

The Atman or soul, Krishna explains, is external and unattainable by man's weapons of destruction. Calling the soul 'This', Krishna says,

> This is never born nor ever dies, nor having been will
> ever not be any more; unborn, eternal, everlasting,
> ancient, This is not slain when the body is slain . . .
> As a man casts off worn-out garments and takes others that
> are new, even so the embodied one casts off worn-out
> bodies and passes on to others new.

Here, succinctly, is the Hindu doctrine of the transmigration of This, of Atman, the soul. Krishna adds:

> This no weapons wound, This no fire burns; This no
> waters wet, This no wind doth dry . . .
> For certain is the death of the born, and certain is the
> birth of the dead; therefore what is unavoidable thou
> shouldst not regret.

Moreover, Krishna insists, Arjuna is a member of the Kshatriya warrior caste, and therefore he must fight: 'Again, seeing thine own duty thou shouldst not shrink from it: for there is no higher good for a Kshatriya than a righteous war.'

Interpreting these texts literally, Orthodox Hindus regard the *Gita* as the historic account of a battle in which one martial leader sought to avoid bloodshed but was soon reminded by God of his caste obligation to commit violence.

Gandhi, apostle of non-violence, obviously had to propound a different version.

On first reading the *Gita* in 1888-89, Gandhi felt that it was 'not a historical work.' Nor, he wrote later, is the *Mahabharata*. The *Gita* is an allegory, Gandhi said. The battlefield is the human soul wherein Arjuna, representing higher impulses, struggles against evil. 'Krishna,' according to Gandhi, 'is the Dweller within, ever whispering to a pure heart . . . Under the guise of physical warfare,' Gandhi asserted, the *Gita* 'described the duel that perpetually went on in the hearts of mankind . . . Physical warfare was brought in merely to make the description of the internal duel more alluring.' Gandhi often questioned doctrinal, and temporal, authority.

The *Gita* was Gandhi's 'spiritual reference book,' his daily guide. It condemned inaction, and Gandhi always condemned inaction. More important, it showed how to avoid the evils that accompany action; this, Gandhi asserted, is the 'central teaching of the *Gita*'. Krishna says:

> Hold alike pleasure and pain, gain and loss, victory
> and defeat, and gird up thy loins for the fight; so
> doing thou shalt not incur sin.

That is one facet of yoga: selflessness in action.

'Act thou, O Dhananjaya [Arjuna], without attachment, steadfast in Yoga, even-minded in success and failure. Even-mindedness is Yoga.'

Then has the yogi no reward? He has, Gandhi replies: 'As a matter of fact he who renounces reaps a thousandfold. The renunciation of the *Gita* is the acid test of faith. He who is ever brooding over results often loses nerve in the performance of duty. He becomes impatient and then gives vent to anger and begins to do unworthy things; he jumps from action to action, never remaining faithful to any. He who broods over results is like a man given to objects of senses; he is ever distracted, he says goodbye to all scruples, everything is right in his estimation and he therefore resorts to means fair and foul to attain his end.' Renunciation gives one the inner peace, the spiritual poise, to achieve results.

But Arjuna could renounce fruit and not hanker after fruit yet obey Krishna and kill. This troubles Gandhi. 'Let it be granted,' he wrote in 1929 in an introduction to his Gujarati translation of the *Gita*, 'that according to the letter of the *Gita* it is possible to say that warfare is consistent with renunciation of fruit. But after forty years' unremitting endeavour fully to enforce the teaching of the *Gita* in my own life, I have, in all humility, felt that perfect renunciation is impossible without perfect observance of ahimsa [non-violence] in every shape and form.' Gandhi decides that loyalty to the *Gita* entitles him to amend it. He often refused to be bound by uncongenial texts, concepts and situations.

The *Gita* says, in effect: since only the body dies and not This, the soul, why not kill when it is your soldierly duty to do so? Gandhi says: since we are all bits of God who is perfect, how can we and why should we kill?

Apart from the summons to action, violent according to the *Gita* and non-violent according to Gandhi, the core of the *Gita* is the description of the man of action who renounces its fruits. Arjuna, still puzzled, asks for the distinguishing marks of the yogi. 'How does he talk? How sit? How move?'

Krishna says: 'When a man puts away, O Partha, all the cravings that arise in the mind and finds comfort for himself only from Atman, then is he called the man of secure understanding.'

Gandhi comments: 'The pleasure I may derive from the possession of wealth, for instance, is delusive; real spiritual comfort or bliss can be attained only if I rise superior to every temptation even though troubled by poverty and hunger.' Krishna continues his definition of the Yogi:

Whose mind is untroubled in sorrow and longeth not for joys, who is free from passion, fear and wrath – he is called the ascetic of secure understanding. The man who sheds all longing and moves without concern, free from the sense of 'I' and 'Mine' – he attains peace.

Yet a person might 'draw in his senses from their objects' and 'starve his senses' and nevertheless brood about them. In this case, attachment returns; 'attachment begets craving and craving begets wrath.' Hence, Krishna teaches, 'The Yogi should sit intent on Me.'

'This means,' Gandhi notes, 'that without devotion and the consequent grace of God, man's endeavour is vain.' Above all, Gandhi says, there must be mental control, for a man might hold his tongue yet swear mentally, or curb sex and crave it. Repression is not enough. Repression must be without regrets; ultimately repression should yield to sublimation.

'He, O Arjuna,' Krishna teaches, 'who keeping all the senses under control of the mind, engages the organs in Karma yoga, without attachment – that man excels.'

Soon after reading the *Gita*, and especially in South Africa, Gandhi began his strivings to become a Karma yogi. Later, defining a Karma yogi, Gandhi wrote, 'He will have no relish for sensual pleasures and will keep himself occupied with such activity as ennobles the soul. That is the path of action. Karma yoga is the yoga [means] which will deliver the self [soul] from the bondage of the body, and in it there is no room for self-indulgence.'

Krishna puts it in a nutshell couplet: 'For me, O Partha, there is naught to do in the three worlds, nothing worth gaining that I have not gained; yet I am ever in action.'

In a notable comment on the *Gita*, Gandhi further elucidates the ideal man or the perfect Karma yogi: 'He is a devotee who is jealous of none, who is a fount of mercy, who is without egotism, who is selfless, who treats alike cold and heat, happiness and misery, who is ever forgiving, who is always contented, whose resolutions are firm, who has dedicated mind and soul to God, who causes no dread, who is not afraid of others, who is free from exultation, sorrow and fear, who is pure, who is versed in action yet remains unaffected by it, who renounces all fruit, good or bad, who treats friend and foe alike, who is untouched by respect or disrespect, who is not puffed up by praise, who does not go under when people speak ill of him, who loves silence and solitude, who has a disciplined reason. Such devotion is inconsistent with the existence at the same time of strong attachments.'

The *Gita* defines detachment precisely:

> Freedom from pride and pretentiousness; non-violence, forgiveness, uprightness, service of the Master, purity, steadfastness, self-restraint.
>
> Aversion from sense-objects, absence of conceit, realization of the painfulness and evil of birth, death, age and disease.
>
> Absence of attachment, refusal to be wrapped up in one's children, wife, home and family, even-mindedness whether good or evil befall . . .

By practising these virtues, the yogi will achieve 'union with the Supreme' or Brahman, 'disunion from all union with pain,' and 'an impartial eye, seeing Atman in all beings and all beings in Atman.'

Gandhi summarized it in one word: 'Desirelessness.'

Desirelessness in its manifold aspects became Gandhi's goal and it created innumerable problems for his wife and children, his followers and himself.

But there is a unique reward. The great yogis, the Mahatmas or 'Great souls,' Krishna declares, 'having come to Me, reach the highest perfection; they come not again to birth, unlasting and and abode of misery.' Thus the yogi's highest recompense is to become so firmly united with God that he need never again return to the status of migrating

mortal man. Several times during his life Gandhi expressed
the hope not to be born anew.

In the end, having learned the art of yoga from Krishna,
the Supreme, who is 'Master of Yoga,' Arjuna abandons
doubt. Now he understands the innermost secrets of action
without attachment. Now therefore he can act. 'I will do thy
bidding,' he promises.

There are devout Hindus, and mystic Hindus, who sit and
meditate and fast and go naked and live in Himalayan caves.
But Gandhi aimed to be ever active, ever useful, and ever
needless. This was the realization he craved. Like everybody
else, Gandhi had attachments. He sought to slough them off.

Hindu detachment includes but also transcends unselfishness; it connotes the religious goal of auto-disembodiment or
non-violent self-effacement whereby the devotee discards his
physical being and becomes one with God. This is not death;
it is Nirvana. The attainment of Nirvana is a mystic process
which eludes most Western minds and is difficult of
achievement even by Hindus who assume, however, that
mortals like Buddha and some modern mystics have
accomplished the transformation. Gandhi did not accomplish
it.

Gandhi did, however, achieve the status of yogi. A yogi
may be a man of contemplation, or he may be a man of action.
Both yogi and commissar may devote their lives to action.
The difference between them is in the quality and purpose of
their acts and the purpose of their lives.

The *Gita* concentrates attention on the purpose of life. In
the West a person may ponder the purpose of life after he has
achieved maturity and material success. A Hindu, if moved
by the *Gita*, ponders the purpose of life when he is still on its
threshold. Gandhi was very much moved by the spirit of the
Gita.

CHAPTER 5

Indian Interlude

In London, Gandhi never got beyond Leviticus and Numbers; the first books of the Old Testament bored him. Later in life he enjoyed the Prophets, Psalms and Ecclesiastes. The New Testament was more interesting, and the Sermon on the Mount 'went straight to my heart.' He saw similarities between it and the *Gita*.

'But I say unto you, that ye resist not evil; but whosoever shall smite thee on thy right cheek, turn to him the other also. And if any man take away thy coat let him have thy cloak too.' These words of Christ 'delighted' Gandhi. Other verses struck a sympathetic chord in the Mahatma-to-be: 'Blessed are the meek . . . Blessed are ye, when men shall revile you and persecute you . . . whosoever is angry with his brother without cause shall be in danger of the judgment . . . Agree with thine adversary quickly . . . whosoever looketh on a woman to lust after her hath committed adultery already in his heart . . . Love your enemies, bless them that curse you . . . forgive men their trespasses . . . Lay not up for yourselves treasures upon earth . . . For where your treasure is, there will your heart be also . . .'

It was thanks to a Bible salesman in England that Gandhi read the Old and New Testaments. At the suggestion of a friend, he read Thomas Carlyle's essay on the prophet Mohammed. Having met Madame H. P. Blavatsky and Mrs Annie Besant in London, he studied their books on theosophy. Gandhi's religious reading was accidental and desultory. Nevertheless, it apparently met a need, for he was not a great reader and, apart from law tomes, had not read much, not even a history of India.

Gandhi refused to join Britain's new theosophist movement, but he rejoiced in Mrs Besant's renunciation of godlessness. He himself had already traversed 'the Sahara of atheism' and emerged from it thirsty for religion.

In this state he returned to India in the summer of 1891. He was more worldly but no more articulate. He quickly recognized his failures yet stubbornly insisted on having his way. He was self-critical and self-confident, temperamentally shy and intellectually sure.

On landing at Bombay, his brother told him that Putlibai, their mother, was dead. The news had been kept from Mohandas because the family knew his devotion to her. He was shocked, but his grief, greater than when his father died, remained under control.

Gandhi's son Harilal was four; his brothers had several older children, boys and girls. The returned barrister led them in physical exercises and walks, and played and joked with them. He also had time for quarrels with his wife; once, in fact, he sent her away from Rajkot to her parents' home in Porbandar; he was still jealous. He performed all the duties of a husband except support his wife and child; he had no money.

Laxmidas Gandhi, a lawyer in Rajkot, had built high hopes on his younger brother. But Mohandas was a complete failure as a lawyer in Rajkot as well as in Bombay where he could not utter a word during a petty case in court.

Laxmidas, who had financed Gandhi's studies in England, was even more disappointed at his brother's failure to carry out a delicate mission for him. Laxmidas had been the secretary and adviser to the throne of Porbandar. He was thus destined, it seemed, to follow in his father's and grandfather's footsteps and become prime minister of the little state. But he lost favour with the British Political Agent. Now Mohandas had casually met the agent in London. Laxmidas therefore wanted his brother to see the Englishman and adjust matters.

Gandhi did not think it right to presume on a slight acquaintance and ask an interview for such a purpose. But he yielded to his brother's importuning. The agent was cold: Laxmidas could apply through the proper channels if he thought he had been wronged. Gandhi persisted. The agent showed him the door; Gandhi stayed to argue; the agent's clerk or messenger took hold of Gandhi and put him out.

The shock of the encounter with the British agent, Gandhi declares in his autobiography, 'changed the course of my entire life.' He had been doing odd legal jobs for the ruling prince. He and his brother hoped he would finally obtain a position as judge or minister in the government which might lead to futher advancement in the tradition of the family. But his altercation with the agent upset these plans. Only a sycophant could succeed and get on. The episode intensified his dislike of the atmosphere of petty intrigue, palace pomp and snobbery which prevailed in Porbandar, Rajkot and the other miniature principalities of the Kathiawar peninsula. It was poison to character. Gandhi yearned to escape from it.

At this juncture a business firm of Porbandar Moslems offered to send him to South Africa for a year as their lawyer. He seized the opportunity to see a new country and get new experiences; 'I wanted somehow to leave India.' So, after less than two unsuccessful years in his native land, its future leader boarded a ship for Zanzibar, Mozambique and Natal. He left behind him his wife and two children; on 28 October, 1892, a second son named Manilal had been born. 'By way of consolation,' Gandhi assured Kasturbai that 'we are bound to meet again in a year.'

In Bombay, Gandhi had met Raychandbai. 'No one else,' Gandhi said, 'has ever made on me the impression that Raychandbai did.' Raychandbai was a jeweller-poet with a phenomenal memory. He was rich, a connoisseur of diamonds and pearls, and a good business man. Gandhi was impressed by his religious learning, his upright character and his passion for self-realization. Raychandbai's deeds, Gandhi felt, were guided by his desire for truth and godliness. Gandhi trusted him completely. In a crisis, Gandhi ran to Raychandbai for confession and comfort. From South Africa, Gandhi sought and obtained Raychandbai's advice. Nevertheless, Gandhi did not accept Raychandbai as his guru. Hindus believe that every man should acknowledge a guru, a superior person, near or far, living or dead, as one's teacher, guide, or mentor. But Raychandbai lacked the perfection that Gandhi sought in a guru. Gandhi never did find a guru; 'The throne has remained vacant,' he said. For a Hindu, this is tremendously significant and for Gandhi it is endlessly revealing. In the presence of prominent men he felt respect, humility and awe, but, wrapped in these sentiments, he sometimes became impervious to their thoughts. With all his diffidence he was spiritually independent. Ideas came to him occasionally through books but chiefly through his own acts. He remade himself by tapping his own inner resources.

Gandhi was a self-remade man and the transformation began in South Africa. It is not that he turned failure into success. Using the clay that was there he turned himself into another person. His was a remarkable case of second birth in one lifetime.

CHAPTER 6

Towards Greatness

When Gandhi landed at Durban, Natal, in May 1893, his mission was simply to win a lawsuit, earn some money and perhaps, at long last, start his career: 'Try my luck in South Africa,' he said. As he left the boat to meet his employer, a Moslem business man named Dada Abdulla Sheth, Gandhi wore a fashionable frock coat, pressed trousers, shining shoes and a turban.

South African society was sharply divided by colour, class, religion and profession, and each group jealously defended the words and symbols which demarcated it from the others. Englishmen called all Indians 'coolies' or 'samis', and they referred to 'coolie teachers', 'coolie merchants', 'coolie barristers', etc., forgetting, deliberately, that if coolie meant anything it meant manual labour. To rise above the coolie level, Parsis from India styled themselves Persians, and Moslems from India chose to be regarded as 'Arabs' which they were not. A turban was officially recognized as part of the costume of an 'Arab' but not of a Hindu.

Several days after arriving, Gandhi went to court. The magistrate ordered him to remove his turban. Gandhi demurred and left the court. To obviate further trouble, he decided to wear an English hat. No, said Dada Abdulla Sheth, a hat on a coloured man is the symbol of a waiter.

The lawsuit required Gandhi's presence in Pretoria, the capital of Transvaal. First class accommodations were purchased for him at Durban where he boarded the train for the overnight journey. At Maritzburg, the capital of Natal, a white man entered the compartment, eyed the brown intruder, and withdrew to reappear in a few moments with two railway officials who told Gandhi to transfer to third class. Gandhi protested that he held a first class ticket. That didn't matter; he had to leave. He stayed. So they fetched a policeman who took him off with his luggage.

Gandhi could have returned to the train and found a place in the third class car. But he chose to remain in the station waiting room. It was cold in the mountains. His overcoat was in his luggage which the railway people were holding; afraid to be insulted again, he did not ask for it. All night long, he sat and shivered, and brooded.

Should he return to India? This episode reflected a much larger situation. Should he address himself to it or merely seek redress of his personal grievance, finish the case, and go home to India? He had encountered the dread disease of colour prejudice. It was his duty to combat it. To flee, leaving his countrymen in their predicament, would be cowardice. The frail lawyer began to see himself in the role of a David assailing the Goliath of racial discrimination.

Many years later, in India, Dr John R. Mott, a Christian missionary, asked Gandhi, 'What have been the most creative experiences in your life?' In reply, Gandhi told the story of the night in the Maritzburg station.

Why, of all people, did it occur to Gandhi to resist the evil? The next morning Indians he met recounted similar experiences. They made the best of conditions; 'You can not strike your head against a stone wall.' But Gandhi intended to test its hardness. His father and grandfather had defied authority. His own meagre contacts with it in India were unhappy. He had rejected the authoritative, time-and-tradition-honoured version of the *Bhagavad Gita* for his own. Was it this inherent anti-authoritarianism that made him rebel against the government colour line? Was he more sensitive, resentful, unfettered and ambitious because his life, so far, had been a failure? Did he aspire to be strong morally because he was weak physically? Did challenging immoral practices in an uncrowded arena present greater opportunity for service than the pursuit of personal gain in crowded courts? Was it destiny, heritage, luck, the *Gita* or some other immeasurable quantity?

That bitter night at Maritzburg the germ of social protest was born in Gandhi. But he did nothing. He proceeded on his business to Pretoria.

The Charlestown-to-Johannesburg lap was negotiated by stage coach. There were three seats on the coach box, usually occupied by the driver, and the 'leader' of the trip. On this occasion, the 'leader' sat inside and told Gandhi to ride with the driver and a Hottentot. There was space for Gandhi inside, but he did not want to make a fuss and miss the coach, so he mounted to the driver's perch. Later, however, the 'leader' decided he wanted to smoke and get some air; he spread a piece of dirty sacking at the driver's feet on the footboard and instructed Gandhi to sit on it. Gandhi complained; why could he not go inside? At this, the 'leader' began to curse and tried to drag him off the coach. Gandhi clung to the brass rail though he felt that his wrists would break. But he did not relax his hold. The 'leader' continued alternately to pummel and pull him until the white passengers intervened: 'Don't beat him,' they shouted. 'He is not to blame. He is right.' The 'leader', yielding to the customers, relented, and Gandhi entered the coach.

The next day, Gandhi wrote to the coach company and received a written assurance that he would not be molested again.

In Johannesburg, Gandhi went to an hotel, but failed to get a room. Indians laughed at his naivety. 'This country is not for men like you,' a rich Indian merchant said to him. 'For making money we do not mind pocketing insults, and here we are.' The same person advised Gandhi to travel third class to Pretoria because conditions in the Transvaal were much worse than in Natal. But Gandhi was obdurate. He ordered the railway regulations to be brought to him, read them, and found that the prohibition was not precise. He therefore penned a note to the station master stating that he was a barrister and always travelled first (it was his ninth day and first journey in South Africa) and would soon apply in person for a ticket.

The station master proved sympathetic. He sold Gandhi the ticket on condition that he would not sue the company if the guards or the passengers ejected him. The collector came to examine the tickets and held up three fingers. Gandhi vehemently refused to move to third class. The sole other passenger, an Englishman, scolded the guard and invited Gandhi to make himself comfortable.

'If you want to travel with a coolie, what do I care,' the guard grumbled.

At the station in Pretoria, Gandhi asked a railway official about hotels, but got no helpful information. An American Negro, who overheard the conversation, offered to take Gandhi to an inn run by an American: Johnston's Family Hotel. Mr Johnston cheerfully accommodated him but suggested, with apologies, that since all the other guests were white, he take dinner in his room.

Waiting for his food, Gandhi pondered the adventures he had had on this strange trip. Not everybody was prejudiced; some whites felt uncomfortable about it all. Presently Mr Johnston knocked and said, 'I was ashamed of having asked you to take your dinner here, so I spoke to the other guests about you, and asked them if they would mind your having dinner in the dining-room. They said they had no objections, and they did not mind your staying here as long as you liked.' Gandhi enjoyed the meal downstairs. But lodgings in a private home were cheaper than Mr Johnston's hotel.

Within a week of his arrival Gandhi summoned all the Indians in Pretoria to a meeting. He wanted 'to present to them a picture of their condition'. He was twenty-four. This was his first public speech. The audience consisted of Moslem merchants interspersed with a few Hindus. He urged four things: Tell the truth even in business; Adopt more sanitary habits; Forget caste and religious divisions; Learn English. A barber, a clerk and a shopkeeper accepted his offer of English lessons. The barber merely wished to acquire the vocabulary of his trade. Gandhi dogged them for months and would not let them be lazy or lax in their studies.

Other meetings followed, and soon Gandhi knew every Indian in Pretoria. He communicated with the railway authorities and elicited the promise that 'properly dressed' Indians might travel first or second class. Though open to arbitrary interpretation, this represented progress. Gandhi was encouraged. The Pretorian Indians formed a permanent organization.

The lawsuit for which Gandhi came to South Africa brought him into contact with Roman Catholics, Protestants, Quakers and Plymouth Brethren. Some of them tried to convert him to Christianity. Gandhi did not discourage their efforts. He promised that if the inner voice commanded it he would embrace the Christian faith. He read the books they gave him and tried to answer their searching questions about Indian religions. When he did not know the answers he wrote to friends in England and to Raychandbai, the jeweller-poet of Bombay.

Once Michael Coates, a Quaker, urged Gandhi to discard the beads which, as a member of the Hindu Vaishnava sect, he always wore around his neck.

'This superstition does not become you,' Coates exclaimed. 'Come, let me break the necklace.'

'No, you will not,' Gandhi protested. 'It is a sacred gift from my mother.'

'But do you believe in it?' Coates questioned.

'I do not know its mysterious significance,' Gandhi said, defensively. 'I do not think I should come to harm if I did not wear it. But I cannot, without sufficient reason, give up a necklace which she put round my neck out of love and in the conviction that it would be conducive to my welfare. When, with the passage of time, it wears away and breaks of its own accord, I shall have no reason to get a new one. But this necklace cannot be broken.' Later in life he did not wear beads.

Gandhi's Christian friends taught him the essence of Christianity. They said if he believed in Jesus he would find redemption. 'I do not seek redemption from the consequences of sin,' Gandhi replied. 'I seek to be redeemed from sin itself.' They said that was impossible. Nor could Gandhi understand why, if God had one son, He could not have another. Why could he go to Heaven and attain salvation only as a Christian? Did Christianity have a monopoly of Heaven? Was God a Christian? Did He have prejudices against non-Christians?

Gandhi liked the sweet Christian hymns and many of the Christians he met. But he could not regard Christianity as the perfect religion or the greatest religion. 'From the point of view of sacrifice, it seemed to me that the Hindus greatly surpassed the Christians.' And Raychandbai assured him that Hinduism was unexcelled in subtlety and profundity. On the other hand, Gandhi doubted whether the sacred Hindu Vedas were the only inspired word of God. 'Why not also the Bible and the *Koran?*' He recoiled from the competitiveness of religions.

He also disliked the competitiveness of lawyers. His client, Dada Abdulla Sheth, and the opposing party, Tyeb Sheth, were relatives, and the cost of the litigation, dragging out for more than a year, was ruining both. Gandhi suggested a compromise out of court. Finally, the plaintiff and defendant agreed on an arbitrator who heard the case and decided in favour of Dada Abdulla. Now a new problem confronted Gandhi. Tyeb was called upon to pay thirty-seven thousand pounds and costs. This threatened him with bankruptcy. Gandhi induced Dada Abdulla to permit the loser to pay in instalments stretched over a very extended period.

In preparing the case, Gandhi learned the secrets of bookkeeping and some of the fine points of law. Above all, it reinforced his opinion that settlements out of court were preferable to trials. He followed this practice during his twenty years as a lawyer. 'I lost nothing thereby – not even money, certainly not my soul.'

The lawsuit settled, Gandhi returned to Durban and prepared to sail for India. He had been in South Africa almost twelve months. Before his departure, his associates gave him a farewell party. During the festivities someone handed him the day's *Natal Mercury*, and in it he found a brief item regarding the Natal government's proposed bill to deprive Indians of their right to elect members of the legislature. Gandhi stressed the necessity of resisting this move. His friends were ready but they were 'unlettered, lame' men, they said, and powerless without him. He consented to stay a month. He remained twenty years fighting the battle for Indian rights. He won.

CHAPTER 7

A Mob Scene

Natal, in 1896, had 400,000 Negro inhabitants, 50,000 whites, and 51,000 Indians. The Cape of Good Hope Colony had 900,000 Negroes, 400,000 Europeans and 10,000 Indians; the Transvaal Republic, 650,000 Negroes, 120,000 whites and about 5,000 Indians. Similar proportions obtained in other areas. In 1914, the five million Negroes easily outnumbered a million and a quarter whites.

Indians or no Indians, the whites were a permanent minority in South Africa. But the Indians were thrifty, able and ambitious, and they worked hard. Given normal opportunities, they became rivals of the whites in business, agriculture, law and the other professions.

Is that why the Indians were persecuted?

The Dutch, who first settled South Africa in the sixteenth century, brought their slaves from Malaya, Java and other Pacific islands; they concentrated in Transvaal and the Orange Free State. The British arrived much later. In Natal, they found they could grow sugar cane, tea and coffee. But the Negroes were reluctant to work for them. Arrangements were accordingly made for the shipment of indentured labourers from India. 'The Indian had come to South Africa', wrote Chancellor Jan H. Hofmeyer of the Witwaterstrand University in Johannesburg, 'because it was deemed to be in the white man's interest that he should. It seemed to be impossible to exploit the Natal coastal belt without indentured labour. So the Indians came – and brought prosperity to Natal.'

The first Indian contract workers landed in Natal on 16 November, 1860. That was the genesis of the Gandhi saga in South Africa.

The indentured Indians were term serfs. They came from India voluntarily or, frequently, involuntarily and not knowing where they were going; many were untouchables snatched from semi-starvation. The system tied them for five years to private farms. They were given free board and lodging for themselves and their families and ten shillings a month in the first year and an additional shilling a month each year after. At the end of five years the contractor paid their passage back to India. He did likewise if they remained an additional five years as free labourers. In numerous cases, the indentured labourers chose to become permanent residents.

When Gandhi had been in South Africa just over twelve months – on 18 August, 1894 – these conditions were altered. At the end of the first five-year period, the indentured labourer was obliged to return to India or to agree to be a serf in South Africa for ever. But if he wished to stay as a free working man, he had to pay an annual tax of three pounds for himself and for each of his dependants. Three pounds was the equivalent of six months' pay of an indentured labourer.

This aroused a storm at the centre of which stood Gandhi.

Indentured Indian immigration drew after it thousands of free Indians who came as hawkers, tradesmen, artisans and members of the professions, like Gandhi. They numbered perhaps fifty thousand in 1900. The pedlars carried their wares on their backs hundreds of miles into Zulu villages where no white man would try to do busines. Gradually, many of them acquired riches and property. Indians even owned steamship lines.

In 1894, 250 free Indians in Natal, being subjects of Her British Majesty, Queen Victoria, and having met the wealth qualification, enjoyed the right to vote. But that year the Natal legislature passed a law explicitly disfranchising Asiatics.

This was the second serious Indian complaint.

Throughout Natal, an Indian had to carry a pass to be in the streets after 9 P.M. Persons without passes were arrested. The Orange Free State, a Boer republic, forbade Indians to own property, to trade, or to farm. In the Crown Colony of Zululand, Indians were not allowed to own or buy land. The same proscription applied in the Transvaal where, moreover, Indians had to pay a three-pound fee for the right to reside; but residence was restricted to slums. In the Cape Colony, some municipalities prohibited Indians from walking on footpaths. Elsewhere, Indians avoided footpaths and pavements because they might be kicked off. Gandhi himself was once so kicked. Indians in South Africa were legally barred from buying South African gold. They were described in statute books as 'semi-barbarous Asiatics'.

In three years in South Africa, Gandhi had become a prosperous lawyer and the outstanding Indian political figure. He was widely known as the champion of indentured labourers. He addressed conferences, drafted memorials to government ministers, wrote letter to newspapers, circulated petitions (one was signed by ten thousand Indians), and made many friends among whites, Indians and Negroes. He learned a few Zulu words and found the language 'very sweet'. He also achieved some knowledge of Tamil, a Dravidian tongue spoken by natives of Madras and other south-Indian provinces. When work permitted he read books, chiefly on religion. He published two pamplets: *An Appeal to Every Briton in South Africa* and *The Indian Franchise, An Appeal*.

'Appeal' was the key to Gandhi's politics. He appealed to the common sense and morality of his adversary. 'It has always been a mystery to me', he says in his autobiography, 'how men can feel themselves honoured by the humiliation of their fellow-beings'. This was the essence of Gandhi's appeal.

Gandhi's struggle in South Africa did not aim to achieve equal treatment for the Indians there. He recognized that the whites thought they needed protection against a coloured majority consisting of Indians and Negroes. He also knew, as he wrote in a letter to the *Times of India* of 2 June, 1918, that 'prejudices cannot be removed by legislation . . . They will yield only to patient toil and education'.

Nor were the Indians protesting against segregation. 'They feel the ostracism but they silently bear it', Gandhi wrote.

This too was a long-range problem.

Gandhi's immediate quarrel with the white governments of Natal, Transvaal, the Orange Free State and Cape Colony was 'for feeding the prejudice by legalizing it.' At least the laws must be just; often they are not. 'I refuse to believe in the infallibility of legislators,' he said. 'I believe that they are not always guided by generous or even just sentiments in their dealings with unrepresented classes.' They may react to non-existent perils; they may serve the interests of white merchants irked by Indian competitors.

Gandhi wished to establish one principle: that Indians were citizens of the British Empire and therefore entitled to equality under its laws. He did not expect fair administration of the laws: the whites would always be favoured. But once the principle of legal equality was fixed he would be content to let life work out its own complicated pattern, trusting honest citizens to brighten the design. If, however, the Indians supinely acknowledged their inferiority they would lose dignity and deteriorate. So would the whites who imposed the inferiority.

Gandhi aimed to save the dignity of Indians and whites.

Thus far in South Africa, Gandhi had displayed unflagging energy, an inexhaustible capacity for indignation, an eagerness to serve the community, honesty which inspired trust, and a talent for easy personal relations with the lowly and the prominent. Zeal and a cause dissolved his timidity and loosened his tongue. Though there was only slight visible evidence, as yet, of the great Gandhi of history, he had proved himself an effective leader and an excellent organizer. His

Indian co-workers felt acutely, and he could not fail to see, that without him the struggle for Indian rights would collapse or at least lag.

Gandhi accordingly took six months' leave and went to India to fetch his family.

Arrived in the homeland in the middle of 1896, the twenty-seven-year-old man with a mission developed a furious activity. In Rajkot Gandhi spent a month in the bosom of his family writing a pamphlet on Indian grievances in South Africa. Bound in green and consequently known as 'The Green Pamphlet', it was printed in ten thousand copies and sent to newspapers and prominent Indians. Many publications reviewed it. To mail the rest of the edition Gandhi, always eager to keep down expenses, mobilized the children of the neighbourhood who wrote the addresses, licked the wrappers and pasted the stamps when there was no school. He rewarded them with used stamps and his blessing. The children were delighted. Two of them grew up to be Gandhi's close disciples.

At this juncture, the bubonic plague appeared in Bombay and Rajkot was in panic. Gandhi volunteered his services to the State and joined the official committee in charge of preventive measures. He stressed the need of supervising toilets and accepted that task himself. 'The poor people', he remarks in his memoirs, 'had no objection to their latrines being inspected and, what is more, they carried out the improvements suggested to them. But when we went to the houses of the upper ten, some of them even refused us admission. It was our common experience that the latrines of the rich were more unclean.' Next, Gandhi urged that the committee investigate the untouchables' quarter. Only one committee member would go with him. It was Gandhi's first visit to the slums. He had never known how outcasts lived. He discovered that they did not have latrines or any enclosed facilities. But their houses were clean.

From Rajkot Gandhi went to Bombay to arrange a public meeting on South Africa. He introduced himself to the leading citizens and enlisted their support. Meanwhile he nursed his sister's husband who was ill, and later moved the dying patient into his own room. Gandhi always boasted of an 'aptitude for nursing which gradually developed into a passion'.

The Bombay meeting was a tremendous success because of the sponsors and the topic. Gandhi had a written speech but could not make himself heard in the big hall. Somebody on the platform read it for him.

At Poona, inland from Bombay, Gandhi interviewed two of the great men of India: Gopal Krishna Gokhale, President of the Servants of India Society, and Lokamanya Tilak, a giant intellect and towering political leader. Tilak, Gandhi said later, was like the ocean and you could not readily launch yourself on it; Gokhale was like the Ganges in whose refreshing, holy waters one longed to bathe. He fell in love with Gokhale but did not take him as his guru. Gandhi described a guru in *Young India* of 6 October, 1921, as a rare combination of 'perfect purity and perfect learning'. Gokhale, as Gandhi saw him, failed to meet those requirements. He did, however, become Gandhi's *political* guru, his ideal in politics.

'They treat us as beasts,' Gandhi cried out at a mass meeting in Madras on 26 October, 1896. 'The policy is to class us with the Kaffir whenever possible,' he said. South Africa depressed the living standards of Indians and locked them up in insanitary districts; then the whites condemned the dirty Indian habits.

'Submission' to these 'insults and indignities', Gandhi told the meeting, 'means degradation'. He urged resistance. He urged too, that if no amelioration took place emigration from India to South Africa be suspended.

At the Bombay, Poona and Madras meetings, Gandhi

quoted from 'The Green Pamphlet' and asked the audience to buy it on the way out. In Madras, the proud author, noting the brochure's success, brought out a second ten thousand edition which, at first, 'sold like hot cakes'; but he had overestimated the market and was left with a remainder.

Gandhi hoped to repeat the performance in Calcutta and talked with newspaper editors and eminent citizens. But a cable recalled him to Natal, South Africa, to cope with an emergency. He therefore rushed back to Bombay where, with his wife, two sons and a widowed sister's only son, he boarded the SS *Courland*, a ship belonging to his client, Dada Abdulla Sheth, who gave the whole family a free trip. The SS *Naderi* sailed for Natal at the same time. The two ships carried about eight hundred passengers.

Gandhi's efforts to arouse Indian public opinion on the South African issue had been reported, with exaggeration, in the South African press. Now he was arriving with eight hundred free Indians. This provoked fierce resentment among the whites: Gandhi, they charged, intended to flood Natal and the Transvaal with unwanted, unindentured coloured people. Gandhi was of course innocent of recruiting or encouraging the travellers.

At first the ships were kept in quarantine, ostensibly because of the plague in Bombay. But after the five-day quarantine period, nobody was permitted to come ashore. In Durban, meetings of whites demanded that the ships and their passengers, including, Ghandi, be returned to India. Dada Abdulla received offers of reimbursement of losses if he sent the steamers back. The offers were accompanied by veiled threats. He stood firm.

On 13 January, 1897, at the end of twenty-three days' rocking outside the harbour (following a three-week voyage from Bombay) the *Courland* and *Naderi* were permitted to dock. But Mr Harry Escombe, Attorney-General of the Natal government, who had openly participated in the anti-Gandhi agitation, sent a message to Gandhi to land at dusk to avoid trouble. Mr F. A. Laughton, an Englishman and legal counsellor of Dada Abdulla, advised against this procedure. Nor did Gandhi wish to enter the city by stealth. Mrs Gandhi, who was pregnant, and the two boys accordingly disembarked in normal fashion and were driven to the home of an Indian named Rustomji, while, by agreement, Gandhi and Laughton followed on foot. The clamouring crowds had dispersed; but two small boys recognized Gandhi and shouted his name. Several whites appeared. Fearing a fight, Laughton hailed a Negro-driven rickshaw. Gandhi had never used one and was reluctant to do so now. The rickshaw boy, in any case, from fright ran away. As Gandhi and Laughton proceeded, the crowd swelled and became violent. They isolated Gandhi from Laughton and threw stones, bricks and eggs at him. Then they came closer, seized his turban and beat and kicked him. Gandhi fainted from pain but caught hold of the iron railing of a house. White men continued to smack his face and strike his body. At this juncture, Mrs Alexander, the wife of the Police Superintendent, who knew Gandhi, happened to pass and she intervened and placed herself between the maddened mob and the miserable Gandhi.

An Indian boy summoned the police. Gandhi refused asylum in the police station but accepted a police escort to Rustomji's house. He was bruised all over and received immediate medical attention.

The city now knew Gandhi's whereabouts. White gangs surrounded Rustomji's home and demanded that Gandhi be delivered to them. 'We'll burn him,' they yelled. Superintendent Alexander was on the scene and tried, vainly, to calm or disperse the howling mob. To humour them, Alexander led the singing of

> And we'll hang old Gandhi
> On the sour apple tree,

but he sensed that the temper of the mob was rising and that the house with all its inmates might be set on fire. Night had set in. Alexander secretly sent a message to Gandhi to escape in disguise. The Superintendent put two detectives at Gandhi's disposal. Gandhi donned an Indian policeman's uniform and a headgear that looked like a turban while the two white detectives painted their skins dark and dressed themselves as Indians. The three then left by the rear of the house and, threading their way through side streets, reached the police station.

When Alexander knew that Gandhi was safe, he informed the crowd of the fact. This new situation required diplomatic handling and fortunately the police chief proved equal to it.

Gandhi remained in the safety of the police station for three days.

News of the assault on Gandhi disturbed London. Joseph Chamberlain, British Secretary of State for Colonies, cabled the Natal authorities to prosecute the attackers. Gandhi knew several of his assailants but refused to prosecute. He said it was not their fault; the blame rested on the community leaders and on the Natal Government. 'This is a religious question with me,' Gandhi told Attorney-General Escombe, and he would exercise 'self-restraint'.

'Gandhi *ought* to have hated every white face to the end of his life,' wrote Professor Edward Thompson of Oxford. But Gandhi forgave the whites in Durban who assembled to lynch him and he forgave those who mauled and beat him. His soul kept no record of past sins against his body. Instead of prosecuting the guilty he pursued the more creative task of lightening his countrymen's lot.

Gandhi had been called back to South Africa to seize a happy opportunity. Under pressure exerted from London by the Colonial Secretary, Joseph Chamberlain, and from the British government in India, the Natal legislature was debating a law to annul racial discrimination and replace it by an educational test. This had been Gandhi's goal. The Natal Act, passed in 1897, met his demand of equal electoral rights for British subjects, Indians included; the attempt to disfranchise the few hundred Indians was abandoned. Gandhi felt some satisfaction. Tempers cooled and tensions relaxed.

CHAPTER 8

Gandhi Goes to War

In the Boer War, which was waged in South Africa from 1899 to 1902 between Dutch settlers and the British, Gandhi's personal sympathies 'were all with the Boers'. Yet he volunteered to serve with the British. 'Every single subject of a state,' he explained, 'must not hope to enforce his opinion in all cases. The authorities may not always be right, but as long as the subjects owe allegiance to a state, it is their clear duty generally to accommodate themselves, and to accord their support, to the acts of the state.'

This is not the language or sentiment of a pacifist. Although the Indians, Gandhi knew, were 'helots in the Empire', they were still hoping to improve their condition within that empire and here was 'a golden opportunity' to do so by supporting the British in the Boer War.

The Indians' claim for equal rights and fair treatment in South Africa, lawyer Gandhi submitted, was based on their status as British subjects, and since they sought the advantages of British citizenship they should also accept its obligations.

Then Gandhi made a fine point: it could be said that this war and any war was immoral or anti-religious. Unless, however, a person had taken that position and actively defended it before the war he could not use it as a justification for abstention after hostilities had commenced.

Gandhi would have been more popular with his countrymen had he advocated a do-nothing neutral policy. But it was unlike Gandhi to be evasive. He accordingly offered to organize Indians as stretcher bearers and medical orderlies at the front or for menial work in hospitals. The

Natal government rejected the offer. Nevertheless, Gandhi and other Indians began, at their own expense, to train as nurses. They conveyed this information to the authorities together with certificates of physical fitness. Another rejection came. But the Boers were advancing, the dead were piling up on the battlefield, and the wounded were receiving inadequate care.

After much procrastination from prejudice, Natal sanctioned the formation of an Indian Ambulance Corps. Three hundred free Indians volunteered together with eight hundred indentured labourers furloughed by their masters. England and South Africa were impressed.

Gandhi led the corps. A photograph taken at the time shows him in khaki uniform and broad-brimmed, jaunty, felt cowboy hat seated in the centre of twenty-one men similarly dressed. Gandhi had a drooping moustache and, like the others, wears a Red Cross armband. He looks stern and small. Next to him is Dr Booth, a bulky English doctor with goatee who trained the volunteers. The man standing above Gandhi had both his hands on Gandhi's shoulders.

The corps members were African-born and Indian-born Hindus, Moslems and Christians who lived together in natural amity. Their relations with the Tommies were very friendly. The public and the army admired the endurance and courage of Gandhi's corps. In one sanguinary engagement at Spion Kop in January 1900, the British were being forced to retire and General Buller, the commanding officer, sent through a message saying that although, by terms of enlistment, the Indians were not to enter the firing line he would thankful if they came up to remove the wounded. Gandhi led his men on to the battlefield. For days they worked under the fire of enemy guns and carried wounded soldiers back to base hospital. The Indians sometimes walked as much as twenty-five miles a day.

Mr Vere Stent, British editor of the *Pretoria News*, wrote an article in the July 1911 issue of the Johannesburg *Illustrated Star* about a visit to the front during the Spion Kop battle. 'After a night's work, which had shattered men with much bigger frames,' he reported, 'I came across Gandhi in the early morning sitting by the roadside eating a regulation army biscuit. Every man in Buller's force was dull and depressed, and damnation was invoked on everything. But Gandhi was stoical in his bearing, cheerful and confident in his conversations, and had a kindly eye. He did one good. It was an informal introduction and it led to a friendship. I saw the man and his small undisciplined corps on many a battlefield during the Natal campaign. When succour was to be rendered they were there. Their unassuming dauntlessness cost them many lives and eventually an order was published forbidding them to go into the firing line.'

Later in 1900 seasoned units arrived from England, fortune smiled on British arms and the Indian Ambulance Corps was disbanded. Gandhi and several comrades received the War Medal, and the corps was mentioned in dispatches.

Gandhi hoped that the fortitude of the Indians in war would appeal to South Africa's sense of fair play and help to moderate white hostility towards coloured Asiatics. Perhaps the two communities would slowly grow closer together. He himself had no unspent belligerence and no further plans or ambitions in South Africa; nothing foreshadowed the epic opportunity for leadership and realization that awaited him there. He yearned to go home to India, and did – at the end of 1901. He took his family. He settled down in Bombay to practise law and enter politics.

Gandhi was forging ahead in both fields. In fact, he was beginning to tread a path which led to the routine success of a mediocre lawyer who made money, joined committees and grew a paunch, when a telegraphic summons from South Africa asked him to return. He had promised to return if called. It pained him to break up his new life but it pleased him to be needed. Kasturbai and the boys remained in Bombay. Gandhi estimated that he might be away four months to a year.

Joseph Chamberlain, the Colonial Secretary, was making a trip to South Africa which the Indian community regarded as fateful, and they wanted their grievances presented to him by Gandhi. Hence the summons.

Gandhi arrived in Durban near the end of 1902.

Chamberlain, Gandhi assumed, had come to get a gift of thirty-five million pounds from South Africa and to cement the post-war bonds between Boers and British. The Colonial Secretary certainly did not propose to antagonize the Boers. On the contrary, every possible concession would be made to them. Very soon, in fact, General Louis Botha, the Boer leader, became Prime Minister of the British-dominated Union of South Africa and Jan Christian Smuts, another Boer general and lawyer, its Minister of Finance and Defence. Britain was tending Boer wounds and did not intend, therefore, to wound Boer susceptibilities by redressing Indian grievances. In British Natal, accordingly, Chamberlain received an Indian delegation, listened to Gandhi's plea and answered with chilling evasiveness; in the former Boer republic of Transvaal Gandhi was not even admitted into Chamberlain's presence, and those Indian representatives who were admitted got no greater satisfaction than seeing him.

From repeated rumblings in the Transvaal it seemed that a political volcano might any day erupt and wipe out the entire Indian settlement. Gandhi therefore pitched his tent close to the crater; he became a resident of Johannesburg, the largest city of the Transvaal, opened a law office there and, without objection from the bar association, won the right to practise before the Supreme Court.

The Transvaal government established an Asiatic Department to deal with Indians. This in itself was ominous;

it suggested a racial approach. The Department, which Gandhi charged with corruption, was manned, in the main, by British army officers who had come from India during the Boer War and elected to stay. Their mentality was that of the white sahib in a colony of coloured inferiors.

One of the top Asiatic Department ideologues was Lionel Curtis, Assistant Colonial Secretary of the Transvaal, who later attained wider fame as a liberal apologist of imperialism. Gandhi went to see him in 1903 and Mr Curtis wrote subsequently: 'Mr Gandhi was, I believe, the first Oriental I ever met'; but ignorance has ever facilitated policy-making. Gandhi, Curtis says, 'started by trying to convince me of the good points in the character of his countrymen, their industry, frugality, their patience'. Still the same Gandhian hope of winning friends by disproving calumnies! But Curtis replied, 'Mr Gandhi, you are preaching to the converted. It is not the vices of Indians that Europeans in this country fear but their virtues.'

If the Indians in South Africa had consented to be 'hewers of wood and drawers of water' they would have had no trouble. But the whites, unprepared to accept the Indians as equals, used their monopoly of political power to handicap the brown men from another part of the Empire. The purpose was unmistakable because frankly avowed. General Botha put it bluntly in an election speech at Standerton in January 1907, when he declared, 'If my party is returned to office we will undertake to drive the coolies out of the country within four years.' And Smuts asserted in October 1906, 'The Asiatic cancer, which has already eaten so deeply into the vitals of South Africa, ought to be resolutely eradicated.' These were the Asiatic Department's marching orders.

Gandhi stopped the whites far short of this goal.

Throughout 1904, 1905 and the first part of 1906, the Transvaal Asiatic Department diligently carried out all anti-Indian regulations and showed special aptitude in inventing new ones. It looked as though the existence of the ten thousand Indians of the Transvaal and of the more than one hundred thousand in South Africa was in jeopardy; the threats of Botha and Smuts appeared on the eve of being translated into actuality.

Gandhi was now the recognized leader of South Africa's Indian community. Tension between whites and Indians was growing. Nevertheless Gandhi forsook the political arena when the Zulu 'rebellion' occurred in the first half of 1906 and joined the British army with a small group of twenty-four Indian volunteers to serve as stretcher bearers and sanitary aids. Gandhi said he joined because he believed that 'the British Empire existed for the welfare of the world'; he had a 'genuine sense of loyalty' to it.

The 'rebellion' was really a punitive expedition or 'police action' which opened with the exemplary hanging of twelve Zulus and continued to the last as a ghastly procession of shootings and floggings. Since white physicians and nurses would not tend sick and dying Zulus, the task was left to the Indians who witnessed all the horrors of black men whipped till their skin came off in strips. Gandhi's party sometimes came on the scene five or six days after the whites had passed by and found the victims suffering agony from open, suppurating wounds. The Indians marched as many as forty miles a day.

After a month's service, the Indian unit was demobilized and each man honoured with a special medal. Gandhi had held the rank of sergeant-major. All members wore khaki uniform, this time with puttees.

When Gandhi returned from this expedition he was obliged to plunge into a cold war with the British which ended in an historic victory for moral force and brought him honour in India and fame throughout the world.

CHAPTER 9

The Transformation Begins

The Gandhi who worsted the South African government in prolonged combat had first conquered himself and transformed his living habits and inner essence. That altered his relations with Kasturbai and their children.

A photograph of Mrs Gandhi on her first arrival in South Africa in 1897 – at twenty-eight – shows her a beautiful woman, elegantly dressed in a rich, silk sari. The fine oval face with eyes wide apart, well-formed nose, delicately curved lips and perfectly shaped chin must have made her very attractive indeed. She was not as tall as Gandhi. He was photographed on the same occasion in a European suit, stiff white collar and stiff white shirt, a gay, striped necktie and a round button in his lapel buttonhole. On his head is a thin skull-cap. In a second exposure he is without head-dress. His full lips begin to reflect the will-power tempered by powerful emotional self-control which they later expressed so eloquently. But on the whole he looks the average Indian, Europeanized by constant imitation of the white world.

Harilal and Manilal, their two sons who came with them to South Africa, were dressed in knee-length coats and long, Western trousers. They wore shoes and stockings; they had not worn them in India. Neither had Kasturbai. All three disliked them and complained to the head of the family that their feet felt cramped and the stockings stank. But Gandhi used his authority to compel obedience. He also inflicted the Western torture of knives and forks at meals; finger-eating had been so much more comfortable and tasty.

Gandhi earned five to six thousand pounds a year from his legal work – a very big income in those days in South Africa.

At one time, in Durban, he rented an English villa at the beach a few doors from the Attorney-General's home, and always his life resembled that of the professional man who had made good.

Before going to study law in London, Gandhi had yearned to be a doctor, and in effect he always was. He offered free medical advice to most of his legal clients. One of them, Lutavasinh, was asthmatic. Gandhi induced him to fast and give up smoking. Later, Gandhi put him on a diet of rice, milk and marmalade for a month. 'At the end of the month,' Gandhi boasted years later, 'he was free from asthma.'

An Indian business man's son became ill suddenly; the doctor advised an operation. Gandhi was summoned. To calm the father, Gandhi agreed to be present at the operation. The child died under the knife; Gandhi never shook off the impression.

Gandhi was also Kasturbai's midwife. He had studied a popular work on childbirth, which constituted a full course in obstetrics and infant care, and, when labour came too swiftly for professional help to be fetched, Gandhi himself delivered his fourth son, Devadas, 22 May, 1900. 'I was not nervous,' he said. For two months after the birth of Devadas and also for a while after the birth of Ramdas, his third son, in South Africa in 1897, Gandhi employed a nurse; she helped Kasturbai in the household. But caring for infants 'I did myself', Gandhi writes.

Gandhi was constantly interfering in household matters; that incensed Kasturbai. He considered himself her teacher, which annoyed her. He imposed new, rigid rules of behaviour. The 'blind, infatuated' love he gave Kasturbai was a diminishing recompense for these tribulations. But 'a Hindu wife', Gandhi declared, 'regards implicit obedience to her husband as the highest religion. A Hindu husband regards himself as the lord and master of his wife who must ever dance attendance upon him.' Gandhi, in this period, was a very Hindu husband. He thought himself 'a cruelly kind' spouse. At times, Kasturbai would have failed to notice the kindness.

Frequently, Gandhi's friends and his law clerks and assistants, whom he treated like sons, stayed with him. Among these non-paying boarders was Sheik Mehtab, his athletic, meat-eating boyhood friend. Gandhi had brought him along on his second trip from India. Mehtab had hardly settled in the Gandhi household when he began secretly to introduce prostitutes into his room. Gandhi was informed but he refused to believe it until on one occasion he caught Mehtab in the act. Mehtab had to leave the house. Later Mehtab married and reformed and wrote mediocre inspirational verse for the Gandhian passive resisters; his wife went to prison as a passive resister.

There was no running water in the Gandhi home; each room had a chamber pot. Gandhi would not employ an untouchable 'sweeper' who in India does all 'unclean' tasks. He and Kasturbai carried out the pots. She had no choice; he insisted. But one clerk had been an untouchable himself and had become a Christian in order to escape the ugly disabilities which Hindus inflict on their 'outcasts'. To the orthodox Kasturbai, however, he remained an untouchable and she balked at cleaning his pot. In fact she hated the whole business and did not see why she, or her husband for that matter, should perform such tasks. Gandhi compelled her obey; he considered it part of her 'education'. But she cried and her eyes were red with anger and tears. He protested; not only must she do this work but she had to do it cheerfully and when he saw her weep, he shouted, 'I will not have this nonsense in my house.'

'Keep your house to yourself and let me go,' she screamed.

Gandhi grabbed her by the hand, dragged her to the gate, opened it and was about to push her out.

'Have you no shame?' she exclaimed through copious tears.

'Where am I to go? I have no parents or relatives here. For Heaven's sake, behave yourself and shut the gate. Let us not be found making scenes like this.'

This brought Gandhi to his senses. He possessed a temper and temperament, and his subsequent Mahatma-calm was the product of training.

In 1901 Gandhi decided to return to India. On the eve of his departure – with his family – the Indian community outdid itself in concrete demonstrations of gratitude. He was presented with numerous gold and silver objects and diamond ornaments. For Kasturbai there was a very valuable gold necklace.

Gandhi had received gifts when he left for India in 1896. They were not like these; they were small, personal tokens of appreciation which he had accepted easily in that spirit. Since then, moreover, his view of personal possessions had been gradually changing. He was beginning to see danger in wealth and property. He had been pleading with people to conquer their infatuation for jewellery. Yet now he himself owned more than anybody whom he had tried to convert.

After the presentation party he went home and spent a sleepless night. The gifts might be construed as payment for services which he had rendered with no thought of material gain. He wanted to give them up. But he saw the advantage of retention. Torn between the yearning for financial security and the desire for the freedom derived from owning nothing, he paced up and down for hours arguing with himself. He was also aware that he faced a family crisis if he decided to return the gifts. Kasturbai would protest; he would be making her unhappy. But by morning his mind was made up: the gifts must go.

He had won his own battle. Could he convince Kasturbai?

First, in order to make the renunciation a fact beyond family dispute, he drafted a letter which elaborated a plan of using the gifts to create a community fund. Then he proceeded to recruit Harilal and Manilal, his first and second born. They were readily persuaded. They had no interest in jewels and no objection to his emerging new philosophy of austerity. Besides, Papa was a compelling debater.

'Let's return them,' they agreed.

'Then you will plead with your mother, won't you?' Gandhi hinted.

'Certainly,' the young boys said with alacrity. 'Just leave it to us. She does not need ornaments. She would want them for us, and if we don't want them why should she not part with them?'

But the boys failed to move Kasturbai. Gandhi came to their aid.

'It's all very well for you,' Kasturbai started calmly. 'You don't care for jewels. You don't wear them. And it's easy enough for you to influence the boys. They'll always dance to your tune. As for me, I have already obeyed your order not to wear trinkets. After all the talking you've done about other people not wearing jewels it would not do for me to wear them. But what about my daughters-in-law?' she said with bitterness and growing determination. 'They will be sure to want them.'

'Well,' Gandhi put in mildly, 'the children aren't married yet. We've always said they must not marry young. When they are grown up they can take care of themselves. And surely we will not chose brides for our sons who are fond of jewellery.'

'Young things like pretty things,' argued Kasturbai.

Gandhi tried to soothe. 'Well,' he said, 'if they do, if after all we have to provide them with ornaments, I shall be here. You will ask me then.'

That infuriated Kasturbai. 'Ask you! I know you by this time. You took my jewellery away from me. Imagine you offering to get jewels for your daughters-in-law! You, who are trying to make monks of my boys.

'No,' she shouted, 'the ornaments will not be returned.'

The Hindu wife was defiant. 'Besides,' she exclaimed, 'the necklace is mine. You have no right to return that.' This was a retreat. She had given up hope of their keeping all the jewels. At least, the necklace.

Eager to mollify her, Gandhi nevertheless was hard. 'Was the necklace given to you for your service or for my service?' he asked rhetorically.

Kasturbai burst into tears. 'It's the same thing,' she sobbed. 'Service rendered by you is as though rendered by me. I have toiled and moiled for you day and night. Is that no service? You forced all and sundry guests upon me, making me weep bitter tears and I slaved for them.'

Gandhi knew this was a just reproach. But he did not admit it at the moment. He was determined to return the jewels and create the community fund. He was 'definitely of the opinion that a public worker should accept no costly gifts'. He was beginning to believe that he should own nothing costly, whether given or earned. Against this powerful impulse which would soon reach full flower and alter his entire mode of life, Kasturbai had no argument. Hers was the instinctive, million-year-old female desire for adornment and the fear, equally primitive, of material want. But a plea for acquisitiveness could not stand against Gandhi's penchant for renunciation, nor could Kasturbai induce him to prefer self-enrichment to community service. In the end, he simply asserted his male authority and announced that the 1901 gifts and those of 1896 would be surrendered to trustees. So it was, and the fund, augmented from other sources, served South African Indians for decades thereafter.

Shortly after this episode, Gandhi, having returned to India and rented a home and chambers in Bombay, received a call at his office from an American insurance agent. The agent had a 'pleasant countenance' and 'a sweet tongue'. He discussed Gandhi's future 'as though we were old friends'. In

America, the agent said, 'a person like you would always carry insurance; life is uncertain'. Moreover, 'It's a religious duty to be insured.' This impressed Gandhi; he had believed that faith in God made an insurance policy superfluous. 'And what about your family?' the agent continued. Gandhi knew that his surrender of the fortune in jewels had intensified Kasturbai's insecurity. What would happen to her and the boys if he died; would it be right again to burden his generous brother who had already spent so much money on them? So Gandhi took out an insurance policy for ten thousand rupees or, roughly, a thousand pound in values of that time. The glib American agent subverted the future Mahatma. The future Mahatma had not yet solved his psychological problems.

Hardly had the family found itself in Bombay than Manilal, aged ten, went down with a severe case of typhoid complicated, before long, by pneumonia. At night, the boy had a very high temperature.

A Parsi doctor was called. He said there was no effective medicine. Everything depended on proper diet and good nursing. He recommended chicken broth and eggs.

'But we are absolute vegetarians,' Gandhi told the doctor.

'Your son's life is in danger,' the doctor cautioned. 'We could give him milk diluted with water but that will not provide enough nourishment.' The Parsi physician said many of his Hindu patients were vegetarians but in serious illness they obeyed his instructions.

Gandhi replied, 'Even for life itself we may not do certain things. Rightly or wrongly it is part of my religious conviction that man may not eat eggs and meat. It is in crises such as this that a person's faith is truly tested.' To be a vegetarian in normal circumstances and take meat when the body is under stress would mock vegetarianism. Gandhi accordingly told the doctor he would persist. 'I propose, in addition,' Gandhi declared, 'to try some hydropathic remedies which I happen to know.' He had been reading pamphlets on water cure by a Dr Kuhne of Leipzig.

Gandhi informed Manilal about this conversation. The boy was too weak to do more than assent. The father now assumed complete charge of the patient. He gave Manilal several three-minute hot hip baths a day and starved him on diluted orange juice for three days.

But the temperature remained at 104. Manilal was delirious. Gandhi worried. He worried about what people would say, what his elder brother, Laxmidas, now the head of the family, would say. And Kasturbai was anxious and angry. Should he try another physician, or perhaps consult an expert in ancient Indian aryuvedic medicine?

On the other hand, he said to himself, 'the thread of life is in God's hand; and God must be pleased by my adherence to vegetarianism and natural cures.'

The boy's condition became extremely critical. Gandhi decided to give him a wet pack. He dipped a bedsheet in water, wrung it out, wrapped it around Manilal's body, covered him with two blankets, and put a wet towel to the head.

Manilal's body was hot and dry. Gandhi was frantic. The boy was not perspiring. Kasturbai fretted. Gandhi put her in charge, telling her strictly not to alter anything; he himself felt he had to leave the house to lessen the tension within him. He walked the streets and prayed, calling, 'God, God, God, God, please, God.'

Excited, exhausted, he returned home.

'It is you Bapu,' Manilal said to his father.

'Yes, darling,' Gandhi replied.

'I am burning, take me out.'

'Just a few more minutes, son. You are perspiring. You will soon be well.'

'No, Bapu, I cannot stand it any longer. I am burning up.'

'Another minute. It will relieve you.'

Gandhi opened the sheet and wiped the body dry. Then they both fell asleep in the same bed. Next morning the fever was down. Gradually, it disappeared. Gandhi kept the boy on diluted milk and fruit juices for forty days until he was completely recovered.

Was it hydropathy? Or diet? It happens that Gandhi did the right thing from the medical point of view. Orange juice and milk were at least as good as, perhaps better than, eggs and chicken. But Gandhi ascribed Manilal's delivery to 'God's grace'.

'God saved my honour,' he said.

Gandhi had settled down in Bombay, but in 1902 he was again recalled to South Africa. He now realized that he would be there for a long time and sent for his wife and three boys; Harilal, the eldest, remained in India. Gandhi resumed his lucrative law practice in Johannesburg.

Gandhi insisted that his clients tell him the whole truth; he dropped many cases when he discovered that he had been deceived. The lawyer's duty, he held, was not to prove the guilty innocent but to help the court to arrive at the truth.

If a person, wishing to retain him, made a confession of wrongdoing, Gandhi would say, 'Why don't you plead guilty and take the penalty?' He thought there was too much litigation for community health and individual morality. 'A true lawyer,' he declared, 'is one who places truth and service in the first place and the emoluments of the profession in the next place only.' But the true lawyer, he found, was a rarity. Lawyers often lied, money talked, and witnesses consciously perjured themselves.

Even as a lawyer his primary impulse was to change men. He respected no precedent, tradition, enactment, or habit that obstructed a change he aspired to introduce. He changed his own habits with the greatest alacrity.

Gandhi suffered from occasional rheumatic inflammation, headaches and constipation. Though a vegetarian he was a heavy eater. He concluded that he overate. Having heard of the formation in England (Manchester) of a No-Breakfast Association, he dispensed with the morning meal and the headaches and other physical ailments disappeared. Thereafter he took no more laxatives or medicines. Instead, if necessary he applied a poultice of clean earth moistened with cold water to his abdomen; this worked alimentary miracles. Simultaneously, he adopted a diet based on sun-baked fruits and nuts. Grapes and almonds, according to his researches, were adequate nourishment for the tissues and nerves.

He walked to and from his law office. As long as the family was in Johannesburg the children accompanied him – a distance of five miles in all. In the office he became an expert typist.

Once a white barber refused to cut Gandhi's hair. Without blaming the barber ('There was every chance of his losing his custom if he should serve black men. We do not allow our barbers to serve our untouchable brethren') Gandhi bought a pair of clippers and thenceforth cut his own hair and that of the boys.

Gandhi wore stiff white collars, but the laundry was expensive and, besides, it returned work so slowly that he had to have several dozen collars. He took to washing and starching them himself. The first time he did it he used too much starch and the iron was not hot enough. In court, the starch began dropping off the collar and Gandhi's colleagues laughed. But 'in the course of time I became an expert washerman'. He saw 'the beauty of self-help'.

In 1903 Gandhi joined a group of Christians and Theosophists called the Seekers' Club. They frequently read the *Bhagavad Gita* together. Spurred by this activity Gandhi began studing the *Gita* again. His morning toilet required thirty-five minutes, 'fifteen minutes for the toothbrush', an old Indian custom, and twenty minutes for bathing. While cleaning his teeth, he memorized the *Gita*. Its outstanding lesson to him now was 'non-possession'. Straightaway he allowed his Bombay American insurance policy to lapse. 'God would take care' of the family.

But 'were not wife and children possessions?'

The discussions at the Seekers led him to introspection. He concluded that his emotions were undisciplined and that he lacked 'equability'. To be equable he would have to treat family, friend and foe alike. This was *Gita* 'detachment'.

One evening Gandhi went to an 'At Home' of the proprietress of his favourite vegetarian restaurant. There he met a young man named Henry S. L. Polak, born at Dover in 1882, who had become a vegetarian after reading Count Leo Tolstoy. Polak also knew Adolf Just's *Return to Nature*, a treatise on nature cures which Gandhi cherished. They talked, found much in common and became friends. Polak was assistant editor of the *Transvaal Critic*. He had 'a wonderful faculty', Gandhi said, 'of translating into practice anything that appealed to his intellect. Some of the changes he had made in his life were as prompt as they were radical'. This description of what Gandhi liked in Polak is a description of Gandhi.

Some months earlier, in 1903, Gandhi had helped to start a weekly magazine called *Indian Opinion*. The paper was in difficulties, and to cope with them at first hand Gandhi took a trip to Durban where the magazine was published. Polak saw him off at the station and gave him a book to read for the long journey. It was John Ruskin's *Unto This Last*.

Ruskin's influence during his lifetime was very great, as art critic, essayist and writer on ethics, sociology and economics. His monumental *Fors Clavigera*, in eight volumes published between 1871 and 1874, preached the dignity of manual labour, urged the simple life, and stressed the debilitating complexities of the modern economic system.

Ruskin was sometimes contemptuous of the society in which he lived. 'How much,' he demanded in *Sesame and*

Lilies, 'do you think we spend on libraries, public and private, as compared with what we spend on our horses? . . . Or, to go lower still, how much do you think the contents of the bookshelves of the United Kingdom, private and public, would fetch, as compared with the contents of its wine-cellars?'

The same iconoclastic spirit permeates *Unto this Last: Four Essays on the First Principles of Political Economy*, first published serially in the London *Cornhill Magazine* and in *Harper's*, New York, in 1860 and later in book form. Of this work, forty years later, Gandhi said that it was written with 'blood and tears'.

'Riches', Ruskin declared, 'are a power like that of electricity, acting through inequalities or negations of itself. The force of the guineas you have in your pocket depends wholly on the default of a guinea in your neighbour's pocket. If he did not want it, it would be of no use to you.' When he is poor and long out of work the guinea is more valuable to you. Therefore, 'what is really desired, under the name of riches, is, essentially, power over men'.

Consequently, men should seek 'not greater wealth, but simpler pleasure; not higher fortune but deeper felicity; making the first of possessions, self-possession; and honouring themselves in the harmless pride and calm pursuits of peace.'

Remembering that 'what one person has, another cannot have', the rich should abstain from luxuries until all, the poorest too, shall have enough, 'until the time come and the kingdom, when Christ's gift of bread and bequest of peace shall be unto this last as unto thee . . .'

To Gandhi it meant: only that economy is good which conduces to the good of all. This Gandhi had known. The second lesson, which he had 'dimly realized', was that 'a lawyer's work has the same value as the barber's, inasmuch as all have the same right of earning their livelihood for their work'. Gandhi derived this interpretation from one sentence in Ruskin's book: 'A labourer serves his country with his spade, just as a man in the middle rank of life serves it with the

sword, the pen, or the lancet.' But Ruskin did not say, as
Gandhi did, that the work of all 'has the same value'. On the
contrary, Ruskin stressed, more than anything else, 'the
impossibility of Equality' between men. He merely
contended that the underprivileged must find protection in
the morality of the fortunate. Ruskin hoped to alleviate the
hardships of inequality by an appeal to the conscience of the
devout.

The third lesson of *Unto This Last* – 'that the life of labour,
that is, the life of the tiller of the soil and the handicraftsman,
is the life worth living' – was completely new to Gandhi. But
these are Gandhi's words; the teaching, though not alien to
Ruskin, is scarcely to be found in the four essays. Ruskin
merely suggested, in a footnote, that the rich would be
healthier with 'lighter dinner and more work' while the poor
could do with more dinner and lighter work.

Gandhi, who had never read Ruskin, started reading *Unto
This Last* the moment the train left Johannesburg and read all
night. 'That book,' he said in October 1946, 'marked the
turning point in my life.' He immediately decided 'to change
my life in accordance with the ideals of the book'. He would
go to live on a farm with his family and associates.

As Gandhi read his deepest convictions into the *Gita*, so he
wove his own notions into Ruskin. Those books appealed to
him most which were closest to his concept of life and, where
they deviated, he brought them closer by interpreting them.
'It was a habit with me,' Gandhi once wrote, 'to forget what I
did not like and to carry out in practice whatever I liked.'

Ruskin, Gandhi observed in 1932, 'was content to
revolutionize his mind' but lacked the strength to change his
life. Gandhi suffered from no such deficiency. Bent on
establishing a Walden on the veldt, he acted quickly. He
bought a farm near Phoenix, a town fourteen miles from
Durban. Situated on a hill, it consisted of a hundred acres
with a well, some orange, mulberry and mango trees and one

dilapidated cottage. It cost a thousand pounds. Several rich Indians helped with the money. One Indian friend contributed quantities of corrugated iron for houses. Gandhi would have preferred mud huts with thatched roofs, but his colleagues vetoed that.

Without delay, the presses and offices of *Indian Opinion* were transferred to the farm. Albert West, the British editor of the magazine, whom Gandhi had met in a vegetarian restaurant, gave instant agreement to the startling project. They fixed a monthly allowance of three pounds for editor, errand boy and compositor. That was in 1904. The magazine is still published in the same place by Manilal Gandhi.

For a while, Gandhi's law practice required his presence in Johannesburg. He could not yet liberate himself for the new life at Phoenix. He wrote much of the matter that went into *Indian Opinion* and personally covered most of its deficits, which amounted to many pounds a month. He did a great deal of legal work for Indians who entrusted him not only with their litigations but also with their savings. The Indian indentured labourers knew Gandhi as their champion with the authorities and in the courts. He also doctored them. Those who became free and accumulated wealth often gave him their money to keep; they had no knowledge of banking and little faith in the whites.

A proprietor was seeking funds to expand a vegetarian dining room. Gandhi had a large sum belonging to Badri, a former serf. 'Badri,' said Gandhi, 'may I use your money to help this restaurant? It requires a thousand pounds.'

'Brother,' Badri replied, 'give away the money if you like. I know nothing in these matters. I know only you.'

Gandhi lent the proprietor the money. In three months the restaurant failed. Gandhi paid back the money out of his own pocket.

Henry Polak was assisting with the magazine, but Gandhi needed him in his law business too, and so Polak, who had settled on the Phoenix farm, came to live in Gandhi's Johannesburg home which always resembled an Indian joint family except that in the Gandhi household not only blood relatives but friends, co-workers, employees and political associates resided under one roof. Gandhi paid the expenses.

Polak wanted to get married; he had postponed it for financial reasons. But having made him a member of the joint Gandhi family, Gandhi urged him to marry. 'You are now mine,' Gandhi said. 'Your concern about yourself and your children is my concern. It is I who am marrying you and I do not see any objection to your marrying immediately.' Polak brought his bride from England. She was a Christian, Polak a Jew, but their real religion, Gandhi said, 'was the religion of ethics'. Ever shaping others' lives, Gandhi also persuaded Albert West to marry. Albert went to Scotland and returned with a wife, a mother-in-law and a sister. They were embraced in the joint family. At this stage of his life, Gandhi was interested in marrying off all his bachelor friends.

The expanding Johannesburg household adopted the practice of maximum manual self-service. Instead of buying bread, unleavened wholemeal biscuits were baked at home after a recipe of the remote but omnipresent Dr Kuhne of Leipzig, author of *The New Science of Healing*. For health and economy reasons, the flour was ground in a handmill with a huge iron wheel. Gandhi, the children and the Polaks took turns at this arduous labour. 'Good exercise for the boys,' said their exacting father. The boys also did the chamber-pot chores.

During 1904 and 1905 Gandhi, Kasturbai and their sons lived now in Johannesburg, now at Phoenix Farm. In both places, the problem of restraint and self-control preoccupied him. He began to fast, like his mother, whenever an occasion presented itself. On the other days, he ate two meagre meals of fruits and nuts. But after a fast he enjoyed his food more and wanted to eat more. Fasts therefore could lead to indulgence! Gandhi's goal was the 'disembodiment' and 'desirelessness' which, in Hindu thought, conduces union with God. Mere abstention does not meet the *Gita* ideal; craving too must be absent. If reduced food consumption stimulated the appetite the restraint was negatived.

His task, therefore, was to conquer the palate. As a minimum, he dispensed with spices and seasoning. Now began his lifelong search for a diet which, while sustaining animal man, lifted the mind above the animal.

If he did not curb his passion for food, how could he curb stronger passions: anger, vanity and sex? We live, Gandhi argued, not in order to provide food, clothing and shelter for the body. We provide food, clothing and shelter for the body in order to live. Material things are only the means to a spiritual end. When they become the end, the sole end, as they usually are, life loses content and discontent afflicts mankind. The soul, alas, needs a temporary abode, but a clean mud hut will do as well as a palace, much better in fact. The body must be kept alive, not pampered. To achieve release for the spirit, the body must be subjected to the discipline of the mind.

The denial of ordinary pleasures is masochism, a Westerner might say. Yet the Christian ethic is ascetic, and sainthood in all religions is related to self-denial.

The year 1906 marked a crisis in Gandhi's struggle with his passions. He had given up the house in Johannesburg, sent the family to Phoenix Farm, and volunteered for medical work in the Zulu 'war'. The suppression of the tribesmen, with its insensate cruelty of man to man, depressed him. The long treks to the hamlets of the suffering Negroes afforded ample opportunity for self-analysis; he must do more to make a better world. Also, he had a premonition of further discriminatory measures against Indians in South Africa. He must dedicate himself completely to public service.

To Gandhi, selfless service did not mean the sacrifice of part

of one's assets; it required the investment of all of one's being.
A dedicated person could not belong to wife or children, for if
he did, then they and not the work would be the first
consideration. To lead others he had to be immune to all
temptations and in command of all his desires.

Gandhi accordingly resolved to give up sexual intercourse.
Twice before, he had tried to become continent. Kasturbai
was willing. They began to sleep in separate beds and he
never retired until he was physically exhausted. Both times he
succumbed to temptation.

This time, however, he took a vow.

On his return from the Zulu uprising, Gandhi went to the
farm and told Kasturbai of his pledge to forswear sex. She
made no protest. 'She was never the temptress,' Gandhi
asserted; he determined the character of their intimate
relations.

Gandhi remained celibate from 1906, when he was thirty-
seven, until his death in 1948.

The Indian word for continence is 'Brahmacharya', and
a celibate man or woman is called a 'Brahmachari'.
Brahmacharya 'fully and properly understood', Gandhi
wrote in 1924, 'means search after Brahma', or God.
'Brahmacharya', he added, 'signifies control of all the senses
at all times and at all places in thought, word and deed.' It
thus includes yet transcends sexual restraint; it embraces
restraint in diet, emotions and speech. It rules out hate,
anger, violence and untruth. It creates equability. It is
desirelessness.

'Perfect Brahmacharis', Gandhi wrote, 'are perfectly
sinless. They are therefore near to God. They are like God.'
To that he aspired. It was the ultimate in self-transformation.

It is difficult to plumb Gandhi's motives; it was difficult
even for him to know them. Gandhi believed his celibacy was
'a response to the calls of public duty'. On the other hand,
'My main object was to escape having more children.'

But why avoid additional children? Phoenix Farm was one big joint family into which Gandhi invited many adults and children. Their care was a common responsibility and expense. More of his own would not have increased the burden.

Kasturbai was anaemic. She was once near death from internal haemorrhage. A gynaecological operation, performed without chloroform because she was too emaciated, brought relief but no cure.

Brahmacharya is encountered frequently in Indian lore and life. But it is unusual for a married man to take the vow at the early age at which Gandhi adopted it. Kasturbai's health and Hinduism are part of the explanation. 'The sight of women', he admitted in the *Harijan* magazine of 15 June, 1947, 'had ceased to arouse any sexual urge in me in South Africa.' That was a third factor. Perhaps, too, he harked back to his behaviour while his father was dying.

In retrospect, Gandhi naturally did not attribute the chastity vow to his own physiology or to Kasturbai's, nor to his psychology. On the contrary, he identified effect with motive and the effect was spiritual. The chaste life apparently reinforced his passion and determination to sacrifice for the common weal. Less carnal, he became less self-centred. He seemed suddenly lifted above the material. A new inner drive possessed him. Storms continued to rage within, but now he could harness them for the generation of more power.

A new Gandhi faced the South African government.

CHAPTER 10

11 September, 1906

Nearly three thousand persons filled the Imperial Theatre in Johannesburg. The big hall throbbed with the din of voices which spoke the Tamil and Telugu languages of southern India, Gujarati and Hindi. The few women wore saris. The men wore European and Indian clothes; some had Hindu turbans and caps, some Moslem headgear. Among them were rich merchants, miners, lawyers, indentured labourers, waiters, rickshaw boys, domestic servants, hucksters and poor shopkeepers. Many were delegates representing the eighteen thousand Indians of the Transvaal, now a British colony; they were meeting to decide what to do about pending discriminatory enactments against Indians. Abdul Gani, chairman of the Transvaal British-Indian Association and the manager of a big business firm, presided. Sheth Haji Habib delivered the main address. Mohandas K. Gandhi sat on the platform.

Gandhi had convened the meeting. On returning from service to the Zulus, and after acquainting Kasturbai with his celibacy vow, he had rushed off to Johannesburg in answer to a summons from the Indian community. The *Transvaal Government Gazette* of 22 August, 1906, had printed the draft of an ordinance to be submitted to the legislature. If adopted, Gandhi decided, it would spell 'absolute ruin for the Indians of South Africa . . . Better to die than submit to such a law.'

'But how are we to die?' Gandhi wondered. He had no idea what to do. He only knew that the ordinance must be resisted; nowhere in the world, he believed, had free men been subjected to such humiliating, restrictive legislation.

The proposed ordinance required all Indian men and

women, and children over eight, to register with the authorities, submit to finger-printing and accept a certificate which they were to carry with them at all times. A person who failed to register and leave his fingerprints lost his right of residence and could be imprisoned, fined, or deported from the Transvaal. An Indian apprehended on the street or anywhere without certificate could likewise be imprisoned, fined or deported even though he owned valuable property or engaged in important commercial transactions.

The Indians were incensed. This act was specifically against Indians and was therefore an affront to them and to India. If passed it would be the beginning of similar laws in other parts of South Africa; in the end, no Indian could remain in South Africa. Moreover, the ordinance would permit a police officer to accost an Indian woman on the street or enter her home and ask for her registration document. In view of the complete or partial aloofness in which Indian women lived, this feature of the measure was highly offensive both to Moslems and Hindus. 'If anyone came forward to demand a certificate from my wife,' exclaimed an irate Indian at a preliminary committee meeting attended by Gandhi, 'I would shoot him on the spot and take the consequences.'

That was the mood of the mass meeting in the Imperial Theatre.

Orchestra, balcony and gallery were crowded long before the chairman opened the proceedings. Angry speeches in four languages stirred the volatile audience to a high emotional pitch and then Sheth Haji Habib read a resolution, which Gandhi had helped to prepare, demanding non-compliance with the registration provisions. Haji Habib called on the assembly to adopt it, but not in the usual manner. They must vote, he urged, 'with God as their witness'.

Gandhi started. A sensitive ear and a keen intuition quickly told him that this was an extraordinary event. An action with God as witness was a religious vow which could not be broken.

It was not the ordinary motion passed by a show of hands at a public function and immediately forgotten.

Gandhi then spoke. He begged them to consider coolly what they were doing. 'Notwithstanding the differences of nomenclature in Hinduism and Islam,' he declared, 'we all believe in one and the same God. To pledge ourselves or to take an oath in the name of God or with Him as a witness is not something to be trifled with. If having taken such an oath we violate our pledge we are guilty before God and man. Personally, I hold that a man who deliberately and knowingly takes a pledge and breaks it forfeits his manhood . . . A man who lightly pledges his word and then breaks it becomes a man of straw and fits himself for punishment here as well as hereafter.'

Having warned them, he tried to stir them. If ever a crisis in community affairs warranted a vow, now was the time. Caution had its place but also its limits. 'The government has taken leave of all sense of decency. We will be revealing our unworthiness and cowardice if we cannot stake our all in the face of the conflagration that envelops us . . .'

The purpose of the resolution was not to impress the outside world. A vote in favour constituted a personal vow and each one of them had to decide whether he possessed the inner strength to keep it. In consequence of the vow, they might be jailed; in prison they might be beaten and insulted. They might go hungry and be exposed to heat and cold. They might lose their jobs, their wealth. They might be deported. The struggle might last a long time, years. 'But I can boldly declare and with certainty,' Gandhi exclaimed, 'that so long as there is even a handful of men true to their pledge, there can be only one end to the struggle – and that is victory.'

The audience applauded. He lowered his voice. Many in the hall, moved by the enthusiasm and indignation which dominated the meeting, might pledge themselves that evening and repent the next morning or the next month.

Perhaps only a handful would be left to face to final contest with the powerful government. To him it would make no difference. 'There is only one course open to me,' Gandhi asserted, 'to die but not to submit to the law. Even if the unlikely happened and everyone else flinched, leaving me to face the music alone, I am confident that I will never violate my pledge. Please do not misunderstand me. I am not saying this out of vanity. But I wish to put you and especially the leaders on the platform, on your guard . . . If you have not the will or the ability to stand firm even when you are perfectly isolated you must not only not take the pledge but you must declare your opposition before the resolution is put . . . Although we are going to take the pledge in a body, no one may imagine that default on the part of one or of many can absolve the rest from their obligation. Every one must be true to his pledge even unto death, no matter what others do.'

Gandhi sat down. The chairman added his sobering words. Then the vote was taken. Everyone present rose, raised his hand and swore to God not to obey the proposed anti-Indian ordinance if it became law.

The next day, 12 September, the Imperial Theatre was completely destroyed by fire. Many Indians regarded it as an omen that the ordinance would meet a similar fate. To Gandhi it was a coincidence. He did not believe in such omens. Fate did not beckon to Gandhi with mute signs. The future spoke to him through that awesome, Himalayan self-assurance which he displayed at the meeting. He knew he could stand alone.

CHAPTER 11

Gandhi Goes to Jail

There was nothing passive about Gandhi. He disliked the term 'Passive Resistance'. Following the collective vow at the Imperial Theatre, Gandhi offered a prize for a better name for this new kind of mass-yet-individual opposition to government unfairness.

Maganlal Gandhi, a second cousin of Gandhi who lived at Phoenix Farm, suggested 'Sadagraha': 'firmness in a good cause'. Gandhi amended it to 'Satyagraha': *satya* is truth, which equals love and *agraha* is firmness or force. 'Satyagraha', therefore, means truth-force or love-force. Truth and love are attributes of the soul.

This became Gandhi's target: to be strong not with the strength of the brute but with the strength of the spark of God.

Satyagraha, Gandhi said, is 'the vindication of truth not by infliction of suffering on the opponent but on one's self'. That requires self-control. The weapons of the Satyagrahi are within him.

Satyagraha is peaceful. If words fail to convince the adversary perhaps purity, humility and honesty will. The opponent must be 'weaned from error by patience and sympathy', weaned, not crushed; converted, not annihilated.

Satyagraha is the exact opposite of the policy of an-eye-for-an-eye-for-an-eye-for-an-eye which ends in making everybody blind.

You cannot inject new ideas into a man's head by chopping it off; neither will you infuse a new spirit into his heart by piercing it with a dagger.

Acts of violence create bitterness in the survivors and brutality in the destroyers; Satyagraha aims to exalt both sides.

Gandhi hoped that if he practised the Sermon on the Mount, Smuts would recall its precepts. Satyagraha assumes a constant beneficent interaction between contestants with a view to their ultimate reconciliation. Violence, insults and superheated propaganda obstruct this achievement.

Several days after the spiritual baptism in Satyagraha at the Imperial Theatre, the Transvaal government released Asiatic women from the necessity of registration under the 'Black Act'. This may or may not have been a result of the new Indian movement, but Indians felt encouraged by the success of Gandhi's tactics.

Before confronting the Government with Satyagraha, Gandhi thought it desirable to go to London. Transvaal was a Crown Colony; the King could, on advice of his ministers, withhold royal assent from legislation. Accompanied by a Moslem soda water manufacturer named H. O. Ali, Gandhi sailed for England. It was his first visit since his shy law-student days. Now he was the vocal lobbyist. He interviewed Lord Elgin, the Secretary of State for the Colonies and Mr John Morley, Secretary of State for India and, like many champions of causes before and since, addressed a meeting of MPs in a committee room of the House of Commons. It gave Gandhi special pleasure to work with Dadabhai Naoroji, 'The Grand Old Man of India'. Dadabhai, as everybody called him, was president of the London Indian Society for more than fifty years, a teacher of Gujarati in University College, London, a past president of the Indian National Congress Party, and on 6 July, 1892, at the age of sixty-one, was elected to the British Parliament as the Liberal Member for Central Finsbury by a majority of three votes. Before the poll, Lord Salisbury, the British Prime Minister, had said, 'I doubt if we have got to that point of view where a British constituency would elect a black man.' The gibe gave Dadabhai his seat and fame. As a student in the Inner Temple, Gandhi once sat, reverent and silent, at the feet of

Dadabhai. Now, autumn 1906, Gandhi and Dadabhai were associates in a political enterprise.

Throughout the six weeks' sojourn, Englishmen assisted Gandhi in winning friends, arranging meetings, licking stamps, pasting envelopes, etc. Their generous co-operation led him to remark that 'benevolence is by no means peculiar to the brown skin'.

When the ship on which they were returning to South Africa stopped at the Portuguese island of Madeira, Gandhi and Ali received a cable from London announcing that Lord Elgin would not sanction the Transvaal anti-Asiatic bill. In the next two weeks on board ship, Gandhi and Ali were happy: they had won.

It transpired, however, that Lord Elgin had employed a 'trick'. He had told the Transvaal Commissioner in London that the King would disallow the registration ordinance. But since the Transvaal would cease to be a Crown Colony on 1 January, 1907, it could then re-enact the ordinance without royal approval. Gandhi condemned this as a 'crooked policy'.

In due course, Transvaal set up responsible government and adopted the Asiatic Registration Act to go into effect on 31 July, 1907. Indians stigmatized it as the 'Black Act', morally black, aimed at black, brown and yellow men. Gandhi, who was light brown, often referred to himself as 'black'.

Gandhi confidently told the Indian community that 'even a crooked policy would in time turn straight if only we are true to ourselves'. The Indians prepared to offer Satyagraha. Uneasy, Prime Minister Botha sent them a message saying he 'was helpless'; the white population insisted on the legislation. Therefore the Government would be firm.

So would the Indians. One Moslem, Ahmad Mohammed Kachhalia, apparently speaking for many Satyagrahis, said, 'I swear in the name of God that I will be hanged but I will not submit to this law.'

Some Indians took out permits under the Act, but most did not. A number of Indians were accordingly served with official notices to register or leave the Transvaal. Failing to do either, they were brought before a magistrate on 11 January, 1908. Gandhi was among them. He had attended the same court as a lawyer. Now he stood in the dock. Respectfully he told the judge that as leader he merited the heaviest sentence. Judge Jordan unobligingly gave him only two months' simple imprisonment 'without hard labour'.

It was Gandhi's first term in jail.

Gandhi recorded this jail experience in an article printed at the time. The prison authorities were friendly, the meals bad, the cells over-crowded. Gandhi went in with four other Satyagrahis. From notes kept in prison with his customary meticulousness, he knew how many joined them each day and the figures are reproduced in the published account. By 29 January, their number had risen to 155.

Gandhi read the *Gita* in the morning and the *Koran*, in English translation, at noon. He used the Bible to teach English to a Chinese Christian fellow prisoner. He also read Ruskin, Socrates, Tolstoy, Huxley, Bacon's essays and Carlyle's *Lives*. He was happy; he believed that 'whoever has a taste for reading good books is able to bear loneliness in any place with great ease'. Indeed, he seemed to regret that his sentence was so short for he had commenced to do a Gujarati translation of a book by Carlyle and of Ruskin's *Unto This Last*, and: 'I would not have become tired even if I had got more than two months.'

Reading and translating were interrupted by a visitor from the outside; he was Albert Cartwright, editor of the Johannesburg *Transvaal Leader* and a friend of Gandhi; he came as an emissary from General Jan Christian Smuts. Cartwright brought a compromise solution drafted by Smuts.

Smuts's proposal required the Indians to register voluntarily. Then the 'Black Act' would be repealed.

On 30 January, the Johannesburg Chief of Police came to the jail and personally conducted Gandhi to Pretoria for a meeting with Smuts. The prisoner, in prison uniform, and the general had a long talk. Gandhi wanted assurances of the repeal and he stipulated that public mention be made of the Indians' resistance.

Smuts said, 'I could never entertain a dislike for your people. You know I too am a barrister. I had some Indian fellow students in my time. But I must do my duty. The Europeans want this law . . . I accept the alterations you have suggested in the draft. I have consulted General Botha and I assure you that I will repeal the Asiatic Act as soon as most of you have undergone voluntary registration.'

Smuts rose.

'Where am I to go?' Gandhi asked.

'You are free this very moment.'

'What about the other prisoners?' Gandhi asked.

'I am phoning the prison officials to release the other prisoners tomorrow morning.'

It was evening and Gandhi did not have a copper in his pockets. Smuts's secretary gave him the fare to Johannesburg.

In Johannesburg Gandhi encountered stormy opposition. 'Why was not the Act repealed first, before registration?' Indians demanded at a public meeting.

'That would not be in the nature of a compromise,' Gandhi replied.

'What if General Smuts breaks faith with us?' they argued.

'A Satyagrahi,' Gandhi said, 'bids goodbye to fear. He is therefore never afraid of trusting the opponent. Even if the opponent plays him false twenty times, the Satyagrahi is ready to trust him for the twenty-first time – for an implicit trust in human nature is the very essence of his creed.'

Optimism about human nature was the starting post of all Gandhi's activities; it sometimes made him sound naive. His optimism sprang from a belief that 'man can change his temperament, can control it' although he 'cannot eradicate it. God has given him no such liberty'. Change and control, therefore, requires constant effort.

Smuts had made the point that unless Indians in the Transvaal registered, there would be no check on Indian immigration, and the State might be inundated with unwanted Asiatics. Gandhi accepted this and told the public meeting that voluntary registration would indicate that 'we do not intend to bring a single Indian into the Transvaal surreptitiously or by fraud'.

Gandhi took into consideration the pressure on the Government from race-prejudiced whites. Therefore he was ready to accept voluntary registration. But he objected to compulsory registration by statute because a government must treat all citizens equally. He did not want Indians to bow to force: that reduced the dignity and stature of individuals. On the other hand, Gandhi explained to the meeting, collaboration freely given – in view of the opponent's known difficulties – was generous and hence ennobling. Smuts had withdrawn the compulsion from registration; that changed the entire situation.

A giant Pathan from the wild mountains of north-west India near the Khyber Pass stood up and said, 'We have heard that you have betrayed the community and sold it to General Smuts for fifteen thousand pounds. We will never give the fingerprints nor allow others to do so. I swear with Allah as my witness that I will kill the man who takes the lead in applying for registration.'

Gandhi's book on Satyagraha records this charge for posterity. He defended himself against it, and declared, despite the threat, that he would be the first to give his fingerprints. Then he added, 'Death is the appointed end of all life. To die by the hand of a brother, rather than by disease or in such other way, cannot be for me a matter of sorrow. And if, even in such a case, I am free from the thought of anger or hatred against my assailant, I know that that will redound to my eternal welfare, and even the assailant will later on realize my perfect innocence.' The audience listened in silence; it could not have foreseen a nearly fatal assault in the immediate future or the death of Gandhi, forty years later, at the hands of a brother.

Gandhi arranged to register on 10 February, the first to do so. He went to his law office in the morning as usual. Outside he saw a group of big Pathans. Among them was Mir Alam, a client of Gandhi's, six feet tall and of powerful build. Gandhi greeted the Pathans, but their response was ominously cold.

After a little while, Gandhi and several companions left the office and commenced walking to the registration bureau. The Pathans followed close behind. Just before Gandhi had reached his destination, Mir Alam stepped forward and said, 'Where are you going?'

'I propose to take out a certificate of registration,' Gandhi replied.

Before he could finish the explanation a heavy blow struck Gandhi on the top of his head. 'I at once fainted with the words "Hey, Rama" (Oh, God) on my lips,' reads his own account. Those were his last words on 30 January, 1948, the day he died.

Other blows fell on Gandhi as he lay on the ground; and the Pathans kicked him for good measure.

He was carried into an office. When he regained consciousness, the Reverend Joseph J. Doke, a bearded Baptist idealist, was bending over him. 'How do you feel? said Doke.

'I am all right,' Gandhi answered, 'but I have pains in the teeth and ribs. Where is Mir Alam?'

'He has been arrested with the other Pathans,' Doke said.

'They should be released,' Gandhi murmured. 'They thought they were doing right, and I have no desire to prosecute them.'

Gandhi was taken to the Doke home, and the wounds in his cheek and lip were stitched. He asked that Mr Chamney, the Registrar for Asiatics, be brought to him so that he could give his fingerprints without delay. The process hurt Gandhi physically; every movement was painful. Chamney began to weep. 'I had often to write bitterly against him,' Gandhi declared, 'but this showed me how man's heart may be softened by events.'

Gandhi remained under the tender care of the 'godly family' for ten days. Several times, Gandhi, feeling the need of comfort, asked Olive, the little Doke daughter, to sing 'Lead, Kindly Light'. It was one of his favourite Christian hymns.

After recovering, Gandhi indefatigably preached loyalty to his registration settlement. Kasturbai and the boys had worried him after Mir Alam's attack; Gandhi visited them at Phoenix Farm and spent most of the time there writing for *Indian Opinion* in explanation of his compromise with Smuts for voluntary finger-printing. Many Indians followed Gandhi without really agreeing, and he tried to convince them.

What was Gandhi's embarrassment, therefore, when Smuts refused to fulfil his promise to repeal the 'Black Act'? Instead, Smuts offered the legislature a bill which validated the voluntary certificates but kept the compulsory-registration law.

'There you are,' the Indians taunted Gandhi. 'We have been telling you that you are very credulous.'

In a charitable and objective mood two decades later, when *Satyagraha in South Africa* was published, Gandhi asserted, 'It is quite possible that in behaving to the Indians as he did in 1908, General Smuts was not guilty of a deliberate breach of faith.' But in the heat of the battle, in 1908, Gandhi contributed articles to *Indian Opinion* under the caption, 'Foul Play', and called Smuts a 'heartless man'.

The Indian community's temper gradually rose to fever pitch. A meeting was called at the Hamidia Mosque in

Johannesburg for four o'clock in the afternoon, 16 August, 1908. A large iron cauldron resting on four curved legs was placed conspicuously on a raised platform.

The speeches finished, more than two thousand registration certificates collected from the spectators were thrown into the cauldron and burned in paraffin as a mighty cheer went up from the brown throng. The London *Daily Mail* correspondent in Johannesburg compared it with the Boston Tea Party.

The issue between the Indians and the Government was now joined.

Under the Smuts-Gandhi compromise, most of the permanent residents registered voluntarily. Thereafter, any Indian discovered without a registration certificate would be subject to deportation as a new, illegal immigrant. The compromise thus stopped immigration, and that was the original purpose of the 'Black Act'.

Then why did Smuts now reintroduce compulsory registration? 'To insult us,' the Indians said. 'To stress our inequality. To force us to admit our inferiority.'

This, Gandhi declared, is one of the virtues of Satyagraha: it uncovers concealed motives and reveals the truth. It puts the best possible interpretation on the opponent's intentions and thereby gives him another chance to discard baser impulses. If he fails to do so, his victims see more clearly and feel more intensely, while outsiders realize who is wrong.

The Indians now decided not to register under compulsion and to defy the ban on immigration into the Transvaal.

For an impending contest with the government of the Transvaal, Gandhi commenced to muster his resources. His law office at the corner of Rissik and Anderson Streets in Johannesburg had now been converted, largely, into a Satyagraha headquarters. It consisted of two small and meagrely furnished rooms, an outer one for a secretary and an inner one where Gandhi worked amidst photographs of his

ambulance unit, of Mrs Annie Besant, and some Indian
leaders, and a picture of Jesus. Gandhi also had an office at
Phoenix Farm, and he spent more time there than before
because he needed the support of the Natal Indians who far
outnumbered the thirteen thousand of the Transvaal. At the
farm, he led a chaste, frugal, Spartan existence. Except when
it rained he slept in the open on a thin cloth. He eschewed all
material pleasures, and concentrated on the coming battle. 'A
Satyagrahi,' he said, 'has to be, if possible, even more single-
minded than a rope dancer.'

To the Johannesburg office and Phoenix Farm came a
steady stream of Indians and whites. Gandhi's circle of friends
was large; he attracted people and they usually remained
loyal to him.

Olive Schreiner, author of *The Story of an African Farm* and
Dreams, was one of Gandhi's best friends in Cape Colony.
'Love was written in her eyes,' he said. Though she came of a
rich, distinguished and learned family, 'she was so simple in
habits that she cleansed utensils in her house herself' and did
her own cooking and sweeping. 'Such physical labour,'
Gandhi held, 'stimulated her literary ability.' Colour
prejudice was repugnant to her. She lent her great influence
in South Africa to the cause of fairness-to-Indians. So did her
brother, Senator W. P. Schreiner, the Attorney-General and,
at one time, the Prime Minister of the Colony. Other
prominent persons and high officials openly aided Gandhi's
movement. Many Christian clergymen supported him. They
saw Satyagraha as Christianity in action against a system that
merely called itself Christian. Gandhi worked through moral
conversion. He preferred it to physical coercion and even to
moral coercion. No true devotee of Christ could resist this.
Christian editors, idealists and ministers atoned for the white
man's sins by helping the little brown Hindu.

Of all Gandhi's South African collaborators – Indian or
white – the most intimate, he said, were Henry S. L. Polak,

Herman Kallenbach, an extremely wealthy Johannesburg architect, and Sonya Schlesin, who came from Scotland.

Kallenbach was a tall, thick-set, squareheaded German Jew with a long handlebar moustache and pince-nez. He met Gandhi by chance; a mutual interest in Buddhism brought them closer together, and thereafter, until Gandhi returned to India, they were inseparable. If anybody can be called Gandhi's second-in-command of the Satyagraha movement it was Kallenbach. Gandhi characterized him as 'a man of strong feelings, wide sympathies, and child-like simplicity.'

When Gandhi needed a private secretary and typist Kallenbach recommended Miss Schlesin, who was of Russian–Jewish origin. Gandhi thought her 'noble' and the finest person among his European associates. She wore boyish-bobbed hair and a collar and necktie. She never married. Though she was young, Indian leaders went to her for advice, and the Reverend Doke, when he ran *Indian Opinion*, liked her to comment on his editorials. Gandhi put her in charge of Satyagraha's treasury and books.

For the financing of the resistance movement, Indians and Europeans in South Africa and Indians in India contributed considerable sums. Gandhi believed that an organization whose cause is just and impersonal, and which operates in full public view, will not lack money. He likewise believed in rigidly economical spending and scrupulous, detailed accounting.

Suggestions poured in on Gandhi to raise the entire question of Indian disabilities in South Africa and to mobilize the whole Indian community of the continent. But he decided that it was against the principles of Satyagraha to expand or even to shift one's goal in the midst of battle. The issue was the right of Indians to live in and enter the Transvaal, nothing else.

Gandhi now made a move of arresting and dramatic simplicity. A Parsi Indian from Natal named Sorabji

Shapurji Adajania, who spoke English and had never visited the Transvaal, was chosen, at his own request, to test the bar on immigrants. He was to notify the Government of his intentions, present himself at the Transvaal frontier station of Volksrust, and court arrest. But the border authorities let him in and he proceeded unmolested to Johannesburg.

When their astonishment subsided, the Indians interpreted this development as a triumph; the Government had refused to fight. Even when Sorabji was sentenced to a month's imprisonment for not leaving the Transvaal, their enthusiasm for the Gandhi method remained strong. It was accordingly decided that a number of English-speaking Indians in Natal, including Harilal, Gandhi's eldest son, who had returned from India, should enter the Transvaal. They were arrested at Volksrust and given three months in jail. 'The Transvaal Indians', Gandhi comments, 'were now in high spirits . . . The movement was now in full swing.' The movement fed on prison sentences.

Gandhi was besieged by people seeking permission to be arrested. He gratified the wish of. some Natal Indians. Transvaal Indians applied for the same privilege; they had only to tell the police that they had no registration certificates.

Gandhi too was arrested and confined in the Volksrust prison. His prison card has been preserved by Manilal. It is cream-coloured and two and seven-eighths inches wide by three and one-eighth. His name is mistakenly given as 'M. S. Gandhi' instead of M. K. Gandhi. 'Trade: Solicitor.' No alias. 'Sentence and date: Twenty-five pounds or two months. 10 October, 1908.' (Like all other Indians, Gandhi preferred prison to fines.) 'Due for discharge: 13 December, 1908.' On the reverse side, under 'Prison Offences', is a blank. He was a model prisoner.

Gandhi had seventy-five compatriots with him in jail, and he became their cook. 'Thanks to their love for me,' he wrote in a contemporary article, 'my companions took without a murmur the half-cooked porridge I prepared without sugar.' In addition he performed hard labour – digging the earth with a shovel – which blistered his hands. The blisters opened and caused pain.

Once the warden wanted two men to clean the latrines. Gandhi volunteered.

He had brought this suffering on himself and, by his agitation, on others. Would it not be better to pay the fine and stay at home?

'Such thoughts,' Gandhi asserted, 'make one really a coward.' Besides, jail has its good sides: only one warden, whereas in the free life there are many; no worry about food; work keeps the body healthy; no 'vicious habits'; 'the prisoner's soul is thus free' and he has time to pray to God. 'The real road to happiness', Gandhi proclaimed, 'lies in going to jail and undergoing sufferings and privations there in the interest of one's country and religion'.

This account of life and reflections in jail ends with a quotation from Thoreau's famous essay on 'Civil Disobedience' which Gandhi had borrowed from the prison library. 'I saw', Thoreau wrote, 'that if there was a wall of stone between me and my townsmen, there was a still more difficult one to climb or break through before they could get to be as free as I was. I did not feel for a moment confined, and the walls seemed a great waste of stone and mortar . . .

'As they could not reach me,' Thoreau continued, 'they had resolved to punish my body . . . I saw that the state was half-witted, that it was timid as a lone woman with her silver spoons, and that it did not know its friends from its foes, and I lost all my remaining respect for it and pitied it.'

Gandhi cherished this excerpt from Thoreau. He studied the entire essay.

It has often been said that Gandhi took the idea of Satyagraha from Thoreau. Gandhi denied this in a letter, dated 10 September, 1935, and addressed to Mr P. Kodanda

Rao of the Servants of India Society; Gandhi wrote, 'The statement that I had derived my idea of Civil Disobedience from the writings of Thoreau is wrong. The resistance to authority in South Africa was well advanced before I got the essay of Thoreau on Civil Disobedience. But the movement was then known as passive resistance. As it was incomplete I had coined the word Satyagraha for the Gujarati readers. When I saw the title of Thoreau's great essay, I began to use his phrase to explain our struggle to the English readers. But I found that even "Civil Disobedience" failed to convey the full meaning of the struggle. I therefore adopted the phrase Civil Resistance.'

Nevertheless, Thoreau's 'Civil Disobedience' essay did influence Gandhi; he called it a 'masterly treatise'; 'it left a deep impression on me,' he affirmed. There is the imprint of Thoreau on much that Gandhi did. Thoreau had read the *Bhagavad Gita* and some of the sacred Hindu *Upanishads*; so had Ralph Waldo Emerson who was Thoreau's friend and frequent host. Thoreau, the New England rebel, borrowed from distant India and repaid the debt by throwing ideas into the world pool of thought; ripples reached the Indian lawyer–politician in South Africa.

Henry David Thoreau, poet and essayist, was born in 1817 and died of tuberculosis at the age of forty-five. He hated Negro slavery and the individual's slavery to the Church, the State, property, customs and traditions. With his own hands he built himself a hut at Walden Pond outside Concord, Massachusetts, and dwelt there alone, doing all the work, growing his food and enjoying full contact with nature.

Two years at Walden proved to Thoreau's own satisfaction that he had the courage and inner strength to be free in isolation. He accordingly returned to Concord to discover whether he could be free inside the community. He decided that the least he could do was 'not lend myself to the wrong which I condemn'. So he refused to pay taxes and was imprisoned. A friend paid the tax for him, and Thoreau came out after twenty-four hours, but the experience evoked his most provoking political essay, 'Civil Disobedience'.

'The only obligation which I have a right to assume', Thoreau declared in 'Civil Disobedience', 'is to do at any time what I think right.' To be right, he insisted, is more honourable than to be law-abiding.

Thoreau democracy was the cult of the minority. 'Why does [the Government] not cherish its wise minority?' he cried. 'Why does it always crucify Christ?'

It was 1849. Thoreau was thinking of Negro slavery and the invasion of Mexico. The majority which tolerated these measures was wrong, and he was right. Could he obey a government that committed such sins? He held that dissent without disobedience was consent and therefore culpable.

Thoreau described civil disobedience in exact terms, as Gandhi understood it: 'I know this well,' Thoreau wrote, 'that if one thousand, if one hundred, if ten men whom I could name – if ten *honest* men only – ay, if one HONEST man, in this state of Massachusetts, *ceasing to hold slaves*, were actually to withdraw from this copartnership, and be locked up in the county jail therefore, it would be the abolition of slavery in America. For it matters not how small the beginning may be: what is once well done is done forever. But we love better to talk about it . . .

'There are thousands who are *in opinion* opposed to slavery and war, who yet in effect do nothing to put an end to them,' Thoreau continued. 'There are nine hundred and ninety-nine patrons of virtue to every virtuous man.' Thoreau despised professions without actions. He asked, 'How does it become a man to behave towards this American government today? I answer, that he cannot without disgrace be associated with it.' His programme was 'peaceful revolution'. 'All men recognize the right to revolution,' he wrote, 'that is, the right to refuse allegiance to, and to resist, the government when its tyranny and efficiency are great and unendurable.'

This is why Gandhi was in jail at the very moment he read 'Civil Disobedience'.

Like Ruskin, Thoreau sought a closer correspondence between man's acts and man's goal. The artist in both required the integration of word and faith with deed. The great poet, the great artist has integrity.

Millions had read Ruskin and Thoreau and agreed with them. Many Hindus had read them and agreed with them. But Gandhi took words and ideas seriously, and when he accepted an idea in principle he felt that not to practise it was dishonest. How can you believe in a moral or religious precept and not live it?

The gulf between word and belief is untruth. The dissonance between creed and deed is the root of innumerable wrongs in our civilization; it is the weakness of all churches, states, parties, and persons. It gives institutions and men split personalities.

In attempting to establish harmony between words, beliefs and acts Gandhi was attacking man's central problem. He was seeking the formula for mental health.

CHAPTER 12

Letter to a Son

Gandhi's second sentence ended on 13 December, 1908, but, since civil resistance against the immigration ban continued, he received a third three-month sentence and was back in Volksrust prison on 25 February, 1909. Five days later, carrying a few possessions on his head and walking in heavy rain, he was escorted to a train for Pretoria where he sat out his term in the newly built local penetentiary. On arriving, the warden said, 'Are you the son of Gandhi?' He apparently looked so youthful that the official mistook him for his son Harilal who was serving a six-month period in Volksrust. Gandhi was forty.

In jail Gandhi received a gift of two religious books from General Smuts; he also read Stevenson's *Dr Jekyll and Mr Hyde*, Carlyle's *French Revolution*, and many Indian religious volumes. 'My books saved me,' he wrote in his reminiscences.

From prison, Gandhi sent a letter to Manilal who has preserved it to this day. It was written by hand, with purple indelible ink pencil, on both sides of five long cream-coloured foolscap sheets of prison stationery and is in English. Normally, Gandhi would have addressed Manilal in Gujarati, but printed instructions in the left-hand margin of each page say, in English, Dutch and Kaffir, that correspondence must be conducted in English, Dutch, German, French and Kaffir. The letter is dated 25 March, 1909; Gandhi's number was 777; the censor initialled it two days later.

Manilal was seventeen and, since nobody else worried, he worried about his profession and future. He had had practically no formal education. Now he was his father's

agent on the farm and in *Indian Opinion*, and probably a very
harassed young man.

My dear son [Gandhi began], I have a right to write one letter
per month and receive also one letter per month. It became a
question with me as to whom I should write to. I thought of
Mr Ritch [the editor of *Indian Opinion*], Mr Polak and you. I
chose you because you have been nearest my thoughts in all
my reading.

As for myself I must not, I am not allowed to say much. I am
quite at peace & none need worry about me.

I hope mother is now quite well. I know several letters from
you have been received but they have not been given to me.
The Deputy Governor however was good enough to tell me
that she was getting on well. Does she walk about freely? I
hope she and all of you would continue to take sago & milk in
the morning.

And how is Chanchi? [The nickname of Harilal's wife,
Gulab.] Tell her I think of her every day. I hope she has got
rid of all the sores she had and that she & Rami [Harilal's little
daughter] are quite well.

I hope Ramdas and Devadas are keeping well, learning their
lessons and not causing any worry. Has Ramdas got rid of his
cough?

I hope you all treated Willie well while he was with you. Any
balance of the food stuff left by Mr Cordes I should wish you
have returned to him.

And now about yourself. How are you? Although I think that
you are well able to bear the burden I have placed on your
shoulders and that you are doing it quite cheerfully, I have
often felt that you required greater personal guidance than I
have been able to give you. I know too that you have
sometimes felt that your education was being neglected. Now
I have read a great deal in prison. I have been reading
Emerson, Ruskin and Mazzini. I have also been reading the

Upanishads. All confirm the view that education does not mean a knowledge of letters but it means character building. It means a knowledge of duty. Our own [Gujarati] word literally means training. If this is the true view, and it is to my mind the only true view, you are receiving the best education-training possible. What can be better than that you should have the opportunity of nursing mother & cheerfully bearing her ill temper, or than looking after Chanchi & anticipating her wants and behaving to her so as not to make her feel the absence of Harilal or again than being guardian to Ramdas and Devadas? If you succeed in doing this well, you have received more than half your education.

I was much struck by one passage in Nathuramji's introduction to the *Upanishads.* He says that the Brahma-charya stage – ie, the first stage, is like the last, ie the sanyasin [monk] stage. This is true. Amusement only continues during the age of innocence, ie, up to twelve years only. As soon as a boy reaches the age of discretion, he is taught to realize his responsibilities. Every boy from such age onward should practice continence in thought & deed, truth likewise and the not-taking of any life. This to him must not be an irksome learning and practice but it should be natural to him. It should be his enjoyment. I can recall to my mind several such boys in Rajkot. Let me tell you that when I was younger than you are my keenest enjoyment was to nurse my father. Of amusement after I was twelve, I had little or none. If you practise the three virtues, if they become part of your life, so far as I am concerned you will have completed your education – your training. Armed with them, believe me you will earn your bread in any part of the world & you will have paved the way to acquire a true knowledge of the soul, yourself and God. This does not mean that you shd not receive instruction in letters. That you shd & you are doing. But it is a thing over which you need not fret yourself. You have plenty of time for it and after all you are to receive such instruction in order that your training may be of use to others.

Remember please that henceforth our lot is poverty. The more I think of it the more I feel it is more blessed to be poor than to be rich. The uses of poverty are far sweeter than those of riches.

There follow one hundred and five lines of instructions, messages, and greetings to persons at Phoenix Farm, then,

And now again yourself. Do give ample work to gardening, actual digging, hoeing, etc. We have to live upon it in future. And you shd be the expert gardener of the family. Keep your tools in their respective places and absolutely clean. In your lessons you shd give a great deal of attention to mathematics and Sanskrit. The latter is absolutely necessary for you. Both these studies are difficult in after life. You will not neglect your music. You shd make a selection of all good passages, hymns, verses, whether in English, Gujarati or Hindi and write them out in your best hand in a book. The collection at the end of a year will be most valuable. All these things you can do easily if you are methodical. Never get agitated and think you have too much to do and then worry over what to do first. This you will find out in practice if you are patient and take care of your minutes. I hope you are keeping an accurate account as it should be kept of every penny spent for the household.

The next paragraph is for a student at the farm. Continuing, Gandhi writes:

Please tell Maganlalbhai that I would advise him to read Emerson's essays. They can be had for nine pence in Durham. There is a cheap reprint out. These essays are worth studying. He shd read them, mark the important passages and then finally copy them out in a notebook. The essays to my mind contain the teaching of Indian wisdom in a western guru. It is interesting to see our own sometimes thus differently fashioned. He should also try to read Tolstoy's *Kingdom of God is Within You*. It is a most logical book. The English of the translation is very simple. What is more Tolstoy practises what he preaches.

Gandhi told Manilal to make copies of this letter and send one to Polak, another to Kallenbach, and a third to a swami who had left for India. He was to wait for Polak's and Kallenbach's replies and incorporate them into his own which, however, 'should not contain any information about the struggle'. The censor did not allow that.

In the last breath Gandhi asked for 'a copy of algebra. Any edition will do'.

And now I close with love to all and kisses to Ramdas, Devadas & Rami.

> from
> > Father.

Solicitude in the writer may be irritation to the recipient. Gandhi's warm and tender concern to mould Manilal into his own image probably sounded like a sermon interlarded with countless obnoxious chores. Gandhi's selfless injunctions were for his son's good, but the prospect of chastity, poverty and hard work under a strict taskmaster who wanted the tools stacked neatly in the storeroom offered few thrills to the young man on the threshold of life.

Married at thirteen, Gandhi never had a boyhood and therefore never understood his own boys. The letter to Manilal showed this. As a blueprint of the future it had the virtue of truth, but the truth was forbidding. The fact that his father had not enjoyed life from the age of twelve would have saddened a sensitive son or, indeed, frightened him. Such a father is difficult to live with. Such a father writes such a letter. The letter said, in effect, 'Your life will remain tied to mine; you cannot go your own way.' Gandhi wanted a helper; Manilal wanted freedom. He thought of becoming a lawyer or doctor. His father was training him to be a minor saint.

Eyes fixed on a distant, glorious goal, Gandhi, at this stage, sometimes failed to see those who were nearest. He expected them to meet the exacting standards he cheerfully imposed on himself. But he was not cruel; very likely, it never occurred to him that his letter conveyed anything but deep love and paternal care.

CHAPTER 13

Tolstoy and Gandhi

In central Russia, a Slav aristocrat grappled with the same spiritual problems that occupied the Hindu lawyer in South Africa. Across continents, Count Leo Tolstoy guided Mohandas K. Gandhi and found solace in his struggle.

In Gandhi's law office there were several books by Tolstoy on religious subjects. But it was only during the leisure of jail that the Indian absorbed the great Russian's teachings.

War and Peace, probably the world's greatest novel, *Resurrection, Anna Karenina*, and other works of art brought Tolstoy colossal success and universal recognition. But his soul was always in torment. The discrepancy between Christ's message and man's way of life troubled him. Born in 1828 to wealth and an ancient title, Tolstoy abandoned high society and, at the age of fifty-seven, adopted the simple life: he went barefoot, wore a plain muzhik smock and trousers, ploughed, harrowed and planted by the side of the peasants, gave up smoking, meat-eating and hunting, and began to take long cross-country walks and bicycle rides. In 1891, in order to escape from 'intolerable luxury', he gave his ample properties to his wife and children and devoted himself to village education, famine relief and writing about vegetarianism, marriage and theology. Though he excoriated church institutions, men and women in search of a faith made his home at Yasnaya Polyana their Mecca; Christians, Jews, Moslems and Buddhists from the four corners of the earth came to sit at the feet of the famous, brilliant nobleman who had drunk his fill of material pleasures and now, nearing seventy, sought God. Among his guests from abroad were Jane Addams, of Hull House, Chicago; William Jennings

Bryan, subsequently United States Secretary of State; Rabbi Joseph Krauskopf of Philadelphia; George Kennan, an American publicist who visited Siberia with the permission of the Tsarist authorities and then denounced their cruelty to prisoners; Rainer-Maria Rilke, the German poet, and Thomas G. Masaryk, later President of Czechoslovakia.

To these pilgrims, Tolstoy was the strong one who had renounced. His attraction was his attempt to create, in his own way of life, a synthesis between creed and conduct. This involved manual labour, minimum needs, no holding of property, no killing. He called landlordism 'a great sin', extolled Henry George's Single Tax, condemned military conscription, defended conscientious objectors, helped the pacifist Dukhobors to emigrate to Canada, denounced the pogromists of Kishenev, praised William Lloyd Garrison's 'non-resistance', taught in a village primary school and refused the Nobel Prize because he did not accept money.

The Orthodox Church of Russia excommunicated him.

To a friend in prison Tolstoy wrote, 'Unfortunately, I am not in prison . . .'

The titles of his tracts reveal his mind: *Thou Shalt Kill No One*, *Love One Another*, *Why Christian People in General and the Russian People Especially Fall into Distress*, *The Teachings of Christ for Children*, *Capital Punishment and Christianity*, *Religious Tolerance*, *Self-Perfection*, and many more like these.

Tolstoy died on 20 November, 1910, after fleeing from his wife in the hope of finding peace in a monastery or a Tolstoyan settlement.

Gandhi came to know Tolstoy through *The Kingdom of God Is Within You*. The name of the volume is the gospel of its author.

'The history of the church', Tolstoy bluntly affirmed, 'is the history of cruelties and horror . . . Every Church, with its doctrines of redemption and salvation, and above all the Orthodox faith with its idolatry, excludes the doctrine of

Christ.' Impartially, and with icy logic and myriad quotations, Tolstoy proved to his own satisfaction that all Christian churches try 'to conceal the true meaning of the doctrine of Christ'.

Tolstoy was equally critical of governments. From the dimmest ages, he declared, 'Peace unto you' has been man's greeting to man, yet in Europe Christian nations keep twenty-eight million men under arms to settle problems by killing. Approvingly he quoted Guy de Maupassant, the French writer: 'It is stupefying that society does not revolt as a unit against the very sound of the word "War".'

Alexander Herzen, Russia's greatest literary critic, has said that mounting militarism made every modern government 'a Genghis Khan with telegraphic equipment'. Tolstoy concurred and added, 'In the matter of oppression, the Christian nations are worse than the pagans.'

'I believe it is Max Mueller [foremost authority on Asia],' Tolstoy recalled, 'who describes the astonishment of an Indian converted to Christianity who, having learned the essence of Christian doctrine, came to Europe and beheld the life of Christians.' This was Tolstoy's, as it was Thoreau's, perpetual theme: the chasm between doctrine and doing.

What to do? Tolstoy's answer was simple: Live as a Christian should. Concretely, 'A Christian enters into no dispute with his neighbour, he neither attacks nor uses violence; on the contrary, he suffers himself, without resistance, and by his very attitude towards evil not only sets himself free, but helps to free the world at large from all outward authority.'

The *Gita* and the Sermon on the Mount had led Gandhi to the same conclusion.

Tolstoy preached peaceful, painful refusal to serve or obey evil governments. He specified: no oath of allegiance, no oath in court 'for an oath is distinctly forbidden by the Gospel', no police duty, no military duty, no payment of taxes.

'What are governments to do with these men?' Tolstoy inquired.

That became Smuts's problem. He did not know what to do with the Indians. 'The position of governments in the presence of men who profess Christianity', Tolstoy wrote, 'is so precarious that very little is needed to shake their power to pieces.' Thoreau said the same thing.

Gandhi began by freeing himself. It was an involved process. For man is bound by many chains, and the stoutest are forged in the inner smithy, not by Church or State. 'The Kingdom of God is within you.' You are what you make yourself. You are not free because you do not free yourself.

'The Kingdom of God,' Tolstoy wrote, 'is attained by . . . sacrificing outward circumstances for the sake of truth.'

Gandhi's path was strewn with the outward possessions and pleasures which he cast off en route to the kingdom of God within him.

Gandhi's first personal contact with Tolstoy was in the form of a long letter, written in English, dated 'Westminster Palace Hotel, 4 Victoria Street, SW, London, 1 October, 1909', and sent from there to Tolstoy at Yasnaya Polyana, in central Russia. In it, he acquainted the Russian novelist with the civil disobedience movement in the Transvaal.

In Tolstoy's diary entry for 24 September, 1909 (the Russian calendar was then thirteen days behind the Western calendar), he wrote, 'Received a pleasant letter from a Hindu of the Transvaal.' Four days later, Tolstoy wrote a letter to Vladimir G. Chertkov, his intimate friend and, later, the editor of his collected works, saying, 'The letter of the Transvaal Hindu has touched me.'

Dating his letter from Yasnaya Polyana, 7 October (20th), 1909, Tolstoy wrote a reply to Gandhi in Russian. The Russian text was translated into English by Tolstoy's daughter, Tatiana, who sent it to Gandhi. Tolstoy wrote, 'I have just received your most interesting letter, which has given me great pleasure. God help our dear brothers and co-workers in the Transvaal. The same struggle of the soft against the harsh, of meekness and love against pride and violence, is making itself felt every year more and more among us here . . . I greet you fraternally and am happy to have contact with you. (signed) Tolstoy.'

Gandhi's second letter to Tolstoy was written in Johannesburg on 4 April, 1910, and was accompanied by a copy of Gandhi's little book, *Hind Swaraj or Indian Home Rule*. In the letter Gandhi said, 'As a humble follower of yours, I send you herewith a booklet which I have written. It is my own [English] translation of a Gujarati writing . . . I am most anxious not to worry you, but if your health permits it, and if you could find the time to go through the booklet, needless to say I shall value very highly your criticism of the writing.'

On 19 April, 1910, Tolstoy wrote as follows in his diary: 'This morning two Japanese arrived. Wild men in ecstasy over European civilization. On the other hand, the book and the letter of the Hindu reveal an understanding of all the shortcomings of European civilization and even of its total inadequacy.'

Next day there was another entry in Tolstoy's diary: 'Yesterday I read Gandhi on civilization. Very good.' And again the next day: 'Read a book about Gandhi. Very important. I must write to him.' The book about Gandhi was the *Biography of Gandhi* by J. J. Doke, which Gandhi had sent to Tolstoy.

A day later, Tolstoy wrote a letter to his friend Chertkov in which he referred to Gandhi as 'a person very close to us, to me'.

Tolstoy replied to Gandhi on 25 April (8 May), 1910, from Yasnaya Polyana. He wrote:

Dear Friend: I just received your letter and your book, *Indian Home Rule*. I read your book with great interest because of the things and questions you treat in it: passive resistance is a question of the greatest importance, not only for India, but for the whole of humanity.

I cannot find your former letter, but came across your biography by J. Doss [this is a mistake made by Tolstoy] which too interested me much and gave me the possibility to know and understand your letter. I am not quite well at present and therefore abstain from writing to you all what I have to say about your book and all your work, which I appreciate very much, but I will do it as soon as I will feel better. Your friend and brother, L. Tolstoy.

This was the English translation, sent to Gandhi, of Tolstoy's perfect Russian.

Gandhi's third letter to Tolstoy is dated '21–24 Court Chambers, corner Rissik and Anderson Streets, Johannesburg, 15 August, 1910'. In it Gandhi acknowledged Tolstoy's letter of 8 May, with thanks, and added: 'I shall look forward to your detailed criticism of the work which you have been so good as to promise in your letter.' Gandhi also informed Tolstoy of the establishment of Tolstoy Farm by Kallenbach and himself. He said that Kallenbach was writing to Tolstoy about the farm. The letters of Gandhi and Kallenbach, accompanied by several issues of Gandhi's weekly, *Indian Opinion*, heightened Tolstoy's interest in Gandhi. In his diary of 6 September (19th), 1910, Tolstoy wrote, 'Pleasant news from Transvaal about the passive resistance colony.' Tolstoy was at this time in a state of serious spiritual depression and physically ill. Nevertheless, he replied to Gandhi's letter on the day he received it. Tolstoy dicatated the letter on the evenings of the 5th and 6th of September (18th and 19th). On the 7th (20th), Tolstoy corrected the letter and sent it in Russian to Chertkov for English translation.

It was Chertkov who posted Tolstoy's letter to Gandhi. Chertkov included in the letter a letter of his own in which he said:

My friend, Leo Tolstoy, has requested me to acknowledge the receipt of your letter to him of 15 August and to translate into English his letter to you of 7 September (new style – 20 September) written originally in Russian.

All you communicate about Mr Kallenbach has greatly interested Tolstoy, who has asked me to answer for him Mr Kallenbach's letter. Tolstoy sends you and your co-workers his heartiest greetings and warmest wishes for the success of your work, his appreciation of which you will gather from the enclosed translation of his letter to you. I must apologize for my mistakes in English in the translation, but living in the country in Russia, I am unable to profit by the assistance of any Englishman for correcting my mistakes.

With Tolstoy's permission his letter to you will be published in a small periodical printed by some friends of ours in London. A copy of the magazine with the letter shall be forwarded to you, as also some English publications of Tolstoy's writings issued by 'The Free Age Press'.

As it seems to me most desirable that more should be known in English about your movement, I am writing to a great friend of mine and Tolstoy, Mrs Mayo, of Glasgow, proposing that she should enter into communication with you . . .

Chertkov sent a separate letter to Mr Kallenbach.

Tolstoy's own letter to Gandhi was the longest in the whole correspondence. Dated 7 September (20th), 1910, and translated into English by Chertkov, it was sent to an intermediary in England for posting to Gandhi. The intermediary was ill at the time and only posted the letter on 1 November, so that Gandhi received the letter in the Transvaal several days after the death of Count Leo Tolstoy.

Tolstoy said:

The longer I live, and especially now when I vividly feel the nearness of death, I want to tell others what I feel so particularly clearly and what to my mind is of great importance – namely, that which is called passive resistance, but which in reality is nothing else than the teaching of love, uncorrupted by false interpretations.

That love . . . is the highest and only law of human life and in the depths of his soul every human being (as we see most clearly in children) feels and knows this; he knows this until he is tangled by the false teachings of the world. This law was proclaimed by all, by the Indian as well as by the Chinese, Hebrew, Greek and Roman sages of the world . . .

In reality, as soon as force was admitted into love, there was no more and there could be no more love as the law of life, and as there was no law of love, there was no law at all, except violence – ie the power of the strongest. Thus Christian mankind has lived for nineteen centuries . . .

This was a very old man on the brink of death writing to a very young man; Gandhi was young, usually twenty-five years younger in spirit than his age. Tolstoy was profoundly unhappy. Anyone with the insight of *War and Peace* yet conscious of humanity's refusal, or inability, to use the key to happiness available in Christ's teachings would have to be unhappy. Gandhi, however, believed he could reform himself and others. He was doing it. It made him happy.

CHAPTER 14

The Shape of Things to Come

Gandhi never despaired of the worst reprobate. During the South African struggle, Gandhi learned that one of his close Indian associates was a government informer. Later the man openly opposed Gandhi, yet when he became ill and impecunious Gandhi visited him and gave him financial aid. In time, the backslider repented.

It was not easy for Gandhi to hold his followers. Government punitive measures caused many Satyagrahis to abandon the movement. Some resisters were deported to India with loss of property. Satyagraha put even the strongest character to a withering test. At one time, of the thirteen thousand Indians in the Transvaal, twenty-five hundred were in jail and six thousand had fled the province. Only as self-abnegating, high-minded, determined and indefatigable a leader as Gandhi could have kept the movement alive. The worst setbacks did not shake his faith in victory. This faith, plus the fact that in and out of jail he shared his followers' hardships and thereby won their love, was the binding cement of the loyal band which at times dwindled alarmingly. Some resisters served five prison terms in quick succession, courting a new sentence the moment they finished the old one. They merely left the Transvaal for Natal and immediately crossed into the Transvaal again. That, under the immigration ban, was their crime.

Presently, a bigger danger loomed: a federal Union of South Africa was projected; it might, probably would, enact anti-Indian legislation like that of the Transvaal. Gandhi decided to lobby in London. Generals Botha and Smuts were already there making arrangements for the creation of the Union.

Gandhi always set his sights high. This time he won the active support of Lord Ampthill, former Governor of Madras and acting Viceroy of India in 1904. From his arrival in England on 10 July, 1909, until his return to South Africa in November, Gandhi met editors, MPs, officials and private citizens of all races; his fervour fascinated and infected many of them.

Liberal Englishmen regretted overt colour discrimination in an empire overwhelmingly non-white. Imperialistic Englishmen were concerned with the effects of South African and anti-Indian legislation on India. While Gandhi worked in England, Henry Polak was in India explaining the Transvaal situation and stirring protests which echoed in Whitehall. The British government in London tried to reconcile the differences between Smuts and Gandhi; but the general yielded too little. Smuts was ready to repeal the compulsory registration act and permit the immigration into the Transvaal of a limited number of English-speaking, educated, professional Indians to serve the Indian community.

Gandhi, however, asked for the removal of the 'badge of inferiority' and the 'implied racial taint'; he wanted 'legal or theoretical equality in respect of immigration'. Small material concessions neither impressed nor mollified him. When, therefore, Lord Crewe, the British Secretary of State for the Colonies, informed Gandhi in writing that 'Mr Smuts was unable to accept the claim that Asiatics should be placed in a position of equality with Europeans in respect of right of entry or otherwise', the militant barrister, admitting defeat in diplomatic negotiation, foresaw a renewal of civil disobedience.

Gandhi's trip to England nevertheless made the South African Indian question a major imperial concern. Therein lay a seed of ultimate triumph in South Africa.

Moreover, and apparently for the first time, Gandhi began, during his London sojourn, to connect himself with the problem of India's independence. In England he sought out Indians of all shades of political belief: nationalists, Home-Rulers, anarchists and advocates of assassination. While he debated with them far into many nights, his own political views and philosophy were taking shape. Some of the tenets which later formed the tissue of the Mahatma's creed found their first expression in a letter addressed to Lord Ampthill by Gandhi on 9 October, 1909, from Westminster Palace Hotel.

Judging by the Indians in England, Gandhi wrote, impatience with British rule was widespread in India as was Indian hatred of the British. Partisans of violence were gaining ground. Against this, repression would be futile. Yet he feared that 'the British rulers will not give liberally and in time. The British people seem to be obsessed by the demon of commercial selfishness. The fault is not of men but of the system . . . India is exploited in the interests of foreign capitalists. The true remedy lies, in my humble opinion, in England discarding modern civilization . . . which is a negation of the spirit of Christianity'. One hears Tolstoy's gentle voice here and echoes, too, of the raucous voices of Indian students in Bloomsbury.

'But this is a large order,' Gandhi admits. 'The railways, machineries and the corresponding increase of indulgent habits are the true badge of slavery of the Indian people, as they are of Europeans. I therefore have no quarrel with the rulers. I have every quarrel with their methods . . . To me the rise of cities like Calcutta and Bombay is a matter of sorrow rather than congratulations. India has lost in having broken up a part of her village system.

'Holding these views,' Gandhi continues, prophetically though unconsciously enunciating the programme of his entire career in India, 'I share the National spirit, but I totally dissent from the methods, whether of the extremists or of the moderates, for either party relies on violence ultimately. Violent methods must mean an acceptance of modern civilization and therefore of the same ruinous competition we notice here and the consequent destruction of morality. I should be uninterested in the fact as to who rules. I should expect rulers to rule according to my wish, otherwise I cease to help them to rule me. I become a passive resister against them.'

Long before Gandhi had any warrant to regard himself as a factor or leader in the liberation of India he knew, and indicated in this letter to Ampthill, that his aim was not merely substitution of Indian rule for British rule. Not governments but methods and objectives interested him, not whether a William or a Chandra sat in the seat of power but whose deeds were more civilized.

This is what distinguished Gandhi from other politicians. The argument – Was Gandhi a saint or politician? – is endless yet barren. Polak quotes Gandhi as having said in South Africa, 'Men say I am a saint losing myself in politics. The fact is that I am a politican trying my hardest to be a saint.' The important fact is that in politics Gandhi always cleaved to religious and moral considerations, and as a saint he never thought his place was in a cave or cloister but rather in the hurly-burly of the popular struggle for rights and right. Gandhi's religion cannot be divorced from his politics. His religion made him political. His politics were religious.

When Gandhi returned from England to South Africa at the end of 1909, political necessity forced him to establish 'a sort of co-operative commonwealth' on a diminutive scale where civil resisters 'would be trained to live a new and simple life in harmony with one another'. There he took further steps towards sainthood, mahatma-ship, and *Gita* detachment.

Previously, when Satyagrahis were imprisoned, the organization attempted to support their dependants in their accustomed style of living. This led to inequality and sometimes to fraud. Gandhi consequently decided that the movement needed a rural commune for civil resisters and their families. Phoenix Farm was thirty hours by train and hence too remote from the epicentre of the Transvaal struggle.

Accordingly, Herman Kallenbach bought 1,100 acres of land at Lawley, twenty-one miles outside Johannesburg and, on 30 May, 1910, gave it to the Satyagrahis free of any rent or charge. Here religion was wed to politics. Gandhi called it The Tolstoy Farm.

The farm had over a thousand orange, apricot and plum trees, two wells, a spring and one house. Additional houses were built of corrugated iron. Gandhi and his family came to live on the farm and so did Kallenbach.

'I prepare the bread that is required on the farm,' Gandhi wrote to a friend in India. 'The general opinion about it is that it is well made. We put in no yeast and no baking powder. We grind our own wheat. We have just prepared some marmalade from the oranges grown on the farm. I have also learned how to prepare caramel coffee. It can be given as a beverage even to babies. The passive resisters on the farm have given up the use of tea and coffee, and taken to caramel coffee prepared on the farm. It is made from wheat which is first baked in a certain way and then ground. We intend to sell our surplus production of the above three articles to the public later on. Just at present, we are working as labourers on the construction work . . .' There were no servants.

Gandhi was baker and caramel and marmalade maker and much more besides. Kallenbach went to stay in a Trappist monastery for German Catholic monks to master the art of sandal making. This he then taught to Gandhi who taught it to others. Surplus sandals were sold to friends. As an architect, Kallenbach knew something of carpentry and headed that department. Gandhi learned to make cabinets, chests of drawers and school benches. But they had no chairs and no beds; everybody slept on the ground and, except in inclement weather, in the open. Each person got two blankets and a wooden pillow. Gandhi likewise sewed jackets for his wife and he later boasted that she wore them.

Gandhi was general manager. The population of the farm, which varied with arrests and other circumstances, consisted originally of forty young men, three old men, five women and between twenty and thirty children, of whom five were girls. There were Hindus, Moslems, Christians and Parsis among them, vegetarians and meat-eaters, smokers and non-smokers and they spoke Tamil, Telugu, Gujarati, etc. As if these conditions did not create enough problems, Gandhi created some more.

Smoking and alcohol drinking were strictly prohibited. Residents could have meat if they wished but, after a little propaganda from the general manager, none ever asked for it. Gandhi assisted in the cookhouse and kept the women there from quarrelling.

He also supervised the sanitation, which was primitive, and taught people not to spit. 'Leaving nightsoil, cleaning the nose, or spitting on the road is a sin against God and humanity,' he told the community.

Occasionally, Kallenbach had business in town and Gandhi still had legal cases. The rule was that if you went on an errand or shopping trip for the commune you could travel by train, third class; but if the journey was private or for fun (children liked to go on picnics to Johannesburg) you had to walk and, for economy, take dry refreshments with you. Gandhi frequently walked the twenty-one miles to the city, starting at 2 A.M. and returning the same night. He said it did them all a lot of good. One day, he recalls, 'I walked fifty miles on foot.'

Gandhi attributed his physical stamina and that of the other communards to pure living and healthy diet. Breakfast was at 7, lunch at 11, dinner at 5.30, prayers at 7.30, bedtime at 9. All meals were light. But to make them lighter still, Gandhi and Kallenbach resolved to avoid cooked food and limit themselves to a 'fruitarian' menu of bananas, dates, lemons, peanuts, oranges and olive oil. Gandhi had read somewhere of the cruelties practised in India to make cows and water buffalo yield the maximum in milk. So he and Kallenbach dispensed with milk. Kallenbach, who owned a beautiful and spacious house on a hilltop above Johannesburg and who always had lived in luxury, shared every deprivation, chore and dietary experiment on the farm. He also divided with Gandhi the task of teaching the children religion, geography, history, arithmetic, etc, and very rudimentary it all was.

Gandhi's ideas on co-education were unconventional. He encouraged boys and girls, some of them adolescents, to bathe at the spring at the same time. For the girls' safety, he was always present and 'My eyes followed the girls as a mother's eye follows a daughter.' No doubt, the boys' eyes did likewise and less innocently. At night, everybody slept on an open veranda and the young folks grouped their sleeping places around Gandhi. Beds were only three feet apart. But Gandhi said the young folks knew he loved them 'with a mother's love', and hadn't he explained the duty of self-restraint to them?

After an incident involving two girls, he searched for a method 'to sterilize the sinner's eye' of males. The quest kept him awake all night, but in the morning he had it: he summoned the girls and suggested that they shave their heads. They were shocked, but he had an irresistible way and finally they consented. He himself did the cutting.

Years later, Gandhi explained this innocence by ignorance, but he did not explain why he should have been ignorant. He dispelled some of the mystery by adding that his 'faith and courage were at their highest in Tolstoy Farm'. Boundless

faith in human beings sometimes blinded him to their faults.
It was the sort of blindness which blots out obstacles and thus
leads to brave ventures. He measured other people's
capacities by his own. This often spurred them to unwonted
effort. It was good pedagogy if it worked; it worked better
with adults and little children than with adolescents.

In October 1912, Gopal Krishna Gokhale, Professor of
English and Economics, President of the Servants of India
Society in India, came to South Africa for a month in order to
assess the Indian community's condition and assist Gandhi in
ameliorating it. Gokhale and Lokamanya Tilak were
Gandhi's forerunners in pre-Gandhian India. Gokhale was a
revered leader of the Indian Nationalist movement, a
brilliant intellectual and an impressive person. Gandhi
acknowledged him an excellent judge of character. In South
Africa, Gokhale once said to Gandhi, 'You will always have
your own way. And there is no help for me as I am here at your
mercy.' The dictum was spoken in friendship and in earnest.

Gandhi's selflessness fortified his assurance. Certain in his
heart that he sought neither material gain, nor power, nor
praise, he had none of the guilty and deterring feeling which
might have prevented him from insisting on his point of view.
Sure he was right, he was sure of victory. Then why yield?
When Gokhale asked for a list of the really reliable civil
resisters, Gandhi wrote down sixty-six names. That was
maximum. The number, however, might sink to sixteen. This
was Gandhi's 'army of peace'. Yet he never flinched; the
Government would surrender.

Gokhale's tour was a triumphal procession through South
Africa. Gandhi was always by his side. In Cape Town, where
Gokhale landed, the Schreiners welcomed him, and
Europeans as well as Indians attended his big public meeting.
From the Transvaal frontier to Johannesburg he travelled by
special train. At every town he stopped for a meeting over
which the local mayor presided. The principal railway

stations had been decorated by Indians. At the Park Terminus in Johannesburg a large ornamental arch designed by Kallenbach was erected. During his stay in Johannesburg Gokhale had the use of the mayor's car. At Pretoria, capital of the Transvaal, the Government entertained him.

The South African authorities wanted Gokhale to carry back a good impression to India.

After making many speeches and talking to many Indians and whites, Gokhale had a two-hour interview with Generals Botha and Smuts, the heads, now, of the Union government. Gandhi, of his own accord, absented himself; he was a controversial figure who might spoil the atmosphere.

When Gokhale came back from the interview, he reported that the racial bar in the Immigration Act would be removed together with the three-pound annual tax collected from indentured labourers who remained in South Africa but did not continue their indenture.

'I doubt it very much,' Gandhi retorted. 'You do not know the Ministers as I do.'

'What I have told you is bound to come to pass,' Gokhale cried. 'General Botha promised me that the Black Act would be repealed and the three-pound tax abolished. You must return to India within twelve months and I will not have any of your excuses.'

Gandhi was glad of the Government's promise; it proved the justice of the Indian cause. But he did not think his job in the Union of South Africa would be completed before many more Indians, and he too, had again gone to prison.

At Gokhale's request, Gandhi and Kallenbach took the steamer with him as far as Zanzibar in Tanganyika. On board, Gokhale talked at length about Indian politics, economics, superstitions, problems. He was introducing Gandhi to the future. Then Gokhale sailed on to India, and Gandhi and Kallenbach returned to Natal for the final struggle.

Addressing an assembly in Bombay Town Hall in December 1912, Gokhale said, 'Gandhi has in him the marvellous spiritual power to turn ordinary men around him into heroes and martyrs.' Gokhale, who looked critically at Gandhi and sometimes rebuked him, added that in Gandhi's presence one is 'ashamed to do anything unworthy', indeed one is 'afraid of thinking anything unworthy'.

Gandhi proved this to the hilt in the final chapter of the South Africa epic.

CHAPTER 15

The Victory

Smuts precipitated the final contest by announcing in the House of Assembly that the Europeans of Natal, who were the original employers of Indian contract labour, would not permit the lifting of the three-pound annual tax on ex-serfs. That was the signal for the renewal of civil disobedience. Indentured labourers and former indentured labourers considered this a breach of the promise given to Professor Gokhale; they volunteered en masse for Satyagraha.

Gandhi closed Tolstoy Farm. Kasturbai, Gandhi, the Gandhi children and several others moved to Phoenix Farm. Adults prepared to go to prison.

There were two issues: the tax and the ban on Asiatic immigrants. Presently, a third was added. On 14 March, 1913, a Justice of the Cape Colony Supreme Court ruled that only Christian marriages were legal in South Africa. This invalidated Hindu, Moslem, or Parsi marriages and turned all Indian wives into concubines without rights.

For the first time, large numbers of women joined the resisters. Kasturbai also joined.

As the opening move in the new campaign, a group of women volunteers were to cross from the Transvaal into Natal and thereby court arrest. If the border police ignored them, they would proceed to the Natal coalfield at Newcastle and urge the indentured miners to go on strike. Simultaneously, a chosen handful of Natal 'sisters', as Gandhi called them, would invite arrest by entering the Transvaal without permission.

The Natal 'sisters' were arrested and imprisoned. Indignation flared and brought new recruits. The Transvaal 'sisters' were not arrested. They went to Newcastle and persuaded the Indian workers to put down their tools. Then the Government arrested these women, too, and lodged them in jail for three months. As a result, the miners' strike spread.

Gandhi hurried from Phoenix Farm to Newcastle.

The miners lived in company houses. The company turned off their light and water.

Gandhi believed the strike would last and therefore counselled the indentured labourers to leave their compounds, taking their blankets and some clothes, and pitch camp outside the home of Mr and Mrs D. M. Lazarus, a Christian couple from India, who had invited Gandhi to stay with them despite the risks such hospitality entailed.

The strikers slept under the sky. Newcastle Indian merchants contributed food and cooking and eating utentils. Before long, five thousand strikers had assembled within sight of the Lazarus house.

Gandhi was astonished and baffled. What could he do with this multitude? They might be on his hands for months. He decided to 'see them safely deposited in jail' in the Transvaal. He informed them of this prospect, described prison at its blackest and urged waverers to return to the mines. None did. It was then agreed that on a fixed day they would all march the thirty-six miles from Newcastle to Charlestown, on the Natal–Transvaal border, walk into the Transvaal and thereby earn jail sentences. A few women with children, and disabled men, were to travel by rail towards the same goal.

While plans were being made, more strikers arrived. Again Gandhi attempted, without success, to dissuade them from following him. Accordingly, 13 October was set as the day of departure from Newcastle. He was able to furnish each 'soldier' with a pound and a half of bread and an ounce of sugar. Instructions were: Conduct yourselves morally, hygienically and pacifically. Submit to police flogging and abuse. Do not resist arrest.

Charlestown was reached without incident. Preparations to receive the Gandhi army had been made in advance by Kallenbach and others. The Indian merchants of Charlestown (normal population one thousand) contributed rice, vegetables, kitchen equipment, etc. Gandhi was chef and head waiter. Complaints about inadequate portions were met with an infectious smile and a report on the total amount of food available and the amount of each person's equal ration.

Women and children were accommodated in houses; the men slept in the grounds of the local mosque.

Before moving on, Gandhi communicated his intentions to the Government. He and his people were coming into the Transvaal to demonstrate against the breach of the Botha–Smuts pledge and assert their self-respect: 'I cannot conceive a greater loss to a man that the loss of his self-respect.' Of course, he added, the Natal government could arrest them in Charlestown and thus spare them further treks. On the other hand, if the Government annulled the three-pound tax the strikers would resume the mining of coal.

The Government did not oblige by arresting them at Charlestown, nor did it eliminate the three-pound levy. In fact, Gandhi suspected that the authorities might not stop the 'army' even if it penetrated into the Transvaal. In that case, he contemplated advancing on Tolstoy Farm by eight day-marches of twenty miles each.

How would he feed his peace troops on the road for eight days? A European baker at Volksrust, the Transvaal border town, undertook to supply them in Volksrust and then to ship the necessary quantity of bread by rail each day to an appointed spot en route to the farm.

Gandhi counted his forces. There were 2,037 men, 127 women and 57 children. At 6.30 on the morning of 6 November, 1913, Gandhi recalls, 'we offered prayers and commenced the march in the name of God'.

From Charlestown on the Natal side to Volksrust is one

mile. A large detachment of Transvaal mounted border
guards was on emergency duty. Two days earlier the
Volksrust whites had held a meeting at which several speakers
declared they personally would shoot any Indian who
attempted to enter the Transvaal. Kallenbach, who attended
to defend the Indians, was challenged to a duel. He was a
pupil of the great Sandow, and an accomplished pugilist and
wrestler, but the Gandhian German arose and said, 'As I have
accepted the religion of peace I may not accept the
challenge . . . The Indians do not want what you imagine . . .
The Indians are not out to challenge your position as rulers.
They do not wish to fight with you or to fill the
country . . . They propose to enter the Transvaal not with a
view to settle here, but only as an effective demonstration
against the unjust tax which is levied upon them. They are
brave men. They will not injure you in person or in property,
they will not fight with you, but enter the Transvaal they will,
even in the face of your gunfire. They are not the men to beat
a retreat from the fear of your bullets or spears. They propose
to melt and I know they will melt, your hearts by self-
suffering.'

Nobody shot anybody; perhaps Kallenbach's speech
turned away the white wrath. Perhaps the police
reinforcements at the border sobered the hotheads. The
guards let the Indians pass.

The first halt was made at Palmford, eight miles beyond
Volksrust. The marchers ate a meagre meal and stretched out
on the earth to sleep. Gandhi had surveyed his slumbering
resisters and was about to lie down when he heard steps and a
moment later saw a policeman approaching, lantern in hand.

'I have a warrant to arrest you,' the officer said politely to
Gandhi. 'I want to arrest you.'

'When?' Gandhi asked.

'Now,' the policeman replied.

'Where will you take me?'

'To the adjoining station first,' the officer explained democratically, 'and to Volksrust when there is a train.'

Gandhi woke Mr P. K. Naidoo, a faithful lieutenant, and gave him instructions for continuing the march to Tolstoy Farm. Gandhi was transported to Volksrust and arraigned in court. The prosecutor demanded imprisonment, but the judge released Gandhi on bail furnished by Kallenbach. Gandhi had asked for release on bail because of his responsibilities to the marchers. Kallenbach, stationed in Volksrust to send on stragglers and new recruits, had a car ready and quickly drove Gandhi back to the Indian 'army'.

The next day the Indians halted at Standerton. Gandhi was handing out bread and marmalade when a magistrate stepped up and said to Gandhi, 'You are my prisoner.'

'It seems I have been promoted,' Gandhi commented with a laugh, 'since magistrates take the trouble to arrest me instead of mere police officials.'

Again Gandhi was freed on bail. Five co-workers were imprisoned.

Two days later, 9 November, as Gandhi and Polak were walking at the head of the long column, a cart came up and the officer in it ordered Gandhi to go with him. Gandhi passed the command to Polak. The officer permitted Gandhi to inform the marchers of his arrest, but when the little 'general' began to exhort the Indians to remain peaceful, the officer exclaimed, 'You are now a prisoner and cannot make any speeches.'

In four days, Gandhi had been arrested three times.

The march continued without the leader.

On the morning of the 10th, on reaching Balfour, the Indians saw three special trains drawn up at the station to deport them from the Transvaal to Natal. At first they refused to submit to arrest, and it was only through the co-operation of Polak, Ahmed Kachhalia and others that the police were able to herd the marchers into the trains.

Polak was thanked for his services and arrested and confined in Volksrust jail. There he found Kallenbach.

On 14 November, Gandhi was brought to trial in Volksrust. He pleaded guilty. The court, however, 'would not convict a prisoner', Gandhi wrote, 'merely upon his pleading guilty'. It therefore requested him to supply the witnesses against himself and Gandhi did so. Kallenbach and Polak testified against him.

Twenty-four hours later, Gandhi appeared as a witness against Kallenbach and two days after that, Gandhi and Kallenbach testified against Polak. Judge Theodore Jooste reluctantly gave each of them three months' hard labour in the Volksrust prison.

Fresh prisoners kept Gandhi informed on Satyagraha developments outside. The arrest of the leaders and marchers had stirred new enthusiasm and the number of resisters throughout South Africa mounted fast. Occasionally, Gandhi could send messages to followers still at liberty. Meanwhile Gandhi rejoiced in congenial company. This was too much of a good thing and the Government shifted him to Bloemfontein where he was with Europeans and Negroes, but no Indians.

The striking miners met a worse fate. Trains carried them back to the mines, where they were forced into wire-enclosed stockades and placed under company employees who had been sworn in as special constables. Despite whips, sticks and kicks, they refused to descend to the coal face.

News of these events was cabled to India and England. India seethed with resentment; the authorities grew alarmed. Lord Hardinge, the British Viceroy, was impelled to deliver a strong speech at Madras in which, breaking precedent, he trenchantly criticized the South African government and demanded a commission of inquiry.

Meanwhile, more indentured labourers left their work in sympathy with the rebellious Newcastle miners. The State regarded such labourers as slaves without the right to strike, and sent soldiers to suppress them. In one place some were killed and several wounded.

The tide of resistance rose higher. Approximately fifty thousand indentured labourers were on strike; several thousand free Indians were in prison. From India came a stream of gold. At a meeting in Lahore, in the Punjab, a Christian missionary named Charles F. Andrews gave all the money he had to the South African movement. Others made similar sacrifices.

By arrangement, several leading Indians and Albert West, who edited *Indian Opinion*, and Sonya Schlesin, Gandhi's secretary, avoided arrest to conduct propaganda, handle finances and communicate with India and England. The Government nevertheless arrested Mr West. Thereupon, Gokhale sent Andrews from India to replace him. He came with W. W. Pearson, another high-minded Englishman.

Cables between the Viceroy's office and London and between London and South Africa hummed with voluminous official messages.

Unexpectedly, the Government liberated Gandhi, Kallenbach and Polak on 18 December, 1913. 'All three of us,' Gandhi writes, 'were disappointed upon our release.' Civil disobedience, properly launched and inspired, needed no leaders.

If Gandhi wanted to be free he need not have gone to jail at all; he could have refrained from opposing the Government. Going into and coming out of prison had to advance the cause and this time coming out did not. Under pressure from the Viceroy and the British authorities in Whitehall, a commission had been appointed to investigate the grievances of the Indians in South Africa and it was hoped that the release of Gandhi and his colleagues would testify to the bona fides of Botha and Smuts in appointing it.

But upon regaining his liberty Gandhi asserted in a public

statement that the commission 'is a packed body and
intended to hoodwink the government and the public opinion
both of England and of India'. He did not doubt the 'integrity
and impartiality' of the chairman, Sir William Solomon, but
Mr Ewald Esselen, he said, was prejudiced. With regard to
the third member, he had, in January 1897, 'led a mob to
demonstrate against the landing of Indians who had arrived
at Durban in two vessels, advocated at a public meeting the
sinking of two ships with all Indians on board and
commending a remark made by another speaker that he
would willingly put down a month's pay for one shot at the
Indians . . . He has consistently been our enemy all these
years'. Gandhi was injured in that 1897 assault.

Three days after leaving prison, Gandhi appeared at a mass
meeting in Durban. He was no longer dressed in shirt and
dungaree trousers. He wore a knee-length white smock, a
white wrapping around his legs (an elongated loincloth) and
sandals. He had abandoned Western clothing. He did so, he
told the meeting, to mourn comrades killed during the
miners' strike.

Reviewing the situation, Gandhi advised 'still greater
purifying suffering until at last the Government may order
the military to riddle us also with bullets.

'My friends,' he exclaimed, 'are you prepared for this?'

'Yes, yes,' the audience shouted.

'Are you prepared to share the fate of those of our
countrymen whom the cold stone is resting upon today?'

'Yes, yes,' they shouted.

'I hope,' Gandhi proceeded, 'that every man, woman and
grown-up child will . . . not consider their salaries, trades, or
even families, or their own bodies . . .'

The struggle, he emphasized, is 'a struggle for human
liberty and therefore a struggle for religion.'

After the meeting Gandhi wrote to Smuts condemning the
choice of two members of the commission. 'Man,' he

philosophized, 'cannot change his temperament all at once. It is against the laws of nature to suppose that these gentlemen will suddenly become different . . .'

Smuts replied three days later, rejecting Gandhi's proposal to add Indians or pro-Indians to the commission.

Gandhi accordingly announced that on 1 January, 1914, he and a group of Indians would march from Durban, Natal, to court arrest. They would not agitate for free immigration into the Union, nor for political franchise in the near future, he declared. They merely wished to regain lost rights.

While this embarrassing threat of an Indian mass march hung over the Government's head, the white employees of all the South African railways went on strike. Gandhi immediately called off his march. It was not part of the tactics of Satyagraha, he explained, to destroy, hurt, humble, or embitter the adversary, or to win a victory by weakening him. Civil resisters hope, by sincerity, chivalry and self-suffering, to convince the opponent's brain and conquer his heart. They never take advantage of the Government's difficulty or form unnatural alliances.

Congratulations poured in on Gandhi; Lord Ampthill wired from England, so did many others; messages of appreciation came from India and many points in South Africa.

Smuts, busy with the railways strike (martial law had been declared), nevertheless summoned Gandhi to a talk. The first talk led to another. The Government had accepted the principle of negotiation. Gandhi's friends warned him against deferring the march again. They recalled Smuts's broken pledge in 1908.

'Forgiveness,' Gandhi replied, quoting the Sanskrit, 'is the ornament of the brave.'

Gandhi's knightly forbearance in cancelling the march created an atmosphere favourable to a settlement. Gandhi's hand, moreover, was strengthened by the arrival, on a fast, special steamer, of Sir Benjamin Robertson, extraordinary envoy of the Viceroy who was worried about hostile reactions in India to South African persecutions.

Gandhi postponed the march a second time.

'Gandhi,' Smuts said at one of their interviews, 'this time we want no misunderstanding, we want no mental or other reservations, let all the cards be on the table and I want you to tell me wherever you think that a particular passage or word does not read in accordance with your own reading.'

This spirit, recognized as friendly by Gandhi, conduced to steady if slow progress in the talks. 'You can't put twenty thousand Indians into jail,' Smuts declared in defence of his new, conciliatory attitude.

Smuts and Gandhi placed their cards and texts on the table. Memoranda passed from one side to the other. For weeks, each word was weighed, each sentence sharpened for precision. On 30 June, 1914, the two subtle negotiators finally exchanged letters confirming the terms of a complete agreement.

This document was then translated into the Indian Relief Bill and submitted to the Union Parliament in Cape Town. Smuts pleaded with Members to approach the problem 'in a non-controversial spirit'. The bill became South African law in July.

The terms were:

1. Hindu, Moslem and Parsi marriages are valid.
2. The three-pound annual tax on indentured labourers who wish to remain in Natal is abolished; arrears are cancelled.
3. Indentured labour will cease coming from India by 1920.
4. Indians could not move freely from one province of the Union to another, but Indians born in South Africa might enter Cape Colony.

Smuts promised publicly that the law would be administered 'in a just manner and with due regard to vested rights' of Indians.

The settlement was a compromise which pleased both sides. Gandhi noted that Indians would still be 'cooped up' in their provinces, they could not buy gold, they could not hold land in the Transvaal, and they had difficulty in obtaining trade licences. But he regarded the agreement as the 'Magna Charta' of South African Indians. The gain, he told a farewell banquet in Johannesburg – he was feted at a dozen dinners – was not 'the intrinsic things' in the law but the vindication of the abstract principle of racial equality and the removal of the 'racial taint'.

The victory, moreover, was a vindication of civil resistance. 'It is a force which,' Gandhi wrote in *Indian Opinion*, 'if it became universal, would revolutionize social ideals and do away with despotisms and the ever-growing militarism under which the nations of the West are groaning and are being almost crushed to death, and which fairly promises to overwhelm even the nations of the East.'

Having won the battle, Gandhi, accompanied by Mrs Gandhi and Mr Kallenbach, sailed for England on 18 July, 1914. Gandhi was in European clothes and looked gentle, thoughtful and tired. Kasturbai wore a white sari with a gay flower design and showed signs of suffering as well as beauty. Like her husband, she was forty-five.

Just before leaving South Africa for ever, Gandhi gave Miss Schlesin and Polak a pair of sandals he had made in prison and asked that they be delivered to General Smuts as a gift. Smuts wore them every summer at his own Doornkloof farm at Irene, near Pretoria. In 1939, on Gandhi's seventieth birthday, he returned them to Gandhi in a gesture of friendship. Invited to contribute to a Gandhi memorial volume on that occasion, Smuts, by then a world-famous statesman and war leader, complied and, graciously calling himself 'an opponent of Gandhi a generation ago', declared that men like the Mahatma 'redeem us from a sense of commonplace and futility and are an inspiration to us not to weary in well-doing . . .

'The story of our clash in the early days of the Union of South Africa,' Smuts wrote, 'has been told by Gandhi himself and is well known. It was my fate to be the antagonist of a man for whom even then I had the highest respect . . . He never forgot the human background of the situation, never lost his temper or succumbed to hate, and preserved his gentle humour even in the most trying situations. His manner and spirit even then, as well as later, contrasted markedly with the ruthless and brutal forcefulness which is the vogue in our day . . .

'I must frankly admit,' Smuts continued, 'that his activities at that time were very trying to me . . . Gandhi . . . showed a new technique . . . His method was deliberately to break the law and to organize his followers into a mass movement . . . In both provinces a wild and disconcerting commotion was created, large numbers of Indians had to be imprisoned for lawless behaviour and Gandhi himself received – what no doubt he desired – a period of rest and quiet in jail. For him everything went according to plan. For me – the defender of law and order – there was the usual trying situation, the odium of carrying out a law which had not strong public support, and finally the discomfiture when the law was repealed.'

Speaking of Gandhi's present, Smuts remarked, 'I have worn these sandals for many a summer since then, even though I may feel that I am not worthy to stand in the shoes of so great a man.' Such humour and generosity proved him worthy of Gandhi's mettle.

Part of Gandhi's effectiveness lay in evoking the best Gandhian impulses of his adversary.

The purity of Gandhi's methods made it difficult for Smuts

to oppose him. Victory came to Gandhi not when Smuts had no more strength to fight him but when he had no more heart to fight him.

Professor Gilbert Murray wrote: 'Be careful in dealing with a man who cares nothing for sensual pleasures, nothing for comfort or praise or promotion, but is simply determined to do what he believes to be right. He is a dangerous and uncomfortable enemy because his body which you can always conquer gives you so little purchase over his soul.'

That was Gandhi, the leader.

Gandhi once recited these verses[1] of Shelley to a Christian gathering in India:

> Stand ye calm and resolute,
> Like a forest close and mute,
> With folded arms and looks which are
> Weapons in unvanquished war.
>
> And if then the tyrants dare,
> Let them ride among you there,
> Slash, and stab, and maim, and hew —
> What they like, that let them do.
>
> With folded arms and steady eyes,
> And little fear, and less surprise,
> Look upon them as they slay
> Till their rage has died away.
>
> Then they will return with shame
> To the place from which they came,
> And the blood thus shed will speak
> In hot blushes on their cheek.

[1] Taken from *The Mask of Anarchy*.

> Rise like lions after slumber
> In unvanquishable number —
> Shake your chains to earth like dew
> Which in sleep has fallen on you —
> Ye are many, they are few.

Those were the followers, the Indian civil resisters in South Africa.

In 1949, the Indian population of South Africa was a quarter of a million, of whom two hundred thousand lived in the province of Natal. Though they had multiplied and prospered, they still did not have the franchise or guaranteed civil rights. They were subject to white and Zulu violence. Their condition was precarious. Manilal Gandhi's *Indian Opinion* of 25 February, 1949, noted that in 1914 passive resistance was 'only suspended' and 'may have to be re-introduced'. Every generation re-enacts the battle for its rights - or loses them. But while individuals in several continents have practised passive resistance, nobody except Mohandas K. Gandhi has ever led a successful, non-violent, mass, civil disobedience campaign. He possessed the personal qualities which aroused the necessary qualities in the community.

PART TWO

Gandhi in India

9 JANUARY, 1915 – 23 MARCH, 1946

CHAPTER 1

Home in India

'Do I contradict myself?' Gandhi asked. 'Consistency is a hobgoblin.' No ism held him rigid in its grip. No theory guided his thoughts or actions. He strove to keep his mind open. He reserved the right to differ with himself.

His life, Gandhi said, was an unending experiment. He experimented even in his seventies. There was nothing set about him. He was not a conforming Hindu nor a conforming nationalist nor a conforming pacifist.

Gandhi was independent, unfettered, unpredictable, hence exciting and difficult. A conversation with him was a voyage of discovery: he dared to go anywhere without a chart.

Under attack, he rarely defended himself. Happily adjusted in India, he never condemned anyone. Humble and simple, he did not have to pretend dignity. Thus relieved of uncreative mental tasks, he was free to be creative.

Nor did he say or do anything merely to gain popularity or win or mollify followers. He upset the applecart frequently. His inner need to perform a given act took precedence over its possible effects on his supporters.

Two days before Gandhi, Mrs Gandhi and Kallenbach reached England from South Africa, the first World War broke out. Gandhi felt that Indians ought to do their bit for Britain. He accordingly volunteered to raise an ambulance corps headed by himself. Eighty Indians, most of them university students in the United Kingdom, volunteered. Gandhi had no delusions: 'Those who confine themselves to attending the wounded in battle cannot be absolved from the guilt of war.'

Then how, Gandhi's friends protested, could he, the man of non-violence, participate in a war?

Gandhi answered in effect: I accept the benefits and protection of the British Empire; I have not tried to destroy it; why should I allow it to be destroyed?

A modern nation is only quantitatively less violent in peace-time than in war-time and unless one collaborates in peace-time one is merely salving one's conscience by non-collaborating in war-time. Why pay taxes to make the arms which kill? Why obey the kind of officials who will make a war? Unless you surrender citizenship or go to jail before the war, you belong in the army during the war.

Gandhi's support of the war was personally painful and politically harmful. But he preferred truth to comfort.

While the minor tempest over his pro-war attitude raged around Gandhi's head, his pleurisy, aggravated by too much fasting, took a serious turn and the doctor ordered him home to India. He arrived in Bombay with Kasturbai on 9 January, 1915. Kallenbach, being a German, was not permitted to travel to India and returned to South Africa.

Except in his native Gujarat region, in the cities of Bombay and Calcutta and in the Madras area, home of the many Tamil indentured · labourers in South Africa, Gandhi's support of the war made little impression. He was not well known in India. Nor did he know India.

Professor Gokhale accordingly 'commanded' Gandhi to spend the first year in India with 'his ears open but his mouth shut'. What he learned in those twelve months about the past and present, Gandhi matched against the hopes for the future which he had formulated as early as 1909 in his first book *Hind Swaraj or Indian Home Rule*. He wrote this brief volume in Gujarati, using right and left hands to do so, while returning from England to South Africa, and had it published in instalments in *Indian Opinion* and then printed as a book in Gujarati and English. He allowed it to be republished in

India in 1921 without change and, in an introduction to still another edition in 1938, he said, 'I have seen nothing to make me alter the views expanded in it.' The seventy-six-page pamphlet, therefore, stands as his social credo.

Indian Home Rule records discussions Gandhi had with Indians in London, one of them an anarchist, some of them terrorists. 'If we act justly,' Gandhi said to them, 'India will be free sooner. You will see, too, that if we shun every Englishman as an enemy, Home Rule will be delayed. But if we are just to them, we shall receive their support . . .' This was prophetic.

Gandhi asked his interlocutors, whom he groups as 'Reader', how they see the future independence of India. 'As is Japan,' Reader replies, 'so must India be. We must own our own navy, our army and we must have our own splendour and then will India's voice ring through the world.'

In other words, Gandhi comments, you want 'English rule without the Englishman. You want the tiger's nature without the tiger . . . You would make India English . . . This is not the Swaraj I want.'

Gokhale told Gandhi in South Africa that the booklet was 'crude and hastily conceived'. Some parts, notably those on British domestic politics, are. On the other hand, Count Leo Tolstoy praised its philosophy. It has abiding interest for Gandhi's definition of Swaraj or home-rule. 'Some Englishmen', Gandhi wrote, 'state that they took and hold India by the sword. Both statements are wrong. The sword is entirely useless for holding India. We alone keep them . . . We like their commerce; they please us by their subtle methods and get what they want from us . . . We further strengthen their hold by quarrelling amongst ourselves . . . India is being ground down not under the British heel but under that of modern civilization.' Then he inveighed against India's use of railways and machinery.

Foreigners, and Indians, frequently challenged Gandhi

on his hostility to the modern machine. The several editions of
Hind Swaraj report some of these discussions. In 1924, for
instance, Gandhi was asked whether he objected to all
machinery?

'How can I,' he replied, 'when I know that even this body is
a most delicate piece of machinery? The spinning wheel is a
machine; a little toothpick is a machine. What I object to is
the craze for machinery, not machinery as such.

'Today,' Gandhi continued, 'machinery merely helps a few
to ride on the back of the millions . . . The machine should
not tend to atrophy the limbs of man. For instance, I would
make intelligent exceptions. Take the case of the Singer
sewing machine. It is one of the few useful things ever
invented and there is a romance about the device itself.' He
had learned to sew on it.

And would you not need big factories to produce little
devices like Singers?

'Yes,' Gandhi agreed.

Then, since he liked to close the circle of every argument
and come back to his starting-point, Gandhi said, 'Ideally, I
would rule out all machinery, even as I would reject this very
body, which is not helpful to salvation and seek the absolute
liberation of the soul. From that point of view I would reject
all machinery, but machines would remain because, like the
body, they are inevitable.' Thus he upheld the principle yet
admitted the contention.

Gandhi was not anti-machine. He merely realized earlier
than many others the dangers and horrors of a civilization in
which the individual is somewhat in the position of a savage
who makes an idol and then makes sacrifices to appease it.
The faster machines move the faster man lives and the greater
his nervous tensions and his cultural and social tributes to
speed. Gandhi would have had less objection to machinery if
it merely served the body; he did not want it to invade the
mind and maim the spirit. He believed that India's mission

was to 'elevate the moral being'. Therefore, 'if the English become Indianized we can accommodate them'.

Such a thing has never happened, Reader objected.

'To believe that what has not occurred in history will not occur at all,' Gandhi replied, 'is to argue disbelief in the dignity of man.' He had the soul of an Eastern prophet and the spirit of a Western pioneer.

Reader scorned Gandhi's moral preoccupations. He wanted India liberated from the British as Mazzini and Garibaldi had liberated Italy from Austria. The analogy enabled Gandhi to drive home the central thesis that guided him to greatness before and especially after India's independence:

'If you believe that because Italians rule Italy the Italian nation is happy you are groping in darkness . . . According to Mazzini [freedom] meant the whole of the Italian people, that is, its agriculturists. The Italy of Mazzini still remains in a state of slavery . . .

'It would be folly to assume,' Gandhi added, 'that an Indian Rockefeller would be better than an American Rockefeller.'

Gandhi saw the flaws in Western culture, but he took much from it. His defence of the individual against the community and of man against the machine is in tune with Ruskin, Thoreau, Mazzini and the Utopian (not Marxist) socialists. Ideologically, Gandhi stood with one foot in the deep individualistic current of the first half of Europe's nineteenth century and the other in the turbulent nationalistic current of the second half of that century; the two streams merged in him and he endeavoured to achieve the same synthesis in the Indian independence movement.

Gandhi asked England to quit India, but he did not want India to quit England. He cultivated cultural and other ties with Britain. In 1936, for instance, he gave an Indian student named Kamalnayan Bajaj a letter of introduction to Henry

Polak in London in which he said, 'However much we may
fight Great Britain, London is increasingly our Mecca . . . I
have advised him to take up a course in the London School of
Economics.' His nationalism lacked the usual concomitants of
nationalism: exclusiveness and hostility towards other
countries. 'My patriotism,' Gandhi declared, 'is subservient
to my religion.' He was too religious to serve one land, one
race, one caste, one family, one person, or even one religion.
His religion was humanity.

Gandhi planted these ideas as he moved up and down India
during that probationary first year Gokhale had enjoined
upon him; he studied and learned, but contrary to orders he
talked. He talked at banquets celebrating his South African
exploits. He attended them with the silent Kasturbai whom
he lauded as his helpful partner.

At a dinner in April 1915, in Madras, he defended his
recruiting campaign for the British army; this speech was pro-
West. 'I discovered,' he said, 'that the British Empire had
certain ideals with which I have fallen in love and one of those
ideals is that every subject of the British Empire has the freest
scope possible for his energy and honour and whatever he
thinks is due to his conscience. I think that is true of the British
government as it is true of no other government . . . I have
more than once said that that government is best which
governs least. I have found that it is possible for me to be
governed least under the British Empire. Hence my loyalty to
the British Empire.'

He took the unpopular side.

Gandhi's speeches were delivered in a weak, unimpressive
conversational tone. He had been heralded as the hero of
Natal and the Transvaal, the person who defeated Smuts.
The Indian nationalists had expected a new giant, a lion of a
man who might lead them to independence. (Gokhale died in
1915.) They were disappointed. Instead of a likely candidate
for the succession, they saw a thin little figure dressed in a

ridiculously large turban and flapping loincloth who could scarcely make himself heard (there were no loudspeakers) and neither thrilled nor stimulated his audience.

Yet Gandhi would soon remake the entire nationalist movement of India.

Simultaneously with Gandhi's departure from Phoenix Farm, his own family, with other families, also left South Africa for India. As the best place for the temporary sojourn of the boys in this group Gandhi chose Shantiniketan, a school in Bengal, eastern India, maintained by Rabindranath Tagore, India's great novelist and poet laureate who won the Nobel Prize for Literature in 1913.

Gandhi and Tagore were contemporaries and closely linked as chief agents of India's twentieth-century regeneration. But Gandhi was the wheat field and Tagore the rose garden, Gandhi was the working arm, Tagore the singing voice, Gandhi the general, Tagore the herald, Gandhi the emaciated ascetic with shaven head and face, Tagore the large, white-maned, white-bearded aristocrat–intellectual with a face of classic, patriarchal beauty. Gandhi exemplified stark renunciation; Tagore felt 'the embrace of freedom in a thousand bonds of delight'. Yet both were united by their love of India and mankind. Tagore wept at seeing his India 'the eternal ragpicker at other people's dustbins' and prayed for 'the magnificent harmony of all human races'.

Tagore believed, with Gandhi, that India's shackles were self-made:

> Prisoner, tell me who was it that wrought this unbreakable chain?
> It was I, said the prisoner, who forged this chain very carefully.

Tagore and Gandhi, the greatest Indians of the first half of the twentieth century, revered one another. It was Tagore, apparently, who conferred on Gandhi the title of Mahatma; 'The Great Soul in beggar's garb,' Tagore said. Gandhi called Tagore 'The Great Sentinel'. Sentimentally inseparable, soulmates to the end, they waged verbal battles, for they were different. Gandhi faced the past and out of it made future history; religion, caste, Hindu mythology were deeply ingrained in him. Tagore accepted the present, with its machines, its Western culture and, despite it, made Eastern poetry. Perhaps, since provincial origins are so important in India, it was the difference between isolated Gujarat and cosmopolitan Bengal. Gandhi was frugal. Tagore was prodigal. 'The suffering millions', Gandhi wrote to Tagore, 'ask for one poem, invigorating food.' Tagore gave them music. At Shantiniketan, Tagore's pupils sang and danced, wove garlands and made life sweet and beautiful. When Gandhi arrived there, shortly after his return to India, to see how his Phoenix Farm boys were faring, he turned the place upside down. With the help of Charles Freer Andrews and William W. Pearson, his friends in South Africa, Gandhi persuaded the entire community of 125 boys and their teachers to run the kitchen, handle the garbage, clean the latrines, sweep the grounds and, in general, forsake the muse for the monk. Tagore acquiesced tolerantly and said, 'The experiment contains the key to Swaraj' or home-rule. But austerity was uncongenial and, when Gandhi left to attend Gokhale's funeral, the experiment collapsed.

Gandhi, however, sought his own hermitage or ashram where he, his family and friends and nearest co-workers would make their permanent home in an atmosphere of renunciation and service. Gandhi's life now had no room for private law practice or private relations with his wife and sons. A foreigner once said to Gandhi, 'How is your family?'

'All of India is my family,' Gandhi replied.

Thus dedicated, Gandhi founded the Satyagraha Ashram first at Kochrab and then, permanently, at Sabarmati, across the Sabarmati River from the city of Ahmedabad. There, rooted in the soil and sand and people of India, Gandhi grew to full stature as the leader of his nation.

Ahmedabad's textile magnates and Bombay's shipping barons supported financially the inmates of Gandhi's ashram. The Sabarmati Ashram consists of a group of low, whitewashed huts in a grove of spreading trees. A mile away stands the Sabarmati prison where fighters for India's freedom were later incarcerated. Below the ashram compound is the river in which women wash their laundry, and cows and buffaloes wade. All around, the scene is gently pastoral, but not too distant are the closely packed houses of Ahmedabad hedged in by ugly factory smokestacks.

Gandhi's room is about the size of a cell; its one window has iron bars. The room opens on to a small terrace where Gandhi slept even in the coldest nights and worked during the day. Except for intervals in prison, Gandhi occupied that cell for sixteen years.

On the high bank which slopes sharply to the river, Gandhi held his daily prayer meetings. Near by is the grave of Maganlal Gandhi, the Mahatma's second cousin, who managed the ashram and died in 1928. 'His death has widowed me. M. K. Gandhi', reads the inscription on the stone.

With the years, new houses were erected to accommodate the Indians who wished to be Gandhi's disciples. Some of the most active leaders of the independence movement began their political careers at the feet of the Mahatma in Sabarmati. The population of the settlement fluctuated from 30 at the start to a maximum of 230. They tended the fruit trees, planted grain, spun, wove, studied and taught in surrounding villages.

In ancient India, ashrams and religious retreats for monks were well-known phenomena. Pilgrimages to four ashrams in different parts of the land signified that one's legs had proved the unity of India. Ashramites resigned from the world and, contemplating themselves inside and out, waited for the end while torturing the body to hasten it. Gandhi and his ashram, however, remained in closest contact with the world. The ashram, in fact, became the navel of India. Contemplating the ashram, Indians attached themselves to its first citizen. Nor did Gandhi ever purposely hurt his body. He had it massaged; he slept adequately; he walked for strength; all his dietetic aberrations, queer to many Westerners and even to many Indians, were designed to make him a biologically perfect instrument for the attainment of spiritual goals. Though he drastically reduced his food consumption he did not want to be famished, and in South Africa he always carried chocolate-coated almonds to still sudden hunger. He remained, until he was killed, a healthy specimen. Who but a very healthy man could have fasted as often and as long as he did yet reach the age of seventy-eight?

A photograph taken shortly after his return to India shows him seated on a platform, legs crossed, nude but for a short loincloth, making a speech while around him stand Indian politicians in European clothes. He soon told them to shed those garments. How could persons in Bond Street suits or Bombay coats and trousers win peasant support?

Peasants? Politicians had nothing to do with peasants. They were hoping to persuade the British to withdraw or, at least, to ameliorate the imperial regime; to achieve this end you either had to shoot well or appear in striped trousers to deliver petitions in impeccable English to English bureaucrats. India's Independence Hall, they thought, would be papered with petitions and memorials addressed to a most gracious sovereign or the sovereign's satrap.

But Gandhi told them to get out among the people. To do so they would have to drop English and use the native languages of India: Hindi, Urdu, Tamil, Telugu, Malayalam, Kannarese, Bengali, Punjabi, etc., each spoken by many millions who had no benefit of Western education or perhaps any education. Village uplift was Gandhi's First Freedom. Over 80 per cent of India lived in villages. India's liberation from England would be vain, he held, without peasant liberation from poverty, ignorance and idleness. The British might go, but would that help the fifty to sixty million outcast untouchables, victims of cruel Hindu discrimination? Independence must mean more than Indian office-holders in the places and palaces of British office-holders.

Gandhi wanted a new Indian today, not just a new India tomorrow.

Gandhi's message touched India with a magic wand. Gradually, a new vision opened. The Indian's heart aches for the lost glory of his country. Gandhi brought it balm. Gandhi in loincloth, imperturbable, prayerful, seated amid trees, not aping the British gentleman but resembling a saint of antiquity, reminded the nation that India had seen many conquerors and conquered them all by remaining true to itself. Gandhi kindled India's pride and faith. His magic wand became a ramrod.

Gandhi's message stood the Indian National Congress party on its head.

The Congress, as Indians call it, was born in Bombay on 28 December, 1885. Its father and first general secretary was an Englishman, Allan Octavian Hume, who had the blessing of Lord Dufferin, the British Viceroy. Hume at first proposed that Indian politicians should meet regularly, under the chairmanship of British governors, as a grievance court, but the Viceroy thought that Indians would speak more freely if one of their number presided. Hume placed both proposals before prominent Indians and they chose the Viceroy's variant. This was the origin of the Congress. Hume remained secretary, sometimes alone, sometimes with Indian colleagues, until 1907. The Congress president for 1888 was George Yule, an Englishman; for 1894, Alfred Webb, an Irish member of the British Parliament; for 1904, Sir Henry Cotton, a retired Indian Civil Service official; and for 1910, Sir William Wedderburn, former Secretary to the Government of Bombay. Gandhi praised Hume and Wedderburn for their devotion to India. They and all the Congressmen of this early period saw India's welfare through constitutional reforms and administrative measures.

The Congress was organized to channel popular protest into legal moderation. But into the channel flowed the fresh waters of national revivalism, spurred, in the second half of the nineteenth century, by the Tagore family, Sri Aurobindo, Swami Vivekananda, a dynamic, eloquent disciple of the mystic Ramakrishna, Dadabhai Naoroji and Raja Rammohan Roy, the first translator of the *Upanishads* into English. The world theosophist movement, which paid permanent tribute to the ancient religious and cultural wealth of India, likewise fed that pride in the past which constituted the foundation of the movement for national regeneration.

Thanks in part to the unification and orderly administration of the country by the British, Indian industrialists, Hindus and Parsis in particular, grew rich and began to buy out their British partners. The emergence of Indian capitalism and of a new Indian middle class gave a powerful impetus to the urge for self-government.

Under these multiple influences, the Congress slowly outgrew its collaborationist boyhood and became a demanding youth. The 'prayers' to British governors were couched in firmer terms, though as late as 1921, Tagore complained of their 'correct grammatical whine'. Polite irritations supplanted polite invitations to high imperial officials to attend Congress functions. Some speeches and resolutions pressed for ultimate home-rule. But only a few 'extremists' dreamt of converting the Congress into an active agent that would win Indian independence by mass action.

Gandhi too was a collaborationist when he returned to

India in 1915. Yet there was a revolutionary, anti-collaborationist potential in his yearning for an India that was Indian instead of a replica of the West in clothing, language, mores and politics. Gandhi craved for his country a cultural regeneration and spiritual renaissance which would give it inner freedom and hence, inevitably, outer freedom, for if the people acquired individual and collective dignity they would insist on their rights and then nobody could hold them in bondage.

The national metamorphosis Gandhi envisaged could not be the achievement of a small upper class or the gift of a foreign power. This made him conscious and critical of the shortcomings of the Congress. Before Gandhi sat securely in the saddle of the Congress he was the burr under the saddle, and it got him into trouble.

CHAPTER 2

'Sit Down, Gandhi'

Under the impact of the first World War, the tide of protest rose higher in India and even moderate Congressmen began to ask for home-rule. In September 1915, Mrs Annie Besant, a remarkable Englishwoman who has written her name permanently into the history of modern India, announced the formation of a Home-Rule League and persuaded the veteran Dadabhai to become its president.

Mrs Besant was then approaching seventy. Born in 1847, she had lived a stormy life as atheist, socialist, women's rights advocate and theosophist. She regarded herself as a reincarnation of Hypathia of Alexandria and Giordano Bruno, both of whom met violent deaths, and in her autobiography she says she longed to be the 'bride of Christ'. Though a foreigner, she was an accepted and respected leader of India. An eloquent speaker, trenchant writer and brave politician, she edited Indian publications and made India her home. She died in 1933.

In 1892, Mrs Besant started a school at Benares, the holy city on the Ganges, and in 1916 this institution, guided by Pandit Malaviya, was expanded into the Hindu University Central College. An illustrious gathering of notables attended the three-day opening ceremonies in February 1916. The Viceroy was there and so were numerous bejewelled maharajas, maharanis, rajas and high officials in all their dazzling panoply.

On 4 February Gandhi addressed the meeting. It broke up before he could finish.

India had never heard such a forthright, unvarnished speech. Gandhi spared no one, least of all those present. 'His

Highness, the Maharaja, who presided yesterday over our deliberations,' Gandhi said, 'spoke about the poverty of India. Other speakers laid great stress upon it. But what did we witness in the great pandal in which the foundation ceremony was performed by the Viceroy [Lord Hardinge]? Certainly a most gorgeous show, an exhibition of jewellery which made a splendid feast for the eyes of the greatest jeweller who chose to come from Paris. I compare with the richly bedecked noblemen the millions of the poor. And I feel like saying to those noblemen: "There is no salvation for India unless you strip yourselves of this jewellery and hold it in trust for your countrymen in India."'

'Hear, hear,' students in the audience exclaimed. Many dissented. Several princes walked out.

Gandhi was not deterred. 'Whenever I hear of a great palace rising in any great city of India,' he went on, 'be it in British India or be it in the India ruled by our great chiefs, I become jealous at once and say, "Oh, it is the money that has come from the agriculturists" ... There cannot be much spirit of self-government about us,' he exclaimed, 'if we take away or allow others to take away from the peasants almost the whole of the results of their labour. Our salvation can only come through the farmer. Neither the lawyers, nor the doctors, nor the rich landlords are going to secure it.' Congress, beware!

Gandhi was unfurling his flag before the mighty ones of India. It was the flag of the lowly.

'If you of the student world to which my remarks are supposed to be addressed this evening,' Gandhi declared, 'consider for one moment that the spiritual life, for which this country is noted and for which this country has no rival, can be transmitted through the lip, pray believe me you are wrong. You will never be able merely through the lip to give the message that India, I hope, will one day deliver to the world ... I venture to suggest to you that we have now reached almost the end of our resources in speech-making and it is not enough that our ears be feasted, that our eyes be feasted, but it is necessary that our hearts have got to be touched and that our hands and feet have got to be moved.

'It is a matter of deep humiliation and shame for us,' Gandhi continued, 'that I am compelled this evening under the shadow of this great college, and in this sacred city, to address my countrymen in a language that is foreign to me.

'Suppose,' Gandhi mused, 'that we had been receiving education during the past fifty years through our vernaculars, what should we be today? We should have a free India, we should have our educated men not as if they were foreigners in their own land, but speaking to the heart of the nation; they would be working amongst the poorest of the poor, and whatsoever they would have gained during the past fifty years would be a heritage of the nation.'

This sentiment provoked scattered applause.

Turning to the essence of his philosophy, Gandhi, using words that shocked the assembled aristocrats, said, 'No paper contribution will ever give us self-government. No amount of speeches will ever make us fit for self-government. It is only our conduct that will fit us for it. And how are we trying to govern ourselves? . . . If you find me this evening speaking without reserve, pray consider that you are only sharing the thoughts of a man who allows himself to think audibly, and if you think that I seem to transgress the limits that courtesy imposes upon me, pardon me for the liberty I may be taking. I visited the Viswanath Temple last evening and as I was walking through those lanes these were the thoughts that touched me . . . I speak feelingly as a Hindu. Is it right that the lanes of our sacred temple should be as dirty as they are? The houses round about are built anyhow. The lanes are narrow and tortuous. If even our temples are not models of roominess and cleanliness what can our self-government be? Shall our temples be abodes of holiness, cleanliness and peace as soon as the British have retired from India . . . ?'

Gandhi stayed close to earth; even the most delicate ears should hear the facts of life. 'It is not comforting to think,' he said, 'that people walk about the streets of Indian Bombay under the perpetual fear of dwellers in the storeyed buildings spitting upon them.' Many Indian eyebrows lifted. Was it right for an Indian to say this with Englishmen present? And what had spitting to do with the Benares University or independence?

Gandhi sensed the audience's antagonism, yet he was relentless. He travelled a good deal in third-class railway carriages, he said. Conditions were not altogether the fault of the management. Indians spat where others had to sleep. Students misbehave in the trains. 'They can speak English,' he commented sarcastically, 'and they have worn Norfolk jackets and therefore claim the right to force their way in and command seating accommodation . . . I am setting my heart bare. Surely we must set these things right in our progress towards self-government.'

The day's ration of unpalatable thoughts was still incomplete. There remained the unmentionable. 'It is my bounden duty,' Gandhi asserted, 'to refer to what agitated our minds these last two or three days. All of us have had many anxious moments while the Viceroy was going through the streets of Benares. There were detectives stationed in many places.' A movement went through the invited guests. This was not to be talked about in public. It was for Gandhi. 'We were horrified,' he revealed. 'We ask ourselves, "Why this distrust? Is it not better that even Lord Hardinge should die than live a living death?" But a representative of the mighty Sovereign may not. He might find it necessary even to live a living death. But why was it necessary to impose these detectives on us?'

Gandhi not only asked the unpalatable question. He gave

the more unpalatable reply. 'We may foam, we may fret,' Gandhi said about the Indian reaction to the detectives, 'we may resent, but let us not forget that the India of today in her impatience has produced an army of anarchists. I am myself an anarchist, but of another type . . . Their anarchism . . . is a sign of fear. If we trust and fear God, we shall have to fear no one, not Maharajas, not Viceroys, not the detectives, not even King George.'

The audience was growing unruly and arguments broke out in various parts of the assembly. Gandhi uttered a few more sentences when Mrs Besant, who presided, called out to him: 'Please stop it.'

Gandhi turned around to her and said, 'I await your orders. If you consider that, by my speaking as I am, I am not serving the country and the empire I shall certainly stop.'

Mrs Besant, coldly: 'Please explain your object.'

Gandhi: 'I am explaining my object. I simply . . .' He could not be heard above the din.

'Go on,' some shouted.

'Sit down, Gandhi,' others shouted.

Decorum restored, Gandhi defended Mrs Besant. It is because 'she loves India so well and she considers that I am erring in thinking audibly before you young men.' But he preferred to speak frankly. 'I am turning the searchlight towards ourselves . . . It is well to take the blame sometimes.'

At this moment, many dignitaries left the platform, the commotion mounted, and Gandhi had to stop. Mrs Besant adjourned the meeting.

From Benares Gandhi went home to Sabarmati.

Distances are great in India and communications bad; few people can read and fewer possess radios. Therefore the ear of India is big and sensitive. In 1916, the ear began to catch the voice of a man who was courageous and indiscreet, a little man who lived like a poor man and defended the poor to the face of the rich, a holy man in an ashram.

Gandhi was not yet a national figure. The hundreds of millions did not know him. But the fame of the new Mahatma was spreading. India stands in awe of power and wealth. But it loves the humble servants of the poor. Possessions, elephants, jewels, armies, palaces win India's obedience. Sacrifice and renunciation win its heart.

Matthew Arnold wrote:

> The East bowed low before the blast
> In patient, deep disdain.

And it bowed low, with the same disdain, before the East that coveted riches and might.

The Indian, therefore, understands as well as appreciates renunciation. India has many monks and ascetics. But Gandhi's renunciation caused a larger echo because he opposed renunciation 'for the mere sake of renunciation'. 'A mother', he observed in a letter, 'would never by choice sleep in a wet bed but she would gladly do so in order to spare the dry bed for her child.'

Gandhi renounced in order to serve.

CHAPTER 3

'Children of God'

'India,' Jawaharlal Nehru said, 'contains all that is disgusting and all that is noble.' Nothing it contains is more disgusting than 'the hideous system', as Gandhi called it, of untouchability, the 'canker eating at the vitals of Hinduism'. Orthodox Hindus did not share this view, nor did they welcome Gandhi's effort to extirpate the evil.

In attempting to eradicate untouchability, Gandhi was tugging at roots several thousand years long. They originated in the prehistoric Aryan invasion of India and grew into the hearts, superstitions and social habits of hundreds of millions of people. Many Western nations have their 'untouchables', but the stubborn Hindu phenomenon of untouchability stems from peculiar historic and economic circumstances which are tied together into an ugly bundle by the sanction of religion.

In the long, unchronicled night before the dawn of history, a fair-skinned folk called Aryans inhabited an area north of India. Perhaps they hailed from the distant Caucasian isthmus between the Caspian and the Black Sea, or from Turkestan, or even from the more remote Russian valleys of the Don and the Terek where exquisite gold ornaments of the ancient Scythians have been unearthed. Nehru notes that Pathan dancing resembles Cossack dancing. Six or seven thousand years ago the Aryans began pushing south; one tide of the migration swept into India about 2000 or 3000 BC, another moved into Iran; a third descended into Europe.

Hence, the 'Indo-European' language family. There is an evident bond between the Sanskrit of India and many Western tongues: Sanskrit *pitri*, Latin *pater*, Greek *pater*, English *father*; Sanskrit *matri*, Latin *mater*, Greek *meter*, English *mother*, Russian *mat*; Sanskrit *duhirti*, English *daughter*, German *Tochter*, Russian *doch*.

Gradually, the Aryans, which means 'noblemen', conquered north-west India. They found there an older civilization related to that of Babylon, Assyria and presumably Egypt.

In 1922, at a place called Mohenjo-daro, about two hundred miles north of Karachi, an Indian archaeologist, examining the ruins of a comparatively new Buddhist temple seventeen hundred years old, found, beneath the temple, proof of a much more antique city. Scientific excavations at the site brought to light a treasure of clay seals, beads, bricks, pots, utensils and ornaments. One jar had a Sumero-Babylonian inscription in the hieroglyphic writing of Mesopotamia which dated it between 2800 and 2500 BC. Many of the discoveries at Mohenjo-daro and other excavated spots in the same area resemble those at Ur of the Chaldees, Kish and Tell-Asmar in the region of the Tigris and Euphrates. Explorers have since traced the abandoned caravan routes over which north-west India and the Biblical Near East exchanged goods and culture.

When the silt, sand and debris were carted away,.the town of Mohenjo-daro, founded fifty-five hundred years ago and continuously inhabited for six centuries, was exposed. It covers more than 240 acres. One can now see its principal avenue, which was thirty-three feet wide, and many broad, straight north–south, east–west streets once lined with burnt-brick homes, two or more storeys high, that had wells and bathrooms. A sewage system using clay pipes helped to keep the city clean.

In a silver jar found under a floor lay a piece of cotton cloth, the oldest in the world. Bronze razors, chairs, spoons, cosmetic boxes, silver drinking cups, ivory combs, bracelets, nose studs for women, necklaces, bronze statuettes showing that ladies wore skirts and girdles, gold beads, gambling dice, and thousands of other historic objects have been retrieved from the dust of ages in this most exciting unveiling of India's past.

Either a flood or an epidemic destroyed this earliest-known Indian civilization. The Aryans brought their own gods and goods and put a new stamp on the country. They used horses and chariots, battle-axes, bows and javelins.

The *Rig-Veda*, consisting of 1,028 hymns and written in liturgical Sanskrit, pictures the life of these conquering Indo-Aryans four to five thousand years ago. Said to be the oldest book in the world, the *Rig-Veda* reveals the origin of the Hindu caste system and of the untouchable outcasts.

No caste divisions, as far as can be ascertained, encumbered the Aryans on their arrival in India. But conquest brought social differentiation. Though the subjugated territory was hardly the home of barbarians, or blacks, the *Rig-Veda* speaks of the inhabitants contemptuously as 'black-skinned', 'noseless', and 'malignant', who did not know enough to appease the gods with burnt offerings of animals. The Aryans employed these 'inferiors' to till their fields, tend their herds, barter their products and fashion their tools and ornaments. The merchants and farmers constituted the Vaisya or third caste, the craftsmen the Sudra or fourth caste.

Power and wealth sowed discord among the Aryans and they called upon a raja or king to rule over their several districts. He and his courtiers and their fighting men and their families constituted the master-warrior Kshatriya caste who served by hymn-singing, *Veda*-writing, ritual-performing, myth-making, animal-sacrificing Brahmans or priests. Such was the ascendancy of religion and intelligence, however, that the Brahmans became the top caste, while the Kshatriyas occupied the next rung down.

The Aryans, who entered India poor in women, intermarried with the local population. This healthy mixing of blood continued even after the conquerors penetrated into south India where they subdued the Dravidians. These races had evolved an interesting culture of their own, but they were dark-skinned, and the colour-conscious Aryans consequently increased the height of their caste barriers. Dravidians became Brahmans, Kshatriyas and Vaisyas, but a larger percentage than in the north were impressed into the Sudra caste, and millions were left outside all castes.

The Aryan invasion frightened many natives into the hills and jungles where they lived by hunting and fishing. In time, they timidly approached the Aryan and Sudra villages to sell their wicker baskets and other handicraft products. Occasionally, they were allowed to settle permanently on the edges of the settlements and do menial tasks, such as handling dead animals and men, removing refuse, etc. These were the untouchables.

Since modern times, vocation no longer follows caste. A Brahman can be a cab driver, a Kshatriya a bookkeeper, and a Vaisya a prince's prime minister. On the other hand, the ban against marriage between castes is observed to this day, and when Gandhi appeared on the scene in 1915 few violated it. Indeed, the four castes are divided into three to four thousand sub-castes, some of them resembling craft guilds, others the equivalent of blood or provincial groups; and parents preferred to find a wife for their son within the sub-castes. Marriage of a caste member with an untouchable was, of course, unthinkable. Love marriages were considered rather indecent, certainly ill-omened. Marriages were arranged by parents; and why would a father demean his family by admitting a pariah bride into it?

Untouchables were confined to tasks which Hindus spurned: street-cleaning, scavenging, tanning, etc. In some regions, wheelwrights, hunters, weavers and potters are considered untouchables. To escape the humiliation, untouchables have adopted Christianity or Islam. Yet forty or fifty million have chosen to stay in the fold even though they are kept outside the pale. Why?

To perpetuate caste it has been clothed in the sacred formula of immutable fate: you are a Brahman or Sudra or untouchable because of your conduct in previous incarnation. Your misbehaviour in the present life might result in caste demotion in the next. A high-caste Hindu could be reborn an untouchable. The soul of a sinner might even be transferred to an animal. An untouchable could become a Brahman.

'The human birth', Mahadev Desai writes in his introduction to the *Gita*, 'is regarded by the Hindu as a piece of evolutionary good fortune which should be turned to the best and noblest account'; then he quotes an old Indian poem:

> I died as mineral and became a plant,
> I died as plant and rose to animal.
> I died as animal and I was man.
> What should I fear? When was I less by dying?

A woman might become a man in the next incarnation, and vice versa. Some Hindus would like to feel that at rebirth they will still be members of the same family though their relationship may be altered; a husband and wife may be brother and sister, for instance, or sister and brother. Men with feminine propensities might turn into women in the coming incarnation; a person who is bloodthirsty and vicious may fall to animal status; a spiritual merchant may be reborn a Brahman. A greedy Brahman may be reborn in the merchant caste. Thus conduct alters inheritance, but once caste rank is fixed in any one incarnation it becomes destiny. According to this doctrine, an untouchable is merely doing penance; to interrupt it by raising his status robs him of a possible ticket to a high caste in the next incarnation. This prospect reconciles religious untouchables to their current misery.

An untouchable is exactly that: he must not touch a caste

Hindu or anything a caste Hindu touches. Obviously, he should not enter a Hindu temple, home, or shop. In villages, the untouchables live on the lowest outskirts into which dirty waters drain; in cities they inhabit the worst sections of the world's worst slums. If, by mischance, a Hindu should come into contact with an untouchable or something touched by an untouchable he must purge himself through religiously prescribed ablutions. Indeed, in some areas, this is incumbent upon him even if the shadow of an untouchable falls on him, for that too pollutes. On the Malabar coast, untouchables are warned by a loud noise to quit the road and its immediate environs at the approach of a caste Indian.

Hindus are expected to bathe once a day, and water for washing their hands and private parts is available in the most primitive toilets. Hindus also take special pride in the cleanliness of the personal pots, pans and drinking vessels. A Hindu will smoke a huka water pipe or a cigarette through his fist without letting it touch his lips, and he often pours water into his mouth instead of sipping it. 'This sense of cleanliness,' Nehru notes, 'is not scientific and the man who bathes twice a day will unhesitatingly drink water that is unclean and full of germs . . . The individual will keep his own hut fairly clean but throw all the rubbish in the village street in front of his neighbour's House . . .' Cleanliness, he adds, is a religious rite, not an end in itself. If it were, Hindus would be concerned with the cleanliness of others, untouchables included.

Untouchability is segregation gone mad. Theoretically a device against contamination, it actually contaminates the country that allows it. Mahatma Gandhi knew this and he fought untouchability for the sake of the castes as well as the outcasts, but in fighting it he defied a thousand taboos and roused a million fears, superstitions, hates and vested interests. Buddhism and many Hindu reformers had attacked untouchability; Gandhi said little against it until he had taken action against it.

In his youth, Gandhi played with an untouchable boy.
Putlibai forbade it. Though he loved her he disobeyed her, his
first rebellion against authority. 'I used to laugh at my dear
mother', he wrote to Charles Freer Andrews, 'for making us
bathe when we brothers touched any pariah.' In South
Africa, too, he associated with untouchables. In May 1918, in
Bombay, he went to a meeting called to improve the lot of
untouchables. When he got up to deliver his address, he said,
'Is there an untouchable here?' No hand was raised. Gandhi
refused to speak.

Now there came to Gandhi's ashram near Ahmedabad an
untouchable family and asked to become permanent
members. He admitted them.

A tempest broke.

The presence of the untouchable father, mother and their
little daughter Lakshmi polluted the entire ashram, and how
could the wealthy Hindus of Bombay and Ahmedabad
finance a defiled place? They withdrew their contributions.
Maganlal, who kept the accounts, reported that he was out of
funds and had no prospects for the next month.

'Then we shall go to live in the untouchable quarter,'
Gandhi quietly replied.

One morning a rich man drove up in a car and inquired
whether the community needed money. 'Most certainly,'
Gandhi replied. Gandhi had met the man only once and that
casually.

The next day the anonymous benefactor put thirteen
thousand rupees in big bills into Gandhi's hand and went
away. That would keep the ashram for a year.

This did not end Gandhi's troubles. The women of the
ashram refused to accept the untouchable woman.
Kasturbai, revolted at the idea of having Danibehn in the
kitchen cooking food and washing dishes, complained to her
husband. Gandhi heard her patiently and appealed to her
reason. But belief in untouchability resides in some remote

nervous recess where, with racial intolerance, dogma and colour prejudice among its neighbours, it eludes common sense and humaneness. Gandhi therefore had to meet Kasturbai on her own terms: she was a loyal Hindu wife; did she wish to leave him and go to live in Porbandar? He was responsible for her acts; if he forced her to commit a sin it was his sin not hers and she would not be punished. Kasturbai was growing accustomed to her husband's strange ways. She could never refute his arguments. He had become a Mahatma; who was she, the almost illiterate Gujarat woman, to question the man of God? He was now the loving teacher, no longer the lustful spouse. She resented him less and listened to him more. Within her nerve tissue, to be sure, the hostility to the untouchables continued to twitch. But her mind was gradually learning hospitality to his ideas. In the worshipful air of India, husband became hero.

Presently, Gandhi announced that he had adopted Lakshmi as his own daughter. Kasturbai thus became the mother of an untouchable! It was like bringing a Negro daughter-in-law into the pre-Civil War mansion of a Southern lady.

Gandhi insisted that untouchability was not part of early Hinduism. Indeed, his war on the 'miasma' of untouchability was conducted in terms of Hinduism. 'I do not want to be re-born,' he stated, 'but if I have to be re-born I should be re-born an untouchable so that I may share their sorrows, sufferings and the affronts levelled against them in order that I may endeavour to free myself and them from their miserable condition.'

If this prayer of the Mahatma has been answered he is now an untouchable child in India and his devout followers might be maltreating him.

But before being transformed into an untouchable in the next incarnation he tried to live like one in this. So he took to cleaning the lavatories of the ashram. His disciples voluntarily joined him. Nobody was an untouchable because everybody did the untouchable's work without considering themselves contaminated thereby.

The outcasts were called 'untouchables', 'pariahs', 'depressed classes', 'scheduled classes'. Gandhi understood; he began calling them 'Harijans' (Children of God), and later named his weekly magazine after them. Gradually, 'harijan' was hallowed by usage.

Fanatic Hindus never forgave Gandhi his love of untouchables and were responsible for some of the political obstructions he encountered during his career. But to vast multitudes he was the Mahatma; they asked his blessing; they were happy to touch his feet; some kissed his footprints in the dust. They accordingly had to overlook, they forgot, that he was as contaminated as an untouchable because he did scavenging and lived with untouchables and had adopted an untouchable as his daughter. Over the years, thousands of high-caste Hindus came to Gandhi's ashram to interview him, to eat with him, to stay with him. A few undoubtedly purged themselves thereafter, but most of them could not be such hypocrites. Untouchability lost some of its curse. Gandhians began to use untouchables in their households; were they better than their saint? He taught by example.

City life and industrialization have had the same effect of weakening the persecution of Harijans. In a village, everybody knows everybody else. But the untouchable does not look different, and in a trolley or train the caste Hindu might be sitting skin-to-skin with a pariah and not realize it. Inescapable contact has reconciled the Hindus to contact.

Nevertheless, the poverty of the Harijans remained, and the discrimination against them was far from overcome by Gandhi's early actions, gestures and statements in their behalf. He therefore continued his efforts unremittingly.

Why did it fall to Gandhi, rather than to somebody else, to lead the movement for the emancipation of untouchables?

Many of the indentured labourers in South Africa were untouchables, and they were the heroes of the final phase of the civil disobedience campaign in 1914. Gandhi's twenty-year struggle in South Africa, moreover, was directed against an evil which, with all its economic overtones, was at bottom a colour prejudice. All men are born with unequal gifts but equal rights, and society owes them an equal or at least unimpeded opportunity to develop their native abilities and live in liberty. How could Gandhi, fresh from his fight for the equality of Indians in South Africa, countenance a cruel inequality imposed by Indians on other Indians in India?

The foundations of freedom are sapped where anybody is denied equal rights because of his religion, the beliefs and deeds of his ancestors or relatives, the shape of his nose, the colour of his skin, the sound of his name, or the place or estate of his birth.

Gandhi's concept of freedom for India excluded Hindu immorality as well as British administrators. 'Swaraj' or independence, he said in *Young India* on 25 May, 1921, 'is a meaningless term if we desire to keep a fifth of India under perpetual subjection . . . Inhuman ourselves, we may not plead before the Throne for deliverance from the inhumanity of others.'

The simplest explanation of Gandhi's attitude towards untouchability is that he just could not stand it. In fact, he loathed this 'inhuman boycott of human beings' so much that he said 'if it was proved to me that it is an essential part of Hinduism I for one would declare myself an open rebel against Hinduism itself'. No man who cared more for popularity than principle would have made such a public statement in a country overwhelmingly and conservatively Hindu. But he made it as a Hindu in an effort, he said, to purify his religion. He regarded untouchability as an 'excrescence', a perversion of Hinduism.

In Hinduism, however, an excrescence is difficult to

distinguish from the essence. Hinduism is more than a doctrine and more than a religion. Certainly, it is not a one-day-a-week religion. It invades homes, farms, schools and shops. It is a way of life which meshes with the mythological prehistory, the history, the economy, the geography and the ethnography of India. In India, religion is the sum total of the national experience. Islam is less absorbent, but Hinduism is a sponge religion, hospitable and without fundamentalism. 'We have no uncontradictable and unquestionable documents, no special revelations, and our scriptures are not final . . .' writes Sir C. P. Ramaswami Aiyar, a Hindu philosopher. Hinduism is simultaneously monotheistic and idolatrous, because it has, at different periods in history, drawn in populations that accepted one or the other. The monotheists tolerate idols and the idolators dance before graven images but pray to one God. Some Hindus sacrifice animals in their temples, and some hold it a religious duty not to kill a worm or germ. The reform movements of Hinduism, like Buddhism and Jainism, have never broken away in schisms. They disappear into the general bloodstream. Hinduism is flexible, capacious, malleable. So is the thinking of many Hindus. So was Gandhi's. He fought untouchability. He abhorred animal sacrifices; the flow of blood in the house of God sickened him. But Hindus who perpetrated these wrongs were his brothers and he was theirs.

India, Nehru has said, is like a palimpsest. A palimpsest is an ancient parchment or canvas which has been written on or painted on and then varnished over at a later period and written on or painted on again and then varnished over and written on or painted on a third, fourth and fifth time. This economic use of materials has unintentionally preserved some precious relics of the past, and experts now know how to wash off the newer coats and reveal the old original inscriptions or drawings. The difference is that in the case of India, the varnish has, so to speak, dissolved, and all the words and figures of the several layers are visible at the same time as one intricate jumble. This explains the complexity of Indian civilization and of those Indians who are permeated by it. 'The human intellect', writes Sir Valentine Chiral, 'has indeed seldom soared higher or displayed deeper metaphysical subtlety than in the great system of philosophy in which many conservative Hindus still seek a peaceful refuge from the restlessness and materialism of the modern world.' No Indian can altogether escape this cultural-intellectual heritage.

At times, however, only one layer of the palimpsest is visible; on such occasions a modern, European-educated Hindu may vanish and become a worshipper of crude, primeval fetishes, even as a Western scientist may accept the irrational abracadabra of a desert cult.

Hinduism amalgamated Mahavira, the founder of Jainism, and Buddha who were regarded as atheists or agnostics. Many Hindus accept Jesus and Mohammed as religious guides. Yet in insane moments, Hindus, Sikhs and Moslems avidly slaughter one another. Then they relax into apathetic tolerance.

Despite its insatiable hunger for oneness, however, Hinduism's 'Live-and-Let-Live' only meant, 'Live separately'. Hinduism has fostered endless division into self-contained villages, self-sufficient joint families comprising two, three, or even four generations in one residence, and self-segregated castes and multitudinous sub-castes whose members did not, until recent times, intermarry or inter-dine. God-fearing Hindus were content to see the 'children of God' in degrading isolation.

Yet the Indian ideal of unity in diversity remains. The binding factors are the three legs of the subcontinent's compact triangle, the unbroken line of culture from the dim past until today, the links of history and the bonds of blood and religion.

Blood connects Hindus with Moslems and Sikhs. Religion weakens the connection. Geography connects; bad communications divide. The multiplicity of languages divides.

Out of these elements, Gandhi and his generation undertook to forge a nation.

CHAPTER 4

Indigo

When I first visited Gandhi in 1942 at his ashram in Sevagram, in central India, he said, 'I will tell you how it happened that I decided to urge the departure of the British. It was in 1917.'

He had gone to the December 1916 annual convention of the Indian National Congress party in Lucknow. There were 2,301 delegates and many visitors. During the proceedings, Gandhi recounted, 'a peasant came up to me looking like any other peasant in India, poor and emaciated, and said, "I am Rajkumar Shukla. I am from Champaran, and I want you to come to my district!"' Gandhi had never heard of the place. It was in the foothills of the towering Himalayas, near the kingdom of Nepal.

Under an ancient arrangement, the Champaran peasants were sharecroppers. Rajkumar Shukla was one of them. He was illiterate but resolute. He had come to the Congress session to complain about the injustice of the landlord system in Bihar, and somebody had probably said, 'Speak to Gandhi'.

Gandhi told Shukla he had an appointment in Cawnpore and was also committed to go to other parts of India. Shukla accompanied him everywhere. Then Gandhi returned to his ashram near Ahmedabad. Shukla followed him to the ashram. For weeks he never left Gandhi's side.

'Fix a date,' he begged.

Impressed by the sharecropper's tenacity and story Gandhi said, 'I have to be in Calcutta on such-and-such a date. Come and meet me and take me from there.'

Months passed. Shukla was sitting on his haunches at the

appointed spot in Calcutta when Gandhi arrived; he waited till Gandhi was free. Then the two of them boarded a train for the city of Patna in Bihar. There Shukla led him to the house of a lawyer named Rajendra Prasad who later became President of the Congress party and of India. Rajendra Prasad was out of town, but the servants knew Shukla as a poor yeoman who pestered their master to help the indigo sharecroppers. So they let him stay on the grounds with his companion, Gandhi, whom they took to be another peasant. But Gandhi was not permitted to draw water from the well lest some drops from his bucket pollute the entire source; how did they know that he was not an untouchable?

Gandhi decided to go first to Muzzafarpur, which was en route to Champaran, to obtain more complete information about conditions than Shukla was capable of imparting. He accordingly sent a telegram to Professor J. B. Kripalani, of the Arts College in Muzzafarpur, whom he had seen at Tagore's Shantiniketan school. The train arrived at midnight, 15 April, 1917. Kripalani was waiting at the station with a large body of students. Gandhi stayed there for two days in the home of Professor Malkani, a teacher in a government school. 'It was an extraordinary thing in those days,' Gandhi commented, 'for a government professor to harbour a man like me.' In smaller localities, the Indians were afraid to show sympathy for advocates of home-rule.

The news of Gandhi's advent and of the nature of his mission spread quickly through Muzzafarpur and to Champaran. Sharecroppers from Champaran began arriving on foot and by conveyance to see their champion. Muzzafarpur lawyers called on Gandhi to brief him; they frequently represented peasant groups in court; they told him about their cases and reported the size of their fees.

Gandhi chided the lawyers for collecting big fees from the sharecroppers. He said, 'I have come to the conclusion that we should stop going to law courts. Taking such cases to the courts does little good. Where the peasants are so crushed and fear-stricken, law courts are useless. The real relief for them is to be free from fear.'

Most of the arable land in the Champaran district was divided into large estates owned by Englishmen and worked by Indian tenants. The chief commercial crop was indigo. The landlords compelled all tenants to plant three-twentieths or 15 per cent of their holdings with indigo and surrender the entire indigo harvest as rent. This was done by long-term contract.

Presently, the landlords learned that Germany had developed synthetic indigo. They thereupon obtained agreements from the sharecroppers to pay them compensation for being released from the 15 per cent arrangement.

The sharecropping arrangement was irksome to the peasants, and many signed willingly. Those who resisted, engaged lawyers; the landlords hired thugs. Meanwhile, the information about synthetic indigo reached the illiterate peasants who had signed, and they wanted their money back.

At this point Gandhi arrived in Champaran.

He began by trying to get the facts. First he visited the secretary of the British landlords' association. The secretary told him that they could give no information to an outsider. Gandhi answered that he was no outsider.

Next Gandhi called on the British official commissioner of the Tirhut division in which the Champaran district lay. 'The commissioner,' Gandhi reports, 'proceeded to bully me and advised me forthwith to leave Tirhut.'

Gandhi did not leave. Instead he proceeded to Motihari, the capital of Champaran. Several lawyers accompanied him. At the railway station, a vast multitude greeted Gandhi. He went to a house and, using it as headquarters, continued his investigations. A report came in that a peasant had been maltreated in a nearby village. Gandhi decided to go and see; the next morning he started out on the back of an elephant.

He had not proceeded far when the police superintendent's messenger overtook him and ordered him to return to town in his carriage. Gandhi complied. The messenger drove Gandhi home where he served him with an official notice to quit Champaran immediately. Gandhi signed a receipt for the notice and wrote on it that he would disobey the order.

In consequence, Gandhi received a summons to appear in court the next day.

All night Gandhi remained awake. He telegraphed Rajendra Prasad to come from Bihar with influential friends. He sent instructions to the ashram. He wired a full report to the Viceroy.

Morning found the town of Motihari black with peasants. They did not know Gandhi's record in South Africa. They had merely heard that a Mahatma who wanted to help them was in trouble with the authorities. Their spontaneous demonstration, in thousands, around the courthouse was the beginning of their liberation from fear of the British.

The officials felt powerless without Gandhi's co-operation. He helped them regulate the crowd. He was polite and friendly. He was giving them concrete proof that their might, hitherto dreaded and unquestioned, could be challenged by Indians.

The government was baffled. The prosecutor requested the judge to postpone the trial. Apparently, the authorities wished to consult their superiors.

Gandhi protested against the delay. He read a statement pleading guilty. He was involved, he told the court, in a 'conflict of duties': on the one hand, not to set a bad example as a lawbreaker; on the other hand, to render the 'humanitarian and national service' for which he had come. He disregarded the order to leave, 'not for want of respect for lawful authority, but in obedience to the higher law of our being, the voice of conscience'. He asked the penalty due.

The magistrate announced that he would pronounce

sentence after a two-hour recess and asked Gandhi to furnish bail for those 120 minutes. Gandhi refused. The judge released him without bail.

When the court reconvened, the judge said he would not deliver the judgement for several days. Meanwhile he allowed Gandhi to remain at liberty.

Rajendra Prasad, Brij Kishor Babu, Maulana Mazharul Huq and several other prominent lawyers had arrived from Bihar. They conferred with Gandhi. What would they do if he was sentenced to prison, Gandhi asked. Why, the senior lawyer replied, they had come to advise and help him; if he went to jail there would be nobody to advise and they would go home.

What about the injustice to the sharecroppers, Gandhi demanded. The lawyers withdrew to consult. Rajendra Prasad has recorded the upshot of their consultations: 'They thought, amongst themselves, that Gandhi was totally a stranger, and yet he was prepared to go to prison for the sake of the peasants; if they, on the other hand, being not only residents of the adjoining districts but also those who claimed to have served these peasants, should go home, it would be shameful desertion.'

They accordingly went back to Gandhi and told him they were ready to follow him into jail. 'The battle of Champaran is won,' he exclaimed. Then he took a piece of paper and divided the group into pairs and put down the order in which each pair was to court arrest.

Several days later, Gandhi received a written communication from the magistrate informing him that the Lieutenant-Governor of the province had ordered the case to be dropped. Civil disobedience had triumphed, the first time in modern India.

Gandhi and the lawyers now proceeded to conduct a far-flung inquiry into the grievances of the farmers. Depositions by about ten thousand peasants were written down, and notes made on other evidence. Documents were collected. The whole area throbbed with the activity of the investigators and the vehement protests of the landlords.

In June, Gandhi was summoned to Sir Edward Gait, the Lieutenant-Governor. Before he went he met leading associates and again laid detailed plans for civil disobedience if he should not return.

Gandhi had four protracted interviews with the Lieutenant-Governor who, as a result, appointed an official commission of inquiry into the indigo sharecroppers' situation. The commission consisted of landlords, government officials, and Gandhi as the sole representative of the peasants.

Gandhi remained in Champaran for an initial uninterrupted period of seven months and then again for several shorter visits. The visit, undertaken casually on the entreaty of an unlettered peasant in the expectation that it would last a few days, occupied almost a year of Gandhi's life.

The official inquiry assembled a crushing mountain of evidence against the big planters, and when they saw this they agreed, in principle, to make refunds to the peasants. 'But how much must we pay?' they asked Gandhi.

They thought he would demand repayment in full of the money which they had illegally and deceitfully extorted from the sharecroppers. He asked only 50 per cent. 'There he seemed adamant,' writes Reverend J. Z. Hodge, a British missionary in Champaran who observed the entire episode at close range. 'Thinking probably that he would not give way, the representative of the planters offered to refund to the extent of 25 per cent, and to his amazement Mr Gandhi took him at his word, thus breaking the deadlock.'

This settlement was adopted unanimously by the commission. Gandhi explained that the amount of the refund was less important than the fact that the landlords had been obliged to surrender part of the money and, with it, part of their prestige. Theretofore, as far as the peasants were concerned, the planters had behaved as lords above the law. Now the peasant saw that he had rights and defenders. He learned courage.

Events justified Gandhi's position. Within a few years the British planters abandoned their estates, which reverted to the peasants. Indigo sharecropping disappeared.

Gandhi never contented himself with large political or economic solutions. He saw the cultural and social backwardness in the Champaran villages and wanted to do something about it immediately. He appealed for teachers. Mahadev Desai and Narhari Parikh, two young men who had just joined Gandhi as disciples, and their wives, volunteered for the work. Several more came from Bombay, Poona and other distant parts of the land. Devadas, Gandhi's youngest son, arrived from the ashram and so did Mrs Gandhi. Primary schools were opened in six villages. Kasturbai taught the ashram rules on personal cleanliness and community sanitation.

Health conditions were miserable. Gandhi got a doctor to volunteer his services for six months. Three medicines were available: castor oil, quinine and sulphur ointment. Anybody who showed a coated tongue was given a dose of castor oil; anybody with malaria fever received quinine plus castor oil; anybody with skin eruptions received ointment plus castor oil.

Gandhi noticed the filthy state of women's clothes. He asked Kasturbai to talk to them about it. One woman took Kasturbai into her hut and said, "Look, there is no box or cupboard here for clothes. The sari I am wearing is the only one I have.'

During his long stay in Champaran, Gandhi kept a long-distance watch on the ashram. He sent regular instructions by mail and asked for financial accounts. Once he wrote to the residents that it was time to fill in the old latrine trenches and dig new ones otherwise the old ones would begin to smell bad.

The Champaran episode was a turning-point in Gandhi's life. 'What I did', he explained, 'was a very ordinary thing. I declared that the British could not order me about in my own country.'

But Champaran did not begin as an act of defiance. It grew out of an attempt to alleviate the distress of large numbers of poor peasants. This was the typical Gandhi pattern: his politics were intertwined with the practical, day-to-day problems of the millions. His was not a loyalty to abstractions; it was a loyalty to living, human beings.

In everything Gandhi did, moreover, he tried to mould a new free Indian who could stand on his own feet and thus make India free.

Early in the Champaran action, Charles Freer Andrews, the English pacifist who had become a devoted follower of the Mahatma, came to bid Gandhi farewell before going on a tour of duty to the Fiji Islands. Gandhi's lawyer friends thought it would be a good idea for Andrews to stay in Champaran and help them. Andrews was willing if Gandhi agreed. But Gandhi was vehemently opposed. He said, 'You think that in this unequal fight it would be helpful if we have an Englishman on our side. This shows the weakness of your heart. The cause is just and you must rely upon yourselves to win the battle. You should not seek a prop in Mr Andrews because he happens to be an Englishman.'

'He had read our minds correctly,' Rajendra Prasad comments, 'and we had no reply . . . Gandhi in this way taught us a lesson in self-reliance.'

Self-reliance, Indian independence and help to share-croppers were all bound together.

CHAPTER 5

First Fast

Gandhi would have remained to assist the sharecroppers of Champaran in getting schools, health service, etc., but unrest among textile workers brought him back to Ahmedabad.

The millhands of Ahmedabad were underpaid and overworked. They wanted more money and better conditions. Their case, Gandhi said, 'was strong'.

Gandhi was a close friend of Ambalal Sarabhai, the biggest textile manufacturer of Ahmedabad. Sarabhai was the leader of the millowners.

Having studied the problem, Gandhi urged the factory owners to arbitrate the dispute. They rejected arbitration.

Gandhi accordingly advised the workmen to go on strike. They followed his advice. Gandhi directed the strike. He was helped actively by Anasuya, sister of Ambalal Sarabhai.

Gandhi had exacted a solemn pledge from the workmen not to return to work until the employers accepted labour's demands or agreed to arbitration. Every day Gandhi met the strikers under a spreading banyan tree by the banks of the Sabarmati. Thousands came to hear him. He exhorted them to be peaceful and to abide by the pledge. From these meetings, they marched off into town carrying banners which read, EK TEK (KEEP THE PLEDGE).

Meanwhile, Gandhi remained in touch with the employers. Would they submit to arbitration? They again refused.

The strike dragged on. The strikers began to weaken. Attendance at meetings dropped, and when Gandhi asked them, as he did each day, to reaffirm the pledge, their reply sounded less resolute. Scabs had been working in some of the mills. Gandhi feared violence. He was also afraid that, pledges notwithstanding, the workers might return to the mills.

To Gandhi it was 'inconceivable' that they should return. 'Was it pride,' he asked, 'or was it my love of the labourers and my passionate regard for truth that was at the back of this feeling – who can say?'

Whatever the feeling, it overpowered Gandhi, and one morning, at the regular strikers' open-air assembly under the banyan branches, he declared that if they did not continue the strike until they won 'I will not touch any food'.

He had not intended announcing the fast. The words just came to him spontaneously without previous thought. He was as surprised as his listeners. Many of them cried. Anasuya Sarabhai was beside herself with grief.

'We will fast with you,' some workers exclaimed. No, said Gandhi, they need merely stay out on strike. As for himself, he would eat nothing until the strike was settled.

Gandhi had fasted before for religious and personal reasons. This was his first fast in a public cause.

On the first day of the fast, Anasuya and several strike leaders fasted too. But Gandhi persuaded them to desist and look after the workmen. With the assistance of Vallabhbhai Patel, a prosperous Ahmedabad lawyer, and others, temporary employment was found for some workers. A number of them helped to erect new buildings at Gandhi's Sabarmati Ashram.

Gandhi saw the dilemma in which the fast placed him. The fast was designed to keep the workers loyal to their pledge. But it constituted pressure on the millowners. Ambalal Sarabhai was a devoted follower of the Mahatma and so was Ambalal's wife, Sarladevi. She, Gandhi wrote, 'was attached to me with the affection of a blood-sister'.

Gandhi told the millowners who called on him that they must not be influenced by his fast; it was not directed against them. He said he was a striker and strikers' representative and should be treated as such. But to them he was Mahatma Gandhi. Three days after the fast commenced, the millowners accepted arbitration, and the strike, which had lasted twenty-one days, was called off.

Gandhi thought he fasted to steady the strikers. The failure of the strike would cow these and other workers, and he disliked cowards. His sympathies were with the poor and downtrodden in whom he wished to arouse a dignified, peaceful protest. Yet he probably would have fasted against the workers had they opposed arbitration. The principle of arbitration is essential to Gandhi's philosophy; it eliminates violence and the compulsion which may be present even in peaceful struggles. It teaches people tolerance and conciliation. Gandhi fasted not for anybody or against anybody, but for a creative idea.

'Fasting for the sake of personal gain is nothing short of intimidation,' Gandhi affirmed. Gandhi obviously had nothing personal to gain from the Ahmedabad fast. The employers knew that. Yet they were probably intimidated by it. They did not want to be the cause of Gandhi's death. But if it had been the Governor of Bombay who was fasting they might have said, 'Let him die'. 'I fasted to reform those who loved me,' Gandhi said on a subsequent occasion, and he added, 'You cannot fast against a tyrant.' The millowners were intimidated because they had a deep affection for Gandhi, and when they saw his selfless sacrifice they may have felt ashamed of their own selfishness. A fast for personal benefit would not arouse such emotions.

'I can fast against my father to cure him of a vice,' Gandhi explained, 'but I may not in order to get from him an inheritance.' Gandhi fasted not so much to raise wages as to cure the employers of their unwarranted objection to a system of arbitration which would promote peace in the textile industry.

The fast, in fact, brought into being a system of arbitration which survives to this day; on a visit to Ahmedabad in 1948, I found capitalists and trade unions convinced of its efficacy. Gandhi had participated in its work as a permanent member of the panel of arbitrators.

In September 1936, for instance, the Millowners Association of Ahmedabad asked the Textile Labour Association to accept a 20 per cent cut in wages. Labour refused, and the case went to arbitration. The employers appointed an owner named Kasturbhai Lalbhai as their representative and labour appointed Mahatma Gandhi; the impartial umpire chairman was Sir Govindrao Madgavkar.

The millowners submitted that their plants, employing approximately 80,000 hands, were suffering from foreign competition and the world economic depression and could not afford to pay existing rates.

Having studied the industry's books and other pertinent data, Gandhi affirmed that 'no cut should be made till the mills have ceased to make any profit and are obliged to fall back upon their capital for continuing the industry. There should be no cut till the wages have reached the level adequate for maintenance.' It is possible to conceive a time when the workmen have begun to regard the industry as if it were their own property and they would then be prepared to help it out of a crisis by taking the barest maintenance consisting of a dry crust and working night and day. That would be a voluntary arrangement. Such cases are irrelevant to the present consideration'.

Moreover, Gandhi wrote, 'It is vital to the well-being of the industry that workmen should be regarded as equals with the shareholders and that they have therefore every right to possess an accurate knowledge of the transactions of the mills.'

Finally, Gandhi suggested a register of all millhands 'acceptable to both parties', after which 'the custom of taking labour through any agency other than the Textile Labour

Association should be stopped'. This approximates to the modern, Western concept of the 'closed shop'.

The impartial chairman agreed with Gandhi and ruled against the wage reduction which, accordingly, was not allowed.

CHAPTER 6

Goat's Milk

'There can be no partnership between the brave and the effeminate. We are regarded as a cowardly people. If we want to become free from that reproach, we should learn the use of arms.'

Mahatma Gandhi spoke those words in July 1918, while recruiting Indians for the British Army during the first World War. 'We should become partners of the Empire,' he added; 'a dominion like Canada, South Africa and Australia. To bring about such a thing,' he declared, 'we should have the ability to defend ourselves, that is, the ability to bear arms and to use them . . . If we want to learn the use of arms with the greatest possible dispatch, it is our duty to enlist ourselves in the Army.'

Gandhi delivered this speech in Kheda district of his native Gujarat region in western India. In March, he had led a Satyagraha movement in Kheda for the remission of taxes on peasants who had suffered a crop failure. The civil disobedience campaign was partly successful: the well-to-do farmers paid taxes but the poor did not.

The peasants had followed him in civil resistance and fed him and given him their carts for transportation. But now, when he came to recruit, they would not even let him hire a cart and they refused to feed him and his small party.

Gandhi records their heckling: 'You are a votary of non-violence, how can you ask us to take up arms?' 'What good has the Government done for India?'

'Partnership in the Empire is our definite goal,' he replied. 'We should suffer to the utmost of our ability and even lay down our lives to defend the Empire. If the Empire perishes, with it perishes our cherished aspirations.'

His audiences said India would fight in return for new freedoms. No, Gandhi insisted, it was evil to take advantage of Britain's war-time predicament. He trusted England.

The district had six hundred villages which averaged one thousand inhabitants each. If every village gave twenty recruits, Gandhi computed, that would make 12,000. 'If they fall on the battlefield,' he exclaimed, 'they will immortalize themselves, their villages and their country.' In the same recruiting-sergeant language, Gandhi asked the women to encourage the men.

His efforts failed and he only succeeded in making himself seriously ill. He had been living on peanut butter and lemons. This slim diet and the exertion, plus, no doubt, the frustration of failure, gave him dysentery.

He fasted. He refused medicine. He refused an injection. 'My ignorance of injections was in those days quite ridiculous,' he said. He thought they were serums.

This was the first important illness in his life. His body was wasting away. His nerves gave way; he felt sure he would die. A medical practitioner ('a crank like myself', Gandhi called him) suggested the ice treatment. Anything, as long as it was outside, Gandhi said.

The ice helped. Appetite returned. The 'crank' suggested sterilized eggs with no life in them. Gandhi remained obdurate; no eggs. Doctors advised milk. But the cruel manner of milking cows and buffaloes had impelled Gandhi to abjure milk for ever. 'No,' he answered. 'I have taken a vow never to drink milk.'

Here Kasturbai put in a stern word. 'But surely,' she said, 'you cannot have any objection to goat's milk.'

Gandhi wanted to live. He was not immune, he confessed, to that 'subtlest of temptations, the desire to serve'. Had he been up to par physically his will might have been strong enough to reject Kasturbai's suggestion. But the very fact that he could not resist the suggestion showed how badly he needed the milk.

Taking milk, he wrote later, was a 'breach of pledge'. It always bothered him; it revealed a weakness. Nevertheless, he continued to be a goat-milk drinker to his last supper.

Kasturbai's insistence is the likely key to Gandhi's willingness to break the vow. Gandhi feared neither man nor government, neither prison nor poverty nor death. But he did fear his wife. Perhaps it was fear mixed with guilt; he did not want to hurt her; he had hurt her enough.

G. Ramchandran, a devoted Gandhian, has written a 'sheaf of anecdotes' about the master for which C. Rajagopalachari, father of Devadas Gandhi's wife and first Governor-General of independent India, vouches as 'true'. Ramchandran, who lived in Sabarmati Ashram for a year, recalls that one day, when Kasturbai had cleaned up the kitchen after lunch and gone into the adjoining room for a nap, Gandhi came to the kitchen and, beckoning to a young male assistant of Ba, or mother, as Kasturbai was called, told him in a whisper that some guests were arriving in an hour and would have to be fed. Putting a finger to his lips as he glanced towards Ba's room, Gandhi told the young man what to do and added, 'Do not disturb her . . . Send for Ba only when she is needed. And mind you, don't irritate her. You will deserve a prize if she does not go for me.'

Gandhi, writes Ramchandran, 'was a little nervous lest Ba should wake up suddenly and burst upon him'. So the husband left the kitchen as quickly as he could, no doubt feeling a husband's relief at getting beyond fury's reach. But Gandhi's hope of escaping from his kitchen crime without detection crashed when a brass platter fell to the floor. After prayers that evening, Ba, arms akimbo, confronted the Mahatma; she had a fierce temper: Why hadn't he wakened her?

'Ba,' Gandhi apologized, 'I am afraid of you on such occasions.'

She laughed incredulously. 'You afraid of me?'

'And yet that was the truth,' Ramchandran comments.

In his debilitated state during the dysentery, he was less than ever inclined to oppose her. Thereafter, for thirty years, Gandhi drank goat's milk.

Gandhi's readiness to recruit for the British army was another weakness. I asked him about it in 1942. 'I had just returned from South Africa,' he explained. 'I hadn't yet found my feet. I was not sure of my ground.' He had come to the unbridgeable gulf between nationalism and pacifism and did not know what to do.

He might have taken the easy course and refused to support the war. Most Indian nationalists did that. They said, India is not free, therefore we will not fight. But this was naked nationalism hiding behind the transparent skirt of pacifism; it meant, if India had self-government we would enlist to kill the enemy.

The issue Gandhi faced in 1918 was universal and eternal: What does a citizen do when his country is invaded? For his conscience' sake, a pacifist may discommode his body and go to jail, or he may bravely attack conscription and other military measures. This can be a valuable educational demonstration. Suppose, however, the entire nation emulated his example and refused to fight? (Suppose the British had refused to fight in 1940?)

For Indians in 1918, two positions were possible.

A 100 per cent Indian pacifist would have abstained from the war and preferred perpetual colonial status, for as a colony India could deny war-time help to the enslaving motherland, whereas India as a nation would have to prepare for war or face destruction.

Gandhi could not take this position because he wanted a free Indian nation.

A 100 per cent Indian nationalist would have abstained from the first World War, saying it was Britain's war, but would have prepared to make war on Britain for the liberation of India.

Gandhi could not take this position because he still hoped for a non-violent settlement with Britain about the future of India.

In 1918, therefore, Gandhi compromised his nationalism by accepting the Empire and hoping to attain freedom gradually and peacefully; having done that, his compelling honesty forced him to compromise his pacifism and recruit for the war.

The political Gandhi was thus caught in the ineradicable conflict between nationalism and pacifism. The religious Gandhi tried to resolve it by preaching and practising non-violence and the universal brotherhood of man.

In this dichotomy lay the tragedies of Gandhi's life.

CHAPTER 7

The History of British Rule in India

Throughout the last thirty years of his life, from 1918 to 1948, Mahatma Gandhi fought three major battles: the battle with himself, the battle with Indians and the battle with Britain.

From remote antiquity to modern times, India has been invaded twenty-six times. The British invasion was the last. Until the end of the fifteenth century, all of India's conquerors came overland and all, except Baber, approached through what is now Russian Turkestan, crossed the Hindu Kush where the passes are from 12,000 to 16,000 feet above sea level and then filed through the narrow Khyber Pass to the Suleiman mountain range and the banks of the Indus and beyond.

Semiramis, Queen of Assyria, sent an army into India via Turkestan twenty-two centuries before Christ. Cyrus of Persia repeated this performance in 530 BC. North-west India remained under Persian domination (Indians probably fought the Greeks at Marathon) until Alexander the Great of Macedon swept out of Greece at the head of an army of 40,000 men, quickly subdued Syria, Egypt and Palestine, defeated Persia at Arbela, marched to the Oxus and Samarkand and then, climbing the Hindu Kush, entered India in 326 BC, at the age of thirty. After a nineteen months' stay, Alexander, a pupil of Aristotle, left for home, taking with him several Indian philosophers. He died two years later in Babylon.

The Greeks, and subsequently the Romans, carried to the West the achievements of Indian science. The so-called 'Arabic' numerals were invented in India. The zero is an Indian concept. An Indian brain likewise evolved the present world-wide system of numeral placement: the system whereby a one with a four after it is fourteen and a four with a one after it is forty-one.

Attracted by the wealth and mystery of India, more fabled conquerors, Genghis Khan, Tamerlane, Nadir Shah and others, added their scratches to Indian history and withdrew with loot and lore.

On 8 July, 1497, five years after Columbus in three Spanish vessels discovered America, Vasco da Gama in three Portuguese ships, the largest of which displaced 150 tons, anchored off the south-west shore of India. Thus began the first seaborne invasion of India.

The Papal bulls of 1493 and an agreement with Spain gave Portugal, then a world power, a Catholic monopoly in south-east Asia. That did not prevent the Dutch from establishing several lucrative trading posts in India early in the sixteenth century. The French followed a few years later. They sent home pepper, cinnamon and other spices.

England hesitated to encroach on the formidable Portuguese. Instead, since they had wool to sell which torrid southern Asia did not need, the British searched for a north-west passage through North America and a north-east passage around northern Europe to the colder regions of China. But when this quest proved vain, England, emboldened by her victory over the Spanish Armada in July 1588, dared to defy Portugal, Spain's confederate, and dispatched her first expedition into the Indian Ocean in 1591. Despite the war with Spain and Portugal, other British expeditions followed. The peace signed with these nations increased the traffic and intensified the commercial competition.

An East India Company was formed in London in 1600; its renewed charter of 1609 gave it a British trade monopoly in Asia unlimited in time and space.

War greased the wheels of business. The Dutch, vigorous and aggressive and supported by all the military might of the homeland, took the offensive against Portuguese settlements in India and, with British co-operation, achieved considerable success. In 1625, an Anglo-Dutch fleet defeated the Portuguese. The victors divided the spoils.

In 1642, England abandoned the Dutch and became Portugal's ally. As reward, British merchants won unhampered trade facilities with all Portuguese possessions in Asia except Macao. Ten years later, Britain went to war with Holland in Europe and Anglo-Portuguese forces fought the Dutch in India. At the cessation of hostilities in 1654, Britain extended her power in India at Holland's expense.

Wars, intrigues with Indian provincial warlords, and shrewd trading filled the coffers of the East India Company and enhanced its power. In the first half of the seventeenth century, England was importing cotton piece-goods, indigo, drugs, lac, sugar and carpets from India. Indian calicoes were a special favourite with British housewives. In return, the Company brought to India broadcloth, industrial metals and gold. In 1668, the Company received from the British King the former Portuguese possession of Bombay with its magnificent undeveloped harbour. With royal assent, a similar British position was established on the eastern coast at Madras. Feuds between the Moslem or Mogul emperors of India and the warlike Maratha Hindus of south-central India, in the area centring on Poona, east of Bombay, enabled the Company to proclaim the fusion of money-making and imperialism; it announced in December 1687, that it proposed to create such civil and military institutions 'as may be the foundation of a large, well-grounded, sure English dominion in India for all time to come.'

The accretion of British power moved with accelerated speed. The process was simple: early in 1749, for instance, Prince Shahji, native potentate of the state of Tajore, on the south-east coast, was dethroned by a rival; he offered the British a town called Devikottai at the place where the

Coleroon River empties into the Bay of Bengal 'on condition' says *The Cambridge History of India*, 'of their helping him to recover the throne'. After a few days of siege, Devikottai surrendered. 'The English kept it with the country belonging to it; and as for Shahji,' the British chronicle notes, 'no one thought of restoring him to his throne.'

Anybody wronged by the British was wooed by the French and vice versa. When Nawab Siraj-ud-daula, exploiting the disintegration of Mogul power at Delhi, took control of Bengal, the British tried to prevent him from getting too strong. In one indecisive skirmish he defeated a force of Europeans and imprisoned some of them overnight in the Black Hole of Calcutta, where an unknown number perished. But on 2 January, 1757, a young British officer named Robert Clive retook Calcutta and forced Siraj-ud-daula to accept humiliating terms. The nawab accordingly conspired with the French. The British Admiral Watson thereupon threatened him: 'I will kindle such a flame in your country,' the Englishman wrote, 'as all the water in the Ganges shall not be able to extinguish.' Sobered by these hot words, the Moslem ruler shrank into a passivity that facilitated the expulsion of his French allies from strategic Bengal areas. But the nawab remained and so did some French advisers. An insurrection, coinciding conveniently with the British attack, enabled Colonel Clive with 800 English and 2,220 mercenary Indian troops to rout the nawab's army of 50,000 at Plassey on 23 June, 1757. Siraj-ud-daula was executed and his rival, necessarily a complacent British puppet, replaced him. The entire province of Bengal was now a British colony. With a frankness born of impunity, Clive wrote to Robert Orme, 'I am possessed of volumes of material for the continuation of your history, in which will appear fighting, tricks, chicanery, intrigues, politics and the Lord knows what.' It was all politics.

Warren Hastings, the Governor-General of Bengal,

continued the policy of British expansion through armed force, enforced tributes and dynastic conspiracies. His trial in England, which lasted from February 1788 to April 1795, showed that the British administration in India was neither scrupulous nor incorruptible, nor concerned with the welfare of Indians.

Gradually, by means mostly foul but considered normal in that age and place, the British established themselves throughout the length and breadth of the vast Indian subcontinent. In some areas, the East India Company ruled directly through its officials. Elsewhere it stood close behind the thrones of Hindu maharajas and Moslem nawabs who pliantly subserved the politics of British empire-building.

The Portuguese had been confined to a few ports. The Dutch ' had been ousted. French power, though still considerable, was waning. In 1786, Mirabeau, the French revolutionary, urged the Russian Czar to help France by invading India. Napoleon's offensive against Egypt was conceived as the first step towards the destruction of the British in India. When the Corsican's campaign in the eastern Mediterranean collapsed he wrote to Emperor Paul I in St Petersburg urging him to march on India and promising men and supplies. Paul agreed and sent instructions to General Orlov, ataman of the Don Cossacks. 'All the wealth of India will be yours as a reward for the expedition,' he wrote. Russia 'would acquire treasure and commerce and strike the enemy in the heart'. The enemy was Britain. 'I am enclosing all the maps I have,' the Emperor added. 'They go only to Khiva and the Oxus.'

Later, Paul sent another map by special courier. General Orlov, however, never got beyond the Urals. Paul was mysteriously murdered and the Russo–French alliance lapsed. But in a few years it was renewed, and when Napoleon met Paul's successor, Alexander I, at Tilsit in East Prussia in 1807, they planned an assault on India. There is a letter in the

Russian archives penned by Napoleon to Alexander on 2 February, 1808, in which the Corsican proposed the formation of a Russo-French army to conquer India. 'England will be enslaved', Napoleon predicted. He promised Stockholm to Russia as a reward for her efforts against England in Asia.

These were idle dreams. The French in India were soon limited to a few maritime dots and when, in 1818, the British crushed the great Maratha empire in south-central India, the last organized challenge to British rule vanished. The rest was a clean-up operation.

While India was being subjugated, the invention of the spinning jenny in 1764, Watt's perfected steam engine in 1768 and the power loom in 1785 were converting England into a maker and exporter of textiles. Indian cotton goods were no longer wanted in Britain; on the contrary, Britain exported textiles and other factory products to the people of India who, in 1800, numbered approximately 140,000,000.

India's industry consequently languished; Indian treasure flowed to the British Isles as profit or plunder. Indian handicrafts suffered too. India was transformed into a purely agrarian country whose villages, overcrowded by the influx of unemployed townsmen, could not produce enough food. According to a British source, the deaths from famine in India between 1800 and 1825 were one million; between 1825 and 1850, four hundred thousand; between 1850 and 1875, five million; and between 1875 and 1900, fifteen million.

Engineered by wit and violence, England's annexations in India in the latter part of the eighteenth century and the first quarter of the nineteenth left many disgruntled and dispossessed native rulers. British attempts to introduce law and order and an equitable system of taxation further irritated innumerable persons nursing innumerable wounds. Widespread economic stringency intensified the general unrest. Only a spark was needed to produce a flame. India had not yet become totally docile, nor had the British learned the technique, which they subsequently mastered, of firm yet smooth and barely visible administration.

It was 1857, and a Hindu prophecy declared that on the centenary of the Battle of Plassey in 1757 British rule would perish. A war, officially called the Mutiny or the Sepoy Mutiny, broke out. The immediate impetus was the distribution among Indian troops of British-made cartridges, greased with cow or pig fat, which had to be bitten off before being loaded into rifles. Since a Hindu must not touch cow fat and a Moslem must not touch pork the provocation was perfect and Indian army units rebelled. But the British authorities admitted that the Bengal Indian force was 'a brotherhood' closely identified with the hungry villages, and the same bond connected all sepoys in British uniform with the ragged, hungry peasants.

Numerous regiments rose; one seized Delhi. Moslems took the lead, but all communities assiduously annulled innovations introduced by the British. Rail and telegraph lines were cut. Both sides committed numerous murders. Indian soldiers killed their British officers, and at Benares, 'rebels, suspects and even disorderly boys', says *The Cambridge History of India*, 'were executed by infuriated officers and unofficial British residents who volunteered to serve as hangmen'. Much blood also flowed in pitched battles and sieges.

The mutiny was unplanned, unco-ordinated, leaderless and hopeless. Inevitably, after many months, the British, aided by loyal Indians, suppressed it. With the restoration of peace, the East India Company, 'upon which', according to *The Cambridge History*, 'all parties in England agreed in throwing the blame of the Mutiny', was abolished. In 1858, Queen Victoria assumed the government of India and appointed Lord Canning her first Viceroy. For eighty-nine years thereafter, until 15 August, 1947, India was a colony of the British Empire.

The blood-and-plunder period was ended. England's ideal of clean government filtered into the British administration of India. The British watered some deserts and improved communications. Many British officials, after twenty or thirty years' service in India, felt at home in India and like foreigners when they went home to England. They were devoted to India. They ate out their hearts and ruined their health coping with difficult problems.

The British in India, however, were a fifth caste, the first caste. They interdined with Indians perfunctorily and intermarried seldom. The British were the super-Brahman-Kshatriyas; all Indians were 'untouchables'. The British were in India, never of India. They were like teachers who keep the class quiet and teach the children to read, write and reckon and to march in twos, but who do not really teach the children anything, nor help them, because they regard themselves as animal trainers and the children as nasty animals.

The British were masters in somebody else's home. Their very presence was a humiliation. Despite the best intentions of the best among them, their every act was a humiliation. Then they complained, with pain, that Indians were 'ungrateful'. The complaint was a measure of the lack of understanding.

The British never deciphered the palimpsest which is India. They merely read the inscription on the surface: India was a weak, dirty, backward country, with some fine monuments to be sure, and some superior brains, but generally inferior, and Asiatic.

Even if the British had converted India into a land flowing with milk and honey they would have been disliked. Imperialism, like dictatorship, sears the soul, degrades the spirit and makes individuals small the better to rule them. Fear and cowardice are its allies. Imperialism is government of other people, by other people, and for other people. What the subjects gain, be it ever so great, is only the by-product of efforts on behalf of a distant master.

The requirements of British prestige hurt Indian pride. All the visible manifestation of the British regime – the ceremonial pomp, the isolated cantonments or villas where the British dwelt, and the use of English – told the Indians that they were a subject race. Subjection stimulated a desire for liberation.

That is why colonial administration never is, and never can be, successful. History has known no good colonizers. Every empire digs its own grave. Imperialism is a perpetual insult, for it assumes that the outsider has the right to rule the insiders who cannot rule themselves; it is thus arrogant nationalism and inevitably begets an opposing nationalism.

Alien rule thwarts the native lovers of power. The British could never forget the Mutiny. 'After all,' Lord Linlithgow, the British Viceroy, said to me in 1942, 'we are the occupying power. Ever since the Mutiny we have hesitated to put arms into the hands of Indians.' Decades after the Mutiny, when the British were secure enough in their power to share it, the share of Indians was small. Real power – the authority to decide, appoint, recall and spend – lay with the British. No matter how high an Indian rose in the government service he remained a British hireling. His power was not merely severely restricted; it lacked one of the sweetest concomitants of power: popularity; for the more the British trusted him the more his own people rejected him.

Unloved and unwanted, the British found it dangerous to arouse too many expectations of self-government and inconvenient to kill too many hopes for it. Hence, all the eighty-nine years of British rule constitute a series of oscillations between bold promises and disappointing performances. When the Queen took over from the Company in 1858 she announced that 'as far as may be' Indians would be given responsible posts in the government. But Lord Lytton, Viceroy from 1876 to 1880, wrote in a secret report, 'Since I am writing confidentially, I do not hesitate to say that both the government of England and of India appear to me up to the present moment unable to answer satisfactorily the charge of having taken every means in their power of breaking to the heart the words of promise they have uttered to the ear.'

This was the complaint by a man who, unfettered by London, would have done better. But the Indians naturally regretted the breach of faith even more keenly than the Queen's first officer in India.

When the demand for broader participation in local government and for redress of grievances grew more insistent, Lord Dufferin, Viceroy from 1884 to 1888, intending to direct upper-class discontent into an artificial canal, sired the Indian National Congress; subsequent Viceroys blessed it. Even if they had foreseen that a callow Indian law student in London in the late 1880s would make Congress an instrument of the downfall of British rule, they could not have helped themselves. The history of the British rule in India is a record of retreats, more graceful in some Viceregal quinquenniums than in others, but always enhancing Indian strength. Torn between their political sagacity and their power lust, the British yielded as much of the appearance of power as circumstances required and as little of its substance as conditions permitted.

Many times, for instance, Indians had been promised equality of employment in the ICS (Indian Civil Service), which was the British administration of India. 'After eighty-two years of equality,' H. N. Brailsford remarks sarcastically, Englishmen held 95 per cent of the posts in the ICS in 1915. In 1923, he declares, using accepted figures, Indian participation was still only 10 per cent.

Jealous of her power, England feared the Indians. Conscious of their white skins and racial superiority, the British scorned the Indians.

Fear, and the administrator's natural wish to administer

with maximum facility, impelled the British to adopt the approved imperialistic tactic of Divide and Rule. Since the Moslems played the leading role in the Mutiny and were thought to harbour dreams of empire, the British at first preferred the Hindus to the Moslems. When unrest and political ambition stirred the Hindus, the British used the Moslems against the Hindus.

Similarly, Britain divided the country between British India, governed directly by England, and native India, governed indirectly by England but directly, and ostensibly, by Indian princes. It was a cynical device, avowed as such by Lord Canning on 30 April, 1860; he wrote, 'It was long ago said by Sir John Malcom that if we made all India into zillahs [or British districts] it was not in the nature of things that our empire should last fifty years; but that if we could keep up a number of native states without political power but as royal instruments, we should exist in India as long as our naval supremacy was maintained. Of the substantial truth of this opinion I have no doubt; the recent events make it more deserving of our attention than ever.' In the twentieth century, these royal instruments without political power numbered over five hundred and fifty. With that number of puppets the British thought they were secure.

Professor Rushbrook Williams, a brilliant Englishman who often served as official intermediary with Indian princes, wrote in the London *Evening Standard* of 28 May, 1930, 'The situations of these feudatory states, chequerboarding all India as they do, are a great safeguard. It is like establishing a vast network of friendly fortresses in debatable territory. It would be difficult for a general rebellion against the British to sweep India because of this network of powerful, loyal, native states.'

Nothing could be more clear.

Lest India become strong enough economically to break from the Empire, and in order, too, to help British industries in the motherland, Indian industries were discouraged and

Indian shipping and shipbuilding were officially restricted. Education was not designed to train a technical staff for industry nor a professional class to serve the country. With a population of approximately 380,000,000, India, in 1939, had only 1,306 students of agriculture, 2,413 of engineering, 719 of veterinary science, 150 of technology, 63 of forestry and only 3,561 in medicine, in her colleges and universities, according to the official *Statistical Abstract for British India.*

In 1939, India, with three times the population of the United States and two-thirds the area, had 41,134 miles of railway track, compared with 395,589 miles in the United States. India produced 2,500,000,000 kilowatt-hours of electric energy in 1935; the United States, 98,464,000,000 kilowatt-hours.

These conditions were not the sole fault of the British; Indians shared the blame. But Indians blamed everything on the British.

Indians delight in criticizing, and autocrats detest criticism. 'All opposition', writes Sir Valentine Chirol, a British authority on India, 'even in the shape of criticism which it can treat as a mere waste of breath, is distasteful to an autocracy and apt to be regarded even as pregnant with sedition, and the British officials in India honestly believed in an autocratic form of government though they tried to make it as paternal as possible.'

British paternalistic autocracy irritated some Indians and embittered others. Towards the end of the nineteenth century, Indian terrorists began to operate in Bengal and other areas. Terror invited repression which provoked more terror.

One school of British politics wished to meet Indian hostility with blood and iron; a second school wished to mollify it with reforms. Each of these had its counterpart inside the Indian National Congress.

The British autocrats did not help the Indian moderates.

Late in the nineteenth century, Field-Marshal Lord Roberts, well known in India, said, 'It is this consciousness of the inherent superiority of the European which has won us India. However well educated and clever a native may be and however brave he may have proved himself, I believe that no rank which we can bestow upon him would cause him to be considered an equal by the British officer.'

Such racialism bred implacable enemies and embarrassed the moderates. The liberal lawyers, publicists and capitalists retained their control of Congress, but not everybody was in Congress. Boys were hurling bombs. Young men with degrees from Oxford and Cambridge were rejecting the West. East is East and West is West, and if the twain cannot meet, they said, it is because East was slave and West was master.

In *Toward Freedom*, an autobiography, Jawaharlal Nehru writes that in 1907, at seventeen, when he had just gone to Cambridge from Harrow, he was an extremist. In fact, speaking of the Indian students, he says, 'Almost without exception we were Tilakites or Extremists.'

Bal Gangadhar Tilak, known as 'Lokamanya' or 'Respected by the People', played a key role in the development of the Indian independence movement and in Gandhi's life.

Tilak was a high-degree Brahman, a Chitpawan Brahman, from Poona in the land of the Marathas, the last Indian folk to be conquered by the British. The Marathas are highlanders who many times in their history descended into the lowlands, notably into Gandhi's homeland Gujarat, to dominate the less bellicose peoples of the plains. Once, these fighting Hindus captured Moslem Delhi; they remained foes of Islam.

Tilak inaugurated an annual festival to celebrate King Shivaji (born 1627, died 1680) who brought new triumphs to the Maratha empire. He wrote a most scholarly commentary on the *Gita* and defended every orthodox tenet and practice of Hinduism, including child marriage. He branded as a puppet any Indian who worked for the British. He exposed the emptiness of British concessions to Indian home-rule aspirations.

Tilak's fierce imprecations, the British charged, stirred a young Chitpawan Brahman to assassinate a British official on 27 June, 1897, the day of Queen Victoria's Diamond Jubilee, and Tilak was condemned to two years in prison. Liberated before the end of his term, he resumed his Hindu-religious agitation which, while aimed at the British, did not, to say the least, improve relations between Hindus and Moslems.

Hindu passions continued to simmer. Indian nationalism found food in numerous events at home and abroad: the hollowness of British reforms nurtured it and so did the Japanese defeat of the Russians in the 1904–05 war (the first time a coloured nation defeated a white one), the 1905 Russian revolution and the rise of the Young Turks.

In 1904 Lord Curzon, considered by some the greatest Viceroy of India, decreed the partition of the province of Bengal. This act may have been the beginning of the end of British rule in India; Indians always mention it as a British atrocity. Curzon, despite his monumental ability and industry, was a bureaucrat, autocrat and aristocrat. He lived close to his files and far from the people. Bengal had a population of over seventy million and Curzon divided it the better to administer it. But the bisection was on religious lines: the Moslem area was separated from the more powerful Hindu area. Bitterness knew no restraint. Curzon was accused of anti-Hindu prejudice and of trying to put the Moslems under a debt which they would have to pay in the coin of submissiveness.

These and similar charges were directed at Curzon until he left India towards the end of 1904. Bengal answered the partition with assassinations. In the land of the Marathas, Tilak whipped his followers into a frenzy. In both provinces

British goods were boycotted; in both, Gandhi always found his most stubborn enemies.

Gandhi and Tilak were opposites. Gandhi was a quiet public speaker, Tilak the consummate orator. Gandhi was wedded to non-violence; Tilak justified violence. Gandhi fostered Hindu–Moslem amity; Tilak favoured Hindu supremacy. Gandhi respected means; Tilak pursued ends. Tilak's work bore bitter fruit.

The 1906 annual session of Congress met in Calcutta, then the capital of India as well as of Bengal. It demanded a reversal of the partition, supported the anti-British boycott and resolved in favour of self-government for India.

Lord Minto, Curzon's successor, let it become known in 1906 that he was contemplating reforms which would give Indians a bigger voice in the provincial legislatures and more jobs in government offices. But the Tilak extremists were not mollified. Violence continued in Bengal and Maharashtra and spread to the Punjab. At the 1907 Congress session in Surat, moderates and extremists threw sandals at one another. After the fray, the Tilakites withdrew from the Congress, leaving the lawyers in control.

The reforms drafted by Lord Minto, with the assistance of John Morley, Secretary of State for India in London, were introduced in 1908 and 1909. They extended Indian participation in the all-Indian and provincial legislative councils and in provincial executive councils as well. One Indian joined the Viceroy's executive council. But Morley made it clear, in the House of Lords debate in December 1908, that 'if it could be said that this chapter of reforms led directly or indirectly or necessarily up to the establishment of a parliamentary system in India, I, for one, would have nothing to do with it'. More Indians sat on legislative councils and they talked more, but they had no more power, for the councils themselves had no power; their function was consultative.

Any joy which Indians might have derived from the Minto–Morley reforms was soured by a concomitant measure: the introduction of separate electorates. In 1906, a Moslem deputation led by the Aga Khan waited upon Lord Minto and urged that in all future elections Hindus vote for Hindu representatives and Moslems for Moslem representatives. Nationalist historians have branded this interview as a 'command performance' rehearsed and conducted under Minto's baton. Whatever the facts, Minto and Morley granted the Moslem request, and in 1909, separate religious electorates, embellished with a device enabling Moslems to obtain more than their proportional number of seats (weightage, this was called), became a permanent Indian institution whose mischief was incalculable, for it made religious differences the decisive factor in every political contest. The central political problem in India was to bridge the gulf between Hindus and Moslems; this widened it.

However, the first though not lasting effect of the separate electorates was to bring more Moslems into the Congress party. Prominent among them was Mohamed Ali Jinnah.

In 1911, the new King, George V, and Queen Mary, visited India amid fantastic pomp. The King announced the removal of the capital to Delhi and the annulment of the partition of Bengal. Nevertheless, and though Tilak had been sentenced for sedition in November 1907 to a long term of imprisonment and was ailing in Mandalay, acts of personal terror continued; in 1912 Lord Hardinge, the Viceroy, narrowly escaped death by a bomb.

The outbreak of war in 1914 found some Indians loyal, some disloyal and a few enthusiastic, but many ready to serve in the British Army. More than half a million Indians fought for England in France, Flanders, Palestine and on other fronts. Indian princes and commoners distinguished themselves in combat on the ground and in the air.

Tilak had returned from exile in 1914 and pledged loyalty.

Gandhi returned from South Africa, via London, in January 1915 and recruited for the British Army. But idleness and the Irish rebellion at Easter, 1916, were too much for Tilak's fiery spirit and he burst forth into a passionate anti-British campaign in favour of home-rule. His companion agitator, who if anything excelled him in oratory and vituperation, was Mrs Annie Besant. They were vigorously assisted by Sir C. P. Ramaswami Aiyar and by Mohamed Ali Jinnah.

The Indian earth rumbled with the noise of the volcano beneath it. Not only the politicians, but the soldiers and even the peasants, felt that the blood Indians were shedding in Britain's battle should be recompensed. On 20 August, 1917, accordingly, Edwin S. Montagu, Secretary of State for India, announced in the House of Commons that British policy envisaged 'not only the increasing association of Indians in every branch of the administration, but also the granting of self-governing institutions with a view to the progressive realization of responsible government in India as an integral part of the British Empire'. This was interpreted as being a pledge of Dominion Status.

Tilak thought that on occasions it might be desirable to occupy positions of power within the state apparatus. He once sent Gandhi a cheque for fifty thousand rupees as a bet that he could recruit five thousand Marathas for the British army if Gandhi extracted a promise from the Viceroy that some of the enlisted personnel would receive officers' commissions. Gandhi returned the cheque. He did not like betting. And he felt that if you do something you do it because you believe in it and nor for what you hope to get out of it.

The war closed victoriously in November 1918. Trouble did not wait long; it came early in 1919.

Tilak had been interned again in August 1918. Mrs Besant was also under arrest. Shaukat Ali and Mohamed Ali, brothers and powerful and prominent Moslem leaders, had been imprisoned during the war. Secret tribunals had been sentencing people in all parts of India. Many newspapers were muzzled by war-time censorship. These measures evoked great bitterness. But with the coming of peace, the country expected the restoration of civil liberties.

Instead, a committee headed by Sir Sidney Rowlatt, who had come from England to study the administration of justice, issued a report on 19 July, 1918, which recommended, in effect, a continuation of the war-time rigours. The Congress party fiercely denounced the Rowlatt findings. In February 1919 a bill embodying them was nevertheless offered by the Government to the Imperial Legislative Council. Gandhi attended the debate and appreciated the attacks levelled by Indian members against the bill but, since a majority of the Council consisted of British government officials, its passage, after what Gandhi called the 'farce of legal formality', was assured.

Gandhi, just recuperating from dysentery and from an operation for fissures necessitated by it, decided that the impending government legislation was 'unjust, subversive of the principle of liberty and destructive of the elementary rights of individuals on which the safety of the community as a whole and of the State itself is based'.

Assuming that the bill would be enacted, Gandhi began preparations for civil resistance on the pattern of his victorious effort in South Africa. Though still so weak that somebody had to read his speeches, he travelled to many cities laying the groundwork for a gigantic, nationwide Satyagraha campaign designed to induce the Government to withdraw repressive legislation. Meanwhile, he appealed to the Viceroy by letter and through the press not to approve the law.

On 18 March, 1919, the Rowlatt Act became the law of the land. An electric shock ran through India. Was this the commencement of Dominion Status? Was this the reward for the blood shed in the war?

The next day, Mahatma Gandhi, who had come to Madras

for a meeting, said to his host, C. Rajagopalachari, 'Last night the idea came to me in a dream that we should call on the country to observe a general hartal.' A hartal is a suspension of economic activity: shopkeepers do not open for business, employees do not report for work, factories stay shut, ships are not loaded or unloaded. Gandhi urged that hartal day be a day of 'fasting and prayer' and of 'humiliation and prayer'. Thereafter Satyagraha would unfold according to the circumstances; resisters might, for example, buy and sell proscribed books, or manufacture salt in contravention of the law which made its production a state monopoly.

The hartal was Gandhi's first act against the British government of India. Indeed, it was his first political act in India. His intervention on behalf of the Champaran sharecroppers had unintentionally involved him in friction with a British court. But now he deliberately appealed for a nation-wide demonstration against the British authorities. It was the beginning of his twenty-eight years of struggle against British rule in India. The end of the struggle was the end of British rule.

CHAPTER 8

Murder

Gandhi's hartal idea spread throughout India. It united vast multitudes in common action; it gave the people a sense of power. They loved Gandhi for it. The hartal paralysed economic life; the dead cities and towns were tangible proof that Indians could be effective. What the Indian people needed most and lacked most, was faith in themselves. Gandhi gave it to them.

Six hundred men and women in Bombay signed the Satyagraha pledge. Gandhi was happy. He had won with fewer numbers in South Africa. Vows were being taken in other cities, and in many villages. 'Even such a mighty government as the Government of India,' Gandhi declared at Bombay, 'will have to yield if we are true to our pledge. For the pledge is no small thing. It means a change of heart. It is an attempt to introduce the religious spirit into politics. We may no longer believe in the doctrine of "tit for tat"; we may not meet hatred with hatred, violence with violence, evil with evil; but we have to make a continuous and persistent effort to return good for evil . . . Nothing is impossible.'

Sceptics mocked. 'I have no desire to argue,' Gandhi replied. 'As the British proverb says, "The proof of the pudding lies in the eating".' The movement had been launched; it would surely spread and surely triumph.

In a further appeal to the Viceroy, the Mahatma put the whole question on a high, universal level. The Satyagraha campaign, he told the Viceroy, 'constitutes an attempt to revolutionize politics and restore moral force to its original station'. He quoted a statement of President Woodrow Wilson at Paris to the effect that if the moral force behind the

League of Nations Covenant did not suffice, physical force would. 'We', Gandhi wrote, 'hope to reverse the process and by our action show that physical force is nothing compared to moral force and that moral force never fails.'

Somebody protested that Gandhi's Satyagraha campaign would abet Bolshevism. (The Bolshevik Revolution had taken place on 7 November, 1917, and made a deep impression on the East.) No, Gandhi said in a speech at Madras on 30 March, 1919, 'if anything can possibly prevent this calamity descending upon our country, it is Satyagraha. Bolshevism is the necessary result of modern materialistic civilization. Its insensate worship of matter has given rise to a school which has been brought up to look upon materialistic advancement as the goal and which has lost all touch with the final things of life . . . I prophesy that if we disobey the law of the final supremacy of spirit over matter, of liberty and love over brute force, in a few years' time we shall have Bolshevism rampant in this land which was once so holy'.

The hartal, a prelude to Satyagraha, was observed in Delhi on 30 March and in Bombay and other cities and villages on 6 April; 'Needless to say,' Gandhi reported, 'the hartal in Bombay was a complete success.' The nationwide hartal, he said, 'was a most wonderful spectacle'.

In Delhi, however, the hartal provoked violence. The Punjab, home of millions of Moslems and Hindus and of five million bearded, turbaned, stoutly built Sikhs whose religion was an offshoot of Hinduism, echoed to riots and shootings. Leaders asked Gandhi to come quickly to Delhi and the Punjab. The British stopped him at the borders of the province on 9 April and escorted him back to Bombay, where he was released. En route to and from Bombay, Gandhi sent messages that he was safe and free; reports of his arrest had inflamed the already heated passions of the people; riots occurred in Bombay and Ahmedabad.

On 11 April, Gandhi admonished his followers in Bombay.

'We have been throwing stones,' he said. 'We have obstructed tramcars by putting obstacles in the way. That is not Satyagraha. We have demanded the release of about fifty men who had been arrested for deeds of violence. But our duty is chiefly to get ourselves arrested. It is a breach of religious duty to endeavour to secure the release of those who have committed deeds of violence . . . If we cannot conduct this movement without the slightest violence from our side,' Gandhi warned, 'the movement might have to be abandoned . . . It may be necessary to go even further. The time may come for me to offer Satyagraha against ourselves . . . I have just heard that some English gentlemen have been injured. Some may even have died from such injuries. If so, it would be a great blot on Satyagraha. For me, Englishmen too are our brethren.'

From Bombay, Gandhi went to his ashram at Sabarmati, where on 14 April he addressed a huge multitude. Ahmedabad citizens too had committed acts of violence of which Gandhi was ashamed; 'a rapier run through my body could hardly have pained me more'. Scathingly he denounced them: 'We have burnt down buildings, forcibly captured weapons, extorted money, stopped trains, cut off telegraph wires, killed innocent people and plundered shops and private houses.' As penance, he announced that he had undertaken a seventy-two-hour fast. He asked the people to fast twenty-four.

Immediately after the Sabarmati meeting, Gandhi left for Nadiad, a town in the Kheda district, twenty-nine miles from Ahmedabad, where he had recruited for the war. There he discovered that violence had spread to small towns as well.

Depressed, Gandhi told the people of Nadiad that the entire Satyagraha campaign was 'a Himalayan miscalculation' on his part. On 18 April he called off the movement.

Many scoffed; the Mahatma, they taunted, had made 'a Himalayan miscalculation'. But Gandhi never regretted a confession of error. 'I have always held', he wrote in his autobiography, 'that it is only when one sees one's own mistakes with a convex lens and does just the reverse in the case of others, that one is able to arrive at a just relative estimate of the two.' What politician would say that?

His miscalculation, Gandhi explained, was in overlooking the fact that a person must be trained in civil obedience before civil disobedience against some laws could succeed. 'I am sorry,' Gandhi said in cancelling the Satyagraha campaign, 'that when I embarked upon a mass movement I underrated the forces of evil and I must now pause and consider how best to meet the situation.' Nobody forsook his leadership because he did not immediately announce a clever new plan to divert attention from the one that failed.

Meanwhile, the Punjab province boiled. Events there culminated in the occurrence in the sacred Sikh city of Amritsar on 13 April, 1919, which Sir Valentine Chirol called 'that black day in the annals of British India'. For Gandhi it was a turning point. Indians never forgot it.

An official commission of inquiry, appointed by the government of India and consisting of seven members, four British and three Indian, with Lord Hunter, Senator of the College of Justice of Scotland, as chairman, investigated the Punjab disturbances for many months and then published its report. It found that in Amritsar 'the Hartal on the thirtieth [of March] was successful beyond expectation and stopped the whole business of the city. There was no collision with the police and no resort to violence'. On 6 April, Amritsar, a city of 150,000 inhabitants, observed another hartal. 'This second time also the Hartal passed off successfully,' the official Hunter Report affirms, 'and Europeans could and did walk unmolested amongst the crowds.'

On 9 April, the Punjab government issued an order for the deportation from the province of the two Congress party leaders, Dr Saifuddin Kitchlew, a Moslem, and Dr Satyapal, a Hindu. It was the day of the Hindu festival Ram Naumi in which, according to the Report, Moslems also joined, shouting 'Mahatma Gandhi ki jai (Long Live Mahatma Gandhi)' and 'Hindu–Mussalman ki jai (Long Live Hindu–Moslem unity)' and 'drinking out of the same cups publicly by way of demonstration'. The police expected that the demonstrators would try to liberate the two leaders and precautions were taken, but 'there was no attempt at rescue'.

The banishing of the leaders removed from Amritsar the two men who might have restrained the populace. 'Starting in anger at the action of the government in deporting the two local politicians,' reads the Hunter Report, a mob raged through the streets. At the National Bank, Mr Stewart, the manager, and Mr Scott, the assistant manager, were beaten to death and at the Alliance Bank, Mr G. M. Thomson, the manager, 'who attempted to defend himself with a revolver, was cruelly murdered'. Other English people were assaulted.

Two days later, Brigadier-General Reginald Edward Henry Dyer arrived in Amritsar. Dyer, born in Simla, India, in 1864, was educated at Middleton College, County Cork, Ireland, and entered the British Army in 1885. He fought on the north-west frontier, in the Burma war and in the first World War. April 1919 found him commanding a brigade at Jullunder, in the Punjab. Ordered to Amritsar on the 11th, he issued a proclamation on the 12th prohibiting processions and meetings. 'The issue of the proclamation which was formally signed by the Brigade-Major on General Dyer's behalf,' says the Hunter Report, 'was left to the police; it does not appear what steps were taken to ensure its publication.'

During the morning of the next day, 13 April, Dyer went through the city reading the proclamation to the people. 'From an examination of the map, showing the different places where the proclamation was read,' the Hunter Report asserts, 'it is evident that in many parts of the city the proclamation was not read.'

The Hunter Report then tells the story of the massacre of 13 April. 'About one o'clock', it reads, 'General Dyer heard that the people intended to hold a big meeting about four-thirty P.M. On being asked why he did not take measures to prevent its being held, he replied: "I went there as soon as I could. I had to think the matter out."'

The meeting took place at Jallianwalla Bagh. Bagh means gardens. 'Jallianwalla Bagh', the Report says, 'is not in any sense a garden as its name would suggest. It is a rectangular piece of unused ground, covered to some extent by building material and debris. It is almost entirely surrounded by walls of buildings. The entrances and exits to it are few and imperfect. It seems to be frequently used to accommodate large gatherings of people. At the end at which General Dyer entered there is a raised ground on each side of the entrance. A large crowd had gathered at the opposite end of the Bagh and were being addressed by a man on a raised platform about 150 yards from where General Dyer stationed his troops.' The Report estimates that there were between ten and twenty thousand persons in the Bagh.

Dyer went to the garden with twenty-five Gurkhas (soldiers from Nepal) and twenty-five Baluchis from Baluchistan armed with rifles, forty Gurkhas armed only with knives and two armoured cars. 'On arriving at Jallianwalla Bagh', the Report declares, 'he [Dyer] entered with this force by a narrow entrance which was not sufficiently wide to allow the cars to pass. They were accordingly left in the street outside.

'As soon as General Dyer entered the Bagh,' the Report continues, 'he stationed twenty-five troops on one side of the higher ground at the entrance and twenty-five troops on the other side. Without giving the crowd any warning to disperse, which he considered unnecessary as they were in breach of his proclamation, he ordered his troops to fire and the firing continued for about ten minutes. There is no evidence as to the nature of the address to which the audience was listening.

None of them were provided with firearms, although some of them may have been carrying sticks.

'As soon as the firing commenced the crowd began to disperse. In all 1,650 rounds were fired by the troops. The firing was individual and not volley firing . . . As a result of this investigation it was discovered that approximately 379 people were killed.' The Report estimates that there were three times as many wounded as dead. This adds up to 379 dead plus 1,137 wounded or 1,516 casualties with 1,650 bullets. The crowd, penned in the low-lying garden, was a perfect target.

Under cross-examination before the Hunter Commission, Dyer revealed his mind and purpose:

'Question: From time to time you changed your firing and directed it to the place where the crowd was thickest?

'Answer: That is so.'

The crowd had rushed to the lowest wall, which was five feet high and that is where the bullets felled many of them.

'Question: Supposing the passage was sufficient to allow the armoured cars to go in, would you have opened fire with the machine-guns?

'Answer: I think, probably, yes.'

'When examined before us', the Hunter Report asserts, 'he [Dyer] explained that his mind was made up as he came along in his motor car; if his orders against holding a meeting were disobeyed he was going to fire at once.'

'I had made up my mind,' Dyer testified, 'I would do all men to death . . .'

General Dyer's own dispatch to his military superior, which is quoted in the Hunter Report with his italics, said, 'I fired and continued to fire until the crowd dispersed and I consider this the least amount of firing which could produce the necessary effect it was my duty to produce if I was to justify my action. *It was no longer a question of merely dispersing the crowd*, but one of producing a sufficient moral effect from a military point of view not only on those who were present, but more especially throughout the Punjab. There could be no question of undue severity.'

The Hunter Commission decided that 'This was unfortunately a mistaken conception of his duty.' It also found that 'in continuing to fire for so long as he did it appears to us that General Dyer committed a grave error'.

Moreover, the Report notes that 'General Dyer's action in not making provision for the wounded at Jallianwalla Bagh has been made the subject of criticism'. Dyer said at the hearings, 'I was ready to help them if they applied.'

Sir Michael O'Dwyer, British Acting Governor of the Punjab, approved of Dyer's action and referred to the disturbances as 'rebellion'. The Hunter Commission commented: 'The action taken by General Dyer has also been described by others as having saved the situation in the Punjab and having averted a rebellion on a scale similar to the Mutiny. It does not, however, appear to us possible to draw this conclusion, particularly in view of the fact that a conspiracy to overthrow British power had not been formed prior to the outbreaks.'

Not only was no insurrection intended or planned, but, according to the Hunter Report, 'It appears that the outburst on the 10 April subsided in a few hours, there was no repetition of any serious incident afterwards either on that date or on subsequent dates. And even with regard to the events on the 10th . . . if the officer in charge . . . had done his duty, the worst crimes, viz., the murders of the bank officers . . . would in all probability have been prevented.'

Amritsar had been calm for two and a half days when Dyer's butchery occurred. His unnecessary massacre was the child of the British military mentality then dominant in India. To characterize this mentality, the Hunter Report quotes an utterance of General Drake-Brockman of Delhi who said, 'Force is the only thing that an Asiatic has any respect for.'

'I thought I would be doing a jolly lot of good,' was Dyer's airy summary of the massacre at Jallianwalla Bagh.

To add humiliation to hurt, General Dyer published his infamous 'crawling order'. On 10 April Miss Sherwood, the headmistress of a girls' school in Amritsar, had been barbarously attacked by the mob. Several days after the Jallianwalla Bagh blood bath, Dyer issued instructions that anybody passing the street where Miss Sherwood was assaulted would have to go on all fours. This applied even to members of families whose only approach to their homes was through that street. Gandhi felt worse about this 'outrage', as he called it, than about the massacre.

At the spot, moreover, on which Miss Sherwood was beaten, Dyer erected a whipping post for the public flogging of those who ignored his order that Indians on animals and vehicles must alight, Indians carrying umbrellas or parasols must lower them, and all Indians must salute or 'salaam' with the hand as they passed British officers in some districts of Amritsar.

The British Secretary of State for India, Edwin S. Montagu, in an official dispatch to the Viceroy, Lord Chelmsford, dated 26 May, 1920, wrote, 'His Majesty's Government repudiate emphatically the doctrine upon which Brigadier-General Dyer based his action' at Jallianwalla Bagh. The crawling order, Montagu added, 'offended against every canon of civilized government'. Innumerable Englishmen were ashamed of Dyer's deed, yet he found many defenders.

Dyer was asked to resign from the army. Towards the end of his life, he invented a range finder for sighting aircraft. He died in retirement at Bristol on 23 July, 1927.

Under the Hunter Commission's cross-examination, General Dyer had said, 'Yes, I think it quite possible that I could have dispersed them perhaps without firing' but 'I was going to punish them. My idea from the military point of view was to make a wide impression.'

'We have no doubt', the official British Hunter Report continued, 'that he succeeded in creating a very wide impression and a great moral effect, but of a character quite opposite from the one he intended.' Jallianwalla Bagh quickened India's political life and drew Gandhi into politics.

CHAPTER 9

Gandhi Enters Politics

Mahatma Gandhi always resisted politics. He regarded his South African work as moral and social, therefore religious. After his return to India in 1915 he attended annual sessions of Congress, but his public activity at such assemblies was usually limited to moving a resolution in support of the Indians in South Africa. Moreover, he regarded the Congress as the unofficial parliament of India in which all political trends and parties were, or could be, represented.

To join one party dedicated to a political goal meant a separation from other parties, and Gandhi disliked anything divisive. He had strong beliefs but no dogmas.

Gandhi's 'readiness to take up the cudgels on behalf of any individual or class whom he regarded as being oppressed', reads a discerning remark in a 1919 British government publication, 'has endeared him to the masses of the country'. He preferred the warm bond of human affection to the cold tongue of a party programme.

Yet in 1920 Gandhi joined the All-India Home Rule League and became its president.

Politics can probably be defined as competition for power. It implies an effort to weaken, destroy, or assume the power of those in power. Gandhi did not wish to weaken, destroy, or supplant Smuts in South Africa. But by becoming leader of the All-India Home Rule League, Gandhi did accept the goal of Indian self-government instead of government by England. The Congress did not yet advocate independence.

Gandhi's early steps in politics were uncertain. Indeed, he remained politically unpredictable throughout life because his mind was a battlefield on which caution contended with passion. Ready to die fighting for a principle, he preferred to arbitrate and compromise. He was a natural fighter and a born peacemaker.

Gandhi's criteria were not the usual criteria of politics. His leadership did not depend on victories. He did not have to save 'face'. In the autobiography, Gandhi tells of incidents that could not have been known but for him, how he visited a brothel, ate meat in stealth, maltreated his wife, etc. Truth had to be the whole truth or it wasn't true. Indians, whom suffering has made suspicious, could not suspect Gandhi because he told them everything; he hated secrets; he was his own harshest critic. He could admit blunders, 'Himalayan' and less, because he did not claim infallibility or superiority.

Gandhi's critics complained that he would withdraw from a political battle before all his forces had been brought to bear on the enemy and, sometimes, when success appeared imminent. But what success? His standards of success were moral and religious. They gave his politics the only consistency and continuity they had.

The road by which Gandhi arrived at the centre of the Indian political world was tortuous. It started at Jallianwalla Bagh; no matter where he went the echo of General Dyer's fusillade pursued him. Following the massacre, Gandhi asked permission to visit the Punjab. He was rebuffed. He pressed his case. Finally, the Viceroy telegraphed him that he could go after 17 October, 1919. The Mahatma's reception at Lahore and other cities was unprecedented in size and warmth. 'The seething mass of humanity', he wrote, 'was delirious with joy.' He had become a symbol of national resistance to the foreign evil.

In the Punjab, Gandhi assisted Indian leaders, among them Motilal Nehru, a veteran Congressman and father of Jawaharlal, in the conduct of an independent inquiry into the Jallianwalla Bagh massacre. He drafted the report; his colleagues felt he would be without bias.

While thus engaged, Gandhi received an invitation to attend a Moslem conference in Delhi. He arrived there 24 November, 1919. The Armistice which ended the first World War had been signed on 11 November, 1918. It sealed the defeat of Turkey, a Moslem country, and of the Turkish Sultan, who, in addition to being a temporal ruler, was the Caliph or religious head of all Islam.

Pan-Islamism has never been a mass movement in India or elsewhere. The fate of the Caliph nevertheless agitated the Moslems in India. The Moslem leaders, notably Mohamed and Shaukat Ali, the brothers who were interned by the British during the war, Jinnah, Asaf Ali and Maulana Abu Kalam Azad had hoped that Indian interest in the Caliph would at least induce England to moderate the peace terms imposed on Turkey. But when it became obvious that the Turks would be shorn of their imperial possessions, and that the Sultan himself would be deposed, concern for the Caliph, added to distaste for the British, produced a powerful Caliphate or, as it is always known in India, Khilafat movement.

The Moslem conference in Delhi, in November 1919, which Gandhi attended, was a Khilafat meeting. Many Hindus were present. This period was the honeymoon of Hindu–Moslem political friendship. The letter of invitation, which reached Gandhi in Lahore, said cow protection as well as the Caliph would be discussed. Gandhi demurred. He told the conference that if, in deference to Hindu regard for the cow as a sacred animal, Mohammedans wanted to desist from slaughtering it, they should do so irrespective of the Hindu attitude towards the Khilafat question. Similarly, if Hindus believed they ought to support Moslems on behalf of the Caliph they should, but not in the expectation of a bargain on cow protection. The cow, therefore, was removed from the agenda.

The conference debated what to do; resolutions

condemning British harshness towards Turkey were not enough. A boycott of British textiles was suggested. But how could buyers distinguish British from other foreign textiles, and might not British goods be sold as Japanese or Italian or Belgian? Perhaps all imported cloth should be boycotted. Could India produce sufficient textiles to supply the domestic market?

Gandhi sat on the platform searching his mind for a plan of action. He was looking for a programme and then for a word that would be alike a slogan and a perfect summary of that programme. Finally, he found it, and when he was called on to speak he said, 'Non-co-operation'. Indians could not simultaneously oppose the Government and work with it. To boycott British exports was inadequate; they must boycott British schools, British courts, British jobs, British honours; they must non-co-operate.

'Non-co-operation' became the name of an epoch in the life of India and of Gandhi. Non-co-operation was negative enough to be peaceful but positive enough to be effective. It entailed denial, renunciation and self-discipline. It was training for self-rule.

Gandhi's advice to the Moslem conference was contingent on the final peace terms dictated to Turkey. If they were as onerous as expected and destroyed the status of the Caliph, then India would non-co-operate. Thus Gandhi left a loophole for a modification of British policy vis-à-vis the Turks.

The annual session of congress took place in the last week of that year, 1919 – at Amritsar. The fact that the Government allowed it to meet near Jallianwalla Bagh and that the Ali brothers were released on the eve of the session so that they could come straight to it from jail, fed Gandhi's congenial optimism.

By design or coincidence, the King-Emperor announced the much-heralded Montagu–Chelmsford reforms ('A new era is opening,' the King declared) the day before Congress met. The announcement, Gandhi asserted, 'was not wholly satisfactory even to me and was unsatisfactory to everyone else'; nevertheless, he favoured acceptance. In November, in Delhi, he urged non-co-operation. In December, in Amritsar, he favoured co-operation.

The Montagu–Chelmsford reforms, approved by the British House of Commons as 'The Government of India Act of 1919' became the new Constitution of India on 9 February, 1921. The British called the new system 'Dyarchy'; monarchy, the rule of one – Great Britain – became dy-archy, the rule of two – Great Britain and India. Indians, however, had no power in the federal government and none was contemplated. In the provinces, Indian ministers would administer agriculture, industries, education, health, excise, roads, building, etc, but the British governor retained complete control of finance and police and he could override any decision of the Indian ministers and of the Indian legislature. Indian participation in the Civil Service was increased and promises of further increases were made. But Indians decided that, on the whole, dyarchy was still the British monarchy.

Nevertheless, Gandhi took kindly to the King's proclamation of the impending constitutional changes and wanted the 1919 Amritsar Congress to accept them. He trusted Britain's good intentions. 'To trust is a virtue,' he said. 'It is weakness that begets distrust.' But when he heard that C. R. Das, the famous Bengal nationalist, Jinnah and Tilak were opposed, he shrank from opposing such well-tried and universally revered leaders. 'I tried to run away from the Congress,' Gandhi reveals in his autobiography.

Gandhi was prevailed upon to stay, for he had become the rock on which Congress rested. The session was attended by 7,031 delegates, an unprecedented number, and many hailed from farms and city shops. Gandhi was their idol. They felt closer to him than to the renowned lawyers. Only Tilak could still question Gandhi's sway.

Tilak advocated acceptance of the Montagu–Chelmsford reforms with a view to proving their inadequacy.

This was not the Gandhian way. If you accepted something, you had to do so without mental reservations and give it a fair trial. If you did not want it, you had to fight it no matter who else wanted it.

The delegates supported Gandhi. But he disliked defeating Tilak. In a dramatic moment, Gandhi turned to Tilak who was sitting on the platform. Gandhi was wearing a small cap of white homespun that resembled an aviator's cap; it later became known as the 'Gandhi Cap' of Indian nationalists. Gandhi dropped his cap on the ground as a gesture of obeisance and pleaded with Tilak to approve a compromise. Tilak succumbed.

The compromise thanked Montagu for his part in the reforms and undertook to co-operate with the new dyarchy scheme in such a manner as to expand it into full parliamentary government, but Lord Chelmsford, who had exonerated General Dyer, was condemned for mismanaging Indian affairs and his recall was demanded. Another resolution denounced British and Indian violence in the Punjab. A third asked for the repeal of the Rowlatt acts.

However, the youth and the new elements activized by Gandhi had expected much faster post-war progress towards self-government; delicately balanced Congress resolutions disappointed them. High post-war prices were pressing additional millions down to starvation level. The Moslems now knew that there would be no amelioration of Turkey's fate; Montagu had sincerely tried, hence the Amritsar Congress tribute to him, but the British Cabinet said no. In England, moreover, Dyer had found many friends; some collected a large purse for him. Gandhi did not want Dyer punished but he resented the fact that Dyer kept his pension.

The Hunter Report fully demonstrated Dyer's guilt yet recommended no measures against the Dyerism of British rulers in India.

Three months after Gandhi had approved the Montagu–Chelmsford dyarchy reforms at the Amritsar Congress session, these development turned him against them.

The Amritsar session was merely a temporary triumph of Gandhian caution. The unmistakable trend of the country was towards non-co-operation. Events moved fast. In April 1920, Gandhi was elected president of the Home Rule League. On 30 June, guided by Gandhi, the Khilafat movement sanctioned the policy of non-co-operation. Gandhi thereupon wrote to the Viceroy, 'I have advised my Moslem friends to withdraw their support from Your Excellency's Government and advised the Hindus to join them.' The Viceroy replied that non-co-operation was 'the most foolish of all foolish schemes'. All Chelmsford's power, however, did not suffice to check it. Gandhi announced that non-co-operation would commence on 1 August, 1920, to be preceded by fasting and prayer on 31 July. That day Tilak died.

With Tilak gone, Gandhi was the undisputed leader of Congress. A special session of Congress, which met at Calcutta between 4 and 9 September, 1920, approved the non-co-operation movement. The annual convention at Nagpur, central India, in December, unanimously confirmed this approval; Gandhi then offered a resolution making the goal of Congress Swaraj, or self-rule, within the British Empire if possible or outside it if necessary. Mr Jinnah, and others, preferred home-rule within the Empire. They lost. Jinnah lost interest in Congress. Gandhi politics were Congress politics.

The Nagpur session adopted a new Congress constitution drafted by Gandhi. Congress had been a golden dome without underpinnings. Gandhi converted it into a democratic mass organization with village units, city district units, provincial sections, an All-India Congress Committee (AICC) of 350 members which made policy, and a Working, or Executive, Committee of fifteen.

Twenty thousand people attended the Nagpur session; it passed resolutions for the removal of untouchability, the revival of hand-spinning and hand-weaving, and the collection of a crore (or ten million) of rupees as a Tilak Memorial Fund.

European clothes were less in evidence at Calcutta and Nagpur than at any previous Congress meeting. Less English was spoken, and more Hindustani. Middle-class delegates predominated. India's poor were there too. The men with great reputations and great fortunes no longer monopolized the limelight. Some drifted away from Congress, but Gandhi's magnetism held many of them; they realized that he had a power over the people to which they never even aspired.

Gandhi was middle caste and middle class. He entered politics just as large numbers of awakened middle-class Indians began to yearn for national freedom. He and they entered politics together.

Everything in Gandhi's personality and record helped the people to identify themselves with him and venerate him. Even sceptics were captivated by his courage, indestructible vitality, good humour, near-toothless smile, selflessness, self-confidence and unlimited faith in people.

In a nation that was powerless, Gandhi became a symbol of strength. In a nation of slaves, he behaved like a free man. Finally, he was a man of God.

His idea of non-co-operation had an instantaneous, mighty appeal because it was so simple: You must not reinforce the walls of the prison that encloses you, you must not forge the fetters that will bind you. He had promised at the Nagpur Congress session in December 1920, that if India non-co-operated non-violently, self-government would come within twelve months. He carried this message to the country. He made non-co-operation so personal as to give each individual the impression that unless he non-co-operated he would delay Swaraj. Gandhi himself returned to the Viceroy his two South African war medals and his Kaiser-i-Hind gold medal for humanitarian work in South Africa. In the accompanying letter, Gandhi said, 'I can retain neither respect nor affection for a government which has been moving from wrong to wrong in order to defend its immorality.' Many Indians renounced their British titles and their decorations. Motilal Nehru abandoned his lucrative law practice, discontinued the use of alcohol and became a total non-co-operator. His son Jawaharlal, C. R. Das, the leader of the Calcutta bar, Vallabhbhai Patel, and thousands of others likewise left the British courts for ever.

Thousands of students dropped their professional duties. The Tilak Memorial Fund benefited from the frenzy of self-sacrifice that seized rich and poor; it was soon oversubscribed. Money was available for the establishment of a chain of permanent Indian institutions of higher learning.

Students, teachers and professional men and women left the cities to go into the villages and teach literacy and non-co-operation. For the peasant, non-co-operation meant non-payment of taxes and no use of intoxicating liquors from which the government derived a large revenue.

Gandhi toured the country incessantly, indefatigably, in torrid, humid weather, addressing mammoth mass meetings of a hundred thousand and more persons who, in those pre-microphone days, could only hope to be reached by his spirit. For seven months he travelled in hot, uncomfortable trains which were besieged at all day and night stops by clamouring multitudes who demanded a view of the Mahatma. The inhabitants of one backwoods area sent word that if Gandhi's train did not halt at their tiny station they would lie down on the tracks and be run over by it. The train did stop there at midnight, and when Gandhi, aroused from deep sleep, appeared, the crowd, until then boisterous, sank to their knees on the railway platform and wept.

During those seven strenuous months the Mahatma took three meals a day; each consisted of sixteen ounces of goat's milk, three slices of toast or bread, two oranges, and a score of grapes or raisins.

In the provinces of Assam, Bengal and Madras, Gandhi and Mohamed Ali, the younger of the Ali brothers, travelled together and addressed meetings together. They told every meeting that if they wanted India to rule herself they had to give up foreign clothing. The audience would burst into applause. At that moment, Gandhi would ask the people to take off the foreign clothing they were wearing and put it on a heap which he would presently set on fire. In some places, men stripped themselves naked. The apparel would be passed to a spot near the dais, and when all the hats, coats, shirts, trousers, underwear, socks and shoes had been heaped high, Gandhi set a match to them.

As the flames ate their way through the imported goods, Gandhi would tell his audiences that they must not substitute Indian mill products for foreign manufacturers; they must learn to spin and weave. Gandhi took to spinning half an hour a day, usually before the midday meal, and required all his associates to do likewise. Before long, few Indians dared to come into his presence wearing anything but homespun.

Daily spinning, Gandhi said, was a 'sacrament' and would turn the spinner's mind 'Godward'. Gandhi had a rosary but he never used it except perhaps at night when he watched the stars in moments of sleeplessness. He found rhythm, instead, in the regular hum of the charka and in the steady chanting of 'Rama, Rama, Rama, Rama, Rama (God)'.

Gandhi's long propaganda circuit for non-co-operation had all the attributes of religious revivalism. Yet wherever he went he talked quietly to small groups about the launching of

branch Congress organizations. He designed a Congress flag
with a charka or spinning wheel in the centre. He recruited
for the Volunteers whose teen-age members, dressed in
civilian uniform, kept order at meetings. And he regularly
wrote several articles for each issue of *Young India*, an English-
language weekly, and *Navajivan*, a Gujarati weekly. Founded
in 1919, they were Gandhi's personal organs; neither took
advertisments; both were published in Ahmedabad.

The year was nearing its close. Gandhi had promised the
nation Swaraj in 1921. But self-rule was nowhere in sight.

One afternoon in September, Gandhi and Mohamed Ali
were walking to a meeting. Two British officers and some
soldiers stepped up and arrested Mohammed Ali. Shortly
thereafter, Mohamed's older brother Shaukat was arrested.
Both were sentenced to two years' imprisonment for trying to
dissuade Moslems from serving in the British Army. Before his
arrest, Mohamed Ali had made plans to proceed to the
Malabar coast in west India where the Moplahs, a Moslem
community, had rebelled against the Government; the affair
had provoked Hindu–Moslem riots.

Mohamed Ali's arrest and the outburst of intercommunity
violence in Malabar upset Gandhi deeply. In his concept, the
achievement of Swaraj depended primarily on Hindu-
Moslem friendship.

His Mohammedan partner gone, Gandhi strained all the
more for results. Spinning became an obsession. He urged it
with mounting persistence. In September, 1921, he
emphasized his devotion to homespun cotton and to
simplicity by discarding, for all time, the cap he had worn, the
sleeveless jacket or waistcoat, and the flowing dhoti or loose
trousers, and adopted the loincloth as his sole garment. In
addition, he carried a homespun bag for writing equipment,
the rosary and a few necessities, possibly some nuts or dried
fruit. This was his 'mendicant's garb'.

Thus attired, to the dismay and amusement of some of his

associates, he arrived in Bombay for decisive consultations with the political leaders of the country. On 5 October, the Congress Working Committee resolved that 'it is the duty of every Indian soldier and civilian to sever his connections with the Government and find some other means of livelihood'. This was a summons to desertion from the army. Congress thus reiterated the seditious statement for which the Ali brothers had been incarcerated. Congress leaders were instructed to return to their districts and practise individual civil disobedience against the Government.

Into this tense situation Britain thrust the Prince of Wales, subsequently King Edward VIII and the Duke of Windsor. India was in no mood for glamour or demonstrations of loyalty. Congress boycotted his tour. He moved through deserted city streets and amidst signs of hostility. In Bombay, those who came out to welcome the Prince were attacked, and bloody riots ensued. Gandhi undertook a fast till the disturbances ended. He fasted five days.

The Government now began to round up political leaders and their followers. C. R. Das, Motilal Nehru, Lajput Rai and hundreds of other leading Congressmen were arrested. When the annual session of Congress convened in Ahmedabad, in December 1921, twenty thousand Indians had been jailed for civil disobedience and sedition. The session elected Gandhi 'the sole executive authority of the Congress'.

During December 1921 and January 1922, ten thousand more Indians were thrown into prison for political offences. In several provinces the peasants spontaneously began no-tax movements. Indians in government offices left their jobs.

The Government responded with increased severity. Citing instances of official action, Gandhi called it 'worse than martial law' and characterized the repression as 'savage, because it is wooden, wild, uncultivated, cruel'. Flogging in prison and out was a daily occurrence.

The year 1921 had passed, but no Swaraj. Gandhi was living at his ashram in Sabarmati, no doubt wondering what to do. He rarely laid long-range plans; he submitted to sudden inspirations. There was dissension in Congress ranks; many ridiculed the Mahatma's emphasis on temperance, home-spun and verbal defiance of the State. They demanded action.

Some nationalists yearned for rebellion. But Gandhi believed in peace even at the price of defeat, though not at the price of cowardice. 'When there is only a choice between cowardice and violence,' he had written in *Young India* of 11 August, 1920, 'I would advise violence.' But there was no cowardice. Non-violence required more bravery than violence, and 'forgiveness is more manly than punishment'. Indians 'have better work to do, a better mission to deliver to the world' than the punishment of the Dyers. 'Non-violence,' he said, 'is the law of our species as violence is the law of the brute.

'If India takes up the doctrine of the sword,' he declared, 'she may gain momentary victory, but then India will cease to be the pride of my heart . . . My religion has no geographical limits. If I have a living faith in it, it will transcend my love for India herself.' He was not an uncritical my-country-right-or-wrong-my-country nationalist.

Lord Reading, the new Viceroy, had arrived in India on 2 April, 1921. He had absolute power over the police and the army. Congress had made Gandhi its dicatator. One word from the Mahatma would have started a conflagration compared with which the 1857 Mutiny would have seemed like a minor affair.

Reading was a Jew who, after a remarkable career at the Bar, became in turn Cabinet Minister, Lord Chief Justice of England, Ambassador to Washington, and now Viceroy. Shortly after his installation at New Delhi, he indicated a desire to talk with Gandhi. 'Rather exciting days lately,'

Reading wrote to his son. '. . . Intermediaries have stepped in and seen me with a view to bringing about a meeting with Gandhi.'

'He certainly is a wonderful person,' Reading said of the rebel he had never met.

Gandhi accepted the Viceroy's invitation. Many Indians objected: Had he become a co-operator, they asked. 'We may attack measures and systems,' Gandhi replied. 'We may not, we must not attack men. Imperfect ourselves, we must be tender towards others and be slow to impute motives. I therefore gladly seized the opportunity of waiting upon his Excellency . . .'

Reading's eager anticipation to see Gandhi was amply rewarded. In the latter part of May, he wrote to his son, he had six talks with the Mahatma, 'the first of four hours and a half, the second of three hours, the third of an hour and a half, the fourth of an hour and a half, the fifth of an hour and a half, and the sixth of three-quarters of an hour; I have had many opportunitities of judging him.'

What did Reading think of Gandhi after thirteen hours of conversation? 'There is nothing striking about his appearance,' he informed his son. 'He came . . . in a white dhoti [loincloth] and cap woven on a spinning wheel, with bare feet and legs, and my first impression on seeing him ushered into the room was that there was nothing to arrest attention in his appearance, and that I should have passed him by in the street without a second look at him. When he talks, the impression is different. He is direct, and expresses himself well in excellent English with a fine appreciation of the value of the words he uses. There is no hesitation about him and there is a ring of sincerity in all that he utters, save when discussing some political questions. His religious views are, I believe, genuinely held, and he is convinced to a point almost bordering on fanaticism that non-violence and love will give India its independence and enable it to withstand the British government. His religious and moral views are admirable and indeed are on a remarkably high altitude, though I must confess that I find it difficult to understand his practice of them in politics . . . Our conversations were of the frankest; he was supremely courteous with manners of distinction . . . He held in every way to his word in the various discussions we had.'

It is not surprising that Reading failed to understand Gandhi's politics. The Mahatma explained to the Viceroy how he expected to defeat Great Britain. 'Ours,' he said he told Reading, 'is a religious movement designed to purge Indian political life of corruption, deceit, terrorism and the incubus of white supremacy.' The major task was to purify India; England's expulsion would come as a by-product. Therefore Indians would non-co-operate non-violently. Reading disapproved.

Many Indians disapproved. To Indians, however, the Mahatma was indispensable, and because he was adamant 'to a point almost bordering on fanaticism', even the Indian champions of violence acquiesced in his non-violence. But why not, they demanded, launch non-violent civil disobedience campaigns simultaneously throughout India? A resolution in support of this measure was actually adopted by the All-India Congress Committee meeting in Delhi on 4 November, 1921, but Gandhi exacted a promise from all leaders not to move without his consent.

Gandhi preferred to try mass civil disobedience in one area, and he chose the county of Bardoli, population 87,000, near Bombay, where he could personally supervise the experiment. On 1 February, 1922, Gandhi informed Reading of this plan.

Why did the Mahatma seek to paralyse the British administration in only one limited territory of 137 tiny villages, thus making himself an easy target for repression, when he might have done the same thing in all provinces and added to the discomfiture of the Government or perhaps even brought it to terms?

Gandhi did not believe that civil disobedience, properly conducted, could be defeated. What did it matter whether the Government was coping with a hundred thousand civil resisters or a hundred million? Could it kill the hundred thousand, or jail them?

Gandhi, moreover, was not contemplating a fight to the finish with the British Empire. He knew that such a struggle would be violent and prolonged, and on both sides it might life into commanding posts men with the least scruples and the greatest capacity for hatred, cruelty, dishonesty and dictatorship. No matter who won the contest, both countries and the world would have lost.

At the Ahmedabad Congress session in December 1921, Gandhi had appealed to the British government 'in all humility': 'No matter what you do,' he said, 'no matter how you repress us, we shall one day wring reluctant repentance from you; and we ask you to think betimes, and take care what you are doing, and see that you do not make the three hundred millions of India your eternal enemies.'

It was because of this spirit that Gandhi chose to work in the Bardoli test tube. A united, restrained, self-disciplined Bardoli, peaceful but not co-operating with British administration, would impress on the people of Great Britain the unpardonable horror of government by massacre, and might induce them to grant India a fuller measure of independence than they now thought Indians deserved or could wisely use. Gandhi always endeavoured to win, convert and convince the adversary, not wrestle with him in a pool of blood. Bardoli was ready for civil disobedience.

But on 5 February something happened in the United Provinces, in Chauri Chaura, eight hundred miles from Bardoli. In that small town, an Indian mob committed murder. There had been a legal procession, Gandhi reported in *Young India* of 16 February, 1921. 'But when the procession had passed, the stragglers were interefered with and abused by the constables. The former cried out for help. The mob returned. The constables opened fire. The little ammunition they had was exhausted and they retired to the Thana [city hall] for safety. The mob, my informant tells me, therefore set fire to the Thana. The self-imprisoned constables had to come out for dear life and as they did so they were hacked to pieces and the mangled remains were thrown into the raging flames.'

The news of this atrocity reached Gandhi in Bardoli on 8 February, and it made him sick and sad. Violence upset him physically and psychologically. 'No provocation,' he exclaimed, 'can possibly justify brutal murder of men who had been rendered defenceless and who had virtually thrown themselves on the mercy of the mob.'

It was a 'bad augury'.

'Suppose,' he asked, 'the non-violent disobedience of Bardoli was permitted by God to succeed and the Government had abdicated in favour of the victors of Bardoli, who would control the unruly elements that must be expected to perpetuate inhumanity upon due provocation?' He was not sure that he could.

He accordingly suspended the campaign in Bardoli and cancelled any defiance of the Government anywhere in India. 'Let the opponent glory in our humiliation or so-called defeat,' he exclaimed. 'It is better to be charged with cowardice and weakness than to be guilty of denial of our oath and to sin against God. It is a million times better to *appear* untrue before the world than to *be* untrue to ourselves.'

Some members of the Congress Working Committee disagreed with Gandhi's move. He saw the justice of their point of view. 'The drastic reversal of practically the whole of the aggressive programme may be politically unsound and unwise,' he affirmed, 'but there is no doubt that it is religiously sound.' And when Gandhi took a religious stand nobody could shake him. Chauri Chaura, he said, 'shows the way India may easily go, if drastic precautions be not taken'. Congress would have to educate itself and educate the people. As for himself, 'I must undergo personal cleansing. I must become a fitter instrument able to register the slightest variation in the moral atmosphere about me.' He fasted for five days.

Meanwhile a sharp struggle was taking place behind the British scenes. It is described by Lord Reading's son and biographer who had at his disposal his father's private letters and unpublished state papers. Official demands had been made for Gandhi's arrest. 'The Viceroy', the biography reads, 'was indeed far from dismissing as unfounded the opinion held by many competent observers, notably Sir George [later Lord] Lloyd [Governor of Bombay], that Mr Gandhi's preaching of non-violence was no more than a cloak for plans aimed at an ultimate revolution by violence. Sir George would have had Mr Gandhi arrested at once, but Lord Reading, as always, opposed arrest for mere speech-making, dangerous as the speeches might be, and awaited some definite act. "I am quite prepared to face the consequences of Gandhi's arrest if he takes action", Reading declared.'

After an interval, the Secretary of State, Edwin Montagu, the biography continues, 'instructed Lord Reading to arrest the principal leaders of the non-co-operation movement, including Mr Gandhi'. Reading, however, resisted this order. His son, in the biography of his father, writes: 'Lord Reading still preferred to wait for some definite move by Mr Gandhi . . . It looked as though the occasion for the arrest would come soon enough, for Mr Gandhi had announced that he was about to start active civil disobedience in the Bardoli tehsil [county] of the Surat district in Bombay Presidency, and on 24 January the Government of India telegraphed to Sir George Lloyd specifically enjoining him to wait until Mr Gandhi openly embarked on the Bardoli campaign . . .'

The biography then relates the events in Chauri Chaura and records Gandhi's cancellation of the Bardoli campaign on 8 February, before it had actually started. However, he continues, 'opinion in England was restive over Mr Gandhi's continued freedom, and Mr Montagu telegraphed early in February saying that he was "puzzled" at the delay in making the arrest. A debate was due to take place in Parliament on the 14th, and both Lord Reading and Mr Montagu were naturally anxious that, as the arrest had to be made, it should be made in time for Parliament to be informed of it as a *fait accompli*. But at this point the Indian members of the Viceroy's Council made the strongest possible representations in favour of delay, and Lord Reading, after careful thought, decided that the risks of a little delay were on the whole less than those of immediate action which would easily be open to misrepresentation both in India and abroad.'

Reading 'postponed the arrest', the biography says, 'but asked the three Presidency Governors, Sir George Lloyd, Lord Willingdon of Madras and Lord Ronaldshay of Bengal to come to Delhi and talk the matter over with him . . .' Ronaldshay could not leave Calcutta, but 'Lord Willingdon was only less disturbed than Sir George by the apparent intention of the Government of India not to proceed at all against Mr Gandhi . . .'

On 1 March, following these talks with the two most important British conservative administrators in India, Reading ordered the arrest of Gandhi, and it took place on Friday, 10 March, 1922, at 10.30 in the evening. A police officer stopped his car on the road, eighty yards from Gandhi's hut in Sabarmati Ashram, and sent polite word by one of his men that the Mahatma should consider himself under arrest and come as soon as he was ready. Standing surrounded by a dozen or more ashramites, Gandhi offered up a prayer and joined in the singing of a hymn. Then, in a gay mood, he walked to the car and was taken to Sabarmati prison. The next morning, Kasturbai sent clothes, goat's milk and grapes to her husband.

Lord Reading had at one time asserted that he would arrest Gandhi only after some overt act. Gandhi had taken none. The Parliamentary debate had come and gone; it did not make the arrest necessary. Reading knew very well what Gandhi had been saying in speeches and articles; they did not convince him of the wisdom of arresting the Mahatma. How then did Sir George Lloyd and Lord Willingdon persuade Reading to act?

'I have had no trouble so far arising from Gandhi's arrest,' the Viceroy wrote in April in a private letter to his son, the biographer. Reading was obviously relieved that Gandhi's arrest had caused no public commotion. The provincial governors could have predicted this.

Hard-boiled considerations of 'law and order' prevailed over the Viceroy's scruples. Gandhi had disarmed himself by suspending the Bardoli civil disobedience; therefore he could be arrested with impunity. Reading's April letter to his son confirms this. Gandhi, he wrote, 'had pretty well run himself into the last ditch as a politician by his extraordinary manifestations in the last month or six weeks before his arrest, when he ran the gamut of open defiance of Government with a challenge of all authority fixed for a certain day, and when the day arrived he went to the opposite extreme and counselled suspension of the most acute activities.

'This of course caused dissension among his followers . . .'

So Gandhi was 'in the last ditch as a politician . . .' Gandhi's political career was finished. The measure of misunderstanding is filled by a remark of the biographer-son: 'The mere fact that Mr Gandhi had been taken into custody and kept in jail like any other ordinary mortal who had run counter to the Law was in itself a real setback to his prestige . . .'

Gandhi had expected arrest and published an article in the 9 March issue of *Young India* entitled 'If I Am Arrested'. 'Rivers of blood shed by the Government cannot frighten me,' he wrote, 'but I should be deeply pained even if the people did so much as abuse the Government for my sake or in my name. It would be disgracing me if the people lost their equilibrium on my arrest.' There were no disorders.

At the preliminary hearings the day after his arrest, Gandhi gave his age as fifty-three and his profession 'farmer and weaver' and pleaded guilty. The charge was writing three seditious articles in *Young India*. Mr S. G. Banker, the printer of the magazine, was arraigned at the same time. Gandhi was kept in prison for trial.

The first of the seditious articles appeared in *Young India* on 19 September, 1921, entitled 'Tampering with Loyalty'. 'I have no hesitation in saying', Gandhi wrote, 'that it is sinful for anyone, either soldier or civilian, to serve this government . . . sedition has become the creed of Congress . . . Non-co-operation, though a religious and strictly moral movement, deliberately aims at the overthrow of the government, and is therefore legally seditious . . . We ask for no quarter; we expect none from the government.'

These words made the Government case easy. If there was doubt, Gandhi made it even more explicit in a second article, 'A Puzzle and Its Solution', in *Young India* of 15 December, 1921. 'Lord Reading,' he wrote, 'must understand that Non-co-operators are at war with the government. They have declared rebellion against it . . . Lord Reading is entitled therefore to put them out of harm's way.'

The third seditious article, 'Shaking the Manes', in *Young India* of 23 February, 1922, cried out in the opening sentence, 'How can there be any compromise whilst the British lion

continues to shake his gory claws in our faces?' Then
sarcastically he informed the British that 'the rice-eating,
puny millions of India seem to have resolved upon achieving
their own destiny without any further tutelage and without
arms'. Adding that 'No empire intoxicated with the red wine
of power and plunder of weaker races has yet lived long in the
world', Gandhi said. 'The fight that was commenced in 1920
is a fight to the finish, whether it lasts one month or one year or
many months or many years . . .'

Gandhi's only surprise was that he had not been arrested
after the first or second of these articles.

'The Great Trial', as it came to be known, was held in
Government Circuit House at Ahmedabad on 18 March,
1922, before Mr Justice C. N. Broomfield, District and
Sessions judge. Sir J. T. Strangman, Advocate-General of
Bombay, prosecuted. Gandhi and Mr Banker had no lawyers.
Heavy military patrols guarded the building and nearby
streets. The little courtroom was crowded. Admission passes
were marked: 'Sessions Case No 45 of 1922. Imperator *vs* (1)
Mr M. K. Gandhi. (2) Mr S. C. Banker.'

After the indictment was read and the Advocate-General
had stated the case against Gandhi, the judge asked the
Mahatma whether he wished to make a statement. Gandhi
had a written statement ready. He introduced it with some
oral, extemporaneous remarks. The Advocate-General,
Gandhi said, 'was entirely fair . . . It is very true and I have
no desire whatsoever to conceal from this court the fact that to
preach disaffection towards the existing system of government
has become almost a passion with me'. Indeed, he had
preached sedition long before the prosecution said he had. 'I
do not ask for mercy. I do not plead any extenuating act. I am
here, therefore, to invite and cheerfully submit to the highest
penalty that can be inflicted upon me for what in law is a
deliberate crime and what appears to me to be the highest
duty of a citizen. The only course open to you, the Judge, is, as

I am going to say in my statement, either to resign your post, or inflict on me the severest penalty if you believe that the system and the law you administer are good for the people. I do not expect that kind of conversion, but by the time I have finished with my statement you will perhaps have a glimpse of what is raging within my breast to run this maddest risk that a man can run.'

Gandhi then read his prepared statement to 'explain why, from a staunch loyalist and co-operator, I have become an uncompromising disaffectionist and non-co-operator'., In South Africa, he began, his contacts with the British were not happy; 'I discovered that I had no rights as a man because I was an Indian.' But he thought this 'was an excrescence upon a system that was intrinsically and mainly good'. So, he criticized the Government but supported it, and joined in two wars which it fought. In India, too, he recruited for the British Army. 'In all these efforts at service,' he explained, 'I was actuated by the belief that it was possible by such services to gain a status of full equality in the Empire for my countrymen.'

In 1919, the shocks commenced: The Rowlatt acts, Jallianwalla Bagh, the crawling order, the floggings, the injustice to the Turkish Caliph. Nevertheless, the Mahatma recalled, 'I fought for co-operation and working the Montagu–Chelmsford reforms'; he still hoped. 'But all that hope was shattered.'

'I came reluctantly to the conclusion,' he told the court, 'that the British connection had made India more helpless than she ever was before, politically and economically . . . She has become so that she has little power of resisting famines. Before the British advent, India spun and wove in her millions of cottages just the supplement she needed for adding to her meagre agricultural resources. This cottage industry, so vital for India's existence, has been ruined by incredibly heartless and inhuman processes as described by

English witnesses. Little do town-dwellers know how the semi-starved masses of India are slowly sinking to lifelessness . . . No sophistry, no jugglery in figures can explain away the evidence that the skeletons in many villages present to the naked eye. I have no doubt that both England and the town-dwellers of India will have to answer, if there is a God above, for this crime against humanity which is perhaps unequalled in history.'

Continuing his indictment of the accuser, the prisoner said, 'I am satisfied that many Englishmen and Indian officials honestly believe that they are administering one of the best systems devised in the world and that India is making steady though slow progress. They do not know that a subtle but effective system of terrorism and an organized display of force on the one hand, and the deprivation of all powers of retaliation and self-defence on the other, have emasculated the people and induced in them the habit of simulation. This awful habit has added to the ignorance and self-deception of the administrators . . .

'I have no personal ill-will against any administrator,' Gandhi assured the judge, 'much less have I disaffection towards the King's person. But I hold it an honour to be disaffected towards a government which in its totality has done more harm to India than any previous system. India is less manly under the British rule than she ever was before . . . it has been a previous privilege for me to be able to write what I have in the various articles tendered in evidence against me . . . In my opinion, non-co-operation with evil is as much a duty as is co-operation with good.'

In conclusion, Gandhi again asked for the 'severest penalty'.

When Gandhi sat down, Mr Justice Broomfield bowed to the prisoner, and pronounced sentence. 'The determination of a just sentence,' the judge declared, 'is perhaps as difficult a proposition as a judge in this country could have to face. The law is no respecter of persons. Nevertheless, it will be impossible to ignore the fact that you are in a different category from any person I have ever tried or am likely to have to try. It would be impossible to ignore the fact that, in the eyes of millions of your countrymen, you are a great patriot and a great leader. Even those who differ from you in politics look upon you as a man of high ideals and of noble and even saintly life.'

The judge then announced that Gandhi must undergo imprisonment for six years, and added that if the Government later saw fit to reduce the term 'no one would be better pleased than I'. Mr Banker received one year in jail and a fine of one thousand rupees.

On hearing the sentence, the Mahatma rose and said that the sentence 'is as mild as any judge could inflict on me, and so far as the entire proceedings are concerned, I must say that I could not have expected greater courtesy'.

When the court was adjourned, most of the spectators in the room fell at Gandhi's feet. Many wept. Gandhi wore a benign smile as he was led away to jail.

Gandhi had no grievance. He knew when he entered Indian politics that it involved going to prison. It meant this for him and for others. Whenever he heard of a friend or colleague who had been arrested he telegraphed congratulations. Going to prison was a basic part of his doctrine of non-co-operation. 'We must widen the prison gates,' he said, 'and we must enter them as a bridegroom enters the bride's chamber. Freedom is to be wooed only inside prison walls and sometimes on gallows, never in the council chambers, courts, or the schoolroom.' Going to prison was essential to arousing the nation for liberation.

The British obliged and sent him to prison often. But this was the last time they tried him.

CHAPTER 10

Gandhi's Families

When he passed through the prison gates, Gandhi left behind him a country full of perplexed politicians and an ashram full of two unhappy families: his personal family and his adopted family of secretaries, disciples, devotees and hangers-on. All of them, including Kasturbai, now called him Father, 'Bapu', or 'Bapuji', the *ji* connoting a Hindu mixture of respect and tenderness. He received and gave a great deal of love.

Love made him indulgent. For himself, he had an extremely strict code of conduct. With others he was tolerant. 'Do not be frightened by the wide implication of these views of mine,' he wrote to the women of the ashram. 'There are always two meanings to everything – one wider the other narrower. We shall not be put out if you understand the wider implications but start with the narrower.'

From young manhood, he was sweet and kind towards everybody except his wife and sons. A tension marred his early relations with Kasturbai, but gradually it waned and he was able to relax with her too. For instance, they frequently joked about their age; they were born six months apart but they were not quite certain who was younger and he would claim that he was and she that she was. Gradually, as lust, in Gandhi's words, yielded to love, they became a model couple, she the acme of service, he a paragon of consideration. 'Ba,' the Mahatma said, referring to Kasturbai, 'takes tea in spite of the fact that she lives with me. She also takes coffee. I would even lovingly prepare it for her.' Tea- and coffee-drinking were rather sinful in Gandhi's eyes. Ba, in other words, retained her personality; yet she attained a high degree of self-effacement. She never behaved like Mrs Gandhi, never asked privileges for herself, never shirked the hardest work, and never seemed to notice the small group of young or middle-aged female disciples who interposed themselves between her and her illustrious husband. Being herself and being at the same time a shadow of the Mahatma made her a remarkable woman, and some who observed them for long years wondered whether she had not come nearer the *Gita* ideal of non-attachment than he. He was too passionate to be the perfect yogi.

As he aged, the passions submitted to more rigid rein, but he never quite learned to be a father to his sons. He had an unGandhian coldness towards them. Perhaps he had an impersonal concept of immortality. 'But may not an artist or a poet or a great genius', insisted an interviewer, 'leave a legacy of his genuis to posterity through his own children?'

'Certainly not,' Gandhi replied in *Young India* of 20 November, 1924. 'He will have more disciples than he can ever have children.'

As he was more severe with himself than with anybody else, so he was severest with his own boys. He expected Harilal, Manilal, Ramdas and Devadas to be chips off the old block, but the block did not chip. He was especially critical of his children when he encountered a young man who did meet a difficult test. In a letter dated Johannesburg, 27 May, 1906, Gandhi wrote to his oldest brother Laxmidas. 'Young Kalyandas Jagmohandas's son is like Prahalad in spirit. He is therefore dearer to me than one who is a son because so born.'

A popular myth, which, like so many other Hindu myths, was tightly woven into Gandhi's culture pattern, makes Prahalad the son of a demon King Hiranya-kashipu. The King hated God, but Prince Prahalad loved God. The King ordered tutors to teach Prahalad that his father was more powerful than God. When the teacher failed to convince the young man, the demon king subjected Prahalad to a series of cruelties: the prince was thrown from a high hill and trampled by elephants and horses. Still he proclaimed the supremacy of God. Finally, Prahalad was forced to embrace a red-hot metal pillar. But when he continued to call in His name, God emerged from the pillar in the form of a creature half lion, half man, and tore King Hiranya-kashipu to pieces.

Gandhi regarded Prahalad as the first Satyagrahi, and the Indian boy in South Africa who behaved like Prahalad was therefore dearer to him than his own sons.

In the same 1906 letter to his brother, Gandhi wrote, 'It is well if Harilal is married; it is well if he is not. For the present at any rate I have ceased to think of him as a son.' Harilal, Gandhi's first born, had remained in India in the hope of achieving personal independence. At eighteen, he wanted to get married; his father thought it was too early and disowned him 'for the present'.

Six years later, still in South Africa, a young Indian married woman successfully assaulted Manilal's continence. When the dereliction was discovered, Gandhi made a public scandal, fasted, persuaded the woman to shave her hair, and said he would never allow Manilal to marry. He only relented under Ba's pressure, in March 1927, when Manilal was thirty-five.

Gandhi leaned over backward to give his sons less than he gave other men's sons. The treatment contained an antidote to the nepotism nourished by the strong Hindu family sense, but it was unfair, and Harilal and Manilal resented it. They felt disgruntled because their father, who had a profession, denied them a professional education. Gandhi contended that character building outranked law and medicine. That was all very well, they thought, but then why did Bapu send Maganlal and Chhaganlal, his second cousins, and other young men to England to study?

When Maganlal died, Gandhi wrote in *Young India* of 26 April, 1928, 'He whom I had singled out as heir to my all is no more.' Why this partiality to a second cousin? 'He closely studied and followed my spiritual career,' Gandhi declared in the same obituary, 'and when I presented to my co-workers brahmacharya [continence] as a rule of life even for married men in search of Truth, he was the first to perceive the beauty and necessity of the practice, and though it cost him to my knowledge a terrific struggle, he carried it through to success, taking his wife along with him by patient argument instead of imposing his views on her . . . He was my hands, my feet and my eyes.

'As I am penning these lines,' Gandhi wrote in a crescendo of lament, 'I hear the sobs of the widow bewailing the death of her husband. Little does she realize that I am more widowed than she. And but for the living God, I should become a raving maniac for the loss of one who was dearer to me than my own sons, who never once deceived or failed me . . .'

The Mahatma thought Manilal had deceived him. In 1916, Manilal had in his keeping several hundred rupees belonging to the ashram, and when he heard that his brother Harilal, who was trying to make his way in business in Calcutta, needed money, he forwarded the sum to him as a loan. By chance, Harilal's receipt fell into Gandhi's hands. The next day, Manilal was banished from the ashram and told to go and apprentice himself as a hand-spinner and weaver but not to use the Gandhi name. 'In addition to this,' Manilal recounts, 'father also contemplated a fast, but I sat all night entreating him not to do so and in the end my prayer was heeded. I left my dear mother and my brother Devadas sobbing. Father did not send me away completely empty-handed. He gave me just sufficient money for my train fare and a little extra.' For two months, Manilal lived incognito. Then the Mahatma sent him a letter of introduction to G. A. Natesan, the Madras publisher, with whom Manilal stayed for seven months. In the letter of introduction, Gandhi recommended that Manilal 'be subjected to discipline and should be made to cook his own food and learn spinning'.

Following this period of penance, Gandhi dispatched Manilal to South Africa to edit *Indian Opinion*. 'During his lifetime,' Manilal wrote after his father's assassination, 'I was able to spend a very few years actually with my father. Unlike my other brothers I had to live away from him in exile, in South Africa.'

Manilal came to India for occasional visits. 'The longest period I was able to spend in India, and most of it with father,' Manilal says, 'was the whole of 1945 and half of 1946. Those were the precious months . . .' At this time, Manilal noticed that Gandhi's attitude . . . had so vastly changed since the time we were under him in our childhood. It seemed to me that he spoilt those near him by his extreme love and affection. They had become his spoilt children, as it were, and much more so after my mother has been called away from his life . . . One of the things that struck me was the extreme softness in father's attitude compared with what it was when we four brothers were under him. He was, of course, always forgiving though he was a very severe task master. But he had grown extremely tolerant, which he was not in our time . . . When I saw this, many a time I chafed and said to father, "Bapu, you have vastly changed from the time we were under you. You never pampered us; I remember how you made us do laundry work and chop wood; how you made us take the pick and shovel in the bitterly cold mornings and dig in the garden, to cook and to walk miles. And I am surprised to see how you now pamper these people around you."

'Bapu would listen and burst out in his usual hearty laughter: "Well, children," he would say, "are you listening to what Manilal is saying?" And yet he would love and caress them.'

How much sorrow there is in all this for many lost years without affection.

Manilal underwent punishment and banishment yet

remained a balanced human being. Harilal, however, suffered an inner trauma. While his wife lived, he was outwardly normal. But when she died in the 1918 influenza epidemic, and when Gandhi frowned on his remarriage, Harilal disintegrated completely. He took to alcohol and women; he was often seen drunk in public. Under the influence of drink, penury and the desire for vengeance, he would succumb to the offers of unscrupulous publishers and attack his father in print, signing 'Abdulla', a Moslem name. He had become a Moslem. Conversion to Islam, drunkenness and profligacy were probably Harilal's effort to hurt his father.

Early in the 1920s, Harilal helped to launch a new firm called All-India Stores, Limited, and became a director. In 1925, Gandhi received a lawyer's letter on behalf of a client who had invested money in the company; it informed the Mahatma that correspondence addressed to the company was being returned and that the whole thing seemed 'a bogus affair'. The client was a Moslem 'whose respect for Mahatmaji led him to become a share-holder'.

Gandhi reproduced the entire letter in *Young India* of 18 June, 1925, and appended his reply.

I do indeed happen to be the father of Harilal M. Gandhi. He is my eldest boy, is over thirty-six years old and is father of four children, the eldest being nineteen years old. His ideals and mine having been discovered over fifteen years ago to be different, he has been living separately from me and has not been supported by or through me. It has been my invariable rule to regard my boys as my friends and equals as soon as they completed their sixteen years . . . Harilal . . . was naturally influenced by the Western veneer that my life at one time did have. His commercial undertakings were totally independent of me. Could I have influenced him he would have been associated with me in my several public activities and earning at the same time a decent livelihood. But he chose, as he had every right to do, a different and independent path. He was and still is ambitious. He wants to become rich, and that too, easily. Possibly he has a grievance against me that when it was open to me to do so, I did not equip him and my other children for careers that lead to wealth and fame that wealth brings . . . I do not know Harilal's affairs. He meets me occasionally, but I never pry into his affairs. I do not know how his affairs stand at present, except that they are in a bad way . . . There is much in Harilal's life that I dislike. He knows that. But I love him in spite of his faults. The bosom of a father will take him in as soon as he seeks entrance . . . Let the client's example be a warning against people being guided by big names in their transactions. Men may be good, not necessarily their children . . . Caveat emptor.

Harilal naturally caused his mother endless tortures. Kasturbai brought up his four children with a grandmother's tenderness. In the 1930s, she could not control her grief, and wrote Harilal an emotional letter; one of his adventures had got into the newspapers.

My dear son Harilal, I have read that recently in Madras policemen found you misbehaving in a state of drunkenness at midnight in an open street and took you into custody. Next day you were produced before a bench of Magistrates and they fined you one rupee. They must have been very good people to treat you so leniently.

Even the Magistrates showed regard for your father in thus giving you only nominal punishment. But I have been feeling very miserable ever since I heard about this incident. I do not know whether you were alone that night or were accompanied by some of your friends, but in any case you acted very improperly.

I do not know what to say to you. I have been pleading with you all these long years to hold yourself in check. But you have been going from bad to worse. Now you are making my very existence impossible. Think of the misery you are causing your aged parents in the evening of their lives.

Your father says nothing to anyone but I know how the shocks you are giving him are breaking his heart. You are committing a great sin in thus repeatedly hurting our feelings. Though born as our son you are indeed behaving like an enemy.

I am told that in your recent wanderings you have been criticizing and ridiculing your father. This does not behoove such an intelligent boy as you. You little realize that you only disgrace yourself by speaking evil of him. He has nothing but love in his heart for you. You know that he attaches the greatest importance to purity of conduct. But you have never paid any heed to advice. Yet he has offered to keep you with him, to feed and clothe you and even to nurse you . . .

I am a frail old woman unable to stand the anguish you are causing . . . You have left no place for me anywhere. For sheer shame, I am unable to move about among my friends or strangers. Your father always pardons you, but God will not tolerate your conduct . . .

Every morning I rise with a shudder to think what fresh news of disgrace the newspapers will bring. I sometimes wonder where you are, where you sleep, what you eat. Perhaps you take forbidden food . . . I often feel like meeting you. But I do not know where to find you. You are my eldest son and nearly fifty years old. I am even afraid of approaching you, lest you humiliate me. I do not know why you have changed your ancestral religion; that is your affair. But I hear that you go about asking innocent and ignorant people to follow your example . . . People are liable to be led away by the fact that you are your father's son. You are not fit to preach religion.

Your daughters and son-in-law also bear with increasing difficulty the burden of sorrow your conduct has imposed upon them.

Gandhi blamed Harilal's misdeeds on himself. 'I was a slave of my passions when Harilal was conceived'; 'I led a carnal and luxurious life during Harilal's childhood,' he would say. But the cause of Harilal's fall could not have been the natural impulses which led to his birth and to that of his brothers. Somewhere deep in Gandhi's psyche there was apparently a protest against having children.

Yet Gandhi loved children and was never as happy as when he played with them. He took time off to play with the youngsters and babies in the ashram. Once, during the week I spent with Gandhi at Sevagram in 1942, he led me to a hut used by a patient of his and then to a neighbouring hut which was empty but for a red wooden cradle. The mother lifted the baby out of the cradle as Gandhi approached. He patted the child's cheeks and said, 'She is not my patient, she is my relaxation.' The baby reacted gleefully and he smacked and pinched it playfully.

There is a delightful photograph showing Gandhi rubbing

noses with a babe in arms. He would amuse the children of the ashram by making funny faces at them and directing funny remarks to them.

Horace Alexander, of the British Society of Friends, who spent years in India and much time with Gandhi, records his first view of the Mahatma. He arrived in Sabarmati one afternoon in March 1928. 'After a rest,' Alexander writes, 'I went to evening prayers. When all were assembled, he came walking quickly and sat down in the centre and the chanting began. When the prayers were over, each member of the ashram gave his or her report on the amount of spinning done. This lasted for fifteen or twenty minutes and was rather tedious. I noticed that the children ran playfully around the Mahatma while this went on and he thrust out his hand as if to catch them as they ran past. Some years later, one of these children, now a grown-up man, told me how difficult he had found it, as he grew up, to realize that the kind old man, so simple and friendly, of his childhood days, was the same as the Mahatma . . .'

Gandhi believed in the goodness of children. 'Children are innocent, loving and benevolent by nature,' he wrote in a letter to the boys and girls of the ashram. 'Evil comes in only when they become older.'

Life at Sabarmati Ashram and, after 1932, at Sevagram in central India, was serene, simple, joyous and unconstrained. Nobody stood in awe of Gandhi. Until he was too old, he sat in the scullery every morning with the ashramites peeling potatoes; he did his share of other chores as well. Petty frictions and rivalries were not absent even in this community of ascetics. There was jealousy for the favour of the Mahatma. He usually succeeded in being above that battle too, but bulletins of its progress came to his attention. In fact, few details of the life and work of the inmates remained hidden from his shrewd ken. He soothed, smoothed and arbitrated impartially.

Gandhi met and expected everybody in the ashram to meet certain rigid requirements: absolute personal and civic cleanliness, undeviating punctuality and physical labour plus one hour or at least thirty minutes a day of spinning. He denounced the 'divorce between intelligence and labour'. Manual work was for him a means of identification with working India, with the working world. His compulsion to economize, though instinctive, also stemmed from his conscious concern for the hundreds of millions who valued a button, a nail and a fraction of a penny.

Gandhi once wrote out a telegram to G. V. Mavalankar, his lawyer, who later become Speaker of the Constituent Assembly. But on learning that there was an extra charge per word because it was a holiday he posted the telegram.

Gandhi was famous for his postcards. Whenever the size and nature of the communication permitted he put it on a postcard instead of into a letter. He frequently wrote letters on the reverse of mimeographed announcements. Any odd piece of scrap paper became an ashram-made envelope. His secretaries' notes and his own memoranda were always written on the backs of letters received from outside. For a brief note he once wrote me to New York he had obviously taken a larger bit of stationery than necessary and carefully torn off the excess.

Miss Slade, daughter of Sir Edmund Slade, a British admiral, who joined Gandhi's ashram in 1925 and lived there for many years until she founded one of her own on the banks of the sacred Ganges, tells how Gandhi lost the little pencil stump he had been cherishing. The staff hunted for the lost treasure but in vain. Somebody brought him a new pencil. No, he insisted that they continue the search for the stump until they recovered it. 'Bapu . . . received it with a beaming smile.'

Gandhi's insistence on economy, cleanliness, punctuality and spinning grew greater, if anything, as he grew older. With all his strictness about the personal conduct of his co-workers, however, he was completely tolerant towards their thinking. Some of his most intimate political collaborators and some who stayed long in the ashram, did not, to his knowledge, believe in non-violence, or in God, or in loving the British or the Moslems. Mrdulla Sarabhai, for instance, said to him, 'I am not Gandhian,' but he laughed and may have smacked her face affectionately. Nobody had to toe a Gandhian 'party line'. There was none.

Gandhi accepted people as they were. Aware of his own defects, how could he expect perfection in others? He believed in the educational and curative value of time and good deeds.

Gandhi took from a person, a book, a religion and a situation that which was congenial to him and discarded the rest. He refused to see the bad in people. He often changed human beings by regarding them not as what they were but as though they were what they wished to be, and as though the good in them was all of them.

His friends knew he forgave them, therefore they frankly confessed. If they hid things from him it was because he would blame himself for their shortcomings. He encouraged familiarity; it never bred contempt. It fostered love. He enjoyed banter even if the point pierced him. A few weeks before Gandhi was arrested in March 1922, Rajagopalachari, already in jail, wrote the Mahatma a letter. He said he was 'completely shut out from all politics, news and newspapers. What an ideal condition which I know you are envying . . . It took me till now to get rid of the boils. I am now quite free from the trouble. It must horrify you to learn that I willingly underwent five injections of vaccine for these boils . . . [Gandhi called vaccine 'filthy'.] Your eyes would flow with delight if you saw me here in my solitary cell spinning, spinning not as a task imposed by a tyrant faddist, but with pleasure'. The 'tyrant faddist' printed the letter as the first item in *Young India* of 9 February, 1922.

Sycophancy repelled Gandhi. He respected and befriended his fiercest antagonists. Though pleased to make a convert, he was not flattered by loud partisans. He encouraged dissent; he helped dissenters. Opponents found comfort in the knowledge that he could reverse himself on even the most important political issue in order to give the alternative policy a fair trial.

Such democratic liberalism made it possible for many members of his political family, some of whom had joined reluctantly in the 1921–22 non-co-operation campaign, to lay plans for co-operation when Gandhi was sentenced on 18 March, 1922, to six years' imprisonment. He had prohibited nothing when he entered prison. From his cell his only injunction was 'peace, non-violence, suffering'. Congress, therefore, was free to flounder and meander in confusion.

CHAPTER 11

Operation and Fast

On the evening of 12 January, 1924, Mahatma Gandhi was hastily carried from Yeravda Central Prison, where he was lodged on 20 March, 1922, to Sassoon Hospital in the city of Poona. He had developed acute appendicitis. The Government was ready to wait for Indian physicians to arrive from Bombay, three hours' distance by train, but shortly before midnight Colonel Maddock, the British surgeon, informed Gandhi that he would have to operate immediately. Gandhi consented.

While the operating theatre was being prepared, V. S. Srinivasa Sastri, head of the Servants of India Society, and Dr Phatak, Poona friend of the Mahatma, were summoned at his request. Together, they drafted a public statement which declared that he had agreed to the operation, that the physicians had treated him well and that, whatever happened, there must be no anti-government agitation. The hospital authorities, and Gandhi, knew that if the operation went badly India might burst into flames.

When the declaration was ready, Gandhi drew up his knees and signed in pencil. 'See how my hand trembles,' he remarked to Colonel Maddock with a laugh. 'You will have to put this right.'

'Oh,' replied the surgeon, 'we will put tons and tons of strength into it.'

Chloroform was administered and a photograph taken. During the operation, a thunderstorm cut off the supply of electricity. Then the flashlight which one of the three nurses had been holding went out, and the operation had to be finished by the light of a hurricane lamp.

The appendicectomy was successful and the Mahatma thanked the surgeon profusely. An abscess formed locally, however, and the patient's progress was too slow. The Government thought it wise or generous in these circumstances to release Gandhi on 5 February.

The operation piqued Gandhi's curiosity, and when Manu Gandhi, the granddaughter of his cousin, had to undergo an appendicectomy at Patna, in Bihar province, during a tour, the Mahatma asked the surgeon, Dr D. P. Bhargava, the same who was first to reach Gandhi's side after the assassination, whether he could be present. Dr Bhargava assented on condition that Gandhi wore a gauze mask, and two snapshots taken during the operation show Gandhi sitting on a chair, an unusual perch, with a white mask covering the lower half of his face and tied around the back of his head. Dr Bhargava says Gandhi did not utter a word during the entire hour. (This was on 15 May, 1947, at 9.30 P.M.)

'The West,' Gandhi once wrote to Miss Slade, 'has always commanded my admiration for its surgical inventions and all-round progress in that direction.'

Nevertheless, Gandhi never quite cast off his prejudices against physicians. Once Gandhi resisted a penicillin injection.

'If I give you penicillin,' the doctor said, 'you will recover in three days. Otherwise it will take three weeks.'

'That's all right,' Gandhi replied. 'I'm in no hurry.'

The doctor said he might infect others.

'Then give them penicillin,' Gandhi advised.

In an unguarded moment, the same physician told Gandhi that if all sick people simply went to bed they'd get well.

'Don't say that aloud,' Gandhi cautioned. 'You will lose all your patients.'

Gandhi liked to be his own doctor. Mahadev Desai, who knew him well, said, 'But for his fundamental objection to vivisection, he might have been a physician and a surgeon.'

Gandhi wrote a book on health, and loved to recommend 'quack' remedies to friends, callers and all of India. Accordingly, when he received his unconditional discharge from Yeravda Jail and went to the beach at Juhu, near Bombay, to recuperate in the home of Shantikumar Morarjee, an industrialist, he decided that since he would be doctoring himself he might as well doctor others too; he converted the seaside villa into a temporary hospital where ailing associates, summoned from near and far, gave Gandhi pleasure by submitting to his mud packs, water baths, food fads and massage. Chiefly, however, he advanced his and their convalescence with the medicine of laughter and companionship.

Others came to Juhu too – unasked – and Gandhi appealed to them through the press to come, if they must, between 4 and 5 in the evening for prayers on the sands. But 'seeing me', he explained, 'is not likely to be of benefit to you. It is an indication of your love for me, but it is an exaggerated indication'. It would be much better to spend the money and time on spinning. If they gave him peace he could husband his 'very small . . . capital of energy' and resume the active editorship of *Young India*, his 'viewspaper', and *Navajivan*, which he did on 3 April, 1924.

To Juhu, too, came C. R. Das and Motilal Nehru for discussions on the ugly situation that had arisen during the twenty-two months Gandhi spent in prison.

First, Hindu–Moslem friendship, the firm rock on which Gandhi hoped to build a united, free India, had been all but submerged in an angry tide of hostility between the two communities. The Khilafat movement was dead, killed not by Britain, but by Kemal Pasha (Ataturk), the master of Moslem Turkey. Wiser than most of his Indian co-religionists, Kemal had created a secular republic, Latinized the cursive Arabic script, proscribed the fez and other Oriental head-dress and, having deposed the Caliph, allowed him to flee to

the island of Malta in a British man-of-war in November
1922. A weak heir clung to the illusion of the Caliph's
religious primacy, but in March 1924 he too became a
refugee.

Left without a cause, the Khilafat movement disintegrated.
Therewith, large-scale Hindu–Moslem political collaboration came to an end.

Second, the non-co-operation movement was dead. 'Scores
of lawyers have resumed practice,' Gandhi said, summarizing
what he was told at Juhu and what he learned first-hand.
'Some even regret having given it up . . . Hundreds of boys
and girls who gave up government schools and colleges have
repented of their action and returned to them.' Moreover,
Motilal Nehru, C. R. Das and their many adherents favoured
a return to the municipal, provincial and national legislative
councils. This, they maintained, would enable them to
participate in elections, keep in touch with the people, air
grievances in the deliberative assemblies and obstruct the
British government. Indeed, in some cases the Government
might lack a majority in the councils and be forced to rule by
administrative fiat, thus unmasking the sham of dyarchy and
showing the British nation that their imperialist leaders were
not ready to share power with Indians. This demonstration
might induce England to alter the system in India.

To carry out their programme, Das and the elder Nehru
had, at the end of 1922, launched the Swaraj (Home-rule)
Party whose 'immediate' aim was Dominion Status within
the Empire.

Those who continued to uphold Gandhi's non-violent non-
co-operation were called No-Changers. The two factions
wanted Swaraj but had been fighting like bitter enemies. A
compromise giving them freedom of action kept both inside
the Congress.

Confronted with this picture at Juhu, Gandhi entered into
the Gandhi–Das pact which confirmed the live-and-let-live

arrangement between the Gandhians and the Swaraj party. He did not want to split Congress.

Gandhi was still a non-co-operator, still a champion of civil disobedience and 'a strong disbeliever in this government', he declared in *Young India* of 10 April, 1924. He would therefore have pressed the boycott of the courts, schools and government jobs and titles. But the Gandhians had grown discouraged during his absence in jail. The boycott involved tremendous personal sacrifice which few could bear. The Swaraj party's policy, on the other hand, was alluring. It meant election victories, membership in legislatures, speech-making, etc. Gandhi had no short-range programme to match it. He accordingly withdrew from Indian politics for several years and devoted himself to purifying India. Swaraj depended on how good India was, not how bad the British were. 'My belief is that the instant India is purified India becomes free and not a moment earlier,' he wrote to 'Charlie' Andrews.

Gandhi's purpose, during this period of withdrawal from politics, was to foster the brotherhood of man among Indians. Looking around, it soon became obvious to him that 'the only question for immediate solution before the country is the Hindu-Moslem question. I agree with Mr Jinnah,' he added, 'that Hindu-Moslem unity means Swaraj . . . There is no question more important and more pressing than this'.

Great editor though he was, Gandhi dedicated the entire 29 May, 1924, issue of *Young India* to his 6,000-word article on 'Hindu-Moslem Tension, its Causes and Cure'. After recording the Hindu charges against Moslems ('Mussulmans', he called them) and the Moslem countercharges and noting the growth of quarrels, disputes and riots between the communities, he expressed the opinion that all this was 'a reaction against the spread of non-violence. I feel the wave of violence coming. The Hindu-Moslem tension is an acute phase of this tiredness'.

What would cure this loss of faith in non-violence, Gandhi asked. Non-violence, he answered.

Gandhi's lengthy article was advocacy rather than analysis. He believed in the immediate possibility of Hindu–Moslem friendship 'because it is so natural, so necessary for both and because I believe in human nature'. That is almost all of Gandhi in one sentence.

'The key to the situation lies with the Hindus,' he wrote. The 'two constant causes of friction' with the Moslems were cow-slaughter and music.

'Though I regard cow protection as the central fact of Hinduism [Gandhi declared], I have never been able to understand the antipathy towards the Mussulmans on that score. We say nothing about the slaughter [of cows] that daily takes place on behalf of Englishmen. Our anger becomes red-hot when a Mussulman slaughters a cow. All the riots that have taken place in the name of the cow have been an insane waste of effort. They have not saved a single cow, but they have on the contrary stiffened the backs of the Mussulmans and resulted in more slaughter. I am satisfied that during 1921 more cows were saved through the voluntary and generous effort of the Mussulmans than through the Hindu effort during all the previous twenty years, say. Cow protection should commence with ourselves. In no part of the world are cattle worse treated than in India . . . The half-starved condition of the majority of our cattle are a disgrace to us. The cows find their necks under the butcher's knife because Hindus sell them. The only effective and honourable way is to befriend the Mussulmans and leave it to their honour to save the cow. Cow protection societies must turn their attention to the feeding of cattle, prevention of cruelty, preservation of the fast disappearing pasture land, improving the breed of cattle . . .'

Then there was the music played in Hindu religious processions as they passed mosques at prayer time. Somehow, the processions contrived to arrive in front of mosques just when the followers of the Prophet were supplicating Allah. Gandhi had heard that Hindus sometimes did this 'with the deliberate intention of irritating Mussulmans'. This was as wrong as the Moslem resort to violence in angry retaliation.

Gandhi's long article ignored the social-economic reasons for the exacerbation of intercommunity relations except in one reference to the Moslem demand that a percentage of jobs in the Government be reserved for them. A Moslem middle class was beginning to emerge in India (and throughout the Arab world); it found itself handicapped in competing with Hindus, Parsis and Christians who had the advantages of better education and better connections. The Moslems therefore wanted a certain number of jobs kept for them irrespective of their qualifications. Gandhi objected. He said,

'For administration to be efficient it must be in the hands of the fittest. There should certainly be no favouritism. If we want five engineers we must not take one from each community but we must take the fittest five even if they were all Mussulmans or all Parsis . . . The educationally backward communities will have a right to favoured treatment in the matter of education at the hands of the national government . . . But those who aspire to occupy responsible posts in the government of the country can only do so if they pass the required test.'

This was logical, fair and sensible, but completely unsatisfactory to the Moslems. And since the economic backwardness of India made government employment one of the major, if not the major industries of the country, the reservation of official jobs for Mohammedans remained a sore point as long as British rule lasted.

In the seven hundred thousand villages of India, Hindus and Moslems had always lived together in peace. The Hindu-Moslem tension of the twentieth century was a man-made, middle-class, urban disease. Indians are often

ambitious and dynamic. A city like Bombay throbs with
vitality. The inhumanly crowded towns, with their herring-
barrel tenements and the frustration which comes from
animal-like poverty and the very limited opportunities to
earn, learn and advance, make urban Indians easily excitable
– especially in the maddening heat of the long summer. In
cities, Gandhi's non-violence contended with nature as well
as human nature.

Gandhi, the optimistic Karma yogi, regarded difficulties as
spurs to greater exertions of will. The editor who gave an
entire issue of his magazine to a problem was the doer who
would give his whole life to solve it. On 18 September, 1924,
therefore, Gandhi started a twenty-one day fast for
Hindu–Moslem friendship.

Gandhi had been ill for months in jail. Then came the
urgent appendicectomy. The wound suppurated and healed
slowly. Convalescence was retarded. Weeks of tense talks
followed by weeks of strenuous touring wore him out. The
political situation depressed him; years of work seemed to
have been lost. At a conference of the All-India Congress
Committee in June, when he realized how many of his
associates did not believe in non-violence, he wept in public.
The steady stream of reports on Hindu–Moslem fighting and
the atmosphere of bickering, hate and gloom weighed heavily
on his body and spirit. He was fifty-five. He knew that a
twenty-one-day fast might be fatal. He did not want to die.
There were too many unfinished tasks. He revelled in life.
Suicide was religiously and physically repugnant to him. The
fast was no tryst with death. It gave him no pleasure to suffer.
The fast was dictated by duty to the highest cause – the
universal brotherhood of man.

For Gandhi, an act had to be right and true. Then he never
counted the cost to himself or even to others; in this sense,
he was without mercy. Service meant sacrifice, renunciation
and detachment. You detach yourself from yourself. All that

remains is duty. On 18 September, 1924, Gandhi felt it his duty to fast.

Gandhi always kept his eye on his objective and when he could not see it he kept his eye on the spot where he thought it would appear. He also had an eye for drama. He fasted in the home of a Moslem, Mohamed Ali, the younger brother of Shaukat. Mohamed Ali was a staunch Congress supporter, a champion of Hindu–Moslem friendship. But the Moslem community was moving away from him. Gandhi had said in his article that 'the key to the situation lies with the Hindus', but with his heart, the senior partner of his mind, he knew that Moslems were the offenders; conditions, he said, were making the Moslem 'a bully'. Gandhi wished to strengthen Mohamed Ali's hand. 'It is our duty', he once wrote, 'to strengthen by our fasting those who hold the same ideals but are likely to weaken under pressure.' For twenty-one days India's attention would be focused on the house where Gandhi lay fasting. Moslems would see that Mohandas and Mohamed were brothers. Hindus, moreover, would note that their saint had confided his life to a Moslem.

No personal benefit could come to Gandhi from the fast; on the contrary. Nor was there any element of compulsion in it. The Moslem in Calcutta or Agra, the Hindu in Amritsar or Allahabad would not be compelled to change their conduct because Gandhi was dying for Hindu–Moslem amity. They would change, if at all, because the Mahatma's great sacrifice established a spiritual bond between him and them, a kind of common wavelength, a means of communication over which he conveyed to them the importance, the necessity, the urgency, the sacredness of the cause for which he was fasting. It was his way of going out to them, of entering their hearts, of uniting himself with them.

In part, this is Eastern, Indian. The bridges of the West are made of concrete, steel, wire, words. Eastern bridges are of spirit. To communicate, the West moves or talks. The East sits, contemplates, suffers. Gandhi partook of West and East. When Western methods failed him, he used Eastern methods.

The fast was an adventure in goodness. The stake was one man's life. The prize was a nation's freedom. If Indians were united as brothers, no outsider could long be their master. The British official report on conditions in India in 1919 remarked, 'One noticeable feature of the general excitement was the unprecedented fraternization between the Hindus and the Mohammedans.' In 1924, Gandhi felt that the fraternization, and with it freedom, was ebbing away. Hence the ordeal under his Moslem brother's roof.

'Nothing evidently which I say or write can bring the two communities together,' he declared in announcing the fast. 'I am therefore imposing on myself a twenty-one-day fast from today and ending Wednesday 6 October. I reserve the liberty to drink water with or without salt. It is both a penance and a prayer . . . I respectfully invite the heads of all communities, including Englishmen, to meet and end this quarrel which is a disgrace to religion and to humanity. It seems as if God has been dethroned. Let us reinstate Him in our hearts.'

Two Moslem physicians were in constant attendance. Charles Freer Andrews, the Christian missionary, served as nurse.

On the second day of the fast, Gandhi wrote a page-long plea for *Young India* on 'unity in diversity'. 'The need of the moment', he stressed, 'is not one religion but mutual respect and tolerance of the devotees of the different religions.' On the sixth day without food he wrote a page article which ended, 'To paraphrase a Biblical verse, if it is no profanation, "Seek you first Hindu–Moslem unity, removal of untouchability and the spinning wheel and Khaddar [homespun] and everything will be added unto you".'

Twelve days after the fast commenced he wrote 112 words for publication: 'Hitherto it has been a struggle and a yearning for a change of heart among Englishmen who compose the government of India. That change has still to come. But the struggle must for the moment be transferred to a change of heart among the Hindus and the Mussulmans. Before they dare think of freedom they must be brave enough to love one another, to tolerate one another's religion, even prejudices and superstitions, and to trust one another. This requires faith in oneself. And faith in oneself is faith in God. If we have that faith we shall cease to fear one another.'

The twentieth day he dictated a prayer: 'Presently from the world of peace I shall enter the world of strife. The more I think of it the more helpless I feel . . . I know that I can do nothing. God can do everything. O! God, make me Thy instrument and use me as Thou wilt. Man is nothing. Napoleon planned much and found himself a prisoner in St Helena. The mighty Kaiser aimed at the crown of Europe and is reduced to the status of a private gentleman. God has so willed it. Let us contemplate such examples and be humble.' The twenty days had been 'days of grace, privilege and peace'.

That evening 'Mahatma Gandhi was wonderfully bright and cheerful,' Andrews wrote. 'Many of his most intimate friends came to see him as he lay upon his bed on the open roof of the house, which was flooded by the moonlight.' They prayed. 'Then followed a long silence. The friends parted one by one and he was left alone.'

The twenty-first day: 'Before four o'clock in the morning . . . we were called for the morning prayers,' Andrews recorded. 'There was no moon and it was very dark. A chill breeze was blowing from the east . . . Bapu was wrapped warmly in a dark shawl and I asked him whether he had slept well. He replied, "Yes, very well indeed." It was a happiness to notice at once that his voice was stronger than the morning before, instead of weaker.' After prayers, many people came for darshan, a sight that blesses.

*　　*　　*

At about 10 A.M. (Andrews writes), Mahatmaji called for me and said, 'Can you remember the words of my favourite Christian hymn?'

I said, 'Yes, shall I sing it to you now?'

'Not now,' he answered, 'but I have in mind that when I break my fast, we might have a little ceremony expressing religious unity. I should like the Imam Sahib to recite the opening verses of the *Koran*. Then I would like you to sing the Christian hymn, you know the one I mean, it begins, "When I survey the wondrous Cross" and ends with the words,

> Love so amazing, so divine,
> Demands my soul, my life, my all.

And then last of all I should like Vinoba to recite from the *Upanishads* and Balkrishna to sing the Vaishnava hymn . . .' He wanted all the servants present.

Now at last the midday hour had come and the fast was to be broken.

The doctors went to Gandhi's room; the Ali brothers, Maulana Abul Kalam Azad, Motilal Nehru, C. R. Das and many others sat on the floor near the bed. Before the actual breaking of the fast, Gandhi spoke, 'and as he spoke his emotion was so deep that in his bodily weakness his voice could hardly be heard except by those who were nearest of all to him'. He asked them to lay down their lives, if need be, for the cause of brotherhood. The Moslem leaders renewed their pledge. Then the hymns were sung. 'Dr Ansari brought forward some orange juice and Mahatma Gandhi drank it. So the fast was broken.'

CHAPTER 12

Funds and Jewels

In the latter part of 1924, the world was subsiding into post-war 'normalcy'. The Dawes Plan undertook to stabilize German economic and political conditions. The big European powers were granting diplomatic recognition to Soviet Russia. Except in south China, where Chiang Kai-shek had an alliance with Moscow, the threat of Bolshevism was on the ebb. Coolidge and complacency presided over America. England had experienced her first Labour government. The British Empire, seriously menaced in 1919–23 by Sinn Fein in Ireland and Near East revolts, was becalmed in stagnant waters.

India, too, relaxed – and pursued the luxuries of division and inaction. The passions of the post-Armistice-post-Amritsar period were spent. Doubts and despondency had replaced faith and fighting spirit. Perhaps Gandhi's non-violence dampened the ardour of belligerent nationalism. His twenty-one-day fast had failed. It impressed many and altered the attitude of some, but Hindu–Moslem tension continued unabated.

Gandhi did not consider this a time for a contest with Britain. It was a time for mending home fences. His programme was: prepare morally for future political opportunities; concretely – Hindu–Moslem unity, the removal of untouchability and spreading the use of homespun or khadi or khaddar. In his propaganda for homespun, Gandhi charged the British with killing India's village industries to help the textile mills of Lancashire. Otherwise, his writings and speeches during 1925, 1926 and 1927 were remarkable for an almost complete absence of denunciations of British rule. He more often criticized Indians. 'I am not interested', he said, 'in freeing India merely from the English yoke. I am bent upon freeing India from any yoke whatsoever.' For this reason, he could never get excited about participation in the legislative or municipal councils: 'Swaraj' he affirmed, 'will come not by the acquisition of authority by a few but by the acquisition by all of a capacity to resist authority when it is abused.' A few hundred Indians were elected to councils, and a few thousand Indians, mostly townspeople, enjoyed the franchise to elect them. In such circumstances, Indians might become tyrants unless the masses were taught to discard docility.

The intellectuals remained unconvinced. 'Though they like me personally,' he wrote, they 'have a horror of my views and methods.' He was not complaining; 'I have simply stated the fact with the object of showing my limitations.'

Educated Indians, he stated, were splitting into parties. 'I confess my inability to bring these parties together', he wrote on 2 September, 1926. 'Their method is not my method. I am trying to work from the bottom upward,' and he warned them that if they did not support his khadi policy, 'educated India will cut itself off from the only visible and tangible tie that binds them to the masses'.

Gandhi put his trust neither in the once-hallowed tradition of Congress petitions and 'prayers' to British officialdom nor in current Swaraj party's desire to become parliamentarians and officials. But having failed to carry the conviction home, 'I must no longer stand in the way of the Congress being developed and guided by educated Indians rather than by one like myself who had thrown in his lot entirely with the masses and who has fundamental differences with the mind of educated India as a body.'

An American clergyman once asked Gandhi what caused him most concern. 'The hardness of heart of the educated,' Gandhi replied.

He still wished to influence the intellectuals, he confessed, 'but not by leading the Congress; on the contrary, by working my way to their hearts, silently so far as possible, even as I did between 1915 and 1919'. He regretted having been dragged into the political leadership of Congress; he was retiring from it.

Loud protests rent the Indian air when he first announced his intention of doing so after coming out of jail in 1924. 'I do not like, I have never liked,' he said in reply, 'this reliance on me for everything. It is the very worst way of managing national affairs. The Congress must not become, as it has threatened to become, one man's show, no matter how good or great that one man be. I often think that it would have been better for the country and for me if I had served the full term of my imprisonment.'

Nevertheless, he was persuaded to take the presidency of Congress for 1925; his friends argued that his aloofness would split Congress between those who followed his constructive programme and the Swaraj party which advocated political work in the councils. He exacted a price: the wearing of khadi as a strict condition of membership in the Congress party; where possible, Congress members should spin each day.

Someone said his retirement from politics would cost him his moral authority. 'Moral authority', was the unequivocal retort, 'is never retained by any attempt to hold on to it. It comes without seeking and is retained without effort.'

In truth, his moral authority was increasing irrespective of anything he did or did not do. It was fed by the Indian soil and Indian mentality. Throughout 1925 he travelled, continuously, across the 1,500-mile width and the 1,900-mile length of India, visiting most provinces and many native states. He no longer lived nor travelled like a poor man, he wailed; his co-workers made him travel in a second-class compartment instead of a third where forty or fifty perspiring people sat squeezed together in an unpartitioned space. He acquiesced because in third class he could not write his articles, or rest, or take an occasional nap.

Wherever he went, he was besieged by hordes. 'They will not leave me alone even when I am taking my bath,' he wrote. At night, his feet and shins were covered with scratches from people who had bowed low and touched him; his feet had to be rubbed with vaseline. His deification had commenced. In one place he was told that a whole tribe, the Gonds, were worshipping him. 'I have expressed my horror and strongest disapproval of this type of idolatry more than once,' he wrote. 'I claim to be a mere mortal, heir to all the weaknesses that human flesh betrays. It would be infinitely better that the Gonds should be taught to understand the meaning of my simple message than that they should indulge in a meaningless deification of me which can do no good either to them or to me and can only intensify the superstitious nature of such simple people as the Gonds.'

Even mere veneration seemed superfluous to him. 'I am no Mahatma,' he cried out. 'My Mahatmaship is worthless,' he wrote.

But the Mahatma was powerless; he had to be a Mahatma. Many regarded him as a reincarnation of God, like Buddha, like Krishna; God descended temporarily to earth. From the mountains, from the plains, from far-off villages, people came to have a glimpse of him, to be sanctified if the eye or, much better, the hand, touched him. Audiences were so large that he would address them standing in front of them, then go to the right side, the rear and the left side, always hoping that they would remain seated on the ground and not stampede towards him. Many times he was in danger of being crushed to death.

At Dacca, in Bengal, a man of seventy was brought before Gandhi. He was wearing Gandhi's photograph around his neck and weeping profusely. As he approached the Mahatma, he fell on his face and thanked Gandhi for having cured him of chronic paralysis. 'When all other remedies failed,' the poor man said, 'I took to uttering Gandhiji's name and one day I found myself entirely cured.'

'It is not I but God who made you whole,' Gandhi rebuked him. 'Will you not oblige me by taking that photograph off your neck?'

Intellectuals too were not immune. One day, Gandhi's train stopped with a jerk; somebody had pulled the emergency cord. It developed that a lawyer had fallen out of the train, head first. When picked up he was unhurt. He ascribed it to being the Mahatma's fellow traveller. 'Then you shouldn't have fallen out at all,' Gandhi laughed. But wit was lost on the devout.

Women, even Hindu women, sometimes sat on their haunches behind a screen when they listened to Gandhi at meetings. Just as Moslems, Christians and even untouchables have borrowed the institution of caste from Hindus, so Hindus have in places succumbed to Islam's purdah or segregation of women. But when a woman came to Gandhi with her face hidden, he said, 'No purdah before your brother,' and she immediately dropped her veil.

Gandhi was an incurable and irresistible fund raiser. He found special relish in stripping women of their jewellery.

'The army of my sweethearts is daily increasing,' he exclaimed during a tour. 'The latest recruit is Ranibala of Burdwan, a darling perhaps ten years old. I dare not ask her age. I was playing with her as usual and casting furtive glances at her six heavy gold bangles. I gently explained to her that they were too heavy a burden for her delicate little wrists and down went her hand on the bangles.'

Ranibala's grandfather encouraged her to give Gandhi the bangles.

'I must confess I was embarrassed,' Gandhi recalled as he told the story. 'I was merely joking as I always do when I see little girls and jokingly create in them a distaste for much

ornamentation and a desire to part with their jewellery for the
sake of the poor. I tried to return the bangles.'

But her grandfather said her mother would consider it an ill
omen to take them back. Gandhi agreed to keep them on one
condition: she was not to ask for new ones.

That day he addressed a ladies' meeting in the same town.
He told them about Ranibala. 'I got quite a dozen bangles
and two or three pairs of earrings, all unasked. Needless to say,
they will all be used for khaddar . . .

'I notify all young girls and their parents and
grandparents,' Gandhi announced gaily, 'that I am open to
have as many sweethearts as would come to me on Ranibala's
terms. They will be handsomer for the thought that they gave
their prized ornaments to be used for the service of the poor.
Let the little girls of India treasure the proverb, "Handsome is
as handsome does".'

Still touring, he came to Bihar. At Kharagdeha, reached
by a branch railway and then a twenty-six-mile journey by
car, the programme began with a ladies' meeting. 'Hitherto,'
Gandhi reported, 'I have restrained myself from criticizing
the heavily ornamental decoration of some of my fair
audiences, oppressive though it has appeared to me. But the
bangled arms from wrist practically to elbow, the huge thick
nose-rings with about a three-inch diameter which could with
difficulty be suspended from two holes, proved beyond
endurance, and I gently remarked that this heavy
ornamentation added nothing to the beauty of the person,
caused much discomfort, must often lead to disease and was, I
could plainly see, a repository of dirt.'

Gandhi feared he might have offended the ladies. But when
he had finished speaking they crowded around him and
brought him money, and many handed him their ornaments.
He hoped Indian women would dispense with 'these articles
of personal furniture'.

Wearing his homespun loincloth, a radiant smile and,

usually, sandals (sometimes he went barefoot), he would stride with long easy steps to the speaker's platform and make his appeal. While the train waited during his meeting at a whistle stop in Bihar, Gandhi made a one-minute speech: 'I have come here to do business,' he said artlessly, 'to collect money for the spinning wheel and khadi and to sell khadi. Who knows, this may be my last visit to Bihar. Let me do as much business as I can.' With that, he moved among the listeners asking for 'ringing testimony' of their devotion to homespun. The people rang the tin bowl with their copper and nickel mites; 526 rupees were collected. (The rupee was one shilling and fourpence.) Then he took an armful of homespun cotton cloth, or loincloths, or women's saris and sold them for as much as he could get. Mahadev Desai, his first secretary, Devadas, his youngest son, and other members of his group did likewise.

It was the custom to present him with a purse collected before his arrival in larger towns. A purse might contain several hundred or even several thousand rupees. At the same time, ceremonial addresses of devotion were given to him. Many of these exquisitely executed documents were enclosed in silver caskets. 'Expensive caskets are not required,' he admonished one committee, 'for I have no use for them, nor do I have any room to keep them in.' He tried selling a casket to the people who gave it to him and not only did they not mind, they paid lavishly for it. So he made a habit of personally auctioning off such caskets; one brought 1,001 rupees. He did the same with floral garlands thrown around his neck. Why kill flowers unnecessarily, he argued, when they could 'garland' him with a ring of yarn. Yarn garlands became an Indian custom.

'Bania', Gandhi's friends called him with amazement. He was the shrewd, successful businessman, but his income and profits were never for himself.

An American friend asked me to get him the Mahatma's

photograph with a personal inscription. I found a photograph
in the ashram, explained the request and asked him to sign.

'If you give me twenty rupees for the Harijan Fund,'
Gandhi said with a smile.

'I'll give you ten.' He autographed it.

When I told Devadas, he said, 'Bapu would have done it for
five.'

In 1924, 1925, 1926 and 1927, the popularizing of khadi
possessed Gandhi's mind. Each issue of the weekly *Young India*
devoted several pages to lists of persons and the exact number
of yards of yarn they had spun. Some spinners gave the yarn to
the fund which gave it to villages, others wove their own.
Gandhi's Sabarmati Ashram was manufacturing simple
spinning wheels, but in 1926 the manager announced that
they had more orders than they could fill. Schools were giving
courses in spinning. At Congress meetings, members would
open a small box like a violin case, take out a collapsible
spinning wheel and spin noiselessly throughout the
proceedings. Gandhi had set the fashion.

Some of Gandhi's closest friends accused him of khadi
extremism; he exaggerated the possibility of restoring India's
village industries and overestimated the benefits that might
accrue even if he were successful; this was the machine age; all
his energy, wisdom and holiness would not avail to turn back
the clock.

'A hundred and fifty years ago,' Gandhi replied, 'we
manufactured all our cloth. Our women spun fine cloths in
their own cottages and supplemented the earnings of their
husbands . . . India requires nearly thirteen yards of cloth per
head per year. She produces, I believe, less than half the
amount. India grows all the cotton she needs. She exports
several million bales of cotton to Japan and Lancashire and
receives much of it back in manufactured calico, although she
is capable of producing all the cloth and all the yarn necessary
for supplying her wants by hand-weaving and hand-

spinning . . . The spinning wheel was presented to the nation for giving occupation to the millions who had, at least for four months of the year, nothing to do . . . We send out of India sixty crores [six hundred million] (more or less) of rupees for cloth . . .'

Many intellectuals sneered at khadi. The stuff was coarse, they said. 'Monotonous white shrouds,' some mocked. 'The livery of our freedom,' Jawaharlal Nehru replied. 'I regard the spinning wheel as a gateway to my spiritual salvation,' Gandhi said.

Gandhi was trying to bridge brain and brawn, to unite city and town, to link rich and poor. What greater service could he perform for a divided country and an atomized civilization? To help the underdog, Gandhi taught, you must understand him and to understand him you must at least sometimes work as he does. Spinning was an act of love, another channel of communication. It was also a method of organization. 'Any single district that can be fully organized for khaddar is, if it is also trained for suffering, ready for civil disobedience.' Thus, khadi would lead to home-rule.

Gandhi asked townspeople and villagers to spend an hour a day at the wheel. 'It affords a pleasant variety and recreation after hard toil.' Spinning does not replace other reforms; it is in addition to them. But he stressed them less than spinning.

'For me,' Gandhi reiterated, 'nothing in the political world is more important than the spinning wheel.' One of India's greatest intellectuals, with a brain as keen as Gandhi's and as habitually sceptical as Gandhi was normally naive, enthusiastically supported the Mahatma's khadi contentions. Chakravarty Rajagopalachari, the famous Madras lawyer, was second only to Gandhi in his sanguine expectations from the nationwide use of homespun. 'Khadi work is the only true political programme before the country,' he declared on 6 April, 1916, in the textile-mill city of Ahmedabad. 'You are living in a great city. You do not really know the amount of poverty that has overtaken the country called India. As a matter of fact, in India there are thousands and tens of thousands of villages where men do not get more than $2\frac{1}{2}$ rupees a month. There is no use shedding tears for them if we won't wear a few yards of khadi which they have manufactured and want us to buy so that they may find a meal. If our hearts were not made of stone we would all be wearing khadi. Khadi means employment for the poor and freedom for India. Britain holds India because it is a fine market for Lancashire . . .'

Motilal Nehru also took to wearing khadi; he peddled it in the streets as Gandhi did. Intellectuals might scoff, but khadi began to have a fascination for them and from the mid-1920s, homespun became the badge of the Indian nationalist. A propagandist for independence would no more dream of going into a village in foreign clothes or foreign cloth or even in Indian mill cloth than he would think of speaking English at a peasant meeting. Apart from its economic value, which has not proved decisive, homespun was Gandhi's peculiar contribution to the education of political India: he made it physically conscious of poor, uneducated, non-political India. Khadi was an adventure in identification between leadership and nation. Gandhi was prescribing for a disease which plagued independent India and most independent countries. He knew that the tragedy of India's history was the canyon between the gold-silver-silk-brocade-jewel-elephant splendour of her palaces and the animal poverty of her hovels; at the bottom of the canyon lay the debris of empires and the bones of millions of their victims.

The work exhausted Gandhi. Three or four stops a day for meetings, a different place to stop every night, heavy correspondence which he never neglected, and unnumbered personal interviews with men and women who sought his word on the biggest political problems and their smallest personal difficulties – all in the great heat and humidity –

wore him down. In November 1925, therefore, he undertook a seven-day fast.

India worried about him and protested. Why a fast? 'The public will have to neglect my fasts and cease to worry about them,' Gandhi stated. 'They are part of my being. I can as well do without my eyes, for instance, as I can without fasts. What the eyes are for the outer world, fasts are for the inner.' He would fast whenever the spirit moved him. The result, to be sure, might be disastrous. 'I may be wholly wrong,' he admitted. 'Then the world will be able to write an epitaph over my ashes: "Well deserved, thou fool." But for the time being, my error, if it be one, must sustain me.' This was a personal fast; 'this fast has nothing to do with the public'. It is said 'I am public property . . . So be it. But I must be taken with all my faults. I am a searcher after truth. My experiments I hold to be infinitely more important than the best-equipped Himalayan expeditions.' He was trying to scale the spiritual heights; he thought fasts conduced to mental ascendancy over the body.

Gandhi's fast brought him a tide of requests for his views on fasting; even in India his frequent abstentions from food were unusual. He gave his response in a *Young India* article. 'With apologies to my medical friends', it read, 'but out of the fullness of my own experience and that of fellow-cranks, I say without hesitation, Fast (1) if you are constipated, (2) if you are anaemic, (3) if you are feverish, (4) if you have indigestion, (5) if you have a headache, (6) if you are rheumatic, (7) if you are gouty, (8) if you are fretting and foaming, (9) if you are depressed, (10) if you are overjoyed, and you will avoid medical prescriptions and patent medicines.' His patent medical prescription for everything was fasting. 'Eat *only* when you are *hungry*,' he added, 'and when you have laboured for your food.'

His highest weight after being discharged from prison in February 1924, he wrote in the same article, was 112 pounds.

He was down to 103 pounds when he started the fast. In the seven days he lost nine pounds but regained it very quickly. Physically, he said, he lost nothing either from this fast or from the twenty-one-day fast in 1924.

Water during fasts nauseated him without a pinch of salt or bicarbonate of soda or a few drops of citrus juice. He never suffered any pangs of hunger during the fast; in fact, 'I broke it half an hour later than I need have.' He spun every day and attended the daily prayer meetings. The first three days of the fast, he wrote, 'I worked practically from four in the morning till eight in the evening,' doing articles, answering letters, giving interviews. On the fourth day, his head ached. He accordingly abandoned work for a day; on the seventh day 'I was able to write with a steady hand my article on the fast.'

The article furnished nine rules for fasting; he himself broke the first which was 'Conserve your energy both physical and mental from the very beginning, (2) You must cease to think of food while you are fasting, (3) Drink as much cold water as you can . . . (4) Have a warm sponge daily, (5) Take an enema regularly during fast. You will be surprised at the impurities you will expel daily, (6) Sleep as much as possible in the open air, (7) Bathe in the morning air. A sun and air bath is at least as great a purifier as a water bath, (8) Think of anything else but your fast, (9) No matter from what motive you are fasting, during this precious time think of your Maker and of your relation to Him and His other creations and you will make discoveries you may not have dreamed of.'

It was for these discoveries that he fasted.

Gandhi's year as president of Congress was now ended and at Cawnpore, in December 1925, he relinquished the gavel to Mrs Sarojini Naidu, mistress of lyric words. Gandhi then took a vow of a year's 'political silence'. 'At least up to twentieth December next,' he announced in *Young India* of 7 January, 1926, 'I am not to stir out of the ashram, certainly not out of Ahmedabad' across the river. Body and soul needed rest.

The Swaraj party, which had sent its people into the legislative councils to obstruct the British government, veered slowly towards a measure of co-operation. A dissident group, headed by M. R. Jayakar and N. C. Kelkar, who believed in still more co-operation with the British, but less with the Moslems, split off from the Swarajists and formed the Responsivist party. It leaned towards the Hindu Mahasabha, a religious political party. In December 1925, the Moslem League session at Aligarh, attended by Jinnah, Mohamed Ali and Sir Ali Imam, moved in the direction of religious politics. Gandhi had hoped to unite India for nationalist liberation. But she was splitting at her religious seam. Political India, Gandhi found, was 'disrupted and demoralized'. It seemed a good time for silence. 'Silence', he quoted, 'is the true language of cosmic adoration.'

CHAPTER 13

The 'Silent' Year

In the 'silent' year there were fifty-two silent Mondays when Gandhi did not speak. On those days, he would listen to an interviewer and occasionally tear off a corner of a piece of paper and pencil a few words in reply. Since this was not the best way to conduct a conversation, the weekly day of silence gave him some privacy.

In 1942, I inquired of Gandhi what lay behind his day of silence.

'It happened when I was being torn to pieces,' he explained. 'I was working very hard, travelling in hot trains, incessantly speaking at many meetings and being approached in trains and elsewhere by thousands of people who asked questions, made pleas and wished to pray with me. I wanted to rest for one day a week. So I instituted the day of silence. Later of course I clothed it with all kinds of virtues and gave it a spiritual cloak. But the motivation was really nothing more than that I wanted to have a day off.'

He liked to laugh at himself. Questioned further, he would have agreed, however, that silence offered an opportunity for spiritual exercise.

Apart from the fifty-two Mondays, the 'silent' year was in no sense silent. He did not travel, he addressed no mass meetings; but he talked, wrote, received visitors and maintained a correspondence with thousands of persons in India and other countries.

On 1 April, 1926, Lord Irwin (who later became Lord Halifax, Foreign Secretary of the United Kingdom and British Ambassador to Washington) arrived in India to succeed Lord Reading as Viceroy. But the fateful change was not mentioned in *Young India*, nor did Gandhi seem to have noted it in any other way. He was still a non-co-operator working on the masses instead of on the Viceroy. His motto was Swaraj from within.

One extremely important change, however, was noticeable in Gandhi's attitude: he began to suspect that Britain's policy militated against Hindu–Moslem friendship. 'The government of India,' he wrote on 12 August, 1926, 'is based on distrust. Distrust involves favouritism and favouritism must breed division.' The Government appeared to prefer Moslems.

Gandhi had thought that Hindu–Moslem amity would bring self-rule to India. Now he felt that Hindu–Moslem amity was almost impossible while the British, 'the third party', were there.

Thus religious peace, the prerequisite of independence, could only follow independence.

This dilemma notwithstanding, Gandhi remained hopeful: 'The unity will come in spite of ourselves . . . Where man's effort may fail God's will succeed and His government is not based upon "divide and rule" policy.' Meanwhile, there had been bloody fighting between the two religious communities in several parts of India.

Gandhi's prescription was better treatment of the Moslem minority by the Hindu majority and non-violence by both. Hindus violently accused him of being pro-Moslem.

But the year's fiercest controversy involved dogs. For months, the storm raged about the Mahatma's head.

Ambalal Sarabhai, the big textile millowner of Ahmedabad, rounded up sixty stray dogs that frequented his large industrial properties and had them destroyed.

Having destroyed the dogs, Sarabhai was disturbed and shared his anguish with the Mahatma. 'What else could be done?' said Gandhi.

The Ahmedabad Humanitarian Society learned of this

conversation and turned on Gandhi. 'Is that true?' it demanded in a letter sent to the ashram. Did he say, 'What else could be done? . . . And if so, what does it mean? . . .

'When Hinduism forbids the taking of the life of any living being,' the letter fumed, 'when it declares it to be a sin, do you think it right to kill rabid dogs for the reason that they would bite human beings and by biting other dogs make them also rabid?'

Gandhi published the letter in *Young India* under the caption 'Is This Humanity?' The letter and his reply filled the entire first page and half the second page. Yes, it was true. He had said, 'What else could be done?' and having thought it over, 'I . . . feel that my reply was quite proper . . .

'Imperfect, erring mortals as we are,' he declared in explanation, 'there is no course open to us but the destruction of rabid dogs. At times we may be faced with the unavoidable duty of killing a man who is found in the act of killing people.'

The next issue of *Young India* gave its front page to the same question under the same caption, 'Is This Humanity?' The first article had brought a deluge of 'angry letters'. Worse, people came to Gandhi to insult him. 'At an hour', he wrote, 'when after a hard day's work I was about to retire to bed, three friends invaded me, infringed the religion of non-violence in the name of humanity and engaged me in a discussion on it.' Gandhi used the word 'friends' only because he considered everybody a friend. One of the 'friends' was a Jain and he 'betrayed anger, bitterness and arrogance'.

Gandhi had grown up under the influence of the absolute non-violence of Jainism. 'Many take me to be a Jain,' Gandhi declared. But Mahavira, the founder of Jainism, 'was the incarnation of compassion, of non-violence. How I wish his votaries were votaries also of non-violence'.

Gandhi stuck to his guns. 'The multiplication of dogs is,' he wrote, 'unnecessary. A roving dog without an owner is a danger to society and a swarm of them is a menace to its very existence.' If people were really religious, dogs would have owners. 'There is a regular science of dog-keeping in the West . . . We should learn it.'

The dog mail continued to come; 'some of the hostile critics have transgressed the limits of decorum', Gandhi asserted in the next *Young India* which devoted almost three pages to the matter. One man had demanded an interview and then, without permission, published the substance of it in a leaflet which he was hawking in the streets. 'Does he seek to teach me in this manner?' Gandhi wondered. He who is angry is guilty of violence. How can such a man teach me non-violence?

'Even so,' Gandhi continued, 'the hostile critics are doing me a service. They teach me to examine myself. They afford me an opportunity to see if I am free from the reaction of anger. And when I go to the root of their anger I find nothing but love.' How did he arrive at that strange conclusion? Because, he said, 'They had attributed to me non-violence as they understand it. Now they find me acting in a contrary manner and are angry with me.

'I do not mind their outburst of anger,' he asserted. 'I appreciate the motive behind it. I must try to reason with them patiently . . .'

He reasoned thus: It is a sin to feed stray dogs. 'It is a false sense of compassion. It is an insult to a starving dog to throw a crumb at him. Roving dogs do not indicate the civilization or compassion of the society, they betray on the contrary the ignorance and lethargy of its members. The lower animals are our brethren. I include among them the lion and the tiger. We do not know how to live with these carnivorous beasts and poisonous reptiles because of our ignorance. When man learns better he will learn to befriend even these. Today he does not even know how to befriend a man of a different religion or from another country.'

Gandhi probably suspected that some of the dog-lovers would howl less if sixty Moslems or Englishmen had been killed.

The humane man, Gandhi wrote, would finance a society to keep the stray dogs; or he would harbour some himself. But if the State did not care for them and if householders would not keep them, the dogs had to be destroyed. 'The dogs in India', Gandhi mourned, 'are today in as bad a plight as the decrepit animals and men in the land.'

(Then why not kill the decrepit cows?)

'Taking life may be a duty,' Gandhi proceeded. 'Suppose a man runs amok and goes furiously about, sword in hand and killing any one who comes his way and no one dares to capture him alive. Anyone who dispatched this lunatic will earn the gratitude of the community . . .'

Many correspondents demanded personal replies and threatened to attack him if they got none. He said he could not answer the mountain of letters that had reached him on this subject, but he would continue to deal with them in his magazines. Four more issues of *Young India* gave several columns each to the dog problem. In one Ahmedabad hospital, Gandhi reported, 1,117 cases of hydrophobia had been treated in 1925 and 990 in 1926. Again he urged India to follow the West in this matter; 'If any one thinks that the people in the West are innocent of humanity he is sadly mistaken.' And then comes a sting: 'The ideal of humanity in the West is perhaps lower, but their practice of it is very much more thorough than ours. We rest content with a lofty ideal and are slow and lazy in its practice. We are wrapped in deep darkness, as is evident from our paupers, cattle and other animals. They are eloquent of our irreligion rather than of religion.'

His pro-dog attitude showed he was under Western influence, correspondents charged. Patiently he reasoned with the furious. He condemned some features of Western civilization and had learned from others, he told them. Moreover, opinions should be judged by content not by their source.

'Letters on this subject are still pouring in,' Gandhi

announced in the third month of the controversy, but since their only contribution was venom he ignored them.

The dog fight established the record for heat in the 'silent' year'. But a little calf also precipitated a storm. A young heifer in the ashram fell ill. Gandhi tended it and watched it suffer and decided it ought to be put to death. Kasturbai objected strenuously. Then she must go and nurse the animal, Gandhi suggested. She did and the animal's torment convinced her. In Gandhi's presence, a doctor administered an injection which killed the heifer. The protest mail was heavy and fierce. Gandhi insisted he had done right.

Frank sex discussions filled many Letters to the Editor. 'My correspondence with young men on their private conduct', Gandhi wrote, 'is increasing.' They asked his advice.

Taking advantage of relative leisure in the 'silent' year, Gandhi read Havelock Ellis, Forel, Paul Bureau's *Toward Moral Bankruptcy* and other European authorities on family and sex. His interest in the sex life of Indians has always remained high. He believed that early and frequent sexual intercourse had a debilitating effect on Indians; he understood the implications of the rapid increase in his country's population. (In the 1940s, the population of India was increasing five million each year.) He wrapped this problem too in a spiritual cloak and, taking a leaf out of sacred Hindu books, advocated chastity for religious reasons. But the biological and economic aspects of the situation did not escape him.

In many articles that came from his pen, or pencil, in 'silent' 1926 and often thereafter, Gandhi consistently opposed the use of contraceptives; they were a Western vice. But he did not oppose birth control. He always advocated birth control. The birth control he favoured, however, was through self-control, through the power of the mind over the body. 'Self-control', he wrote, 'is the surest and only method of regulating the birth rate.' Without such discipline, he contended, man was no better than a brute. He maintained that abstinence for ever or for long periods was neither physically nor psychologically harmful. Gandhi and his closest ashram associates practised Brahmacharya, complete continence; people in general, he said, might indulge in sex for purpose of procreation, but not to gratify animal passion. He denied 'that sexual indulgence for its own sake is a human necessity'.

A correspondent wrote: 'In my case, three weeks seem to be the utmost period of beneficial abstention. At the end of that period I usually feel a heaviness of body, a restlessness both of body and mind, leading to bad temper. Relief is obtained either by normal coitus or nature herself coming to the rescue by an involuntary discharge. Far from feeling weak or nervous, I become the next morning calm and light and am able to proceed to my work with added gusto.' Many similar cases were brought to Gandhi's notice.

Dipping into his personal experience, Gandhi said in reply, 'Ability to retain and assimilate the vital liquid is a matter of long training.' Once achieved, it strengthens body and mind. The vital liquid, 'capable of producing such a wonderful being as man, cannot but, when properly conserved, be transmuted into matchless energy and strength'.

Realistically, in *Harijan* magazine of 14 September, 1935, Gandhi wrote, 'Assuming that birth control by artificial aids is justifiable under certain conditions, it seems to be utterly impracticable of application among the millions.' India was poor and ignorant because she was too poor and ignorant to apply birth control by contraceptives. Therefore, Gandhi urged other means of reducing the population. Contraceptives led to over-indulgence with the result that a 'society that has already become enervated through a variety of causes will become still further enervated by the adoption of artificial methods'.

Gandhi endeavoured to delay the marriage of his own sons. Times without number, he attacked the institution of child marriage: 'Early marriages are a fruitful source of life, adding to the population . . .' He conceded, of course, that the earth should produce enough to support all who are born on it, but, as a religious man with a strong practical sense, he saw the necessity of population limitation. 'If,' he wrote to Charles Freer Andrews, 'I could find a way of stopping procreation in a civil and voluntary manner whilst India remains in the present miserable state I would do so today.' The only manner he countenanced was mental discipline. To the strong and saintly he proposed lifelong Brahmacharya; to the mass, he proposed late marriage, in the mid-twenties if possible and self-control thereafter. In the ashram, the minimum marriage age for girls was twenty-one. He recognized human frailties but insisted that unspiced food, the right kind of clothes, the right kind of work, walking, gymnastics, unspiced literature, prayer, pure films (Indian films to this day prohibit kissing on the screen) and devotion to God would relieve the tension in modern life and conduce to the sexual self-control which most persons unthinkingly consider unnatural. Gandhi's writings on these matters, though they appeared in his small-circulation *Young India* and Gujarat *Navajivan*, were, like almost everything he said, reprinted in the entire Indian press.

A cognate question attracted Gandhi's special attention during the 'silent' year: child widows. According to the official British census for 1921, which he cited, there were in India 11,892 widows less than five years old; 85,037 widows between the ages of five and ten; and 232,147 widows between ten and fifteen; together 329,076 widows under sixteen.

'The existence of girl widows', Gandhi exclaimed, 'is a blot on Hinduism.' Parents would marry their baby daughters to baby sons of other families, or even to old men and if the husband died, either in infancy or of senility, the widow could not, under Hindu law, remarry. Defiantly, Gandhi declared, 'I consider the remarriage of virgin widows not only desirable but the bounden duty of all parents who happen to have such widowed daughters.' Some of these youthful widows were no longer virgins but prostitutes. 'The remedy in anticipation,' he wrote, 'is to prevent early marriages.' To those bigoted Hindus who, loyal to every immoral custom, defended the proscription against second marriage of child widows, Gandhi retorted, 'They were never married at all.' The wedding of a child is a sacrilege, not a sacred rite. His deepest feeling about child widows was expressed in one sweet sentence, 'They are strangers to love.' Chastity had to be the deliberate and voluntary act of a mature person, not the imposition of cruel parents on children. Gandhi wanted all human beings to know love. But a widow, or widower, who had married as an adult should not remarry, he said; they had tasted love. This proscription constituted another birth-control technique.

Protection of the cow, protection of Indians in South Africa where race hate was again rampant, prohibition and world peace also excited Gandhi's reforming zeal during his Sabbatical year.

Occasionally, some proverbs dropped from his pen: 'Any secrecy hinders the real spirit of democracy'; 'If we could erase the "I's" and "Mine's" from religion, politics, economics, etc., we should be free and bring heaven on earth.' Occasionally, too, he made brief excursions into religion, but there was remarkably little discussion in print about God, metaphysics and kindred topics. One thought he did leave with his readers: 'Rationalists are admirable beings,' he wrote in an article on the efficacy of prayer; 'rationalism is a hideous monster when it claims for itself omnipotence. Attribution of omnipotence to reason is as bad a piece of idolatry as is worship of stick and stone believing it to be God . . . I do not know a single rationalist who has never done anything in simple faith . . . But we all know millions of human beings living their more or less orderly lives because of their childlike faith in the Maker of us all. That very faith is a prayer . . . I plead not for the suppression of reason, but for due recognition of that in us which sanctions reason itself.'

'Mankind cannot live by logic alone, but also needs poetry,' he once wrote. Gandhi frequently left the field of sensory perception and rational mental processes for that middle zone of faith, instinct, intuition and love, but he never wandered away from it into the rarefied realm of mystic messages, miracles, hallucinations, prophecy and other unaccountable manifestations of mind and body. 'Whilst he did not rule out the authenticity of supra-sensuous phenomena,' says one of his closest disciples, 'he very strongly disapproved of pursuing them.' He judged men and events by the criteria of cold facts and invited others to judge him rationally. He did not wish to influence people by mystic radiation. His estimate of himself was severely sober. His work was practical and its goal was practical success. He told Muriel Lester, an Englishwoman, that he 'never heard a voice, saw a vision, or had some recognized experience of God'. No mystic experience had been vouchsafed to him. His guide was reason on the wing of faith.

Gandhi's reputation abroad was spreading. Romain Rolland, the French author, wrote a book about him. Many invitations reached him, especially from America, to come on a visit. He rejected them. 'My reason is simple,' he explained, 'I have not enough self-confidence to warrant my going to America. I have no doubt that the movement for non-violence has come to stay. I have no doubt whatsoever about its final success. But I cannot give an ocular demonstration of the efficacy of non-violence. Till then, I feel I must continue to preach from the narrower Indian platform.'

Two American women, Mrs Kelly and Mrs Langeloth, representing the Fellowship of Faith, the League of Neighbours and the Union of East and West, actually came to Sabarmati to invite the Mahatma. First they cross-examined him: 'Is it true that you object to railways, steamships and other means of speedy locomotion?'

'It is and it is not,' Gandhi replied patiently, for the thousandth time, and urged them to read his *Indian Home-Rule*. More conversation of the same kind followed. He was afraid, in the end, that they did not understand his attitude to the machine and speed, because they had to catch a train and left early.

Gandhi was in no hurry either personally or politically, and sat still for a year. He seemed to enjoy his 1926 moratorium from politics. It gave his body time to rest and his spirit a chance to roam. He played more with the children. He participated in an ashram spinning contest. He and Kasturbai, the oldest members of the community, were beaten by the youngest, their granddaughter. The announcement evoked great hilarity.

He cultivated his friends, Rajagopalachari, the lawyer with the razor-edge brain; Mahadev Desai, who was a secretary and an apostle; and 'Charlie' Andrews, two years Gandhi's junior, whom Gandhi called 'The Good Samaritan'. He 'is more than a blood brother to me,' Gandhi said. 'I do not think that I can claim a deeper attachment to anyone than to Mr Andrews.' The Hindu saint had found no better saint than Andrews. The Christian missionary had found no better Christian than Gandhi. Perhaps the Indian and Englishman were brothers because they were truly religious. Perhaps religion brought them together because nationality did not separate them. 'Each country,' Andrews said, speaking of England and India, 'has become equally dear to me.' Gandhi declared, 'I would not hurt England or Germany to serve India.' In a letter to Andrews dated Calcutta, 27 December, 1928, Gandhi wrote, 'The most forward nationalists in India have not been haters of the West or of England or in any other way narrow ... but they have been internationalists under the guise of nationalism.'

Where nationalism does not divide, religion can make men brothers.

CHAPTER 14

Collapse

Gandhi emerged from the year of silence with views unchanged. His programme was still Hindu–Moslem unity, the removal of untouchability and the promotion of homespun. Indeed, Gandhi's programme in its simplest terms remained the same for decades. The vision of the future of India which he outlined in 1909 in his booklet *Indian Home-Rule* guided him to the end of his days. In 1921, at the height of the non-co-operation movement, he had sent Andrews to tell the Viceroy that if the Government would help promote home spinning and weaving in the villages and suppress alcohol and opium he would drop non-co-operation. The Government did not reply. He would have settled for khadi and prohibition at any time in his career. But khadi struck at British trade and prohibition at government revenue.

Leaving Sabarmati Ashram in December 1926, Gandhi worked his way from meeting to meeting till he reached Gauhati, in north-east India, in the province of Assam, to attend the annual session of Congress. En route, he received word of a tragedy which horrified India. A young Moslem named Adbul Rashid had called on Swami Shraddhanand, a well-known Hindu nationalist, and said he wished to discuss religious problems with him. The Swami, or priest, was ill in bed; his doctor had ordered complete repose. When the Swami heard the altercation outside his room between his servant and the insistent visitor he ordered the man to be admitted. Inside, the Swami told Abdul Rashid that he would be glad to talk with him as soon as he felt stronger. The Moslem asked for water. When the servant left to fetch him a drink, Abdul Rashid pulled out a revolver and fired several bullets into the Swami's breast, killing him.

The Moslem press had been attacking the Swami as a proponent of Hindu domination of India. In an address to the Congress, Gandhi assured the Moslems that the Swami had not been their enemy. He said Abdul Rashid was not guilty. The guilty ones were 'those who excited feelings of hatred against one another'. He referred to the assassin repeatedly as his 'brother'.

The British too were brothers. Extreme nationalists at the Congress session moved a resolution in favour of independence and the severance of all ties with England. Gandhi opposed it. 'They betray want of faith in human nature and therefore in themselves,' he said. 'Why do they think there can never be a change of heart in those who are guiding the British Empire?' If India were dignified and strong, England would change.

Gandhi accordingly continued his efforts to strengthen the nation from within; otherwise, resolutions in favour of independence were empty words and vain gestures.

Again, therefore, Gandhi toured the country. At meetings where he saw a sector of the grounds set apart for untouchables he squatted among them and challenged Brahmans and other caste Hindus to come and do likewise. The Mahatma on active service for India could not be disobeyed.

During some speeches, he would lift his left hand and open up the five fingers. Taking the first finger between two fingers of his left hand he would shake it and say, 'This is equality for untouchables,' and even those who could not hear him would ask for and get an explanation later on from those who had. Then the second finger: 'This is spinning.' The third finger was sobriety; no alcohol, no opium. The fourth was Hindu–Moslem friendship. The fifth was equality for women. The hand was bound to the body by the wrist. The wrist was non-violence. The five virtues, through non-violence, would free the body of each one of them and, hence, India.

Sometimes, if he was too tired or the crowd too noisy, he would sit on the platform in silence till the audience, which often numbered two hundred thousand, became quiet. He then continued to sit in silence, and the men and women sat in silence, and he touched his palms together to bless them, and smiled, and departed. This was communication without words, and the mass silence was an exercise in self-control and self-searching, a step therefore towards self-rule.

Thousands of townspeople came to meetings wearing khadi. In one locality, the laundry men, the indispensable men of India, refused to wash anything but homespun. A primitive tribe gave up alcohol when they heard it was the Mahatma's wish. His attacks on child marriage met with wider acceptance. Women mixed with men at meetings.

But the Hindu–Moslem problem defied Gandhi's efforts. 'I am helpless,' he admitted. 'I have now washed my hands. But I am a believer in God . . . Something within tells me that Hindu–Moslem unity will come sooner than we might care to hope, that God will one day force it on us, in spite of ourselves. That is why I said that it has passed into the hands of God.' This formula comforted him, but it did not relax the tension. Hindus and Moslems were kidnapping one another's womenfolk and children and forcibly converting them.

From Calcutta, Gandhi moved down through Bihar to the country of the Marathas, Tilak's country. At Poona, the students demanded that he should speak English; their language was Marathi which Gandhi did not command. He started in English and then switched to Hindustani, which he wanted to have accepted as the national language. Some students were friendly; one sold his gold medal for khadi. Some students were hostile. In Bombay, however, the people overwhelmed him with kindness and money. It was his own Gujarat region. Thence he returned to Poona to take the train for Bangalore and a tour of the Carnatic, in south-east India.

At the Poona station, Gandhi felt so weak he had to be carried into the Bangalore train. His vision was blurred and he could scarcely scribble an urgent note. Sleep that night refreshed him, and the next day, at Kolhapur, in the Deccan princely states, he addressed seven meetings: the untouchables insisted on their own meetings and dragged Gandhi to their school. The women had a special affair; the children too; the non-Brahmans; the Christians; the khadi workers; the students. At the close of the final meeting, Gandhi collapsed.

Yet he went on. The next day, he felt too ill to make speeches, but he sat on the porch of his host's house while multitudes passed. Then he drove to a meeting to receive a purse of 8,457 rupees for khadi. At Belgaum, over a hundred miles from Kolhapur, he also attended a meeting, but did not speak. Finally, a doctor persuaded him that his condition was serious and he had to rest. He was taken to a hill town swept by sea breezes.

Under pressure from his friend and physician, Dr Jivraj Mehta, and others, Gandhi agreed to rest for two months. But why couldn't he go home to Sabarmati where his upkeep would cost less money? He was told that the altitude and salubrious climate would help him to recover more quickly. He said he did not wish 'to vegetate'. Well, he could continue working on his autobiography and do light reading.

'What is light reading?' Gandhi asked.

'You must not spin,' the doctor continued. 'Your blood pressure is too high.' This raised a fierce protest.

'Take my blood pressure before and after spinning,' Gandhi urged. 'Besides, what a glorious death to die spinning.' He did spin. But he agreed not to answer correspondence, not to work.

'Well, my cart has stuck in the mire,' he wrote to the women of Sabarmati Ashram. 'Tomorrow it might break down beyond hope of repair. What then? Gitaji [the *Bhagavad Gita*] proclaims that everyone that is born must die, and everyone that dies must be born again. Eveyone comes, repays part of his obligation and goes his way.'

The sale of khadi was medicine to Gandhi. The chief of the native state and his wife came for a visit and bought some homespun. Devadas and Mahadev Desai went out to peddle khadi and came back with purses full.

Soon Gandhi commenced to write articles for his two magazines. His blood pressure was down, he reported, 'from 180 to 155, and from 155 to 150 which is normal for my age. I have been walking for the last theee days over one mile a day in two periods . . .' He suggested a fast; that would cure him. The doctors dissuaded him with difficulty. They suggested recreation instead.

'Like backgammon, or whist or bridge, or pingpong?' Gandhi laughed.

They could propose nothing definite.

'So your proposal has ended in smoke,' he teased. 'It cannot be otherwise. What can you suggest where all work is play . . .?' He had a proposition. 'Get me a carpenter's box of tools and broken spinning wheels and I shall repair them, or crooked spindles and I shall make them straight.'

During April 1927, he remained in the native state of Mysore, recuperating. The prime minister of the state appeared for a visit, and in the course of the conversation he assured Gandhi that he had no objection to the wearing of homespun by Mysore officials. Gandhi went to inspect the Methodist Mission School for girls at Bangalore, capital of Mysore. He told the teachers that E. Stanley Jones, the American missionary, had promised him to introduce spinning in the Methodist mission schools. He joked with the pupils and asked them to wear khadi.

Dr B. C. Roy, Gandhi's physician in later years, and Dr Manchershah Gilder, an Indian who practised medicine in Bombay and London, have stated that Gandhi had a 'slight stroke' at Kolhapur in March 1927. Neither found any

physical after-effects. Dr Gilder, who was Gandhi's heart
specialist after 1932, said that the Mahatma's heart was
stronger than in an average man his age. He never knew
Gandhi's blood pressure to rise except when an important
decision was in the making. On one occasion, Gandhi went to
bed with high blood pressure; in the morning it was normal,
because, during the night, he had made up his mind on a
crucial question. The presence of irritating persons, or public
attacks on him, or concern about his work, Dr Gilder
declared, never affected Gandhi's blood pressure; only the
self-wrangling that preceded a decision brought on a rise.

The 'slight stroke' of 1927, accompanied by high blood
pressure, may have been due to overwork at a time when the
political situation did not permit Gandhi to reach a decision
in favour of a new civil disobedience campaign. From the
moment he came out of jail in 1924, Gandhi watched for an
opportunity to renew non-co-operation. This was his goal.
Everything else was preparation for it. More than ever, co-
operation with the British, or even obstruction to the British
in the legislative assemblies, appeared to him a waste of time.

Most co-operators were loyal to Gandhi. Vithalbhai Patel,
president of the national Legislative Assembly at New Delhi,
brother of Vallabhbhai Patel, Gandhi's closest associate, had
been sending more than half his handsome British salary to
Gandhi by cheque every month for constructive work. Others
did likewise. Civil disobedience, Gandhi felt, would unite co-
operators and non-co-operators. Only civil disobedience
would impel the British to yield real power; under dyarchy
they yielded the semblance of power.

But 'the present look of things' between Hindus and
Moslems, Gandhi wrote in *Young India* on 16 June, 1927, was
'ugly'. He yearned to do something, perhaps to fast, in order
to 'melt and change the stony hearts of Hindus and Moslems.
But I have no sign from God within to undertake the penance.'

Hindu–Moslem dissension, Gandhi said, proved that

Indians could not regulate their own affairs. Then what claim had they on the British for more power? It was not enough to reply that British made use of their division or even created it. Why did Indians give England this advantage?

Gandhi put his faith in God; when all seemed lost perhaps the British would help. They did.

Lord Irwin, the new Viceroy, had arrived in India in April 1926, at the age of forty-five, to relieve Reading. From his grandfather, the first Viscount Halifax, who had served in India and as Secretary of State for India in Whitehall, he inherited a bond with India. From his father he acquired an attachment to the Church of England and High Church views. In fact, on his arrival, on Good Friday, in Bombay, he postponed the ceremonies that accompany the advent of a new Viceroy and went to church.

The choice of a religious man as Viceroy was regarded in some quarters as auspicious for his five-year reign over a religious country in which a Mahatma led the opposition.

But for nineteen months, Irwin sent no invitation to Gandhi nor indicated any desire to discuss the Indian situation with the most influential Indian. On 26 October, 1927, while filling speaker engagements at Mangalore, on the west coast, a message reached Gandhi that the Viceroy wished to see him on 5 November.

The Mahatma immediately broke off his tour and travelled the 1,250 miles – a two-day train journey – to New Delhi. At the appointed hour he was ushered into the presence of Lord Irwin. He did not enter alone. The Viceroy had also asked Vithalbhai Patel, the president of the national Legislative Assembly, S. Srinivasa Iyengar, the president of the Congress party for 1927, and Dr M. A. Ansari, the president-elect of Congress for 1928.

When the Indians had been seated, Irwin handed them a paper announcing the impending arrival of an official British commission, led by Sir John Simon, to report on Indian conditions and make recommendations for political reforms.

Having read the text, Gandhi looked up and waited. The Viceroy said nothing.

'Is this the only business of our meeting?' Gandhi asked.

'Yes,' replied the Viceroy.

That was the end of the interview. Silently, Gandhi returned to southern India and from there went on to Ceylon to collect money for khadi.

In the days following Irwin's confrontation with Gandhi, other Indian leaders were informed, in similar fashion, of the forthcoming visit of the Simon Commission. In no case was there any discussion or elaboration. The Viceroy simply said that under Section 84a of the Government of India Act of 1919, which provided for ten-year surveys, a Statutory Commission consisting of Sir John Simon and six other members of the British House of Commons and the House of Lords would soon arrive in India to investigate and to suggest changes, if any were necessary, in the Indian political system. Irwin expected Indians to testify before the commission and submit proposals to it.

Irwin's biographer, Alan Campbell Johnson, describes this episode as 'a deplorable lack of tact in the handling of the Indian leaders'. The blame was shared by Irwin and Lord Birkenhead, the Secretary of State for India in the British government. Birkenhead, a brilliant lawyer, made Indian policy in Whitehall. In doing so he was guided by an attitude epitomized in his pronouncement in the House of Lords in 1929. 'What man in this House', Birkenhead asked rhetorically, 'can say that he can see in a generation, in two generations, in a hundred years, any prospect that the people of India will be in a position to assume control of the Army, the Navy, the Civil Service, and to have a Governor-General who will be responsible to the Indian government and not to any authority in this country?' The legal mind had no eyes; yet he, with Irwin, ruled India.

The Simon Commission was the premature child of Birkenhead's brain. Under the Act of 1919, the commission might have been created a year or two later, but a national election was imminent in Britain, and Birkenhead feared that his Tory party might be defeated by Labour, as indeed it was, in 1929. This being the case, the Indians were all the more disappointed that the Labour party should have lent itself to Birkenhead's manoeuvre by allowing Major Clement R. Attlee, then a less-known MP, to serve with Simon.

The news of the Simon Commission astounded India. The Commission would determine the fate of India, but it had no Indian member. The British explained that it was a commission of Parliament and must therefore consist of peers or MPs. But there was an Indian peer, Lord Sinha. No, India did not accept the explanation. Indians were being treated as 'natives'; the whites would come, look around, and decide the fate of the dumb, brown Asiatics. Are these the fruits of co-operation, the Gandhian non-co-operators scoffed.

Spontaneously, a movement sprang up throughout India not to help the Simon Commission in its studies, nor to lay plans before it. Sir Tej Bahadur Sapru, a great Indian constitutional lawyer, former member of the Viceroy's Advisory Council, persuaded the Liberal party of India to vote for boycott. The Hindu Mahasabha wavered for a moment and then followed the lead of Pandit Madan Malaviya into the boycott camp. Congress was of course unanimous for boycott, and needed no prompting from Gandhi. Mr Jinnah, of the revived Moslem League, also seemed inclined to join the boycott. Irwin, according to his biographer, 'did his utmost to bring Jinnah back into the fold and made a substantial offer to him'. But a rude speech by Birkenhead challenging Indians to produce 'an agreed scheme' of future government convinced Jinnah that the British were playing on Indian religious divisions and caused him to spurn the Viceroy's 'substantial offer'. One touch of

Birkenhead made all Indians non-co-operate.

Upon its arrival in Bombay on 3 February, 1928, the Simon Commission was greeted with black flags and processions shouting, 'Go back, Simon.' This slogan, chanted by Indians who sometimes knew no other English words, rang in the commissioners' ears throughout their stay in India. The boycott was political and social. The commission was isolated.

Simon tried his hand at compromise. Irwin tempted and cajoled. A few bitter or ambitious untouchables and a handful of very minor politicians were induced to come before the Simonites. But no representative Indian would see them. They toiled honestly, and produced an intelligently edited compendium of valuable facts and statistics. It was a learned epitaph on British rule.

The first Gandhi-Irwin interview of 5 November, 1927, stood for inequality; the composition of the Simon Commission stood for exclusion. Both principles angered Gandhi and the Indian people.

By 1930, however, Gandhi had changed the relationship between India and England to one of negotiation between hard bargainers. By 1930, automatic Indian obedience to British fiat was a thing of the past. Imperceptibly, in 1928, 1929 and 1930, unknown even to themselves, and scarcely noticed by outsiders, Indians became free men. The body still wore shackles; but the spirit had escaped from prison. Gandhi had turned the key. No general directing armies against an enemy ever moved with more consummate skill than the saint armed with righteousness as his shield and a moral cause as his spear. All of Gandhi's years in South Africa were preparation for the 1928–30 struggle; all his work in India since 1915 prepared the Indian people for it. He did not plan it that way. But in perspective his activities make a delicate design.

CHAPTER 15

Prologue

Gandhi moved into battle very slowly. Unlike most rebels he did not get ammunition from his adversary. The British merely provided him with an opportunity to use his special, self-made weapons: civil disobedience.

The savage massacre of policemen in Chauri Chaura in February 1922, by a Congress mob, had induced Gandhi to suspend civil disobedience in the county of Bardoli. But he did not forget. He waited six years, and on 12 February, 1928, he gave the signal for Satygraha in the same place: Bardoli.

Gandhi did not conduct it himself. He watched from afar, wrote lengthy articles about it, and supplied the general direction and inspiration. The actual leader was Vallabhbhai Patel, assisted by a Moslem named Abbas Tyebji.

In 1915, Sardar Vallabhbhai Patel, a prosperous Ahmedabad lawyer, was playing bridge in his club when Gandhi entered. Patel looked at the visitor with a side glance of his heavy-lidded eyes, smiled under his thick moustache at the little man with the big, bulbous, loose turban and the long Kathiawar coat with the sleeves rolled up, and turned back to his cards. He had heard of Gandhi's exploits but was not impressed by this first view.

A week later, however, he dropped in at a conference on peasant taxation convened by Gandhi and stayed to admire the newcomer's logic. Patel had a precise, scientific, steel-trap mind. In later years, his clean-shaven pouchy face, his round, nut-brown bald head, and his broad body wrapped down to the knees in white khadi gave him the appearance of a classic Roman senator. If he had any sentiments, he hid them successfully. He became the 'Jim Farley', as Americans called him, of the Congress party, the machine 'box' who remembered everybody's name and navigated with supreme confidence among the numerous jutting reefs of Indian politics.

Gandhi won Patel's loyalty by the common sense of his position: to win freedom you needed peasant backing, for India was more than 80 per cent peasant. To win peasant backing you had to speak the peasant's language, dress like him, and know his economic needs.

In 1928 Patel was mayor of Ahmedabad. At Gandhi's suggestion, he left the post and went to Bardoli, in Bombay province, to guide the 87,000 peasants in a peaceful revolt against a 22 per cent increase in taxes decreed by the British government.

The villagers, responding to Patel's leadership, refused to pay taxes. The collector seized their water buffaloes which worked and gave milk. Cultivators were driven off their farms. Kitchens were invaded and pots and pans confiscated for delinquency. Carts and horses were also taken. The peasants remained non-violent.

'At the rate the forfeitures are being served,' Gandhi observed in *Young India*, 'practically the whole of the county of Bardoli should soon be in the government's possession, and they can pay themselves a thousand times over for their precious assessments. The people of Bardoli, if they are brave, will be none the worse for dispossession. They will have lost their possessions but kept what must be the dearest of all to good men and women – their honour. Those who have stout hearts and hands need never fear loss of belongings.'

Apparently, the Mahatma thought every hungry peasant was a Gandhi. Strangely enough, the judgement did not err. A spark of Gandhism lifted the peasantry into a mood of sacrifice.

Months passed. Bardoli stood its ground. Hundreds were arrested. The Government was accused of 'lawlessness'; no one called it terror, for no one was terrorized.

India began to take notice. Voluntary contributions flowed

in for the maintenance of the struggle.

Government officials drove through the countryside in motorcars. 'Why not barricade the roads,' some peasants whispered to Sardar Patel, 'or place spikes on them to burst the tyres of the officials' cars and give a "non-violent" shake-up to some fellow who has made himself a veritable nightmare to the people?'

'No,' Patel admonished, 'your fight is not for a few hundred thousand rupees, but for a principle . . . You are fighting for self-respect which ultimately leads to Swaraj.'

The Government undertook to denude whole villages of movable property. The peasants barricaded themselves in their huts with their animals. The collectors then made off with carts. 'Pull your carts to pieces,' the Sardar ordered. 'Keep the body in one place and the wheels in another. Bury the shaft.'

The Government stated in a public announcement that some seized land had been sold to new occupants and that all farms in Bardoli would be auctioned if taxes remained unpaid. Vallabhbhai Patel's elder brother Vithalbhai, president of the national Legislative Assembly, wrote to the Viceroy with the charge that 'the measures adopted have crossed in several instances the bounds of law, order and decency'. Gandhi hailed the letter as breaking 'that unhealthy and slavish tradition' of neutrality when the people defied the Government.

At the instance of Gandhi, India celebrated a hartal, or cessation of work and business, on 12 June, in honour of Bardoli. Huge sums were thrust upon Sardar Patel by Indians at home and abroad.

Gandhi went on a brief visit to Bardoli. Processions greeted him everywhere.

Indians of national importance, Sir Tej Bahadur Sapru, the great constitutional lawyer, K. M. Munshi, a member of the Legislative Council of Bombay, and others expressed sympathy with the Bardoli resisters and demanded that justice be done by the Government. On 13 July, with the Satyagraha movement at its height, the Governor of the province of Bombay went to Simla to consult Lord Irwin. He returned five days later and summoned Vallabhbhai Patel, Abbas Tyebji and four other leading Satyagrahis to a conference. Negotiation is always welcome to the civil resister; it may lead to compromise. No compromise on Bardoli was possible, however, and on 23 July, Sir Leslie Wilson, opening the session of the Bombay Legislative Council, declared the issue was 'whether the writ of his Majesty the King-Emperor is to run in a portion of His Majesty's dominions'.

The press in England awoke to the Bardoli revolt. Questions were asked in the House of Commons where Lord Winterton was firmly in favour of 'enforcing compliance with law and crushing the movement . . ' The Satyagrahis and Patel ignored this 'sabre rattling'.

From all over India, Gandhi was urged to start civil disobedience in other provinces. He counselled patience. 'The time has not yet come for even limited sympathetic Satyagraha. Bardoli has still to prove its mettle. If it can stand the last heat and if the Government go to the farther limit, nothing I or Vallabhbhai can do will stop the spread of Satyagraha or limit the issue . . . The limit will then be prescribed by the capacity of India as a whole for self-sacrifice and self-suffering.' Meanwhile, the people of Bardoli 'are safe in God's hands'.

The arrest of Patel was expected hourly. On 2 August, accordingly, Gandhi moved to Bardoli. On 6 August, the Government capitulated. It promised to release all prisoners, return all confiscated land, return the confiscated animals or their equivalent, and, the essence, to cancel the rise in taxes. Patel promised that the peasants would pay their taxes at the old rates. Both sides kept the agreement.

Gandhi had shown Irwin and India that the weapon worked.

Would he use it on a vaster scale?

India was in turmoil. From 3 February, 1928, when the Simon Commission landed at Bombay, India boycotted it. Gandhi's boycott was so complete that he never mentioned the commission. For him, it did not exist. But others demonstrated against it. At a huge anti-Simon meeting in Lahore, Lajpat Rai, the chief political figure of the Punjab, a man of sixty-four whom Gandhi called the 'Lion of the Punjab', was struck with a lathi or four-foot wooden staff swung by the policeman in charge, and died soon afterwards. About the same time, Jawaharlal Nehru was beaten with lathis during an anti-Simon protest meeting in Lucknow. In December 1928, several weeks after Lajpat Rai's death, Assistant Police Superintendent Saunders of Lahore was assassinated. Gandhi branded the assassination 'a dastardly act'. Bhagat Singh, the suspected assassin, eluded arrest and quickly achieved the status of hero.

During the autumn of 1928, the Government moved against the growing labour organizations of India. Trade union leaders, and Socialists and Communists, were arrested en masse. Labour was unhappy and anti-British for nationalist as well as class reasons.

In Bengal, always the hearth of turbulence and of opposition to the Government as well as to the Congress leadership, Subhas Chandra Bose, a stormy petrel whose philosophy was, 'Give me blood and I promise you freedom', had won great popularity and a big, restive following.

Gandhi sensed the crisis atmosphere. The existing British system was, he said, 'an unmitigated evil'. One word from him and a thousand Bardolis would spring into action throughout India. But as a good field-commander, Gandhi was always careful to choose the right time and place for battle. He knew India's strength; he also knew its weakness, and the weaknesses of Congress. Perhaps, if he was patient, the battle could be avoided; even a non-violent contest should not be undertaken before every possibility of averting it had been exhausted.

In this mood of uncertainty, Gandhi approached the annual Congress session which met in Calcutta in December 1928. En route to the meeting, friends put some searching and significant questions to him when the train stopped at Nagpur.

'What would be your attitude towards a political war of independence?' they asked.

'I would decline to take part in it,' Gandhi answered.

'Then you would not support a national militia?'

'I would support the formation of a national militia under Swaraj,' Gandhi said, 'if only because I realize that people cannot be made non-violent by compulsion. Today I am teaching the people how to meet a national crisis by non-violent means.'

The Congress session demanded action. But Gandhi had an eye for organization and a nose for reality. Congress talked war. Was it an effective army? Gandhi wanted Congress 'overhauled'. 'The delegates to the Congress', he wrote, 'are mostly self-appointed ... As at present constituted, the Congress is unable to put forth real united and unbreakable resistance.'

The Congress, however, would not be gainsaid. Caution was not on its agenda. Subhas Chandra Bose and Jawaharlal Nehru, leading the young men, wanted a declaration of immediate independence to be followed, implicitly, by a war of independence. Gandhi suggested a two years' warning to the British. Under pressure, he finally cut it down to one year. If by 31 December, 1929, India had not achieved freedom under Dominion Status, 'I must declare myself an Independence-walla.

'I have burnt my boats,' Gandhi announced.

The year 1929 would be crucial and decisive.

As preparation for 1930, Gandhi toured India in 1929. He no longer allowed himself to be cooped up in first or second class, however. He travelled third again and found that the passengers were just as slovenly about personal sanitation as they were five years before.

While touring in the west-of-India province of Sindh, in February, Gandhi was summoned to New Delhi to accept the chairmanship of the Congress Committee for the Boycott of Foreign Cloth. He did not believe in boycotting British books or surgical instrument, etc. Nor would he countenance a boycott of British cloth only. Imported textiles from any country must be boycotted in favour, not of Indian mill products, but of khadi. He regarded the universal use of khadi as a prime requisite for the battle of 1930. Indians would go into that struggle wearing uniforms of homespun.

During his days in Delhi, Gandhi went to a tea party, and it became the subject of much rumour. The party was given by Speaker Patel of the Legislative Assembly, and among the guests were Gandhi, Lord Irwin, Jinnah, Motilal Nehru, Pandit Malaviya, the Maharaja of Bikaner and the Maharaja of Kashmir. Surely, press and politicians speculated, the tea party was arranged to initiate conversations between Indians and Englishmen with a view to avoiding the 1930 clash. Speculation became so lush that Gandhi honoured the afternoon party with an inimitable paragraph in *Young India*. Gandhi admitted that Patel, a partisan of Swaraj, staged the tea party 'to break the ice as it were. But there cannot be much breaking of ice at a private, informal tea party. And in my opinion it cannot lead to any real advance or action unless both are ready. We know that we are not yet ready. England will never make any advance so as to satisfy India's aspirations till she is forced to it. British rule is no philanthropic job, it is a terribly earnest business proposition worked out from day to day with deadly precision. The coating of benevolence that is periodically given to it merely prolongs the agony. Such occasional parties are therefore good only to the extent of showing that the bringing together of parties will be easy enough when both are ready for business. Meanwhile let the reader rest satisfied with the assurance that no political significance attaches to the event. The party was one of Speaker Patel's creditable freaks.'

During the first four months of 1929, while Gandhi was lighting bonfires of foreign textiles in Calcutta and keeping longstanding speaking engagements in Burma, no longer a part of India, Irwin, according to his biographer, 'was largely absorbed with finding administrative remedies to meet the perils of political terrorism and industrial strife'. Alas, the remedy did not lie in administrative measures. It required statesmanship.

On 8 April, Bhagat Singh, the Sikh who killed Assistant Police Superintendent Saunders in Lahore in December 1928, walked into the Legislative Assembly in New Delhi while the chamber was filled with its British and Indian members, tossed two bombs into their midst, and then began firing from an automatic pistol. The bombs exploded with a mighty impact but burst into large fragments instead of small splinters, and only one legislator was seriously wounded. Sir John Simon saw the outrage from the gallery. It was his last big impression of India; that month the commission went home.

In May 1929, national elections in Britain gave Labour a minority in the House of Commons, but as the largest party it took office and Ramsay Macdonald became Prime Minister. In June, Irwin sailed for England to consult the new government and especially the new Secretary of State for India, Mr Wedgwood Benn. Gandhi, who had said, 'You know, there is one thing in me, and this is that I love to see the bright side of things and not the seamy side,' hoped for a change that would obviate the expected showdown in 1930.

But though he looked for the silver lining, his head was never in the clouds; he kept his bare feet on the earth of India. In an unconditional condemnation of terrorist acts, Gandhi reiterated that the Government could stop them 'by conceding the national demand gracefully and in time. But that is hoping against hope. For the Government to do so would be a change of heart, not merely of policy. And there is nothing on the horizon to warrant the hope that any such change is imminent'.

He feared a bloody clash. 'If India attains what will be to me so-called freedom by violent means she will cease to be the country of my pride,' he wrote in *Young India* of 9 May, 1929. Prophetically, he pictured the ideal: freedom should come non-violently 'through a gentlemanly understanding with Great Britain. But then,' he added, 'it will not be an imperialistic haughty Britain manoeuvring for world supremacy but a Britain humbly trying to serve the common end of humanity'.

That day was not yet.

With the fateful test of strength only a few months away, Gandhi continued to concern himself with the things that normally concerned him. In a leading article entitled 'A National Defect', the Mahatma returned to the question of cleanliness. He was travelling by car through the country and crossed the Krishna River. 'The car,' he wrote, 'practically passed by hundreds of men and women evacuating themselves not many yards from the river bank. It is the stream in which people bathe and from which they drink. Here there was a breach of the code of decency and a criminal disregard of the most elementary laws of health. Add to this the economic waste of the precious manure, which they would save if these evacuations were made in a field and buried in the living surface of the earth and well mixed with loosened soil . . . Here is work for the municipalities.'

He worried about the expenses of his party while on tour. He asked for an accounting and found that 'these expenses do not amount to more than 5 per cent of the collections . . . Having said this in defence of the expense, I must confess that even though the sums collected may be large, we cannot afford to fly from place to place and pay high motor charges'. (He never flew in his life. 'Fly' meant move fast in cars.)

Editorial offices and homes were being searched, presumably for seditious material. Individuals sent Gandhi reports of such measures. 'Let us thank the police,' he commenced, 'that they were courteous.' The purpose of the raids, he declared, was 'to overawe and humiliate a whole people. This studied humiliation is one of the chosen methods which the ruling race consider necessary in order that they – though less than one hundred thousand – may rule three hundred million people. It is a state of things we must strain every nerve to remedy. To command respect is the first step to Swaraj'.

This was Gandhi's refrain: dignity, discipline and restraint would bring Indians self-respect, therefore respect, therefore freedom.

1 January, 1930, was not far off.

Irwin returned to India in October after conferences lasting several months with members of the Labour government, his predecessor Lord Reading, Lloyd George, Churchill, Stanley Baldwin, Sir John Simon and many others. The Viceroy found the situation in India 'bordering on a state of alarm'. Everything was ready for the great challenge of 1930.

On the last day of October 1929, accordingly, Irwin made 'his momentous statement' envisaging a Round Table Conference in which British government representatives would sit with delegates from British India and from the native states. (The idea of such a conference with Indian participants had been broached before the Simon Commission was appointed, but Irwin would not listen to it.) The statement declared that 'the natural issue of India's constitutional progress . . . is the attainment of Dominion Status'.

By thus anticipating the recommendations of the Simon Commission, Irwin suggested in effect that its labours were vain and its life ended. Indians, to whom it had become a red flag, were expected to appreciate this aspect of the Viceroy's move.

A few days later, in Delhi, Gandhi met Dr Ansari, Mrs Annie Besant, Motilal Nehru, Sir Tej Bahadur Sapru, Pandit Malaviya, Srinivasa Sastri and others, and issued a 'Leaders' Manifesto'. Their response to the Viceroy's announcement was favourable, but, they said, steps should be taken to induce 'a calmer atmosphere', political prisoners should be released and the Indian National Congress should have the largest representation at the forthcoming Round Table Conference. They added a gloss: they understood the Viceroy to have said that the purpose of the conference was not to determine whether or when Dominion Status would be introduced but rather to draft a constitution for the Dominion.

The conciliatory attitude of Gandhi and the elder statesmen precipitated a storm of protest, especially from Jawaharlal Nehru, president-elect of the Congress party for 1930, and Subhas Chandra Bose. Undeterred, confident that a peaceful agreement with the British would be accepted by the nation, Gandhi and his colleagues continued their probings. They made an appointment with Lord Irwin for the afternoon of 23 December.

That morning, Irwin returned by train from a tour of south India. At 7.40 A.M. the white cars of the Viceroy's train appeared out of the mist and approached New Delhi station. Three miles from the terminus, where the track is single, a bomb exploded under the train. Only one person was hurt, and Irwin did not know what happened until informed by his aide-de-camp.

A far deadlier bomb had been prepared for the Viceroy in Westminster. Lord Reading led the attack in the House of Lords, and the Tories and Liberals combined in the House of Commons to condemn Irwin's promise of a Round Table Conference and Dominion Status. Wedgwood Benn and other Labourites defended the Viceroy, but the result of the

debate was to bring majority parliamentary pressure to bear
against any commitment in favour of Dominion Status.

When Jinnah, Gandhi, Sapru, Motilal Nehru and
Vithalbhai Patel entered the Viceroy's office on the afternoon
of 23 December, Gandhi congratulated the Viceroy on his
escape and then proceeded to detonate the long-fuse torpedo
made in Parliament. The audience lasted for two and a half
hours; Irwin and Gandhi did most of the talking.

Could His Excellency, Gandhi demanded, promise a
Round Table Conference which would draft a constitution
giving India full and immediate Dominion Status including
the right to secede from the Empire?

Reflecting the Parliamentary debate, Irwin replied, in the
words of his biographer, 'that he was unable to prejudge or
commit the [Round Table] conference at all to any particular
line . . .'

These events formed the overture to the historic annual
Congress party convention which met, late in December, in
Lahore, under the presidency of Jawaharlal Nehru who had
celebrated his fortieth birthday the month before.

At the second of time when the year 1929 ended and 1930
was born, the Congress, with Gandhi as stage director,
unfurled the flag of freedom and acclaimed a resolution in
favour of unabridged independence and secession. 'Swaraj,'
Gandhi declared, 'is now to mean complete independence.'
The Congress convention instructed its members and friends
to withdraw from all legislatures, and sanctioned civil
disobedience including the non-payment of taxes. The All-
India Congress Committee was authorized to decide when
Satyagraha would commence but, as Gandhi said, 'I know
that it is a duty devolving primarily on me.' Everyone
realized that Gandhi would have to be the brain, heart and
directing hand of any civil disobedience movement, and it
was therefore left to him to choose the hour, the place and the
precise issue.

CHAPTER 16

Drama at the Seashore

Gandhi was a reformer of individuals. Hence his concern for the means whereby India's liberation might be achieved. If the means corrupted the individual the loss would be greater than the gain.

Gandhi knew that the re-education of a nation was a slow process and he was not usually in a hurry unless prodded by events or by men reacting to those events. Left to himself, he would not have forced the issue of independence in 1930. But now the die was cast; Congress had decreed a campaign for independence. The leader therefore became an obedient soldier.

During the weeks after the stirring New Year's Eve independence ceremony, Gandhi searched for a form of civil disobedience that left no opening for violence.

Gandhi's monumental abhorrence of violence stemmed from the Jainist and Buddhist infusions into his Hinduism but, particularly, from his love of human beings. Every reformer, crusader and dictator avows his undying devotion to the anonymous masses; Gandhi had an apparently endless capacity to love the individual men, women and children who crowded his life. He gave them tenderness and affection; he remembered their personal needs and he enjoyed catering for their wants at the unnoticed expense of his limited time and energy. H. N. Brailsford, the humane British Socialist, explains this by 'the fact that female tendencies were at least as strong in his mental make-up as male. They were evident, for example, in his love of children, in the pleasure he took in playing with them, and in the devotion he showed as a sick-nurse. His beloved spinning wheel has always been a woman's tool. And is not Satyagraha, the method of conquering by self-suffering, a woman's tactic?' Perhaps. But maybe Brailsford is being unfair to men and too fair to the fair. Like Brailsford, everyone will interpret Gandhi's loving kindness according to his own experience. It wrapped the Mahatma's iron will and austerity in a downy softness; one touch of it and most Indians forgave his blunders, quirks and fads. It ruled out anything that could lead to violence. In the successful Bardoli Satyagraha in 1928, for instance, there was no violence, but there might have been. The peasants might have allowed themselves to be goaded into the use of force. The civil disobedience campaign of 1930, Gandhi felt, had to preclude such potentials, for if it got out of hand no one, not even he, could control it.

Rabindranath Tagore, for whom Gandhi had the deepest veneration, was in the neighbourhood of Sabarmati Ashram and came for a visit on 18 January. He inquired what Gandhi had in store for the country in 1930. 'I am furiously thinking night and day,' Gandhi replied, 'and I do not see any light coming out of the surrounding darkness.'

The situation made Gandhi apprehensive. 'There is a lot of violence in the air,' he said. The British government had altered the exchange rate of the rupee so that India might import more from Lancashire; the Indian middle class suffered. The Wall Street crash of October 1929, and the spreading world economic depression hit the Indian peasant. Working-class unrest was mounting for all these reasons, and because of the Government's persecution of labour organizers. Again, as in 1919 to 1921, a number of young Indians saw an opportunity of striking a bloody blow for freedom.

Civil disobedience in these circumstances involved 'undoubted risks', but the only alternative was 'armed rebellion'. Gandhi's confidence remained unshaken.

For six weeks, Gandhi had been waiting to hear the 'Inner

Voice'. This, as he interpreted it, had no Joan-of-Arc connotations. 'The "Inner Voice",' he wrote, 'may mean a message from God or from the Devil, for both are wrestling in the human breast. Acts determine the nature of the voice.'

Presently, Gandhi seemed to have heard the Voice, which could only mean that he had come to a decision, for the 27 February issue of *Young India* opened with an editorial by Gandhi entitled 'When I am Arrested', and then devoted considerable space to the iniquities of the salt tax. The next number of the magazine quoted the penal sections of the Salt Act. And on 2 March, 1930, Gandhi sent a long letter to the Viceroy serving notice that civil disobedience would begin in nine days.

It was the strangest communication the head of a government ever received.

Dear Friend, Before embarking on Civil Disobedience and taking the risk I have dreaded to take all these years, I would fain approach you and find a way out.

My personal faith is absolutely clear. I cannot intentionally hurt anything that lives, much less human beings, even though they may do the greatest wrong to me and mine. Whilst, therefore, I hold the British rule to be a curse, I do not intend harm to a single Englishman or to any legitimate interest he may have in India . . .

And why do I regard the British rule as a curse?

It has impoverished the dumb millions by a system of progressive exploitation and by a ruinous expensive military and civil administration which the country can never afford.

It has reduced us politically to serfdom. It has sapped the foundations of our culture. And by the policy of cruel disarmament, it has degraded us spiritually . . .

I fear . . . there never has been any intention of granting . . . Dominion Status to India in the immediate future . . .

It seems as clear as daylight that responsible British statesmen do not contemplate any alteration in British policy that might adversely affect Britain's commerce with India . . . If nothing is done to end the process of exploitation India must be bled with an ever increasing speed . . .

Let me put before you some of the salient points.

The terrific pressure of land revenue, which furnishes a large part of the total, must undergo considerable modification in an Independent India . . . the whole revenue system has to be so revised as to make the peasant's good its primary concern. But the British system seems to be designed to crush the very life out of him. Even the salt he must use to live is so taxed as to make the burden fall heaviest on him, if only because of the heartless impartiality of its incidence. The tax shows itself still more burdensome on the poor man when it is remembered that salt is the one thing he must eat more than the rich man . . . The drink and drug revenue, too, is derived from the poor. It saps the foundations both of their health and morals.

The iniquities sampled above are maintained in order to carry on a foreign administration, demonstrably the most expensive in the world. Take your own salary. It is over 21,000 rupees [about £1,750] per month, besides many other indirect additions . . . You are getting over 700 rupees a day against India's average income of less than two annas [twopence] per day. Thus you are getting much over five thousand times India's average income. The British Prime Minister is getting only ninety times Britain's average income. On bended knee, I ask you to ponder over this phenomenon. I have taken a personal illustration to drive home a painful truth. I have too great a regard for you as a man to wish to hurt your feelings. I know that you do not need the salary you get. Probably the whole of your salary goes for charity. But a system that provides for such an arrangement deserves to be summarily scrapped. What is true of the Viceregal salary is true generally of the whole administration . . . Nothing but organized non-violence can check the organized violence of the British government . . .

This non-violence will be expressed through civil disobedience, for the moment confined to the inmates of the Satyagraha [Sabarmati] Ashram, but ultimately designed to cover all those who choose to join the movement . . .

My ambition is no less than to convert the British people through non-violence, and thus make them see the wrong they have done to India. I do not seek to harm your people. I want to serve them even as I want to serve my own . . .

If the [Indian] people join me as I expect they will, the sufferings they will undergo, unless the British nation sooner retraces its steps, will be enough to melt the stoniest hearts.

The plan through Civil Disobedience will be to combat such evils as I have sampled out . . . I respectfully invite you to pave the way for the immediate removal of these evils, and thus open a way for a real conference between equals . . . But if you cannot see your way to deal with these evils and if my letter makes no appeal to your heart, on the eleventh day of this month I shall proceed with such co-workers of the Ashram as I can take, to disregard the provisions of the Salt Laws . . . It is, I know, open to you to frustrate my design by arresting me. I hope that there will be tens of thousands ready, in a disciplined manner, to take up the work after me . . .

If you care to discuss matters with me, and if to that end you would like me to postpone publication of this letter, I shall gladly refrain on receipt of a telegram . . .

This letter is not in any way intended as a threat but is a simple and sacred duty peremptory on a civil resister. Therefore I am having it specially delivered by a young English friend who believes in the Indian cause . . .

I remain,

Your sincere friend,
M. K. Gandhi.

The messenger was Reginald Reynolds, a British Quaker who later wrote a book on beards. Clad in khadi and a sun helmet, he entered the Viceroy's house and delivered the letter to Irwin who had flown back from the polo matches at Meerut to receive it.

Irwin chose not to reply. His secretary sent a four-line acknowledgement saying, 'His Excellency . . . regrets to learn that you contemplate a course of action which is clearly bound to involve violation of the law and danger to the public peace.'

This law-and-order note, which disdained to deal with matters of justice and policy, caused Gandhi to say, 'On bended knee I asked for bread and I received stone instead.' Irwin refused to see Gandhi. Nor did he have him arrested. 'The government,' Gandhi declared, 'is puzzled and perplexed.' It was dangerous not to arrest the rebel, and dangerous to arrest him.

As 11 March neared, India bubbled with excitement and curiosity. Scores of foreign and domestic correspondents dogged Gandhi's footsteps in the ashram; what exactly would he do? Thousands surrounded the village and waited. The excitement spread abroad. Cables kept the Ahmedabad post office humming. 'God guard you,' the Reverend Dr John Haynes Holmes wired from New York.

Gandhi felt it was the 'opportunity of a lifetime'.

On 12 March, prayers having been sung, Gandhi and seventy-eight male and female members of the ashram, whose identities were published in *Young India* for the benefit of the police, left Sabarmati for Dandi, due south of Ahmedabad. Gandhi leaned on a lacquered bamboo staff one inch thick and fifty-four inches long with an iron tip. Following winding dirt roads from village to village, he and his seventy-eight disciples walked two hundred miles in twenty-four days. 'We are marching in the name of God,' Gandhi said.

Peasants sprinkled the roads and strewed leaves on them. Every settlement in the line of march was festooned and decorated with India's national colours. From miles around, peasants gathered to kneel by the roadside as the pilgrims passed. Several times a day the marchers halted for a meeting where the Mahatma and others exhorted the people to wear khadi, abjure alcohol and drugs, abandon child marriage, keep clean, live purely and – when the signal came – break the Salt Laws.

He had no trouble in walking. 'Less than twelve miles a day in two stages with not much luggage,' he said. 'Child's play!' Several became fatigued and footsore, and had to ride in a bullock cart. A horse was available for Gandhi throughout the march but he never used it. 'The modern generation is delicate, weak, and much pampered,' Gandhi commented. He was sixty-one. He spun every day for an hour and kept a diary and required each ashramite to do likewise.

In the area traversed, over three hundred village headmen gave up their government posts. The inhabitants of a village would accompany Gandhi to the next village. Young men

Gandhi photographed with his wife Kasturbai after his return
from South Africa

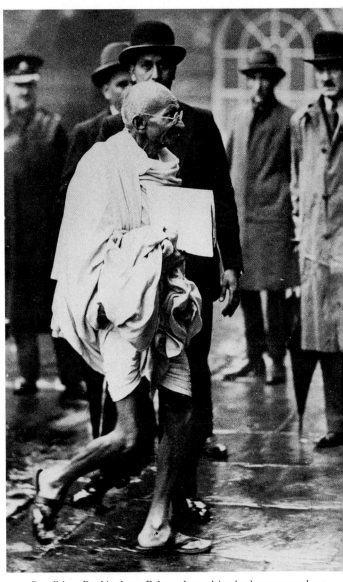

Gandhi at Buckingham Palace dressed in the homespun sheet
that was his uniform

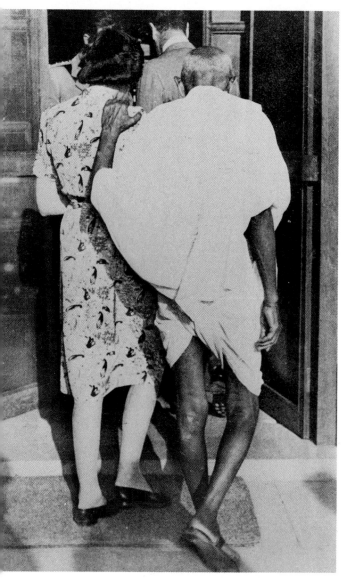

Gandhi leans his hand on the shoulder of Lady Mountbatten as
they enter the Viceregal Lodge, New Delhi

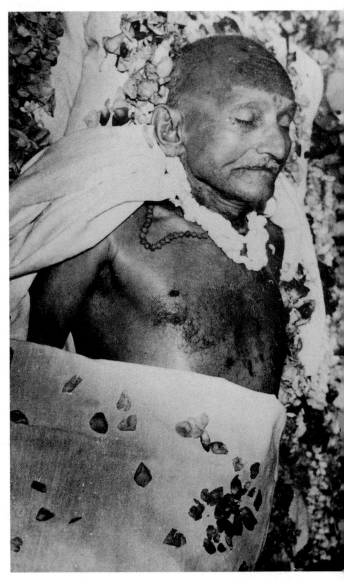

The 'Father' of India lying in state in New Delhi
following his assassination

and women attached themselves to the marching column; when Gandhi reached the sea at Dandi on 5 April, his small ashram band had grown into a non-violent army several thousand strong.

The entire night of 5 April, the ashramites prayed, and early in the morning they accompanied Gandhi to the sea. He dipped into the water, returned to the beach, and there picked up some salt left by the waves. Mrs Sarojini Naidu, standing by his side, cried, 'Hail, Deliverer'. Gandhi had broken the British law which made it a punishable crime to possess salt not obtained from the British government salt monopoly. Gandhi, who had not used salt for six years, called it a 'nefarious monopoly'. Salt, he said, is as essential as air and water, and in India all the more essential to the hard-working, perspiring poor man and his beasts because of the tropical heat.

Had Gandhi gone by train or motor-car to make salt, the effect would have been considerable. But to walk for twenty-four days and rivet the attention of all India, to trek across a countryside saying, 'Watch, I am about to give a signal to the nation,' and then to pick up a pinch of salt in publicized defiance of the mighty Government and thus become a criminal, that required imagination, dignity and the sense of showmanship of a great artist. It appealed to the illiterate peasant and it appealed to a sophisticated critic and sometime fierce opponent of Gandhi's like Subhas Chandra Bose who compared the Salt March to 'Napoleon's march to Paris on his return from Elba'.

The act performed, Gandhi withdrew from the scene. India had its cue. Gandhi had communicated it by lifting up some grains of salt.

The next act was insurrection without arms. Every villager on India's long sea coast went to the beach or waded into the sea with a pan to make salt. The police began mass arrests. Ramdas, third son of Gandhi, with a large group of ashramites, was arrested. Pandit Malaviya and other moderate co-operators resigned from the Legislative Assembly. The police began to use violence. Civil resisters never resisted arrest; but they resisted the confiscation of the salt they had made, and Mahadev Desai reported cases where such Indians were beaten and bitten in the fingers by constables. Congress volunteers openly sold contraband salt in cities. Many were arrested and sentenced to short prison terms. In Delhi, a meeting of fifteen thousand persons heard Pandit Malaviya appeal to the audience to boycott foreign cloth; he himself bought some illegal salt after his speech. The police raided the Congress party headquarters in Bombay where salt was being made in pans on the roof. A crowd of sixty thousand assembled. Hundreds were handcuffed or their arms fastened with ropes and led off to jail. In Ahmedabad, ten thousand people obtained illegal salt from Congress in the first week after the act at Dandhi. They paid what they could; if they had no money they got it free. The salt lifted by Gandhi from the beach was sold to a Dr Kanuga, the highest bidder, for 1,600 rupees. Jawaharlal Nehru, the president of Congress, was arrested in Allahabad under the Salt Acts and sentenced to six months' imprisonment. The agitation and disobedience spread to the turbulent regions of the Maharashtra and Bengal. In Calcutta, the Mayor, J. M. Sengupta, read seditious literature aloud at a public meeting and urged non-wearing of foreign textiles. He was put in prison for six months. Picketing of liquor shops and foreign cloth shops commenced throughout India. Girls and ladies from aristocratic families and from families where purdah had been observed came out into the streets to demonstrate. Police became vindictive and kicked resisters in sensitive parts. Civil resistance began in the province of Bihar. Seventeen Bihar Satyagrahis, including resigned members of Legislative Councils, were sentenced to periods of from six months to two years in prison. A Swami who had lived in South Africa received two and a half years. Teachers, professors and students made salt at the sea and inland, and were marched off to jail in batches. Kishorlal Mashruwala, a faithful disciple of Gandhi, and Jamnalal Bajaj, a rich friend of Gandhi's, were sentenced to two years' imprisonment. In Karachi, the police fired on a demonstration; two young Volunteers were killed. 'Bihar has been denuded of almost all its leaders,' Mahadev Desai wrote, 'but the result has been the opening of many more salt centres.' Congress distributed literature explaining simple methods of producing salt. B. G. Kher and K. M. Munshi, leaders of the National Congress, were arrested in Bombay. Devadas Gandhi was sentenced to three months' imprisonment in Delhi. The salt movement and the arrests and imprisonments spread to Madras, the Punjab and the Carnatic (Karnatak). Many towns observed hartals when Congress leaders were arrested. At Patna, in Bihar, a mass of many thousands moved out of the city to march to a spot where salt would be made. The police blocked the highway. The crowd stayed and slept on the road and in the fields for forty hours. Rajendra Prasad, who was present and told the story, received orders from the police officer to disperse the crowd. He refused. The officer announced that he would charge with cavalry. The crowd did not move. As the horses galloped forward, the men and women threw themselves flat on the ground. The horses stopped and did not trample them. Constables then proceeded to lift the demonstrators and place them in trucks for transportation to prison. Other demonstrators replaced them. Mahadev Desai was arrested for bringing in a load of salt. In villages, millions of peasants were preparing their own salt. The British pressed local officials to cope with the problem. The officials resigned. Vithalbhai Patel, the speaker of the Legislative Assembly, resigned. A large group of prominent women appealed to Lord Irwin to prohibit the sale of intoxicating beverages. At Karachi, fifty thousand people watched as salt was made on the seashore. The crowd was so dense the policemen were surrounded and could make no arrests. At Peshawar, the key to the volatile north-west Frontier Province, an armoured car, in which the Deputy Commissioner was seated, first ran full-tilt into a crowd then machine-gunned it, killing seventy and wounding about a hundred. In parts of Bengal, in the United Provinces and in Gujarat, peasants refused to pay rent and the land tax. The Government tried to place all nationalist newspapers under censorship, whereupon most of them voluntarily suspended publication. Congress provincial offices were sealed and their property and office paraphernalia confiscated. Rajagopalachari was arrested in Madras and given a nine months' sentence. The wild Afridi tribe, in the north-west frontier Tribal Area, attacked British patrols. In the city of Chittagong, Bengal, a band of violent revolutionists raided the arsenal to seize arms. Some were killed.

The Viceroy, says Irwin's biographer, 'had filled the jails with no less than sixty thousand political offenders'. Estimates ran as high as a hundred thousand. 'A mere recital of the action taken by him during this time', the biography affirms, 'belies once for all the legend that he was a weak Viceroy. Those who were responsible for executing his orders testify that his religious convictions seemed to reinforce the very ruthlessness of his policy of suppression . . .'

A month after Gandhi touched salt at the Dandi beach, India was seething in angry revolt. But, except at Chittagong, there was no Indian violence, and nowhere was there any Congress violence. Chauri Chaura in 1922 had taught India a lesson. Because they treasured the movement Gandhi had conjured into being, and lest he cancel it, they abstained from force.

On 4 May, Gandhi's camp was at Karadi, a village near Dandi. He had gone to sleep on a cot under a shed beneath the branches of an old mango tree. Several disciples slept by his side. Elsewhere in the grove, other ashramites were in deep slumber. At 12.45 A.M., in the night of 4 to 5 May, heavy footsteps were heard. Thirty Indian policemen armed with rifles, pistols and lances, two Indian officers, and the British District Magistrate of Surat invaded the leafy compound. A party of armed constables entered Gandhi's shed and the English officer turned the flashlight on Gandhi's face. Gandhi awoke, looked about him, and said to the Magistrate, 'Do you want me?'

'Are you Mohandas Karamchand Gandhi?' the Magistrate asked for the sake of form.

Gandhi admitted it.

The officer said he had come to arrest him.

'Please give me time for my ablutions,' Gandhi said politely.

The Magistrate agreed.

While brushing his few teeth, Gandhi said, 'Mr District Magistrate, may I know under which charge I am arrested. Is it Section 124?'

'No, not under Section 124. I have got a written order.'

By this time, all the sleepers in the compound had crowded around the shed. 'Please, would you mind reading it to me?' Gandhi asked.

The Magistrate (reading): 'Whereas the Governor-in-Council views with alarm the activities of Mohandas Karamchand Gandhi, he directs that the said Mohandas Karamchand Gandhi should be placed under restraint under Regulation XXXV of 1827, and suffer imprisonment during the pleasure of the Government, and that he be immediately removed to the Yeravda Central Jail.'

At 1 A.M., Gandhi was still cleaning his teeth. The officer told him to hurry. Gandhi packed some necessities and papers in a small bag. Turning to the officer, he said, 'Please give me a few minutes more for prayer.'

The officer nodded in assent, and Gandhi requested Pandit

Khare to recite a famous Hindu hymn. The ashramites sang.
Gandhi lowered his head and prayed. Then he stepped to the
side of the Magistrate who led him to the waiting vehicle.

There was no trial, no sentence and no fixed term of
imprisonment. The arrest took place under an ordinance,
passed before a British government existed in India, which
regulated the relations between the East India Company and
Indian potentates.

The prison authorities measured Gandhi and noted his
height: five feet five inches. They also made sure to have his
special identification marks in case they needed to find him
again: a scar on the right thigh, a small mole on the lower
right eyelid, and a scar about the size of a pea below the left
elbow.

Gandhi loved it in jail. 'I have been quite happy and
making up for arrears in sleep,' he wrote Miss Madeleine
Slade, a week after his imprisonment. He was treated
extremely well; the prison goat was milked in his presence. On
his day of silence he wrote a letter to the little children in the
ashram.

Little birds, ordinary birds cannot fly without wings. With wings, of
course, all can fly. But if you, without wings, will learn how to fly,
then all your troubles will indeed be at an end. And I will teach you.
See, I have no wings, yet I come flying to you every day in thought.
Look, here is little Vimala, here is Hari and here is Dharmakurmar.
And you can also come flying to me in thought . . . Tell me too who
amongst you are not praying properly in Prabhubhai's evening
prayer.
Send me a letter signed by all, and those who do not know how to
sign may make a cross.
					Bapu's blessings.

Just before his arrest, Gandhi had drafted a letter to the
Viceroy announcing his intention, 'God willing', to raid the
Dharasana Salt Works with some companions. God,
apparently, was not willing, but the companions proceeded to

effect the plan. Mrs Sarojini Naidu, the poet, led twenty-five hundred Volunteers to the site one hundred and fifty miles north of Bombay and, after morning prayers, warned them that they would be beaten 'but', she said, 'you must not resist; you must not even raise a hand to ward off a blow'.

Webb Miller, the well-known correspondent of the United Press who died in England during the second World War, was on the scene and described the proceedings. Manilal Gandhi moved forward at the head of the marchers and approached the great salt pans which were surrounded by ditches and barbed wire and guarded by four hundred Surat policemen under the command of six British officers. 'In complete silence the Gandhi men drew up and halted a hundred yards from the stockade. A picked column advanced from the crowd, waded the ditches, and approached the barbed-wire stockade.' The police officers ordered them to retreat. They continued to advance. 'Suddenly,' Webb Miller reported, 'at a word of command, scores of native policemen rushed upon the advancing marchers and rained blows on their heads with their steel-shod lathis. Not one of the marchers even raised an arm to fend off the blows. They went down like nine-pins. From where I stood I heard the sickening whack of the clubs on unprotected skulls. The waiting crowd of marchers groaned and sucked in their breath in sympathetic pain at every blow. Those struck down fell sprawling, unconscious or writhing with fractured skulls or broken shoulders . . . The survivors, without breaking ranks, silently and doggedly march on until struck down.' When the first column was laid low, another advanced. 'Although everyone knew,' Webb Miller wrote, 'that within a few minutes he would be beaten down, perhaps killed, I could detect no signs of wavering or fear. They marched steadily, with heads up, without the encouragement of music or cheering or any possibility that they might escape serious injury or death. The police rushed out and methodically and mechanically beat down the second column. There was no fight, no struggle; the marchers simply walked forward till struck down.'

Another group of twenty-five advanced and sat down. 'The police,' Webb Miller testifies, 'commenced savagely kicking the seated men in the abdomen and testicles.' Another column advanced and sat down. Enraged, the police dragged them by their arms and feet and threw them into the ditches. 'One was dragged to a ditch where I stood,' Miller wrote, 'the splash of his body doused me with muddy water. Another policemen dragged a Gandhi man to the ditch, threw him in, and belaboured him over the head with his lathi. Hour after hour stretcher-bearers carried back a stream of inert, bleeding bodies.'

A British officer approached Mr Naidu, touched her arm, and said, 'Sarojini Naidu, you are under arrest.' She shook off his hand. 'I'll come,' she declared, 'but don't touch me.' Manilal was also arrested.

'By eleven [in the morning],' Webb Miller continued, 'the heat had reached 116 and the activities of the Gandhi volunteers had subsided.' He went to the temporary hospital and counted three hundred and twenty injured, many of them still unconscious, others in agony from the body and head blows. Two men had died. The same scenes were repeated for several days.

India was now free. Technically, legally, nothing had changed. India was still a British colony. Tagore explained the difference. 'Those who live in England, far away from the East,' he told the *Manchester Guardian* of 17 May, 1930, 'have now got to realize that Europe has completely lost her former moral prestige in Asia. She is no longer regarded as the champion throughout the world of fair dealing and the exponent of high principle, but as the upholder of Western race supremacy and the exploiter of those outside her own borders.

'For Europe this is, in actual fact, a great moral defeat that has happened. Even though Asia is still physically weak and unable to protect herself from aggression where her vital interests are menaced, nevertheless she can now afford to look down on Europe where before she looked up.' He attributed the achievement in India to Mahatma Gandhi.

Gandhi did two things in 1930: he made the British people aware that they were cruelly subjugating India, and he gave Indians the conviction that they could, by lifting their heads and straightening their spines, lift the yoke from their shoulders. After that, it was inevitable that Britain should some day refuse to rule India and that India should some day refuse to be ruled.

The British beat the Indians with batons and rifle butts. The Indians neither cringed nor complained nor retreated. That made England powerless and India invincible.

CHAPTER 17

Parleys with the Rebel

Many British Labour ministers and their supporters were champions of Indian independence. Prime Minister Ramsay MacDonald could be faced with his own unequivocal statements in favour of India's freedom. It was embarrassing for Labour to keep Gandhi and tens of thousands of Indian nationalists in jail. To Lord Irwin, Gandhi's imprisonment was more than an embarrassment; it paralysed his administration. Revenues dropped steeply. Unrest mounted. When the news of Gandhi's arrest reached industrial Sholapur, in the Bombay Presidency or province, the population overpowered the police, raised the national flag, and declared themselves independent of British rule. In Peshawar, the police surrendered the city to the non-violent, religious 'Red Shirts', an organization led by Khan Abdul Ghaffar Khan, the 'Frontier Gandhi'. The army appeared three days later and machine-gunned peaceful citizens. But a platoon of Garhwal Rifles, famous Hindu regiment of the British Army, mutinied, refused to fire on Moslems, and were court-martialed and sentenced to ten to fourteen years' hard labour. On 30 June, Motilal Nehru was arrested. More than a hundred thousand Indians, and almost all Congress first-, second-, third-rank leaders were in prison.

The situation was politically intolerable for MacDonald and Irwin. Gandhi in jail was as much a nuisance as Gandhi on the march or at the beach or in the ashram.

Conscious of their dilemma and of the growing revolt, the authorities permitted George Slocombe, handsome, red-bearded correspondent of the London Labour paper, the *Daily Herald*, to interview Gandhi in prison, on 19 and 20

May, only two weeks after the Mahatma's arrest. Gandhi gave Slocombe the terms on which he would be ready to negotiate with the British government. In July, with the Viceroy's consent, Sir Tej Bahadur Sapru and Mr M. R. Jayakar, leaders of the moderates, went to Gandhi's cell for parleys. Gandhi was glad to talk to them but said he could not reply to overtures before he consulted the Congress Working Committee. Motilal and Jawaharlal Nehru, father and son, and Syed Mahmound, the acting secretary of Congress, were accordingly transported in a special train, with every comfort and courtesy, from their jail in the United Provinces to Gandhi's jail at Poona where Mrs Naidu and Vallabhbhai Patel were also confined. Irwin willingly brought his prisoners together, but Working Committee members still at liberty were not allowed to participate in these prison conversations.

After two days' discussion (14–15 August), the leaders announced publicly that 'an unbridgeable gulf' separated them from the British position.

The first Round Table Conference opened in London on 12 November, 1930; Jinnah, the Maharaja of Bikaner, Srinivasa Sastri and others were there. No Congress representative attended. The Conference accomplished nothing. But the Labour government's conciliatory attitude was apparent throughout; indeed, at the closing session, on 19 January, 1931, Ramsay MacDonald expressed the hope that Congress would send delegates to the second Round Table Conference.

Irwin gladly took the hint – or the command – and unconditionally released Gandhi, the Nehrus, and more than twenty other Congress leaders on 26 January, Independence Day. In appreciation of this graceful gesture, Gandhi wrote a letter to the Viceroy asking for an interview. 'Face-saving' was an unintelligible concept to Gandhi. He did not believe in ending a relationship that could be mended, and since he had an undying faith in mending, he tried never to end a personal or political relationship.

The first meeting between Irwin and Gandhi began on 17 February, at 2.30 P.M., and lasted till 6.10 P.M. 'So the stage was set', writes Irwin's biographer, 'for the most dramatic personal encounter between a Viceroy and an Indian leader in the whole seething history of the British raj.'

It was more than dramatic; the mere fact of the encounter was historically decisive. Winston Churchill, always clear-eyed, saw this better than anyone. He was revolted by 'the nauseating and humiliating spectacle of this one-time Inner Temple lawyer, now seditious fakir, striding half-naked up the steps of the Viceroy's palace, there to negotiate and to parley on equal terms with the representative of the King-Emperor'.

A fakir is an Indian mendicant monk.

Churchill realized that it was not an ordinary interview. Gandhi did not come, like most of the Viceroy's visitors, to ask favours. He came as the leader of a nation to negotiate 'on equal terms' with the leader of another nation. The Salt March and its aftermath had proved that England could not rule India against or without Gandhi. The British Empire was at the mercy of the half-naked fakir, and Churchill did not like it. Churchill saw that Britain was conceding India's independence in principle while withholding it, for the time being, in practice.

The negotiations between Irwin and Gandhi took place in the Viceroy's new palace, designed by the gifted British architect Sir Edward Lutyens. Rising suddenly, high, expensive and resplendent, out of the flat Delhi plains amidst the ruins of Mogul mosques and forts, it symbolized the towering might of the British raj. But almost the first act within its halls marked the beginning of the end of that power.

Gandhi and Irwin conferred again for three hours on 18 February, and for half an hour on the 19th. Meanwhile Irwin was cabling his superiors six thousand miles away in London, while Gandhi held long meetings with the Congress Working

Committee members in New Delhi. (The great Motilal Nehru had died on 6 February.) Shuttling between the two parties, Sapru, Jayakar and Sastri strove to prevent a deadlock.

Once, during a conference, Irwin asked Gandhi whether he would have tea. 'Thank you,' said Gandhi, taking a paper bag out of a fold in his shawl, 'I will put some of this salt into my tea to remind us of the famous Boston Tea Party.' Both laughed.

Difficulties arose. There were no talks for seven days. On 27 February they were resumed. On 1 March, Gandhi came to Irwin at 2.30 P.M. The discussions continued till his dinner time, so Miss Slade had brought his dinner – forty dates and a pint of goat's milk – to the palace and Gandhi ate it in the presence of the Viceroy. At 5.50 P.M. Gandhi left the Viceroy, but that same evening he walked, unescorted, from Dr Ansari's house, where he was staying, to the palace, a distance of five miles, and remained closeted with Irwin till after midnight. 'Good night,' Irwin said to him as he departed to trudge home alone in the darkness. 'Good night, Mr Gandhi, and my prayers go with you.' Gandhi reached home at 2 A.M. The Working Committee was waiting for him.

Finally, after further wrangling between the two men and between each of them and their colleagues, the Irwin–Gandhi Pact, or The Delhi Pact as Irwin's biographer calls it, was signed after breakfast on 5 March. The key word is 'Pact'. Two national statesmen had signed a pact, a treaty, an agreed text, every phrase and stipulation of which had been hammered out in tough bargaining. British spokesmen maintained that Irwin won the battle, and a good case could be made for the contention. But in the long-range terms in which the Mahatma thought, the equality that had been established, in principle, between India and England was more important than any practical concession which he might have wrung from the reluctant Empire. A politician would have sought more substance. Gandhi was satisfied with the essence: a basis for a new relationship.

For the millions, and for history, the thousands of words of the Pact with its many articles, headings and subheadings which appeared in the official *Gazette of India Extraordinary* of 5 March, 1931, meant: civil disobedience would be called off, prisoners released, and salt manufacture permitted on the coast; Congress would attend the next Round Table Conference in London. Independence was not promised. Dominion Status was not promised.

In an address to American and Indian journalists that day, Gandhi paid tribute to the Viceroy. 'I am aware,' he told the newsmen, 'that I must have, though quite unconsciously, given him cause for irritation. I must also have tried his patience, but I cannot recall an occasion when he allowed himself to be betrayed into irritation or impatience.' The settlement, Gandhi said, was 'provisional' and 'conditional'; a 'truce'. The goal remained: 'complete independence . . . India cannot be satisfied with anything less . . . The Congress does not consider India to be a sickly child requiring nursing, outside help and other props'.

One has a feeling, in reviewing Gandhi's 1930 negotiations, that he viewed them at the time in the perspective of several decades later. What does the phraseology or even content of Article Two matter now? Seventeen years after the Delhi Pact, India was an independent nation. What are seventeen years in the life of an old nation like India?

Subhas Chandra Bose, a critic of the Mahatma, watching the public reaction during a tour with Gandhi after the Pact was signed, wrote, 'I wonder if such a spontaneous ovation was ever given to a leader anywhere else.' And Bose admitted that Irwin, 'though a prominent Member of the Conservative Party . . . had proved himself to be a well-wisher of India'. To Gandhi, who was often guided in politics by his responses to persons, this warranted the signing of the Pact.

The moment the Pact was signed, complaints of non-fulfilment were levelled against the Government, and soon Gandhi was again negotiating, this time with the new Viceroy, Lord Willingdon. Adjustments made, the Congress convention at Karachi which, according to Bose, was 'the pinnacle of the Mahatma's popularity and prestige', elected Gandhi its sole delegate to the second Round Table Conference.

At noon on 29 August, Gandhi sailed from Bombay aboard the SS *Rajputana*. Accompanying him in various capacities were Pandit Malaviya, Mrs Naidu, his son Devadas, Mahadev Desai who, Gandhi said, 'out-Boswelled Boswell', Pyarelal Nayyar, a secretary and disciple, Miss Slade, who had made India her permanent home and Gandhi her spiritual father, and G. D. Birla, the big Indian industrialist. 'There is every chance of my returning empty-handed,' he said on embarking.

Gandhi had given orders that he and his party should travel by the lowest class. When he discovered how much luggage they had brought he saw to it that seven suitcases and trunks were sent back from Aden. He himself spent most of the day and all night on deck, spinning, writing, sleeping, eating, praying, talking and playing with child passengers. Like so many steamship passengers the world over, he was the Captain's guest on the bridge, where he looked through the sextant and steered the ship for a minute.

Gandhi arrived in London on 12 September, and remained in England until 5 December. He stayed in an East End Settlement House called Kingsley Hall as guest of Muriel Lester who had visited him in 1926. Kingsley Hall is five miles from the centre of the city and from St James's Palace where the Round Table Conference sat.

Friends told him that he would save many hours for work and sleep if he lived in an hotel, but he did not want to spend the money. Nor would he avail himself of the hospitality of

Indians and Englishmen who had big houses nearer the heart of London. He would come home to Kingsley Hall every evening, often very late, because, he said, he enjoyed living among his own kind, the poor people. To spare interviewers the necessity of coming all the way to the East End, however, he agreed, under pressure, to keep a little office at 88 Knightsbridge. (The building was destroyed in the second World War.)

In the mornings, he walked through the slum streets around Kingsley Hall, and women and men going to work would smile and greet him and some would join him for conversation; he visited several in their homes. Children ran up and held his hand. 'Uncle Gandhi', they called him. One mischievous youngster yelled, 'Hey, Gandhi, where's your trousers?' The Mahatma laughed heartily.

Questioned by a reporter about his dress, Gandhi said, 'You people wear plus-fours, mine are minus fours.' Gandhi was wonderful newspaper copy, and journalists covered every move he made. The dailies and weeklies in Europe and America eagerly sought special features about him. George Slocombe wrote a story about Gandhi's generosity and as an illustration said that when the Prince of Wales visited India the Mahatma prostrated himself before him. The next time Gandhi saw Slocombe, he smiled and said, 'Well, Mr Slocombe, this does not even do credit to your imagination. I would bend the knee before the poorest untouchable in India for having participated in crushing him for centuries, I would take the dust off his feet. But I would not prostrate myself, not even before the King, much less before the Prince of Wales, for the simple reason that he represented insolent might.' Gandhi went to Buckingham Palace to have tea with King George V and Queen Mary. On the eve of the event, all England was agog over what he would wear. He wore a loincloth, sandals, a shawl and his dangling watch. Later, someone asked Gandhi whether he had had enough on. 'The

King,' he replied, 'had enough on for both of us.'

David Lloyd George, Britain's war-time Prime Minister, invited Gandhi to his farm at Churt, in Surrey. They talked for three hours. In 1938, when I saw Lloyd George at Churt, he mentioned the Gandhi visit. He said the servants did what no guest had ever inspired them to do: they all came out to meet the holy man.

Four years later, I told Gandhi that Lloyd George had talked to me about his visit. 'Yes,' Gandhi queried eagerly. 'What did he say?'

'He told me that you squatted on his couch and just as you got settled a black cat they had never seen before entered through the window and rested in your lap.'

'That's correct,' Gandhi recalled.

'And when you left, Lloyd George said, the cat disappeared.'

'Ah,' Gandhi said, 'that I don't know.'

'Lloyd George,' I continued, 'said that the same cat returned when Miss Slade visited him at Churt.'

'That too I don't know,' Gandhi declared.

As soon as Gandhi reached England he inquired about Colonel Maddock who had performed the operation on him for appendicitis in 1924, and the moment he found some leisure he went down to spend some hours at the home of Colonel and Mrs Maddock near Reading where they sat in the beautiful garden and reminisced and told one another they did not look a year older.

Charlie Chaplin asked to see Gandhi. Gandhi had never heard of him; he had never seen a moving picture. On being enlightened, Gandhi said no, he had no special interest in actors. But when told that Chaplin came from a poor family in the London East End, he received him at the home of Dr Katial. The encounter turned into a competition between toothless and toothsome smiling and the inevitable discussion about Gandhi's attitude to the machine, which was Chaplin's first question. The answer may have inspired one of the actor's subsequent films.

George Bernard Shaw also paid his respects. With unusual modesty he gave the palm to Gandhi and called himself 'Mahatma Minor'. 'You and I,' he said, 'belong to a very small community on earth.' They touched on a score of subjects and Shaw's humour immensely amused 'Mahatma Major', but it cannot be said that Gandhi liked the playwright's love of the word that shocks. Neither had Tolstoy.

Gandhi met Lord Irwin, General Smuts, the Archbishop of Canterbury, the Dean of Canterbury, Harold J. Laski, C. P. Scott, the retired editor of the *Manchester Guardian*, Arthur Henderson and hundreds of others. Churchill declined to see him. Smuts said, apropos South Africa, 'I did not give you such a bad time as you gave me.'

'I did not know that,' Gandhi apologized.

At the Montessori Training College Gandhi joyously drank in the beautiful rhythmic exercises of the healthy, happy children who made him think, with sadness, of 'the millions of children in semi-starved Indian villages'. Madame Maria Montessori introduced him as 'Noble Master'. 'Thought of world civilization and thought of the child,' she said, 'that is what links us . . .' In his speech, Gandhi declared, 'I believed implicitly that the child is not born mischievous in the bad sense of the term. If parents behave themselves while the child is growing, the child will instinctively obey the law of truth and the law of love . . . From my experience of hundreds – I was going to say thousands – of children, I know that they have a finer sense of honour than you and I have . . . Jesus never uttered a loftier or grander truth than when he said that wisdom cometh out of the mouths of babes. I believe it . . .'

With what is regarded as typical American enterprise, the Columbia Broadcasting System arranged for a radio address to the United States the day after Gandhi's arrival in

England. He refused to prepare a script and spoke extemporaneously. In the studio, he eyed the microphone, and said, 'Do I have to speak into that?' He was already on the air.

India's struggle, Gandhi stated, had drawn the attention of the world not because Indians were fighting for their freedom, but because 'the means adopted by us for attaining that liberty are unique, and as far as history shows us, have not been adopted by any other people . . . Hitherto, nations have fought in the manner of the brute. They have wreaked vengeance upon those whom they have considered to be their enemies . . . We in India,' Gandhi continued, 'have endeavoured to reverse the process. We feel that the law that governs brute creation . . . is inconsistent with human dignity. I personally would wait, if need be for ages, rather than seek to attain the freedom of my country through bloody means. I feel in the innermost recesses of my heart . . . that the world is sick unto death of blood-spilling. The world is seeking a way out and I flatter myself with the belief that perhaps it will be the privilege of the ancient land of India to show the way out to the hungering world . . .

'It is a matter of deep humiliation to confess that we are a house divided against itself, that we Hindus and Mussulmans are flying at one another. It is a matter of still deeper humiliation that we Hindus regard several million of our own kith and kin as too degraded even for our touch.'

He then elaborated on the curse of drink and of drugs and on the destruction, by the East India Company, of village industries for the benefit of British manufacturers. At this juncture, a note was passed to Gandhi saying his time was almost up and New York would cut him off in three minutes. Unperturbed, he delved still further into the economics of British rule, and closed with a plea: 'May I not, then, on behalf of the semi-starved millions, appeal to the conscience of the world to come to the rescue of a people dying to regain its liberty?'

The CBS producer signalled him to stop. 'Well, that's over,' Gandhi said. He was still on the air. His voice was clear and the reception perfect.

In his eighty-four days in England, Gandhi visited Eton, Cambridge, where he sentimentally asked to be taken to Trinity, which was Jawaharlal Nehru's and C. F. Andrews's college, and Oxford, and addressed scores of public meetings of women's organizations, Quakers, Indian students, Indian merchants, British students, Labourites, Members of Parliament, the London School of Economics, The American Journalists Association, which arranged a vegetarian luncheon at the Savoy in deference to his habits, Friends of India, Temperance Society, Vegetarians, etc. etc.

Gandhi's two weekends at Oxford were memorable. He stayed with Professor Lindsay, the Master of Balliol, who later became a peer, Lord Lindsay of Birker. 'Both my wife and I said', Lindsay wrote in 1948, 'that having him in our house was like having a saint in the house. He showed that mark of a great and simple man that he treated everyone with the same courtesy and respect whether one were a distinguished statesman or an unknown student. Anyone who was in earnest in wanting an answer to a question got a real one.'

Another view of Gandhi at Oxford was expressed by Dr Edward Thompson, at whose home, on his second Oxonian weekend, Gandhi had a discussion with a group that included the Master of Balliol, Gilbert Murray, Professor S. Coupland, Sir Michael Sadler, P. C. Lyon and other trained minds. 'He can be exasperating,' Professor Thompson remarked after Gandhi's visit.

Describing the intellectual joust, Thompson said, 'For three hours he was sifted and cross-examined . . . It was a reasonably exacting ordeal, yet not for a moment was he rattled or at a loss. The conviction came to me, that not since Socrates has the world seen his equal for absolute self-control and composure; and once or twice, putting myself in the place of men who had to confront the invincible calm and imperturbability, I thought I understood why the Athenians made "the martyr-sophist" drink the hemlock. Like Socrates, he had a "daemon". And when the "daemon" has spoken, he is as unmoved by argument as by danger.'

Apparently, not all those present possessed the Socratic imperturbability, for Professor Thompson says, 'I can still hear Lindsay's desperate tones, as he cited Cromwell's appeal to the Presbyterian ministers – "In the bowels of Christ, I beseech you to think it possible that you may be mistaken" – and added, "Mr Gandhi! think it *possible* that you may be *mistaken*!" Mr Gandhi did not think it possible.'

But Mahadev Desai was there, taking notes as usual, and he records Gandhi as pleading for 'the liberty to make mistakes'. On the other hand, Gandhi was adamant in defending civil disobedience; he would never give it up. 'I will not purchase my country's freedom at the cost of non-violence,' he told the professors who thought they could not be mistaken. 'You may be justified', Gandhi admitted, 'in saying that I must go more warily, but if you attack the fundamentals you have to convince me.' They failed.

In all Gandhi's public and private, official and unofficial utterances during his eighty-four days in England, he tried, above all else, to clarify what he meant by the independence of India.

'How far would you cut India off from the Empire?' a member of the audience at the Raleigh Club asked.

'From the Empire entirely,' Gandhi replied. 'From the British nation not at all, if I want India to gain and not to grieve. The Emperorship must go and I should love to be an equal partner with Britain sharing her joys and sorrows and an equal partner with the Dominions. But it must be a partnership on equal terms.'

He advocated 'an honourable partnership . . . We can have a partnership between England and India . . . I still aspire to be a citizen not in the Empire, but in a Commonwealth, in a partnership if possible; if God wills it, an indissoluble partnership, but not a partnership superimposed upon one nation by another . . . The Congress does not stand merely for isolated independence which may easily become a menace to the world . . . I would heartily welcome the union of East and West provided it is not based on brute force . . . England and India [should be] bound by the silken cord of love . . . India as an independent partner would have a special contribution to make in a world which is getting weary of war and bloodshed. In case of an outbreak of war it would be the common effort of India and Great Britain to prevent war, not indeed by force of arms, but by the irresistible force of example'.

In these statements, Gandhi described precisely, and with remarkable prevision, the status which independent India voluntarily assumed in the Commonwealth in 1948. More, the protagonists of that move used the very argument – and almost the exact words – which Gandhi had used in London seventeen years earlier. Gandhi saw that the only beneficent independence was the kind that led to interdependence. 'Isolated independence is not the goal,' he said. 'It is a voluntary interdependence.' He arrived at this conclusion through no abstruse theorizing about internationalism or world government. Gandhi was addicted to love; it was the basis of his relations with people. Love is creative interdependence. And since Gandhi regarded nations not as abstract legal entities but as agglomerations of human beings with names, noses, aches and smiles, he believed that international relationships should be founded on interdependence and love.

Gandhi had been criticized for acquiescing in Article Two of the Irwin–Delhi Pact of 5 March, 1931, which stated that in the contemplated constitution of India, England would retain control over defence, foreign affairs, minority problems and

financial obligations to foreign creditors. It was a severe
limitation on freedom. Gandhi took the criticism to heart.
Indeed, the Congress convention in Karachi at the end of
March 1931, instructed Gandhi to change his position on this
key question. Gandhi, accordingly, told British audiences
that 'it is part of the mandate given me by Congress that
complete independence would be meaningless unless it was
accompanied by complete control over finance, defence and
external affairs'. This reversal in Gandhi's attitude
exasperated the British; he had gone back on his signature.
Gandhi had a technical justification in the mandate of
Congress, his master. Actually, he attached no political
importance to the stipulation in the Delhi Pact and only
propaganda importance to his advocacy of the opposite in
London. England was not yet parting with power in India.
That was the crucial fact. Hair-splitting over who would
control what was therefore futile.

This being his approach, Gandhi concentrated more on
convincing the British people than on debating with the
British government at the Round Table Conference. 'I find
that my work lies outside the Conference,' he told one
audience. Referring to his efforts to explain India to England,
he said, 'This to me is the real Round Table Conference . . .
The seed which is being sown now may result in softening the
British spirit . . . and in preventing the brutalization of
human beings.' He made friends through his charm,
frankness, humanity and accessibility. He won the hearts of
the Christians in England who recognized him as a big
brother and ally. He touched what was Christian in all
Englishmen. He found an echo in their common sense; it was
clear after his visit that some day, sooner than some thought,
sooner than Churchill wished, India would be liberated.
Many considered him 'difficult', and he undoubtedly could
be. But he moderated the hostility of the most rabid. He even
walked into the lion's den and went to Lancashire where his

agitation against foreign cloth and in favour of khadi had caused unemployment and loss of profits. At a meeting, one man said, 'I am one of the unemployed, but if I was in India I would say the same thing that Mr Gandhi is saying.' There is a telling photograph, taken outside the Greenfield Mill at Darwen, Lancashire, showing Gandhi, wrapped in white cotton from neck to knee, overcome with coyness and squeezed in amidst cotton factory workers, most of them women, one of them holding his hand, and all of them, young, old, male, female, cheering the Mahatma and smiling. He made friends among those whom he hurt.

The Government assigned two Scotland Yard detectives, Sergeant Evans and Sergeant Rogers, to guard Gandhi; they were special policemen, giants in stature, usually assigned to protecting royalty. They grew to like 'the little man'. Unlike most prominent personalities in such circumstances, Gandhi did not keep them at arm's length or ignore them. He talked to them and visited their homes. Before leaving England, he begged that they be allowed to accompany him to Brindisi, Italy. The bureaucrat asked the reason for this strange request.

'Because they are part of my family,' Gandhi answered.

From India he sent each a watch engraved 'With love from M. K. Gandhi'.

Between lectures, speeches, forums, press interviews, trips, innumerable individual appointments, and answering a mountain of mail – all with a view to conquering Britain's heart – he attended to the official business which had brought him to London: the second Round Table Conference. His official and unofficial activities usually kept him busy twenty-one hours a day; diaries preserved show that he sometimes got to bed at 2 A.M., awoke at 3.45 A.M. for prayers, rested again from 5 to 6 A.M., and had no respite from then till the next morning at 1 or 2 A.M. The schedule wore him out; he delighted in driving his body to the maximum of endurance

and beyond. As a result, what he gave the Round Table
Conference was not of his best quality, yet the participants
heard some remarkable, and certainly unique, utterances
from his lips. He attended regularly, although most plenary
sessions and committee meetings bored him; they were so
political that he lost all sense of their reality. Often he sat with
eyes closed. He may have slept a few winks.

The purpose of the Round Table Conference was
'constitution-building' for India. Lord Reading, a member of
the British delegation, formulated the British purpose in one
sentence: 'I believe that the true policy between Britain and
India is that we should in this country strive all we can to give
effect to the views of India while preserving at the same time
our own position, which we must not and cannot abandon.'

How could England give effect to the view of India while
remaining the mistress of India?

The Round Table Conference was worse than a failure. By
intensifying the religious divisions of India it exercised a
sinister, tragic influence on the future.

The Conference consisted of 112 delegates: 20 representing
the Government of the United Kingdom, 23 from princely
India – rajas, maharajas, nawabs and their subordinates –
and 64 from British India. The Viceroy appointed the
princes, and, with the exception of Gandhi, Mrs Naidu and a
few others, he appointed the visitors from British India.

His selections were careful and purposeful. The British
government advocated a federation of princely India, which
was roughly a third of India, with British India. This would
have introduced the weight of the autocratic princes, British
puppets all, into the government of India. Thus what seemed
like the unification of the two Indias was calculated to
strengthen feudal, medieval reaction and reinforce British
rule.

The delegation from British India included the Aga Khan
and others like him. It included British merchants,

Anglo-Indians, Christians, Hindus, Moslems, landlords, Labourites, untouchables and Parsis (but not one peasant), and each of these groups demanded a separate electorate for itself. In other words, a number of seats in the legislative assemblies would be reserved for Englishmen resident in India, for landlords, for Moslems, etc., and the Englishmen would be elected only by the votes of the Englishmen of India who could vote for no one else, the landlords would be elected by landlords, the Moslems could vote only for Moslem candidates, and so on. Every divisive tendency in India was encouraged.

The Conference set up a Minorities Committee comprising six Englishmen from England, thirteen Moslems, ten Hindus, two untouchables, two Labourites, two Sikhs, one Parsi, two Indian Christians, one Anglo-Indian (Anglo-Indians are descendants of mixed marriages between British men and Indian women), two Englishmen domiciled in India and four women. Only the women did not ask for a separate electorate. Of the thirteen Moslems in the Committee only one was a nationalist Moslem who was an Indian politically and a follower of the Prophet religiously. The remaining twelve mingled Church and State and put the political interests of their religious community above the welfare of India as a whole.

Mr Fazl-ul Huq, a Moslem, was addressing the Plenary Session of 28 November, 1931. 'I wonder', he said, 'if Sir Austen Chamberlain has come across two such incongruous specimens of humanity as Dr Moonje [a Hindu member of the Conference] and myself – professing different religions, worshipping different Gods.'

'The same God,' a member interjected.

'No,' Mr Fazl-ul Huq demurred, 'no, it cannot be the same God. My God is for separate electorates; his God is for joint electorates.'

The Moslem delegate was partitioning God. But Gandhi

would not partition God or India. He told the conference he
rejected all separate electorates. In an independent India, he
said, Indians would vote as Indians for Indians. The virtue of
Indian nationalism and its appeal to outsiders was not that it
would create new national barriers – there were already too
many – but rather that it would rid England and the world of
the incubus of imperialism and take religion out of politics in
India. Instead, the Round Table Conference, under British
management, intensified the old and attempted to introduce
new fissiparous influences. 'Divide and Rule' is the law of
Empire; the more the rule is threatened the more diligently
that law is applied.

The solution for India would have been to banish religious
considerations from politics. But with all its twentieth-
century vitality, Indian nationalism still lacked the strength
to unite that which religion, provincial loyalties and
economic differences separated. The Indian national
movement was faced with the task of liberation before the
Indians had been welded into a nation.

The caste system was a further divisive influence which
weakened nationalism. The Harijans or untouchables feared
and often hated the Hindus who had harnessed so many
brutal disabilities upon them. They, too, through their gifted
and ambitious representative at the Conference, Dr Bhimrao
Ramji Ambedkar, a lawyer who studied at Columbia
University of New York under a scholarship from the
Gaekwar Maharaja of Baroda, demanded a separate
electorate or at least a right to a specified number of Hindu
seats in the legislative assemblies.

Mahatma Gandhi, a supremely devout Hindu, was
incapable of discriminating against anyone on account of
religion, race, caste, colour, or anything. His contribution to
the equality of untouchables and to the education of a new
generation which was Indian instead of Hindu or Moslem or
Parsi or Christian had world significance. But at the time of

the Round Table Conference of 1931, and especially with the British government pulling in the opposite direction, his arm lacked the power to draw the Hindu, Moslem and Harijan communities together into an Indian unity which could have commanded the British raj to go home.

At the last plenary sitting of the Round Table Conference, on 1 December, 1931, the chairman, James Ramsay MacDonald, Prime Minister, since the general elections of 27 October, 1931, not of a Labour government but of a Tory government in which he and J. H. Thomas were prisoners, referred to Gandhi as a Hindu.

'Not Hindu,' Gandhi exclaimed.

To his God, Gandhi was a Hindu. To the British Prime Minister, and in politics, he was an Indian. But there were few such Indians at the Round Table Conference and too few in India.

That was the upshot of the Round Table Conference. It was completely abortive. It made the situation in India worse. Gandhi left it and England with a heartache, for though he had charmed and convinced many English people, he had failed to bridge or even to narrow the gulf that separated Hindus from Moslems; and the British government was holding on to India.

CHAPTER 18

On the Way Home

Gandhi sent apologies to persons and groups in almost every free country of the world; he could not visit them because he had work to do in India. On the way home, he stopped for a day in Paris. Sitting on a table, he addressed a large meeting in a cinema theatre, and then took the train for Switzerland, where he stayed five days with Romain Rolland at Villeneuve, at the eastern end of Lake Leman.

Rolland, whose *Jean Christophe* is a literary masterpiece of the twentieth century, had come under the influence of Count Leo Tolstoy, author of the finest novel of the nineteenth. Rolland made a shrewd comparison between Tolstoy and Gandhi. 'With Gandhi,' he said in 1924, 'everything is nature – modest, simple, pure – while all his struggles are hallowed by religious serenity, whereas with Tolstoy everything is proud revolt against pride, hatred against hatred, passion against passion. Everything in Tolstoy is violence, even his doctrine of non-violence.'

Tolstoy was storm-tossed, Gandhi was calm and equable. Gandhi could not have fled from his wife, or from anything. The market place in which he sat was criss-crossed by hundreds of millions of persons with their wares and carts and cares and thoughts, but he sat still and there was silence in him and around him. Gandhi would have suffocated in an ivory tower or on an Olympian height.

Tagore was different. 'But where am I in a great crowd, squeezed in at all sides?' Romain Rolland quoted Tagore as saying. 'And who can understand the noise I hear? If I hear a song, my sitar can catch the melody, and I can join the chorus, for I am a singer. But in the mad clamour of the crowd, my voice is lost, and I become dizzy.'

Rolland and Gandhi had never met before 1931. Rolland knew Gandhi from long conversations with Tagore and C. F. Andrews who had lived for fifteen years with Tagore. He had also read Gandhi. Like Tagore, Rolland was a singer. He was the author of books on Beethoven, Handel, Goethe and Michelangelo. He wrote a book on Ramakrishna, the Hindu mystic.

Rolland regarded Gandhi as a saint. In fact, he wrote in his 1924 biography of the Mahatma, 'Gandhi is too much of a saint; he is too pure, too free from the animal passions that lie dormant in man.' Rolland and Tagore were afraid of the evil in human beings. Tagore feared that when Gandhi lit bonfires of foreign cloth he would kindle uncontrollable emotions in men; Rolland agreed; Andrews agreed.

This estimate omits Gandhi's faith in the basic goodness and corrigibility of man which is the essence of Gandhi. In South Africa, Gandhi believed that the ordinary, illiterate, indentured labourer in a mine or on a farm could rise to the purity and restraint required of a Satyagrahi. He trusted the peasant of backward Bardoli to resist provocation and violence. His trust exalted them. Gandhi did not regard nobility as a monopoly of the great man or the artist or the elite. Gandhi's uniqueness lay in working with common clay and finding the soul-spark in it.

Before Gandhi's arrival on 5 December, Rolland had received hundreds of letters connected with the Mahatma's visit: an Italian wanted to know from Gandhi what numbers would win in the next national lottery; a group of Swiss musicians offered to serenade Gandhi under his window every night; the Syndicate of the Milkmen of Leman volunteered to supply 'the King of India' with dairy products during his stay. Journalists sent questionnaires and camped around Rolland's villa; photographers laid siege to the house; the police reported that the hotels had filled with tourists who hoped to see the Indian visitor.

The two men, Gandhi sixty-two, Rolland sixty-five, met

like old friends and treated one another with the tenderness of mutual respect. Gandhi arrived on a cold rainy evening with Miss Slade, Mahadev Desai, Pyarelal Nayyar and Devadas. The next day was Monday, Gandhi's day of silence, and Rolland delivered a ninety-minute talk on the tragic moral and social state of Europe since 1900. Gandhi listened and pencilled some questions.

On Tuesday, they discussed Gandhi's trip to Rome. He wanted to see Mussolini and other Italian leaders as well as the Pope. Rolland warned him that the Fascist regime would exploit his presence for its sinister purposes. Gandhi said he would break through the cordon they might throw around him. Rolland suggested that he put certain conditions. Gandhi replied that it was against his convictions to make such arrangements in advance. Rolland persisted. Gandhi said, 'Then tell me, what is your final opinion on my plan to stop in Rome?' Rolland advised him to stay with some independent persons. Gandhi promised and kept that promise.

Rolland asked Gandhi to comment on his remarks about Europe. Gandhi said it showed him how vast had been Rolland's suffering. Speaking English which Rolland's sister translated into French, Gandhi said he had learned very little from history. 'My method is empiric,' he explained. 'All my conclusions are based on personal experience.' This, he admitted, could be dangerous and misleading, but he had to have faith in his own views. All his trust was in non-violence. It could save Europe. In England, friends tried to show him the weakness of his non-violent method; 'but even though the whole world doubt it, I will continue to believe in it'.

The next two days Gandhi spent in Lausanne where he addressed a public meeting and in Geneva where he spoke in Victory Hall. At each he was heckled for hours by atheists and others. He answered them in perfect calm, 'not a muscle of his face twitching', Rolland wrote.

On 10 December, they resumed their conversation.

Rolland recalled Gandhi's statement at Geneva: 'Truth is God.' He gave Gandhi a brief sketch of his life, his childhood, how cramped he felt in the small French town, how he became a writer and struggled with the problem of the truth in art. 'If it is correct', Rolland said, 'that "Truth is God", it appears to me that it lacks one important attribute of God: joy. For – and on this I insist – I recognize no God without joy.'

Gandhi replied that he did not distinguish between art and truth. 'I am against the formula, "Art for art's sake". For me, all art must be based on the truth. I reject beautiful things if, instead of expressing truth, they express untruth. I accept the formula "Art brings joy and is good" but on the condition I mentioned. To achieve truth in art I do not expect exact reproductions of external things. Only living things bring living joy to the soul and must elevate the soul.'

Rolland did not differ but he stressed the pain of searching for truth and for God. He took a book from his shelf and read from Goethe. Rolland later confessed that he thought Gandhi's God found pleasure in man's sorrow; Rolland was trying to modify this Gandhian view.

They talked about the perils of another war. 'If one nation possessed the heroism to submit without answering violence with violence,' Gandhi declared, 'it would be the most effective lesson. But for this an absolute faith is necessary.'

Rolland: 'Nothing should be done by halves, no matter whether it is bad or good.' Rolland's sister, Madeleine, and Miss Kondachev, a Russian secretary, were taking notes. Neither recorded Gandhi's reaction to this assertion.

The last day, 11 December, Rolland requested Gandhi to deal with some questions submitted by Pierre Monatte, the editor of a Paris magazine called *The Proletarian Revolution*. In response to one query, Gandhi asserted that if labour was perfectly organized it could dictate conditions to the employers; 'labour is the only power in the world'. But Rolland interposed that the capitalists might divide the workers; there might be scabs; 'then the conscious minority of labour must set up a dictatorship of the proletariat and force the mass of labour to unite in its own interest'.

'I am absolutely opposed to that,' Gandhi affirmed. Rolland dropped the subject and quickly introduced several others: non-violence in relation to criminals, etc. etc., and 'What do you call God? Is it a spiritual personality or a force which rules over the world?'

'God,' Gandhi replied, 'is not a person . . . God is an eternal principle. That is why I say that Truth is God . . . Even atheists do not doubt the necessity of truth.'

The last evening Gandhi asked Rolland to play some Beethoven. Rolland played the Andante from the Fifth Symphony and, as an encore of his own accord, Gluck's 'Elysian Fields'.

The theme of the Fifth Symphony is considered to be man's struggle with fate, man's harmony with fate, the brotherhood of man. The second movement, the Andante, is melodious and suffused with tender lyrical emotions, quiet nobility and optimism. Rolland chose it because it came closest to his concept of Gandhi's personality. It is gentle and loving. In the Gluck piece one almost hears the angels singing to the strains of the flute. It is celestial music, full of purity and clarity. The *Gita* might be set to it.

Rolland was frail and had just recovered from bronchitis, but he insisted on taking Gandhi and his party to the railway station. Then they embraced, as they did when they first met; Gandhi pressed his cheek against Rolland's shoulder and threw his right arm around Rolland; Rolland touched his cheek to Gandhi's head. 'It was the kiss of St Dominic and St Francis,' Rolland said.

The Italian government wished Gandhi to be its guest and made the corresponding preparations. Gandhi politely refused and stayed with General Moris, a friend of Rolland's,

who had lived in India. The day of his arrival, the Mahatma
went to see the Duce. An official communiqué said the
interview lasted twenty minutes. Gandhi's companions recall
that it lasted only ten minutes. Gandhi could establish no
psychological contact with Mussolini. 'He has the eyes of a
cat,' Gandhi said later; 'they moved about in every direction
as if in constant rotation. The visitor would totally succumb
before the awe of his gaze like a rat running directly into the
mouth of a cat out of mere fright.

'I was not to be dazed like that,' Gandhi testified, 'but I
noticed that he had so arranged things about him that a
visitor would easily get stricken with terror. The walls of the
passage through which one has to pass to reach him are all
overstudded with various types of swords and other weapons.'
Mussolini's office, too, Gandhi noted, was hung with
weapons, but, he added, 'he keeps no arms on his person'.

The Pope did not see Gandhi. Several members of
Gandhi's entourage thought the Holy Father might have
been acting in deference to Il Duce's wishes, but they did not
know. Some suggested that the interview failed to materialize
not only on account of Mussolini's relations with the Vatican
but also because of Anglo–Italian relations; Gandhi, after all,
was an anti-British rebel.

Gandhi was taken to the Rome–Naples rugby match and to
a parade of the young Balilla Musketeers where he was
received with a salvo of cannon. He was more interested in the
Vatican Library, and spent two happy hours in St Peter's. In
the Sistine Chapel he stood before Christ on the Cross and
wept. 'One cannot help being moved to tears,' he said to
Mahadev Desai. If he could have lingered 'two or three
months' in the museums and observed the statues and
paintings every day, Gandhi wrote to the ashram, he might
have an opinion that was worth while. Even then, 'I am
hardly qualified as an art critic.'

Romain Rolland, however, had directed his attention to

art. 'I do not think that European art is superior to Indian art,' Gandhi boasted. 'Both these arts have developed on different lines. Indian art is based entirely on the imagination,' he wrote to a friend; he was probably recalling the Indian statues with many arms and heads. 'European art is an imitation of nature. It is therefore easier to understand but turns our attention to the earth, whereas Indian art, when understood, tends to direct our thoughts to Heaven.'

Then he checked himself. 'This is only for a person like you,' he cautioned. 'I attach no importance to these views. It may be that my unconscious partiality for India or perhaps my ignorance that makes me say this.'

To Gandhi, art had to be spiritual. 'True beauty,' he said in his autobiography, 'consists in purity of heart.'

'Jesus₁[he wrote in *Young India*] was to my mind a supreme artist, because he saw and expressed Truth . . . But I know that many call themselves artists, and are recognized as such, and yet in their work there is absolutely no trace of the soul's upward surge and unrest . . . True art is thus an expression of the soul . . . All true art must help the soul to realize its inner self. In my own case, I find that I can do entirely without external forms in my soul's realization. I can claim, therefore, that there is truly sufficient art in my life, though you might not see what you call works of art about me. My room may have blank walls. And I may even dispense with the roof, so that I may gaze upon the starry heavens overhead that stretch in an unending expanse of beauty . . . Is a woman with fair features necessarily beautiful? . . . Socrates, we are told, was the most truthful man of his time and yet his features are said to have been the ugliest in Greece. To my mind he was beautiful because he was struggling after truth . . . Truth is the first thing to be sought for, and beauty and goodness will then be added unto you . . . True art takes note not merely of form but also of what lies beyond. There is an art that kills and an art that gives life. True art must be evidence of the happiness, contentment and purity of its authors.'

Before Gandhi left Rome he sought out Tolstoy's daughter. As he sat spinning on the floor of her apartment, Princess Maria, a daughter of the King of Italy, entered with a lady-in-waiting, and brought the Mahatma a large basket of figs.

'Her Majesty the Queen packed them for you,' said the lady-in-waiting.

Nobody exploited Gandhi's presence for pro-Fascist purposes although the *Giornale d'Italia* did print an interview with him which he never gave by a journalist he had never seen. Altogether, from Swiss border to the Italian heel, Gandhi spent forty-eight hours in Italy. At Brindisi, he bade farewell to his two Scotland Yard men, but not to Professor and Mrs Edmond Privat.

The professor and his wife were friends of Romain Rolland and accompanied Gandhi from Villeneuve to the Italian frontier. As they were saying goodbye they remarked that they would like some day to visit India. Gandhi asked why they didn't come along with him. They replied that they could not afford it.

'You probably think in terms of first and second class,' Gandhi said, 'but we only pay ten pounds each for our passage on deck, and once there, many Indian friends would open their houses to you.'

The Privats counted the money in their pockets and purse and decided to go. At Rome they bought bedding, sent telegrams to the University of Neuchatel, where the professor taught, that he would not be back for his lectures, and on 14 December boarded the SS *Pilsna* at Brindisi with the Gandhi party. Two weeks later they landed at Bombay.

A mammoth crowd cheered Gandhi's arrival on the morning of 28 December. 'I have come back empty-handed,' he told them, 'but I have not compromised the honour of my country.' That was his summary of how India had fared at the Round Table Conference. But things were blacker than he thought.

CHAPTER 19

Climax

Never was deck passenger accorded such a regal welcome; 'judging from the warmth, cordiality and affection displayed at the reception, one would think that the Mahatma had returned with Swaraj in the hollow of his hand', Subhas Chandra Bose remarked caustically. He had returned with his integrity; he had not stepped down from the role of half-naked fakir who parleyed as an equal with the mighty British Empire. This was the next best thing to freedom, for it reflected the liberation of India's spirit. Since the Salt March, and especially since the Irwin–Gandhi Pact, India felt free. Gandhi fed that feeling, and Indians were grateful. Moreover, their Mahatma had come back safely from the cold world across the sea.

India's partial liberation was achieved in 1930–31, thanks to Gandhi, Irwin and the British Labour government. But Irwin was gone; and in October 1931, Ramsay MacDonald's Labour government had been supplanted by a Cabinet, headed by MacDonald, in which Conservatives predominated. Sir Samuel Hoare, 'an honest and frank-hearted Englishman,' according to Gandhi, and an honest and frank Conservative, was Secretary of State for India.

The new British government proceeded to attack India's new sense of freedom.

A full report was poured into Gandhi's ear from the moment he set foot on the Bombay quay on 28 December. By evening he had a detailed picture of the ugly situation and conveyed it to the two hundred thousand listeners whom he addressed, with the aid of loudspeakers, on the vast Azad Maidan.

Jawaharlal Nehru and Tasadduq Sherwani, Moslem president of the Congress organization of the United Provinces, had been arrested two days earlier while travelling to Bombay to greet Gandhi. Emergency Powers Ordinances had been promulgated early in December in the United Provinces and in the North-west Frontier Province and Bengal to deal with a widespread no-rent movement; they authorized the military to seize buildings, impound bank balances, confiscate wealth, arrest suspects without a warrant, suspend court trials, deny bail and habeas corpus, withdraw mailing privileges from the press, disband political organizations, and prohibit picketing and boycotting. 'We are not playing a game with artificial rules,' Sir Harry Haig, Home Member (Minister of Interior) of the government of India, said in the Assembly. 'The question is whether the Congress is going to impose its will on the whole country.'

'All this,' Gandhi told his Bombay audience, 'I learned after my landing here. I take it these are all Christmas gifts from Lord Willingdon, our Christian Viceroy. For is it not a custom during Christmas to exchange greetings and gifts? Something had to be given me and this is what I have got.' (He had not yet unwrapped all the packages.)

The same evening he spoke to the Welfare of India League in the Hotel Majestic. 'I am not conscious of a single experience throughout my three months' stay in England and Europe,' he asserted, 'that made me feel that after all East is East and West is West. On the contrary, I have been convinced more than ever that human nature is much the same, no matter under what clime it flourishes, and that if you approached people with trust and affection you would have ten-fold trust and thousand-fold affection returned to you.'

The members of the British government were friendly to him; 'we parted as the best of friends . . . But when I come here I find a different order of things altogether . . .' He summarized the extraordinary ordinances. 'The Congress is

charged with trying to run a parallel government . . . I assure
you that I shall strain every nerve to see if I would not tender
co-operation on honourable lines to induce the Government
to withdraw or revise these ordinances.'

The Government had no intention of letting Gandhi offer
anything.

The day after his arrival, Gandhi telegraphed the Viceroy
deploring the ordinances and arrests and suggesting an
interview. The Viceroy's secretary replied on the last day of
the year; the ordinances were justified by the activities of
Congress against the Government. The Viceroy would be
'willing to see you and to give you his views as to the way in
which you can best exert your influence', the secretary said.
'But His Excellency feels bound to emphasize that he will not
be prepared to discuss with you measures which the
Government of India, with the full approval of His Majesty's
Government, have found it necessary to adopt in Bengal, the
United Provinces and the NWFP.'

The British raj would no longer parley with the rebel.

Gandhi's rejoinder defended Congress and intimated that
he might have to start a civil disobedience campaign. The
Viceroy's secretary answered sharply on 2 January, 1932.
'His Excellency and the government', he wrote, 'can hardly
believe that you or the Working Committee [Executive
Committee of Congress] contemplate that His Excellency can
invite you, with the hope of any advantage, to an interview
held under the threat of the resumption of civil
disobedience . . . nor can the Government of India accept the
position implied in your telegram that its policy should be
dependent on the judgement of yourself as to the necessity of
measures which the government has taken . . .'

Willingdon was right. No autocracy can permit a private
citizen or organization to question its acts.

Gandhi replied on the same day. He had not threatened; he
had expressed an opinion. Moreover, he had negotiated with

Irwin, prior to the Delhi Pact, while civil disobedience was actually in progress. He never thought the Government had to depend on his judgement, 'But I do submit,' Gandhi wired, 'that any popular and constitutional government would always welcome and consider sympathetically suggestions made by public bodies and their representatives . . .'

The Government 'has banged the door in my face', Gandhi informed the nation on 3 January. The next day, the Government banged an iron door in his face: he was arrested – again, as after the Salt March, under Regulation XXXV of 1827; again he was His Majesty's guest in Yeravda Jail. A few weeks earlier he had been the guest of His and Her Majesty in Buckingham Palace.

The Government attack on Congress was fierce. Congress organizations were closed and almost all leaders imprisoned; in January, 14,800 persons were jailed for political reasons; in February, 17,800. Winston Churchill declared that the repressive measures were more drastic than any since the 1857 Mutiny.

Mahatma Gandhi enjoyed a special regime in prison. In 1930, in the same Yeravda Jail, the chief warden came to him and asked how many letters he needed to receive from the outside each week.

'I do not need to receive a single letter,' Gandhi replied.

'How many letters do you wish to write?' the warden inquired.

'Not one,' Gandhi said.

He was given unlimited privileges to write and receive correspondence.

Major Martin, the prison governor, brought furniture, crockery and other utensils for Gandhi. 'For whom have you brought all this', Gandhi protested. 'Take it away, please.'

Major Martin said he had permission from the central authorities to spend a minimum of three hundred rupees a month on such an honoured guest. 'That is all very well,'

Gandhi declared, 'but this money comes from the Indian treasury, and I do not want to increase the burdens of my country. I hope that my boarding expenses will not exceed thirty-five rupees a month'. The special equipment was removed.

At Yeravda an official named Quinn asked Gandhi to teach him Gujarati and he used to come every day for his lesson. One morning, Quinn failed to appear, and on inquiry Gandhi was told that the official was busy at a hanging in the prison. 'I feel as though I am going to be sick,' Gandhi said.

Vallabhbhai Patel too was arrested and lodged at Yeravda. In March, Mahadev Desai was transferred from another jail to Yeravda: Gandhi had asked for his companionship. When Mahadev arrived he laid his head on Gandhi's feet, and Gandhi patted his head and shoulders affectionately. The three enjoyed numerous conversations together in which other prisoners and British wardens and physicians sometimes joined.

Gandhi read the newspapers more carefully than he did outside, washed his own clothes, spun, studied the stars at night, and read many books; he liked Upton Sinclair's *The Wet Parade*, Goethe's *Faust*, Kingsley's *Westward Ho!* and others. He also put the finishing touches on a tiny book most of which he had written in Yeravda in 1930 in the form of letters to Sabarmati Ashram. He entitled it *From Yeravda Mandir*; 'mandir' is a temple; the prison was a temple for he worshipped God in it. The booklet, supplemented by occasional articles and pronouncements at other times, furnishes a key to Gandhi's thinking on the nature of God and the ideal conduct of a man.

'God is,' Gandhi said.

The word *satya* means 'truth', and it derives from *sat* which means 'to be'. *Sat* also denotes God. Therefore, God is that which is. 'And since', according to Gandhi, 'nothing else I see merely through the senses can or will persist, He alone is'.

Everything else is illusion. God is the only truth.

Over the years Gandhi tried many times to prove the existence of God. 'There is an indefinable mysterious Power', he wrote, 'which pervades everything. I feel it, though I do not see it. It is this unseen Power which makes itself felt and yet defies all proof, because it is so unlike all that I perceive through my senses. It transcends the senses.

'But', he added optimistically, 'it is possible to reason out the existence of God to a limited extent . . . There is an orderliness in the Universe, there is an unalterable law governing everything and every being that exists or lives. It is not a blind law, for no blind law can govern the conduct of human beings . . . That law then which governs all life is God . . . I do dimly perceive that whilst everything around me is ever changing, ever dying, there is underlying all that change a living Power that is changeless, that holds all together, that creates, dissolves, and recreates. That informing Power or spirit is God . . . In the midst of death life persists, in the midst of untruth truth persists, in the midst of darkness light persists. Hence I gather that God is Life, Truth, and Love. He is Love. He is the supreme God.'

After this valiant rational effort, Gandhi says, 'But He is no God who merely satisfies the intellect, if He ever does. God to be God must rule the heart and transform it. He must express Himself in every smallest act of His votary. This can only be done through a definite realization more real than the five senses can ever produce. Sense perceptions can be, often are, false and deceptive, however real they may appear to us. Where there is realization outside the senses it is infallible. It is proved not by extraneous evidence but in the transformed conduct and character of those who have felt the real presence of God within.'

That was another attempt at proof, this time not by logic but by the palpable testimony of human behaviour. But 'faith transcends reason', he confessed; consequently, 'the safest course is to believe in the moral government of the world and therefore in the supremacy of the moral law, the law of truth and love ... If we could solve all the mysteries of the Universe, we would be co-equal with God. Every drop of ocean shares its glory but is not the ocean'. Every human being, in other words, partakes of the nature of God but is not God and cannot know what He is. Even the greatest Hindu sage, Sankara, did not know more than that God is 'Not this' and 'Not that'.

Except as a youth, Gandhi never doubted the existence of God as Jains and Buddhists may. 'I literally believe', he said, 'that not a blade of grass grows or moves without His will ... God is nearer to us than fingernails to the flesh ... I can tell you this, that I am surer of His existence than of the fact that you and I are sitting in this room ... You may pluck out my eyes, but that cannot kill me. You may chop off my nose, but that will not kill me. But blast my belief in God, and I am dead.'

Gandhi, moreover, was convinced of the large and intimate role which God played in his work. 'Whatever striking things I have done in life', he declared, 'I have not done prompted by reason but prompted by instinct – I would say God. Take the Dandi Salt March of 1930. I had not the ghost of a suspicion how the breach of the Salt Law would work itself out. Pandit Motilalji and other friends were fretting and did not know what I would do, and I could tell them nothing as I myself knew nothing about it. But like a flash it came, and as you know it was enough to shake the country from one end to the other.'

'Do you feel a sense of freedom in your communion with God?' someone asked.

'I do,' Gandhi replied. 'I have imbibed through and through the teaching of the *Gita* that man is the maker of his own destiny in the sense that he has freedom of choice as to the manner in which he uses that freedom. But he is no controller of results. The moment he thinks he is, he comes to grief.

'I have no special revelation of God's will', Gandhi explained. 'My firm belief is that He reveals Himself daily to every human being, but we shut our ears to the "still small voice" . . . God never appears to you in person but in action.'

How did Gandhi worship God? He believed in the efficacy of prayer. 'Prayer is the key of the morning and the bolt of the evening . . . As food is necessary for the body, prayer is necessary for the soul . . . No act of mine is done without prayer . . . I am not a man of learning, but I humbly claim to be a man of prayer. I am indifferent to the form. Every man is a law unto himself in that respect.' But 'it is better in prayer to have a heart without words than words without a heart'. One can pray in the silence that has banished words.

Nevertheless, the highway to God was through action. For ten days Gandhi and E. Stanley Jones, an American missionary, discussed a variety of topics, chiefly religion. One day Gandhi said, 'If one is to find salvation, he must have as much patience as a man who sits by the seaside and with a straw picks up a single drop of water, transfers it and thus empties the ocean.' Salvation, according to Gandhi, comes – as Dr Jones understood it – 'through one's strict, disciplined efforts, a rigid, self-mastery'.

'But I,' E. Stanley Jones declares, 'look on salvation, not as an attainment through one's efforts, but as an obtainment through grace. I came to God morally and spiritually bankrupt with nothing to offer except my bankruptcy. To my astonishment He took me, forgave me, and sent my soul singing its way down the years. By grace was I saved through faith, and that not of myself; it was the gift of God . . . It was at this point that the Christians and the Mahatma never got together.

'I know,' Dr Jones adds, 'that salvation by grace seems too cheap and easy, but it is not cheap; for when you take the gift, you belong for ever to the Giver.'

Gandhi took the hard road. His doctrine was: By their works shall ye know them. His God required him to live for humanity. 'If I could persuade myself', Gandhi wrote, 'that I should find Him in a Himalayan cave I would proceed there immediately. But I know I cannot find him apart from humanity . . . I claim to know my millions. All the hours of the day I am with them. They are my first care and last because I recognize no God except that God that is to be found in the hearts of the dumb millions.'

Gandhi's relation with God was part of a triangle which included his fellow man. On this triangle he based his system of ethics and morality.

The first duty of the God-worshipper is truth: for truth is God. This Gandhi repeated thousands of times: 'Truth is God.'

'There should be Truth in thought, Truth in speech and Truth in action,' Gandhi wrote in *From Yeravda Mandir*. 'Devotion to Truth is the sole justification of our existence.' This Truth is honesty, and also something else: 'It is impossible for us to realize perfect Truth so long as we are imprisoned in this mortal frame . . . if we shatter the chains of egotism, and melt into the ocean of humanity, we share its dignity. To feel that we are something is to set up a barrier between God and ourselves; to cease feeling that we are something is to become one with God. A drop in the ocean partakes of the greatness of its parent, although it is unconscious of it. But it is dried up as soon as it enters upon an existence independent of the ocean.'

Truth is identification with God and humanity. From Truth, non-violence is born. Truth appears different to different individuals. 'There is nothing wrong in every man following Truth according to his lights,' says *From Yeravda Mandir*. Each person must be true to his own truth. But if the seeker after Truth began to destroy those who saw Truth in their way he would recede from the Truth. How can one realize God by killing or hurting? Non-violence, however, is more than peacefulness or pacifism; it is love, and excludes evil thought, undue haste, lies, or hatred.

First, Truth; second, non-violence or Love; and third, chastity. 'If a man gives his love to one woman, or a woman to a man, what is there left for all the world besides? It simply means "We two first, and the devil take the rest of them." . . . Such persons cannot rise to the height of Universal Love.'

Then are married people lost for ever? No, 'if the married couple can think of each other as brother and sister, they are freed for universal service'. This is the maximum programme for the monks and nuns of the ashram. For the rank and file of humanity 'Sex urge is a fine and noble thing. There is nothing to be ashamed of in it. But it is meant only for the act of creation. Any other use of it is a sin against God and humanity . . . Indulgence interfered with my work.'

The next injunction to the ashramites is 'Non-stealing' which implies non-possession. 'Civilization, in the real sense of the term, consists not in the multiplication, but in the deliberate and voluntary reduction of wants . . .

'Anxiety about the future,' Gandhi said to a friend, 'is sheer atheism. Why should we fear that our children will be less efficent or successful than we are? To save money for the sake of children is to show lack of faith in them,' and in God. Attachment to money or possessions is the product of fear. Violence is the result of fear. Dishonesty is fear. Fearlessness is the key to Truth, to God, to Love; it is the king of virtues.

The remaining virtues are: the removal of untouchability which 'means love for, and service of, the whole world'; 'bread-labour' or regular productive manual work; tolerance of all religions; humility; and, finally, spinning and the encouragement of domestic national economy without 'ill-will towards the foreigner.'

Few inside or outside the ashram ever lived up to Gandhi's austere code; only he approached his ideal.

*   *   *

While Gandhi was editing these simple epistles on God and ethics in his prison-'temple', India moved towards its tensest fortnight in modern history.

It centred around saving Gandhi's life.

'To find a parallel for the anguish of September 1932', wrote Rajagopalachari, 'we have to go back to Athens twenty-three centuries ago when the friends of Socrates surrounded him in prison and importuned him to escape from death. Plato has recorded the questions and answers. Socrates smiled at the suggestion . . . and preached the immortality of the soul.'

The 'Anguish of September 1932' began for Gandhi early that year. He had gathered from the newspapers that the proposed new British constitution of India would grant separate electorates not only to Hindus and Moslems as in the past but to untouchables, or 'Depressed Classes'. He accordingly wrote a letter on 11 March, 1932, to Sir Samuel Hoare, the Secretary of State for India.

'A separate electorate for the Depressed Classes', Gandhi wrote, 'is harmful for them and for Hinduism . . . So far as Hinduism is concerned, separate electorates would simply vivisect and disrupt it . . . The political aspect, important though it is, dwindles into insignificance compared to the moral and religious issue.' If therefore the Government decided to create a separate electorate for untouchables, 'I must fast unto death'. That, he knew, would embarrass the authorities whose prisoner he was, but 'for me the contemplated step is not a method, it is part of my being.'

The minister replied to the prisoner on 13 April, saying that no decision had yet been taken and that his views would be considered before it was taken.

No new developments occurred until 17 August, 1932, when Prime Minister Ramsay MacDonald announced Britain's decision in favour of separate electorates.

'I have to resist your decision with my life,' Gandhi wrote to

Ramsay MacDonald the next day. 'The only way I can do it is by declaring a perpetual fast unto death from food of any kind save water with or without salt and soda.' The fast would commence at noon, 20 September.

In a very long reply, dated 10 Downing Street, 8 September 1932, Prime Minister MacDonald said he had received Gandhi's communication 'with much surprise and, let me add, with very sincere regret'. Gandhi had misunderstood; they had considered his known friendship for the untouchables and his letter to Sir Samuel Hoare. 'We felt it our duty to safeguard what we believed to be the right of the Depressed Classes to a fair proportion of representation in the legislature' and 'we were equally careful to do nothing that would split off their community from the Hindu world.'

Then MacDonald cogently defended the Government's decision: 'Under the government scheme the Depressed Classes will remain part of the Hindu community and will vote with the Hindu electorate on an equal footing.' That is what Gandhi wanted. 'But for the first twenty years, while still remaining part of the Hindu community, they will receive through a limited number of special constituencies, means of safeguarding their rights and interests . . .'

In other words, MacDonald emphasized, the untouchables would have one vote in the Hindu electorate, and many of them would have a second vote in their special untouchable electorate. They will 'have two votes', he wrote. Surely Gandhi, their champion, could not object.

The alternative method, 'reservation of seats', MacDonald declared, had been rejected because, though it would reserve a number of seats for untouchable legislators within the larger block of Hindu seats, 'in practically all cases, such members would be elected by a majority consisting of higher caste Hindus'. That being the case, the Prime Minister implied, they might be stooges of caste Hindus: they would have to keep in the good graces of caste Hindus, and might not be 'in a position to speak for themselves'.

So, MacDonald reasoned, 'you propose to adopt the extreme course of starving yourself to death not in order to secure that the Depressed Classes should have joint electorates with other Hindus, because that is already provided, nor to maintain the unity of Hindus, which is also provided, but solely to prevent the Depressed Classes, who admittedly suffer from terrible disabilities today, from being able to secure a limited number of representatives of their own choosing to speak on their behalf in the legislatures . . .' Therefore, MacDonald could only think that Gandhi's proposal to fast was based on a misapprehension. The Government's decision would stand.

Gandhi's letter of 9 September, from Yeravda Central Prison to 10 Downing Street, was typical.

Without arguing, I affirm that to me this matter is one of pure religion. The mere fact of the Depressed Classes having double votes does not protect them or Hindu society in general from being disrupted. You will please permit me to say that no matter how sympathetic you may be, you cannot come to a correct decision on a matter of vital and religious importance to the parties concerned. I should not be against even over-representation of the Depressed Classes. What I am against is their statutory separation, even in a limited form, from the Hindu fold, so long as they choose to belong to it. Do you realize that if your decision stands and the constitution comes into being, you arrest the marvellous growth of the work of Hindu reformers who have dedicated themselves to their suppressed brethren in every walk of life?

Gandhi added that he was also opposed to the other separate electorates 'only I do not consider them to be any warrant for calling from me such self-immolation as my conscience has prompted me in the matter of the Depressed Classes'.

That ended Gandhi's correspondence with London.

MacDonald was not alone in his bewilderment. Many

Indians, some Hindus, were perplexed. Jawaharlal Nehru was in prison when he heard Gandhi would fast. 'I felt angry with him', he writes in his autobiography, 'at his religious and sentimental approach to a political issue, and his frequent references to God in connection with it.' Nehru 'felt annoyed with him for choosing a side issue for his final sacrifice'. Untouchability was a side issue, independence the central issue. For two days, Nehru 'was in darkness'. He thought with sorrow of never seeing Bapu any more.

'Then a strange thing happened to me,' Nehru continues, 'I had quite an emotional crisis, and at the end of it I felt calmer, and the future seemed not so dark. Bapu had a curious knack of doing the right thing at the psychological moment, and it might be that his action – impossible as it was from my point of view – would lead to great results not only in the narrow field in which it was confined, but in the wider aspects of our national struggle . . . Then came the news of the tremendous upheaval all over the country . . . What a magician, I thought, was this little man sitting in Yeravda Prison, and how well he knew how to pull the strings that move people's hearts.'

Even Nehru had underestimated Gandhi's magic and Gandhi's political sagacity.

The Government's fierce repressions against the civil resisters were breaking the back of the movement; it was petering out into pessimism. Gandhi's fast rescued nationalist India from the political doldrums. But compared with the big result, this was a minor by-product.

All Gandhi's adult life he had fought against the 'bar sinister' between caste Hindus and Harijans; even as a boy he laughed at his mother's idea that the touch of an untouchable defiles. Now the British Empire was erecting a political reservation for Harijans. With his congenital impulse to assume the best motives, he was ready to believe that MacDonald and Hoare were acting in the interest, as they saw it, of the Depressed Classes. But he knew India better. Legalisms do not make life; Hindus and Harijans might form a joint electorate, but the Harijans' additional separate electorate would blot out the good psychological effect of the joint electorate. Given a separate electorate, Harijan candidates and elected representatives would stress what divided them from the caste Hindus. A political machine would arise with a vested interest in perpetuating the rift between Harijans and caste Hindus; its political capital would be Hindu injustice. Gandhi felt passionately that untouchability was a perversion which would kill the soul of Hinduism and, in turn, poison the soul of the Harijans. The MacDonald award threatened to give long life to India's worst sin.

Harmony in diversity, love despite differences, was Gandhi's way of eliminating violence in thought and action. To divide is to invite war. Gandhi had fasted for Hindu–Moslem unity; he did not want two Indias. Now he was faced with the prospect of three Indias. He regarded Hindu–Moslem enmity as politically disastrous. The Hindu–Harijan division was politically disastrous and religiously suicidal. Gandhi could not countenance the widening of the Hindu–Harijan gulf.

The fast, Gandhi said, 'is aimed at a statutory separate electorate, in any shape or form, for the Depressed Classes. Immediately that threat is removed once for all, my fast will end'. He was not fasting against the British, for the Government had stated that if Hindus and Harijans agreed on a different and mutually satisfactory voting arrangement it would be accepted. The fast, Gandhi declared, 'is intended to sting Hindu conscience into right religious action'.

On 13 September Gandhi announced that he would commence his fast un.to death on the 20th. India now witnessed something the world had never seen.

On the 13th, political and religious leaders went into

action. Mr M. C. Rajah, an untouchable spokesman in the
Legislative Assembly, identified himself with Gandhi's
position; Sir Tej Bahadur Sapru, the great constitutional
leader, petitioned the Government to release Gandhi; Yakub
Husain, a Moslem leader in Madras, urged the Harijans to
renounce the separate electorate; Rajendra Prasad suggested
that Hindus save Gandhi by giving Harijans access to their
temples, wells, schools and the public roads; Pandit Malaviya
convoked a conference of leaders for the 19th; Rajagopalachari asked the country to pray and fast on the 20th.

Several deputations asked to see Gandhi in jail. The
Government opened the gates and allowed full consultations
with him. Devadas Gandhi arrived to act as intermediary
with negotiators. Journalists also enjoyed unobstructed access
to Gandhi.

Meanwhile Gandhi wrote copious letters to many friends in
India and abroad. 'There was no escape from it,' he said in a
letter to Miss Slade. 'It is both a privilege and a duty. It comes
rarely to someone in a generation or generations.' He had
been observing the cat family in the prison, he told Miss Slade
in the same communication. 'We have an addition to the
family, did I tell you? There was a human touch about the
mother whilst she was in pain and two or three days after
delivery. She would caress us and insist on being caressed. It
was a pathetic sight. The care she bestows on the "baby" is
very wonderful. Love from us all to you all, Bapu.'

On the 20th, Gandhi awoke at 2.30 A.M. and wrote a letter to
Tagore whose approval he craved. 'This is early morning, 3
o'clock of Tuesday,' the Mahatma began. 'I enter the fiery
gates at noon. If you can bless the effort I want it. You have
been a true friend because you have been a candid friend
often speaking your thoughts aloud . . . Though it can now
only be during my fast, I will yet prize your criticism, if your
heart condemns my action. I am not too proud to make an
open confession of my blunder, whatever the cost of the

confession, if I find myself in error. If your heart approves of the action I want your blessing. It will sustain me . . .'

Just as Gandhi posted this letter he received a telegram from Tagore: 'It is worth sacrificing precious life', it read, 'for the sake of India's unity and her social integrity . . . I fervently hope that we will not callously allow such national tragedy to reach its extreme length stop our sorrowing hearts will follow your sublime penance with reverence and love.'

Gandhi thanked Tagore for 'your loving and magnificent wire. It will sustain me in the midst of the storm I am about to enter'.

At 11.30 the same morning, Gandhi took his last meal; it consisted of lemon juice and honey with hot water. Millions of Indians fasted for twenty-four hours. Throughout the country prayers were sung.

That day, Rabindranath Tagore, whom India and Gandhi affectionately called 'The Poet', addressed his school at Shantiniketan and said, 'A shadow is darkening today over India like a shadow cast by an eclipsed sun. The people of a whole country is suffering from a poignant pain of anxiety, the universality of which carries in it a great dignity of consolation. Mahatmaji, who through his life of dedication has made India his own in truth, has commenced his vow of extreme self-sacrifice.'

Tagore explained the Mahatma's fast:

'Each country has its own inner geography where her spirit dwells and where physical force can never conquer even an inch of ground. Those rulers who come from the outside remain outside the gate . . . But the great soul . . . continues his dominion even when he is physically no longer present . . . The penance which Mahatmaji has taken upon himself is not a ritual but a message to all India and to the world . . . Let us try to understand the meaning of his message . . . No civilized society can thrive upon victims whose humanity has been permanently mutilated . . . Those whom we keep down inevitably drag us down . . . we insult our own humanity by insulting man where he is helpless and where he is not of our own kin . . . Mahatmaji has repeatedly pointed out the danger of those divisions in our country . . . Against that deep-seated moral weakness in our society Mahatmaji has pronounced his ultimatum . . . We have observed that the English people are puzzled at the step that Mahatmaji has been compelled to take. They confess that they fail to understand it. I believe that the reason of their failure is mainly owing to the fact that the language of Mahatmaji is fundamentally different from their own . . . I ask them to remember the terrible days of atrocities that reddened in blood at their door when dismemberment was being forced between Ireland and the rest of Great Britain. Those Englishmen, who imagined it to be disastrous to the integrity of their empire, did not scruple to kill and be killed, even to tear into shreds the decency of civilized codes of honour.'

The British, Tagore explained, were ready to indulge in the 'Black and Tan' blood bath in Ireland to prevent dismemberment of the Empire. Gandhi was immolating one person, himself, to prevent dismemberment of Indian society. This was the language of non-violence. Is that why the West could not decipher it?

Tagore saw the possibility of losing Gandhi in the fast. The very thought sent a shiver through the spine of the nation. If nothing were done to save him, every Hindu would be Mahatmaji's murderer.

Gandhi lay on a white iron cot in the shade of a low mango tree in the quiet prison yard. Patel and Mahadev Desai sat near him. Mrs Naidu had been transferred from the women's ward of Yeravda Jail to nurse and guard him from excessive exertion. On a stool were some books, writing paper, bottles of water, salt and soda bicarbonate.

Outside, the negotiators in conference were racing with

death. Hindu leaders gathered in Birla House in Bombay on
20 September. There were Sapru, Sir Chunilal Mehta,
Rajagopalachari, the president of Congress for that year, G.
D. Birla, a very wealthy industrialist and friend of Gandhi,
Rajendra Prasad, Jayakar, Sir Purshottamdas Thakurdas, a
millionaire patron of schools, and others. The untouchable
delegates were Dr Solanki and Dr Ambedkar.

Ambedkar, a distinguished lawyer with international
experience who had played a big part at the Round Table
Conferences in London, owned a powerfully built body and
strong, stubborn, superior intellect. His father and
grandfather saw service in the British Army. The
accumulated bitterness against Hindus that rankled for
centuries in millions of Harijan breasts found expression in
Ambedkar's Himalayan hatred. He preferred British raj to
Hindu raj; he preferred Moslems to Hindus and once thought
of leading the untouchable community, as a body, into the
Mohammedan Church. Age-long Hindu cruelty to his
unhappy brethren filled him with anger, spite and
vindictiveness. If anybody in India could have contemplated
with equanimity the death of Gandhi, Ambedkar was the
man. He called the fast 'a political stunt'. At the conference,
he faced the great Hindu minds, and he must have derived
sweet pleasure watching them court him in order to save their
beloved Mahatma.

Gandhi had always wanted one electorate for Hindus and
Harijans, which would jointly elect a solid block of Hindu and
Harijan members of the legislative councils. He even
opposed reserving a fixed number of seats in that block for
Harijans because it would accentuate the cleavage between
the two communities. But on the 19th Gandhi told a
deputation – much to its relief – that he had become
reconciled to reserved seats.

Ambedkar, however, demurred: the Harijans who would
occupy the reserved seats in the legislatures would be elected

jointly by Hindus and Harijans and would, therefore, feel
considerable restraint in airing Harijan grievances against
Hindus. If a Harijan denounced Hindus too fiercely the
Hindus might defeat him in the next election and elect a more
docile untouchable.

To meet this legitimate objection, Sapru had evolved an
ingenious plan which he presented to the conference on 20
September: all Hindu and Harijan members of the
legislatures would be elected jointly by Hindu and Harijan
voters. A number of the Hindu–Harijan seats would be
earmarked in advance for Harijans. The candidates for a
portion of these reserved Harijan seats would be nominated in
private consultations between Hindus and Harijans. But for
the remainder of the reserved seats, Sapru introduced
something new: primaries in which only Harijans would vote.
In those primary elections, a panel of three Harijan
candidates would be chosen for each reserved seat. Then in
the final or secondary elections, Harijans and Hindus would
vote jointly for one of those three Harijan candidates. The
Hindus would have no choice but to vote for one of them.
That would enable the Harijans to place their bravest and
best champions in the legislatures while retaining the system
of joint electorates.

Anxiously, the Hindus waited for Ambedkar's views on the
scheme. He examined it minutely. He sought the advice of
friends. Hours drifted by. Finally he accepted, but stated that
he would draft his own formula to incorporate his own ideas
plus the Sapru plan.

Encouraged, but still not quite sure of Ambedkar, the
Hindu leaders now wondered about Gandhi; would he
sanction the Sapru innovation? Sapru, Jayakar, Rajagopalachari, Devadas, Birla and Prasad took the midnight train
and were in Poona the next morning. At 7 A.M. they were taken
into the prison office. Gandhi, already weak after less than
twenty-four hours without food, came into the office with a

laugh, and taking a place at the centre of the table, announced cheerfully, 'I preside'.

Sapru explained the plan of the primaries. Others amplified. Gandhi asked some questions. He was non-committal. Half an hour passed. Finally Gandhi said, 'I am prepared to consider your plan favourably . . . But I should like to have the whole picture before me in writing.' In addition, he asked to see Ambedkar and Rajah.

Urgent invitations were sent to Ambedkar and Rajah. A memorandum on the Sapru plan was prepared. Rajah, representing Gandhi's untouchables following, accepted it. Ambedkar promised to come.

A troubled night passed. The morning of the 22nd Gandhi expressed displeasure with the scheme: Why should only some candidates for the reserved Harijan seats be elected in the Harijan primaries? Why not all? Why create two sets of Harijan candidates, one chosen by Harijans in the primaries, the other selected by Hindus and Harijans? He wanted no distinctions between Harijans. Nor did he want Harijan legislators to be under any political debt to Hindus.

The negotiators were overjoyed. Gandhi was offering Ambedkar more than Ambedkar had already accepted.

Ambedkar appeared at Gandhi's cot late that afternoon; he did most of the talking. He was ready to help to save the Mahatma's life, he said. But 'I want my compensation'.

Gandhi had already commenced to sink. In previous fasts he had taken water regularly, on the hour. Now he was listless and drank it irregularly. In previous fasts, massage moderated his aches. This time he refused massage. Sharp pains racked his wasting body. He had to be moved to the bath on a stretcher. The least movement, sometimes even speaking, gave him nausea.

When Ambedkar said, 'I want my compensation,' Gandhi propped himself up painfully and spoke for many minutes. He mentioned his devotion to the Harijans. He discussed the

Sapru scheme point by point. He did not like it, he said. All Harijans should be nominated by Harijans and not just some of them, Gandhi declared. Weakened by the effort, the Mahatma subsided to his pillow.

Ambedkar had expected to be put under pressure in the presence of the dying Mahatma to recede from his position. But now Gandhi out-Harijaned the Harijan Ambedkar.

Ambedkar welcomed Gandhi's amendment.

That day, Mrs Gandhi arrived; she had been transferred from Sabarmati Prison to Yeravda. As she slowly moved towards her husband, she shook her head from side to side reprovingly and said, 'Again, the same story!' He smiled. Her presence cheered him. He submitted to massage by her, and by a professional, more for her sake than because he wanted it.

Friday, 23 September, the fourth day of the fast, Dr Gilder, Gandhi's heart specialist, and Dr Patel came from Bombay, and in consultation with prison physicians diagnosed the prisoner's condition as dangerous. Blood pressure was alarmingly high. Death was possible at any moment.

The same day, Ambedkar conferred at length with the Hindu leaders and presented his new demands for compensation: MacDonald's award had given the Depressed Classes 71 seats in the provincial legislatures. Ambedkar asked for 197. Sapru had suggested a panel of three Harijan candidates. Gandhi suggested five; Ambedkar suggested two. There was also the question of a referendum of Harijan voters to decide when the reserved seats should be abolished and the political distinction thus wiped out between Hindus and Harijans; that would be a step towards the merger of the two communities in life. Gandhi wanted the primaries abolished after five years. Ambedkar held out for fifteen. Ambedkar did not believe that untouchability would be destroyed in five years.

Later in the day, Ambedkar came to Gandhi. It was a hot sultry day and not a mango leaf stirred in the prison yard.

Gandhi's blood pressure was rising. He could hardly speak above a whisper. Ambedkar bargained hard. The outcome was indecisive.

Saturday, 24 September, the fifth day, Ambedkar renewed his talks with the Hindu leaders. After a morning's wrangling, he visited Gandhi at noon. It had been agreed between Ambedkar and the Hindus that the Depressed Classes would have 147 reserved seats instead of the 197 Ambedkar had demanded and the 71 MacDonald ordered. Gandhi accepted the compromise. Ambedkar was now ready to abolish the separate primaries after ten years. Gandhi insisted on five. 'Five years or my life,' Gandhi said. Ambedkar refused.

Ambedkar returned to his Harijan colleagues. Later, he informed the Hindu leaders that he would not accept the abolition of primaries in five years: nothing less than ten.

Rajagopalachari now did something which probably saved Gandhi's life. Without consulting Gandhi, he and Ambedkar agreed that the time of the abolition of the primaries would be determined in further discussion. This might make a referendum superfluous.

Rajagopalachari rushed to the jail and explained the new arrangement to Gandhi.

'Will you repeat it?'

Rajagopalachari repeated it.

'Excellent,' Gandhi murmured; he may not have understood precisely what Rajagopalachari was saying; he was faint. But he had acquiesced.

That Saturday, the Yeravda Pact, as Indian history knows it, was drafted and signed by all the chief Hindu and Harijan negotiators except Gandhi.

On Sunday it was ratified in Bombay at a full conference of the negotiators and others.

But the pact was no pact and Gandhi would not abandon his fast unless the British government consented to substitute it for the MacDonald Award. Its verbatim text had been telegraphed to London where Charles Andrews, Polak and other friends of Gandhi laboured to get quick action from the Government. It was Sunday and ministers had left town, and Ramsay MacDonald was in Sussex attending a funeral.

On hearing of the agreement in Poona, MacDonald hurried back to 10 Downing Street; so did Sir Samuel Hoare and Lord Lothian who had helped to formulate the MacDonald Award. They pored over the text until midnight on Sunday.

Gandhi's life was fast ebbing away. He told Kasturbai who should get the few personal belongings that lay around his cot. Early Monday, Tagore arrived from Calcutta and sang a selection of his own songs to the Mahatma. They soothed Gandhi. Friends from Poona were admitted to play on musical instruments and chant devotional hymns. He thanked them with a nod and a faint smile. He could not speak.

A few hours later, the British government announced simultaneously in London and New Delhi that it had approved the Yeravda Pact. Gandhi could break his fast.

At 5.15 on Monday afternoon, in the presence of Tagore, Patel, Mahadev Desai, Mrs Naidu, the negotiators and journalists, Gandhi accepted a glass of orange juice from Kasturbai and broke his fast. Tagore sang Bengali hymns. Many eyes were wet.

Dr Ambedkar made an interesting speech at the Bombay conference on Sunday, 25 September, which ratified the Yeravda Pact or Poona Agreement. Praising Gandhi's conciliatory attitude, Ambedkar said, 'I must confess that I was surprised, immensely surprised, when I met him, that there was so much in common between him and me. In fact whenever any disputes were carried to him – and Sir Tej Bahadur Sapru has told you that the disputes that were carried to him were of a very crucial character – I was astounded to see that the man who held such divergent views

from mine at the Round Table Conference came immediately
to my rescue and not to the rescue of the other side. I am very
grateful to Mahatmaji for having extricated me from what
might have been a very difficult situation.'

This was not only a polite tribute at a moment of relaxation
after hectic days, but also a correct description of Gandhi's
attitude. Gandhi did favour the Harijan position over the
Hindu position. Indeed, Gandhi had gone so far in his desire
to meet the Harijans 100 per cent of the way, that he reversed
himself on the key issue of reserved seats. 'My only regret is,'
Dr Ambedkar stated in that same speech, 'why did not
Mahatmaji take this attitude at the Round Table
Conference? If he had shown the same consideration for my
point of view then, it would not have been necessary for him to
go through this ordeal. However,' he added generously, 'these
are things of the past. I am glad that I am here now to support
this resolution' of ratification.

At the Round Table Conference in September–December
1931, Gandhi had opposed Harijan reserved seats in the
Hindu block because it divided the two communities. But on
13 September, 1932, and again on the 19th, Gandhi had
accepted the idea of reserved seats as an unavoidable and, he
hoped, passing evil.

He accepted the reservation of seats as something infinitely
preferable to the segregation that would arise out of the
separate electorate which MacDonald wanted to introduce.
But if Gandhi had done so at the Round Table Conference or
months before the fast he might not have carried the orthodox
Hindus with him. One of the negotiators of the Poona
Agreement subsequently told me that he had always opposed
Gandhi's policies, but Gandhi was God descended to earth
and 'the gates of Heaven were waiting to receive him'. The
threat of the Mahatma's death won over the Hindu leaders
for Gandhi's policies.

Suppose, however, that the Hindu leaders had adopted

reservation of seats before the fast. Would the fast have been superfluous? Was the Mahatma's torment unnecessary?

The answer to this question is crucial to an understanding of Gandhi's role in India's history. By the criterion of cold logic and arid legalisms, Gandhi need not have fasted to reach an agreement with Ambedkar. But Gandhi's relationship with the Indian people was not based on logic and legalism. It was a highly emotional relationship. For the Hindus, Gandhi was Mahatma, The Great Soul, a piece of God. Were they going to kill him? The moment the fast began, texts, constitutions, awards, elections, etc., lost their significance. Gandhi's life had to be saved.

From 13 September, when the fast was announced, to the afternoon of 26 September, when Gandhi drank his first orange juice, every change in Gandhi's physical condition, every word pronounced by anyone who had seen him, every journey of the least of the negotiators was broadcast to every corner of the country. A mother hovering over the crib of a tender child during a high-temperature crisis could be no more anxious than the India that watched the white cot of the sinking Mahatma. No mystic himself, Gandhi affected others mystically. They became one with him, as one as mother and babe. Reason withdrew; passionately, frantically, because the end might have come at any instant, Hindus were reacting to a single throbbing wish: The Mahatma must not die.

Gandhi had made each Hindu personally responsible for his life. On 15 September, in a statement widely disseminated, Gandhi said, 'No patched-up agreement between Caste Hindus and rival Depressed Class leaders will answer the purpose. The agreement to be valid has to be real. If the Hindu mass mind is not yet prepared to banish untouchability root and branch it must sacrifice me without the slightest hesitation.'

While the negotiators parleyed, therefore, the Hindu community – close to a quarter of a billion persons –

experienced a religious–emotional upheaval. At the very beginning of the fast week, the famous Kalighat Temple of Calcutta and the Ram Mandir of Benares, citadel of Hindu orthodoxy, were thrown open to untouchables. In Delhi, Caste Hindus and Harijans demonstratively fraternized in streets and temples. In Bombay, a nationalist women's organization organized a poll in front of seven big temples. Ballot boxes, watched by volunteers, were placed outside the gates, and worshippers were asked to cast their votes on the admission of untouchables. The tally was 24,797 for, 445 against. As a result, temples in which no Harijan foot had ever trod were opened to all.

The day before the fast started, twelve temples in Allahabad were made accessible to Harijans for the first time; on the first day of the fast, some of the most sacred temples throughout the country opened their doors to untouchables. Every subsequent day, until 26 September, and then every day from the 27th to 2 October, Gandhi's birthday, which was Anti-Untouchability Week, scores of holy places lowered the bars against Harijans. All temples in the native states of Baroda, Kashmir, Bhor and Kolhapur cancelled temple discrimination. The newspapers printed the names of the hundreds of temples that lifted the ban under the impact of Gandhi's fast.

Mrs Swarup Rani Nehru, Jawaharlal's very orthodox mother, let it be known that she had accepted food from the hand of an untouchable. Thousands of prominent Hindu women followed her example. At the strictly Hindu Benares University, Principal Dhruva, with numerous Brahmans, dined publicly with street cleaners, cobblers and scavengers. Similar meals were arranged in hundreds of other places.

In villages, small towns and big cities, congregations, organizations, citizens' unions, etc., adopted resolutions promising to stop discriminating against untouchables; copies of these resolutions formed a man-high heap in Gandhi's prison-yard.

Villages and small towns allowed untouchables to use water wells. Hindu pupils shared benches formerly reserved for untouchables. Roads and streets, from which they were previously excluded, were opened to Harijans.

A spirit of reform, penance and self-purification swept the land. During the six fast days, most Hindus refrained from going to cinemas, theatres, or restaurants. Weddings were postponed.

A cold political agreement between Gandhi and Ambedkar, without a fast, would have had no such effect on the nation; it might have redressed a legal Harijan grievance, but it would have remained a dead letter as far as the Hindu's personal treatment of untouchables was concerned. Most Hindus would never have heard of it. The political pact was important only after the emotional churning which Gandhi's fast gave the country.

The fast could not kill the curse of untouchability, which was more than three thousand years old. Access to a temple is not access to a good job. The Harijans remained the dregs of Indian society. Nor did segregation end when Gandhi slowly drank his orange juice.

But after the fast, untouchability forfeited its public approval; the belief in it was destroyed. A practice deeply imbedded in a complicated religion full of mystic overtones and undercurrents was recognized as morally illegitimate. A taboo hallowed by custom, tradition and ritual lost its potency. It had been socially improper to consort with Harijans; in many circles now it became socially improper not to consort with them. To practise untouchability branded one a bigot, a reactionary. Before long, marriages were taking place between Harijans and Hindus; Gandhi made a point of attending some.

Gandhi's 'Epic Fast' snapped a long chain that stretched back into antiquity and had enslaved tens of millions. Some links of the chain remained. Many wounds from the chain remained. But nobody would forge new links, nobody would link the links together again. The future promised freedom.

The Yeravda Pact said, 'No one shall be regarded as untouchable by reason of his birth . . .' Orthodox Hindus, with large religious followings, signed that statement. It marked a religious reformation, a psychological revolution. Hinduism was purging itself of a millennial sickness. The mass purified itself in practice. It was good for India's moral health. The perpetuation of untouchability would have poisoned India's soul just as the retention of its economic remnants must hamper India's progress.

If Gandhi had done nothing else in his life but shatter the structure of untouchability he would have been a great social reformer. In retrospect, the wrestling with Ambedkar over seats, primaries and referendums seems like that year's melted snow on the Himalayas. The real reform was religious and social, not political.

Five days after the end of the fast Gandhi's weight had gone up to ninety-nine and three-quarter pounds, and he was spinning and working for many hours. 'The fast was really nothing compared with the miseries that the outcasts have undergone for ages,' he wrote to Miss Slade. 'And so', he added, 'I continue to hum "God is great and merciful".'

He remained in prison.

Gandhi's fast touched Hindu India's heart. Gandhi had a compelling need to communicate with the hearts of men; he had an artist's genius for reaching the heart strings of the inner man. But how does one communicate with a hundred or two hundred or three hundred million persons most of whom are illiterate and only five thousand of whom have radios? Gandhi's fasts were means of communication. The news of the fast was printed in all papers. Those who read told those who did not read that 'The Mahatma is fasting'. The cities knew, and peasants marketing in the cities knew, and they carried the report to the villages, and travellers did likewise.

'Why is the Mahatma fasting?'

'So that we Hindus open our temples to the untouchables and treat the untouchables better.'

India's ear was listening for more news.

'The Mahatma is sinking.' 'The Mahatma is dying.' 'We must hurry.'

Gandhi's agony gave vicarious pain to his adorers who knew they must not kill God's messenger on earth. It was evil to prolong his suffering. It was blessed to save him by being good to those whom he had called 'The Children of God'.

CHAPTER 20

Without Politics

The 'Epic Fast' enabled Gandhi to break through a thick, high wall into the immense neglected field of social reform. Many of his friends were unhappy because he allowed himself to be 'sidetracked' into welfare work for Harijans and peasants. Politicians wanted him to be political. But to Gandhi vitamins for villages were the best politics and Harijan happiness the highroad to independence.

Social reform was ever his favoured activity. 'I have always held', he declared on 25 January, 1942, in *Harijan*, 'that a parliamentary programme at all times is the least of a nation's activity. The most important and permanent work is done outside.' He wanted the individual to do more so that the State would do less. The more work at the bottom, the less dictation from the top.

Gandhi's revulsion against government was indeed so strong that he promised in the 27 April, 1940, *Harijan* not to participate in the government of free India. He would do his share, he said, 'outside the official world'. He was too religious to identify himself with any government.

This being Gandhi's philosophy, he depended for the success of his social reform work on special-purpose voluntary organizations with many active members.

In February 1933, Gandhi, still in prison, had started the Harijan Sevak Sangh, a society to help Harijans, and *Harijan*, a new weekly which replaced *Young India*, suspended by the Government. On 8 May, he undertook a three weeks' fast for self-purification and to impress the ashram with the importance of service rather than indulgence; the presence of an attractive American woman visitor had caused some backsliding. The first day of the fast the Government released him. It seemed certain, after the physical agony of the seven days of the 'Epic Fast', that twenty-one days without food would kill him. And Britain did not want a dead Gandhi within prison walls.

He survived.

Why was the short fast almost fatal and the other, three times as long, easy to endure? During the former, he negotiated incessantly and was consumed by a desire, to remove the taint of untouchability; his body burned simultaneously. In the twenty-one-day fast, spirit and mind were relaxed. His little body was the creature of a powerful will.

As a gesture of friendship to the Government for his release, Gandhi suspended for six weeks the civil disobedience campaign which had commenced in January 1933. On 15 July he asked Willingdon for an interview. The Viceroy declined. On 1 August, Gandhi proposed to march from Yeravda, where he had been residing, to the village of Ras. That night, he was arrested with thirty-four ashramites, but released three days later and ordered to remain in the city of Poona. Half an hour later, he disobeyed the order, and was arrested again and sentenced to a year's imprisonment. He commenced to fast 16 August, was removed to hospital in a precarious condition on 20 August, and unconditionally released on the 23rd. He nevertheless regarded himself as serving the year's sentence and announced he would not resume civil disobedience before 3 August, 1934.

Until 1939, except for a month's silence to catch up with his work and several long periods of physical breakdown, Gandhi was completely at the disposal of the organizations he had founded for mass welfare and education. He gave Sabarmati Ashram to a Harijan group and established headquarters in Wardha, a small town in the Central Provinces. From there, on 7 November, 1933, he commenced a ten-month tour for

Harijan welfare; he visited every province in India without once going home to relax or rest.

On 15 January, 1934, a large section of Bihar province suffered a severe earthquake. Gandhi interrupted his tour and visited the stricken area in March; he walked barefoot from village to village, comforting, teaching and preaching. The earthquake, he told the public, 'is a chastisement for your sins', chiefly 'the sin of untouchability'. Such superstition angered Tagore and other enlightened Indians; the poet denounced the Mahatma. '... physical catastrophes', Tagore declared in a statement to the press which he first sent to Gandhi, 'have their inevitable and exclusive origin in certain combinations of physical facts ... If we associate ethical principles with cosmic phenomena then we shall have to admit that human nature is morally superior to the Providence that preaches lessons in good behaviour in orgies of the worst behaviour possible ... As for us, we feel perfectly secure in the faith that our sins and errors, however enormous, have not enough force to drag down the structure of creation to ruins ... We who are immensely grateful to Mahatmaji for inducing by his wonder-working inspiration a freedom from fear and feebleness in the minds of his countrymen, feel profoundly hurt when any words from his mouth may emphasize the elements of unreason in those very minds ...'

Gandhi was not shaken. 'There is an indissoluble marriage', he replied, 'between matter and spirit ... The connection between cosmic phenomena and human behaviour is a living faith and draws me nearer to God.' The moment Gandhi invoked God there was no arguing with him. In effect, the overzealous Mahatma was harnessing God to his propaganda chariot; he was Arjuna using Krishna as a charioteer to fight for the common people.

Gandhi's paramount compulsion was to help the poor, and since Gandhi and Gandhi's God were partners, the Mahatma enlisted the Almighty in the task. 'To a people famishing and idle', he wrote, 'the only acceptable form in which God can dare appear is work and promise of food and wages.'

'India lives in her villages, not in her cities,' he wrote in *Harijan* on 26 August, 1936; and several issues later, 'When I succeed in ridding the villages of their poverty, I have won Swaraj . . .' The idea that Gandhi favoured poverty is fiction; he merely urged select idealists to serve the people through self-abnegation. For the nation as a whole, 'No one has ever suggested that grinding pauperism can lead to anything else but moral degradation,' which is the last thing he wanted. Gandhi insisted that 'If we do not waste our wealth and energy, the climate and natural resources of our country are such that we can become the happiest people in the world,' which is what he did want.

Gandhi decried the extreme of pauperism and the extreme of wealth.

Between 1933 and 1939, Gandhi allowed few matters to deflect him from welfare work. It was not smooth sailing . On 25 June, 1935, at Poona, in the heart of the late Tilak's Maratha country, a Hindu suspected of opposing equality for Harijans threw a bomb into a car thinking mistakenly that the Mahatma was in it. Shortly thereafter, a Gandhi supporter belaboured an anti-Harijan with a lathi. Gandhi fasted seven days in July 1934 to do penance for both.

On 26 October, 1934, the All-India Village Industries Association was launched with Gandhi as a patron and Gandhi's millionaire industrialist friends as backers.

At village meeting and in *Harijan*, Gandhi was now giving the farming population rudimentary instructions about food. 'Milk and banana make a perfect meal,' he wrote. *Harijan* of 15 February, 1935, contained an article by Gandhi entitled 'Green Leaves and their Food Value' in which he reported, 'For nearly five months I have been living on uncooked foods. The addition of green leaves to their meals will enable villagers to avoid many diseases from which they are now suffering.' He devoted another article to the debate on 'Cow's Milk versus Buffalo's', and still a third to the supreme Indian problem: rice. In his booklet, *Key to Health*, and elsewhere, Gandhi gave warning against machine-polished rice. Polishing removes an overcoat rich in vitamins, especially B_1, he explained; lacking those vitamins, Indians, for most of whom rice is the chief staple food, are subject to numerous debilitating diseases, notably beriberi which means 'I cannot'. Hand-pounded rice, Gandhi explained, retains the vitamin-rich coating.

At other times, Gandhi expatiated on the nutritional value of the mango kernel and the groundnut or peanut. Peanuts were politics to him, as political as primaries. Repeatedly, too, he gave detailed information on how to prepare animal manures and how to cure snake bites and malaria.

Gandhi knew that the improvement of seed, the proper use of fertilizer and the proper care of cattle could solve basic political problems. Many a civil war in Asia might have been prevented by an additional daily bowl of rice per person.

Gandhi also paid attention to non-agrarian aspects of village life. 'We have to concentrate on the village being self-contained, manufacturing mainly for use,' he wrote in *Harijan* on 29 August, 1936. 'Provided this character of village industry is maintained, there would be no objection to villagers using even the modern machines and tools that they can make and afford to use. Only they should not be used as a means of exploiting others.'

In *Harijan* of 26 July, 1942, Gandhi described the ideal Indian village: 'It is a complete republic, independent of its neighbours for its vital wants, and yet interdependent for many other wants in which dependence is a necessity. Thus every village's first concern will be to grow its own food crops and cotton for its cloth. It should have a reserve for its cattle, recreation and playground for adults and children. Then if there is more land available, it will grow *useful* money crops, thus excluding . . . tobacco, opium and the like. The village will maintain a village theatre, school and public hall. It will have its own water works ensuring clean supply. This can be done through controlled wells and tanks [reservoirs]. Education will be compulsory up to the final basic course. As far as possible, every activity will be conducted on a co-operative basis . . .' To this modest blueprint, which, however, seemed like a sketch of Heaven to India's permanently underfed farmers, Gandhi added another wild dream: electricity in every village home.

Did Gandhi advocate a land reform for India which would give landless or land-poor peasants the redistributed estates of the big landlords?

In the 2 January, 1937, issue of *Harijan*, Gandhi wrote, 'Land and all property is his who will work it'; but he admitted the landlords into that category though he knew that the landlord class included a large percentage of absentee owners, intermediaries, agents, moneylenders and other unproductive elements.

'I cannot picture to myself a time when no man shall be richer than another,' Gandhi said. 'Even in the most perfect world, we shall fail to avoid inequalities, but we can and must avoid strife and bitterness. There are numerous examples extant of the rich and the poor living in perfect friendliness. We have but to multiply such instances.'

Gandhi would have done it by 'trusteeship'.

In Bengal once, Gandhi was the guest of a landlord who served him milk in a gold bowl and fruit on gold plates.

'Where did he get these golden plates from?' Gandhi said to himself.

'From the substance of the peasants,' Gandhi answered. 'Where their life is one long-drawn-out agony, how dare he have these luxuries?'

Gandhi spared his host, but he shared these thoughts with a meeting of landlords in 1931 and added, 'Landlords would do well to take time by the forelock. Let them cease to be mere rent collectors. They should become trustees and trusted friends of their tenants . . . They should give the tenants a fixture of tenure, take a lively interest in their welfare, provide well-managed schools for their children, night schools for adults, hospitals and dispensaries for the sick, look after the sanitation of the villages, and in a variety of ways make them feel that they, the landlords, are their true friends taking only a fixed commission for their manifold services.'

'Exploitation of the poor can be extinguished,' Gandhi wrote in *Harijan* on 28 July, 1940, 'not by effecting the destruction of a few millionaires, but by removing the ignorance of the poor and teaching them to non-co-operate with their exploiters. That will convert the exploiters also.'

Gandhi reminded the peasants and workers of their power.'There is in English a very potent word, and you have it in French also,' he said. 'All the languages of the world have it – it is "No" . . . Immediately Labour comes to recognize that it has got the choice of saying "Yes" when it wants to say "Yes", and "No" when it wants to say "No", Labour is free of Capital, and Capital must woo Labour.' The worker can strike; the peasant can refuse rent.

Nevertheless, he declared in *Young India* of 7 October, 1926, 'capital and labour need not be antagonistic to each other'.

But the passage of time and all Gandhi's persuasiveness produced few trustees. No report of 'voluntary abdication' by a landlord or millowner reached Gandhi before the day of his death. No one answered his 1929 appeal to the 'model landlord' to 'reduce himself to poverty in order that the peasant may have the necessities of life'.

Gradually, therefore, Gandhi's economic views changed. He continued to advocate class collaboration. But as he moved nearer the end of his life and further from the nineteenth century, he sought new means of removing poverty. He became reconciled to more state participation in economic affairs. He wanted the law to help in the levelling process. Equality grew more attractive.

In *Harijan* of 31 July, 1937, Gandhi noted that British income surtaxes amounted to 70 per cent. 'There is no reason why India should not go to a much higher figure.' And, he added, 'Why should there not be death duties?' In an article published 13 April, 1938, he went still further: 'A trustee has no heir but the public.' The millionaire's wealth should go to the community, not to his son who would only lose morally by inheriting material riches, Gandhi declared.

One of the first acts of a free India would be to give grants to the untouchables, he said, out of the pockets of 'the moneyed classes'. And if the rich complain, 'I shall sympathize with them, but will not be able to help them, even if I could possibly do so, because I would seek their assistance in that process, and without their assistance it would not be possible to raise these people out of the mire.'

In 1941, and again in 1945 in his *Constructive Programme*, Gandhi warned the Indian capitalists. 'A non-violent system of government', he wrote, 'is clearly an impossibility so long as the wide gulf between the rich and the hungry millions persists. The contrast between the palaces of New Delhi and the miserable hovels of the poor labouring class nearby cannot last one day in a free India in which the poor will enjoy the same power as the richest in the land. A violent and bloody revolution is a certainty one day unless there is a voluntary abdication of riches and the power that riches give, and sharing them for the common good.'

The response was nil.

'The power that riches give' troubled him. He began to search for means of diffusing it. 'Key industries, industries which the state needs', he wrote on 28 June, 1939, 'may be centralized.' He was opposed, however, to concentration of economic power in the hands of the Government. He therefore added, 'But supposing the state controlled paper-making and centralized it, I would expect it to protect all the paper that villages can make.' Power houses, he wrote, should be owned 'by village communities or the state', preferably by the villages.

'What would happen in a free India?' I asked Gandhi in 1942. 'What is your programme for the improvement of the lot of the peasantry?'

'The peasants would take the land,' he replied. 'We would not have to tell them to take it. They would take it.'

'Would the landlords be compensated?' I asked.

'No,' Gandhi said. 'That would be fiscally impossible.'

An interviewer told Gandhi that the number of textile mills was increasing. 'That is a misfortune,' he remarked. Better that textiles be made in the homes of the millions of partially employed peasants.

'God forbid', Gandhi exclaimed in *Harijan* on 28 January, 1939, 'that India should ever take to industrialism after the manner of the West. The economic imperialism of a single tiny island kingdom [England] is today keeping the world in chains. If an entire nation of three hundred millions took to similar economic exploitation, it would strip the world bare like locusts.'

Nor did Gandhi regard the mere multiplication of material wants and of objects to gratify them as the highroad to happiness or godliness. He drew no line between economics and ethics. 'An economics', he said in *Harijan* of 9 October, 1937, 'that inculcates Mammon worship, that enables the strong to amass wealth at the expense of the weak, is a false and dismal science. It spells death. True economics . . . stands for social justice' and moral values. Gandhi knew that people with full refrigerators, crowded clothes closets, cars in every garage and radios in every room may still be psychologically insecure and unhappy. 'Rome,' he said, 'suffered a moral fall when it attained high material affluence.' 'What shall it avail a man if he gain the whole world and lose his soul?' Gandhi quoted. 'In modern terms,' he continued, 'it is beneath human dignity to lose one's individuality and become a mere cog in the machine. I want every individual to become a full-blooded, fully developed member of society.' Next to God, Gandhi's supreme being was man the individual. He accordingly regarded himself as 'the born democrat'.

'No society can possibly be built on a denial of individual freedom. It is contrary to the very nature of man,' Gandhi wrote. 'Just as man will not grow horns or a tail so he will not exist as a man if he has no mind of his own.' Therefore, 'democracy is not a state in which people act like sheep'.

Gandhi disliked the word 'tolerance' but he found no substitute, 'For me,' he said, 'every ruler is alien who defies public opinion . . . Intolerance betrays want of faith in one's cause . . . We shut the door of reason when we refuse to listen to our opponents or, having listened, make fun of them.

'Always keep an open mind,' he admonished.

There could, however, be no democracy without discipline. 'I value individual freedom,' he wrote, 'but you must not forget that man is essentially a social being. He has risen to his present status by learning to adjust his individualism to the requirements of social progress. Unrestricted individualism is the law of the beast of the jungle. We must learn to strike a mean between individual freedom and social restraint.' It could be done by self-discipline. If the individual did not discipline himself the state would try to discipline the individual, and too much official discipline kills democracy.

'We cannot learn discipline by compulsion,' Gandhi affirmed. A dictatorship can exact obedience; it can implant the habit of robot compliance; it can, by fear, convert man into a cringing, kowtowing pigmy. None of that is discipline.

Gandhi discouraged the notion that democracy meant economic freedom at the expense of personal liberty, or political freedom without economic freedom. 'My conception of freedom is no narrow conception,' he declared in *Harijan* of 7 June, 1942. 'It is coextensive with the freedom of man in all his majesty.

'If the individual ceases to count, what is left of society?' he asked. To those who argued that dictatorships reduce illiteracy, he replied, 'Where a choice has to be made between liberty and learning, who will not say that the former has to be preferred a thousand times to the latter?'

Democracy means majority rule, Gandhi agreed. But, 'In matters of conscience,' he said, 'the law of majority has no place; . . . it is slavery to be amenable to the majority no matter what its decisions are.'

Nor was freedom Gandhi's highest law. 'Not even for the freedom of India would I resort to an untruth,' he said. 'We do not seek our independence out of Britain's ruin.'

Gandhi's hostility to violence and untruth, his objection to the omnipotent State which embodies both, and his economic ideas made him anti-Communist.

'India does not want Communism,' Gandhi said as early as 24 November, 1921.

'All Communists are not bad, as all Congressmen are not angels,' Gandhi declared on 26 January, 1941. 'I have, therefore, no prejudice against Communists as such. Their philosophy, as they have declared it to me, I cannot subscribe to.'

The Communists sent spokesmen to convert him. But his instincts led him to reject their teachings.

'I am yet ignorant of what exactly Bolshevism is,' he wrote on 11 December, 1924. 'I have not been able to study it. I do not know whether it is for the good of Russia in the long run. But I do know that in so far as it is based on violence and denial of God, it repels me . . . I am an uncompromising opponent of violent methods even to serve the noblest of causes.'

In 1926, he received some enlightenment and declared,

'Let no one think that the people in Russia, Italy and other countries are happy or are independent.'

In 1927, Shapuri Saklatwala, an Indian Communist who was a member of the British House of Commons, appealed to Gandhi to forsake his mistaken ways and join the Communists. Gandhi replied to the 'impatient comrade' in *Young India* of 17 March, 1927. 'In spite of my desire to offer hearty co-operation,' the Mahatma said, 'I find myself against a blind wall. His facts are fiction and his deductions based upon fiction are necessarily baseless . . . I am sorry, but we stand at opposite poles.'

Communists accused him of consorting with capitalists and taking their money. He did not reply that Communists were tarred with the same brush. He said he took money from the rich to help the poor. He consorted with capitalists to convert them. He consorted with Communists as often as they wished to come.

'You claim to be Communists,' he said to one group of Communists, 'but you do not seem to live the life of Communism.' Then he berated them for their discourtesy in debate. On another occasion, he attacked their lack of scruples. 'I have it from some of the literature that passes under the name of Communist literature,' he wrote in *Harijan* on 10 December, 1930, 'that secrecy, camouflage, and the like are enjoined as necessary for the accomplishment of the Communist.' This repelled him.

Was Gandhi a Socialist?

The Communists call themselves Socialists. The full name of Hitler's Nazi party was National Socialist Workers' Party, and Mussolini spoke of his regime as 'proletarian'. The French Radical Socialists are mild and middle class. Socialism is an overworked word.

Gandhi read Karl Marx's *Capital* in prison and remarked, 'I think I could have written it better, assuming, of course, that I had the leisure for the study he has put in.' If Gandhi meant the style he was certainly right. But Gandhi was no Marxist; he did not believe in class war.

Minoo Masani, Indian author and India's first Ambassador to Brazil, asked Gandhi's opinion of the programme of the Indian Socialist Party. Gandhi replied in a letter dated 14 June, 1934. 'I welcome the rise of the Socialist Party in the Congress,' the Mahatma wrote. 'But I can't say I like the programme as it appears in the printed pamphlet. It seems to me to ignore Indian conditions and I do not like the assumption underlying many of its propositions which go to show that there is necessarily antagonism between the classes and the masses or between the labourers and capitalists, such that they can never work for mutual good. My own experience covering a fairly long period is to the contrary. What is necessary is that labourers or workers should know their rights and should also know how to assert them. And since there never has been any right without a corresponding duty, in my opinion, a manifesto is incomplete without emphasizing the necessity of performance of duty and showing what duty is.' He invited Masani and friends for a discussion.

Gandhi opposed the Socialists for their class-war doctrine, and he condemned them when they used violence. Yet as he observed disturbing trends, he became more pro-Socialist and more favourably disposed to equality. 'Today', Gandhi wrote in the 1 June, 1947, *Harijan*, 'there is gross economic inequality. The basis of socialism is economic equality. There can be no rule of God in the present state of iniquitous inequalities in which a few roll in riches and the masses do not get enough to eat. I accepted the theory of Socialism even while I was in South Africa.' His, however, was a moral Socialism.

If India were to carry out most of Gandhi's numerous economic prescriptions the result, two or three decades after his death, might be an economy pivoting on a fully employed, self-governing village enjoying maximum self-sufficiency and minimum mechanization; a city where capitalists and municipal, provincial and federal governments shared industry and trade; strong trade unions and co-operatives; and one-generation capitalists whose wealth, since they could not bequeath it, would revert to the community.

Gandhi's loyalty to truth exceeded his loyalty to political dogma or party. He allowed truth to lead him without a map. If it took him into an area where he had to discard some intellectual baggage or walk alone without past associates, he went. He never impeded his mind with STOP signs. Many groups have claimed him. But he was the private property of none, not even of Congress. He was its leader for years, yet at the Congress convention in Bombay in December 1934, having immersed himself in Harijan and peasant uplift work, he ceased to be a dues-paying member, let alone an officer, of the Congress party. 'I need complete detachment and absolute freedom of action,' he said.

Gandhi's individualism meant maximum freedom from outward circumstances and maximum development of inner qualities. His antagonism to British rule was part of a larger antagonism to fetters of all kinds. His goal was *Gita* detachment, in politics as in religion.

Gandhi's intellectual receptivity and flexibility are characteristics of the Hindu mind. There is a Hindu orthodoxy but it is not characteristic of Hinduism. In Hinduism it is the intensity and quality of the religious zeal, not so much its object, which constitutes religion.

In 1942, when I was Gandhi's houseguest for a week, there was only one decoration on the mud walls of his hut: a black and white print of Jesus Christ with the inscription, 'He is Our Peace.' I asked Gandhi about it. 'I am a Christian,' he replied. 'I am a Christian, and a Hindu, and a Moslem, and a Jew.'

'All faiths', Gandhi wrote in *From Yeravda Mandir* in an unintended definition of religious tolerance, 'constitute a revelation of Truth, but all are imperfect, and liable to error. Reverence for other faiths need not blind us to their faults. We must be keenly alive to the defects of our own faith also, yet not leave it on that account, but try to overcome those defects. Looking at all religions with an equal eye, we would not only not hesitate, but would think it our duty to blend into our faith every acceptable feature of other faiths.'

That paragraph is a portrait of the Gandhi mind: he was the conservative who would not change his religion, the reformer who tried to alter it, and the tolerant believer who regarded all faiths as aspects of the divine. He was loyal yet critical, partisan yet open-minded, devout yet not doctrinaire, inside yet outside, attached yet detached, Hindu yet Christian, yet Moslem, yet Jew.

Next to Hinduism he was most attracted by Christianity. He loved Jesus. Hindu bigots even accused him of being a secret Christian. He considered this 'both a libel and a compliment – a libel because there are men who believe me to be capable of being secretly anything . . . a compliment in that it is a reluctant acknowledgment of my capacity for appreciating the beauties of Christianity. Let me own this. If I could call myself, say, a Christian or a Moslem, with my own interpretation of the Bible or the *Koran*, I could not hesitate to call myself either. For then Hindu, Christian and Moslem would be synonymous terms. I do believe that in the other world there are neither Hindus, nor Christians or Moslems.'

Gandhi was more specific, however, in an address at the YMCA in Colombo, Ceylon, in 1927. 'If then,' he said, 'I had to face only the Sermon on the Mount and my own interpretation of it, I should not hesitate to say, "Oh, yes, I am a Christian." . . . But negatively I can tell you that much of what passes as Christianity is a negation of the Sermon on the Mount. And please mark my words. I am not at the present moment speaking of the Christian conduct. I am speaking of Christian belief, of Christianity as it is understood in the West.'

Many Christian missionaries came to Gandhi often, and he had long friendly talks with Dr John R. Mott, Bishop Fisher who lived in India for years, and others. But Gandhi frowned on proselytizing, whether by Christians, Hindus, or Moslems. He said, 'I do not believe in people telling others of their faith, especially with a view to conversion . . . Faith does not permit of telling. It has to be lived and then it is self-propagating.'

S. K. George, a Syrian Christian of India and lecturer at Bishop's College, Calcutta, wrote a book entitled, *Gandhi's Challenge to Christianity* and dedicated it 'To Mahatma Gandhi who made Jesus and His Message real to Me'. The Reverend K. Mathew Simon, of the Syrian Orthodox Church of Malabar, India, writes of Gandhi, 'It was his life that proved to me more than anything else that Christianity is a practicable religion even in the twentieth century.' This suggests how relevant Gandhi is to the problems of our times.

Gandhi presented a perplexing problem to Christians in India: he was the world's most Christ-like person yet not a Christian. 'And so,' exclaims E. Stanley Jones, 'one of the most Christlike men in history was not called a Christian at all.' Missionaries frequently tried to convert him to Christianity. (He, speaking softly, tried to do the same for them.) But why enrol a saint in a church?

Gandhi protested that the missionaries fed the starving and healed the sick in order to convert them to Christianity. 'Make us better Hindus,' he pleaded. That would be more Christian.

Christianity has had a good effect on Hinduism. 'The indirect influence of Christianity has been to quicken Hinduism into life,' Gandhi asserted. The fact that the missionaries' richest recruiting field was the embittered Harijan community may have awakened some Hindus to the necessity of supporting Gandhi's Harijan work. And Gandhi probably had a good effect on Christianity. Dr E. Stanley Jones says, 'God uses many instruments, and he may have used Mahatma Gandhi to help Christianize unchristian Christianity.'

Gandhi never tried to convert Christians to Hinduism.

Although Gandhi was a Hindu reformer and welcomed the play of outside influences on Hinduism, he departed from Hindu customs and beliefs with reluctance. In 1927, Devadas fell in love with Lakshmi, the daughter of Rajagopalachari, and wanted to marry her. But Rajagopalachari was a Brahman and Gandhi a Vaisya, and members of different castes should not marry. Nor should young folks choose their mates; marriages are arranged by parents. But the man and maid persisted, and finally the illustrious fathers agreed to sanction the union if the couple still wanted one another after five years of separation. So Devadas, who was born in 1900, and Lakshmi waited five painful years and married with pomp in Poona on 16 June, 1933, in the presence of both happy fathers. Gandhi's wedding gift was a hymn book and garland of yarn which he had spun.

The conservative traditionalist and the radical iconoclast merged in Gandhi into a tantalizing unpredictable mixture. The Mahatma's successful assault on untouchability produced the most revolutionary change in Hinduism's millennial existence. It would seem that the corollary of the abolition of untouchability was the abolition of caste, for if one mingled with outcasts surely the barriers between the higher castes should crumble. Yet for many years Gandhi defended caste restrictions.

Defending the four Hindu castes, Gandhi said in 1920, 'I consider the four divisions to be fundamental, natural and essential.' 'Hinduism,' he wrote in *Young India* of 6 October, 1921, 'does most emphatically discourage interdining and intermarriage between divisions . . . . Prohibition against intermarriage and interdining is essential for the rapid evolution of the soul.'

The same man said, 'Restriction on intercaste dining and intercaste marriage is no part of the Hindu religion. It crept into Hinduism when perhaps it was in its decline, and was then probably meant to be a temporary protection against the disintegration of Hindu society. Today those two prohibitions are weakening Hindu society.' This was on 4 November, 1932.

In 1921, the prohibition of intermarriage and interdining was 'essential' to the soul; in 1932, it was 'weakening Hindu society'.

Even this, however, was not Gandhi's final position. Having broken with the orthodox tradition, he characteristically continued to travel further and further away from it, and on 5 January, 1946, he declared, in the *Hindustan Standard*, 'I therefore tell all boys and girls who want to marry that they cannot be married at Sevagram Ashram unless one of the parties is a Harijan.' Earlier, he had refused to attend a wedding unless it was an intercaste marriage.

From 1921 to 1946 Gandhi had gone full circle: from utter disapproval of intercaste marriages to approval of only intercaste marriages.

He had opposed marriages between religions. But he came to favour those too. He congratulated Dr Humayun Kabir, a Moslem writer, on taking a Hindu wife, and approved of B. K. Nehru's marrying a Hungarian Jewess.

Caste is as deeply ingrained in India as the family is in the Western world. Yet Gandhi could change his views on it. In later years, his ideas on celibacy also moderated. In 1935, Professor J. B. Kripalani, a disciple of Gandhi who had first met the Mahatma at Shantiniketan in 1915 and again in Champaran in 1917, fell in love with a Bengali girl and wanted to marry her. Gandhi summoned the girl, Sucheta, and tried to dissuade her. 'Marriage will ruin him,' he said. It would weaken his concentration on social problems. Gandhi advised her to marry somebody else.

A year later, however, Gandhi called Sucheta and gave his approval to the marriage. 'I shall pray for both of you,' he said. Subsequently, he treated her as a daughter.

In the ashram, too, Gandhi became more tolerant of marriage and stopped insisting that marriages be sexless.

As a crusader, Gandhi had to be positive about his opinions. As a devotee of the truth, he had to be able to change them. He sometimes defended his position with a persistence that seemed immodest; yet he also altered it, when necessary, with a completeness that embarrassed his followers but never him. Though he usually tried to prove his consistency, he admitted his inconsistencies. He could be adamant and softly yielding. He dictated to Congress in one period and left it to its fate and follies in another. Tremendous power was at his command but it often remained unused; in very crucial issues he bowed to the wishes of opponents whom he could have broken with a crook of a finger. He had the might of a dictator and the mind of a democrat. Power gave him no pleasure; he had no distorted psychology to feed. The result was a relaxed man. The problem of maintaining an impression of omniscience, infallibility, omnipotence and dignity never occupied him.

Part of every leader's equipment is a wall. It may be high and made of brick and a battalion of guards or it may consist of an unanswered question and an enigmatic smile. Its purpose is to lend distance and awe and to obscure frailties and secrets. There was no wall around Gandhi. 'I say without the least hesitation,' he once declared, 'that I have never had recourse to cunning in all my life.' His mind and emotions were even more exposed than his body.

'My darkest hour', Gandhi wrote in *Harijan* of 26 December, 1936, at the age of sixty-seven, 'was when I was in Bombay a few months ago. It was the hour of my temptation. Whilst I was asleep I suddenly felt as though I wanted to see a woman. Well a man who had tried to rise superior to the instinct for nearly forty years was bound to be intensely pained when he had this frightful experience. I ultimately conquered the feeling, but I was face to face with the blackest moment of my life and if I had succumbed to it, it would have meant my absolute undoing.' Most people are incapable of such nudity and many would think it unnecessary. But it is the supreme manifestation of life without a wall. He wanted the world to know him, all of him; less than that would not have been the truth. And he told the truth about his inner struggles and outer contacts so that others might learn from them. 'As I have all along believed that what is possible for one is possible for all, my experiments have not been conducted in the closet, but in the open,' Gandhi asserted. To say this sounds somewhat boastful; not to say it would have meant suppressing an inspiring message.

Gandhi was the eternal teacher. He accordingly made himself accessible to all. The accessibility was not only complete, it was creative.

In the 1930s, a young Indian named Atulananda Chakrabarti wrote a pamphlet on the increasingly envenomed Hindu–Moslem problem. He of course sent a copy to the Mahatma. Usually a prominent person in any country limits his exertion in such cases to the sending of a formal, polite acknowledgment. Gandhi read the brochure and wrote the unknown author a detailed criticism of its ideas and proposals. He also referred to minor matters. For instance, 'At page 151, you say India is "thousands of miles wide". Is it? As a matter of fact not more than 1,500. Then you have not given the dates to your quotations in the appendix except in one case ... And think of the spelling mistakes. Unpardonable! But the book should serve a useful purpose in spite of the defects, if you have adhered to the truth.'

Encouraged by this unexpected attention, Atulananda asked whether he could come and live in the ashram for a while. Gandhi invited him and he stayed for several weeks. They became friends and corresponded regularly thereafter. Atulananda kept sending his articles to Gandhi for comments; he suggested a culture league to bring Hindus and Moslems together. In one reply, dated 3 August, 1937, Gandhi wrote:

Dear Atulananda, I hope your daughter is well and wholly out of danger. I have gone through your articles carefully. I still do not see light. It seems to me that no culture league will answer the purpose you and I have in view. It has got to be done by individuals who have a living faith and who would work with missionary zeal. Try again, if I have not seen what you see in your proposal. I shall be patient and attentive. I want to help if I can see my way clear.

Yours sincerely,

M. K. Gandhi

The letter was written by hand in ink on a small sheet of handmade paper.

Atulananda continued to concentrate on the Hindu-Moslem tension and suggested a book about it. Replying by postcard on 17 June, 1939, the Mahatma said, 'The disease has gone too deep for books to help. Some big action is necessary. What I do not know as yet, Sincerely, M. K. Gandhi.'

Gandhi was in correspondence with many thousands of persons in India and elsewhere. In most cases, a letter became the seed of a prolonged personal relationship; he remembered members of the correspondent's family and mentioned them by name. Originally approached on a general political or religious question he would soon be asked for advice on private matters. He was a motherly father to multitudes.

In August 1947, Gandhi was in Calcutta coping with one of the ugliest crises in Indian history. City streets were running with Hindu and Moslem blood. One morning, Amiya Chakravarty came to see him. Amiya had been the literary secretary of Tagore. A cousin who was very dear to him had just died of an illness, and for comfort he wanted to share his sorrow with the Mahatma. He stood close to the wall in a corner of Gandhi's room; Gandhi was writing. When he lifted his head, Amiya stepped forward and told him of his cousin's passing. Gandhi made a friendly remark and invited him to the prayer meeting that evening. When Amiya arrived in the evening, Gandhi handed him a slip of paper and whispered, 'It came straight from the heart so it may have some value.' The note read:

Dear Amiya, I am sorry for your loss which in reality is no loss. 'Death is but a sleep and a forgetting.' This is such a sweet sleep that the body has not to wake again and the dead load of memory is thrown overboard. So far as I know, happily there is no meeting in the beyond as we have it today. When the isolated drops melt, they share the majesty of the ocean to which they belong. In isolation they die but to meet the ocean again. I do not know whether I have been clear enough to give you any comfort. Love, Bapu.

The fact that he cared would have been comfort enough. He cared for one little person in the midst of his cares for the whole nation. He was convinced that politics is worth less than zero unless it is an integral part of the everyday life of human beings. Gandhi's unwalled existence was directed to the welfare of mankind through concern for green vegetables in village diet, the aching heart of a bereaved relative, the choice of a girl's husband, a mud pack for a sick peasant and an author's spelling. Nobody rises above such little things; they constitute life; nobody lives in the rarefied air of isms and theological principles.

Over a long period of years, Gandhi's daily post averaged a hundred letters, often with enclosures. He answered about ten of them himself by hand, dictated the replies to some, and instructed his secretaries how to answer others. No communication remained without a response. In numerous instances, where the correspondent did not object, Gandhi replied in *Harijan*. His weekly contributions to that magazine invariably took him two days of solid work. These too he wrote by hand; very rarely he dictated them.

All the remainder of his long day he gave himself to visitors. Ashram members had their personal and general problems; workers in the organizations which Gandhi had established for Harijan and peasant welfare, the popularization of khadi, the development of a nationwide language, and for Indian-sponsored education wanted guidance; journalists wanted interviews; foreigners asked his views on every variety of subject; and, always, whether he was in politics or, as in the 1933 to 1939 period, officially withdrawn from politics, the great and small leaders of the Indian national movement sought his advice, approval and support. A few times in his life he spoke on the telephone. Usually, his conversations were face-to-face. It was not difficult to obtain an appointment with him. Except with a few important Indians or Englishmen, an interview might be attended by ten or more persons, but active participation was limited to Gandhi and the interviewer. Mrs Margaret Sanger, birth-control advocate, visited Gandhi in December 1935; Yone Noguchi, the Japanese author, in January 1936; Lord Lothian, the British statesman, spent three days in Gandhi's village in January 1938. The list of the Mahatma's non-Indian guests looked like an international Who's Who. Outsiders felt that their sojourn in India was incomplete without a visit to Gandhi.

They were right; he came as near being India as one person could be. He called himself a Harijan, Moslem, Christian, Hindu, farmer, weaver. He wove himself into the texture of India. He had the gift of identification with large masses and with many individuals. He aimed to free India the hard but lasting way: by freeing the human beings of India. This would be more difficult than political liberation from England. How could it be done? 'I can indicate no royal road for bringing about the social revolution,' he wrote in 1945, 'except that we should represent it in every detail of our lives.' Gandhi's battlefield, therefore, was the hearts of men. There he made his home. He knew better than anybody how little of the battle had been fought and won. Yet without the social revolution in man's daily conduct, he said, 'we will not be able to leave India happier than when we were born'. The social revolution could not produce a new man. A new type of man would make the social revolution.

CHAPTER 21

Descent into War

Jawaharlal Nehru was president of the Congress for 1936 and 1937 – an unusual honour and a heavy burden. But he himself admitted that Gandhi was 'the permanent Super-President' of Congress. It obeyed him. Thanks to Gandhi's suggestion, for instance, the twenty-five thousand persons who attended the Haripura annual convention in February 1938 were fed with hand-pounded rice, hand-ground flour, cow's (not buffalo's) milk and cow's butter; of course everybody wore khadi. In politics or out of politics, Gandhi could, by virtue of his hold on the people and on most Congress leaders, dictate the actions and veto the decisions of Congress if he wished.

Only after Gandhi gave his consent did Congress participate in the elections to the provincial and central legislatures held early in 1937, under the new British constitution, the Act of India of 1935. 'The boycott of the legislatures, let me tell you,' Gandhi explained in *Harijan* of 1 May, 1937, 'is not an eternal principle like that of truth and non-violence.'

Congress swept the elections in six of India's eleven provinces (Bombay, Madras, United Provinces, Bihar, Central Provinces and Orissa), was the largest single party in Assam, Bengal and the North-west Frontier Province, but obtained a very small minority of the votes in Sind and the Punjab.

Should the Congress accept office in the provinces where it had won a majority? In March 1937, on the advice of Gandhi, it decided in the affirmative on the understanding, however, that the British governors of the provinces would not interfere, and in the hope of using office to organize the country for independence.

The total Congress membership rose from 3,102,113 at the beginning of 1938, to 4,478,720 at the beginning of 1939. But Gandhi, never impressed by mere numbers, warned the party of being corrupted by power and office-seekers. He saw 'decay' setting in, and confessed that he could not undertake civil disobedience because, 'though there is non-violence enough among the masses, there is not enough among those who have to organize the masses'.

This reflected his disappointment with Congress leaders. When, therefore, the convention of 1939 elected Subhas Chandra Bose as president of Congress – he was president too in 1938, and rode to that session in an ancient vehicle drawn by fifty-one bulls – Gandhi stepped in and forced Bose to resign. Bose openly advocated violence and dreamed of an armed revolt against Britain. He was dynamic and popular and threatened to seize control of Congress from the Vallabhbhai Patel machine.

Gandhi also condemned the Congress provincial governments for using force during strikes and religious riots. As the 1930 decade advanced, Gandhi became more uncompromising in his pacifism. But neither Nehru, nor Bose, nor Maulana Abul Kalam Azad, the outstanding Moslem leader of Congress, was a pacifist. Of all India's prominent nationalists, the only one who earned the title of 'Gandhi' was Khan Abdul Ghaffar Khan, known to the country as 'The Frontier Gandhi'. He is a Pathan from the wild, legendary north-west frontier region near the Khyber inhabited by the unruly Afridis, Wazirs and other mountain tribes; the British subsidized but never subdued them. Ghaffar Khan is six feet four, with a fine, perfectly oval head and a powerful muscular body. Grey-black stubble covers his head and face. He was sixty when I saw him in Devadas's home in New Delhi in 1942; his dark, penetrating, flashing eyes were those of a young man of thirty. His father and he were rich, but he renounced wealth to follow the Mahatma. He lives in a village (when he is not in jail) and lives like the villagers. He wears a long, blue-grey blouse and very wide-seat trousers made of homespun. His feet are bare. His feet are beautifully moulded and his big hands are almost white. After he shook hands he touched his hand to his heart. As Gandhi was of the soil and sand of India, Ghaffar Khan is of its rocks and crags and raging torrents. The hot blood of sharpshooting, trigger-happy mountaineers courses in his veins but he has adopted the philosophy of complete non-violence and so have the thousands of brother Pathans whom he organized as the Khudai Khidmatgar or Servants of God.

Millions obeyed Gandhi, myriads adored him, multitudes accounted themselves his followers, only a handful did as he did. He knew it. The knowledge did not diminish his volcanic energy or break his steel will. On the contrary; as he watched the darkness advance during the 1930s across China, Abyssinia, Spain, Czechoslovakia and above all Germany, his zeal for pure pacifism grew. 'My faith is brightest in the midst of impenetrable darkness,' he said on 6 February, 1939. He saw the second World War approaching.

In 1921, he had written that 'under independence too I would not hesitate to advise those who would bear arms to do so and fight for the country'. In 1928, answering the Frenchman the Rev B. de Ligt, Tolstoy's friend Chertkov and other European pacifists who criticized him for supporting the two South African wars and the first World War, Gandhi declared, 'I did participate in the three acts of war. I could not, it would be madness for me to, sever my connection with the society to which I belong.'

It would have been normal for Gandhi to be a pacifist from the very beginning of his public career. But basic attitudes rarely came to Gandhi through cogitation. The absolute pacifism at which he arrived in the mid-1930s was partly the result of his less hopeful relationship towards the British Empire in which he had believed earlier. But chiefly,

Gandhi's pacifism came out of his own inner development.

Once, when Gandhi was in prison, a scorpion stung a fellow prisoner; Gandhi sucked out the poison. A leper named Parchure Sastri, who was a Sanskrit scholar, asked to be admitted to Sevagram Ashram. Some members objected; they feared infection. Gandhi not only admitted him; he gave him massage ... In March 1939 Gandhi undertook a fast unto death on behalf of the civil liberties of the people of Rajkot, where he had gone to school as a boy. The doctors sought to dissuade the Mahatma. He showed symptoms of myocarditis, an inflammation or hardening of the muscles of the heart.

But it was a Gandhian principle to subordinate the flesh to the spirit. When moral considerations made an act imperative, the body had no veto. If the flesh was weak it suffered or even died; it could not say no.

This was the source of Gandhi's pacifism. In the past, he had fought in the wars. He had allowed sympathy for Britain and duty to a country to guide him. Nor had he risen above Indian Nationalism. Morality did not yet completely command him.

However, by the time the second World War approached, he had achieved more complete detachment. Also, he said, 'I was not so disconsolate before [between 1914 and 1918] as I am today.' He envisaged the second war as a 'greater horror' than the first; 'the greater horror would prevent me from becoming the self-appointed recruiting sergeant that I had become during the last war'.

He had little hope of persuading others. But whereas in the past he had resisted all proddings from abroad and pleaded that he could not carry non-violence to the West while India remained violent, he advised the Abyssinians in 1935 not to fight.

'If the Abyssinians had adopted the attitude of non-violence of the strong,' Gandhi said, 'that is, the non-violence which breaks to pieces but never bends, Mussolini would have had no interest in Abyssinia. Thus if they had simply said: "You are welcome to reduce us to dust and ashes, but you will not find one Abyssinian ready to co-operate with you," what could Mussolini have done? He did not want a desert . . . If the Abyssinians had retired from the field and allowed themselves to be slaughtered, their seeming inactivity would have been much more effective though not for the moment visible. Hitler and Mussolini on the one hand and Stalin on the other are able to show the immediate effectiveness of violence. But it is as transitory as that of Genghis Khan's slaughter.'

The tragedy of Czechoslovakia and of Germany's Jews touched him even more deeply. 'The peace of Europe gained at Munich', where Chamberlain and Daladier betrayed Czechoslovakia to Hitler in September 1938, Gandhi wrote, 'is a triumph of violence; it is also a defeat . . . England and France . . . quailed before the combined violence of Germany and Italy. But what have Germany and Italy gained? Have they added anything to the moral wealth of mankind?' These words make more sense today than on 8 October, 1938, when they were published in *Harijan*. 'The war is only postponed,' Gandhi continued prophetically. 'During the breathing time, I present the way of non-violence for acceptance by the Czechs. They do not yet know what is in store for them. They can lose nothing by trying the way of non-violence. The fate of Republican Spain is hanging in the balance. So is that of China. If in the end they all lose, they will do so not because their cause is not just . . . I suggest that, if it is brave, as it is, to die as a man fighting against odds, it is braver still to refuse to fight and yet to refuse to yield to the usurper . . .'

While touring with Ghaffar Khan in October 1938, among the Pathans of the frontier, Gandhi wrote a *Harijan* article entitled 'If I were a Czech'. 'Democracy dreads to spill blood,' he said. 'The philosophy for which the two dictators stand calls it cowardice to shrink from carnage . . . Science of war leads one to dictatorship pure and simple. Science of non-violence can alone lead one to pure democracy . . . Russia is out of the picture just now. Russia has a dictator who dreams of peace and thinks he will wade to it through a sea of blood . . .

'It was necessary to give this introduction to what I want to say to the Czechs and through them to all those nationalities which are called "small" or "weak". I want to speak to the Czechs because their plight moved me to the point of physical and mental distress.' His advice was: 'Refuse to obey Hitler's will and perish unarmed in the attempt. In so doing, though I lose the body, I save my soul, that is, my honour.'

Usually, the pacifist says, 'It is evil to kill.' He therefore abstains from war. He is answered by those who say, 'I'd rather kill than be killed.' To which, Gandhi replied, 'No, I'd rather be killed.'

'Man may and should shed his own blood for establishing what he considers to be his "right",' Gandhi wrote in *Harijan*. 'He may not shed the blood of his opponent who disputes his "right".'

In December 1938 the International Missionary Conference took place at Tambaram, near Madras, and when it was over, Christian clergymen, including Dr John R. Mott, Reverend William Paton, secretary of the International Missionary Council, Reverend Leslie B. Moss, secretary of the Conference of Missionary Societies of North America, and many others sat at Gandhi's feet in his ashram in Sevagram. Pyarelal Nayyar took notes. Soon they were cross-examining him on his formula for the Czechs. 'You do not know Hitler and Mussolini,' one missionary said. 'They are incapable of any moral response. They have no conscience, and they have made themselves impervious to world opinion. Would it not be playing into the hands of these dictators if, for instance, the Czechs, following your advice, confronted them with non-violence?'

'Your argument,' Gandhi objected, 'presupposes that the

dictators like Mussolini and Hitler are beyond redemption.'

Discussions of a similar and even more challenging character were provoked by Gandhi's counsel to the Jews.

Gandhi wrote in *Harijan*, 11 November, 1938:

'My sympathies are all with the Jews. They have been the untouchables of Christianity . . . A Jewish friend has sent me a book called *The Jewish Contribution to Civilization*, by Cecil Roth. It gives a record of what the Jews have done to enrich the world's literature, art, music, drama, science, medicine, agriculture, etc. . . . the German persecution of the Jews seems to have no parallel in history. The tyrants of old never went so mad as Hitler seems to have done. If there ever could be a justifiable war in the name of and for humanity, war against Germany to prevent the wanton persecution of a whole race would be completely justified. But I do not believe in any war. . .

'Can the Jews resist this organized and shameless persecution? . . . If I were a Jew and were born in Germany and earned my livelihood there, I would claim Germany as my home even as the tallest gentile German might, and challenge him to shoot me or cast me in the dungeon . . . And for doing this I should not wait for the fellow Jews to join me in civil resistance, but would have confidence that in the end the rest were bound to follow my example. If one Jew or all the Jews were to accept the prescription here offered, he or they cannot be worse off than now . . . The calculated violence of Hitler may even result in a general massacre of the Jews by way of his first answer to the declaration of such hostilities. But if the Jewish mind could be prepared for voluntary sacrifice, even the massacre I have imagined could be turned into a day of thanksgiving that Jehovah had wrought deliverance of the race even at the hands of a tyrant. For to the God-fearing, death has no terror . . .

'The Jews of Germany can offer Satyagraha under infinitely better auspices than the Indians of South Africa.

The Jews are a compact, homogeneous community in Germany. They are far more gifted than the Indians of South Africa. And they have organized world opinion behind them. I am convinced that if someone with courage and vision can arise among them to lead them in non-violent action, the winter of their despair can in the twinkling of an eye be turned into the summer of hope. And what has today become a degrading man hunt can be turned into a calm and determined stand offered by unarmed men and women possessing the strength of suffering given to them by Jehovah . . . The German Jews will score a lasting victory over the German gentiles in the sense that they will have converted the latter to an appreciation of human dignity.'

The Nazi press assaulted Gandhi savagely for these words. It threatened reprisals against India. 'I should rank myself a coward,' he replied, 'if for fear of my country or myself or Indo-German relations being harmed, I hesitated to give what I felt in the innermost recesses of my heart to be one hundred per cent sound advice.'

The missionaries questioned him closely on his statements about the Jews. 'To be truly non-violent,' he said, 'I must love [my adversary] and pray for him even when he hits me.' The Jews should pray for Hitler. 'If even one Jew acted thus, he would save his self-respect and leave an example which, if it became infectious, would save the whole of Jewry and leave a rich heritage to mankind besides.'

Herman Kallenbach was living in Sevagram Ashram at the time. 'He has an intellectual belief in non-violence,' Gandhi remarked, 'but he says he cannot pray for Hitler . . . I do not quarrel with him over his anger. He wants to be non-violent, but the sufferings of his fellow Jews are too much for him to bear. What is true of him is true of thousands of Jews who have no thought even of "loving the enemy". With them, as with millions, "revenge is sweet, to forgive is divine".' There were few divine Jews or Christians or Hindus. Only one little Hindu and very few of his friends were capable of divine forgiveness.

Jewish Frontier, a New York magazine, riddled Gandhi's proposal in March 1939, and sent him a copy. He quoted at length from the attack. 'I did not entertain the hope . . . that the Jews would be at once converted to my view,' Gandhi replied. 'I should have been satisfied if even one Jew had been fully convinced and converted . . . It is highly probable that, as the [*Jewish Frontier*] writer says, "A Jewish Gandhi in Germany, should one arise, could function for about five minutes and would be promptly taken to the guillotine." But that does not disprove my case or shake my belief in the efficacy of non-violence. I can conceive the necessity of the immolation of hundreds, if not thousands, to appease the hunger of dictators . . . Sufferers need not see the result during their lifetime . . . The method of violence gives no greater guarantee than that of non-violence . . . ' Millions sacrifice themselves in war without any guarantee that the world will be better as a result or even that the enemy will be defeated. Yet who does not fiercely resent the suggestion that anybody should die in deliberate non-violent sacrifice?

I mentioned the subject to Gandhi in 1946 when Hitler was dead. 'Hitler,' Gandhi said, 'killed five million Jews. It is the greatest crime of our time. But the Jews should have offered themselves to the butcher's knife. They should have thrown themselves into the sea from cliffs . . . It would have aroused the world and the people of Germany . . . As it is they succumbed anyway in their millions.'

Gandhi in 1938 and 1939 was seeking a moral substitute for the impending war. He knew his ideas would be rejected. But he had to express them.

In December 1938 Mr Takaoka, a member of the Japanese Parliament, came to Sevagram. He deliberately avoided the subject of the Sino-Japanese war; he asked how unity could be achieved between India and Japan.

'It can be possible,' Gandhi replied harshly, 'if Japan ceases to throw its greedy eyes on India.'

Takaoka requested a message for the Japanese party which advocated Asia for the Asiatics. 'I do not subscribe to the doctrine of Asia for the Asiatics if it is meant as an anti-European combination,' Gandhi affirmed. (Pyarelal published the interview in the 24 December, 1938, *Harijan*.) 'How can we have Asia for the Asiatics unless we are content to let Asia remain a frog in the well? . . .'

A lady cabled from London to Gandhi on 24 August, the day after the Stalin–Hitler pact was signed. 'Please act. World awaiting lead.' The war was a week off. Another woman wirelessed from England, 'Urge you consider immediate expression of your unshakable faith in reason not force to rulers and all peoples.' Similar urgent messages poured into Sevagram.

It was too late. On 1 September, 1939, the Nazi Army invaded Poland.

Sunday, 3 September, 1939, 11 A.M., British churches were filled; the British government declared war on Germany. I spent that afternoon in the country outside Paris. At 5 P.M. a lone plane flew overhead. The radio announced that France had gone to war. We drove back to town. Women stood in the streets of little towns gazing morosely into nowhere, into the bleak future. Some bit their fingernails. Our car paused for a long line of farm horses requisitioned by the army – heavy, well-groomed, powerful horses. A farmer put his arms around the neck of his horse, put his cheek against its head, and talked into its ear. The horse shook its head up and down. They were saying goodbye. Before it was over in 1945, more than thirty million persons in all parts of the world said goodbye to life. More than thirty million dead men, women and children; more than a hundred million wounded, hurt and incapacitated; millions of homes smashed; atom bombs dropped on two cities; hopes destroyed; ideals soured; moral values questioned.

'We have too many men of science, too few men of God,' General Omar N. Bradley, Chief of Staff, United States Army, said in Boston on 10 November, 1948. 'We have grasped the mystery of the atom and rejected the Sermon on the Mount . . . The world has achieved brilliance without wisdom, power without conscience. Ours is a world of nuclear giants and ethical infants. We know more about war than we know about peace, more about killing than we know about living.'

Gandhi rejected the atom and grasped the Sermon on the Mount. He was a nuclear infant and an ethical giant. He knew nothing about killing and much about living in the twentieth century.

Only those who have no doubts can reject Gandhi completely.

CHAPTER 22

Winston S. Churchill versus
Mohandas K. Gandhi

The day the second World War started, England took India into the war by proclamation without consulting any Indians. India resented this additional proof of foreign control. The next day, nevertheless, Gandhi boarded the first Delhi train to Simla in response to a telegraphic summons from the Viceroy, Lord Linlithgow, to come to the summer capital. 'We Do Not Want Any Understanding', the public at the station chanted as the Mahatma walked to the train. It was his day of silence, so he smiled and departed.

The Viceroy and the Mahatma discussed the nature of the coming hostilities, 'and as I was picturing before him the House of Parliament and the Westminster Abbey and their possible destruction, I broke down. I have become disconsolate. In the secret of my heart I am in perpetual quarrel with God that He should allow such things to go on'.

Gandhi had a 'daily quarrel' with God; non-violence had failed; God had failed. But at the end of each quarrel, the Mahatma decided that 'neither God nor non-violence is impotent. Impotence is in men. I must try on without losing faith'.

Gandhi blamed Hitler for the war. 'Rightly or wrongly, and irrespective of what the other powers have done before under similar circumstances,' he wrote in *Harijan* of 16 September, 1939, 'I have come to the conclusion that Herr Hitler is responsible for the war. I do not judge his claim. It is highly probable that his right to incorporate Danzig is beyond question if the Danzig Germans desire to give up their independent status. It may be that his claim to appropriate the Polish Corridor is a just claim. My complaint is that he will not let the claim be examined by an independent tribunal.'

Critics said he had talked 'sentimental twaddle' in the Simla interview with the Viceroy. 'My sympathy for England and France,' Gandhi replied, 'is not the result of momentary emotion or, in cruder language, of hysteria.' Equally, 'My whole heart is with the Poles in the unequal struggle in which they are engaged for the sake of their freedom.'

Hitlerism, Gandhi declared, 'means naked ruthless force reduced to an exact science and worked with scientific precision'. It was thoroughly abhorrent to him.

But what could he do? In addition to his daily debate with God, Gandhi was in an interminable argument with Congress which, he admitted, echoed the views of most articulate Indians. With Gandhi non-violence was a creed, with Congress it 'was always a policy'. Congress adopted non-violence for the expected gains. Gandhi wanted non-violence irrespective of the fruits.

The day after war's beginning, Gandhi pledged publicly that he would not embarrass the British government. He would also lend moral support to England and her allies; even one who disapproves of war should distinguish between aggressor and defender. Further than this, however, he could not go; he could not participate in the war effort nor would he defend India against an aggressor. He did not want India to have an army or to use police against Hindu–Moslem rioters. A constabulary to deal gently with bandits and professional hooligans was the maximum violence he might countenance.

Congress, on the other hand, was ready to support the war effort if specified conditions were satisfied.

From these different positions, Gandhi and Congress fought a friendly but hard battle.

On 14 September, 1939, the Working or Executive Committee of Congress issued a manifesto which condemned Fascist aggression in Poland yet recalled that the Western democracies had condoned or not opposed similar developments in Manchuria, Abyssinia, Spain and Czecho-slovakia; it said the Western democracies must shed their own imperialism before they could convincingly contend that they were fighting imperialism and not merely rivals. 'A free democratic India will gladly associate herself with other free nations for mutual defence against aggression and for economic co-operation . . .'

Gandhi was present, as a guest, during the four days of discussion that fathered this manifesto. After its adoption, he revealed that Jawaharlal Nehru had drafted it. 'I was sorry,' Gandhi commented, 'to find myself alone in thinking that whatever support was to be given to the British should be given unconditionally' and non-violently. Gandhi disliked the tit-for-tat offer: India will fight if you make India free. Nevertheless, he commended the manifesto to the country: 'I hope that the statement will receive the unanimous support of all parties among Congressmen.'

How could he do this, the critics howled; how could he appeal for support of a view he had opposed? 'I would not serve the cause of non-violence,' he replied, 'if I deserted my best co-workers because they could not follow me in an extended application of non-violence. I therefore remain with them in the faith that their departure from the non-violent method will be confined to the narrowest field and will be temporary.'

Haven't you changed your mind since 1918, some chided.

'At the time of writing,' he retorted, 'I never think of what I have said before. My aim is not to be consistent with my previous statements on a given question, but to be consistent with the truth as it may present itself to me at a given moment. The result is that I have grown from truth to truth . . .'

Gandhi went beyond his plea for support of a manifesto that conflicted with his views; he made himself its spokesman in an interview with the Viceroy on 26 September. Lord

Linlithgow replied on 17 October; England could not yet define her war aims. He cautioned India against a too rapid advance towards self-government. After the war, there would be changes in the direction of Dominion Status, he said.

Five days later, accordingly, the Working Committee voted against aiding Britain. It also instructed the Congress ministries of the provinces to resign. Gandhi saw Congress coming closer to him.

Hitler overran Norway, Denmark, Holland and Belgium. France was next. Britain's stock was low in India. 'Let us strike now,' many Indians urged.

Gandhi replied in *Harijan* on 1 June, 1940: 'I am of the opinion that we should wait till the heat of the battle in the heart of the Allied countries subsides and the future is clearer than it is. We do not seek our independence out of Britain's ruin. That is not the way of non-violence.'

Time was working for Indian independence. 'We are nearing our goal without having fired a single shot,' Gandhi said. He wanted only the right to preach non-violence.

France surrendered to Hitler. Panic, and in places hope, seized India. There were runs on banks. Gandhi called for order. Soberly he predicted that 'Britain will die hard and heroically even if she has to. We may hear of reverses, but we will not hear of demoralization.'

Whenever Congress rejected Gandhi's pacifism and volunteered to aid the British, he did not interfere. Whenever Congress agreed with him and wanted to hinder the war effort, he objected.

The Working Committee met in Wardha to review the war crisis: On 21 June, 1940, it plainly stated that it could not 'go to the full length with Gandhi' on non-violence. 'So, for the first time,' Nehru wrote in his autobiography, Gandhi 'went one way and the Congress Working Committee another . . .'

'I am both happy and unhappy over the result,' Gandhi affirmed. 'Happy because I have been able to bear the strain of the break and have been given the strength to stand alone. Unhappy because my word seemed to lose the power to carry with me those whom it was my proud privilege to carry all these many years.'

The Viceroy summoned the Mahatma for another audience on 29 June. Lord Linlithgow recognized Gandhi's indestructible influence; he intimated that Britain was ready to grant Indians a broader share in the Indian government.

The Working Committee met in Delhi early in July to weigh the offer. Gandhi had no use for it. He encountered the astute opposition of Rajagopalachari, the Mahatma's warm friend. Rajagopalachari converted Sardar Vallabhbhai Patel, the Mahatma's loyal lieutenant. Only Ghaffar Khan, the 'Frontier Gandhi', sided with the Mahatma.

Gandhi printed a report of the proceedings: Rajagopalachari 'thinks that I suffer from obsession owing to too much brooding on non-violence. He almost thinks that my vision is blurred. It was no use returning the compliment though half-joking I did . . . I at once saw as clear as daylight that, if my position was not acceptable, Rajaji's was the only real alternative. I therefore encouraged him to persist in his effort, though all the time I held him to be hopelessly in the wrong'. Rajaji, or Rajagopalachari, won a big majority; five abstained.

Gandhi failed to convince Congress of the wisdom of pure pacifism in the midst of a war. All acknowledged that he could have killed Rajaji's resolution; indeed, one firm request from the Mahatma and Rajaji would probably have withdrawn it. That would have been dictation, however, and Gandhi believed too much in personal liberty to exploit his power to make men vote or act against their will. He preferred to break with Congress rather than break its leaders.

The Rajaji resolution, adopted, despite Gandhi's disapproval, on 7 July, announced that if India were given complete independence and a central Indian government 'it will enable Congress to throw its full weight in the efforts for the effective organization of the defence of the country'; free India would wage war as one of the allies.

Winston Churchill was Prime Minister of Great Britain and stirring England to gallant resistance. He had, through the years, made numerous statements against Indian independence. He now had the power to prevent it. On 8 August, accordingly, Linlithgow stated that he would invite a number of Indians to join his Executive Council and establish a War Advisory Council to meet regularly, but, in the paraphrase of Lord Pethick-Lawrence who became Secretary of State for India in 1945, 'Britain could not divest herself of the responsibilities which her long association with India had imposed on her.' This foreshadowed Churchill's famous dictum of 10 November, 1942: 'I have not become the King's First Minister in order to preside at the liquidation of the British Empire.'

Nor, said Linlithgow, could His Majesty's Government contemplate the transfer of their present responsibilities to any Indian government whose authority was directly denied by large and powerful elements of the population. This indicated that Britain would not allow Congress to rule India without Moslem consent. It was the first time Britain gave the Moslem community a veto on India's political future.

Thoroughly incensed, the Working Committee, according to Lord Pethick-Lawrence's summary of its resolution, 'accused the British government of rejecting their friendly and patriotic offer of co-operation and making the issue of the minorities an insuperable barrier to India's progress'.

Thanks to Churchill, Congress again came back to Gandhi.

Gandhi explained the new position in a speech to the All-India Congress Committee on 15 September, 1940, in Bombay: 'I do not want England to be defeated or humiliated. It hurts me to find St Paul's Cathedral damaged . . . It is not because I love the British nation and hate the German. I do not think the Germans as a nation are any worse than the English or the Italians. We are all tarred with the same brush; we are all members of the vast human family. I decline to draw any distinctions. I cannot claim any superiority for Indians . . . I can keep India intact and its freedom intact only if I have goodwill towards the whole of the human family and not merely for the human family which inhabits this little spot of the earth called India.'

He would ask to see the Viceroy. 'I will tell him that this is the position to which we have been reduced: We do not want to embarrass you and deflect you from your purpose in regard to the war effort. We go our way and you go yours . . .' But Congress must have freedom to preach. 'If we carry the people with us, there will be no war effort on the part of our people. If, on the other hand, without using any but moral pressure, you find that the people help the war effort, we can have no cause for grumbling. If you get assistance from the Princes, from the landlords, from anybody high or low, you can have it, but let our voice also be heard. If you accept my proposal . . . it will certainly be a feather in your cap. It will be honourable of you, although you are engaged in a life and death struggle, that you have given us this liberty . . .

'The Viceroy', Gandhi anticipated, 'may say, "you are a visionary". I may fail in my mission, but we will not quarrel. If he says he is helpless, I will not feel helpless.'

The Viceroy said no, orally and in a confirming letter.

Rebuffed and eager to protest against the war and India's helplessness, Gandhi proposed to fast, but he allowed himself to be dissuaded by Mahadev Desai and chose instead the alternative of civil disobedience. He did not, however, launch a campaign of mass Satyagraha. He adopted a milder symbolic form which could not impede the war effort; he called on individuals selected by him by name to defy the official ban on propaganda against the war. He first pointed to Vinoba Bhave, a quiet, scholarly Gandhian. Bhave engaged in anti-war propaganda, was arrested, tried and sentenced to three months' imprisonment.

Next, Gandhi designated Nehru. He was arrested and tried. The judge gave him four years.

Patel was chosen next; he informed the Government of his intention and was arrested before he could make his speech.

As a Christmas gesture and in order that harassed British officials might enjoy their holiday without being called out to make arrests, Gandhi suspended the civil disobedience from 25 December, 1940, to 4 January, 1941. In the interval, however, the Government seized Maulana Abul Kalam Azad, the president of Congress.

After a while, provincial and local Congress committees started submitting to Gandhi lists of potential resisters. In sum, 23,223 persons were arrested, most of them in Nehru's United Provinces. Gandhi had promised Congress to stay out of jail.

The person-by-person civil disobedience continued for about a year to the end of 1941. It generated little public enthusiasm. People were tired of going to jail.

In December 1941, the British government released those members of the Working Committee who had been imprisoned. The second World War had taken a menacing turn.

On 7 December, Japan struck at Pearl Harbor; the next day, Japanese forces occupied Shanghai and Siam (Thailand) and made a landing in British Malaya. Twenty-four hours later, the Tokyo navy sank two British battleships, the *Repulse* and the *Prince of Wales*, thus crippling England's naval strength in the Pacific.

The war was moving closer to India. The situation uncovered the old split in Congress between the Gandhian non-violent non-co-operators and those who would barter support of the war effort for an Indian national government. Gandhi, accordingly, withdrew once more from the Congress leadership.

Hong Kong fell to the Japanese late in December 1941. The great British base of Singapore surrendered to the Japanese in February 1942. In March, Japan occupied most of Java, Sumatra and other islands of the Dutch East Indies. On 9 March, an imperial Tokyo communiqué announced that Rangoon, the capital of Burma, India's neighbour, had been seized.

In North Africa, Nazi General Rommel was moving east towards Egypt. The Arabs of Palestine were preparing a friendly welcome for him. Observers talked of a possible German–Japanese junction in India. From Cairo to Calcutta gloom brooded over the fortunes of the United Nations at war.

The American public was disturbed by the low war morale of the Indian people; having been a colony of Britain the United States understood India's aspirations despite the propaganda fog. President Roosevelt sent Colonel Louis Johnson as his personal envoy to India; this was an extraordinary act, for India was not a sovereign state, and therefore all the more calculated to impress the British government with America's concern. In London, United States Ambassador John G. Winant tried unsuccessfully to dissuade Prime Minister Churchill from stating publicly that the Atlantic Charter's self-government clause did not apply to India. Face-to-face at the White House and in transatlantic telephone conversations, Roosevelt had discussed India with Churchill and urged him to make an acceptable offer to the Indian people. Churchill never appreciated these prods.

Chiang Kai-shek, then in a key war position, made direct representations to President Roosevelt and to the British government in favour of Indian independence.

The Labour party was in the British war-time coalition government. Many of its members were friends of Indian freedom; Labour ministers reflected this attitude in Cabinet deliberations.

Pressed on all sides, Churchill consented to send Sir Stafford Cripps to New Delhi with a proposal. But though the British Empire and the Dutch had lost valuable outposts, the optimistic, resilient British Prime Minister had more faith than ever in ultimate military victory, and for the cogent reason that Russia and the United States were now England's partners. He was neither depressed nor defeatist about war prospects when Cripps went out to India.

Tall, thin, austere vegetarian, son of a Labour Lord and nephew of Beatrice Webb, the famous Fabian Socialist writer, Stafford Cripps attended exclusive schools and became an unorthodox, left-wing Labour Member of Parliament. A brilliant lawyer, he gave a large part of his huge professional income to political causes.

When the second World War opened, Sir Stafford abandoned his lucrative law practice and in November 1939 undertook a trip around the world to discover what people were thinking. He spent eighteen days in India, saw Jinnah, Linlithgow, Tagore, Ambedkar, Jawaharlal Nehru and Gandhi. (Cripps was the same age as Nehru and twenty years younger than Gandhi.) The Mahatma lay ill on the floor of his hut, but as 'a concession to your English bones' he provided a stool for Cripps.

Sir Stafford drafted a plan for Indian constitutional changes which he presented to Lord Halifax, the former Lord Irwin, now British Foreign Secretary, who filed it in the archives. Cripps's interest in India was recalled when crisis clouds darkened the horizon of Asia in the winter of 1942. Meanwhile, his prestige had risen enormously because he was serving as British Ambassador in Moscow when Hitler invaded Russia. He had been appointed to the small inner War Cabinet and was often mentioned as Churchill's successor.

Cripps arrived in New Delhi on 22 March, 1942, and the same day commenced his conferences with British officials.

On the 25th, Maulana Abul Kalam Azad called at 3 Queen Victoria Road, where Cripps was staying. Therewith began the negotiations with representative Indians.

Gandhi was in his ashram. He received a telegram from Cripps politely asking him to come to Delhi. 'I did not wish to go,' Gandhi said to me in June 1942, when I interviewed him at Sevagram, 'but I went because I thought it would do some good.'

On 27 March, at 2.15 P.M., Gandhi arrived at 3 Queen Victoria Road and remained with Cripps until 4.25 P.M. Sir Stafford showed the Mahatma the as-yet-unpublished proposals of His Majesty's Government. 'After a brief study,' Gandhi told me in Sevagram, 'I said to Cripps, "Why did you come if this is what you have to offer? If this is your entire proposal to India, I would advise you to take the next plane home."'

'I will consider that,' Cripps replied.

Cripps did not go home. He proceeded with the conversations. Gandhi went home to Sevagram. After that first talk, he had no further contact with Cripps.

The deliberations continued until 9 April when Congress finally rejected the Cripps offer. Later, the Moslem League, the Sikhs, Hindu Mahasabha, the Harijans and Liberals rejected it. Nobody accepted it. The Cripps Mission failed.

On 12 April, Sir Stafford went home.

The 'Draft Declaration by His Majesty's Government' brought to India by Cripps consisted of Articles A, B, C and D which dealt with the post-war period and Article E which dealt with India's war effort. The first four articles provided for a full-fledged Dominion which, as Cripps explained to a press conference, could vote itself out of the Commonwealth.

Congress, and Gandhi, would have accepted that.

An assembly consisting entirely of Indians would, after the war, frame a constitution for India; the representatives in that body of British India would be elected. But one-third of the constituent assembly would be appointed by the princes of India with whom the British had considerable influence.

This did not satisfy Indians who feared that England would seek to retain power in India by manipulating the autocratic maharajas.

Moreover, any province could, if it did not like the future constitution, refuse to accede to the Indian Union. 'With such non-acceding Provinces,' reads the Draft Declaration, 'should they desire, His Majesty's Government will be prepared to agree upon a new constitution, giving them the same full status as the Indian Union . . .'

This could have led to the establishment of many Indias, a Hindu India, a Moslem India, a Princely India, perhaps a Sikh India. But Gandhi had said that the vivisection of India was a sin.

The Cripps terms of the future post-war settlement violated basic Congress and Gandhian principles. That Azad, Nehru and Rajagopalachari, the Congress spokesmen, should nevertheless have negotiated with Cripps shows how eager they were to come to an agreement about the present.

Article E regarding the immediate war-time arrangement stated: 'His Majesty's Government must inevitably bear the responsibility for and retain control and direction of the defence of India as part of the total war effort' but invited the leaders of the Indian people to participate in it.

Gandhi did not wish to fight this war and therefore Article E was to him unacceptable. Congress did wish to contribute to the war effort. But it found Article E vague and restrictive. All documents show that throughout the *pourparlers* with Cripps the efforts of Azad, Nehru and Rajagopalachari were directed to expanding the responsibility and activity of Indians in the war effort; the British, on the other hand, sought to limit them. It was on this point that the talks broke down.

Official British sources blamed the failure of the Cripps

mission on Gandhi's pacifism. Others blamed Cripps and Churchill. Nehru said, 'After Gandhiji left Delhi there was no consultation with him of any kind and it is entirely wrong to imagine that the rejection was due to his pressure.' Nehru reiterated this view in his book, *The Discovery of India*, published in 1946, years after the heat of the Cripps controversy had died away.

In 1946, Gandhi said to me, 'They have asserted that I had influenced the negotiations after I left Delhi. But that is a lie.'

'Englishmen have told me,' I informed him, 'that you telephoned from Sevagram to Delhi and instructed Congress to reject the Cripps offer. They declare they have a record of that conversation.'

'It is all a tissue of lies,' he declared. 'If they have a record of the telephone conversation let them produce it.'

It is easy to see how Gandhi's pacifism would mislead people in interpreting the collapse of the Cripps talks. Gandhi rejected the Cripps offer because of his pacifism and, too, out of devotion to the idea of a united India. Since Gandhi could at all times, whether or not he actively led Congress, bend it to his will, it would be natural to deduce that in rejecting the Cripps proposal, Congress obeyed Gandhi. This appears logical but it omits Gandhi's psychology. On numerous occasions before Cripps, and on one subsequent occasion which determined the fate of India, Gandhi gave Congress a free hand even when he disliked the intended act of Congress. That was his non-violence. Non-violence was more than non-killing to Gandhi, more than non-hurting. It was freedom. Had he coerced his followers, he would have been a violent dictator. He knew that many Congress leaders wished to participate in the conduct of the war. He would not interfere.

Some day the official British and American reports on the Cripps mission (Louis Johnson functioned as intermediary at one stage) will be published. Several interesting documents have already been published.

On 10 March, the day before Churchill announced that Cripps was going to India, Roosevelt sent a long cable to Churchill about India. Dipping into American history between 1783 and 1789 for an analogy, the President suggested a stopgap government that would function for 'five or six years'. 'Perhaps', Roosevelt declared, 'some such method . . . might cause the people of India to forget hard feelings and to become more loyal to the British Empire . . .'

India, Roosevelt added in the cable to Churchill, is 'none of my business' and 'for the love of Heaven do not bring me into this, though I do want to be of help'.

Robert E. Sherwood, who quotes this dispatch in his book *Roosevelt and Hopkins*, declares, 'It is probable that the only part of the cable with which Churchill agreed was Roosevelt's admission that it is "none of my business" . . . 'Hopkins', Sherwood continues, 'said a long time later that he did not think that any suggestions from the President to the Prime Minister in the entire war were so wrathfully received as those relating to the solution of the Indian problem. As one of Churchill's closest and most affectionate associates has said to me, "The President might have known that India was the one subject on which Winston would never move a yard".' An inch would be more like it.

On Sunday, 12 April, 1942, Harry Hopkins was at Chequers, the Prime Minister's country residence, when he received a cable request from Roosevelt to do everything possible to prevent the breakdown of the Cripps negotiations; the President also wired Churchill saying,

I am unable regretfully to agree with the point of view you express in your message to me that the American public believes the negotiations have failed on general broad lines. The general impression here is quite the contrary. The almost universal feeling is that the deadlock has been due to the unwillingness of the British government to concede the right of self-government to the Indian people notwithstanding the Indians' willingness to entrust technical military and naval defence control to the competent British authorities. American public opinion cannot understand why, if the British government is willing to permit component parts of India to secede from the British Empire after the war, it is not willing to permit them during the war to enjoy what is tantamount to self-government.

Roosevelt added, 'I gather that last Thursday night [9 April], agreement was almost reached.'

Cripps had been working eagerly for an agreement, and when the British government's Draft Declaration was rejected he made a new offer to Congress. 'Cripps', Churchill told Hopkins, 'had presented a new proposal to Nehru without consultation with the Governor General [Viceroy].'

The new offer brought an understanding measurably near. 'It was perfectly clear,' Hopkins reported, 'that the Governor General was irritated with the whole business.' The Viceroy telegraphed Churchill. Churchill ordered Cripps to withdraw the new unauthorized proposal and return to England.

Louis Johnson informed Roosevelt. Roosevelt wired Hopkins to see Churchill and try to reopen the negotiations.

Churchill, 'probably with some vehemence', Sherwood suspects, replied to Roosevelt through Hopkins. The upshot of it was that he did not trust Congress. 'Churchill said that he personally was quite ready to retire to private life if that would be any good in assuaging American public opinion . . .' In any case, the negotiations could not be reopened because Cripps had already left India. 'India was one area', Hopkins felt, 'where the minds of Roosevelt and Churchill would never meet.'

Obviously, the minds of Gandhi and Churchill would never meet.

In 1935, Churchill had declared, 'Gandhism and all that it stands for must ultimately be grappled with and finally crushed.' It stood for India's independence. For the first time since 1935, Churchill was in office. Cripps, the Labour anti-imperialist, was the victim of Churchill. He was the envoy of the Churchill government, and 'We mean to hold our own' was Churchill's policy on India. Churchill regarded India as Britain's property. How could he have authorized Cripps to give it away? Only when Churchill was replaced by Cripps's Labour party did India win independence.

Churchill and Gandhi were alike in that each gave his life to a single cause. A great man is all of one piece like good sculpture. Churchill's absorbing purpose was the preservation of Britain as a first-class power. During the war he showed little interest in peace aims. He was bound to the past. He was a product of the nineteenth century and he loved it. He loved Empire, royalty and caste. Lloyd George despised the British upper classes, the generals, the nobility. He fought them. Churchill wanted to perpetuate them. His attachment was not so much to them as to the nineteenth century that made them. The nineteenth century was the British century, the century of Pax Britannica after the defeat of Napoleonic France and before the rise of the Kaiser's Germany, the century of the flowering of the British Empire under Queen Victoria. Britain's past glory was Churchill's god. The upper classes were synonymous to him with the greatness of his country. So was parliamentary democracy. So was India.

Churchill fought the second World War to preserve the heritage of Britain. Would he permit the half-naked fakir to rob her of that heritage? If Churchill could help it, Gandhi would not be striding up the steps of the Viceroy's palace to negotiate or parley.

From the time he became the King's First Minister in 1940 to the day his party went out of office in 1945, Churchill was in conflict with Gandhi. It was a contest between the past of England and the future of India.

A British cartoonist once drew Churchill in a loincloth and, in the next panel, Gandhi in top hat, frock coat and striped trousers, smoking a long cigar and carrying a cane and brief-case. The device suggested how different they were under the surface.

Churchill is the Byronic Napoleon. Political power is poetry to him. Gandhi was the sober saint to whom such power was anathema. The British aristocrat and the brown plebeian were both conservatives, but Gandhi was a non-conformist conservative. As he grew older Churchill became more Tory, Gandhi more revolutionary. Churchill loved social traditions. Gandhi smashed social barriers. Churchill mixed with every class, but lived in his own. Gandhi lived with everybody. To Gandhi, the lowliest Indian was a child of God. To Churchill, all Indians were the pedestal for a throne. He would have died to keep England free, but was against those who wanted India free.

CHAPTER 23

My Week With Gandhi

What an unhappy country! That was my first impression of India in May 1942, and the impression was deepened by my two months' stay. Rich Indians were unhappy, poor Indians were unhappy, the British were unhappy.

One did not have to be in India for more than a few days to realize how abysmally poor the people were. American and many European farmers would consider it bad for business to keep their livestock in accommodation as unhealthy as the tenements I visited with Dr Ambedkar in Bombay; hundreds of thousands lived in them. Gandhi was fully dressed compared to the nakedness of peasants one saw in villages. The vast majority of Indians are always, literally always, hungry.

'The expectation of life,' says the 1931 British official census report on India, is '26.56 years for females and 26.91 for males.' The average person born in India could look forward to only twenty-seven years of life.

According to British figures, one hundred and twenty-five million Indians contracted malaria annually and only a few could afford a grain of quinine. Half a million Indians died of tuberculosis each year.

Climate is only part of the explanation; an Indian community had a death rate five times higher than a neighbouring British settlement.

Despite disease and mortality, India's population was increasing by five million each year. This was the biggest problem of the nation. In 1921, India had 304,000,000 inhabitants; in 1931, 338,000,000; in 1941, 388,000,000. In the same twenty years the area under cultivation was practically stable and industry did not appreciably expand. The poorer the country the higher the birth rate. The higher the birth rate the poorer the country.

The British in India stressed their achievements. But they did not deny the cankers. They blamed the Hindu religion and Moslem backwardness; Indians blamed England. It was an atmosphere in which work and life were becoming increasingly unsatisfactory for the British.

Englishmen whose families had made India their career for more than a century knew that there was no future for them here. India did not want them and they sensed it and were sad. Sir Gilbert Laithwaite, the Viceroy's private secretary, and Major-General Molesworth, Assistant to Wavell as Commander-in-Chief, bicycled to and from work under the hot Indian sun to save petrol though they had cars and drivers. Many of the British were good men, but India preferred to be ruled by bad Indians. Governing unwilling India was no longer 'fun'; the British officials were as sick of India as India was of them. Twenty years of Gandhi's non-violence had destroyed their faith in the future of the Empire.

A typical New Delhi university student delivered a passionate diatribe against Britain. I said to him, 'Tell me, since you dislike the British so violently, would you want Japan to invade and conquer India?'

'No,' he replied, 'but we Indians pray that God may give the British enough strength to stand up under the blows they deserve.'

Some Indians went to the length of preferring Japan to England.

No Indian party or group was supporting the war except the Communists. After Hitler invaded Russia in June 1941, they supported Britain, and the British imperialists in India supported them but did not relish the unnatural liaison.

I heard Nehru address a hundred thousand in Bombay. The Communists formed a heckling island in the vast ocean of brown faces and white clothes. 'This is a people's war,' they chorused.

'If you think it is a people's war go and ask the people,' Nehru shouted. That and the public's hostile reaction silenced them. They knew he told the truth and the British knew it too.

'I would fight Japan sword in hand,' Nehru declared, 'but I can only do so as a free man.'

India could have been held if it had had no freedom, just as a dictator can rule by complete suppression. But the moment Nehru was free enough to say he was not free, India's freedom was inevitable. That is why Gandhi always insisted on freedom of speech as the irreducible minimum. The British administrators in India saw this even when London did not.

'We will be out of here two years after the war ends,' Sir Reginald Maxwell, Home Member in the Viceroy's Council, told me in his home at dinner. He was in charge of police and internal order, and the Indians hated him, but he had no illusions because to him Empire was a daily grind while to Churchill it was romance.

The Viceroy said to me, 'We are not going to remain in India. Of course, Congress does not believe this. But we will not stay here. We are preparing for our departure.'

When I reported these opinions to Indians they did not believe them. They argued bitterly: Churchill and many lesser Churchills in New Delhi and the provinces will obstruct independence or vitiate it by vivisecting the country.

Nehru said to me, 'Gandhi has straightened our backs and stiffened our spines.'

You cannot ride a straight back.

Independence was near. But the present was so black that few could see the future. History had stood still so long in India that nobody foresaw how fast it was about to move. Indians resented the stagnation; it gave them a sense of frustration.

In Bombay I talked to J. R. D. Tata, the head of the big steel-chemicals-airlines-textiles-hotels trust. His father was Parsi, his mother French; he speaks excellent English and French and is intelligent and cultured. He said he was unhappy because strangers ruled his country. On his desk stood several brightly polished two-inch anti-tank shells which a Tata mill was making for the British – and a plastic plaque of Mahatma Gandhi.

An American general stationed in India said 'the British are like a drop of oil in a bucket of water'.

The Viceroy talked about Gandhi. 'Make no mistake about it,' he asserted. 'The old man is the biggest thing in India . . . He has been good to me . . . If he had come from South Africa and been only a saint he might have taken India very far. But he was tempted by politics. Make no mistake. His influence is very great.'

Gandhi, he said, was now contemplating some kind of civil disobedience campaign. 'I have been here six years,' Lord Linlithgow declared, 'and I have learned restraint. I sit here until late in the evening studying reports and carefully digesting them. I will not take precipitate action. But if I felt that Gandhi was obstructing the war effort I would have to bring him under control.' He struck the desk with his hand and the four telephones tinkled.

I said it would be bad if Gandhi died in jail.

'I know,' the Viceroy agreed. 'He is old, and you know you can't feed the old man. He is like a dog and can empty his stomach at will . . . I hope none of this will be necessary but I have a grave responsibility and I cannot permit the old man to interfere with the war effort.'

Nehru was going down to Sevagram to consult the Mahatma about the contemplated civil disobedience action. I asked him to arrange an interview for me. Soon I received a telegram reading: 'Welcome. Mahadev Desai.'

I got out of the train at the small town of Wardha, was met by an emissary from Gandhi and slept on the roof of a Congress hostel; all night the orange-white-green Congress flag played a Morse code in the breeze. Early in the morning, I took a tonga with Gandhi's dentist for Sevagram. (A tonga is a one-horse, two-wheel vehicle in which passengers sit behind the driver with their backs to the horse.) I tried to make him talk about Gandhi's teeth. He talked about British politics.

The tonga stopped where the dirt road met the village. There stood Gandhi. He said, 'Mr Fischer,' with a British accent and we shook hands. He greeted the dentist and turned round and I followed him to a bench. He sat down, put his palm on the bench and said, 'Sit down.' The way he sat down first and the way he touched the bench with his hand was like saying, 'This is my house, come in.' I felt at home immediately.

Each day I had an hour's interview with Gandhi; there was also an opportunity for conversation at meals; in addition, I walked with him once or twice a day. I usually arrived for the morning constitutional while he was still sitting on his bed in the open air eating mango pulp. Between spoonfuls he plunged into serious discussion. Breakfast finished, he accepted a towel and a long, rectangular, narrow-necked, corked bottle of water from Kasturbai and washed his hands before starting on the stroll across nearby fields. Kasturbai, with sunken face, straight mouth and square jaw, seemed to listen attentively, but I did not hear or see her say a single word to her husband during the entire week, nor he to her. At meals and prayers she sat slightly behind his left shoulder fanning him solicitously. She always looked at him; he rarely looked at her, yet he wanted her nearest to him and there appeared to be perfect understanding between them.

During walks, Gandhi kept his arms on the shoulders of two young girls or boys but moved forward with long quick strides and kept up a rapid conversation without losing breath or, apparently, tiring. The walk lasted not less than half an hour. When he returned I was ready for rest and leaned against a post while he continued to speak.

Gandhi was well built, with fine muscular bulging chest, thin waist, and long thin firm legs, bare from sandals to short, tight loincloth. His knees were pronounced bulges and his bones wide and strong; his hands were big and the fingers big and firm. His chocolate-coloured skin was soft, smooth and healthy. He was seventy-three. His fingernails, hands, feet, body were immaculate; the loincloth, the cheesecloth cape he occasionally wore in the sun, and the folded, moistened kerchief on his head were bright white. Once a drop of yellow mango juice stained his loincloth and he scratched it intermittently during an hour.

His body did not look old. He did not give one a feeling that he was old. His head showed his age. His head was large, wide at the top and tapering down to a small face; big ears extended away from it abruptly. His upper lip, covered with a black-and-white stubble moustache, was so narrow that it almost met the fat, down-pointed nose. The expression of his face came from his soft and gentle eyes, the sensitive lower lip which combined self-control with strength and showed suffering, and the ever-present smile revealing naked gums. (He wore his dentures only for eating and took them out and washed them in public; he wore gold-rimmed bifocals; he shaved his face every day with a straight razor, but sometimes one of the men or women disciples shaved him.)

His facial features, with the exception of his quiet, confident eyes, were ugly and in repose his face would have been ugly, but it was rarely in repose. Whether he was speaking or listening, it was alive and registering actively. He spoke with a low, singsong, undistinguished voice (many Indians have the same singsong when they speak English) and he gestured eloquently, but not always, with the fingers of one hand. His hands were beautiful.

Lloyd George looked like a great man. One could not help seeing that Churchill and Franklin D. Roosevelt had stature and distinction. Not Gandhi. (Nor Lenin.) Outwardly he had nothing remarkable about him; perhaps the lower lip. His personality was in what he was and what he had done and what he said. I felt no awe in Gandhi's presence. I felt I was in the presence of a very sweet, gentle, informal, relaxed, happy, wise, highly civilized man. I felt, too, the miracle of personality, for by sheer force of personality, without an organization – Congress was a loose organization – or government behind him, Gandhi had radiated his influence to the far ends of a disunited country and, indeed, to every corner of a divided world. He did it not through his writings; few people anywhere had read his books, and his articles, though known abroad and republished widely in India, were not the source of his hold on people. He reached people through direct contact, action, example and loyalty to a few simple, universally flouted principles: non-violence, truth, and the exaltation of means above ends.

The big names of recent history: Churchill, Roosevelt, Lloyd George, Stalin, Lenin, Hitler, Woodrow Wilson, the Kaiser, Lincoln, Napoleon, Metternich, Talleyrand, etc., had the power of states at their disposal. The only non-official figure comparable to Gandhi in his effect on men's minds is Karl Marx whose dogma, however, was a prescription for a system of government. One has to go back centuries to find men who appealed as strongly as Gandhi did to the conscience of individuals. They were men of religion, in another era. Gandhi showed that the spirit of Christ and of some Christian fathers, and of Buddha and of some Hebrew prophets and Greek sages, could be applied in modern times and to modern politics. He did not preach about God or religion; he was a living sermon. He was a good man in a world where few resist the corroding influence of power, wealth and vanity. There he sat, four-fifths naked, on the earth in a mud hut in a tiny Indian village without electricity, radio, running water, or telephone. It was a situation least conducive to awe, pontification, or legend. He was in every sense down-to-earth. He knew that life consists of the details of life.

'Now put on your shoes and hat,' Gandhi said. 'Those are two indispensable things here. Don't get a sunstroke.' It was 110° with practically no shade except inside the huts, which were like heated ovens. 'Come along,' he said in a friendly tone of mock command. I followed him to the common dining hall which consisted of two long walls of matting connected by a third back wall of the same material. Where one entered, the building was open to the elements.

Gandhi sat down on a cushion near the entrance. At his left was Kasturbai, on his right Narendra Dev, an Indian Socialist leader whom the Mahatma had undertaken to cure of asthma. I was Dev's neighbour. There were about thirty diners. Women sat apart. Several bright-eyed, brown-faced youngsters, between the ages of three and eight, were opposite me. Everyone had a thin straw mat under him and a brass tray in front of him on the ground. Male and female waiters, members of the ashram, moved noiselessly on bare feet, depositing food on the trays. A number of pots and pans were placed near Gandhi's legs. He handed me a bronze bowl filled with a vegetable stew in which I thought I discerned chopped spinach leaves and pieces of squash. A woman poured some salt on my tray and another gave me a metal tumbler with warm water and another with warm milk. Then she came back with two little boiled potatoes in their jackets and some soft, flat wheatcakes baked brown. Gandhi handed me one hard, paper-thin wheatcake from a metal container in front of him.

A gong sounded; a robust man in white shorts stopped waiting on the trays, stood erect, closed his eyes leaving only a white slit open – it made him look blind – and started a high-pitched chant in which all others, including Gandhi, joined. The prayer ended with 'Shahnti, Shahnti, Shahnti' which, Dev said, means 'Peace'.

Everyone started eating with their fingers, fishing out the vegetable stew with a wheatcake folded in four. I was given a teaspoon and then some butter for the cake. Gandhi munched busily, stopping only to serve his wife, Dev and me.

'You have lived in Russia for fourteen years,' was his first political remark to me. 'What is your opinion of Stalin?'

I was very hot, and my hands were sticky, and I had commenced to discover my ankles and legs from sitting on them, so I replied briefly, 'Very able and very ruthless.'

'As ruthless as Hitler?' he asked.

'At least.'

After a pause, he turned to me and said, 'Have you seen the Viceroy?' I told him I had, but he dropped the subject.

'You can have all the water you want,' he told me. 'We take good care that it is boiled. And now eat your mango.' I began to peel it and several people, Gandhi too, laughed. He explained that they usually turned it in their hands and squeezed it to make it soft and then sucked on one end, but he added that I was right to peel it to see whether it was good.

Lunch was at eleven and dinner just before sundown. Kurshed Naoriji, a member of the ashram and granddaughter of Dadabhai Naoriji, brought my breakfast – tea, biscuits or bread with honey and butter and mango – to the mud-walled, bamboo-roofed guest hut where I lived.

At lunch on the second day, Gandhi handed me a tablespoon for the vegetable dish. He said the tablespoon was more commensurate with my size. He offered me a boiled onion from his pot. I asked for a raw one instead; it was a relief from the flat food of the menu.

At lunch on the third day, Gandhi said, 'Fischer, give me your bowl and I will give you some of the vegetables.' I said I had eaten the mess of spinach and squash four times in two days and had no desire for more.

'You don't like vegetables,' he commented.

'I don't like the taste of these vegetables three days running.'

'Ah,' he exclaimed, 'you must add plenty of salt and lemon.'

'You want me to kill the taste,' I interpreted.

'No,' he laughed, 'enrich the taste.'

'You are so non-violent you would not even kill a taste,' I said.

'If that were the only thing men killed, I wouldn't mind,' he remarked.

I wiped the perspiration from my face and neck. 'Next time I'm in India . . .' Gandhi was chewing and seemed not to have heard me so I stopped.

'Yes,' he said, 'the next time you are in India . . .'

'You either ought to have air-conditioning in Sevagram or live in the Viceroy's palace.'

'All right,' Gandhi acquiesced.

He encouraged banter. One afternoon when I came to his hut for the daily interview, he was not there. When he arrived he lay down on his bed. 'I will take your blows lying down,' he said, inviting questions. A Moslem woman gave him a mud pack for his abdomen. 'This puts me in touch with my future,' he said. I did not comment.

'I see you missed that one,' he noted.

I said I had not missed it but thought he was too young to think about returning to the dust.

'Why,' he declared, 'you and I and all of us, some in a hundred years, but all sooner or later, will do it.'

On another occasion he quoted a statement he had made to Lord Sankey in London; 'Do you think,' he had said, 'I would have reached this green old age if I hadn't taken care of myself? This is one of my faults.'

'I thought you were perfect,' I ventured.

He laughed and the eight or ten members of the ashram who usually sat in on the interviews laughed. (He had asked me whether I objected to their presence.) 'No,' he declared. 'I am very imperfect. Before you are gone you will have discovered a hundred of my faults and if you don't, I will help you to see them.'

Usually the hour's interview began with his finding the coolest place in the hut for me to sit. Then with a smile he would say, 'Now', inviting 'blows'. As the hour was about to end he would, with an unerring time sense, look at his big 'dollar' watch and proclaim, 'Now, your hour is up.' He was minutely punctual.

One day when I was leaving his hut after a talk, he said, 'Go and sit in a tub.' I wondered whether that was the Indian equivalent of 'go sit on a tack'. But crossing the sun-baked hundred yards between Gandhi's hut and the guest hut, the heat made the inside of my head feel dry and I decided that sitting in a tub would be a very good idea. In fact I thought I could improve on it. Adjoining the one living-room-bedroom of the guest hut was a small water room with cement floor on which stood a variety of pots, pitchers, tubs and bowls; an old woman kept them filled with water. Six or seven times a day I would step into this bathroom, slip off the two pieces of clothing and sandals I wore, and take a standing splash bath with the aid of a cup.

The worst ordeal of the day was typing the complete record of my conversations with Gandhi and others in the ashram, and with Nehru who came for two days of that week. After five minutes I was tired and wet all over with perspiration. Stimulated by Gandhi's suggestion to sit in a tub, I placed a small wooden packing case in one of the tin wash-tubs filled with water, put a folded Turkish towel on the packing case, then set a somewhat larger wooden packing case just outside the tub and placed my portable typewriter on it. These arrangements made, I sat down on the box in the tub and typed my notes. At intervals of a few minutes, when I began to perspire, I dipped a bronze bowl into the tub and poured the water over my neck, back and legs. By that method I was able to type a whole hour without feeling exhausted. The innovation stirred the ashram to mirth and jolly comment. It was not a glum community. Gandhi saw to that. He made eyes at the little children, provoked adults to laughter and joked with all and sundry visitors.

I asked Gandhi to be photographed with me. 'If a photographer is around by accident,' he replied, 'I have no objection to being seen in a photograph with you.'

'That,' I said, 'is the biggest compliment you have paid me.'

'Do you want compliments?' he inquired.

'Don't we all?'

'Yes,' Gandhi agreed, 'but sometimes we have to pay too dearly for them.'

During the week he inquired whether I knew Upton Sinclair, Dr Kellogg, the food specialist of Battle Creek, Michigan, and Mrs Eleanor Roosevelt. But I noticed no general curiosity. He focused his attention on issues which he could affect and on questions put to him.

I said I had been told that the Congress party was in the hands of big business and that he himself was supported by Bombay millowners. 'What truth is there in these assertions?' I probed.

'Unfortunately they are true,' he affirmed. 'Congress hasn't enough money to conduct its work. We thought in the beginning to collect four annas from each member per year and operate on that. But it hasn't worked.'

'What proportion of the Congress budget,' I pressed, 'is covered by rich Indians?'

'Practically all of it,' he admitted. 'In this ashram, for instance, we could live much more poorly than we do and spend less money. But we do not and the money comes from our rich friends.'

(There is a famous quip attributed to Mrs Naidu, which Gandhi enjoyed tremendously. to the effect that 'it costs a great deal of money to keep Gandhiji living in poverty'.)

'Doesn't the fact that Congress gets its money from the moneyed interests affect Congress politics?' I asked. 'Doesn't it create a moral obligation?'

'It creates a silent debt,' he stated. 'But actually we are very little influenced by the thinking of the rich. They are sometimes afraid of our demand for full independence . . . The dependence of Congress on rich sponsors is unfortunate. I use the word "unfortunate". It does not pervert our policy.'

'Isn't one of the results that there is a concentration on

nationalism almost to the exclusion of social and economic problems?'

'No,' he replied. 'Congress has from time to time, especially under the influence of Pandit Nehru, adopted advanced social programmes and schemes for economic planning. I will have those collected for you.'

Most of the money for the maintenance of Gandhi's ashram and of Gandhi's organizations for Harijan and peasant uplift and the teaching of a national language came from G. D. Birla, millionaire textile manufacturer at whose house in New Delhi the Mahatma sometimes lived. Birla first saw Gandhi in 1920 in Calcutta. On Gandhi's arrival at the railway station, Birla, then a young broker, and several friends unhitched the horses of the Mahatma's landau and pulled it through the streets. Birla became a devotee. He did not agree with some of the Mahatma's policies, but that did not matter; Gandhi was his 'father', he says. Had Birla believed in the spinning wheel he would have had to close his mills, but he did not believe in it. After the death of Birla's wife, he never remarried and became a Brahmachari; that was probably part of the bond between him and Gandhi. Gandhi first went to Birla's house in 1933 for ten days. Subsequently, he stayed a number of times for shorter or longer periods. Often, however, Gandhi preferred to make his headquarters in the Delhi Harijan colony near Kingsway; his upkeep there cost Birla fifty rupees a day. The ashram, including its hospital and dairy, cost Birla an estimated fifty thousand rupees a year and he supported it after 1935; he never kept accounts of what he gave Gandhi. But Gandhi wrote out in his own hand every smallest item of expenditure and presented it to Birla who tore it up before Gandhi's eyes without examining it. In addition, Birla backed many welfare institutions in which Gandhi was interested. His outlay for Gandhian enterprises ran into millions of rupees. Gandhi's friendship gave Birla prestige and satisfaction and perhaps even business advantages, for he learned many political secrets from the Mahatma. But had the occasion demanded, Gandhi might have led a strike of Birla's mill workers, as he did in the case of his friend and financial backer, Ambalal Sarabhai of Ahmedabad. Gandhi was tolerant of capitalists even when he opposed capitalist exploitation; he was equally tolerant of Englishmen after he turned against the British Empire. He would undoubtedly have stayed in Churchill's house. He was too sure of his purity and purpose to think he could be contaminated. To Gandhi nobody was an untouchable, neither Birla, nor a Communist, nor a Harijan, nor an imperialist. He fanned the spark of virtue wherever he discovered it. He allowed for the diversity of human nature and the multiplicity of man's motives.

Early in the week I spent at the ashram in June 1942, it became obvious that Gandhi was determined to launch a civil disobedience campaign with a view to making England 'Quit India'. That was to be the slogan.

Gandhi felt that unless England purged herself by leaving India the war could not be won and the peace could not be won.

One afternoon, after Gandhi had talked at length about the reasons that were prompting him to start civil disobedience against the British government, I said, 'It seems to me that the British cannot possibly quit India altogether. That would mean making a present of India to Japan; England would never agree, nor would the United States approve. If you demand that the British pack up and go bag and baggage, you are simply asking the impossible; you are barking up a tree. You do not mean, do you, that they must also withdraw their armies?'

For at least two minutes Gandhi said nothing. The silence in the room was almost audible.

'You are right,' Gandhi said at last. 'No, Britain and America and other countries too can keep their armies here and use Indian territory as a base for military operations. I do not wish Japan to win the war. But I am sure that Britain cannot win unless the Indian people become free. Britain is weaker and Britain is morally indefensible while she rules India. I do not wish to humiliate England.'

'But if India is to be used as a military base by the democracies, many other things are involved. Armies do not exist in a vacuum. For instance, the western allies would need good organization on the railroads.'

'Oh,' he exclaimed, 'they could operate the railroads. They would need order in the ports where they received their supplies. They could not have riots in Bombay and Calcutta. These matters would require co-operation and common effort.'

'Could the terms of this collaboration be set forth in a treaty of alliance?'

'Yes,' he agreed, 'we could have a written agreement . . .'

'Why have you not said this?' I asked. 'I must confess that when I heard of your proposed civil disobedience movement I was prejudiced against it. I believe that it would impede the prosecution of the war. I think the war has to be fought and won. I see complete darkness for the world if the Axis wins. I think we have a chance for a better world if we win.'

'There I cannot quite agree,' he argued. 'Britain often cloaks herself in the cloth of hypocrisy, promising what she later does not deliver. But I accept the proposition that there is a better chance if the democracies win.'

'It depends on the kind of peace we make,' I said.

'It depends on what you do during the war,' he corrected. 'I am not interested in future promises. I am not interested in independence after the war. I want independence now. That will help England win the war.'

'Why,' I again inquired, 'have you not communicated your plan to the Viceroy? He should be told that you have no objection now to the use of India as a base for Allied military operations.'

'No one has asked me,' he replied weakly.

Several of Gandhi's most intimate disciples were unhappy over his readiness to tolerate British and other armed forces in India. They felt his statement to me a serious blunder. He himself admitted publicly that he had changed his mind. 'There was obviously a gap in my first writing,' he said in *Harijan* shortly after my interview with him. 'I filled it in as soon as it was discovered by one of my numerous interviewers. Non-violence demands the strictest honesty, cost what it may. The public have therefore to suffer my weakness, if weakness it be. I could not be guilty of asking the Allies to take a step which would involve certain defeat . . . Abrupt withdrawal of the Allied troops might result in Japan's occupation of India and China's sure fall. I had not the remotest idea of any such catastrophe resulting from my action . . .'

Before I left the ashram Mahadev Desai asked me to tell the Viceroy that Gandhi wished to see him. The Mahatma was prepared to compromise and perhaps to abandon the projected civil disobedience movement. In New Delhi, later, I received a letter from Gandhi for transmission to President Roosevelt. The accompanying note said, characteristically, 'If it does not commend itself to you, you may tear it to pieces.'

He was malleable. 'Tell your President I wish to be dissuaded,' he told me. He was deeply convinced, however, that India should be granted self-government during the war; if the anti-Axis powers did not understand this he would call it to their attention by a civil disobedience campaign. 'Your President,' Gandhi declared one afternoon, 'talks about the Four Freedoms. Do they include the freedom to be free?'

Gandhi felt that the democratic position on India was morally indefensible. Roosevelt or Linlithgow could dissuade him by changing the position. Otherwise he had no doubts. Nehru and Azad did. Rajagopalachari had resigned from the Congress leadership because of his differences with the Mahatma. Gandhi could not be shaken. He convinced Nehru and Azad. Nehru had considered the foreign and domestic situation inopportune. 'I argued with him for days together,' Gandhi reported. 'He fought against my position with a passion which I have no words to describe.' Nehru's personal contacts, Gandhi explained, 'make him feel much more the misery of the impending ruin of China and Russia . . . In that misery he tried to forget his old quarrel with [British] imperialism'. But before Nehru left the ashram 'the logic of facts', as Gandhi put it, 'overwhelmed him'. Indeed, Nehru became such a staunch supporter of the proposed civil disobedience campaign that when I asked him subsequently in Bombay whether Gandhi ought to see the Viceroy, he replied, 'No, what for?' Gandhi was still hoping for an audience with Linlithgow.

I left the ashram on 10 June in the car that took Azad and Nehru to the Congress hostel in Wardha. Several hours later, the car returned to Sevagram to fetch Gandhi for further consultations with the two Congress leaders. At three in the afternoon, Gandhi entered the hostel alone. Three-quarters of a mile from Wardha the car had broken down. Gandhi got out and walked the distance in the broiling Indian afternoon June sun. When he reached the house he was in a gay mood; if he suffered from fatigue it was not noticeable and must have retreated before the pleasure of being able to comment on the unreliability of 'these new-fangled technical achievements of the industrial age'.

He had great charm. He was a remarkable natural phenomenon, quiet and insidiously overwhelming. Intellectual contact with him was a delight because he opened his mind and allowed one to see how the machine worked. He did not attempt to express his ideas in finished form. He thought aloud; he revealed each step in his thinking. You heard not only words but also his thoughts. You could therefore follow him as he moved to a conclusion. This prevented him from talking like a propagandist; he talked like a friend. He was interested in an exchange of views, but much more in the establishment of a personal relationship.

Even when evasive Gandhi was frank. I was asking him about his dreams of the post-independence India. He argued back and forth. 'You want to force me into an admission,' he said, 'that we would need rapid industrialization. I will not be forced into such an admission. Our first problem is to get rid of British rule. Then we will be free, without restraints from the outside, to do what India requires. The British have seen fit to allow us to have some factories and also to prohibit other factories. No, for me the paramount problem is the ending of British domination.'

That, obviously, was what he wanted to talk about; he did not conceal his desire. His brain had no blue pencil. He said, for instance, that he would go to Japan to try to end the war. He knew, and immediately added, that he would never get an opportunity to go and, if he went, Japan would not make peace. He knew too that his statement would be misinterpreted. Then why did he make it? Because he thought it.

Gandhi asserted that a federal administration would be unnecessary in an independent India. I pointed out the difficulties that would arise in the absence of a federal administration. He was not convinced. I was baffled. Finally he said, 'I know that despite my personal views there will be a central government.' This was a characteristic Gandhi cycle: he enunciated a principle, defended it, then admitted with a laugh that it was unworkable. In negotiation, this faculty could be extremely irritating and time-wasting. In personal conversation, it was attractive and even exciting. He himself was sometimes surprised at the things he said. His thinking was fluid. Most persons like to be proved right. So did Gandhi. But frequently he snatched a victory out of an error by admitting it.

Old people are prone to reminiscences. Lloyd George would commence to answer a question on current events and soon be talking about his conduct of the first World War or a campaign for social reform early in the century. At seventy-three, Gandhi never reminisced. His mind was on things to come. Years did not matter to him because he thought in terms of the unending future. Only the hours mattered because they were the measure of what he could contribute to that future.

Gandhi had more than influence, he had authority, which is less yet better than power. Power is the attribute of a machine; authority is the attribute of a person. Statesmen are varying combinations of both. The dictator's constant accretion of power, which he must inevitably abuse, steadily robs him of authority. Gandhi's rejection of power enhanced his authority. Power feeds on the blood and tears of its victims. Authority is fed by service, sympathy and affection.

One evening I watched Mahadev Desai spin. I said I had been listening carefully to Gandhi and studying my notes and wondering all the time what was the source of his hold on people; I had come to the tentative conclusion that it was his passion.

'That is right,' Desai said.

'What is the root of his passion?' I asked.

'This passion,' Desai explained, 'is the sublimation of all the passions that flesh is heir to.'

'Sex?'

'Sex and anger and personal ambition . . . Gandhi is under his own complete control. That generates tremendous energy and passion.'

It was a subdued, purring passion. He had a soft intensity, a tender firmness and an impatience cotton-wooled in patience. Gandhi's colleagues and the British sometimes resented his intensity, firmness and impatience. But he retained their respect, often their love, through his softness, tenderness and patience.

Gandhi sought approval; he was very happy when the great Tagore agreed with him. But he could defy the whole world and his political next-of-kin.

Gandhi was a strong individual, and his strength lay in the

richness of his personality, not in the multitude of his possessions. His goal was To be, not To have. Happiness came to him through self-realization. Fearing nothing, he could live the truth. Having nothing, he could pay for his principles.

Mahatma Gandhi is the symbol of the unity between personal morality and public action. When conscience dwells at home but not in the workshop, office, classroom and market-place, the road is wide open to corruption and cruelty and to dictatorship.

Gandhi enriched politics with ethics. He faced each morning's issues in the light of eternal and universal values. He always distilled a permanent element out of the ephemeral. Gandhi thus broke through the framework of usual assumptions which cramp a man's action. He discovered a new dimension of action. Unconfined by considerations of personal success or comfort, he split the social atom and found a new source of energy. It gave him weapons of attack against which there was often no defence. His greatness lay in doing what everybody could do but doesn't.

'Perhaps he will not succeed,' Tagore wrote of the living Gandhi. 'Perhaps he will fail as the Buddha failed and as Christ failed to wean men from their iniquities, but he will always be remembered as one who made his life a lesson for all ages to come.'

CHAPTER 24

Will-Power

In May, June and July 1942, one felt a suffocating airlessness in India. Indians seemed desperate. British generals, US General Joseph W. Stilwell and a small armed remnant, and thousands of Indian refugees were straggling out of Burma to escape the conquering Japanese. Japan was next door to India. England apparently lacked the strength to protect India from invasion. Vocal Indians were irritated and exasperated by their utter helplessness. There was the national emergency; tension was mounting; danger threatened; opportunity knocked; but Indians had no voice and no power to act.

Gandhi found the situation intolerable. Resignation was alien to his nature. He believed and had taught a vast following that Indians must shape their own destiny.

The Cripps mission awakened many hopes; India might gain the right to guide her fate. Now the hopes were dashed. Indians were to be supine spectators in an hour of decision. Anger swept the country.

In the light of subsequent events, it appears clear that 1942 or 1943 or 1944 was the best time to grant India independence. For, since Britain and other United Nations would keep their troops in the country as long as the war lasted, the transfer of power to a provisional Indian government could be achieved smoothly and with the least likelihood of riots, chaos, or attempts at a separate peace with Japan. Real power would remain in British hands. This would have avoided the hundreds of thousands of deaths and the millions of human torments and tragedies which attended the liberation of India in 1947.

Gandhi could not have foreseen the black future, but he did

sense the urgent need of an immediate change. He was determined to exert maximum pressure on England for the early establishment of an independent national government.

Gandhi's formula was: 'not to put any obstacle in the way of the British forces'; not to assist the British actively; and to offer complete passive resistance to the Japanese.

'If the Japanese come,' Indians asked, 'how are we to resist them non-violently?'

'Neither food nor shelter is to be given,' Gandhi replied in the 14 June, 1942, *Harijan*, 'nor are any dealings to be established with them. They should be made to feel that they are not wanted But of course things are not going to happen quite so smoothly as the question implies. It is a superstition to think that they will come as friendlies . . . If the people cannot resist fierce attack and are afraid of death, they must evacuate the infested place in order to deny compulsory service to the enemy.'

On 26 July, answering similar questions in *Harijan*, Gandhi wrote, 'I would rather be shot than submit to Japanese or any other power.' He recommended the same preference to his friends.

Gandhi, the absolute pacifist, would have wished India to give an unprecedented demonstration of a successful non-violent defeat of an invading army. Yet he was not so unrealistic as to forget that a fierce war to the death of countries raged. In *Harijan* of 14 June, 1942, Gandhi declared, 'Assuming that the National government is formed and if it answers my expectations, its first act would be to enter into a treaty with the United Nations for defensive operations against aggressive powers, it being common cause that India will have nothing to do with any of the Fascist powers and India would be morally bound to help the United Nations.'

Asked by Reuters in London to amplify this encouraging pronouncement, Gandhi cabled, 'There can be no limit to what friendly independent India can do. I had in mind a treaty between the United Nations and India for the defence of China against Japanese aggression.'

Would Gandhi, then, assist the war effort? No. United Nations armies would be tolerated on Indian soil and Indians could enlist in the British Army or render other help. But if he had anything to say, the Indian Army would be disbanded and the new Indian national government would use 'all its power, prestige and resources' to bring about world peace.

Did he expect this to happen? No. 'After the formation of the National Government', he said, 'my voice may be a voice in the wilderness and nationalist India may go war-mad.'

Nationalist India might well have gone 'war-mad' if only to shake off the oppressive frustration of inaction. Nehru, Azad and Rajagopalachari were eager to have a national government for its own sake, to be sure, but also in order to fight the war. They were militantly anti-fascist. Nehru said, 'We would fight in every way possible with non-violence and with arms, by making it a people's war, by raising a people's army, by increasing production . . .' But if Britain did not enable them to do these things, they must continue the struggle for independence. 'Passivity on our part at this moment', Nehru declared, 'would be suicidal . . . It would destroy and emasculate us.' Fear of India's emasculation was an everpresent motive. 'Today the whole of India is impotent,' Gandhi complained in the same context. In different ways, both Nehru and Gandhi were concerned with building up the manhood of their people. Gandhi wanted to give them inner strength through confidence. He inspired that feeling in his Indian and foreign visitors.

As the summer of 1942 wore on, it became clear that London would not depart from the spurned Cripps proposal. Nehru had waited for a sign from Washington; he had hoped Roosevelt would prevail upon Churchill to make another move in India. No sign came. Some Congressmen wondered whether the country would respond to a call for civil disobedience, and some feared that it would respond violently. Gandhi had no doubts. He was registering a nation's blind urge to self-assertion.

He did not contemplate the overthrow of the British government. 'A non-violent revolution,' he explained, 'is not a programme of seizure of power. It is a programme of transformation of relationships ending in a peaceful transfer of power...'

'British rule in India must end immediately,' the Working Committee of Congress resolved in Wardha on 14 July; foreign domination 'even at its best' is an evil and a 'continuing injury'. The frustration left by the Cripps Mission 'has resulted in a rapid and widespread increase of ill-will against Britain and a growing satisfaction at the success of Japanese arms. The Working Committee view this development with grave apprehension, as this, unless checked, will inevitably lead to a passive acceptance of aggression. The Committee hold that all aggression must be resisted ... The Congress would change the present ill-will against Britain into good-will and make India a willing partner in a joint enterprise ... This is only possible if India feels the glow of freedom'.

Congress, the resolution continued, did not wish to embarrass the Allied powers; it is therefore 'agreeable to the stationing of the armed forces of the Allies in India . . .'

If this appeal failed, the resolution concluded, Congress will 'be reluctantly compelled' to start a civil disobedience campaign which 'would inevitably be under the leadership of Mahatma Gandhi'.

The resolution still required the approval of the larger All-India Congress Committee summoned to convene in Bombay early in August. From Sevagram, meanwhile, Gandhi issued an appeal 'To Every Japanese'. 'I must confess', he began, 'that though I have no ill-will against you, I intensely dislike your attack upon China ... you have descended to imperial ambition. You will fail to realize that ambition and may become the authors of the dismemberment of Asia, thus unwittingly preventing world federation and brotherhood without which there can be no hope for humanity.'

He warned Tokyo not to exploit the situation to invade

India. 'You will be sadly disillusioned if you believe that you will receive a willing welcome from India . . . we will not fail in resisting you with all the might that our country can muster . . .'

Then he went to Bombay. To A. T. Steele, of the *New York Herald Tribune*, Gandhi said, 'If anybody could convince me that in the midst of war, the British government cannot declare India free without jeopardizing the war effort, I should like to hear the argument.'

'If you were convinced,' Steele asked, 'would you call off the campaign?'

'Of course,' Gandhi replied. 'My complaint is that all these good people talk *at* me, swear *at* me, but never condescend to talk *to* me.'

Linlithgow had talked to him in 1939 and 1940, but not thereafter.

Several hundred Congress leaders assembled for the AICC session on 7 August, and after deliberating all day of the 7th and 8th, they adopted a slightly modified version of the Wardha resolution; they dotted one *i* by declaring that an Indian government would resist aggression 'with all the armed as well as the non-violent forces at its command' – this was an un-Gandhian touch inserted by the Nehru–Azad school – and crossed one bridge before they reached it by cautioning the Congress rank and file that if their leaders were arrested and prevented from issuing instructions they must obey the general instructions which read, 'non-violence is the basis of this movement.'

Shortly after midnight of 8 August, Gandhi addressed the AICC delegates. 'The actual struggle does not commence this very moment,' he emphasized. 'You have merely placed certain powers in my hands. My first act will be to wait upon His Excellency the Viceroy and plead with him for the acceptance of the Congress demand. This may take two or three weeks. What are you to do in the meanwhile? I will tell you. There is the spinning wheel . . . But there is something more you have to do . . . Every one of you should, from this very moment, consider himself a free man or woman and even act as if you are free and no longer under the heel of this imperialism . . .' He was reversing the materialistic concept that conditions determine psychology. No, psychology could shape conditions. 'What you think, you become,' he once said.

The delegates went home to sleep. Gandhi, Nehru and scores of others were awakened by the police a few hours later – before sunrise – and carried off to prison. Gandhi was sent into a palace of the Aga Khan at Yeravda, near Poona. Mrs Naidu, Mirabehn, Mahadev Desai and Pyarelal Nayyar, arrested at the same time, were quartered with him. The next day, Kasturbai got herself arrested by announcing that she would address a meeting in Bombay at which Gandhi had been scheduled to speak. She and Dr Sushila Nayyar, who had been giving her medical care, joined the Gandhi jail company. The British were very accommodating.

In an interview with the Viceroy after my week with Gandhi I conveyed the message entrusted to me at Sevagram: Gandhi wished to talk with Linlithgow. The Viceroy replied, 'That is a matter of high policy and will have to be considered on its merits'; 1942 was Churchill's first opportunity in office to cope with a civil disobedience movement in India. The British government preferred suppression to discussion.

The moment the prison doors closed behind Gandhi the sluice gates of violence opened. Police stations and government buildings were set on fire, telegraph lines destroyed, railroad ties pulled up and British officals assaulted; a number were killed. Individuals and groups dedicated to destruction roamed the countryside. Soon a powerful underground movement sprang into existence led, in most cases, by members of the Socialist party, a segment of the Congress party. Socialist leaders Jaiprakash Narayan, Mrs Aruna Asaf Ali and others, political children of Gandhi but recent students of Karl Marx, acquired the halos of heroes as they moved secretly across the land fomenting rebellion. Staid citizens harboured and financed them while the British police hunted them. His Majesty's writ no longer ran and his officials no longer appeared in many areas where Indians set up independent village, town and district governments. These were, in most cases, skeleton structures whose propaganda value exceeded their administrative effectiveness. Yet in some regions, notably in Tilak's traditionally militant Maharashtra, it was not till 1944 that the British returned to rule.

Even Gandhi was in a bellicose mood. With that irrepressible ability to take the centre of the stage, the jailed Mahatma's personality broke through the walls of the Aga Khan's desolate palace and besieged the mind first of the British government and then of the Indian people.

He was no sooner in jail than he wrote a letter to Sir Roger Lumley, the governor of Bombay, protesting against his own transportation from the train to the prison by car while his comrades went by motor truck. He wanted no privileges, he said, 'except for the special food'. The palace, he wrote, was 'commodious'; could not Sardar Patel, who had been ill, and his daughter who nursed him, be moved into it? The final point: on the train he had seen in a paper the Government's justification of its policy; it contained 'some grossly inaccurate statements which I ought to be allowed to correct. This and similar things I cannot do, unless I know what is going on outside the jail'. Yet newspapers had been forbidden to him.

Lumley's secretary replied he could not have newspapers or Patel. He might write personal letters to his family.

Didn't the Government know, Gandhi answered, that 'for over thirty-five years I have ceased to live a family life' and had been living an ashram life? He wanted to be in touch with the various voluntary organizations he had founded for Harijan uplift, khadi, the development of a national language, etc. The Government then made a concession: he could write to ashram members on personal questions but not about the organizations. Gandhi refused to avail himself of the privilege.

Gandhi now turned on the Viceroy. Ever since President Roosevelt's intervention in the Indian crisis and Churchill's offer to 'assuage' United States public opinion by resigning, a gigantic propaganda battle had been going on to win American approval of British policy in India. Gandhi knew this. In his first letter from jail to the Viceroy on 14 August, Gandhi accused the Government of 'distortions and misrepresentations'. The letter was many pages long. Linlithgow, addressing 'Dear Mr Gandhi', answered in a paragraph that 'it would not be possible for me either to accept your criticism' or change the policy.

Gandhi waited several months. On New Year's Eve, 1942, he wrote, 'Dear Lord Linlithgow, This is a very personal letter . . . I must not allow the old year to expire without disburdening myself of what is rankling in my breast against you. I have thought we were friends . . . However what has happened since 9 August makes me wonder whether you still regard me as a friend. I have not perhaps come in such close touch with any occupant of your throne as with you.' Then he voiced what apparently hurt him most: 'Why did you not, before taking drastic action, send for me, tell me your suspicions and make yourself sure of your facts? I am quite capable of seeing myself as others see me.' The Government had made the charge that he was responsible for the violence throughout the country and expected him to condemn it. How could he when he had only the official version? By accusing him without giving him freedom to reply, by holding him and his followers in prison despite their good intentions, the Government had 'wronged innocent men'.

Therefore, Gandhi concluded, he had decided to 'crucify the flesh by fasting'. This was a last resort and he would be glad not to fast. 'Convince me of my error or errors and I shall make ample amends. You can send for me . . . There are many other ways if you have the will . . . May the New Year bring peace to us all! I am, Your sincere friend, M. K. Gandhi.'

The Viceroy received this letter fourteen days later; minor officials had delayed it. He answered in a letter marked 'Personal'. It was a two-page letter. Newspapers had been supplied to Gandhi's prison after the early period without them. He knew of the arson and murders. Linlithgow was therefore 'profoundly depressed . . . that no word of condemnation for that violence and crime should have come from you'. If Gandhi wished to dissociate himself from these acts 'You know me well enough after these many years to believe that I shall be only too concerned to read with the same close attention as ever any message which I receive from you . . . Yours sincerely, Linlithgow.'

'I had almost despaired of ever hearing from you,' Gandhi's reply began. 'Please excuse my impatience. Your letter gladdens me to find that I have not lost caste with you. My letter of December 31st was a growl against you. Yours is a counter-growl . . . Of course I deplore the happenings that have taken place since August 9th. But have I not laid the blame for them at the door of the Government of India? Moreover, I could not express any opinion on events which I cannot influence or control and of which I have but a one-sided account . . . I am certain that nothing but good could have resulted if you had stayed your hand and granted me the interview which I had announced, on the night of August 8th, I was to seek . . . convince me that I was wrong and I will make ample amends . . .'

Linlithgow responded quickly saying he had no choice 'but to regard the Congress movement and you as its authorized and fully empowered spokesman . . . as responsible for the sad campaign of violence and crime'. He repelled Gandhi's charge that the Government was at fault. He asked the Mahatma to 'repudiate or dissociate yourself from the resolution of August 8th and the policy which the resolution represents' and to 'give me appropriate assurances as regards the future . . .' He had asked the Governor of Bombay to forward Gandhi's letter without delay.

It was the Government, Gandhi's return letter stated, that 'goaded the people to the point of madness'. The Congress resolution of 8 August was friendly to the United Nations and to England. The Government's violence was 'leonine'. The arrests started the trouble. Yet the Viceroy blamed him for the violence though he had worked all his life for non-violence. 'If then I cannot get soothing balm for my pain, I must resort to the law prescribed for Satyagrahis, namely, a fast according to capacity.' It would commence on 9 February and end twenty-one days later. 'Usually, during my fasts, I take water with the addition of salt. But nowadays, my system refuses water. This time therefore I purpose to add juices of citrus fruit to make water drinkable. For my wish is not to fast unto death, but to survive the ordeal, if God so wills. The fast can be ended sooner by the government giving the needed relief.'

The Viceroy replied immediately, on 5 February, with a many-page letter. He still held Congress responsible for 'the lamentable disorders'. Sir Reginald Maxwell, the Home Member of Linlithgow Executive Council, had made a full statement of this charge in the assembly and this would be sent to the prisoner. The letter reiterated the charge and added details. 'Let me in conclusion say how greatly I regret, having regard to your health and age, the decision' to fast. He hoped he would not fast. But it was Gandhi's responsibility. 'I regard the use of a fast for political purposes as a form of political blackmail for which there is no moral justification, and understood from your own previous writings that this was also your view.'

Besides, Gandhi had written that one may fast only against those who love you, not against a tyrant.

By return post, Gandhi denied that his decision to fast was contrary to his previous writings. 'I wonder whether you yourself have read those writings . . . Despite your description of it as "a form of political blackmail", it is on my part an appeal to the Highest Tribunal for justice which I have failed to secure from you. If I do not survive the ordeal I shall go to the Judgement Seat with the fullest faith in my innocence. Posterity will judge between you as a representative of an all-powerful government and me a humble man who tried to serve his country and humanity through it.'

Two days before the fast was to commence the Government offered to release Gandhi for its duration. He and his associates in prison could go wherever they liked. Gandhi refused. If he was released, he said, he would not fast. Thereupon, the Government announced that he would be responsible for any results; meanwhile, he could invite into the jail any doctors he wanted to have and also friends from the outside.

The fast commenced on 10 February, 1942, a day later than scheduled. The first day he was quite cheerful and for two days he took his customary morning and evening half-hour walks. But soon the bulletins became increasingly disquieting. On the sixth day, six physicians, including British official doctors, stated that Gandhi's condition had 'further deteriorated'. The next morning Sir Homi Mody, Mr N. R. Sarker and Mr Aney, three Indians in the Viceroy's Executive Council, whose membership indicated their pro-government and anti-Congress attitude, resigned from the Council in protest against the government accusations which had caused Gandhi to undertake the fast. A debate on the fast took place in the Central Legislature. From all over the country, the Government was bombarded with demands to release the Mahatma. Eleven days after the fast began, Linlithgow rejected all suggestions to liberate Gandhi.

Dr B. C. Roy came from Calcutta to attend Gandhi. The British physicians urged intravenous feeding to save the Mahatma. The Indian physicians said it would kill him; he objected to injections. The body could reject medicines taken orally, Gandhi always argued, but it was helpless before injections, and his mind therefore rebelled against them; they were violence.

Crowds gathered around Yeravda. The Government allowed the public to come into the palace grounds and file through Gandhi's room. Devadas and Ramdas, his sons, arrived.

Horace Alexander, the British Friend, attempted to intervene with the Government. He was rebuffed. Mr Aney, who had just resigned from the Viceroy's Council, visited the sinking Mahatma.

Gandhi had been taking water without salt or fruit juice. Nausea plagued him. His kidneys began to fail and his blood became thick. On the thirteenth day of the fast the pulse grew feeble and his skin was cold and moist. Kasturbai knelt before a sacred plant and prayed; she thought his death was near.

Finally, the Mahatma was persuaded to mix a few drops of fresh moosambi fruit juice with the drinking water. Vomiting stopped; he became more cheerful.

On 2 March, Kasturbai handed him a glass containing six ounces of orange juice diluted with water. He sipped it for twenty minutes. He thanked the doctors and cried copiously while doing so. He lived on orange juice for the next four days and then went on a diet of goat's milk, fruit juice and fruit pulp. His health improved slowly.

India's prominent non-Congress leaders now started agitating for Gandhi's release and for a new government policy of conciliation. Sir Tej Bahadur Sapru and others asked permission to see Gandhi; Linlithgow refused.

On 25 April, William Phillips, Roosevelt's personal envoy in India and former United States Under-Secretary of State, said to foreign correspondents before leaving for home, 'I should have liked to meet and talk with Mr Gandhi. I requested the appropriate authorities for permission to do so and I was informed that they were unable to grant the necessary permission.'

Linlithgow's behaviour had induced unwonted bitterness

in Gandhi, and when the Viceroy, whose usual five-year term had been prolonged because of the war emergency, was finally preparing to leave India, Gandhi wrote to him on 27 September, 1943, as follows:

Dear Lord Linlithgow, On the eve of your departure from India I would like to send you a word.
Of all the high functionaries I have had the honour of knowing none has been the cause of such deep sorrow to me as you have been. It has cut me to the quick to have to think of you as having countenanced untruth, and that regarding one whom you at one time considered your friend. I hope and pray that God will some day put it into your heart to realize that you, a representative of a great nation, have been led into a grievous error. With good wishes, I still remain your friend, M. K. Gandhi.

Linlithgow replied on 7 October:

Dear Mr Gandhi, I have received your letter of September 27th. I am indeed sorry that your feelings about any deeds or words of mine should be as you describe. But I must be allowed, as gently as I may, to make plain to you that I am quite unable to accept your interpretation of the events in question.
    As for the corrective virtues of time and reflection, evidently they are ubiquitous in their operation and wisely to be rejected by no man. I am sincerely, Linlithgow.

Before and after the fast, Gandhi wrote long letters, some of which were of pamphlet length, to Sir Reginald Maxwell, Lord (formerly Sir Herbert) Samuel and others, seeking to controvert their public assertions about events and conditions in India. But none of them was published and his letter to Samuel, sent on 15 May, 1943, was not delivered in London until 25 July, 1944. Throughout, Gandhi continued to maintain that he could 'accept no responsibility for the unfortunate happenings' in India, that he was neither anti-British nor pro-Japanese and that he could have been dissuaded from taking any steps against the Government.
    The facts are: Gandhi never launched the civil

disobedience movement. Congress had merely authorized
him to launch it, but he had stated that it would not begin
until he gave the order. First he would seek an interview with
the Viceroy. The country was in a violent mood; Gandhi
knew it; conceivably he might have chosen a form of civil
disobedience, like the Salt March, which did not lend itself to
mass violence. Had Gandhi remained at liberty he might
have prevented his followers from engaging in the destruction
of property and persons. He might have fasted against them.
At least, he could have curbed the general violence. He would
not have added to it. The British gained nothing from
Gandhi's arrest except the satisfaction, tempered by
headaches, of having him under lock and key. Gandhi's
freedom would have mollified many Indians. His arrest
inflamed them. It deepened the wide-spread impression that
England did not intend to part with power in India. Hence
the revolt. It was intensified by the 1943 famine in Bengal in
which, according to British official figures, a million and a
half Indians died. Indians said the Government might have
prevented the famine or, at a minimum, undertaken
emergency feeding. That was one of Wavell's first steps on
ascending the Viceroy's throne in October 1943.

For Gandhi, this stay in prison was an unrelieved tragedy.
The widespread violence and his inability to deal with it made
him unhappy. The Government's accusation that he was to
blame for the disturbances when it knew his devotion to non-
violence and when it knew that he had never actually started
civil disobedience impressed him as unfair and untrue; the
injustice pained him. It was to protest against the charge – not
to force the British to release him – that he had fasted. A
perfect yogi might have remained indifferent to what others
said. Gandhi was not completely detached.

The tragedy was deepened by personal loss. Six days after
Gandhi entered the Aga Khan's palace, Mahadev Desai, who
was arrested with him, had a sudden heart attack and lost
consciousness. 'Mahadev, Mahadev,' Gandhi called.

'If only he would open his eyes and look at me he would not die,' Gandhi said.

'Mahadev, look, Bapu is calling you,' Kasturbai exclaimed.

But it was the end.

Mahadev Desai, who was past fifty, had served Gandhi devotedly and efficiently for twenty-four years as secretary, adviser, chronicler, friend and son. The Mahatma was stunned by the death. He went daily to the spot in the palace grounds where the ashes were buried.

Soon a still greater personal sorrow overtook Gandhi.

Gandhi spent much time in prison teaching his wife Indian geography and other subjects. She failed, however, to memorize the names of the rivers of the Punjab, and on examination by Gandhi she said Lahore, which is the capital of the Punjab, was the capital of Calcutta, a city which is the capital of Bengal. He had little success in his persistent efforts to improve her reading and writing of Gujarati. She was seventy-four.

Ba, or Mother, as everybody called Mrs Gandhi, still paid homage to Brahmans for their high-caste status and regarded them as possessing special endowments; she asked one Brahman who worked in the jail when they would be released. But she had rid herself of anti-untouchable prejudices, was a regular spinner and a sincere but not uncritical Gandhian. One day she was annoyed with Gandhi and said to him, 'Didn't I tell you not to pick a quarrel with the mighty Government? You did not listen to me and now we all have to pay the penalty. The Government is using its limitless strength to crush the people.'

'Then what do you want me to do . . . write to the Government and ask for their forgiveness?'

No, she did not ask that. But, she exclaimed, 'Why do you ask the British to leave India? Our country is vast. We can all live there. Let them stay if they like, but let them stay as brothers.'

'What else have I done?' Gandhi replied. 'I want them to go as rulers. Once they cease to be our rulers, we have no quarrel with them.'

Ah, yes, she agreed with that. She apparently worshipped him without understanding.

Kasturbai had been ailing, and in December 1943 she became seriously ill with chronic bronchitis. Dr Gilder and Dr Nayyar tended her, but she asked for Dr Dinshah Mehta, a nature cure expert who had treated Gandhi, and an Aryuvedic or Indian-medicine practitioner. In deference to her wishes, Gandhi bombarded the Government with letters to admit them. The practitioner tried all his art for a number of days during which the modern-medicine physicians withdrew from the patient. When he confessed defeat, Dr Gilder, Dr Nayyar and Dr Jivraj Mehta resumed their efforts, but they too failed. The Government gave permission for her sons and grandsons to visit her. Ba especially asked for her first-born, Harilal, who had been estranged from his parents.

Gandhi sat by his wife's bed for many hours. He ordered all medicines to be stopped and all food except honey and water. It was more important, he said, for her to have peace with God. 'If God wills it,' he said, 'she will pull through, else I would let her go, but I won't drug her any longer.'

Penicillin, then rare in India, was flown from Calcutta; Devadas had insisted on it. 'Why do you not trust God?' Gandhi said to him. 'Do you wish to drug your mother even on her deathbed?'

Gandhi had not known that penicillin was given by injection. On being told, he forbade it. Most of the day, Gandhi sat on her bed, holding her hand. Fellow prisoners sang Hindu hymns. On 21 February Harilal arrived, summoned hastily by the Government. He was drunk and had to be removed from Kasturbai's presence. She cried and beat her forehead. (Harilal attended his father's funeral without being recognized and spent that night with Devadas. He died, a derelict, in a tuberculosis hospital in Bombay on 19 June, 1948.)

The next day, her head resting in Gandhi's lap, she died. At the funeral, Gandhi offered a prayer borrowed from Hindu,

Parsi, Moslem and Christian scriptures. Devadas lit the pyre. The ashes were buried beside those of Mahadev Desai in the prison grounds.

When Gandhi returned from the cremation, he sat on his bed in silence and then, from time to time, as the thoughts came, he spoke: 'I cannot imagine life without Ba . . . Her passing has left a vacuum which never will be filled . . . We lived together for sixty-two years . . . If I had allowed the penicillin it would not have saved her . . . And she passed away in my lap. Could it be better? I am happy beyond measure.'

Gandhi had been in correspondence on political issues with the new Viceroy, Lord Wavell. Immediately after Kasturbai's death, Wavell said in a letter to the Mahatma, 'I take this opportunity to express to you deep sympathy from my wife and myself at the death of Mrs Gandhi. We understand what this loss must mean to you after so many years of companionship.'

Gandhi was touched. In his reply he wrote, 'Though for her sake I have welcomed her death as bringing freedom from living agony, I feel the loss more than I had thought I should.' Then he explained their intimate relationship to Wavell, whom he had never met. 'We were a couple outside the ordinary,' he said. Their continence, after the age of thirty-seven, 'knit us together as never before. We ceased to be two different entities . . . The result was that she became truly my *better* half'.

Six weeks after Kasturbai's passing, Gandhi suffered a severe attack of benign tertian malaria, during which he was delirious. His temperature rose to 105. A blood count showed a very high germ content. At first he thought he could cure it with a fruit-juice diet and fasting; he accordingly refused to take quinine. After two days he relented; he took a total of thirty-three grains of quinine in two days and the fever disappeared. In all subsequent examinations, parasites were absent and the malaria never recurred.

On 3 May Gandhi's physicians issued a bulletin saying his anaemia was worse and his blood pressure low. 'His general condition is again giving rise to severe anxiety.' Agitation for his release swept India. A heavy armed guard was placed around the prison. At 8 A.M., 6 May, Gandhi and his associates were released. A subsequent analysis showed that he had hookworm (ankylostomiasis) and amoebiasis of the intestines.

This was Gandhi's last time in jail. Altogether, he spent 2,089 days in Indian and 249 days in South African prisons.

Gandhi went to Juhu, by the sea near Bombay, where he stayed in the home of Shantikumar Morarji, whose father was from Porbandar, Gandhi's birthplace. Mrs Naidu and Mrs Pandit, Jawaharlal Nehru's sister, were there at the same time.

Mrs Morarji suggested that the Mahatma see a moving picture film; he had never seen either a silent movie or a talkie. After some urging, he agreed. *Mission to Moscow* was being exhibited in a nearby suburb. Mechanical equipment and the film were brought to the Morarji home and, together with about one hundred other persons, Gandhi viewed *Mission to Moscow*.

'How did you like it?' Mrs Morarji asked.

'I didn't like it,' he said. He hadn't liked the ballroom dancing and the women in scanty dresses; he considered it improper.

Friends complained that he had viewed a foreign picture, not one of Indian manufacture. He accordingly saw *Ram Rajya*, based on an ancient legend of an ideal moral king.

For his relaxation, somebody read Gandhi a delightful, tranquil children's book by Pearl S. Buck entitled *The Chinese Children Next Door*.

The doctors were curing Gandhi and he was curing himself with silence, 'medical silence', he called it. At first it was total; after a few weeks, he would speak between 4 P.M. and 8 P.M., which was prayer-meeting time.

After several weeks he plunged into work again.

CHAPTER 25

Jinnah and Gandhi

Mohamed Ali Jinnah, who considered himself Gandhi's opposite number, lived in a large, crescent-shaped marble mansion from which a classic flight of marble stairs and a series of carefully moulded terraces led down to the sea at Bombay. He had built it during the second World War and he apologized, when I saw him in 1942, that it was still inadequately furnished. His little study, however, and other parts of the great house on Malabar Hill revealed the cultured and opulent touch.

Jinnah was over six feet tall and weighed nine stone. He was a very thin man. His well-shaped head was covered with thick, long, silver-grey hair brushed straight back. His shaven face was thin, the nose long and aquiline. The temples were sunken and the cheeks were deep holes which made his cheekbones stand out like high horizontal ridges. His teeth were bad. When not speaking, he would pull in his chin, tighten his lips, knit his big brow. The result was a forbidding earnestness. He rarely laughed.

Jinnah wore a knee-length straw-coloured tunic, tight white Indian trousers that clung to his bony legs and black patent-leather pumps. A monocle dangled from a black cord. He often dressed in European clothes. He was, wrote George E. Jones in the *New York Times* of 5 May, 1946, 'undoubtedly one of the best dressed men in the British Empire'.

Jinnah, the first child of a rich skins, hide and gum-arabic merchant, was born on Christmas Day 1876 – seven years later than Gandhi – in the Kathiawar peninsula, Gandhi's birthplace; his native language was Gujarati. 'Jinnah' is a Hindu name; the family were recent converts to Islam. Jinnah was a Khoja Moslem. Many Khojas carry Hindu names and maintain the Hindu joint family system. In the eighteenth and nineteenth centuries, the Khojas attempted to return to Hinduism but were rebuffed.

Hinduism and Mohammedanism are dissimilar religions, but Hindus and Mohammedans are far less dissimilar. Most Moslems of India are converted Hindus, converted by the invading Arabs, Afghans and Persians who began thrusting into India during the eighth century. Jinnah said converted Hindus were 75 per cent of the Moslem community; Nehru put it at 95 per cent. In parts of India, Moslems worship in Hindu temples. There are castes among some Indian Moslems. In many areas, Hindus and Moslems are indistinguishable from one another in appearance, costume, customs and language. Hindi and Urdu, the predominant tongues of Hindus and Moslems respectively, are written with different scripts and the former has absorbed more Sanskrit words while the latter uses more Persian words, but Hindus understand Urdu and Moslems understand Hindi. Hinduism is an insidious, emotional religion, native to India, which clings to the descendants of those who were converted to the *Koran* by the sword. Religious leaders have succeeded in widening the gulf and poisoning the relations, yet ties remain. Jinnah, Gandhi, Nehru, the Viceroy, Wavell and all the British officials, Hindus and Moslems one met in India agreed that Hindus and Moslems lived peacefully side by side in the villages – and the village is 80 per cent of India. In the Indian Army, moreover, Hindus, Moslems, Sikhs, Christians, in fact all religions and races, ate, slept, trained and waged war side by side without friction.

I suggested to Jinnah that religious hatreds, nationalism and boundaries plagued humanity and had caused the war; the world needed harmony, not new discords.

'You are an idealist,' he replied. 'I am a realist. I deal with what is. Take, for instance, France and Italy. Their customs and religion are the same. Their languages are similar. Yet they are separate.'

'Do you want to create here the mess we have in Europe?' I asked.

'I must deal with the divisive characteristics which exist,' he said.

Jinnah was not a devout Moslem. He drank alcohol and ate pork, which are un-Islamic acts. He seldom visited the mosque and knew no Arabic and little Urdu. In his forties, he went outside his religion to marry a Parsi girl of eighteen; when his only child, a beautiful daughter, married a Parsi turned Christian, he disowned her. His wife left him and died shortly thereafter in 1929. In the remaining years, his sister Fatima, a dental surgeon who looked like him, was his constant companion and adviser. 'Moslem women are the real force behind their men,' she said.

Early in his career, Jinnah tried to unite Hindus and Moslems. On returning from London where he studied law at Lincoln's Inn, and after establishing a lucrative practice in Bombay, he threw himself into politics. Addressing the Moslem League in 1917 on the alleged threat of Hindu domination, he said, 'Fear not. This is a bogey which is put before you to scare you away from the co-operation and unity which are essential to self-government.'

Jinnah was once a leader of the Congress party. 'I have been in this movement for thirty-five years,' he said to me in the first of two interviews at his home. 'Nehru worked under me in the Home-Rule Society. Gandhi worked under me. I was active in the Congress party. When the Moslem League was organized I persuaded Congress to congratulate the League as a step towards Indian freedom. In 1915, I induced the League and Congress to meet at the same time in Bombay so as to create the feeling of unity. My goal was Hindu–Moslem unity. The British, seeing a danger in such unity, broke up an open meeting. The closed sessions, however, continued. In 1916, I again persuaded the two organizations to meet simultaneously in Lucknow and was instrumental in bringing about the Lucknow Pact in which both agreed on elections and weightage. So it was until 1920 when Gandhi came into the limelight. A deterioration of Hindu–Moslem relations set in. In 1931, at the Round Table Conference, I had the distinct feeling that unity was hopeless, that Gandhi did not want it. I was a disappointed man. I decided to stay in England. I did not even go back to India to sell my possessions but sold them through an agent. I remained in England until 1935. I took up law practice before the Privy Council, and contrary to my expectations, I was a success. I had no intention of returning to India. But each year friends came from India and told me of conditions and told me how much I could do. Finally, I agreed to go back.'

He had been speaking breathlessly, with excitement. He paused, puffed on his cigarette. 'I tell you all this,' he continued, 'to show that Gandhi does not want independence. He does not want the British to go. He is first of all a Hindu. Nehru does not want the British to go. They want Hindu raj.'

'Writing 'In Memory of Jinnah', in the London *Economist* of 17 September, 1949, a correspondent, who knew Jinnah well, declared that while Jinnah was practising law in London someone 'repeated to him that Nehru, whom he despised and hated, had imprudently said at a private dinner party that "Jinnah was finished". Outraged, Jinnah packed up and sailed back to India at once just to "show Nehru" . . . To Cleopatra's nose as a factor in history one should perhaps add Jinnah's pride'.

George E. Jones, the *New York Times* correspondent who interviewed Jinnah several times, writes in his book, *Tumult in India*, 'Jinnah is a superb political craftsman, a Machiavelli in the amoral sense of that description . . . His personal defects are a somewhat hostile reserve, conceit and a narrow outlook . . . He is an extremely suspicious man, who feels that he has been wronged many times in his life. His repressed intensity borders on the psychotic. Withdrawn and isolated, Jinnah is arrogant to the point of discourtesy . . .'

Jinnah withdrew from the Congress party just when Gandhi, backed by the masses, ousted the rich lawyers from control. He never liked Gandhi. At public meetings in those days, he would refer to Gandhi as 'Mr Gandhi' which most Indians regarded as less respectful than Mahatma or Gandhiji; yet when members of the audience protested he persisted. Later, after he returned to India and became the undisputed leader of the anti-Congress Moslem League, he zealously guarded his prestige. In 1939, upon the outbreak of the war, the Viceroy invited Gandhi and Jinnah to the palace. Gandhi offered to come to Jinnah's house to fetch him. Jinnah welcomed that appearance of an obeisance. But he refused to go in Gandhi's car. They both rode in his. Subsequently, when they conferred, Jinnah insisted that the meetings take place in his home. Gandhi, who was completely indifferent to such considerations, gladly complied.

Vanity, jealousy and dislike undoubtedly play a major role in politics. Some of the great political feuds of history were personal before they became political. The Hindu-Moslem problem, to be sure, would have existed Jinnah or no Jinnah. His intensity and hates blew on the coals and brought forth flames.

Apart from Jinnah, all the leading figures in his Moslem League were large estate owners and landholding noblemen. They watched the rising tide of peasant discontent with mounting concern. In the North-west Frontier Province, the Congress party, led by Khan Abdul Ghaffar Khan, the 'Frontier Gandhi', was a popular movement of Moslem peasants directed against Moslem landowners. In the United Provinces, Moslem and Hindu peasants made common cause against Moslem and Hindu landlords.

The landlords who financed the Moslem League used

religion to divide Moslem from Hindu peasants.

Owing to Islamic precept, the bulk of Moslem wealth was invested in land instead of trade or industry. Hindu and Parsi business men often preferred to engage their own co-religionists. Mohammedans, moreover, encountered considerable difficulty in entering government employ; their education was usually inferior to that of Hindus, Parsis and Christians. The Moslem urban middle class, which began to emerge in the twentieth century, looked to Jinnah to get them British government jobs, and he did so by persuading the authorities to establish quotas for Moslems irrespective of qualifications.

The Moslem upper class (the landlords) and the Moslem middle class were ready for Jinnah. But they needed the peasantry for numbers. They soon discovered that they could win it by arousing religious passions. The formula was Pakistan, a separate Moslem state. Such a state would be officered by Moslems and in it Hindu and Parsi firms would be at a disadvantage. The landlords believed they had less to fear from a country they controlled than from an independent, liberal, secular India where a land reform that would dispossess them was expected to be one of the first pieces of legislation.

One hundred million compared to three hundred million Hindus, the Moslems could never hope to win a political majority unless religious aims ceased to dominate politics. The separate religious electorates, introduced by Lord Minto in 1909, militated against such a consummation. In a number of districts, however – the North-west Frontier, Punjab, Sind, Baluchistan, Kashmir and Bengal – Moslems formed a majority. Pakistan, as Jinnah conceived it, would embrace the sixty million Mohammedans thickly settled in these Moslem-majority provinces where they were safe from Hindu domination. But to achieve Pakistan, Jinnah would have to inflame Moslem religious and nationalistic sentiments and risk inflaming in turn similar feelings among Hindus at the cost of the forty million Moslems dispersed in provinces where Hindus were the majority.

Jinnah was prepared to take this plunge.

The irreligious Jinnah wished to build a religious state. Gandhi, wholly religious, wanted a secular state.

The hope of religious peace in India lay in the unifying nationalism written on the Gandhi-Nehru-Azad-Raja-gopalachari banner. No doubt, the relations between Hindus and Moslems required adjustments and mutual concessions and depended greatly on economic expansion which would lessen the competition for government posts and increase business opportunities. Gandhi had enough faith in man to think that, with patience, it could be done.

Jinnah, on the other hand, urged immediate bisection. Herbert L. Matthews, a veteran foreign correspondent of the *New York Times*, quotes a frank admission by Sikander Hyat Khan, the Moslem prime minister of the Punjab, 'that he considered a Bengal Moslem as foreign as a Chinese'. Yet Jinnah believed that the Punjab and Bengal yearned to be one in Pakistan.

The fact is that India, a backward country without adequate communications, still lived in the grip of provincialism, like Europe in the Middle Ages. Gandhi wanted to use the cement of nationalism to make it one; Jinnah wanted to use the dynamite of religion to make it two.

The bisection of India could not be done gently with a surgeon's scalpel. It could only be achieved with a blunt butcher's knife and heavy cleaver, and leave broken bones, mutilated muscles, severed nerves and bruised brain matter robbed of the capacity to think. The partitioning of the United States or France would be no more painful.

The tragedy of partition hung over Gandhi's head from the time of his liberation in 1944 to the day of his death in 1948.

In June 1944 Gandhi, partially recuperated from his illness, came back into the political arena. He asked Viceroy

Wavell to receive him. Wavell replied, 'In consideration of the radical difference in our points of view, a meeting between us at present could have no value.'

Gandhi now focused his attention on Jinnah. Gandhi had always felt that if Congress and the Moslem League came to an agreement, the British would have to grant India independence.

Spurred by Rajagopalachari, who evolved a formula for a Congress–League understanding, Gandhi wrote to Jinnah on 17 July, 1944, suggesting talks. Gandhi addressed Jinnah as 'Brother Jinnah' and signed, 'Your brother, Gandhi'. Jinnah's reply was addressed to 'Dear Mr Gandhi' and was signed 'M. A. Jinnah'. In subsequent letters, Gandhi addressed Jinnah as 'Qaid-e-Azam' or Great Leader, a recently assumed title. Jinnah still wrote, 'Dear Mr Gandhi'.

The correspondence was voluminous. Gandhi arrived at Jinnah's Bombay house for the first meeting at 3.55 P.M. on 9 September and remained till 7 P.M. He returned at 5.30 P.M. on the 11th and stayed for two hours. The two men conferred a third time on the 12th for two and a half hours, twice on the 13th for a total of three and a half hours, again on the 14th, again on the 15th and so on. After each conversation they wrote long letters to one another confirming and continuing the oral arguments. At one stage, Gandhi suggested that he be allowed to address the executive council of the Moslem League and, if the council rejected his proposal, that he should go before an open convention of the League. Jinnah called the suggestion 'most extraordinary and unprecedented', and repulsed it.

The talks broke down on 26 September and then the entire correspondence was published in the newspapers.

The wall between Gandhi and Jinnah was the two-nation theory. 'By all the canons of international law, we are a nation,' Jinnah wrote. 'We are a nation with our own distinctive culture and civilization, language and literature, art and architecture, names and nomenclature, sense of value and proportion, legal laws and moral codes, customs and calendar, history and traditions, aptitudes and ambitions.'

Gandhi did not make an effort to controvert this large statement. He merely said, 'I find no parallel in history for a body of converts and their descendants claiming to be a nation apart from the parent stock.' Do people change their characteristics when they change their religion? Would there be a third nation in India if several million people adopted Christianity and a fourth if several million joined the Jews?

The cleavage on this cardinal issue was known in advance. Then why the discussions?

'Can we not agree to differ on the question of "two nations",' Gandhi pleaded, 'and yet solve the problem on the basis of self-determination?'

Gandhi proposed that Baluchistan, Sind, the North-west Frontier Province where Moslems constituted a majority, and those parts of Bengal, Assam and the Punjab where Moslems were a majority, should vote on whether to secede from the Indian Union. 'If the vote is in favour of separation,' Gandhi explained, 'it shall be agreed upon that these areas shall form a separate state as soon as possible after India is free.' The two states, he urged, would then set up one, unified 'administration of foreign affairs, defence, internal communications, customs, commerce and the like'.

Jinnah said 'No' three times: he wanted the partition while the British were in India, not after India was free; he wanted complete separation with no unified administration; and he had his own remarkable plan for a referendum.

According to Jinnah's plan, only Moslems would vote in the plebiscite and if the majority of the voting Moslems voted for separation then the entire province would go to Pakistan. 'Separation', according to an analysis of Jinnah's views made by the British Embassy in Washington 'for the information of British officials,' 'must be decided on by the votes of Moslems only.'

But the British census gave the Moslem population of Assam as 3,442,479, the non-Moslem 6,762,254. Yet Jinnah was demanding that a majority of the 3,442,479 determine the fate of the entire province.

The Moslem population of the Punjab was 16,217,242, the non-Moslem 12,201,577; the Moslems were not more than 56 per cent of the total. Actually, two or three million Moslems, at most, would have been entitled to cast votes. And if a majority of the two or three million voted for Pakistan then the entire province of over twenty-eight million would become a part of Pakistan.

In Bengal, Moslems were 52 per cent of the population. A Moslem majority for secession would necessarily be a minority of the total number of inhabitants.

Gandhi, obviously, could not agree to such a proposition. Jinnah did not have the power to effect it by force. Only the British could give it to him.

'Mr Jinnah', reads the 'Note on the Gandhi–Jinnah Conversations' compiled by the British Embassy in Washington (Lord Halifax was Ambassador), 'is in a strong position; he has something to give which Mr Gandhi wants very badly and without delay, Moslem co-operation in putting pressure on the British government to hand over a substantial instalment of power at once . . . Mr Gandhi, on the other hand, has got nothing to give which Mr Jinnah is not prepared to wait for; in Mr Jinnah's eyes, the prospect of independence a year or two earlier is as nothing compared with security for Moslems. It is obvious that Mr Jinnah is content to wait and see how near Mr Gandhi will come to the price for which he is holding out.'

This is a shrewd analysis of the tactics of a shrewd bargainer. Jinnah could wait for independence. Gandhi felt this was the best time to get independence.

History now intervened to upset Jinnah's calculations. Then the able Jinnah upset history.

PART THREE

The Birth of Two Nations

23 MARCH, 1946 – 30 JANUARY, 1948

CHAPTER 1

On the Eve of Independence

On 30 August, 1944, Wendell Willkie received me in his law office overlooking New York harbour. He was a good man. His death in September 1944 left America poorer.

'The war is about seven-tenths won,' he said, 'and the peace is about nine-tenths lost.' He had toured the East and noted the perpetuation of old conflicts between Europe and Asia, white man and coloured man, free man and colonial slaves. He realized that there would either be a new world or a new world war.

Others too were beginning to see that war with a dictatorship creates a moral obligation to expand the area of freedom.

The nearer England came to victory the clearer it became that political changes in India could not be delayed.

By 1945, India was too restive to hold, and Britain had suffered too heavily in the war to contemplate the colossal expenditure of men and treasure that would have been required to suppress another non-violent contest with Gandhi or a violent contest if he lost control. The exhaustion which compelled Britain to cut her commitments in Greece, Turkey, the Arab countries and other strategic regions after the war was apparent during the war.

It was especially apparent to Lord Wavell. 'The Indian administration,' Leopold S. Amery, Secretary of State for India, said in the House of Commons on 14 June, 1945, 'overburdened by great tasks laid upon it by the war against Japan and by planning for the post-war period, is further strained by the political tension that exists.' Wavell directed the Indian administration.

Wavell was a general and a poet and an unusual person. During my first talk with him in New Delhi in 1942, I remarked that he looked tired. 'Yes,' he agreed, 'I am tired after three years of military defeats and setbacks.' Then he paid a tribute to Nazi Marshal Rommel who administered the defeats. At each subsequent meeting, Wavell brought the conversation round to Rommel and praised his genius.

Wavell had a body like a solid thick tree trunk. His legs were thick and bent outward. His hair was dense and grey-black. All the wrinkles and deep lines of his gnarled face seemed to end in his blind left eye which was partly open and riveted one's attention. Five rows of ribbons made a bright patch on the left breast of his khaki uniform.

He talked philosophy and quoted Matthew Arnold. When I walked with him once in the immense garden behind his house in New Delhi he reminisced about service in the Caucasus during the first World War and sang a verse of 'Allahverdi', a popular Georgian drinking song. He was informal and friendly and did not behave like a commander-in-chief or an imperial administrator.

Wavell's hero was General Allenby under whom he had fought in the first World War. He was writing a long biography of Allenby and allowed me to read part of the neatly typed manuscript tied in red ribbons. The prose was exquisite. The most dramatic episode of the book was Allenby's first conflict with the British government over the political status of Egypt. Allenby was High Commissioner of Egypt after the first World War. While serving in that capacity he became convinced that Britain should end her protectorate and grant Egypt independence. But his pleas from Cairo failed to sway the men in Whitehall. He accordingly appeared in London to face an all-star Cabinet which included Lloyd George, Lord Curzon, Milner and Winston Churchill, all of them opponents of Egyptian independence and 'the most determined', Wavell wrote, 'had been Winston Churchill'. Allenby's arguments did not move the ministers. He threatened to resign. He was the conqueror of Jerusalem, the man who broke the back of the Turks in the war, and had a strong hold, consequently, on the loyalty and the imagination of the British people. Lloyd George did not want to risk an open break with Allenby and capitulated.

I wrote to Wavell, 'Lloyd George, Curzon and Churchill probably adduced as plausible objections to the independence of Egypt as those one can hear today in British circles in New Delhi against the independence of India, yet Allenby stood his ground and won. You are convinced that he was right and the Cabinet wrong. Governments are often wrong. The whole history of Europe between 1919 and 1939 is a record of wrong policies. There is little in the recent acts of British Cabinets to suggest that London's present attitude to India is a pillar of wisdom.'

Wavell was then Commander-in-Chief and he limited himself to military affairs. In 1944, however, Churchill appointed him Viceroy.

Wavell went to London in March 1945.

An editorial in *The Times* of 20 March,1945, summarizing numerous letters in its correspondence columns and its own views, said, 'There is a general conviction that it is for this country to resume the political initiative . . . First, it is proposed that Britain should now begin a gradual remodelling of the structure, staffing and procedure of the governmental machine in preparation for the complete transfer of power to Indian hands; and, secondly, that the persistence of the antagonisms now sundering the parties and interests of India constitute a reproach to British as well as Indian statesmanship . . .'

British opinion, even conservative opinion, was deserting Churchill's intransigent stand on India.

Wavell stayed in London for nearly two months. Prophets were predicting a Labour party triumph in the impending

British general election. Policy abroad usually reflects politics at home. And Wavell still had four years as Viceroy.

In April 1945, on the eve of the San Francisco Conference to draft the charter of the United Nations, Indian and foreign correspondents sought a statement from Mahatma Gandhi. 'India's nationalism spells internationalism,' he declared.

'There will be no peace for the Allies or the world,' he asserted, 'unless they shed their belief in the efficacy of war and its accompanying terrible deception and fraud, and are determined to hammer out a real peace based on the freedom and equality of all races and nations . . .' Freedom of India will demonstrate to all the exploited races of the earth that their freedom is near and that in no case will they henceforth be exploited.

'Peace,' Gandhi added, 'must be just. In order to be that it must neither be punitive nor vindictive. Germany and Japan should not be humiliated. The strong are never vindictive. Therefore the fruits of peace must be shared equally. The effort then will be to turn them into friends. The Allies can prove their democracy by no other means.'

But he feared that behind the San Francisco Conference 'lurk the mistrust and fear which breed war'.

Gandhi saw that freedom was the twin of peace, and fearlessness the parent of both. Who could doubt that India would be free before 1960 and most of south-east Asia as well? Who could doubt that until they were free they could make the West's life a nightmare and Europe's recovery impossible? To prevent another war the victors would have to remove the ills which conduce to the 'rotten world' of which Sumner Welles had spoken.

These ideas were beginning to shape Britain's attitude towards India.

Government policy is like a ticker tape; the old message is still visible when the first words of the new message appears. A country can have two conflicting policies or parts of two conflicting policies. Actually there is no such thing as a government; there are many men and women in a government and some may pull in one direction and some in another.

Wavell brought back to New Delhi the British government's approval of a new plan for India which he broadcast on 14 June. The same day he released Maulana Abul Kalam Azad, the president of the Congress party, Jawaharlal Nehru and other leaders who had been in prison since the morning of 9 August, 1942. He also summoned India's outstanding politicians to Simla, the summer capital, for 25 June.

Congress leaders showed no bitterness about their long imprisonment without trial. They agreed to come. Jinnah attended as president of the Moslem League and Liaquat Ali Khan as secretary of the League. Khizr Hyat Khan and Kwaja Sir Nazimuddin were invited in their capacity of former prime ministers of their provinces. In addition, Master Tara Singh represented the Sikhs and Mr Sivaraj the Harijans. Gandhi was not a delegate but he went to Simla and remained throughout the discussions.

According to the Wavell plan the Viceroy and the Commander-in-Chief would be the only Englishmen in the Viceroy's Executive Council. All the others would be Indians. Indians would thus take charge of foreign affairs, finance, police, etc.

The Viceroy would appoint the Indian members of his Council but he undertook to do so from lists of names submitted by the several parties. The Viceroy would still have the right to veto the decisions of the Council, but he promised publicly that the veto power 'will of course not be exercised unreasonably'. Most political Indians took him at his word, for if he abused the veto the Indians could withdraw from the Council and forbid any of their party members to succeed them; that would have put an end to the Wavell plan and to government with popular support.

The Simla conference nevertheless failed. Wavell placed the blame on Jinnah.

The plan provided for 'equal proportions of Moslems and Caste Hindus' in the Viceroy's Council. The Congress objected. Congress was a much larger organization than the Moslem League. The whole history of Congress was a battle against differentiating between caste and outcast Hindus. So eager was Congress for a settlement, however, that it accepted the formula.

Wavell, who worked indefatigably at Simla, then asked the party leaders for their lists. All complied except Jinnah. 'I therefore,' Wavell said in a public statement, 'made my provisional selections, including certain Moslem League names ... When I explained my solution to Mr Jinnah, he told me that it was not acceptable to the Moslem League, and he was so decided that I felt it would be useless to continue the discussions.'

Jinnah torpedoed the Simla conference for one discernible reason; he insisted that all Moslems in the Viceroy's Council must be designated by him as the leader of the Moslems of India.

The Moslem League had gained strength during the war and won most elections against Moslem candidates who were not in the League. But neither Wavell nor Gandhi, who made Congress policy behind the Simla scenes, could admit Jinnah's claim to represent Moslem India. There were many Moslems in Congress; President Azad was a Moslem and Congress wanted him in the Viceroy's Council. Khizr Hyat Khan, former premier of the Punjab, was anti-Jinnah and anti-Pakistan; so were other outstanding Moslems.

Moreover, Congress would have been untrue to its secular nature and to Gandhi's principles if it had accepted the role of a purely Hindu organization. Congress aspired to be a national not a religious body; it could not allow itself to be identified with one religious community.

On this rock, the Simla conference foundered. The British authorities in India, or Britain, were not ready to act without Jinnah's co-operation.

During the Simla conference, the war in Europe had come to an end. On 26 July, the Labour party decisively defeated the Conservatives; Clement R. Attlee replaced Winston Churchill as Prime Minister.

On 14 August Japan's surrender was accepted by the Powers.

The British Labour government immediately announced that it sought 'an early realization of self-government in India' and summoned Wavell to Whitehall. Their conclusions were announced by Attlee in London and Wavell in New Delhi on 19 September, 1945.

Elections to the central and provincial legislatures were the first step. Then Wavell would renew his efforts to form an Executive Council supported by the main Indian parties and to restore popular goverment in the provinces. Guided by the results at the polls, he would convene an assembly to draft a constitution for a united India.

The All-India Congress Committee, habitually distrustful, considered the proposals 'vague, inadequate and unsatisfactory'. But the Government was conciliatory; more Congress prisoners were released; three high officers of the Indian National Army who had deserted in Malaya and Burma and joined the Japanese were brought to trial in Delhi Fort, defended by Nehru and other lawyers, sentenced to life imprisonment and then set free.

All parties agreed to contest the elections.

Congress won the overwhelming majority of the non-Moslem seats in the legislatures, the Moslem League the overwhelming majority of the Moslem seats.

The deadlock remained unbroken.

In December 1945, Wavell, speaking in Calcutta, appealed to the Indian people to avoid strife and violence when they stood 'at the gate of political and economic opportunity'.

Gandhi was in Calcutta, too. He spent many hours with Richard Casey, the Australian who served as British Governor of Bengal. He also spent an hour with the Viceroy. As he left the Viceroy's house in Calcutta a vast multitude blocked the road and would not allow his car to advance until he had spoken. He stood up in the car and said, 'India has attained her great position in the East because of her message of peace.' Thereupon the crowd opened a corridor for him so that he could drive to his ashram eight miles outside the city. Along the entire route, Indians touched the dust of the road before and after he passed.

The same day, Jinnah made a statement in Bombay. 'We could settle the Indian problem in ten minutes,' he declared, 'if Mr Gandhi would say, "I agree that there should be Pakistan; I agree that one-fourth of India, composed of six provinces – Sind, Baluchistan, the Punjab, the North-west Frontier Province, Bengal and Assam – with their present boundaries, constitute the Pakistan state".'

But Gandhi could not say that and did not say it; he regarded the vivisection of India as 'blasphemy'.

CHAPTER 2

India in Suspense

Gandhi had been saying that he wanted to live a hundred and twenty-five years but without becoming 'an animated corpse, a burden to one's relations and society'. How would he keep physically fit? He first explained how he had kept physically fit. In 1901 he threw away the medicine bottle and substituted nature cures and regular habits of eating, drinking and sleeping. More important, he developed 'detachment of mind', the key to longevity. 'Everyone,' Gandhi said, 'had a right and should desire to live 125 years while performing service without an eye to result.' Dedication to service and renunciation of the fruits thereof are 'an ineffable joy', a 'nectar' which sustains life. It leaves 'no room for worry or impatience'. Egoism is the killer; unselfishness the life preserver.

The Mahatma now adopted an additional cause: nature cure. He called it his 'latest born'; the older children – khadi, village industries, the development of a national language, food-growing, independence for India, freedom for Indians and world peace – continued to receive his energetic care. For the new baby, a trust was set up with Gandhi as one of three trustees. Dr Dinshah Mehta, Gandhi's physician, had a nature-cure clinic in the city of Poona and it was therefore agreed, as the trust's first venture, to expand the clinic into a nature-cure university.

But one silent Monday Gandhi abruptly decided to abandon the project. It 'dawned upon me', he confessed, 'that I was a fool to think that I could ever hope to make an institute for the poor in a town'. He had to carry nature cure to the poor and not expect the poor to come to him. This mistake had a moral: 'Never take anything for gospel truth even if it comes from a Mahatma unless it appeals to both . . . head and heart.' Gandhi disliked automatic obedience.

He would start nature-cure work in a village; 'that is real India,' he wrote, 'my India, for which I live'. He did so immediately. He settled down for a short while in Uruli, a village of three thousand inhabitants on the Poona-Sholapur railway line with plenty of water, a good climate, fruit farms, a telegraph and post office, but no telephone.

The first day, thirty peasants appeared at the nature cure centre. Gandhi himself examined six. In each case, he prescribed the same thing: the continuous recitation of God's name, sun baths, friction and hip baths, cow's milk, buttermilk, fruit juices and plenty of water. The reciting of God's name, however, should be more than lip movement; it must absorbe the entire being throughout the recitation and throughout life. 'All mental and physical ailments,' Gandhi explained simply, 'are due to one common cause. It is therefore but natural that there should be a common remedy.' Almost everyone is sick in body or mind, he said. Repeating 'Rama, Rama, Rama, Rama, Rama' while intensively concentrating on godliness, goodness, service and selflessness paves the way for the remedial functions of mudpacks, sitz baths and massage.

Gandhi was himself a proof of the power of mind and mood over matter.

Gandhi was occupied with health throughout his entire adult life and indeed in his youth when he nursed his dying father. He doctored everyone within reach. Pain in others pained him. He was capable of boundless compassion.

The loving mother fervently yet vainly wishes she could take her child's illness upon herself. Gandhi's fasts were suffering self-inflicted in the hope of alleviating the sufferings of untouchables, strikers, Hindus and Moslems. He did penance for those who inflicted pain.

The inner compulsion to relieve misery and assuage pain comes very close to being Gandhi's deepest urge. It is the kin of love, the root of non-violence, the spur to service. Gandhi believed his mission was to heal. He was India's doctor. The India of the last two years of his life gave him ample work.

There was famine in the land, food and clothing famine. 'Grain and cloth dealers must not hoard, must not speculate,' he wrote on 17 February, 1946. 'Food should be grown on all cultivable areas wherever water is or is made available . . . All ceremonial functions should be stopped . . .'

He had been wandering over Bengal, Assam and Madras. In one locality, six hundred thousand people came to a meeting. 'Grow More Food' was his slogan. 'Spin,' he begged. 'Every pint of water, whether from bathing and ablution or from the kitchen should be turned into backyard vegetable beds,' he told townspeople. 'Vegetables could be grown in earthen pots and even in old discarded tins.'

Hunger raised the question of the nation's high birth rate. 'Let me say,' he stated, 'that propagation of the race rabbit-wise must undoubtedly be stopped, but not so as to bring greater evils in its train. It should be stopped by methods which in themselves ennoble the race,' by 'the sovereign remedy of self-control.'

Shortages provoked looting of shops and other violent outbursts. Heavy rioting took place in Bombay. In Calcutta, Delhi and other cities mobs engaged in arson, compelled passers-by to shout slogans, and forced Englishmen to remove their hats. Gandhi reprimanded them severely. Indian sailors in the British navy in the harbour of Bombay mutinied and were only with difficulty persuaded by Congress leaders to desist.

'Now that it seems we are coming into our own,' Gandhi wrote on 10 February, 1946, 'indiscipline and hooliganism', which were increasing, 'ought to go, and calmness, rigid discipline, co-operation and goodwill must take their place . . . I hug the hope', he continued, 'that when real responsibility comes to the people and the dead weight of a foreign army of occupation is removed, we shall be natural, dignified and restrained . . .

'Let me affirm that I love the Englishman as well as the Indian,' he wrote in March.

Prime Minister Attlee announced that a British Cabinet Mission, consisting of Lord Pethick-Lawrence, the Secretary of State for India; Sir Stafford Cripps, President of the Board of Trade; and Albert V. Alexander, First Lord of the Admiralty, were coming to India to settle the terms of liberation. 'Emphatically,' Gandhi affirmed, 'it betrays want of foresight to disbelieve British declarations and precipitate and quarrel in anticipation. Is the official deputation coming to deceive a great nation? It is neither manly nor womanly to think so.'

The Cabinet Mission arrived from England in New Delhi on 23 March and immediately began to interview Indian leaders. Gandhi came to Delhi to meet the British ministers and 'at my request,' writes Pethick-Lawrence, 'in spite of the trying weather conditions in Delhi during the ensuing months, he remained in touch with us and with the Congress Working Committee during the whole progress of the negotiations'. Gandhi stayed in the untouchables' slums where Cripps, Pethick-Lawrence and Alexander, as well as many Indians, visited him regularly. Sometimes, too, Gandhi went to 2 Willingdon Crescent, the house occupied by the Mission, and on one occasion, by arrangement, he encountered Pethick-Lawrence on his evening walk and thus avoided the publicity that attended every one of Gandhi's acts.

After weeks of goings and comings with no definite result, the Cabinet Mission invited the Congress and the Moslem League to send four delegates each to a conference in Simla. Gandhi was not a delegate but he made himself available in the summer capital for consultation. At a subsequent stage

Nehru and Jinnah wrestled with the issues privately. There was no agreement. The two Indian parties did not wish to accept the onus of devising a plan or of agreeing with one another.

Finally, Gandhi told the Cabinet Mission to suggest a plan to the Indian parties.

The Cabinet Mission's plan, published on 16 May, 1946, was Britains's proposal for the liquidation of British power in India. 'Whether you like the Cabinet delegation's announcement or not,' Gandhi told his prayer meeting that day, 'it is going to be the most momentous one in the history of India and therefore requires careful study.'

Gandhi pondered the announcement for four days and then stated that after 'searching examination . . . my conviction abides that it is the best document the British government could have produced in the circumstances'.

Rejecting a facile and popular Indian charge, Gandhi said in *Harijan* of 26 May, 1946, 'The Congress and the Moslem League did not, could not agree. We would err grievously if at this time we foolishly satisfy ourselves that the differences are a British creation.'

The British government's 'one purpose', the Mahatma said, 'is to end British rule as early as can be'.

'Voluminous evidence', the Cabinet Mission's statement declared, 'has shown an almost universal desire, outside the supporters of the Moslem League, for the unity of India.'

Nevertheless, 'We were greatly impressed by the very genuine and acute anxiety of the Moslems lest they should find themselves subjected to a perpetual Hindu-majority rule. This has become so strong and widespread amongst the Moslems that it cannot be allayed by mere paper safeguards. If there is to be internal peace in India it must be secured by measures which will insure to the Moslems a control in all matters vital to their culture, religion and economic and other interests.'

The Mission therefore examined 'closely and impartially the possibility of a partition of India'.

What was the result?

On the basis of statistics given in the statement, the Cabinet Mission proved that in the north-western area of Pakistan the non-Moslem minority would constitute 37.93 per cent, and in the north-eastern area it would amount to 48.31 per cent, while twenty million Moslems would remain outside Pakistan as a minority in the other India. 'These figures show', the statement said, 'that the setting up of a separate sovereign State of Pakistan on the lines claimed by the Moslem League would not solve the communal minority problem.'

The Mission then considered whether a smaller Pakistan, which excluded non-Moslem areas, was feasible. 'Such a Pakistan', the statement noted, 'is regarded by the Moslem League as quite impracticable.' It would have necessitated the division of the Punjab, Bengal and Assam between the two new states, whereas Jinnah demanded those three provinces in their entirety. 'We ourselves', the Ministers affirmed, 'are also convinced that any solution which involves a radical partition of the Punjab and Bengal, as this would do, would be contrary to the wishes of a very large percentage of the inhabitants of these Provinces. Bengal and the Punjab each has its own common language and a long history and tradition. Moreover, any division of the Punjab would of necessity divide the Sikhs, leaving substantial bodies of Sikhs on both sides of the boundary.'

The division of India, the Mission said, would weaken the country's defences and violently tear in two its communications and transport systems. 'Finally there is the geographical fact that the two halves of the proposed Pakistan State are separated by some seven hundred miles and the communications between them both in war and peace would be dependent on the goodwill of Hindustan . . .

'We are therefore unable to advise the British government', the statement announced, 'that the power which at present resides in British hands should be handed over to two entirely separate sovereign States.'

Instead, the British Ministers recommended a united India, embracing both British India and the native states, with one federal government to deal with foreign affairs, defence and communications. In the national legislature, a majority of those voting and a majority of the Hindus as well as a majority of the Moslems voting would be required to decide any major communal or religious issue.

Newly elected provincial legislatures would elect the members of a national Constituent Assembly. It would draft India's constitution.

Meanwhile, the Cabinet Mission announced, Lord Wavell would proceed with the formation of an interim or provisional government.

In a peroration, the Cabinet statement declared that the Indian people now had 'the opportunity of complete independence ... in the shortest time and with the least danger of internal disturbance and conflict'.

That same day, 16 May, 1946, Cripps, Pethick-Lawrence and Wavell, speaking on the radio, explained and extolled the plan. Cripps called attention to the danger of nationwide famine and the need of preventing a breakdown of administrative machinery. 'Let no one doubt for one moment our intention,' he begged. Pethick-Lawrence addressed his audience as 'a great people'. This term had political significance, for the Moslem leaders always spoke of 'peoples'. He pleaded with the Moslems to accept the plan; it gave them the advantages of a Pakistan without its disadvantages. Wavell spoke of the necessity of maintaining the union of India and closed with a verse from Longfellow:

Thou too, sail on, O Ship of State,
Sail on, O Union, strong and great,
Humanity with all its fears,
With all the hopes of future years
Is hanging breathless on thy Fate.

Jinnah criticized the Cabinet Mission on 21 May. He insisted that Pakistan was the only solution and deplored the 'common-place and exploded arguments aimed at it by Pethick-Lawrence, Cripps and Alexander . . . It seems', he charged, 'that this was done by the Mission simply to appease and placate the Congress'. Jinnah said he would have preferred a Union with no Union legislature and an executive branch with an equal number of Moslems and Hindus. If there was to be a national legislature, it too should, he felt, consist of as many representatives from Pakistan as from Hindustan; and 'in regard to any matter of a controversial nature', a three-fourths majority would be necessary in the executive and the legislature. All these ideas were ignored by the British ministers, he complained. Small wonder. They would have made government impossible.

On 4 June, nevertheless, the Moslem League accepted the Cabinet Mission's plan.

Everything depended on what the Congress party would do.

The Congress Working Committee withdrew to Mussoorie, a summer resort in the hills, to escape the debilitating heat and suffocating dust storms of Delhi, and took Gandhi with them.

India's eyes were on Mussoorie. The Working Committee deliberated with Gandhi. The meetings were more fateful than they knew.

Foreign correspondents followed Gandhi to Mussoorie. 'What would you do if you were dictator of India for a day?' one of them asked.

If the journalist had expected Gandhi's answer to contain

some hint of the long-delayed Congress decision, he was disappointed. 'I would not accept it,' Gandhi replied, but if he did he would spend the day cleaning out the hovels of the Harijans in New Delhi and converting the Viceroy's palace into a hospital. 'Why does the Viceroy need such a big house?' he exclaimed.

'Well, sir,' the journalist persisted, 'suppose they continue your dictatorship for a second day?'

'The second day,' Gandhi said with a laugh, 'would be a prolongation of the first.' This provoked general gaiety among the Indians present.

Still no word of the Congress response to the Cabinet Mission's proposal!

On 8 June, refreshed by the pine-scented breezes that blew down from the cool, wooded slopes, Gandhi returned in a car to New Delhi where the Congress deliberations would be continued. Rajagopalachari, no longer a member of the Working Committee (nor was Gandhi), had come from Madras to Delhi to urge acceptance of the British plan.

A week passed and still no word from Congress on whether it would accept or reject the Cabinet Mission's proposal.

On 16 June Lord Wavell announced that Congress and the Moslem League had failed to agree on the composition of a provisional government and he was therefore appointing fourteen Indians to posts in that government.

Congress now had to answer two questions: to join or not to join the provisional government; to enter or not to enter the Constituent Assembly and draft a new constitution for a free united India.

CHAPTER 3

Gandhi Revisited

I arrived at the New Delhi airport on 25 June, 1946, and drove to the Imperial Hotel. I was tired from the flight from Cairo; I needed a bath and shave. But I had an uncontrollable impulse to see Gandhi immediately. My first act in India, I felt, should be to have a word with Gandhi. So instead of making sure I had a room in the hotel, I left my luggage in the lobby and took a taxi to Gandhi's little stone hut in the Harijan colony.

He was at his evening prayer meeting in an open space outside the hut. Approximately a thousand persons were at the services. Gandhi in loincloth, a moist white-pad on his head, his feet on his thighs, sat in the centre of a large elevated wooden platform with several disciples. His eyes were closed. Occasionally he opened them and beat time with his hands to the singing. On the ground, in front of the platform, sat the women worshippers; behind them the men. The curious stood around on the periphery of the congregation. The Indian and foreign correspondents were there, also Mrdula Sarabhai, Nehru and Lady Cripps.

I posted myself at the foot of the three wooden steps where Gandhi would descend from the prayer platform. 'Ah, there you are,' he said; 'well, I have now grown better-looking in these four years.'

'I would not dare to differ with you,' I replied. He threw back his head and laughed. Taking me by the elbow, he walked towards his hut; he asked about my trip, my health and my family. Then, probably sensing that I would like to stay for a talk, he said, 'Lady Cripps is here to see me. Will you walk with me tomorrow morning?'

Later that evening I went to the house of Abul Kalam Azad, the Congress president, for dinner with him, Nehru, Mr Asaf Ali and other members of the Congress Working Committee. They seemed tense, and listened with special attention to the government news broadcast. Earlier that day, Congress had finally communicated its decisions to the Cabinet Mission and Wavell, but no public announcement had yet been made.

The Working Committee had decided, I learned, to accept the British plan for the future constitution of India but not to participate in the provisional government.

The next morning I was up early enough to sip a cup of lukewarm black tea and eat a banana and find a taxi which brought me to Gandhi's hut at 5.30. We talked for half an hour. He talked most of the time about the negotiations with the Cabinet Mission.

I lunched with Patel and Rajagopalachari in Birla House, talked for an hour in the same mansion with Miss Slade, and spent the evening with Patel.

The following day, 27 June, I went to Gandhi again at 5.30 A.M. and walked with him for thirty minutes. Sir Stafford and Lady Cripps received me at 9.30 for a friendly and helpful interview. I kept the taxi because I had an appointment with Jinnah for 10.30.

After going a short distance, the taxi coughed and coughed and stood still. The Sikh driver tinkered under the bonnet, but as the time of my meeting with Jinnah drew near I became increasingly alarmed and finally, after trying in vain to persuade the chauffeur of a government car to earn some extra money, hired a tonga. Hunger had apparently made the horse unresponsive to whips and oaths and I arrived at Jinnah's house thirty-five minutes late. I was admitted into his study after a short wait. I offered profuse apologies, explained that my taxi had broken down, that no other taxi was available, that the tonga was slow and that I loathed being unpunctual. He said frigidly, 'I trust you are not hurt.' I said it was not that kind of breakdown; the mechanism had simply refused to function. He was sympathetic but formal and continued to talk about the incident.

When I could disentangle myself from the discussion of taxi and tonga I remarked, 'It seems India is about to become independent.'

He did not answer. He did not say anything. He pulled in his chin, looked sternly at me, stood up, extended his hand and said, 'I will have to go now.'

I once more apologized for keeping him waiting, I had not reckoned with the taxi difficulty and could I see him another day in New Delhi? No, he would be busy. He was going to Bombay and I would soon be in Bombay; could I see him there? No, he would be too busy. He had by this time brought me to the door. I shall never know whether he was offended by my being late or by my statement on the imminence of India's freedom.

Over the week-end, I absorbed as much as possible about the political situation. Patel's sharp mind was my best help. On Monday, 1 July, I flew to Bombay and on Tuesday evening I commenced a three-day sojourn at Dr Dinshah Mehta's nature-cure clinic in Poona where Gandhi was staying. Part of the time, Nehru was there.

I travelled with Gandhi to Bombay on 5 July and spent the 6th and 7th at the sessions of the All-India Congress Committee which debated the Working Committee's decisions on the Cabinet Mission plan and listened to the Mahatma on the subject.

Later that month I toured Maharashtra with Jaiprakash Narayan, the Socialist leader, and arrived at Panchgani, in the rain-soaked hills, on 16 July, for a forty-eight-hour visit to Gandhi.

Gandhi did not seem to have aged since 1942; his stride was not as long and lusty, but walking did not tire him nor did days of interviews. He was in almost constant good humour.

At the beginning of my first morning stroll with him in New Delhi he asked about the rumours of war with Russia. I said there was a good deal of talk about war but perhaps it was only talk. 'You should turn your attention to the West,' I added.

'I?' he replied, 'I have not convinced India. There is violence all around us. I am a spent bullet.'

Since the end of the second World War, I suggested, many Europeans and Americans were conscious of a spiritual emptiness. He might fill a corner of it. India needs material goods and perhaps had the illusion that they brought happiness. We had the material goods but knew they did not bring happiness. The West was groping for a solution.

'But I am an Asiatic,' he commented. 'A mere Asiatic.' He laughed; then after a pause, 'Jesus was an Asiatic.'

In this, and in subsequent conversations, I thought I detected a despondent note with an optimistic undertone: if he lived 125 years he would have enough time to finish his work.

It was 8.30 in the evening when I arrived at the stone building of the Poona nature-clinic. I was shown his room and walked in. He was sitting on a pallet; a white shawl enveloped him from neck to ankles. He did not look up. When he finished writing the postcard, he raised his head and said, 'Ah.' I knelt in front of him and we shook hands. He had a way, which none of his heirs has inherited, of figuratively putting his arms around you and making you feel welcome to his house and India.

'You have come by the *Deccan Queen*,' he remarked. 'On that train there is no food.'

I said I didn't mind, I had already been promised dinner. 'The weather here seems wonderful,' I volunteered. 'You tortured yourself in the summer heat of Sevagram,' where I had seen him in 1942.

'No,' he objected, 'it wasn't torture. But in New Delhi I would melt ice in the bath and sit in it as you did in Sevagram. I was even unashamed to receive people in my bath and dictate in the bath. Here in Poona the weather is delightful.' He appeared very relaxed.

Presently, without any question from me, he spoke at length about violence. 'First,' he said, 'there is South Africa. A man has been killed there in connection with the recent disturbances. He was innocent. Also, they have tied Indians to trees and whipped them. This is lynch law. And now these riots in Ahmedabad between Hindus and Moslems. The trouble is that one side begins stabbing and killing and then the other does likewise. If one side did not avenge its deaths the thing would stop. It is the same in Palestine. The Jews have a good case. I told Sidney Silverman, the British MP, that the Jews have a good case. If the Arabs have a claim to Palestine the Jews have a prior claim, because they were there first. Jesus was a Jew. He was the finest flower of Judaism. You can see that from the four stories of the four apostles. They had untutored minds. They told the truth about Jesus. Paul was not a Jew, he was a Greek, he had an oratorical mind a dialectical mind and he distorted Jesus. Jesus possessed a great force, the love force, but Christianity became disfigured when it went to the West. It became the religion of kings.'

He reverted to the Jewish question in Hitler's Germany. 'But I did not intend talking with you tonight,' he declared, 'and you have not eaten.'

I rose to go. 'Sleep well,' I said.

'I always sleep well. Today was my day of silence and I slept four times. I fell asleep while I was on the rack.'

'During his massage,' a woman doctor interpreted.

'You must get massage here,' Gandhi urged.

After dinner, I passed Gandhi's bed on the open-air stone terrace. Two women disciples were massaging his feet and shins. His bed was a mattress-covered wooden plank with two bricks under it to raise the head higher than the feet. A mosquito net hung over the bed. Several young women were sitting on the mats near him and laughing. He called out to me, 'I hope you will be up in time to have breakfast with me.' He said first breakfast was at 4.

'I'd rather be excused from that one.'

'Then second breakfast at 5.'

I made a face and everybody laughed.

'You had better have third breakfast with me at 9,' he said. 'Get up at 6.'

I was up at 6.30. When I stepped out into the courtyard, Gandhi was chatting with an Indian. He greeted me and we started on his morning walk.

'You said last night,' I recalled, 'that Paul altered the teachings of Jesus. Will the people around you do the same?'

'You are not the first to mention this possibility,' he replied. 'I see through them. Yes, I know they may try to do just that. I know India is not with me. I have not convinced enough Indians of the wisdom of non-violence.'

Again he talked at length about the persecution of coloured races in South Africa. He inquired about the treatment of Negroes in the United States. 'A civilization,' he said, 'is to be judged by its treatment of minorities.'

After a massage by a powerful Ceylonese who kneaded the muscles till they ached, I felt better and looked into Gandhi's room. It had no door, only a curtain which I pushed aside. He noticed me and said, 'Come in, you are always welcome.' He was writing an article for *Harijan* and submitting to questions in the vernacular by three Indians. I went in and out until 11 A.M. Rajkumari Amrit Kaur, a Christian princess who served him as first English-language secretary, was reading Reuters news bulletins to him. Now and then he muttered 'Hm'. The South African items made him shake his head sadly. 'President Truman', a flash radiogram stated, 'yesterday signed the Indian immigration and naturalization bill.'

Gandhi asked about the provisions of the new law. How many Indians would be granted citizenship and how many would immigrate? Are Chinese and Japanese admitted into the United States?

'More than anyone else,' I said to Gandhi, 'the man who is responsible for the passage of the bill is the President of the India League of America, J. J. Singh. Would you write him a letter?' He promised and gave me the letter a few days later.

Gulbai, Dr Mehta's wife, brought me a heaped bowl of peeled and sliced fruit and placed it on the mat. Gandhi had already had his third breakfast, so I ate while he talked. He said he was trying to create a classless and casteless India. He yearned for the day when there would be only one caste and Brahmans would marry Harijans. 'I am a social revolutionist,' he asserted. 'Violence is bred by inequality, non-violence by equality.' Gandhi's religion merged with his sociology.

I said I knew that the mounting prejudice against coloured peoples in South Africa disturbed him; he had fought it for twenty years. 'But I hope,' I added, 'you will do nothing violent in this connection. You are a violent man.' He laughed. 'Some of your fasts are violent,' I continued.

'You want me to confine myself to violent words,' he commented.

'Yes.'

'I do not know when I am going to fast,' he explained. 'It is God who determines that. It comes to me suddenly. But I will not act rashly. I have no desire to die.'

Sudhir Ghosh, a youthful Cambridge University graduate, came in to bid Gandhi goodbye. He was going to England and the Mahatma was giving him a letter of introduction to Prime Minister Attlee. Gandhi's go-between with the Cabinet Mission, Ghosh had so distinguished himself by his intelligent and gracious handling of delicate diplomatic tasks that Gandhi was asking him to be his liaison with Attlee, Cripps, Pethick-Lawrence and others in London. Like many a head of state, Gandhi wished to be his own 'foreign minister'. Usually, the official foreign minister resents the intrusion.

That afternoon, before the prayer meeting, an Indian in his twenties approached me and said he was the editor of a Hindu Mahasabha weekly published in Poona and would I give him a message. I said I did not approve of the Hindu Mahasabha any more than I approved of the Moslem League; both stood for religion in politics. 'The Hindu Mahasabha,' I declared with acerbity, 'stands for Hindu supremacy. Do you like white supremacy?' We parted.

Hundreds of Poona citizens stood in a field on the other side of the clinic's low fence while Gandhi and his friends conducted the services on a wooden platform on this side of the fence. During the singing it commenced to rain; worshippers put up their black umbrellas. A murmur of protest arose from those in the rear and all umbrellas were lowered. Somebody held one over Gandhi. A few hundred yards away two Indian teams in white flannels were playing cricket.

Before dinner, Gandhi invited me to walk with him. 'Surely you are not going to walk in the rain,' I protested lightly.

'Come along, old man,' he said and stretched out his arm.

I had been given a private room that opened on the terrace where Gandhi slept. Late in the evening, when I was about to retire, I passed Gandhi's bed. I greeted him silently with a raised hand but he called out, 'You must sleep well tonight. But we will disturb you with our prayers at 4.'

'I hope not,' I said and approached him.

He addressed himself to Mrs Mehta in Hindustani or Gujarati, and I thought he was scolding her. 'We are talking about you and you are curious,' Gandhi remarked.

'Somehow I knew it,' I replied. 'Now you have made it worse by telling me but not disclosing what you were talking about. I should offer Satyagraha against you until you tell me.'

'All right,' he laughed.

'I will sit by your bed all night.'

'Come along,' he said with a lilt.

'I will sit here and sing American songs.'

'All right, you will sing me to sleep.'

Everybody was enjoying the fun.

Gandhi's laughter was physical and mental; it was amusement plus agreement or at least amusement plus tolerance. It was the laughter of a man who is not afraid to be caught with his visor up and his guard down.

It had grown late and I wished them good night. I talked to Mrs Mehta. Gandhi had scolded her because she served my breakfast in his room at 11 instead of 9 and this had held up the noonday meal of the others and besides she had given me special food; no one should receive privileged treatment.

I awoke very fit and went to Gandhi's room. He invited me to walk. I requested his views on the next step in the Indian political situation. 'The British,' he answered with alacrity, 'must ask Congress to form a coalition government. All the minorities will co-operate.'

'Would you include members of the Moslem League?'

'Of course', he replied. 'Mr Jinnah can have a highly important post.'

He left me for a while to talk to a young Indian woman. I had noticed him walking up and down the terrace with her the day before in agitated conversation. Then she had gone away and a young man stepped to Gandhi's side and they talked together for about a quarter of an hour. Pyarelal told me who they were. She was an untouchable and limped from an accident. The young man, likewise a Harijan, was her husband and he had had a forearm amputated. They were having marital difficulties and Gandhi wanted to patch up their relations.

When we resumed our consitutional, he began a discussion of Europe and Russia. I said Moscow had nothing to give the world; it had gone nationalistic, imperialistic and Pan-Slav. This could not feed the West. The democracies were beginning to realize that world peace would only come with internationalism and spiritual regeneration.

'Why do you want me to go to the West?'

'Not go to the West, but speak to the West.'

'Why does the West need me to tell them that two times two are four? If they realize that the way of violence and war is evil why am I necessary to point out the obvious truth? Besides, I have unfinished work here.'

'Nevertheless,' I said, 'the West needs you. You are the antithesis to materialism and therefore the antidote to Stalinism and statism.' He talked about the increase of the spirit of violence in India since 1942.

Pedestrians gathered to watch Gandhi as we moved to and fro on the path that led to the city. There were factories near by and occasionally their whistles blew, but he never stopped talking; nor did he lift his voice; he talked through the noise.

I asked whether he had read my book *A Week with Gandhi*. He had, and apart from a few minor errors (I mis-stated Kasturbai's age, for instance) he thought well of it. He had also read my *Men and Politics*; he read it in his 'library', as he called the lavatory where he kept a shelf of books.

Nehru arrived at the clinic with Krishna Menon who later became Indian High Commissioner in London. 'Nehru,' Gandhi said to me, 'had an oratorical mind.' Menon, Nehru, I and several others lunched together in the large common dining-room. I was served mutton chops. By request, I shared my portion with Nehru.

Gandhi knew that Nehru ate meat and smoked; he did not object. But Nehru never smoked in Gandhi's presence. (Only Maulana Abul Kalam Azad did, and Gandhi always reminded the girls in advance to bring in an ashtray.) Nehru has infinite charm, grace, tenderness and talent to express himself in words. Gandhi called him an artist. His years at

Harrow and Cambridge made him very British and other years in prison made him very bitter. During his long imprisonment between 1942 and 1945 he had grown completely grey and completely bald but no less handsome. In his private life and public life he had suffered much. His smile, which reveals two rows of fine white teeth, melts the heart alike by its cheer and its unintended sadness.

Gandhi loved Nehru as a son and Nehru loved Gandhi as a father. Nehru never hid the deep difference between his outlook and Gandhi's. He spoke and wrote about it frequently. Gandhi welcomed the frankness. Their affection for one another did not depend on agreement.

Something far down in Nehru's psyche rebels against surrender. He was repelled by the unquestioning obedience which most Indian leaders gave Gandhi. He questioned and argued and resisted – and finally surrendered. He fights for the independence of his personality. He balks against conquest. When he submits he does so with meekness and grace. Gandhi knew his frailties and he himself has come to recognize his limitations. In politics all his life, Nehru never mastered the intricacies of party politics as the Mahatma and Patel did. He is the tribune not the organizer, a spokesman to the outside, not the manipulator inside. He appeals most to intellectuals but not with intellect; his appeal is to the heart. In India, that is an asset. He is an aristocrat whose love for aristocrats is no impediment to his love of the people. One of the world's foremost statesmen, he is not a statesman at all. He is a good person lost among statesmen. The people give him adulation; he lends it to those who run the machine of government.

In India Nehru is addicted to gusts of temper and bursts of indignation. On occasions, he bodily assaulted men who aroused his indignation. He has endless physical courage. Sometimes, in press conferences, he makes unconsidered statements of defiance. These may all be strivings towards strength. There can be no doubt that it was Gandhi's vast inner strength and clarity, among other things, that so fascinated and captivated Jawaharlal.

Nehru's books show beauty of soul, nobility of ideal and egocentrism. Gandhi seemed entirely extrovert; he was no burden to himself. Nehru must always cope with his own problem.

In the afternoon of that second day at the nature-cure clinic, Nehru sat cross-legged on my bed for an hour while I occupied the chair. He had gone to his beloved native Kashmir on a visit; the Maharaja forbade his entry. He grappled with an Indian soldier, equipped with bayoneted rifle, who barred his way at the frontier post. Now he said, 'I am convinced that the British Agent would not have kept me out of Kashmir while I was engaged in the Cabinet Mission negotiations without first consulting the Viceroy, and, that being so, it does not appear that they are getting ready to leave India.'

Krishna Menon shares his scepticism.

I asked Nehru whether he considered himself a Socialist. 'I am a Socialist but not a Marxist,' he replied. 'I am a Socialist but I don't believe in any dogma.' (In 1948, in New Delhi, he told me that as he grew older he judged people 'more by their personal character than their isms' and that he had moved 'closer to Christ and Buddha, especially Buddha', and further, therefore, from Marx, Lenin and Stalin and closer to Gandhi.)

Nehru spent several hours of the afternoon alone with Gandhi; nobody disturbed them. Late in the afternoon, I went to Gandhi's room and found him spinning. I said I thought he had abandoned spinning. 'No, how could I?' he asked. 'There are four hundred million Indians. Subtract one hundred million children, waifs and others; if the remaining three hundred million would spin an hour each day we would have Swaraj.'

'Because of the economic or spiritual effect?' I asked.

'Both,' he said. 'If three hundred million people did the same thing once a day not because a Hitler ordered it but because they were inspired by the same ideal we would have enough unity of purpose to achieve independence.'

'When you stop spinning to talk to me you are delaying Swaraj.'

'Yes,' he agreed, 'you have postponed Swaraj by six yards.'

Prime Minister Kher of Bombay province and Morarji Desai, the Home Member of the province, visited Gandhi to report on the continuing Ahmedabad intercommunity riots. At nine in the evening I accompanied Nehru and Menon to Desai's residence in Poona. Desai blamed Moslems for the disturbances. Shortly before midnight, Nehru and Menon took the train to Bombay.

The next morning Gandhi and about ten companions and I walked to the Poona station and boarded the express to Bombay. The party had the use of a special third-class carriage with a hard wooden bench down the length of each outer wall and another down the centre of the carriage. It rained heavily throughout the journey, and soon water began to pour from roof and through openings in the window frames and door. Large puddles formed on the floor. At a number of stops en route, local Congress leaders boarded a train for conferences with Gandhi. Between times, he wrote a brief article for *Harijan* and corrected another article. He looked up at me once and smiled and we exchanged a few remarks. When his editorial work was finished he stretched out on the wooden bench and in a moment he was sleeping serenely. He slept for about fifteen minutes.

Gandhi occupied a place near a window. At all stations immense crowds gathered despite the downpour. At one stop, two boys, about fourteen years of age, wet to their brown skins, their hair dripping, jumped up and down outside Gandhi's window, moved their bent arms up and down and yelled, 'Gandhiji, Gandhiji, Gandhiji.' He smiled.

I said, 'What are you to them?'

He put his fists with thumbs upward to his temples and replied, 'A man with horns, a spectacle.'

Gandhi left the train at a suburban station to avoid the crowd at the Bombay terminus. He and the other Congress leaders were congregating in Bombay for a meeting of the All-India Congress Committee (AICC) which would debate the Working Committee decisions to accept the Cabinet Mission's long-term plan for a constitution but to refuse participation in the interim government.

The two-day session took place in a hall built like a theatre. The floor of the stage was covered with white cotton homespun. Leaders clothed in somewhat finer white homespun sat on the floor of the stage and leaned on large bolsters placed against the scenery. To the left and rear of the centre of the stage was a big divan covered with white homespun. It was unoccupied. Nehru, in clinging white cotton trousers, a white blouse reaching half way down his thighs and an apricot-coloured sleeveless vest, presided. He used a microphone erected near his chair. Two hundred and fifty-five voting delegates sat in the hall together with hundreds of visitors and several score Indian and foreign journalists.

Access to the stage from the well of the theatre was by a short flight of wooden steps. A speaker would mount to the top step, leave his or her sandals there and walk barefoot to the microphone.

During the deliberations, a woman came on the stage from behind the scenes and put a flat box on the divan. Shortly after, Gandhi walked on, sat down on the divan, opened the box and started spinning. His entrance was applauded briefly by the standing delegates. He acknowledged their welcome with a smile. It is considered undignified to make too much noise with hand-clapping or exclamations.

The second day, Sunday, 7 July, Gandhi, in loincloth, addressed the Committee from a sitting position on the white divan. He spoke Hindustani into a microphone but the mechanism was defective and he was barely audible.

The speech, delivered extemporaneously, was published verbatim in *Harijan* and all Indian dailies. It consisted of about 1,700 words and he pronounced them slowly, in approximately fifteen minutes, as though he were talking to one person in his hut.

He said:

'I have been told that some of my previous remarks about the Cabinet Mission's proposals have caused a good deal of confusion in the public mind. As a Satyagrahi it is always my endeavour to speak the whole truth and nothing but the truth. I never have a wish to hide anything from you. I hate mental reservations. But language is at best an imperfect medium of expression. No man can express fully in words what he feels or thinks. Even seers and prophets of old have suffered under that disability . . .

'I did say in one of my speeches at Delhi in regard to the Cabinet Mission's proposals that I saw darkness where I saw light before. That darkness has not yet lifted. If possible it has deepened. I could have asked the Working Committee to turn down the proposal about the Constituent Assembly if I could see my way clearly. You know my relations with the members of the Working Committee. Babu Rajendra Prasad might have been a High Court Judge, but he chose instead to act as my interpreter and clerk in Champaran. Then there is the Sardar [Patel]. He has earned the nickname of being my Yes-man. He does not mind it. He even flaunts it as a compliment. He is a stormy petrel. Once he used to dress and dine in the Western style. But ever since he decided to cast his lot with me my word has been law to him. But even he cannot see eye to eye with me in this matter. They both tell me that whereas on all previous occasions I was able to support my instinct with reason and satisfy their head as well as heart, this time I have failed to do so. I told them in reply that whilst my own heart was filled with misgivings I could not adduce any reason for it or else I would have asked them to reject the proposals straightaway. It was my duty to place my misgivings before them to put them on their guard. But they should examine what I had said in the light of reason and accept my point of view only if they were convinced of its correctness.'

They were not convinced of its correctness and therefore the Working Committee took a middle course by approving the provisions for the future constitution of India but holding aloof from the interim government. The Socialist fraction of the AICC, and some others, were fighting the Working Committee's compromise. They advocated abstention from the Constituent Assembly as well as from the interim government. They wished to follow Gandhi's instinct even though he had not supported it with rational argument.

'. . . I am surprised that Jaiprakash Narayan said yesterday' Gandhi continued, 'that it would be dangerous to participate in the proposed Constituent Assembly and therefore you should reject the Working Committee's resolution. I was not prepared to hear such defeatist language from the lips of a tried fighter like Jaiprakash . . . A Satyagrahi knows no defeat.

'Nor would I expect a Satyagrahi to say that whatever Englishmen do is bad. The English are not necessarily bad. There are good men and bad men among the English people as among any other people. We ourselves are not free from defects. The English could not have risen to their present strength if they had not some good in them. They have come and exploited India because we quarrelled amongst ourselves and allowed ourselves to be exploited. In God's world unmixed evil never prospers. God rules even where Satan holds sway because the latter exists on His sufferance.' Then he talked about non-violence and the 1942 civil disobedience movement.

'We must have patience and humility and detachment . . . The Constituent Assembly is going to be no bed of roses but only a bed of thorns. You may not shirk it . . .

'Let us not be cowardly, but approach our task with confidence and courage . . . Never mind the darkness that fills my mind. He will turn it into light.'

Everybody handclapped two or three times.

The vote was 204 in favour of the Working Committee's compromise and 51 against. The negative poll was considered large; it reflected the doubts present in Gandhi's, Nehru's, in fact most members' minds about British intentions. After more than a hundred and fifty years of British tutelage and eighty-nine years of the British Empire, no Indian could completely divest himself of distrust.

I spent a number of days in the hot, dank Bombay of the monsoon summer and then left with Jaiprakash Narayan and his wife Prabhavati to tour the Maharashtra en route to Gandhi's new residence in Panchgani. We travelled to Poona by train and thence by car.

The ancient car broke down several miles outside the town and we proceeded by a commercial passenger bus. Arrangements had been made for Socialist delegations to greet Jaiprakash along the road. Wherever they appeared – six times during the journey – the bus stopped, Jaiprakash, Prabhavati and I stepped out, the local folks made little speeches, each of us received a garland of most fragrant blooms placed around the neck and a tightly packed bouquet or an armful of bananas to carry. In several places, after we had returned to the bus, a woman came in and touched our knuckles with a tiny metal hand covered with a colourless, perfumed cream. We rode in a cloud of scent. Throughout the repeated ceremonies, the passengers in the bus and the driver waited patiently without demur.

Jaiprakash stayed over to address an evening meeting in Satara while Prabhavati and I, in a borrowed car, drove over the hills and through the mists to Panchgani. We arrived near midnight; the town was dark and dead. Stray pedestrians could not tell us where Gandhi was stopping. We were compelled to get out of the car at every stone summer villa, walk up the steps to the porch and see whether anybody was sleeping there. On one porch, we saw Gandhi lying among his disciples.

In the morning Prabhavati put her head on Gandhi's feet and he patted her with sweet affection. About lunchtime, Jaiprakash arrived. He and I were the only visitors so I had ample opportunity for conversation with Gandhi.

He began by asking me what I had learned. I had noticed a sharp cleavage between those who believed in the Constituent Assembly and those who did not.

Gandhi: 'I do not consider the Constituent Assembly non-revolutionary. I am convinced that it is a perfect substitute for civil disobedience.'

L.F.: 'You think the British are playing the game?'

Gandhi: 'I think the British will play the game this time.'

L.F.: 'You believe they are withdrawing from India?'

Gandhi: 'Yes.'

L.F.: 'I believe it, too, but I cannot convince Jaiprakash. But supposing the British do not leave, you will offer your kind of protest, not Jaiprakash's?'

Gandhi: 'No, Jaiprakash will have to join me. I will not pit myself against him. In 1942, I said I was sailing out on uncharted waters. I will not do it now. I did not know the people then. I know now what I can do and what I cannot.'

L.F.: 'You did not know in 1942 that there would be violence?'

Gandhi: 'Correct.'

L.F.: 'So if the Constituent Assembly fails you will not stage a civil disobedience campaign?'

Gandhi: 'Not unless the Socialists and the Communists are subdued by that time.'

L.F.: 'That is not likely . . .'

Gandhi: 'I cannot think of civil disobedience when there is so much violence in the air in India. Today some Caste Hindus are not playing the game by the untouchables.'

L.F.: 'By some Caste Hindus you mean some Congressmen?'

Gandhi: 'Not many Congressmen. But there are some who have not banished untouchability from their hearts. That is the tragedy . . . The Moslems also feel they are wronged. In an orthodox Hindu house a Moslem will not be permitted to sit on the same carpet with a Hindu and have his meal. That is false religion. India is falsely religious. It must get true religion.'

L.F.: 'You have not succeeded with Congress?'

Gandhi: 'No, I have not. I have failed. Something, however, has been accomplished. The Harijans are admitted to the temples in Madura and in many other holy places, and the Caste Hindus worship in the same temples.'

That was the end of our morning talk. Gandhi was 'turning the searchlight inward' and instead of finding fault with others the beam helped him to find the faults of Congress and the Hindus. Some Hindus did not like it. They preferred to blame Jinnah and England.

In the early afternoon, Jaiprakash had an hour with Gandhi. One of the secretaries translated to me part of her notes.

Jaiprakash: 'Congress is not organizing the strength of the country. Merit does not count in Congress today. Caste and family relationships count. This is the main reason we Socialists will not go into the Constituent Assembly. We felt that the Working Committee was overcome by a kind of helplessness. "If we do not accept the British proposal what can we do?" they were saying. This is an attitude of weakness.

They expect the British to devise ways and means of bringing about an agreement between Congress and the Moslem League. We should have said to the British, "You go. We will settle this ourselves!" If the British do not like it they can put us in jail.'

Gandhi: 'Jail is jail for thieves and bandits. For me it is a palace. I was the originator of jail-going even before I read Thoreau. Tolstoy wrote that I had discovered something new, he wrote it in a Russian daily paper. A Russian woman translated it for me. I have fought the government from inside jails. Jail-going can bring Swaraj if the philosophy behind it is correct . . . But today jail-going would be a farce.'

Jaiprakash: 'Today we should send Englishmen to jail.'

Gandhi: 'Why? How? There is no need of it. This is a mere figure of speech and should not come from lips like yours. Even after violent warfare it would not be necessary. This is how Churchill talked of what he would do to Hitler. And witness the folly and the wickedness of the trial of the Nazi war criminals. Some of those who try the criminals are just as criminal.'

Congress had formed the governments of a number of provinces, and Jaiprakash and Gandhi saw mounting corruption and nepotism there. The Socialists, moreover, together with many non-Socialist Congressmen, would have gloried in one last struggle to oust the British. They believed freedom is not real unless you forcibly expel your master. They suspected that the British would, with Moslem League connivance, seek to maintain a foothold in India. Jaiprakash therefore was in an anti-constitutional, anti-legal mood, a militant mood, whereas Gandhi, disillusioned by the Socialist and other violence in 1942, 1943 and 1944, was less militant than ever before in his career. That made his 'misgivings' about the Cabinet Mission's plan all the more painful. Widespread violence had knocked from his hand the special weapon he had forged: civil disobedience. The Constituent Assembly, consequently, was his only alternative.

Gandhi had entered on the road of anguish that led to his death.

Gandhi gave me more than an hour in the afternoon. He reverted to the Negro question in America. After a while, I said, 'Since my arrival in India, I have met some intelligent people . . .'

Gandhi: 'Ah, have you? Not many.'

L. F.: 'You and two or three others.' He laughed. 'And some say Hindu–Moslem relations are better and some say they are worse.'

Gandhi: 'Jinnah and other Moslem leaders were once members of Congress. They left it because they felt the pinch of Hindu patronizing. In the beginning, the leading Congressmen were theosophists. Mrs Annie Besant attracted me very much. Theosophy is the teaching of Madame Blavatsky. It is Hinduism at its best. Theosophy is the brotherhood of man. They took me to Mrs Besant's [in London]. I was just a student from Bombay. I could not understand the British accent. It was an ordeal for me. I felt quite unworthy of going to Mrs Besant. Cultivated Moslems joined the theosophists. Later, Congress membership grew and with it the Hindu patronizing attitude. The Moslems are religious fanatics, but fanaticism cannot be answered with fanaticism. Bad manners irritate. Brilliant Moslems in Congress became disgusted. They did not find the brotherhood of man among the Hindus. They say Islam is the brotherhood of man. As a matter of fact, it is the brotherhood of Moslems. Theosophy is the brotherhood of man. Hindu separatism has played a part in creating the rift between Congress and the League. Jinnah is an evil genius. He believes he is a prophet.'

L.F.: 'He is a lawyer.'

Gandhi: 'You do him an injustice. I give you the testimony of my eighteen days of talks with him in 1944. He really looks upon himself as the saviour of Islam.'

L.F.: 'The Moslems are rich in temperament and spirit. They are warm and friendly.'

Gandhi: 'Yes.'

L.F.: 'But Jinnah is cold. He is a thin man. He pleads a case, he does not preach a cause.'

Gandhi: 'I agree he is a thin man. But I don't consider him a fraud. He has cast a spell over the Moslem, who is a simple-minded man.'

L.F.: Sometimes I think the Moslem–Hindu question is the problem of finding a place for the new Moslem middle class in an underdeveloped India. India is even too underdeveloped to offer a place to the poor. Jinnah won over the middle class because he helped it to compete with the other entrenched Hindu middle class. Now he is bridging the chasm between the landlord and peasant. He has done it with Pakistan.'

Gandhi: 'You are right. But Jinnah has not won the peasant. He is trying to win him. The peasant has nothing in common with the landlord or middle class. Landlords crush the peasants. The franchise does not reach the poor. Even the British electorate is not informed.'

L.F.: 'I think it is. It is better informed than ever.'

Gandhi: 'It is better informed but not well informed.'

L.F.: 'How can Congress, with its Hindu stamp, win the Moslems?'

Gandhi: 'In the twinkling of an eye, by giving equality to untouchables. Hinduism has to reform itself. I have every hope. Improvement is very gradual . . .'

L.F.: 'I understand there is less contact between Hindus and Moslems.'

Gandhi: 'Political contact in the upper stratum is breaking down . . .'

L.F.: 'Jinnah told me in 1942 you did not want independence.'

Gandhi: 'And what do I want?'

L.F.: 'He said you want Hindu rule.'

Gandhi: 'He is utterly wrong. That is absurd. I am a Moslem, a Hindu, a Buddhist, a Christian, a Jew, a Parsi. He does not know me when he said I want Hindu rule. He is not speaking the truth. He is speaking like a pettifogging lawyer. Only a maniac resorts to such charges . . . I believe that the Moslem League will go into the Assembly. But the Sikhs have refused. They are stiff-necked like the Jews.'

L.F.: 'You are stiff-necked too.'

Gandhi: 'I?'

L.F.: 'You are a stiff-necked man. You are stubborn. You like everything your way. You are a sweet-tempered dictator.' This aroused general laughter among the secretaries and disciples in which Gandhi heartily joined.

Gandhi: 'Dictator? I have no power. I have not changed Congress. I have a catalogue of grievances against it.'

L.F.: 'What did you learn from your eighteen days with Jinnah?'

Gandhi: 'I learned that he was a maniac. A maniac leaves off his mania and becomes reasonable at times. I have never regretted my talks with him. I have never been too stubborn to learn. Every one of my failures has been a stepping stone. I could not make any headway with Jinnah because he is a maniac, but many Moslems were disgusted with Jinnah for his behaviour during the talks.'

L.F.: 'What is the solution?'

Gandhi: 'Jinnah has twenty-five years more to work.'

L.F.: 'He wants to live as long as you do.'

Gandhi: 'Then he must live till I am 125.'

L.F.: 'You had better not die, it would kill him and then you would be a murderer.' (Laughter.) 'He will die the day after you.'

Gandhi: 'Jinnah is incorruptible and brave . . . If Jinnah stays out of the Constituent Assembly the British should be firm and let us work the plan alone. The British must not yield to Hitler.'

L.F.: 'The British do not yield to force but they yield to the force of circumstances . . .'

The next morning, I heard Sushila Pie, a schoolteacher who had joined Gandhi's staff, singing in the next room. When she came out on the veranda I asked why she had been singing.

'Because I am happy,' she replied.

'And why are you happy?'

'We are happy because we are near Bapu,' she said.

Jaiprakash and I were leaving that day for Bombay; Prabhavati was staying with Gandhi. She had worked with Gandhi for many years. The women in the Mahatma's entourage – Miss Slade, Rajkumari Amrit Kaur, Sushila Nayyar, Prabhavati Narayan and others – loved Gandhi and he loved them. It was a father–daughter relationship of more than usual warmth and interdependence. Miss Slade became physically ill on a number of occasions when she was separated from Bapu or when she was worried about his health. Her bond with him was one of the remarkable platonic associations of our age. He often said to her, 'When this body is no more there will not be separation, but I shall be nearer to you. The body is a hindrance.'

Rajkumari and Miss Slade would kiss his hand; he would stroke their cheeks. He said that he deliberately surrounded himself with women to prove that his mastery over 'lust' was not achieved by avoiding women. But after his 'lust dream' in 1936 he took a six weeks' silence and did not put his hand on women's shoulders. He told his women secretaries about that dream before he wrote of it in *Harijan*. He shared his innermost thoughts with them.

Some of the female disciples were jealous when Gandhi appeared to favour one above the other. He was aware of it and tried to be impartial. He enjoyed their company and devotion. Whether they did not marry because of attachment to him or whether they were attached to him because they would not marry it is folly to guess. One was married but remained continent. They were all valiant Amazons of his causes.

Tagore, who loved Gandhi, wrote of the Mahatma, 'He condemns sexual life as inconsistent with the moral progress of man and has a horror of sex as great as that of the author of *The Kreutzer Sonata*, but, unlike Tolstoy, he betrays no abhorrence of the sex that tempts his kind. In fact, his tenderness for woman is one of the noblest and most consistent traits of his character and he counts among the women of his country some of his best and truest comrades in the great movement he is leading.'

On 18 July, I had my last talk with the Mahatma. 'If the Working Committee had responded to your 'groping in the dark', or your instinct, as you also called it, they would have rejected the Cabinet Mission's plan for the Constituent Assembly?' I began.

Gandhi: 'Yes, but I did not let them.'

L.F.: 'You mean you did not insist.'

Gandhi: 'More than that. I prevented them from following my instinct unless they felt likewise. It is no use conjecturing what would have happened. The fact is, however, the Dr Rajendra Prasad asked me, "Does your instinct go so far that you would prevent us from accepting the long term proposals whether we understand you or not?" I said, "No, follow your reason since my own reason does not support my instinct. My instinct rebels against my reason. I have placed my misgivings before you because I want to be faithful to you. I myself have not followed my instinct unless my reason backed it".'

L.F.: 'But you told me that you follow your instinct when it speaks to you on occasions, as, for instance, before certain fasts.'

Gandhi: 'Yes, but even in these cases my reason was there before the fast began . . .'

L.F.: 'Then why do you inject your instinct into the present political situation?'

Gandhi: 'I did not. But I was loyal. I wanted to retain my faith in the bona fides of the Cabinet Mission. So I told the Cabinet Mission that my instinct had misgivings. "Supposing" I said to myself, "they meant ill; they would be ashamed. They will say, 'He says his instinct tells him this, but we know the reason.' Their guilty conscience would prick them".'

L.F.: 'It did not. Does that mean the Cabinet Mission's intentions were honest?'

Gandhi: 'I do not retract anything from the original certificate I gave them . . .'

L.F.: 'You are strongly constitutionalist now because you fear violence?'

Gandhi: 'I say we must go into the Assembly and work it. If the British are dishonest they will be found out. The loss will not be ours but theirs and humanity's.'

L.F.: 'I think you are afraid of the spirit of the Indian National Army and Subhas Chandra Bose [its hero who went to Germany and Japan during the second World War]. It is widespread. He has captured the imagination of the youth and you are aware of it and you fear that mood. The young generation is indocentric.'

Gandhi: 'He has not captured the imagination of the country. It is too wide a term, but a section of the youth and of the women follow him . . . The Almighty has reserved mildness for India. "The mild Hindu" is used as a term of reproach. But I take it as a term of honour, just like Churchill's "Naked Fakir". I appropriated it as a compliment and even wrote about it to Churchill. I told Churchill I would love to be a naked fakir but was not one as yet.'

L.F.: 'Did he answer?'

Gandhi: 'Yes, he acknowledged my letter through the

Viceroy in a courteous manner. But to resume . . . The unsophisticated woman, untouched and unspoiled by civilization, so-called, are with me.'

'L.F.: 'But you admire Bose. You believe he is alive.' [He had been reported killed in an aeroplane accident.]

Gandhi: 'I do not encourage the Bose legend. I did not agree with him. I do not now believe he is alive. Instinct made me believe to the contrary at one time, because he had made himself into a legendary Robin Hood.'

L.F.: 'My point is this: Bose went to Germany and Japan, both fascist countries. If he was pro-fascist you can have no sympathy with him. If he was a patriot and believed that India would be saved by Germany or Japan, especially in 1944, he was stupid and statesmen cannot afford to be stupid.'

Gandhi: 'You have a high opinion of statesmen. Most of them are stupid . . . I have to work against heavy odds . . . There is an active mood of violence that has to be combated and I am doing it in my own way. It is my implicit faith that it is a survival which will kill itself in time . . . It cannot live. It is so contrary to the spirit of India. But what is the use of talking? I believe in an inscrutable Providence that presides over our destinies – call it God or by any name you like.'

CHAPTER 4

Pilgrim's Progress

Congress would not participate in the provisional government because Lord Wavell had, on Jinnah's insistence, refused to allow it to nominate a Moslem for one of the government posts. True, Wavell had stipulated publicly that the composition of the interim government would not constitute a precedent. Congress feared it would, and refused adamantly to recognize Jinnah's right to veto a Congress Moslem's appointment to the Cabinet.

Wavell accordingly again asked Congress and the League to submit lists of its candidates for positions in the Government, but, in deference to Congress, stressed that no side could bar the nominees of the other. Jinnah thereupon declined the invitation to participate in the provisional government. On 12 August, 1946, Wavell commissioned Nehru to form the government. Nehru went to see Jinnah and offered him a choice of places in the Government for the Moslem League. Jinnah refused. Nehru then organized a government consisting of six Congressmen, of whom five were caste Hindus and one a Harijan, and, in addition, one Christian, one Sikh, one Parsi and two Moslems who were not of the Moslem League. Wavell announced that it was open to the Moslem League to name five of its members to the provisional government. Jinnah was not interested.

The Moslem League declared 16 August 'Direct Action Day'. Savage riots lasting four days broke out in Calcutta. 'Official estimates', writes Lord Pethick-Lawrence, 'placed the casualties at some five thousand killed and fifteen thousand wounded, and unofficial figures were higher still.'

Sir Shafaat Ahmed Khan, a Moslem who had resigned

from the Moslem League to join Nehru's interim government, was waylaid in a lonely spot in Simla at dusk on 24 August and stabbed seven times. 'Obviously political', high British authorities said of the assault.

On 2 September, Nehru became Prime Minister of India. 'Our representatives and leaders have broken into the citadel of power,' J. B. Kripalani, the new president of Congress, declared.

Gandhi was living in the untouchables' quarter in New Delhi on 2 September. He woke very early that morning and wrote a letter to Nehru on the duties of the new Government. This was a red-letter day in India's history, he told his evening prayer meeting and he felt grateful to the British but in no mood for jubilation. 'Sooner, rather than later, complete power will be in your hands,' he promised the audience, 'if Pandit Nehru, your uncrowned king and Prime Minister, and his colleagues, did their part.' The Moslems were the brothers of the Hindus even if they were not in the Government as yet, Gandhi continued, and a brother does not return anger with anger.

But Jinnah proclaimed 2 September a day of mourning and instructed Moslems to display black flags. The next day in Bombay; Jinnah said: 'The Russians may have more than a spectator's interest in Indian affairs, and they are not very far from India either.'

Sir Firoz Khan Noon, a big Punjab landowner and a Moslem League leader, had spoken in the same vein. 'If our own course is to fight,' he asserted, 'and if in that fight we go down, the only course for the Moslems is to look to Russia.'

Gandhi did not misread these signs. 'We are not yet in the midst of civil war,' he stated on 9 September, 'but we are nearing it.' Shootings and stabbings occurred in Bombay throughout September. A Moslem black flag was like a red flat to a Hindu. Trouble spread to the Punjab. Violence shook Bengal and Bihar.

The Moslem League announced that it would abstain from the national Constituent Assembly.

Alarmed by the disturbed state of the nation, Wavell redoubled his efforts to win Moslem League adherence to the new Government. Jinnah finally agreed, and appointed four Moslem League members and one untouchable who was an opponent of Gandhi. The Moslem League always proclaimed itself a religious body representing the Moslems of India. Why then should it have appointed an untouchable, a Hindu? Obviously to annoy Congress and the caste Hindus. It was a bad augury for the new Government. And, in fact, Nawabzada Liaquat Ali Khan, Finance Member and foremost League spokesman in the Government, announced that he and his colleagues did not recognize the Government as a coalition and felt no obligation to co-operate with Nehru and the other Congress ministers. The Government was a house divided – by religion.

Every day Gandhi preached against the uninterrupted violence between the two communities. 'Some people even rejoice,' he said, 'that Hindus are now strong enough to kill in return those who tried to kill them. I would far rather that Hindus died without retaliation . . .'

At the same time he remembered his other causes and stressed the need for more khadi production; he protested against maltreatment of Harijans: 'If there is an epidemic they are beaten and cannot draw water from the wells. They live in hovels.' He wanted the Salt Tax completely annulled, but he asked the people to be patient in this regard: the new ministers were overwhelmed with unaccustomed tasks.

Most Congress ministers and many of the assistants as well as provincial officials came to Gandhi's hut in the Harijan quarter for frequent visits – sometimes daily – to ask his advice and approval. Gandhi was 'super-Prime Minister'.

He wrote on leprosy and the need of collective prayer, on the regime on Indian jails and discrimination in South Africa, on lagging food production and the good in the Hindu pantheon. Each day he gave instructions for his meals the next day. Whenever possible, he made diary entries. 'It seems to be so very hard', he wrote one night, 'to maintain detachment of mind in the midst of raging fire.' And he told a friend 'Why could I not suffer this anguish with unruffled calmness of spirit? I am afraid I have not the detachment required for living to 125 years.'

The raging fire of Hindu-Moslem strife gave him no rest. Yet his faith in human beings persisted. 'In Bombay a Hindu gave shelter to a Moslem friend the other day,' he wrote on 15 October. 'This infuriated a Hindu mob who demanded the head of the Moslem friend. The Hindu would not surrender his friend. So both went down literally in deadly embrace. This was how it was described to me authentically. Nor is this the first instance of chivalry in the midst of frenzy. During the recent blood bath in Calcutta, stories of Moslems having, at the peril of their lives, sheltered their Hindu friends and vice versa were recorded. Mankind would die if there were no exhibition at any time and anywhere of the divine in man.'

Gandhi now went in search of the divine in maddened man.

Widespread Moslem attacks on Hindus had taken place during October in the distant Noakhali and Tippera rural areas of east Bengal. These seemed to alarm the Mahatma more than urban disturbances. Hitherto, inter-religious amity had prevailed in India's villages. If now community hatred invaded the countryside it might doom the nation to destruction. Gandhi decided to go to the scene of the trouble. Unless he could stem the violence, life would have no attraction for him. Friends tried to dissuade him. His health was poor. The Congress members of the Government wanted him near by. 'All I know is that I won't be at peace with myself unless I go there,' he replied. He wondered whether he would accomplish anything. But he had to try. He told people not to come to the station to see him off and get his blessing. He was in no mood for it.

They came in hordes. The Government gave him a special train (the British had done likewise) because when he went by the regular express the crowds that wanted to catch a glimpse of him delayed the train for hours and disrupted all traffic schedules. At the big cities where the special stopped, vast multitudes beleaguered the stations and swarmed over the tracks. They mounted the roof of the station, broke glass windows and wooden shutters, and created an ear-splitting din. Several times the conductor gave the signal for departure but someone pulled the emergency cord and the train stopped with a jerk. At one station the railway authorities turned the fire hose on the people but the water flooded Gandhi's compartment. He arrived in Calcutta five hours late, tired from the noise and commotion, and sad.

The day he left New Delhi, thirty-two persons were killed in another inter-religious riot in Calcutta; military reinforcements rushed to the scene. Police and troops were kept busy night and day dispersing bands of hooligans who attacked one another with kerosene bombs, bricks and soda-water bottles. The day after his arrival in Calcutta, Gandhi paid a brief courtesy call on Sir Frederick Burrows, the British governor, and a longer visit to Mr H. S. Suhrawardy, the Moslem prime minister of Bengal province. The next day, 31 October, he again saw Suhrawardy and together they drove through deserted streets piled two-feet high with uncollected garbage and saw many rows of stores and houses gutted in the most recent as well as in the August disturbances. He was overcome, Gandhi said, by 'a sinking feeling at the mass madness that can turn man into less than a brute'. Yet he remained an optimist. This could not go on much longer; he thought the citizens of Calcutta were already beginning to sicken at their own hideous excesses.

He was going to Noakhali, the rural area where Moslems

had killed Hindus, forcibly converted Hindus to Islam, ravished Hindu women and burned Hindu homes and temples. 'It was the cry of outraged womanhood,' he told his prayer meeting, 'that has peremptorily called me to Noakhali . . . I am not going to leave Bengal until the last embers of the trouble are stamped out. I may stay on here for a whole year or more. If necessary, I will die here. But I will not acquiesce in failure. If the only effect of my presence in the flesh is to make people look up to me in hope and expectation which I can do nothing to vindicate, it would be far better that my eyes were closed in death.'

Many members of the congregation wiped tears from their eyes.

But worse woes were in store for the sorrowing Mahatma. In the neighbouring province of Bihar, with a population of 31,000,000 Hindus and 5,000,000 Moslems, the events in Noakhali and Tippera had incensed the majority community; 25 October was declared 'Noakhali Day'. Speeches by Congressmen and sensational newspaper headlines whipped the Hindus into hysteria and thousands paraded the streets and country lanes shouting 'Blood for blood'. In the next week, 'the number of persons officially verified as killed by rioters' wrote the Delhi correspondent of the London *Times*, was 4,580; Gandhi later put the total at more than ten thousand. They were preponderantly Moslem.

The news of the Bihar atrocities reached Gandhi in Calcutta and filled him with grief. He addressed a manifesto to the Biharis: 'Bihar of my dreams seems to have falsified them . . . The misdeeds of the Bihari Hindus may justify Qaid-e-Azam Jinnah's taunt that the Congress is a Hindu organization in spite of its boast that it has in its ranks a few Sikhs, Moslems, Christians, Parsis and others . . . Let not Bihar, which has done so much to raise the prestige of Congress, be the first to dig its grave.'

As penance, Gandhi announced, he would keep himself 'on

the lowest diet possible', and this would become 'a fast unto death if the erring Biharis have not turned over a new leaf'.

Expecting vengeance in Bengal for the horrors of Bihar, Nehru and Patel, and Liaquat Ali Khan and Abdur Rab Nishtar, two Moslem members of the interim government, hurried by air from Delhi to Calcutta. Lord Wavell also came. The sacred Islamic festival of the Id impended when Moslems might rise to fervour and frenzy. The ministers appealed to the populace to remain calm. Soldiers patrolled the city and countryside.

Nehru and Patel begged Gandhi not to fast unto death; they, and the nation, needed him.

From Calcutta, the four ministers flew to Bihar. Infuriated by what he saw and heard, Prime Minister Nehru threatened to bomb Bihar from the air if the Hindus did not desist from killings. 'But that was the British way,' Gandhi commented. 'By suppressing the riots with the aid of the military they would be suppressing India's freedom,' he said. 'And yet what was Panditji to do if Congress had lost control over the people?'

Nehru announced he would remain in Bihar until the province became calm. On 5 November, Gandhi sent a letter to him there saying, 'The news from Bihar has shaken me . . . If even half of what one hears is true, it shows that Bihar has forgotten humanity . . . My inner voice tells me, "You may not live to be a witness to this senseless slaughter . . . Does it not mean that your day is over?" The logic of the argument is driving me irresistibly towards a fast.'

The Id holiday passed quietly in Calcutta and elsewhere. Reassuring messages reached the Mahatma from Bihar. His duty lay in Noakhali where frightened Hindus were fleeing before Moslem violence. Fear is the enemy of freedom and democracy. Non-violent bravery is the antidote to violence. He would teach the Noakhali Hindus to be brave by being brave with them. Equally important, Gandhi wanted to know whether he could influence Moslems. If they were not accessible to the spirit of non-violence and non-retaliation and brotherhood, how could there be a free, united India?

'Supposing someone killed me,' Gandhi said. 'You will gain nothing by killing someone in retaliation. And if you think over it, who can kill Gandhi except Gandhi himself? No one can destroy the soul.'

Did he think a Moslem in Noakhali might murder him and was he afraid that in revenge Hindus would massacre Moslems throughout India?

The impulse to go to Noakhali was irresistible. He abandoned the idea of a fast for Bihar.

Gandhi left Calcutta on the morning of 6 November. Noakhali is one of the least accessible areas of India. It lies in the water-logged delta of the Ganges and Brahmaputra Rivers. Transport and daily living present gigantic difficulties. Many villages can be reached only by small boats. Even the bullock cart, symbol of retarded India, cannot traverse the roads of the district. Phillips Talbot, correspondent of the Institute of Current Affairs of New York, spent four days travelling by rail, steamer, bicycle, hand-poled ferry and on foot from Calcutta to a settlement where the Mahatma had pitched his camp. The region, forty miles square, is thick with human beings, 2,500,000 of them; 80 per cent are Moslem. It was rent by civil strife and steeped in religious bitterness. Some villages had been laid in ruins.

Gandhi deliberately accepted the physical and spiritual challenge presented by this remote region. Month after month he persevered. 'My present mission', he wrote from Noakhali on 5 December, 'is the most difficult and complicated one of my life ... I am prepared for any eventuality. "Do or Die" has to be put to the test here. "Do" here means Hindus and Mussulmans should learn to live together in peace and amity. Otherwise, I should die in the attempt.'

Several ministers of the Bengal government and a group of Gandhi's secretaries and assistants had accompanied him to Noakhali. He dispersed his disciples among the villages and remained alone with Professor Nirmal Bose who was his Bengali interpreter, Parasuram, his permanent stenographer, and Manu Gandhi. He said he would prepare his own food and do his own massage. Friends protested that he needed police protection against Moslems; Sushila Nayyar, his doctor, should remain near him, they said. No, she and her brother Pyarelal and Sucheta Kripalani and even young Abha, the wife of Kanu Gandhi and Kanu himself, each of them must settle alone in a village, often a hostile, isolated village and by their example and love wean it from the ways of violence. Pyarelal was laid low with malaria. He sent a note to Gandhi asking whether Sushila could not come to nurse him. 'Those who go to the villages have to go there with a determination to live or die there,' Gandhi replied. 'If they must fall ill they have to get well there or die there. Then alone could the going have any meaning. In practice this means that they must be content with home remedies or the therapy of nature's "five elements". Dr Sushila has her own village to look to. Her services are not at present meant for the members of our party. They are pre-mortgaged to the village folk of East Bengal.' He was subjecting himself to the same cruel, unyielding discipline.

Gandhi lived in forty-nine villages during his Noakhali pilgrimage. He would rise at four in the morning, walk three or four miles on bare feet to a village, stay there one or two or three days talking and praying incessantly with the inhabitants and then trek to the next village. Arrived in a place, he would go to a peasant's hut, preferably a Moslem's hut, and ask to be taken in with his companions. If rebuffed he would try the next hut. He subsisted on local fruits and vegetables and goat's milk if he could get it. This was his life from 7 November, 1946, to 2 March, 1947. He had just passed his seventy-seventh birthday.

The walking was difficult. Gandhi developed chilblains. But he rarely put on sandals. The Noakhali troubles arose because he had failed to cure the people by non-violence. This was therefore a pilgrimage of penance and in penance the pilgrim wears no shoes. Sometimes hostile elements strewed broken glass, brambles and filth in his path. He did not blame them; they had been misled by their politicians. In many places, walking involved the crossing of bridges built over low, marshy land. The bridges stood on bamboo stilts often ten or fifteen feet high and consisted of four or five bamboo poles about four inches in diameter lashed together with jute ropes or vines. These crude, shaking structures occasionally had one side-rail for support, often not. Once Gandhi's foot slipped and he might have fallen to the muddy earth far below, but he nimbly regained his balance. To become proficient and fearless in such crossings he practised, wherever he could, on bridges a few inches above the ground.

Mr Arthur Henderson told the House of Commons on 4 November, 1946, that the dead in the Noakhali and contiguous Tippera districts had not yet been counted but 'will', according to estimates, 'be low in the three figures category'. The Bengal government put the number of casualties at 218; some families, however, hid their victims out of fear. Over ten thousand houses were looted in the two districts. In Tippera 9,895 persons were forcibly converted to Islam; in Noakhali inexact data suggested that the number of converts was greater. Thousands of Hindu women were abducted and married to Moslems against their will. Gandhi was deeply depressed by the conversions and abductions.

To convert Hindu women Moslems broke their bangles and removed the 'happiness mark' on their foreheads which showed they were not widows. Hindu men were compelled to grow beards, to twist their loincloths the Moslem instead of the Hindu way, and to recite the *Koran*. Stone idols were smashed and Hindu temples desecrated. Worst of all, Hindus were made to slaughter their cows if they had any or, in any case, to eat meat. It was felt that the Hindu community would not accept back into its fold one who had killed a sacred beast or partaken of its flesh.

In the beginning, several of Gandhi's associates suggested that he should urge Hindus to abandon the affected areas and settle in other provinces. He passionately rejected such defeatism. To exchange populations would be a recognition of the impossibility of keeping India united. Moreover, it would deny a basic tenet of Gandhi's faith: that an affinity exists or can easily be established between people who are different or think themselves different. Love and tolerance between the unlike are greater virtues than between the like.

After he had studied the problem in Noakhali, Gandhi decided it was necessary to choose one Moslem and one Hindu in each village who would guarantee the safety of all the inhabitants and die, if need be, in their protection. With this in view, he interviewed members of both religious communities. He was once sitting on the floor of a hut in the midst of a group of Moslems and discoursing on the beauties of non-violence. Sucheta Kripalani passed a note to the Mahatma saying that the man on his right had killed a number of Hindus in the recent riots. Gandhi smiled faintly and went on speaking. Unless you hang the murderer – and Gandhi did not believe in hanging – you must try to cure him with goodness. If you imprison him there will be others. Gandhi knew he was dealing with a social disease; the liquidation of one or many individuals could not extirpate it. The criminals who feared retribution would remain on the highway and repeat their crimes. Gandhi therefore forgave them and told them so, and told the Hindus to forgive them; indeed he told them that he shared their guilt because he had failed to remove Hindu–Moslem antagonisms.

The world is full of such antagonisms and the ordinary

individual is their victim as well as their agent. 'But I say unto you, Love your enemies, bless them that curse you, do good to them that hate you and pray for them which despitefully use you and persecute you . . . For if ye love them which love you, what reward have ye?' Thus Jesus spoke. Thus Gandhi lived.

Generations back, the ancestors of many Noakhali Moslems to whom Gandhi was appealing had been Hindus and were forcibly converted to the *Koran* by the sword. Either they retained part of the Hindu temper or the Gandhian method has a universal application. To one village, for instance, Gandhi had sent a young Moslem disciple, Miss Amtul Salam. She found that Moslems continued to mistreat their Hindu neighbours. 'In the Gandhian tradition', reports Phillips Talbot, 'she decided not to eat until Moslems returned a sacrificial sword which during the October upheaval had been looted from a Hindu home. Now, a fast concentrates very heavy social pressure on its objects, as Indians have long since learned. The sword was never found. Possibly it had been dropped into a pond. Whatever had happened, the nervous Moslem residents were almost ready to agree to anything when Gandhi arrived in that village on the twenty-fifth day of Miss Salam's fast. Her doctor reported that life was ebbing. After hours of discussion (which . . . Gandhi took as seriously as the Cabinet Delegation negotiations) Gandhi persuaded the village leaders to sign a pledge that they would never molest Hindus again.'

The return of the sword would have symbolized amity, Gandhi explained.

Gandhi and his associates were working against heavy odds. In the beginning of his tour, Moslems flocked to his prayer meetings. But politicians in Calcutta discouraged this practice. And Mohammedan priests inveighed against it. They made the charge that the Mahatma was suborning the faithful. Sometimes Gandhi would interrupt his services to let the Moslems withdraw temporarily to the fringe of the congregation and turn west to Mecca and say their prayers. He had an attraction for Moslems which neither political Moslems nor religious Moslems relished.

Gandhi addressed his meetings in Hindustani. Then an interpreter gave the Bengali translation. Gandhi would sit on the prayer platform during the translation and make notes of his own speech which he would then publish: 'Some Moslems feared that he had come to suppress them. He could assure them that he had never suppressed anyone in his life.'

'I have told our people,' Gandhi said in an interview, 'not to depend on military and police aid. You have to uphold democracy, and democracy and dependence on the military and police are incompatible.' He wanted to restore a sense of popular security by changing the minds of the people. 'For me,' he told a friend, 'if this thing is pulled through it will be the crowning act of my life . . . I don't want to return from Bengal in a defeatist way. I would rather die, if need be, at the hand of an assassin.'

At times, his closest co-workers were afraid of what might happen to them alone in remote villages. 'You are not to rush into danger unnecessarily,' he instructed them, 'but unflinchingly face whatever comes in the natural course.'

6 January was Gandhi's day of silence and his prayer meeting address was read to the congregation while he sat and listened and nodded assent. They were in the little village of Chandipur and he told them why he was there: 'I have only one object in view and it is a clear one: namely that God should purify the hearts of Hindus and Moslems and the two communities should be free from suspicion and fear of one another. Please join with me in this prayer and say that God is the Lord of us both and that He may give us success.'

Why did he have to come such a long way to do this? 'My answer is that during my tour I wish to assure the villagers to the best of my capacity that I bear not the least ill-will towards any. I can prove this only by living and moving among those who mistrust me.'

In this village Gandhi received information that Hindus who had fled during the riots were beginning to return. On the other hand, attendance at prayer meetings was dwindling. 'But', Gandhi wrote, reporting his own speech, 'he said that even then there would be no reason for him to give up his mission in despair. He would then roam from village to village taking his spinning wheel. With him it was an act of service to God.'

On 17 January the newspapers stated that during the last six days Gandhi had been working twenty hours out of every twenty-four. He had spent each of those days in a different village and the people were flocking to his hut for advice, comfort and confessions.

At Narayanpur village, a Moslem gave him shelter for the night and food during the day. Gandhi thanked him publicly. Such hospitality was becoming more frequent.

His Moslem host asked Gandhi why he did not come to an understanding with Jinnah instead of subjecting himself to such a strenuous pilgrimage. A leader, he replied, was made by his followers. The people must make peace among themselves and 'then their desire for neighbourly peace would be reflected by their leaders . . . If a neighbour was ailing would they run to the Congress or the League to ask them what should be done?'

Would not literacy help, Gandhi was asked. He held that it was not enough. The Germans were literate yet they succumbed to Hitler. 'It is not literacy or learning that makes a man,' Gandhi said, 'but education for real life. What would it matter if they knew everything but did not know how to live in brotherliness with their neighbours?'

'If the question is between taking one's own life or that of the assailant, which would you advise?'

'I have no doubt in my mind', Gandhi declared, 'that the first should be the choice.'

Five thousand persons came to his prayer meeting on 22 January in the village of Paniala where, several weeks earlier, a large intercommunity dinner had taken place with Hindus, Moslems and untouchables sitting shoulder to shoulder. 'What in your opinion is the cause of the communal riots?' someone asked.

'The idiocy of both communities,' he replied.

The prayer meeting at Muraim on 24 January was the largest of the pilgrimage. Gandhi attibuted it to the successful fast of Miss Amtul Salam, who was a devout Moslem and a member of the Mahatma's ashram.

'What should a woman do if she is attacked?' Gandhi was asked at Palla on 27 January. 'Should she commit suicide?'

'Surrender' he answered, 'has no room in my plan of life. A woman should most certainly take her own life rather than surrender.'

Was she to carry poison with her or a knife?

'It is not for me to prescribe the means,' Gandhi said. 'And behind the approval of suicide in such circumstances is the belief that one whose mind is prepared for even suicide will have the requisite courage for such mental resistance and such internal purity that her assailant will be disarmed.'

Sometimes economic questions were raised at prayer meetings. Did Gandhi think the landowner's share in crops should be reduced from one-half to one-third?

Yes, he welcomed the move. 'The land belongs to the Lord of us all and therefore to the worker on it. But until that ideal state of things came about the movement towards the reduction of the landlord's portion was in the right direction.' Many of the landlords were Hindus, and the riots were partly caused by resentment against high rents.

Dr Sushila Nayyar was stationed in the village of Changirgaon. She wanted to go to the hospital in the

Sevagram Ashram which she had set up, but the Moslem patients begged her to stay and she stayed. She also reported that Moslems were, of their own accord, returning some of the loot they took in October. 'A happy omen,' Gandhi called it. If the infection spread, the courts would have less work to do. He aspired to no truce imposed by the military; he wanted a change of heart.

Four young Moslem men came to Gandhi's hut for an exchange of views. Their visit gave him joy; he sought intimate contact with the people. He told them, incidentally, that the figures on Moslem killings of Hindus in Noakhali had been exaggerated; there were not thousands. The Hindus had behaved much worse in Bihar.

At Srinagar village on 5 February the volunteers had erected a platform and canopy. This was a waste of labour and money, Gandhi chided them. 'All I need,' he told the prayer meeting 'is a raised seat with something clean and soft to rest my fatless and muscleless bones.' Then he laughed and showed his toothless gums.

He lectured next day's congregation on cleanliness. He liked to walk barefoot on the village streets and on the road, but why did they spit and clear their noses on them? He sometimes had to wear sandals. No doubt, chronic poverty was responsible for the prevalence of disease in India, but chronic breach of the laws of sanitation was no less responsible, he said.

The poorer Moslems attended Gandhi's meetings in larger numbers than the rich. Tales reached him that the propertied and educated Moslems were threatening the poor with economic sanctions. They displayed anti-Gandhi posters. Returning from Bishkatali in the Tippera district on 20 February, Gandhi walked through beautiful bamboo woods and coconut groves. Hanging from trees he saw placards reading, 'Remember Bihar, Leave Tippera Immediately'; 'Repeatedly you have been warned, Yet you insist on roaming from house to house. You must leave for you own good'; 'Go where you are needed. Your hypocrisy will not be tolerated. Accept Pakistan.'

Yet crowds at meetings grew in size.

In Raipura, on a Sunday, Gandhi was present at a dinner given by Hindu merchants to two thousand persons, including caste Hindus, Moslems, Harijans and Christians. The local Moslem priest took Gandhi to the village mosque.

Elsewhere a student asked Gandhi whether it was not true that Christianity and Islam were progressive religions and Hinduism static or retrogressive. 'No,' he replied, 'I have noticed no definite progress in any religion. The world would not be the shambles it has become if the religions of the world were progressive.'

'If there is only one God,' a questioner said, 'should there not be only one religion?'

'A tree has a million leaves,' Gandhi replied. 'There are as many religions as there are men and women, but they are all rooted in God.'

A written query was handed to the Mahatma: 'Should religious instruction form part of the school curriculum as approved by the State? Do you favour separate schools for children belonging to different denominations for facility of religious instruction?'

Gandhi replied, 'I do not believe in state religion even though the whole community has one religion. State interference will probably always be unwelcome. Religion is purely a personal matter . . . I am also opposed to State aid partly or wholly to religious bodies. For I know that an institution or group which does not manage to finance its own religious teaching is a stranger to true religion. This does not mean that State schools would not give ethical teaching. The fundamental ethics are common to all religions.'

Moslem critics warned him not to discuss purdah. How dare a Hindu tell their women to expose their faces? He nevertheless discussed it. Segregation of women was a species of violence and led to other forms of compulsion.

On 2 March, 1947, Gandhi left Noakhali for Bihar province. He promised to return some day. He promised to return because his mission had not been completed. He had not established the brotherhood of Hindus and Moslems in Noakhali. Relations had improved perceptibly but insufficiently.

Gandhi's task in Noakhali consisted in restoring inner calm so that the refugee Hindus could return and feel safe and so that Moslems would not attack them again. The malady was deep; the violent eruptions, however, were infrequent and ephemeral. Gandhi, therefore, did not despair. He felt that the local communities, undisturbed by outside political propaganda, could live in peace.

The call of Noakhali had been insistent. Gandhi might have sent a message from Delhi or preached a sermon. But he was a man of action, a Karma yogi. He believed that the difference between what we do and what we could do would suffice to solve most of the world's problems. All his life he endeavoured to eliminate that difference. He gave his maximum.

CHAPTER 5

Asia's Message to the West

Late in November 1946 Prime Minister Attlee summoned Nehru, Defence Minister Baldev Singh, Jinnah and Liaquat Khan to 10 Downing Street for an extraordinary conference. The Constituent Assembly was to meet in New Delhi on 9 December; Jinnah had repeatedly declared that the Moslem League would boycott it. The object of the Downing Street conference was to bring the Moslem League into the Constituent Assembly. For if the Assembly was a predominantly Congress affair, with the Moslems outside, how, the argument ran, could England transfer power to it and leave India?

Originally, the Moslem League had accepted the Cabinet Mission's plan of 16 May, 1946, and thereby agreed to go into the Constituent Assembly. Later, however, it had withdrawn.

The issue on which Jinnah withdrew from the Assembly provoked hot discussions and fierce hatreds. What was it?

Article 19 of the Cabinet Mission's plan stipulated that the Constituent Assembly would first meet in New Delhi for a short, formal session and then break up into three sections corresponding to three groups of provinces: Group A comprised the centre, the heart of India and was overwhelmingly Hindu; Group B included the North-west Frontier Province, Sind and the Punjab and was largely Moslem in population; Group C, in the north-east, consisted of Bengal and Assam.

Each section would draft a constitution for its group of provinces. But if a province did not like the constitution it could stay out of the group.

Thus Hindu Assam would be required to sit in Section C

with Moslem Bengal and participate in the drafting of a constitution for Group C. But should Assam dislike the final constitution it could secede from Group C and stand alone, or, possibly, join Group A. The sections were compulsory, the groups voluntary.

Gandhi objected. He said it was compulsion and a waste of effort. Suppose Bengal which would have a big majority in Section C, drew up a constitution that tied Assam to Group C. And why should the North-west Frontier Province, which though predominantly Moslem had always been anti-Jinnah, be forced to sit with the Punjab and Sind?

The sections and groups were introduced into the Cabinet Mission's plan in order to satisfy Jinnah; they were half-way or perhaps quarter-way to Pakistan. They divided India into three federated units. For that very reason Gandhi rejected them.

While Gandhi was in Noakhali, the Congress organizations of neighbouring Assam sent emissaries to him to ask for guidance. He told them bluntly to refuse to go into the sections even if the national Congress leaders told them to go in.

It was to resolve this difficulty that Nehru, Baldev Singh, Jinnah and Liaquat Ali Khan made their hasty aeroplane trip to London early in December.

During his stay in London, Jinnah declared publicly that he expected India to be divided into a Hindu state and a Moslem state. He shared Mr Churchill's apprehensions, he added, 'regarding the possibility of civil strife and riots in India'. Both halves of the declarations were programme rather than prophecy.

There had already been enough riots to lead the British to expect more unless Jinnah got the half-Pakistan or quarter-Pakistan implicit in the sections and groups. But although Attlee succeeded, after great exertion, in bringing the Congress and League ministers into his Downing Street office, the conference ended in disagreement.

Attlee thereupon announced on 6 December that if the Constituent Assembly adopted a constitution without the co-operation of the Moslem League 'His Majesty's Government could not, of course, contemplate . . . forcing such a constitution upon any unwilling parts of the country.'

This meant that one part of India would accept the constitution and another part might reject it. Again India faced partition.

Soon after Nehru's return from London he made the long journey from New Delhi to the village of Srirampur in Noakhali and, on 27 December, 1946, reported to the Mahatma on the historic failure to agree in Downing Street.

But Gandhi repeated his advice to Assam and to the Sikhs, to remain aloof from the constitutional sections and groups. He regarded them as devices to split India and refused to countenance anything that contributed to division.

The All India Congress Committee, however, resolved on 6 January, 1947, by a vote of 99 against 52, to accept the sections.

Gandhi's influence in Congress was waning.

Gandhi had gone to Noakhali to reinforce the human bond between Hindus and Moslems before politics and legal enactments tore it asunder. He dreaded the consequences of the bisection of India. In New York, on 16 October 1949, Prime Minister Nehru stated that he would have fought to the end against the establishment of Pakistan if he had foreseen the dire results that flowed from it.

Perhaps Gandhi intuitively anticipated these results. The division of India caused the violent death of hundreds of thousands of Indians. It caused fifteen million refugees to wander unhappily from their homes into distant uncertainty. It provoked the war in Kashmir. It brought gigantic economic losses to all parts of the country. It fed a continuing religious–nationalistic bitterness with disastrous potentialities.

Even though the Congress leaders were not as perceptive as Gandhi they knew that no good could come of partition. Why then did they acquiesce in Attlee's 6 December statement?

In 1942, Congress President Maulana Azad said to me in Nehru's presence that Congress abhorred the idea of the division of India but could not reject it indefinitely if the Moslems wanted it. He was opposed, however, he said, to 'divorce before marriage'. First they must try to live together in a united independent India and if it did not work then there would be time enough to separate.

Now Nehru, Patel, Azad and the other Congress members had had a taste of marriage; they had been sitting in the Government with Moslem Leaguers who obviously entered the Cabinet to disrupt it. The experience was a harrowing one. It frayed the nerves of the Congress leaders. It destroyed their faith in Congress–League collaboration.

Gandhi still believed in Hindu–Moslem friendship. Nehru and Patel were reconciled to the constitutional sections knowing that this might be the beginning of Pakistan but seeing no way out except civil war. They hoped Jinnah would be happy with the division into three federated states and forgo Pakistan.

The next step was a statement by Prime Minister Attlee in the House of Commons on 20 February, 1947, that England would leave India 'by a date not later than June 1948'. Simultaneously, it became known that Lord (Admiral Louis) Mountbatten, a great-grandson of Queen Victoria, would succeed Lord Wavell as Viceroy; he would be the twentieth and last British Viceroy of India.

To whom would Britain transfer power? On this key question Attlee, according to Lord Pethick-Lawrence, 'was less precise'. His Majesty's Government, Attlee asserted, would have to determine whether power should be handed over 'to some form of central government' or in some areas 'to the existing provincial governments' or 'in some other way as may seem most reasonable and in the best interests of the Indian people'.

Nehru found this rather vague but he welcomed the whole statement as 'wise and courageous'; it removed 'all misconception and suspicion'.

The Working Committee, in its session during the first week of March, officially approved of Attlee's new utterance and, in view of the impending 'swift transfer of power', invited the Moslem League to talks. Simultaneously, the Committee took cognizance of the widespread bloodshed in the populous Punjab. Indeed, it took such a sombre and serious view of events there that it envisaged 'a division of the Punjab into two provinces, so that the predominantly Moslem part may be separated from the predominantly non-Moslem part'.

The Punjab situation was ominous. According to a reply given on 21 May, 1946, in the House of Commons by the Earl of Listowel, the Secretary of State for India and Burma, 4,014 persons had been killed in disturbances in India between 18 November, 1946, and 18 May, 1947, and of these, 3,024 were killed in fighting between Moslems and Sikhs and Hindus in the Punjab.

Disturbed by events further west, Gandhi left east Bengal for Bihar. Without a day's respite, he began a tour of the province. In village and city, he chastised the Bihari Hindus. They 'had forgotten in a fit of insanity that they were human beings'.

One day he listened for hours to reports by Moslems and Hindus about continued tension. Nobody could assure him 'that things had completely settled down to complete normality'. The recital so tired him mentally that he had to take a brief nap before services.

Another day he apologized for coming to prayers in a car; the Biharis 'should know the art of welcoming people in a quiet and dignified manner instead of the present embarrassing manner'. Thousands had tried to come near enough to touch him or kiss his feet.

Wherever he went he preached repentance and restitution. All kidnapped Moslem women should be returned. Compensation should be paid for property looted or destroyed.

A telegram arrived from a Hindu warning the Mahatma not to condemn Hindus for what they had done. Gandhi mentioned the telegram at this prayer meeting and said, 'I would forfeit my claim to being a Hindu if I bolstered the wrongdoing of fellow Hindus or of any other fellow being'. He cautioned them against avenging the killings of Hindus in the Punjab.

He knew that even worshipful Hindus were irritated by his message of love. Nevertheless, he began collecting money at all his meetings for the relief of aggrieved Moslems. In Patna, two thousand rupees were gathered at one assembly and a number of women contributed their personal jewellery.

Before he spoke in any locality, Gandhi visited the ruined homes of Moslems or Moslem families who had suffered death or physical injury. The deeper he penetrated into the Bihar tragedy the more it obsessed him; he would not leave the province until 'both the communities had become friendly with one another and no longer needed his services'. He insisted that Hindus should call back the Moslems who had fled and rebuild their huts and re-establish them in business. He summoned Hindus guilty of atrocities to surrender.

The day Gandhi arrived in the town of Masurhi 'fifty persons' he reported, 'who were wanted in connection with the riot cases' surrendered to the police. He welcomed that, and hoped others would follow suit. If the criminals lacked the courage to surrender to the authorities they should come to him or to Ghaffar Khan, 'the Frontier Gandhi', or to General Shah Nawaz of the Indian National Army, who were accompanying him on the tour, and confess.

As his car moved across the countryside, groups of Hindus signalled him to stop and gave him purses for Moslems. This was the way to stop violence, not with the aid of the military and the police.

Hindus were boycotting Moslem stores and firms. He begged them to abandon such intolerance. He asked them to recant publicly in order to reassure the Moslems. 'But he was sorry to say that not one Hindu got up to give the needed assurance . . . There was little cause for wonder, therefore, if the Moslems were afraid to return to their villages.' He warned them that 'Indians might lose the golden apple of independence'. There was renewed agitation among Biharis to avenge the Moslem attacks on Hindus and Sikhs in the Punjab. 'If ever you become mad again,' he cried out, 'you must destroy me first.' It was his fourth week in Bihar.

On 22 March, 1947, Lord Mountbatten, handsome in white naval uniform, arrived in New Delhi with his wife, Edwina, the Vicereine; their charm and informality and his first political declaration made a fine impression. Twenty-four hours later, Jinnah stated publicly that partition was the only solution; otherwise there would be 'terrific disasters'.

Within four days of his arrival, Mountbatten invited Gandhi and Jinnah to the palace. Gandhi was deep in Bihar. Mounbatten offered to bring him out by aeroplane. Gandhi said he preferred a means of locomotion used by the millions. At the station, before the train left Patna, the Mahatma collected money for Harijan relief.

Gandhi conferred with Mountbatten for two and a quarter hours on 31 March.

The next day Gandhi visited the Asian Relations Conference which had been sitting in New Delhi since 23 March; delegates attended from most countries of Asia and from five constituent republics of the Soviet Union. Asked to speak, he said he would deliver an address at the closing session the next day, but if there were any questions now he would try to answer them.

Did he believe in One World and could it succeed under present conditions?

'I will not like to live in this world if it is not to be one,' Gandhi replied. 'Certainly I should like to see this dream realized in my lifetime. I hope that all the representatives who have come here from the Asian countries will strive their level best to have only one world.' If they worked with 'fixed determination' the dream could come true.

Answering a Chinese delegate's question about a permanent Asia Institute, he drifted far from the subject and discussed what was uppermost in his mind. 'I am sorry,' he said, 'that I have to refer to the conditions we see today [in India]. We do not know how to keep peace between ourselves . . . We think we must resort to the law of the jungle. It is an experience which I would not like you to carry to your respective countries.'

He turned to the problem of Asia. 'All the Asian representatives have come together,' he began. 'Is it in order to wage a war against Europe, against America, or against other non-Asiatics? I say most emphatically, "No," this is not India's mission . . . It will be a sorry thing if we go away from this conference without a fixed determination that Asia shall live and live as free as every Western nation. I just wanted to say that conferences like the present should meet regularly and if you ask me where, India is the place.'

The next day he delivered his promised address before the conference. He first apologized for speaking English. He admitted that he had hoped to collect his thoughts but had no time. On the way to the meeting he had asked Ghaffar Khan for a piece of paper and pencil to make some notes. 'I got a pen instead of a pencil. I tried to scribble a few words. You will be sorry to hear that that piece of paper is not by my side though I remember what I wanted to say.'

Then he rambled: They were assembled in a city, but cities were not India. The real truth was in the villages and in the untouchable homes of the villages. The villages, to be sure, were dungheaps full of 'miserable specimens of humanity with lustreless eyes'. But in them was wisdom.

The East, he proceeded, had submitted to a cultural conquest by the West. Yet the West had originally received its wisdom from the East: Zoroaster, Buddha, Moses, Jesus, Mohammed, Krishna, Rama and lesser lights.

He asked the conference to understand the message of Asia. 'It is not to be learned through Western spectacles or through the atomic bomb. If you want to give a message to the West it must be the message of love and the message of truth. I do not want merely to appeal to your head,' he said suddenly. 'I want to capture your heart.'

He hoped Asia's message of love and truth would conquer the West. 'This conquest will be loved by the West itself. The West is today pining for wisdom.'

It was structurally a poor speech but full of essential wisdom and of the essence of Gandhi. Most of the delegates had probably not heard such simple, sincere words for many years.

Between 31 March and 12 April Gandhi conferred with Mountbatten six times. Jinnah had an equal number of talks with the hard-working Viceroy.

What did they talk about? 'Before I would get down to any actual solution of the problem,' Mountbatten said in an address before the Council of the Royal Empire Society in London on 6 October, 1948, when his task in India was done, 'I just wanted to talk to them to get to know them, to get together and gossip. Thus Gandhi told me about his early life in South Africa, Mr Jinnah about his early life in London and I told them a bit about my early life. Then, when I felt I had some sort of understanding with the men I was dealing with, I started talking to them about the problem before us.'

The problem was the fate of 400,000,000 people, the fate of India, perhaps the fate of Asia. Mountbatten's assignment was to take Britain out of India by June 1948. The schedule required him to propose a solution by the end of 1947. This would allow the British Parliament enough time to pass the necessary legislation for the liberation of India by June 1948. But on the spot, he told the Royal Empire Society, he and his advisers agreed that this would be too slow. Trouble had started, he said, on 16 August, 1946, Jinnah's Direct Action Day. There followed the massacres of Hindus in Noakhali and Hindu reprisals in Bihar; then 'the Moslems massacred the Sikhs at Rawalpindi [in the Punjab]' and a rising took place in the North-west Frontier Province. 'I arrived out there,' Mountbatten stated, 'to find this terrible pendulum of massacres swinging wider and wider; if it was not stopped there was no telling where India might end . . .

'Personally,' Mounbatten continued, 'I was convinced that the right solution for them would have been to keep a United India' under the 16 May, 1946, plan of the British Cabinet Mission. But the plan presupposed the co-operation and goodwill of all parties. 'Mr Jinnah,' however, Lord Mountbatten told the Royal Empire Society, 'made it abundantly clear from the first moment that so long as he lived he would never accept a United India. He demanded partition, he insisted on Pakistan.' Congress, on the other hand, favoured an undivided India. But, Mountbatten stated, the Congress leaders agreed that they would accept partition in order to avoid a civil war. The Viceroy 'was convinced that the Moslem League would have fought'.

But how was India to be divided? Congress refused to let large non-Moslem areas go to Pakistan. 'That automatically meant,' Mountbatten explained, 'a partition of the great provinces of the Punjab and Bengal.'

'When I told Mr Jinnah,' Mountbatten said in his historic review before the Royal Empire Society, 'that I had their provisional agreement to partition he was overjoyed. When I said that it logically followed that this would involve partition of the Punjab and Bengal he was horrified. He produced the strongest arguments why these provinces should not be partitioned. He said they had national characteristics and that partition would be disastrous. I agreed, but I said how much more must I now feel that the same considerations applied to the partitioning of the whole of India. He did not like that and started explaining why India had to be partitioned and so we went round and round the mulberry bush until finally he realized that either he could have a United India with an unpartitioned Punjab and Bengal or a divided India with a partitioned Punjab and Bengal and he finally accepted the latter solution.'

Gandhi did not approve of any kind of partition in April 1947 and refused until his death to approve of it.

On 15 April, at the request of Mountbatten, Gandhi and Jinnah issued a joint statement deploring the 'recent acts of lawlessness and violence that have brought the utmost disgrace on the fair name of India' and denouncing 'for all time the use of force to achieve political ends'. This came at the end of a fortnight in which Jinnah had convinced Mountbatten that if he did not achieve his political ends India would be rent by civil war.

During that fortnight, Gandhi lived in the untouchables' quarter on Kingsway, Delhi, and conducted a public prayer meeting there every evening. The first evening he asked those present whether they would object to the recitation of some verses from the *Koran*. Several objectors raised their hands. They said he had no authority to intone an Islamic holy book at Hindu services. Gandhi thereupon broke off the meeting. He put the same question the second evening. Again there were objectors; again he refused to pray with the congregation. The same thing happened the third evening.

The fourth evening nobody objected. The objectors had withdrawn. If all members of the congregation on the previous three days had objected, Gandhi explained, he would have read from the *Koran* and been prepared 'to die at their hands with the name of God on his lips if they wanted to kill him. But he wished to avoid a clash on the prayer ground between those who wanted the prayers to be held and those who objected. In the end non-violence prevailed.'

He received angry letters, threatening letters, some of them anonymous. He was a bad Hindu, one said. He was a Moslem 'fifth columnist' in Hinduism, another said. A third was addressed to 'Mohamed Gandhi'.

'How can it be a sin to chant God's name in Arabic?' he argued. Hindu–Moslem unity was his life's goal. 'If Hindustan meant a land only for the Hindus and Pakistan only for Moslems, Pakistan and Hindustan would then be lands flowing with poison.'

On 13 April Gandhi returned to Bihar.

Action for non-violence and against hate was now the only political work that made sense. Unless Gandhi could prove that Hindus and Moslems lived in peace, Jinnah was right and Pakistan inevitable. Mountbatten would not succumb to the most brilliant debating points; Hindu–Moslem tolerance had to be demonstrated in life.

A victory for non-violence in Bihar or Bengal or the Punjab would spell success in the battle for the mind of Mountbatten and Britain and of those in Congress who had lost faith in a united India. This was a case where the people would really decide a major issue – not by their votes but by their behaviour, and Gandhi still hoped to alter their behaviour. The question was: Is India a nation or a country inhabited by warring religious communities?

One of the world's worst curses is the influence of past centuries. In India, the seventeenth, eighteenth and nineteenth centuries have survived to plague the twentieth. Religious passions, provincial loyalties and princely states exercised the same debilitating, divisive influence they had in Europe before the modern age of industrialism and nationalism. India, with four hundred million inhabitants, had only three million industrial workers. The country lacked cohesion because nobody possessed enough unifying power or a sufficiently attractive unifying idea to overcome the centrifugal trends of a backward land. Gandhi, the towering symbol of unifying nationalism, was himself a mingling of an obsolete past, a struggling present and the unborn world of his high ideals.

Jinnah's strength was the threat of civil war. The riots were a preview. The only hope of preserving the unity of India was to pacify the people and thus prove Jinnah's threat an empty one.

Gandhi approached this task without flinching and alone. History was asking whether India was a nation.

CHAPTER 6

Tragic Victory

It was very hot in Bihar in April, and Gandhi could not stand the strain of extensive travel among the villages. But he would have to go if the Hindus did not repent and bring back the Moslems who had fled in fear. He received a letter suggesting that he should retire to the forest as Krishna had done; the country had lost faith in non-violence, the correspondent stated, and the *Bhagavad Gita*, moreover, did not teach non-violence. He reported this to his prayer meeting in Patna.

He heard of renewed rioting in Noakhali.

Yet several developments encouraged him. At Gandhi's request General Shah Nawaz, a Moslem and hero of the Indian National Army, had remained in Bihar. Shah Nawaz now said the Moslems were returning to their villages and that Hindus and Sikhs were helping them. A Sikh had been invited to a mosque.

This information made Gandhi feel that 'if the Hindus were true Hindus and befriended the Moslems the present all-enveloping fire would be extinguished'. Bihar was a big province. Its example would inspire others. Peace in Bihar would 'dissolve' the trouble in Calcutta and elsewhere. His mother, 'an illiterate village woman', Gandhi said, had taught him that the atom reflected the universe; if he took care of his immediate surroundings the universe would take care of itself.

Nehru telegraphed Gandhi to come back to Delhi. The Congress Working Committee was convening on 1 May for a great historic decision. Gandhi made the five-hundred-mile trip by hot train.

Mountbatten had been extremely active, visiting provinces, talking to leaders, steeping himself in the problems of India's future. As his thoughts crystallized he saw no escape from Pakistan.

Mountbatten accordingly put the question to the Congress party: Would they accept the partition of India? Nehru had already told a United Provinces Political Conference on 21 April that 'The Moslem League can have Pakistan if they wish to have it, but on condition that they do not take away other parts of India which do not wish to join Pakistan.'

Would the Working Committee take the same stand?

Gandhi was opposed to it. Patel wavered; he would have put Jinnah's threats to the test of force. He would have used the central government to suppress Moslem violence. But in the end he too acquiesced. 'I agreed to partition as a last resort when we reached a stage when we would have lost all,' he revealed two and a half years later. Rather than risk a civil war or the loss of independence, Congress was reconciled to Pakistan.

Gandhi made no secret of his chagrin. 'The Congress', he told his prayer meeting in the untouchables' colony in Delhi on 7 May, 'has accepted Pakistan and demanded the division of the Punjab and Bengal. I am opposed to any division of India now as I always have been. But what can I do? The only thing I can do is to dissociate myself from such a scheme. Nobody can force me to accept it except God.'

Gandhi went to see Mountbatten. His advice to the British was to leave with their troops and 'take the risk of leaving India to chaos or anarchy'. If the British left India, Gandhi explained, there might be chaos for a while; 'We would still go through the fire no doubt but that fire would purify us.'

Mountbatten's mind was too precise and military to build the future on a chance. Yet not only do most individuals do exactly that; in a war, nations often gamble with their lives. Every battle is a 'calculated risk' in which the calculation is quite theoretical. To Gandhi, the division of India was an absolute evil, as evil as Britain's submission to Hitler would have been in 1940, and rather than resign himself to it he would have accepted all the possible material losses.

This, however, was only the abstract aspect of Gandhi's suggestion. In concrete form, its simplicity concealed its astuteness. The British could not abandon India without a government. Gandhi's advice to England to leave India to chaos meant give India to Congress. If England refused, Gandhi wanted Congress to leave the Government. The burden of maintaining peace in the country would then have rested solely on the British, who sought no such responsibility.

The choice that Gandhi put to the British therefore was: Let Congress rule India or rule it yourself in these troubled times.

Gandhi saw that no Pakistan was possible unless the British created it, and the British would not create Pakistan until Congress accepted it; they could not split India and antagonize the majority in order to placate Jinnah and the minority. Therefore Congress should not accept it.

Nobody listened to Gandhi. 'Our leaders were tired and short-sighted,' writes an intimate collaborator of Gandhi. The Congress leaders were afraid to delay independence. Gandhi would have delayed it in the hope of ultimately winning freedom for a united country instead of independence for two hostile Indias.

In the summer of 1948, I asked Nehru, Patel and others in India why Gandhi had not attempted to prevent Congress from accepting Pakistan; if nothing less had availed he might have coerced them by fasting.

It was not Gandhi's way, their composite reply ran, to compel agreement even on the most crucial issue. That is true, but the complete answer goes deeper. Congress acquiesced in Pakistan and stayed in the Government. The only alternative would have been to reject Pakistan, leave the Government and stake everything on a restoration of the people's sanity and peaceful inclinations. But Gandhi saw that the leaders had no faith in his alternative. He might have induced them to vote for his view in committee; he could not have infused them with faith in it except by proving that Hindus and Moslems could live together amicably. The burden of proof was on Gandhi. And time was running out fast.

Gandhi hurried across the continent to Calcutta. To get Pakistan, Bengal would have to be partitioned between Pakistan and Hindustan. If he could impress the Bengal Moslems with the painful results of such vivisection and if he could check the rising Hindu sentiment for the division of Bengal, he might prevent Pakistan.

'When everything goes wrong at the top,' Gandhi asked in Calcutta, 'can the goodness of the people at the bottom assert itself against the mischievous influence?' This was his hope.

Bengal has one culture, one language, he argued. Let it stay united. They had reunited Bengal after Lord Curzon partitioned it; could they not rebuff Jinnah before he partitioned it?

After six days in Calcutta, Gandhi went to Bihar. Despite the torrid heat, he travelled to the villages. His refrain was the same: 'If the Hindus showed the spirit of brotherliness, it would be good for Bihar, for India and for the world.'

On 25 May, in response to a summons from Nehru, Gandhi again returned to New Delhi. Mountbatten, his mind made up, had flown to London. Rumour had it that India would be partitioned, that the plan would be announced soon. But why, Gandhi wondered. The Cabinet Mission had rejected partition and Pakistan on 16 May, 1946. What had happened since then to alter the situation? The riots? Were they yielding to hooliganism? 'I must cling to the hope,' Gandhi said, 'that Britain will not depart a hair's breadth from the spirit and letter of the Cabinet Mission's statement of 16 May of last year . . .'

'He is burning the candle at both ends,' Dr Sushila Nayyar

reported. He was still striving to reverse the tide towards partition. If the effort killed him what did it matter? 'In the India that is shaping today there is no place for me,' he said; his voice shook with emotion. 'I have given up the hope of living 125 years. I may last a year or two. That is a different matter. But I have no wish to live if India is to be submerged in a deluge of violence as it is threatening to do.'

Yet he could not be a pessimist for long. Nehru brought Dr Lo Chia-luen, the Chinese Ambassador, to Gandhi's untouchable hut. 'How do you think things will shape themselves?' Dr Lo asked.

'I am an irrepressible optimist,' Gandhi said. 'We have not lived and toiled all these years that we should become barbarians as we appear to be becoming, looking at all the senseless bloodshed in Bengal, Bihar and the Punjab. But I feel that it is just an indication that, as we are throwing off the foreign yoke, all the dirt and froth is coming to the surface. When the Ganges is in flood, the water is turbid; the dirt comes to the surface. When the flood subsides, you see the clear, blue water which soothes the eye. That is what I hope for and live for. I do not wish to see Indian humanity becoming barbarian.'

Mountbatten, meantime, had been working in London on a plan to divide India.

The Mountbatten plan provided for the division not only of India but of Bengal, the Punjab and Assam if their people wished. In the case of Bengal and the Punjab, the recently elected provincial legislatures would decide. If Bengal voted to partition itself, then the Moslem-majority district of Sylhet in Assam would determine by popular referendum whether to join the Moslem part of Bengal.

'Nor is there anything in this plan', the text read, 'to preclude negotiations between communities for a united India.'

The scheme was thus permissive and involved no legal

compulsion by Britain. Bengal and the Punjab might vote to remain united, in which case there would be no partition and no Pakistan. But even if Pakistan came into being, it and the other India could subsequently unite.

Before leaving England, Mountbatten saw Churchill who promised to support the plan in the House of Commons.

On 2 June, 1947, Herbert L. Matthews, telegraphing to the *New York Times* on the eve of the announcement of the plan, said, 'Mr Gandhi is a very real worry, since if he decides to go on a "fast unto death" it would well wreck the whole plan.'

The next day, Prime Minister Attlee announced the plan in the House of Commons and Mountbatten revealed it on the New Delhi radio. In his broadcast, the last Viceroy said frankly, 'I am, of course, just as much opposed to the partition of provinces as I am to the partition of India herself.' The plan, he knew, was imperfect, especially because of its effect on the five million fighting Sikhs of the Punjab. Any conceivable line through that province would leave some Sikhs in Pakistan against their wishes.

Nehru, Patel and the Working Committee had approved the plan; their approval became official when the All-India Congress Committee, sitting in New Delhi, on 15 June voted 153 for the plan, 29 against, with some abstentions.

After the resolution had been adopted, Professor J. B. Kripalani, the president of Congress, delivered a brief speech which explained why Congress had abandoned Gandhi.

The Hindu and Moslem 'communities', Kripalani said, 'have vied with each other in the worst orgies of violence . . . I have seen a well where women with their children, 107 in all, threw themselves to save their honour. In another place, a place of worship, fifty young women were killed by their menfolk for the same reason . . . These ghastly experiences have no doubt affected my approach to the question. Some members have accused us that we have taken this decision out of fear. I must admit the truth of this charge, but not in the

sense in which it is made. The fear is not for the lives lost or of
the widows' wail or the orphans' cry or of the many houses
burned. The fear is that if we go on like this, retaliating and
heaping indignities on each other, we shall progressively
reduce ourselves to a state of cannibalism and worse. In every
fresh communal fight the most brutal and degraded acts of the
previous fight become the norm.' This is the cruel truth of all
violence.

'I have been with Gandhiji for the last thirty years,'
Kripalani continued. 'I joined him in Champaran. I have
never swayed in my loyalty to him. It is not a personal but a
political loyalty. Even when I have differed with him I have
considered his political instinct to be more correct than my
elaborately reasoned attitudes. Today also I feel that he with
his supreme fearlessness is correct and my stand defective.

'Why then am I not with him? It is because I feel that he has
as yet found no way of tackling the problem on a mass basis.'
The nation was not responding to Gandhi's plea for peace
and brotherhood.

Gandhi knew this. 'If only non-Moslem India were with
me,' he declared, 'I could show the way to undo the proposed
partition . . . Many have invited me to head the opposition.
But there is nothing in common between them and me except
the opposition . . . Can love and hate combine?'

Ninety-five per cent of Gandhi's mail was abusive and
hateful. The Hindu letters asked why he was partial to
Moslems and the Moslem letters demanded that he stop
obstructing the creation of Pakistan.

A Marathi couple from the Tilak country came up to
Delhi, camped near the untouchables' quarter and
announced to Gandhi that they had begun a fast which would
last until Pakistan was abandoned. He addressed them at two
successive prayer meetings. Are you fasting against Pakistan,
he asked, because you hate Moslems or love Moslems? If you
hate Moslems you may not fast. If you love Moslems, you

should go and teach other Hindus to love them. The young couple abandoned the fast.

The Hindus did not love Moslems enough and the Moslems did not love Hindus enough. India would therefore be divided between them.

Gandhi considered partition 'a spiritual tragedy'. He noted preparations for bloody strife. He saw the possibility of a 'military dictatorship' and then 'goodbye to freedom'. 'I do not agree with what my closest friends have done or are doing,' he said.

Thirty-two years of work, Gandhi stated, have come to 'an inglorious end'. On 15 August, 1947, India would become independent. But the victory was a cold, political arrangement: Indians would sit where Englishmen had sat; a tricolour would wave in place of the Union Jack. That was the hollow husk of freedom. It was victory with tragedy, victory that found the army defeating its own general.

'I cannot participate in the celebrations of 15 August,' Gandhi announced.

Independence brought sadness to the architect of independence. The Father of his Country was disappointed with his country. 'I deceived myself into the belief that people were wedded to non-violence . . .' he said. Indians had betrayed non-violence which was more important to him than Indian independence.

Mountbatten told the Royal Empire Society on 6 October, 1948, that in India Gandhi 'was not compared with some great statesman like Roosevelt or Churchill. They classified him simply in their minds with Mohammed and with Christ'. Millions adored the Mahatma, multitudes tried to kiss his feet or the dust of his footsteps. They paid him homage and rejected his teachings. They held his person holy and desecrated his personality. They glorified the shell and trampled the essence. They believed in him but not in his principles.

Independence Day, 15 August, found Gandhi in Calcutta fighting riots. He fasted all day and prayed. He issued no message to the nation. Invited to the capital to participate in the formal inauguration of the nation's life, he refused to attend. 'There is disturbance within,' he wrote to Rajkumari Amrit Kaur the next day. In the midst of festivities, he was sad. 'Is there something wrong with me,' he asked, 'or are things really going wrong?'

Freedom had come to India and Gandhi was perplexed and perturbed; his *Gita* detachment was impaired. 'I am far away from the condition of equipoise,' he declared.

But faith never left him, nor did he contemplate retiring to a cave or a wood. 'No cause that is intrinsically just can ever be described as forlorn,' he asserted.

'You must not lose faith in humanity,' he wrote Amrit Kaur on 29 August. 'Humanity is an ocean. If a few drops of the ocean are dirty, the ocean does not become dirty.'

He had kept his faith in man. He had kept his faith in God. He had therefore kept his faith in himself. 'I am a born fighter who does not know failure,' he assured a prayer-meeting audience.

Partition was a fact, but 'it is always possible by correct conduct to lessen an evil and eventually even to bring good out of evil', Gandhi said.

He still hoped his faith would move people, but how? 'I am groping today,' he declared. He was full of 'searching questions' about himself. 'Have I led the country astray?'

A lesser man might have sulked or grown bitter or plotted the discomfiture of those who thwarted him. Gandhi turned the searchlight inward; perhaps it was his fault.

'I can echo your prayer that I may realize peace and find myself,' he wrote in a letter to Kurshed Naoroji. 'It is a difficult task but I am after it.'

'O Lord,' he exclaimed, 'Lead us from darkness into light.'

He was approaching his seventy-eighth birthday. The

world he had built lay partly in ruins all around him. He must begin building anew. Congress was too much a political party; it must become an instrument for the constructive uplift of the people. He wrote two articles in *Harijan* on the virtues of non-violent, non-revolutionary, God-loving, equalitarian Socialism. He was seeking new directions. He was old in body and young in spirit, old in experience and young in faith. Future plans lifted past troubles from his back.

He had gone to Calcutta and been taken into a Moslem house in an area were the stones were slippery with fresh blood and the air acrid with the smoke of burning homes. The Moslem family to whom the house belonged were friendly to him. 'For the moment I am no enemy,' he wrote Amrit Kaur. He rejoiced more in the smallest triumph of brotherhood than in the political independence of a country.

The bereaved came to him in the lowly house and he wiped their tears. He found solace in the balm he gave others. He had discovered his new task. It was his old task: to assuage pain, to spread love, to make all men brothers.

St Francis of Assisi, hoeing his garden, was asked what he would do if he were suddenly to learn that he was to die at sunset that day.

He said: 'I would finish hoeing my garden.'

Gandhi continued to hoe the garden in which he had worked all his days. Sinners had thrown stones and filth into the garden. He continued to hoe.

Pertinacity was Gandhi's antidote to frustration and tragedy. Action gave him inner peace.

CHAPTER 7

Gandhi Hoes His Garden

The British had left India. Politically literate, they had read the handwriting on the Indian wall: 'Your day is done.' The handwriting was Gandhi's.

By the will of Indians, Lord Mountbatten remained as Governor-General of the Indian Union. It had been agreed that Mountbatten would also be Governor-General of Pakistan and thus a symbol of unity. But Jinnah substituted himself.

Pakistan bisected India. Pakistan itself was bisected. It counted 38,000,000 inhabitants in north-west India and 45,000,000 in north-east India. Between the two parts lay nearly 800 miles of the Indian Union.

In Moslem Pakistan there were many million Hindus and Sikhs. Of the 330,000,000 residents of the Indian Union, some 42,000,000 were Moslems.

Five hundred and fifty of the 565 native states quietly acceded to the Indian Union. Three joined Pakistan. Most of the maharajas and nawabs became overpaid pensioned puppets. Elephants went begging.

The frontier that divided India in two divided families in two; it separated factories from raw materials, crops from markets. The army was divided; the treasury was to be divided. The non-Moslems of Pakistan were worried about their future. The Moslems of the Indian Union were anxious. In each of the new Dominions, fighting broke out between ruling majority and frightened minority.

One India could have lived in peace. Vivisection sundered vital arteries; out of them flowed human blood and the poison of religious hate.

Calcutta and the western part of Bengal province remained in the Indian Union. Eastern Bengal went to Pakistan. Twenty-three per cent of the population of Calcutta was Moslem. The Hindus and Moslems fought.

How does a religious riot commence? On 17 April, 1938, three Hindus and a Moslem were sitting on their haunches in the Northbrook Gardens in Bombay and playing cards. They had been drinking. They quarrelled over the game. 'Rumours of a Hindu–Moslem disturbance', reads an official report, 'spread in the city resulting in panic which was taken advantage of by hooligans and stray assaults, stabbing and stone-throwing commenced . . . Orders were issued prohibiting the carrying of lethal weapons and prescribing the routes for Hindu and Moslem funeral processions. Troops were also asked to stand by . . . A clash that threatened to assume serious proportions was soon brought under control. Sporadic assaults, however, continued for a few days and altogether there were fourteen deaths and injuries to ninety-eight persons.' The police arrested 2,488 persons.

That was in the quiet, normal, pre-Pakistan days of 1938. With tension at its peak in 1947, especially in a city like Calcutta where the inhabitants are squeezed together herring-barrel fashion in filthy slums, a little Moslem girl pulling a Hindu girl's hair or a Hindu boy calling a Moslem boy names might precipitate a mortal riot. Passion and poverty converted men into tinder.

On this inflammable material, Gandhi undertook to sprinkle the sweet waters of peace.

Gandhi had arrived in Calcutta on 9 August, 1947. For an entire year, ever since Jinnah's Direct Action Day on 16 August, 1946, Calcutta had been torn by bloody strife. Gandhi and H. S. Suhrawardy, the former prime minister of Bengal, walked arm in arm through streets tense with religious frenzy. Suhrawardy drove a car with Gandhi as his passenger through riotous areas. Violence seemed to melt away wherever they passed. Thousands of Moslems and Hindus embraced one another shouting 'Long Live Mahatma Gandhi', 'Long Live Hindu-Moslem unity'. Huge crowds fraternized at Gandhi's daily prayer meetings. After 14 August no disturbances were reported in Calcutta. Gandhi had calmed the storm. The press paid tributes to the magician in loincloth.

On the night of 31 August Gandhi had gone to bed in the Moslem house. At about 10 o'clock he heard angry noises. He lay still. Suhrawardy and several female disciples of the Mahatma could be heard attempting to pacify some intruders. Then glass crashed; window panes had been broken with stones and fists. A number of young men entered the house and commenced kicking in doors. Gandhi got out of bed and opened the door of his room. He was face to face with enraged rioters. He touched his palms together in greeting. A brick was thrown at him. It hit a Moslem friend standing by his side. One of the rioters swung a lathi stick which narrowly missed Gandhi's head. The Mahatma shook his head sorrowfully. The police arrived; the police chief appealed to Gandhi to retire to his room. Then the officers hustled the intruders out of the house. Outside, tear gas was used to disperse an unruly mob of Moslems infuriated by the presence of a bandaged Moslem who, they alleged, had been stabbed by Hindus.

Gandhi decided to fast.

In a statement to the press on 1 September, he said, 'To put in an appearance before a yelling crowd does not always work. It certainly did not that night. What my word in person cannot do, my fast may. It may touch the hearts of all the warring factions in the Punjab if it does in Calcutta. I therefore begin fasting from 8.15 tonight to end only if and when sanity returns to Calcutta.'

It was a fast unto death. Unless sanity returned, the Mahatma would die.

On 2 September, groups and delegations commenced streaming to Gandhi's residence. They would do anything to save his life, they said. That was the wrong approach, he explained. His fasts were 'intended to stir the conscience and remove mental sluggishness'. Saving his life must be incidental to a change of heart.

Leaders of all communities and many organizations called on the Mahatma. He received them all and talked with them. He would not desist from the fast until communal harmony had been restored. Prominent Moslems and an official of the Pakistan Seamen's Union visited Gandhi and assured him they would work to keep the peace. More Moslems came. The fast impressed them; it was for their safety and for the rehabilitation of their destroyed homes.

On 4 September, municipal officials reported to Gandhi that the city had been absolutely quiet for twenty-four hours. They also told him that as a proof of their wish for communal peace 500 policemen of North Calcutta, including the British police officers, had commenced a twenty-four-hour sympathy fast while remaining on duty. The leaders of hooligan bands, burly ruffians, came and sat at Gandhi's bedside and wept and promised to refrain from their usual depredations. Hindu, Moslem and Christian representatives, workers, merchants and shopkeepers gave a pledge in Gandhi's presence that there would be no more trouble in Calcutta. He believed them, he said, but this time he wanted a written promise. And before they signed the promise they must know this: if the promise was broken he would commence 'an irrevocable fast' which nothing on earth could stop until he died.

The city leaders withdrew to deliberate. It was a serious moment and they were conscious of the responsibility. They nevertheless drafted and signed the pledge. At 9.15 P.M. on 4 September, Gandhi drank a glass of sweet lime juice which Suhrawardy handed him. He had fasted seventy-three hours.

From that day, through the many months when the Punjab

and other provinces shook with religious massacres, Calcutta and both parts of Bengal remained riot-free. Bengal remained true to its plighted word.

On 7 September, Gandhi left Calcutta for New Delhi en route to the Punjab. Another part of the garden needed hoeing.

At the station Gandhi was met by Sardar Vallabhbhai Patel, Rajkumari Amrit Kaur and others. Gloom covered their faces. Riots were raging through Delhi. Sikh and Hindu refugees from the fires of the Punjab were flooding the city. They had occupied the untouchables' colony where the Mahatma used to stay. He would have to live in the 'palatial Birla House', as Gandhi called it.

Gandhi's room in Birla House was on the ground floor, about a foot above the earth. It was approximately 25 feet by 16 feet in area and some 10 feet high. A bathroom adjoined it. When Gandhi arrived he had all the furniture removed. Visitors sat on the floor and he slept on the terrace outside the room. An electric heater and electric lamp were available for use. The room was where the prayer meetings were held on the right side of the house and furthest from the area of the Birla grounds. To go to prayers Gandhi would step down to the earth through a high window and then walk under a long row of red sandstone pergolas covered with luxurious vines.

On arriving at the house Gandhi learned that no fresh fruit or vegetables were available; vital services had been disrupted by the riots in Delhi which, he said, resembled a 'city of the dead'.

With passion and without restraint, Gandhi now gave himself to the task of bringing Delhi to its senses – it and the Punjab. Nothing else mattered. In former years, he had permitted doctors to measure his blood pressure. Now he said, 'Leave me alone. I must work and do not want to know about my blood pressure.' His circulatory system, the physicians said, had not deteriorated in ten years, not did he have more wrinkles on his face or body. A cataract discovered in 1939 by an eye specialist had not progressed. His ears had become very sensitive to loud noises. He slept five to six hours every night and half an hour to an hour during the day; he always slept soundly and rarely talked in his sleep. On one occasion, he made arm motions during his sleep and when he woke, Dr Nayyar asked him what had happened and he said he had dreamt he was scaling a wall. He was always fresh and keen in the morning.

Despite acute distress over the political situation, Gandhi continued to take excellent care of his body. He enjoyed lying for ten to twenty minutes in a very hot bath at a temperature of 100 or 101 Fahrenheit. Sometimes it made him giddy. If a shower-bath was available he finished with a cold one.

In these months of hard travel and tremendous mental pressure, he ate less. His formula was: Under-eat when overworked. There was much work to be done.

The very first day in Birla House Gandhi visited Dr Zakir Hussain at Okla, a village fourteen miles outside New Delhi.

Zakir Hussain, a stately scholar with a noble head and character, presided over the Jamia Millia Islamia, a Moslem religious academy at Okla. Gandhi had collected money for the school. He had also appointed Dr Zakir Hussain chairman of the national society for basic education; he did it at a conference where everybody except Hussain had accepted Gandhi's ideas on training for children.

The Okla academy, a collection of small, new, clean-looking buildings, lies in a region redolent with Moslem tradition and rich in ruins of ancient Mogul forts and mosques. But in August 1947 it found itself engulfed in a sea of angry Hindus and Sikhs to whom everything Moslem, whether man or building, was hateful. At night the teachers and students of the academy stood guard, expecting an assault. All lights were out. In a circle around them they could see Moslem villages in flames and Moslem homes burning like torches. Nearby is the Jumna River. Night after night they could hear Moslems jumping into the river to escape their pursuers. But the pursuers would jump in after them and then there was a scuffle and splash and the victim would be held down till he drowned or gave one last anguished scream as the knife cut his throat. Nearer and nearer the ring of attackers came. One dark night a taxicab arrived at the Jamia Millia grounds; out of it stepped Jawaharlal Nehru. He had driven alone through the belt of madmen that circled Delhi in order to stay with Dr Hussain and his students and protect them if harm came.

The moment Gandhi heard of the danger that threatened the Moslem academy he went out in a car and spent an hour with Zakir Hussain and talked with the teachers and the boys. His presence hallowed the academy; after that it was safe.

The same day Gandhi visited several refugee camps; he was urged to go with an armed guard; the Hindus and Sikhs might attack him as pro-Moslem and the Moslems might attack him as a Hindu and anybody crazed by deaths or abductions in the family might attack him without reasons. He went without escort.

Throwing caution and health considerations to the wind, Gandhi now developed inordinate energy, criss-crossing the city many times each day to tour riotous area, visit refugee camps in and outside the city and speak several times a day to thousands of embittered, uprooted specimens of humanity. 'I think of the poor refugee in Delhi in both East Punjab [Indian Union] and West Punjab [Pakistan] today while it is raining,' he told his prayer meeting on 20 September. 'I have heard that a convoy of Hindus and Sikhs fifty-seven miles long is pouring into the Indian Union from West Punjab,' he said. 'It makes my brain reel to think how this can be. Such a happening is unparalleled in the history of the world and it makes me, as it should make you, hang my head in shame.'

Gandhi was not exaggerating; the fifty-seven-mile long convoy was one of several in the Great Migration in which at least 15,000,000 people trekked hundred of miles not to new homes and opportunities but to homelessness, sometimes to death and disease. Out of the part of the Punjab assigned to Pakistan, moving in the general direction of New Delhi, came millions of Hindus and Sikhs fleeing the knives and clubs of Moslems. Out of the Indian Union, moving towards Pakistan, came millions of Moslems fearing the daggers and lathis of Hindus and Sikhs. Police protection had become a thing of the past. Police and even military were animated by the same passions as the aggressors and often helped them to loot and kill.

A few tired policemen and groups of young volunteers were all that distinguished the 'convoys' from disorganized flights of panicked people. They fled in their bullock carts or, if they had never owned a cart or it was taken from them, they fled on foot, whole families, adults carrying children, carrying the sick in baskets, carrying the aged on their shoulders. Frequently the sick were abandoned and left to die on the dusty road. Cholera, smallpox and other diseases scourged the migrant hordes. For days and weeks the convoys crawled forward leaving corpses behind to mark their route. Vultures hovered over the line of march waiting for weary wanderers to drop to the ground. Few families had salvaged enough food to support health. If they did it was stolen or fought for; the losers starved, the victors existed a little longer. Sometimes hostile convoys, advancing in opposite directions, camped during the night in the vicinity of one another and continued their senseless vendetta.

The Nehru government set up camps outside Delhi to catch the migrants before they entered the city and care for them. But endless thousands escaped the cordons. They took what they could seize in the town. They slept in doorways and courtyards, on pavements, in gutters, on streets. They lay on the asphalt, exhausted. Unheeding drivers might run over them. The Delhi home of a Moslem gone to Pakistan was considered legitimate booty; the refugees occupied it. Moslem stores were looted. Where Moslems resisted, riots occurred. Reduced to primitive living, the displaced persons yielded to primitive passions.

In this city of the dead and the mad, Mahatma Gandhi tried to spread the gospel of love and peace. Moslems must remain even if they were molested, he said; 'the Hindus and Sikhs who molested them discredited their religion and did irreparable harm to India'. He urged holders of unlicensed arms to surrender them to him; 'driblets have been coming to me voluntarily'.

'I must be pardoned for putting first blame on the Hindus and Sikhs,' he told a prayer audience consisting chiefly of Hindus and Sikhs. 'I will not rest till every Moslem in the Indian Union who wishes to be a loyal citizen of the Union is back in his home living in peace and security and until the Hindus and Sikhs have returned to their homes.' But the Hindus and Sikhs were afraid to return to Pakistan, nor did they wish to relinquish the homes of Moslems, who had fled to Pakistan and whom Gandhi was inviting to return.

Gandhi had planted himself, alone, athwart a raging torrent.

He went to a meeting of about five hundred members of the Rashtriya Sevak Sangha or RSS, a highly disciplined organization of young militant Hindus. They were fiercely anti-Moslem, and many of them were fiercely opposed to him because he tried to protect Moslems. But he told them that they would kill Hinduism by their intolerance. If Pakistan was maltreating Hindus that was no justification for their maltreating Moslems. 'There is no gain in returning evil for evil.' He was indeed a friend of the Moslems, but also a friend of the Sikhs and Hindus. 'Both sides appear to have gone crazy. The result can be nothing but destruction and misery' for both sides. The RSS, Gandhi said, was 'a well-organized, well-disciplined body. Its strength could be used in the interests of India or against it'. Allegations had been made against the RSS, Gandhi declared; it had been accused of fomenting riots and planning assassinations. 'It is for you to show by your uniform behaviour that the allegations are baseless.'

After his speech, Gandhi invited questions. One question and answer was recorded.

'Does Hinduism permit killing an evil-doer?'

'One evil-doer cannot punish another,' Gandhi replied. 'To punish is the function of the Government, not of the public.'

2 October, 1947, was the Mahatma's seventy-eighth birthday. Lady Mountbatten and foreign diplomats came to congratulate him; sheaves of telegrams were delivered from abroad and all parts of India. Many Moslems sent greetings. The rich sent money. Refugees sent flowers. 'Where do congratulations come in?' Gandhi asked. 'Would it not be more appropriate to send condolences? There is nothing but anguish in my heart. Time was whatever I said the masses followed. Today, mine is a lone voice . . . I have lost all desire to live long, let alone 125 years . . . I cannot live while hatred and killing mar the atmosphere . . . I therefore plead with you to give up the present madness.'

He did not feel depressed; he felt helpless. 'I invoke the aid of the all-embracing Power to take me away from this "vale of tears" rather than make me a helpless witness of the butchery by man become savage . . . If He wants me He will keep me on earth yet awhile.'

He visited refugee camps that were filthy. Refugees who were not untouchables refused to clean. He chastised that weakness in Hindus. Cold weather was approaching. He appealed for blankets, quilts and cotton sheets for the homeless.

The Punjab is the granary of India. The turmoil in it had stamped the harvest into the dust and the Indian Union was feeling greater hunger than usual. Gandhi nevertheless opposed rationing because it entailed centralization, red tape, speculation and corruption.

Each evening he announced how many blankets he had

received. Blankets were better than quilts because quilts got wet with dew. But quilts, he said, could be covered with old newspapers at night.

Gandhi hoped to leave for the Punjab. But Delhi was not at peace. A Moslem shopkeeper, thinking that things had settled down, opened the shutters of his shop. The same instant a bullet killed him.

One evening Gandhi went to the Delhi Central Jail and conducted a prayer service for three thousand prisoners. 'I am a seasoned ex-prisoner myself,' he told them with a laugh.

'What should jails be like in free India?' he asked. 'All criminals should be treated as patients and the jails should be hospitals admitting this kind of patients for treatment and cure.' He closed by expressing the wish that Hindu, Moslem and Sikh prisoners live together in fraternity.

The news from Calcutta was good. Why, he asked his prayer meeting at Birla House, could Delhi not follow the peaceful example of Calcutta?

Each evening Gandhi asked his prayer congregation whether anybody objected to the reading of some verses from the *Koran*. Usually there were two or three objectors. Then he asked whether the other worshippers would harbour any ill feeling for the objectors. They said they would not. Would the objectors remain quiet during the *Koran* readings? They would. He read the verses. This was a lesson in tolerance and discipline. He did not expect all to agree. He expected all to remain non-violent despite disagreements.

With the refugees came harrowing tales of savagery. A man swung an infant by its foot and bashed its head against a wall. Two men stood a child by the feet and tore its body in two down the middle. A Moslem mob laid siege to a village; after long resistance, the Hindu and Sikh men came out and surrendered; the women had huddled inside the stockade which enclosed the village well. The Moslems were coming to fetch them; a woman jumped into the well; another woman jumped after her; in the next four minutes, seventy-three women had drowned themselves on top of one another in the well.

These memories bred new atrocities. Assume that some Moslems had killed Hindus because they were Hindus and that most Moslems condoned those killings. To hate, suspect and wish to hurt all Moslems because they were Moslems made the Hindus as immoral as the Moslems. (The argument could also be applied to Hindu killings of Moslems.) Moreover, if Hindus sought to justify their actions by proving that the Moslems had commenced the atrocities it merely meant that the Hindus had allowed themselves to become as evil as the Moslems whom they abominated because of that evil; they had been conquered by the spirit of their tormentors.

Fearing retaliation, Moslems in the Indian Union decided to escape to Pakistan. Fearing reprisals, the Hindus and Sikhs in Pakistan were trekking to the Indian Union. A vast region was churning with hate, murder and migrating millions. In the midst of the upheaval stood the little man in the loincloth. A reprisal for a reprisal, a death for a death, he was saying, means death for India.

Lady Mountbatten visited a refugee camp; she brought Gandhi a message; the refugees wanted to see him. Similar messages arrived from other camps, Hindu camps and Moslem camps. He went as often as he could. Two hundred thousand displaced persons were packed into Kurukshetra Camp in east Punjab and more were pouring in each day from west Punjab. Gandhi had a session of the Congress Working Committee to attend so he addressed the camp by radio on 12 November, 1947: 'I can serve you best by drawing attention to your shortcomings. That has been my life's motto, for therein lies true friendship and my service is not only to you or to India; it extends to the world, for I know no barriers of race or creed. If you can get rid of your failings, you will benefit not only yourself but the whole of India.

'It hurts me to know that so many of you are without

shelter. This is a real hardship particularly in the cold weather . . . You must help in the maintenance of discipline . . . You must take the sanitation of the place in your hands. I ask you . . . everyone of you, men, women and children to keep Kurukshetra clean . . . share your rations, be content with what you get . . . You must live for others and not only for yourselves. Idleness is demoralizing.' He urged them to spin.

Sporadic violence in Delhi continued. In the early disturbances 137 mosques had been damaged; some had been converted into Hindu temples with idols. Gandhi considered 'such desecration a blot on Hinduism and Sikhism'. He went to a Sikh celebration attended by 100,000 bearded Sikhs and their families. He condemned their violence against Moslems. Sikhs, he said, had been drinking and rioting. 'Keep your hearts clean and you will find that all other communities will follow you.'

Gandhi also criticized the Indian government. 'Our statesmen', he wrote in a letter to Madame Edmond Privat, 'have for over two generations declaimed against the heavy expenditures on armaments under the British regime, but now that freedom from political serfdom has come, our military expenditure has increased and still threatens to increase and of this we are proud. There is not a voice raised against it in our legislative chambers.' He called it 'mad imitation of the tinsel of the West'. But he still hoped that India would 'survive this death dance' and 'occupy the moral height that should belong to her after the training, however imperfect, in non-violence for an unbroken period of thirty-two years since 1915'.

'When it is relevant,' Gandhi wrote, 'truth has to be uttered, however unpleasant it may be . . . Misdeeds of the Hindus in the Indian Union have to be proclaimed by the Hindus from the housetop if those of the Moslems in Pakistan are to be arrested or stopped.' As a Hindu he was sternest with Hindus.

CHAPTER 8

The Future of India

Gandhi seldom made an adverse criticism without suggesting a concrete cure. He had criticized the Congress party and the new government of independent India. What did he propose?

Gandhi was quick to see that the freedom of India raised the question of freedom in India. How could India remain a democracy?

There was only one major party, the Congress party, and it enjoyed vast prestige as the party of Gandhi, Nehru and Patel, the party which had fought and won the battle for liberation from Britain. Other parties like the Hindu Mahasabha and the Communists were insignificant.

The question Gandhi pondered was: Could the Congress party guide and curb the Government? He had not studied political conditions in the Soviet Union or Franco Spain or other totalitarian countries, but by intuition he arrived at conclusions which others had reached after long experience and analysis: he realized that a one-party system could actually be a no-party system, for when the Government and party are one, the party is a rubber stamp and leads only a fictitious existence.

If the one important party of India, the Congress, did not maintain an independent, critical attitude towards the Government, who could act as a brake on any autocratic tendencies that might develop in the Government?

Without free criticism and potent opposition, a democracy dies.

Without political criticism and opposition, a nation's intellect, culture and public morality stagnate; big men are purged and small men become kowtowing pygmies. The leaders surround themselves with cowards, sycophants and grovelling yes-men whose automatic approval is misread as a tribute to greatness.

Could the Congress party, with aid from Gandhi and from the free press, prevent such a development in India?

On 15 November, 1947, in the presence of Gandhi, Professor J. P. Kripalani, president of Congress, informed the All-India Congress Committee that he was resigning his position. He had not been consulted by the Government nor been taken into its full confidence. Although 'it is the party from which the government of the day derives its power', Kripalani said, the Government ignored the party. Gandhi, Kripalani revealed, felt that in these circumstances the resignation was justified.

Nehru and Patel were the heads of the Government. They were also leaders of the Congress party. Their popularity and hold on the Congress machine enabled them to dominate the party. They identified themselves with the party. Why then should they accept the Congress president as a curb on their power? Why should they give him a veto on their proposals?

The choice of a successor to Kripalani assumed key importance. The election of a puppet who obeyed the Government would signalize the elimination of effective political opposition.

Gandhi attended the meeting of the Congress Working Committee which was to elect the new president. It was the Mahatma's day of silence. When nominations were opened, he wrote the name of his candidate on a small piece of paper and passed it to Nehru. Nehru read the name aloud: Narendra Dev, the Socialist leader. Nehru supported Narendra Dev's candidature. Others opposed it.

The Socialists were then still inside the Congress party. But their ideological, political and personal differences with right-wing Congressmen presumably encouraged Gandhi in the belief that they might be able to control and check certain trends within the Government.

The morning session of the Working Committee closed at 10 A.M.; no vote was taken.

At noon, Nehru and Patel summoned Rajendra Prasad and, without consulting Gandhi, urged him to be a candidate for the presidency of Congress. Dr Prasad, a member of the Working Committee, was a lawyer who first met Gandhi in Champaran in 1917 during the struggle for the indigo sharecroppers.

Prasad went to Gandhi in Birla House at 1 P.M. and told the Mahatma about the offer. 'I don't like it,' Gandhi said.

'I cannot remember ever having dared to oppose Gandhi,' Dr Prasad stated in recounting these events. 'Even when I differed with him I felt he must be right and followed him.'

On this occasion, too, Prasad agreed with Gandhi and promised to withdraw his candidacy.

Subsequently, however, Prasad was persuaded to change his mind. He became the new Congress president. He was a gentle, modest, compliant, retiring, well-intentioned, high-minded person more inclined to serve than to lead. He was sixty-three.

Gandhi had been defeated by the Congress machine and by the key men in the Government.

Gandhi now tried a different approach.

During the first half of December 1947 he held a series of conferences with his most trusted collaborators outside the Government. They were the Constructive Workers, the men and women who directed the several organizations set up by Gandhi over the years to remove untouchability, spread the use of Hindustani as the national language, extend basic education, improve food cultivation, develop village industries and encourage hand spinning. The Constructive Workers were devoted to non-violence; they believed in

Gandhi not merely because he was the chief instrument of India's political independence but because they considered him the chief agent for India's social reform.

Gandhi wanted all these organizations to combine. But he did not want the Constructive Workers 'to go into power politics; it would spell ruin. Or else why,' Gandhi asked, 'should not I myself have gone into politics and tried to run the Government my way? Those who are holding the reins of power today would easily have stepped aside and made room for me, but whilst they are in charge they carry on only according to their own lights.

'But I do not want to take power into my hands,' Gandhi assured his friends. 'By abjuring power and devoting ourselves to pure, selfless service of the voters we can guide and influence them. It would give us far more real power than we shall have by going into the government. A stage may come when the people themselves may feel and say that they want us and no one else to wield power. The question could then be considered. I shall most probably not be alive then.'

Unable to guide Congress, Gandhi planned to build a new vehicle which would push the Government and, in an emergency, carry the Government's load. It would be in politics without seeking political power except as a last resort. Instead of trying to win votes it would teach the masses 'to use their votes intelligently', Gandhi said.

'Under adult suffrage,' he declared, 'if we are worth our salt, we should have such a hold on the people that whomsoever we choose would be returned.' To assist in this task Gandhi wanted to attract more intellectuals. 'Our intelligentsia', he told the conference of Constructive Workers, 'are not lacking in sympathy. Reason, as a rule, follows in the footsteps of feeling. We have not sufficiently penetrated their hearts to convince their reason.' That is a key to Gandhi: heart and mind were one, but heart ruled.

Why could not the constructive welfare work be done by

the Congress party or by the Government? a delegate asked.

'Because Congressmen aren't sufficiently interested in constructive work,' Gandhi replied simply. 'We must recognize the fact that the social order of our dreams cannot come through the Congress party of today . . .

'There is so much corruption today,' Gandhi asserted, 'that it frightens me. Everybody wants to carry so many votes in his pocket, because votes give power.' (Kripalani described the trouble as 'red-tapism, jobbery, corruption, bribery, black-marketing and profiteering'.) Therefore, Gandhi emphasized, 'banish the idea of the capture of power and you will be able to guide power and keep it on the right path . . . There is no other way of removing the corruption that threatens to strangle our independence at its very birth'.

He who is immune to the temptation of power can best oppose the men in power, Gandhi felt. His limited experience told him that legislators and judges were too close to the machinery of power to check-and-balance the executive; only those outside government, he contended, could check-and-balance those in government.

Yet even his own high authority was no match for the power of a government born of his efforts and whose members touched his feet in obeisance.

CHAPTER 9

The Last Fast

Richard Symonds, a British friend who had met Gandhi in Bengal while doing relief work there, fell ill with typhoid in New Delhi in November 1947. Gandhi invited the patient to Birla House.

Once the doctor advised brandy for the sick man. The house was searched and a bottle of brandy found; on being asked, Gandhi, a strict prohibitionist, said he had no objection to it being given to Symonds. He took the same attitude subsequently when sherry was recommended to Symonds.

On the approach of Christmas, Gandhi asked a group of Indian Christian girls to decorate Symonds's room with holly and gay festoons; on Christmas Eve, at the Mahatma's suggestion, the girls came and sang carols.

Gandhi spent at least a few minutes and often much longer, with the patient each day. His only interference in the cure was to urge the application of mud packs to the abdomen. For the rest, his chief contribution to the restoration of the Englishman's health was to make him laugh whenever he was with him.

Symonds had been to Kashmir and wanted to discuss the situation with Gandhi, but except on the Mahatma's day of silence he never got a chance, for Gandhi entertained Symonds with funny stories and jokes from the moment he came into the room till the moment he left. The Kashmir problem was too grave for a patient.

Kashmir, including the beautiful Vale of Kashmir, is at the top of the world, in northernmost India. Its Hindu maharaja had ruled his 800,000 Hindu subjects and 3, 200,000 Moslem subjects with equal disregard of their welfare and freedom. In September 1947 the Pakistan government abetted incursions into Kashmir by the wild warriors of the tribal area between the north-west frontier and Afghanistan; subsequently Pakistan regular troops invaded Kashmir. Alarmed and helpless, the maharaja asked that his state be admitted into the Indian Union. On 29 October the accession was officially announced, and the maharaja thereupon appointed as his prime minister Sheik Abdulla, a Moslem, whom he had held in prison for protracted periods. Simultaneously, the New Delhi authorities rushed troops to Kashmir by air and road. Without the airlift, Kashmir would have been overrun and annexed by Pakistan. Soon Kashmir and neighbouring Jammu, likewise the realm of the maharaja, became the scene of a small war between India and Pakistan which seriously drained the financial resources, patience and military establishments of both Dominions. Moslems called it 'Holy War'.

In a Christmas Day broadcast, Gandhi approved of India's action in sending troops to Kashmir to repel the tribal invaders. He condemned suggestions to partition the State between India and Pakistan. He regretted the fact that Nehru had submitted the dispute to the United Nations. At the UN, he told Horace Alexander, the British pacifist, considerations of international 'power politics' rather than merit would determine the attitude of countries towards the Kashmir issue. Gandhi therefore urged India and Pakistan to 'come to an amicable settlement with the assistance of impartial Indians'; that, he said, would 'enable the Indian Union's representation to the UN to be withdrawn with dignity'. If direct negotiations failed, Gandhi contemplated mediation by one or two Englishmen; in his talk with Horace Alexander, the Mahatma mentioned Philip Noel-Baker, a member of the

British Labour government, as an acceptable mediator. He also envisaged the possibility of a plebiscite or referendum among the inhabitants of the disputed region.

The Indian government, however, rejected mediation and arbitration; bitter UN debates continued interminably while tempers and military expenditures rose.

Gandhi always combined high politics with low politics. He talked Kashmir with Nehru one day, and the next day he went to a village and told the peasants how to mix 'the excreta of animals and human beings' with rubbish to make 'valuable manure'. They must improve their cattle, he advised further. Hindus complained that Moslems killed cows, Gandhi said, but Hindus killed cows 'by inches through ill treatment'. The villagers' address to him had lauded the virtues of non-violence. 'But I know how such an address is prepared,' he stated in his reply. 'Someone writes it out and someone else reads it parrotwise and that is the end of it.' Did they practise non-violence? 'There must be consistency between one's thoughts, words and actions.'

By this touchstone, Gandhi was great; greater in fact after India became independent than before. On the eve of his departure from India after several months' sojourn, the Reverend Dr John Haynes Holmes, of the Community Church in New York, wrote to Gandhi saying, 'I count these last months to be the crown and climax of your unparalleled career. You were never so great as in these dark hours.' Dr Holmes had talked with Gandhi and knew his mood. 'Of course,' he wrote to the Mahatma, 'you have been sad, well-nigh overborne, by the tragedies of recent months, but you must never feel that this involves any breakdown of your life work.'

Gandhi printed the praise in *Harijan* of 11 January, 1948, under the caption: 'Is It Deserved?' His answer was, 'I wonder if the claim can be proved.' In the same issue of the paper, Gandhi printed another letter, from a European friend, who had written to comfort him. 'I for one, and I am sure I speak the heart of untold millions,' the friend declared, 'feel it my bounden duty to express my deepest gratitude to you for giving the whole of your life to what you felt to be the one way to salvation for mankind', non-violence.

'I must not flatter myself with the belief, nor allow friends like you to entertain the belief,' Gandhi replied, 'that I have exhibited any heroic and demonstrable non-violence in myself. All I can claim is that I am sailing in that direction without a moment's stop . . .'

Gandhi's views on these matters were sober and modest. But he was too involved emotionally in his life work to be objective about it. He could not see himself in historic perspective. He was too disappointed by the failure of others to judge his own success correctly.

Would it be right to judge Christ by his crucifiers and detractors?

Gandhi was too great to succeed. His goals were too high, his followers too human and frail.

Gandhi did not belong to India alone. His failures in India in no wise detract from his message and meaning to the world. He may be very dead in India and very alive outside India. Ultimately he may live there and here.

It is the manner of Gandhi's life that matters, not his immediate effect on his immediate neighbours.

Jesus may have thought that God had forsaken Him and Gandhi may have thought his people had forsaken him. The verdict of history cannot be anticipated by those who make it.

The stature of a man is in the eye of the beholder. Harassed, unhappy, thwarted by those who adored him, Gandhi could not have seen what heights he attained in the last months of his life. In that period he did something of endless value to any society: he gave India a concrete, living demonstration of a different and better life. He showed that men could live as brothers and that brute man with blood on his hands can respond, however briefly, to the touch of the spirit. Without such moments humanity would lose faith in itself. For ever after, the community must compare that flash of light with the darkness of normal existence.

The fact that Gandhi's fast restored Calcutta to its senses and peace, the fact that his presence reduced the mass killings in Delhi to occasional outbursts, the fact that his fleeting visit to Dr Zakir Hussain's Okla academy gave it immunity to violence, that fact that hardened bandits laid their arms at his feet, the fact that Hindus would listen to *Koran* verses and that Moslems would not object to hearing the holy words of Islam from the mouth of a Hindu – all this remains to inspire or haunt those whose actions would suggest that they have forgotten it. It is the seed of conscience and the source of hope.

On 13 January, 1948, Mahatma Gandhi commenced his last fast. It engraved an image of goodness on India's brain.

The killings in Delhi had ceased. Gandhi's presence in the city had produced its effect. But he was still in 'agony'. 'It is intolerable to me,' he said, 'that a person like Dr Zakir Hussain, for instance, or for that matter Shaheed Suhrawardy [the ex-prime minister of Bengal] should not be able to move about in Delhi as freely and with as much safety as I myself.' Gandhi wanted to go to Pakistan to help the Hindus and Sikhs there, but how could he when the Moslems of Delhi had not obtained full redress? 'I felt helpless,' he said. 'I have never put up with helplessness in all my life.'

He therefore fasted; it was an 'all-in fast', to death. 'It came to me in a flash.' He had not consulted Nehru or Patel or his doctors. To the charge that he had acted impatiently when the situation was improving, he replied that he had waited patiently since the riots started a year ago; the spirit of interreligious killing was still abroad in the land. 'It was only when in terms of human effort I had exhausted all resources . . . that I put my head on God's lap . . . God sent me the fast . . . Let our sole prayer be that God may vouchsafe me strength of spirit during the fast that the temptation to live may not lead me into a hasty or premature termination of the fast.'

The fast, Gandhi declared on the first day, was directed to 'the conscience of all', to the Hindus and Moslems in the Indian Union and to the Moslems of Pakistan. 'If all or any one of the groups respond fully, I know the miracle will be achieved. For instance, if the Sikhs respond to my appeal as one man I shall be wholly satisfied.' He would go and live among the Sikhs of the Punjab.

'We are steadily losing hold in Delhi,' Gandhi asserted; he feared a recrudescence of violence in the capital, and 'if Delhi goes, India goes and with that the last hope of world peace'. Hindus had been murdered in Karachi, the capital of Pakistan, and elsewhere in the Moslem Dominion. With his fingertips, the Mahatma sensed the danger of a new wave of riots. In Delhi refugees were ejecting Moslems from their homes, and demands had been heard to banish all the Moslem inhabitants of the city. 'There is storm within the breast,' Gandhi said; 'it may burst forth any day.'

He had brooded over the situation for three days without telling anybody. When at last he decided to fast 'it made me happy'. He felt happy for the first time in months.

He knew he might die, 'but death for me would be a glorious deliverance rather than that I should be a helpless witness to the destruction of India, Hinduism, Sikhism and Islam'. His friends, he announced, must not rush to Birla House to try to dissuade him. Nor must they be anxious. 'I am in God's hands.' Instead of worrying about him they should 'turn the searchlight inward; this is essentially a testing time for all of us.'

The first day of the fast he walked to the evening prayer meeting and conducted the services as usual. 'A fast weakens nobody during the first twenty-four hours after a meal,' he told the congregation with a smile. A written question passed to him on the platform asked who was to blame for the fast. No one, he replied, 'but if the Hindus and Sikhs insist on turning out the Moslems of Delhi they will betray India and their religions; and it hurts me'. Some taunted him, he said, with fasting for the sake of the Moslems. They were right. 'All my life I have stood, as everyone should stand, for minorities and those in need . . .

'I expect a thorough cleansing of hearts,' he declared. It did not matter what the Moslems in Pakistan were doing. Hindus and Sikhs should remember Tagore's favourite song: 'If no one responds to your call, Walk alone, Walk alone.'

He would break his fast when Delhi became peaceful 'in the real sense of the term'.

The second day of the fast the doctors told Gandhi not to go to prayers, so he dictated a message to be read to the congregation. But then he decided to attend and addressed the worshippers after the hymns and holy scriptures had been chanted. He had been deluged with messages, he said. The most pleasant was from Mrdulla Sarabhai in Lahore, Pakistan. She wired that his Moslem friends, including some in the Moslem League and Pakistan government were anxious for his safety and asked what they should do.

His answer was: 'The fast is a process of self-purification and is intended to invite all who are in sympathy with the mission of the fast to take part in the process of self-purification . . . Such a Pakistan can never die. Then, and only then, shall I repent that I ever called partition a sin, as I am afraid I must hold today . . .'

As a child, he revealed, after listening to his father's discussions with friends of other communities, he had dreamed of real amity between religions. 'In the evening of my life, I shall jump like a child to feel that the dream has been fulfilled.' Then his wish to live 125 years would be revived.

'I have not the slightest desire that the fast should be ended as soon as possible,' he assured the congregation. 'It matters little if the ecstatic wishes of a fool like me are never realized and the fast is never broken. I am content to wait as long as it may be necessary, but it will hurt me to think that people have acted merely to save my life.'

In this fast Gandhi did not wish to be examined by the physicians. 'I have thrown myself on God,' he told me. But Dr Gilder, the heart specialist of Bombay, said that doctors wished to issue daily bulletins and could not tell the truth unless they examined him. That convinced the Mahatma and he relented. Dr Sushila Nayyar told him there were acetone bodies in his urine.

'This is because I haven't enough faith,' Gandhi said.

'But this is a chemical,' she protested.

He looked at her with a faraway look and said, 'How little science knows. There is more in life than science and there is more in God than in chemistry.'

He could not drink water; it caused nausea. He refused to add some drops of citrus juice or honey to the water to prevent nausea. The kidneys were functioning poorly. He had lost much strength; his weight dropped two pounds each day.

The third day he submitted to a high colonic irrigation. At 2.30 in the morning he awoke and asked for a hot bath. In the tub he dictated a statement to Pyarelal asking the Indian Union government to pay the government of Pakistan 550,000,000 rupees, or approximately £40,000,000. This was Pakistan's share in the assets of pre-partition India; the New Delhi authorities had delayed payment, and Gandhi was demanding immediate transfer of the money. Having dictated the memorandum, he felt giddy and Pyarelal lifted him out of the water and sat him in a chair. The Mahatma's weight was down to 107 pounds, his blood pressure 140.98.

The Indian Union government paid out the money.

That day, Gandhi occupied a cot which stood in an enclosed porch at the side of Birla House. Most of the time he lay in a crouched position, like an embryo, with his knees pulled up towards his stomach and his fists under his chest. The body and head were completely covered with a white khadi cloth which framed the face. His eyes were closed and he appeared to be asleep or half conscious. An endless queue filed past at a distance of ten feet. Indians and foreigners in the line were moved to pity as they observed him; many wept and murmured a prayer and touched their palms together in a greeting which he did not see. Acute pain was written on his face. Yet even in sleep or semi-consciousness, the suffering seemed to be sublimated; it was suffering dulled by the exhilaration of faith, suffering moderated by an awareness of service. His inner being knew that he was making a contribution to peace and he was therefore at peace with himself.

Before prayers at 5 P.M. he was fully awake but he could not walk to the prayer ground and arrangements were made for him to speak from his bed into a microphone connected with a loud-speaker at the prayer ground and with the All-India Radio which would broadcast his remarks throughout the country.

'Do not bother about what others are doing,' he said in a weak voice. 'Each of us should turn the searchlight inward and purify his or her heart as much as possible. I am convinced that if you purify yourselves sufficiently you will help India and shorten the period of my fast . . . No one can escape death. Then why be afraid of it? In fact, death is a friend, who brings deliverance from suffering.'

He could speak no further. The rest of his message was read for him. Journalists had submitted questions to him and he was answering them orally.

'Why have you undertaken a fast when there was no disturbance of any kind in any part of the Indian Dominion?'

'What was it if not a disturbing disturbance', he replied, 'for a crowd to make an organized and a determined effort to take forcible possession of Moslem houses? The disturbance was such that the police had reluctantly to resort to tear gas and even a little shooting, if only overhead, before the crowd dispersed. It would have been foolish for me to wait till the last Moslem had been turned out of Delhi by subtle, undemonstrative methods which I would describe as killing by inches.'

The charge had been made that he was fasting against Vallabhbhai Patel, the assistant Prime Minister and Home Minister, whom some regarded as anti-Moslem. Gandhi denied it and said this seemed like an attempt to create a gulf between him and Nehru on the one hand and Patel on the other.

The fourth day, Gandhi's pulse was irregular. He allowed the doctors to take an electro-cardiogram and give him another irrigation. Maulana Abul Kalam Azad pleaded in vain with the Mahatma to drink some water with citrus juice. Gandhi had been drinking no water and passing no urine. They physicians warned him that even if he survived the fast he would suffer permanent, serious injury. Unheeding, he spoke to the prayer meeting by microphone from his cot and boasted that his voice was stronger than the day before. 'I have never felt so well on the fourth day of a fast,' he stated. 'My sole guide, even dictator, is God, the Infallible and Omnipotent. If he has any further use for this frail body of mine He will keep it in spite of the prognostications of medical men and women. I am in His hands. Therefore I hope you will believe me when I say that I dread neither death nor permanent injury even if I survive. But I do feel that this warning of medical friends should, if the country has any use for me, hurry the people up to close their ranks.'

He insisted on addressing the prayer meeting by microphone for two minutes. This was followed by the reading of a statement which he had dictated earlier. The government of the Indian Union was paying Pakistan 550,000,000 rupees. This, Gandhi, hoped, would lead to an honourable settlement of the Kashmir question and all outstanding differences between the two Dominions. 'Friendship should replace the present enmity . . . What will be Pakistan's counter gesture?'

On 17 January, Gandhi's weight was stabilized at 107 pounds. He was accumulating water apparently from the irrigations. He suffered from nausea and was restless. But for hours he rested quietly or slept. Nehru came and cried. Gandhi sent Pyarelal into the city to ascertain whether it was safe for Moslems to return. Hundreds of telegrams arrived from princes, from Moslems in Pakistan, from every corner of India. Gandhi felt gratified, but his written statement that day was a warning: 'Neither the Rajas nor Maharajas nor the Hindus or Sikhs or any others will serve themselves or India as a whole if at this, what is to me sacred juncture they mislead me with a view to terminating my fast. They should know that I never feel so happy as when I am fasting for the spirit. This fast has brought me higher happiness than hitherto. No one need disturb this happy state unless he can honestly claim that in his journey he has turned deliberately from Satan towards God.'

On 18 January, Gandhi felt better. He permitted some light massage. His weight remained at 107 pounds.

Ever since 11 A.M. on the 13th when Gandhi commenced to fast, committees representing numerous communities, organizations and refugee groups in Delhi had been meeting in the house of Dr Rajendra Prasad, the new Congress president, in an effort to establish real peace among divergent elements. It was not a matter of obtaining signatures to a document. That would not satisfy Gandhi. They must make concrete pledges which they knew their followers would carry out. If the pledges were broken Gandhi could easily and quickly ascertain the fact and then he would fast irrevocably to death. Conscious of the responsibility, some representatives hesitated and went away to consult their conscience and subordinates.

At last, on the morning of the 18th, the pledge was drafted and signed and over a hundred delegates repaired from Prasad's home to Birla House. Nehru and Azad were already there. The Chief of Police of Delhi and his deputy were also present; they too had signed the pledge. Hindus, Moslems, Sikhs, Christians and Jews attended. The Hindu Mahasabha and the RSS were represented.

Jarab Zahid Hussain-Saheb, the High Commissioner (Ambassador) of Pakistan in Delhi, was also present.

Prasad opened the conference with the fasting Mahatma by explaining that their pledge included a promise and programme for implementation. The undertakings were definite. 'We take the pledge that we shall protect the life, property and faith of the Moslems and that the incidents which have taken place in Delhi will not happen again.'

Gandhi listened and nodded.

'We want to assure Gandhiji,' Point Two, 'that the annual fair at Kwaja Qutab-ud-Din Mazar will be held this year as in previous years.' This was a reference to a fair held regularly at a Moslem shrine outside the city.

The specific nature of this promise seemed to brighten Gandhi's face.

'Moslems will be able to move about in Subzimandi, Karol Bagh, Paharganj and other localities just as they could in the past.

'The mosques which have been left by Moslems and which are now in the possession of Hindus and Sikhs will be returned. The areas which have been set apart for Moslems will not be forcibly occupied.'

Moslems who had fled could return and conduct their business as before.

'These things,' they assured him, 'will be done by our

personal efforts and not with the help of the police or military.'

Prasad accordingly begged the Mahatma to discontinue the fast.

A Hindu representative then reported to Gandhi on the touching scenes of fraternization that had taken place that morning when a procession of 150 Moslem residents of Subzimandi was given an ovation and then feted by the Hindus of the locality.

Gandhi had been kept informed of the deliberations in Rajendra Prasad's house; he had originally formulated several of the points which the delegates were presenting to him as adopted.

Gandhi now addressed the group before him. He was moved, he said, by their words. But 'your guarantee is nothing worth and I will feel and you will one day realize that it was a great blunder for me to give up the fast if you hold yourself responsible for the communal peace of Delhi only.' The press had reported inter-religious troubles in Allahabad. Representatives of the Hindu Mahasabha and RSS, Gandhi continued, were in the room and had signed the pledge for Delhi. 'If they are sincere about their professions surely they cannot be indifferent to outbreaks of madness in places other than Delhi.' This was a clear implication of the guilt of these two organizations. 'Delhi,' Gandhi continued, 'is the heart of the Indian Dominion and you are the cream of Delhi. If you cannot make the whole of India realize that the Hindus, Sikhs and Moslems are all brothers, it will bode ill for the future of both Dominions. What will happen to India if they both quarrel?'

Here Gandhi, overcome with emotion, broke down; tears streamed down his hollow cheeks. Onlookers sobbed; many wept.

When he resumed his voice was too weak to be heard and Dr Sushila Nayyar repeated aloud what he whispered to her.

Were they deceiving him, Gandhi asked. Were they merely trying to save his life? Would they guarantee peace in Delhi and release him so he could go to Pakistan and plead for peace there? Did Moslems regard Hindus as infidels who worshipped idols and who should therefore be exterminated?

Maulana Azad and other Moslem scholars spoke and assured Gandhi that this was not the Islamic attitude. Ganesh Dutt, speaking for the RSS and the Hindu Mahasabha, pleaded with Gandhi to break his fast. The Pakistan Ambassador also addressed a few friendly words to the Mahatma. A Sikh representative added his pledge.

Gandhi sat on the cot, silent and sunk in thought. The assembly waited. Finally he announced that he would break the fast. Parsi, Moslem and Japanese scriptures were read and then the Hindu verse:

> Lead me from untruth to truth,
> From darkness to light,
> From death to immortality.

The girls of Gandhi's entourage sang a Hindu song and 'When I survey the Wondrous Cross', Gandhi's favourite Christian hymn.

Thereupon, Maulana Azad handed Gandhi a glass filled with eight ounces of orange juice which Gandhi slowly drank.

If the pledge was kept, Gandhi said, it would revive his wish to live his full span of life and serve humanity. 'That span, according to learned opinion,' he declared, 'is at least 125 years, some say 133.'

The same afternoon, Gandhi had a talk with Arthur Moore, former editor of the British-owned daily *Statesman*. 'He was lightsome and gay,' Moore wrote, 'and his interest while he talked with me was not in himself but in me, whom he plied with probing questions.'

When he awoke that morning, Nehru had decided to fast

until evening in sympathy with Gandhi. Then the Prime Minister was summoned to Birla House where he witnessed the giving of the pledge and the breaking of the fast. 'See here,' Nehru said to Gandhi in mock censure, 'I have been fasting; and now this will force me to break my fast prematurely.'

Gandhi was pleased. In the afternoon he sent some documents to Nehru with a note saying he hoped he had ended his fast. 'May you long remain the jewel of India,' Gandhi added. *Jawahar* is 'jewel' in Hindustani.

Gandhi told his evening prayer meeting that he interpreted the pledge as meaning, 'Come what may, there will be complete friendship between the Hindus, Moslems, Sikhs, Christians and Jews, a friendship not to be broken.'

Sir Mohamed Zafrullah Khan, the Foreign Minister of Pakistan, informed the UN Security Council at Lake Success that 'a new and tremendous wave of feeling and desire for friendship between the two Dominions is sweeping the subcontinent in response to the fast'.

The national boundary between Pakistan and the Indian Union is an unhealed cut through the heart of India and friendship is difficult to achieve. Nevertheless, Gandhi's last fast did perform the miracle not merely of pacifying Delhi but of putting an end to religious riots and violence throughout both Dominions.

That partial solution of a problem which is world wide stands as a monument to the moral force of one man whose desire to serve was greater than his attachment to life. Gandhi loved life and wanted to live. But through the readiness to die he recovered the capacity to serve, and therein lay happiness. In the twelve days that followed the fast he was happy and jolly; despondency had fled and he was full of plans for further work. He courted death and found a new lease on life.

CHAPTER 10

The Last Act

The first day after the fast Gandhi was carried to prayers in a chair. In his speech, which was only faintly audible, he reported that an official of the Hindu Mahasabha, which believed in Hindu supremacy and was the parent of the militant anti-Moslem RSS, had repudiated the Delhi peace pledge. Gandhi said he was sorry.

The second day he again had to be carried to prayers. In the course of his usual remarks, he declared he hoped to recuperate rapidly and then go to Pakistan to pursue the mission of peace.

At question time, a man urged Gandhi to proclaim himself a reincarnation of God. 'Sit down and be quiet,' Gandhi replied with a tired smile.

While Gandhi was speaking, the noise of an explosion was heard. 'What is it?' he asked. 'I don't know.' The audience was agitated. 'Don't worry about it,' he said. 'Listen to me.'

A hand-made bomb had been thrown at the Mahatma from the nearby garden wall.

The next day Gandhi, having walked to the prayer meeting, told the worshippers that congratulations had poured in on him for remaining unruffled during the incident. He said he deserved no praise; he had thought it was military practice. 'I would deserve praise,' he asserted, 'only if I fell as a result of such an explosion and yet retained a smile on my face and no malice against the doer. No one should look down on the misguided youth who had thrown the bomb. He probably looks upon me as an enemy of Hinduism.'

The young man, Gandhi continued, should realize that 'those who differ with him are not necessarily evil'. He urged the supporters of such young people to desist from their activity. 'This is not the way to save Hinduism. Hinduism can only be saved by my method.'

Sikhs visited Gandhi and assured him that the would-be assailant was not a Sikh. 'What does it matter,' Gandhi asked, 'whether he was a Sikh or a Hindu or a Moslem? I wish all perpetrators well.'

An illiterate old woman had grappled with the grenade-thrower and held him till the police came. Gandhi commended 'the unlettered sister on her simple bravery'. He told the Inspector General of Police not to molest the young man. Instead, they should try to convert him to right thinking and right doing. Nor should the worshippers be angry with the 'miscreant'. 'You should pity him,' Gandhi said.

The young man's name was Madan Lal. He was a refugee from the Punjab, had found shelter in a mosque in Delhi and been evicted when the police, under pressure of Gandhi's wishes, commenced clearing Moslem places of worship.

'I had seen with my own eyes horrible things in Pakistan,' Madan Lal testified at his trial. 'I had also been an eye-witness to the shooting down of Hindus in Punjab towns and in Delhi by troops from the south.'

Aroused, Madan Lal had joined a group of men who were plotting to kill Gandhi. When the grenade failed to reach its target and Madan Lal was arrested, his fellow conspirator, Nathuram Vinayak Godse, came to Delhi. Godse, age thirty-five, was the editor and publisher of a Hindu Mahasabha weekly in Poona, in Tilak's Maratha country, and he was a high-degree, Chitpawan Brahman.

Subsequently, Godse, Madan Lal and seven others were tried together. The trial lasted more than six months. Among other things, Madan Lal said he was angered by the Indian Union's payment of 550,000,000 rupees to Pakistan. This exasperated Godse.

'I sat brooding intensely on the atrocities perpetrated on

Hinduism and its dark and deadly future if left to face Islam outside and Gandhi inside,' Godse testified, 'and ... I decided all of a sudden to take the extreme step against Gandhi.'

The success of Gandhi's last fast especially infuriated Godse. He resented the Mahatma's insistence that refugees be evacuated from the mosques. He was bitter because no demands were made on the Moslems.

Godse began hovering around Birla House. He wore a khaki jacket. In a pocket of the jacket he kept a small pistol.

Gandhi's prayer meeting on Sunday, 25 January, 1948, had an unusually heavy attendance. Gandhi was pleased. He told the people that they should bring straw mats or thick khadi to sit on because the ground in winter was cold and damp. It gladdened his heart, he continued, to be told by Hindu and Moslem friends that Delhi had experienced 'a reunion of hearts'. In view of this improvement, could not every Hindu and Sikh who came to prayers bring along 'at least one Moslem'? To Gandhi this would be concrete evidence of brotherhood.

But Hindus like Madan Lal and Godse and their ideological sponsors were incensed by the presence of Moslems at Hindu services and the reading of selections from the *Koran*. Moreover, they seemed to hope that the death of Gandhi might be the first step towards the violent reunification of India. They wished, by removing him, to make the Moslems defenceless, little realizing that his assassination would have the opposite effect by showing the country how dangerous and undisciplined extreme anti-Moslems could be.

Despite the relaxation that followed his fast, Gandhi knew the great difficulties facing the new, inexperienced Government. He had lost confidence in the ability of Congress. Much, very much, now depended on the two top government leaders: Prime Minister Nehru and Deputy

Prime Minister Patel. They did not always see eye to eye. They were temperamental opposites. There had been friction between them. It worried Gandhi. Indeed, things had come to such a pass that Gandhi wondered whether Nehru and Patel could work together in the Government. Forced to make a choice, the Mahatma might have preferred Nehru. He appreciated Patel as an old friend and skilled administrator, but loved Nehru and was sure of his equal friendship for Hindus and Moslems. Patel had been suspected of political pro-Hinduism.

In the end, Gandhi decided that Nehru and Patel were indispensable to one another. The Government would be seriously weakened if it lost either. Gandhi accordingly wrote Nehru a note in English saying he and Patel 'must hold together' for the good of the country. At 4 P.M. on 30 January, Patel came to see Gandhi in Birla House to hear the same message.

At 5.05, Gandhi, troubled because he was late, left Patel and leaning his arms on Abha and Manu, hurried to the prayer ground. Nathuram Godse was in the front row of the congregation, his hand in his pocket gripping the small pistol. He had no personal hatred of Gandhi, Godse said at his trial, at which he was sentenced to be hanged: 'Before I fired the shots I actually wished him well and bowed to him in reverence.'

In response to Godse's obeisance and the reverential bows of other members of the congregation, Gandhi touched his palms together, smiled and blessed them. At that moment, Godse pulled the trigger. Gandhi fell, and died murmuring, 'Oh, God.'

PART ONE

The pages that follow contain notes and comments on sources. They indicate how this book was written.

CHAPTER 1

Eye-witness observations of Gandhi's assassination, funeral and cremation were supplemented by accounts in the New Delhi *Hindustan Times* and the Bombay *Times of India*, a full file of which for the period from 30 January, 1948, to 24 February, 1948, I brought home with me from India in the autumn of 1948 . . . The 15 February, 1948, issue of *Harijan*, Gandhi's English-language weekly, contains two invaluable articles, by Devadus Gandhi and by Pyarelal, Gandhi's chief secretary, which enabled me to piece together and enrich the account in this chapter . . . Under the imprint of the *Hindustan Times*, Devadus, its managing editor, published in 1948 a one-hundred page, large-format picture book, *Memories of Bapu*, whose contents are also a record of the funeral and cremation . . . A personal letter from Sardar Vallabhbhai Patel gave me several details about Gandhi's last day . . . Two letters from Dr D. P. Bhargava supplied important medical data included in the chapter . . . General Sir Roy Bucher, whom I met in New Delhi, sent me a most exact military report on the funeral procession, giving distances, names of units, numbers of planes, numbers of vehicles, etc. . . . The account of the special memorial meeting of the United Nations Security Council is based on the official stenographic record . . . Tributes and eulogies were found in the newspapers of various countries, the bulletins of the Government of India Information Services in Washington, DC, *Homage to Mahatma Gandhi*, a pamphlet published by the Indian government in New Delhi and other publications . . . Several letters from Krishna Nehru Hutheesing, who was in New Delhi the day of the murder and the day of the funeral, were very helpful.

CHAPTER 2

The chief source of information on Gandhi's early life is his

autobiography. The introduction appeared in *Young India*, Gandhi's
English-language weekly, on 3 December, 1925, and thereafter he
wrote a short chapter for publication in each issue. He wrote in
Gujarati, his native tongue, which was rendered into English by
Mahadev Desai, his loyal secretary and Boswell. In 1927, Part One
of the autobiography appeared in book form and in 1929, Part Two.
Subsequently they were bound in a single volume entitled *An
Autobiography or the Story of My Experiments with Truth*, by M. K.
Gandhi (London: Phoenix House Ltd, 1949) 616 pp.

Gandhi's autobiography is as indispensable as it is inadequate. It
begins at birth and ends in 1920, but the twenty-one crucial years he
spent in South Africa are covered so poorly as to be unintelligible
without an earlier book by Gandhi, *Satyagraha in South Africa*
(Madras: S. Ganesan, 1928). Other periods likewise receive scant
attention.

Moreover, the autobiography was written and published to
preach morals to the Mahatma's followers and it suffers from all the
disadvantages of that approach.

Some facts about Gandhi's boyhood not found in the
autobiography were obtained in interviews with Raliatbehn,
Gandhi's sister. The data on the house in which Gandhi was born,
the census figures for 1872, the names of rulers served by Gandhi's
father, etc., were sent to me by Mr N. M. Buch, of Rajkot, acting on
instructions from Sardar Vallabhbhai Patel, India's Deputy Prime
Minister and Minister of States.

Information about Mrs Gandhi is contained in *Sati Kasturba, a
Life-Sketch with Tributes in Memoriam*, edited by R. K. Prabhu;
Foreword by M. R. Masani (Bombay: Hind Kitabs, 1944) and
Kasturba, Wife of Gandhi, by Sushila Nayyar (Wallingford,
Pennsylvania: Pendle Hill, 1948). In her old age, Kasturbai was
called Kasturba, the 'Ba' meaning 'mother'.

CHAPTER 3

The autobiography furnished most of the material for this chapter.
Also *A Sheaf of Gandhi Anecdotes*, by C. Ramchandran, with a
Foreword by C. Rajagopalachari (Bombay: Hind Kitabs, 1945),
p 33; *The Middle Span*, by George Santayana, vol. 2; *Persons and Places*
(London: Constable & Co, 1947), p 187, etc.; and *Harijan*, a weekly
magazine founded by Gandhi, of 20 February, 1949. The dates of

Gandhi's enrolment in the Inner Temple and London University
were ascertained from the records at my request ... Dr Sinha,
whose description of Gandhi is quoted in this chapter, is the only
contemporary of Gandhi, the law student, whom I have been able to
discover. He was still living in Patna, province of Bihar, in 1949, at
the ripe age of eighty. He was good enough to send me a long account
of all his encounters with Gandhi.

CHAPTER 4

In the preparation of this chapter several translations of the *Gita* have
been used. They are *The Bhagavadgita*, by S. Radhakrishnan
(London: George Allen & Unwin Ltd, 1948); *The Bhagavad Gita*, by
Swami Nikhilananda (New York: Ramakrishna-Vivekananda
Centre, 1944); and *The Gospel of Selfless Action, the Gita According to
Gandhi*, by Mahadev Desai (Ahmedabad: Navajivan Publishing
House, 1946). *Gita* quotations in the chapter are from this last book
not only because they are from the English version of Gandhi's
Gujarati translation but because they sound so good.

Among other books used in the preparation of the chapter are
Hinduism and Buddhism by Ananda K. Coomaraswamy (New York:
Philosophical Library); *Essence of Hinduism* by Swami Nikhilananda
(Boston: Beacon Press, 1948); *Vedanta for the Western World*, edited
with Introduction by Christopher Isherwood (London: George
Allen & Unwin Ltd, 1945); *The Pageant of Indian History*, vol. 1, by
Gertrude Emerson Sen (New York: Longmans Green & Co, 1948);
and *In the Path of Mahatma Gandhi* by George Catlin (London:
Macdonald & Co, 1948).

This chapter was read in manuscript by Swami Nikhilananda, the
leader of the Ramakrishna-Vivekananda Centre, New York. He
likewise gave me the benefit of his views on chapters 1, 9, 18, 22, 34,
35 and 47. I also borrowed books from the Centre's rich library.

CHAPTER 5

The facts in the chapter are from Gandhi's autobiography.

CHAPTER 6

Books used: *Satyagraha in South Africa* by M. K. Gandhi; the autobiography; and a rare volume entitled *Speeches and Writings of Mahatma Gandhi* (Madras: G. A. Natesan & Co, 1933).

CHAPTER 7

Chancellor Jan. H. Hofmeyer and Professor Edward Thompson of Oxford are quoted from their contributions to *Mahatma Gandhi: Essays and Reflections on his Life and Work. Being Tributes from Sixty-two Friends and Admirers, Presented to him on his Seventieth Birthday*, edited by S. Radhakrishnan (London: Allen & Unwin Ltd, 1939). *Satyagraha in South Africa*, the autobiography and *Speeches and Writings* were found indispensable.

In recounting the mob assault on Rustomji's house, Gandhi states in the autobiography that he fled in the company of two policemen, and in *Satyagraha in South Africa* that he was accompanied by one disguised policeman. I have assumed that the autobiography gives the correct version.

CHAPTER 8

Lionel Curtis's statement is quoted in *Mahatma Gandhi, Essays and Reflections*, edited by S. Radhakrishnan . . . The photographs of Gandhi's Ambulance Corps appear in 'The Mahatma Gandhi Memorial Number' of *Indian Opinion* (Phoenix, Natal: March 1948) . . . The Botha and Smuts anti-Indian declarations are reproduced in the 'Golden Number' of *Indian Opinion*, entitled *Souvenir of the Passive Resistance Movement in South Africa, 1906-1914* (Phoenix, Natal: 1914) . . . The narrative follows Gandhi's *Satyagraha in South Africa*. The autobiography supplies general guidance and a few facts.

CHAPTER 9

All conversations between Gandhi and Kasturbai and their children and others which are quoted in this and other chapters are taken verbatim from printed records. There is no fictionalized or imagined conversation in this book. The argument on the jewellery, for instance, is in Gandhi's own words.

Satyagraha in South Africa by M. K. Gandhi, as well as the autobiography, supplied invaluable material for this chapter. Further data were found in *Self-Restraint versus Self-Indulgence* by M. K. Gandhi (Ahmedabad: Navajivan Publishing House, 1947); *Selections from Gandhi* by Nirmal Kumar Bose, another helpful Navajivan book which appeared in 1948; and *The Teachings of Mahatma Gandhi*, edited by Jag Parvesh Chander (Lahore: Indian Printing Works, 1947) . . . The story of the Indian boy who died of an operation is from Mrs Millie Graham Polak's contribution to a volume called *Incidents of Gandhiji's Life*, edited by Chandrashanker Shukla (Bombay: Vora & Co, 1949). The Ruskin quotations are from *The Political Economy of Art; Unto This Last; Sesame and Lilies; The Crown of Wild Olive* by John Ruskin (London: George Allen & Unwin Ltd). Discussions with Joseph Freeman, author of *American Testament* and of several novels, helped to clarify the philosophy of Ruskin . . . Gandhi's statement to Polak about marriage appears in the weekly *Harijan* of 5 September, 1948.

The name of the Moslem boy who taught Gandhi to eat meat and later misbehaved in Gandhi's house was given to me by Manilal Gandhi. K. Kalelkar, a disciple of Gandhi, asked the Mahatma, many years later, why he had omitted the name from the autobiography. Gandhi replied that the man was still alive at the time and he added that he left many other things out of the autobiography.

How Gandhi cured the asthma sufferer he told in a letter, published in *Harijan* of 6 February, 1949, which he wrote in jail in 1932 to a person who asked him how to get rid of asthma.

Gandhi's 1946 statement on the effect of *Unto This Last* on his life was made to Andrew Freeman of the *New York Post* and was printed in *Harijan* of 17 November, 1946.

CHAPTER 10

The text of the speeches and the temperature of the audience at the Imperial Theatre meeting are recorded in *Satyagraha in South Africa* by M. K. Gandhi.

CHAPTER 11

Gandhi's articles on his jail experiences are reprinted in *Speeches and Writings of Mahatma Gandhi* ... Gandhi's letter on Thoreau was placed at my disposal by Mrs Ellen Watumull of Los Angeles, California ... *Satyagraha in South Africa*, the autobiography and the 'Golden Number' of *Indian Opinion* were as indispensable to the preparation of this chapter as of preceding ones ... Gandhi's prison card was sent to me from Phoenix by his son Manilal ... Thoreau quotations are from *The Portable Thoreau*, edited and with an Introduction by Carl Bode (New York: Viking Press, 1947); *Thoreau* by Henry Seidel Canby (Boston: Houghton Mifflin Co, 1939) contains an illuminating discussion of the influence of Hindu scriptures on Thoreau's mind ... Additional bibliography: *The Story of an African Farm*, a novel by Olive Schreiner; *Dadabhai Naoroji, the Grand Old Man of India* by R. P. Masani, with a Foreword by Mahatma Gandhi (London: George Allen & Unwin Ltd, 1939).

CHAPTER 12

The original Gandhi letter was posted to me from Phoenix on 29 November, 1948, by Manilal in answer to a request for material about his father. It was folded horizontally in four divisions. Despite its age – thirty-eight years – it was perfectly and easily legible. Manilal wrote me that he had no copy. Lest something happen to it, I had it photostated immediately and then returned it. I subsequently discussed it with Manilal.

The letter came with several other valuable hitherto unpublished pieces of Gandhiana which were listed by Manilal with a meticulousness which would have pleased Papa.

Other data in the chapter are culled from *Speeches and Writings of Mahatma Gandhi; Satyagraha in South Africa*; and Mahadev Desai's 1932 diary, published by Navajivan Press, Ahmedabad, in Gujarati, in 1948, portions of which were translated for me by Mahadev's younger brother Parmanand, a student at Columbia University.

CHAPTER 13

The Kingdom of God is Within You was unobtainable as a separate publication but is included in all standard collections of Count Leo Tolstoy's works. These collections also include biographical data.

The texts of Gandhi's three letters in the original English and Russian translations, as well as the Russian originals of Tolstoy's three letters and the English translations of the first two, plus the several entries in Tolstoy's diary, appeared in a Soviet collection entitled *Literaturnoye Nasledstovo* (Literary Heritage), vols 37-8 (Moscow, 1939), pp 339-52.

Gandhi's three letters to Count Leo Tolstoy are in the Archive of Vladimir G. Chertkov in Moscow.

CHAPTER 14

The central narrative in this chapter follows Gandhi's own story in *Satyagraha in South Africa*. To this the autobiography adds only a few details. Gokhale's speech in Bombay is quoted from *Gandhi As We Know Him*, edited by C. Shukla (Bombay: Vora & Co, 1949), p 144.

Gandhi's boast of his prowess as a carpenter and dressmaker for Mrs Gandhi is found in *Young India*, 12 May, 1927.

Gandhi's confidential and hitherto unpublished letters to Lord Ampthill were graciously offered to me by Benarsi Das Chaturvedi, an Indian writer who stayed with Gandhi in India.

CHAPTER 15

The Smuts tribute to Gandhi is quoted from *Mahatma Gandhi, Essays and Reflections on his Life and Work*. The copy I used was lent to me by Leilamani Naidu, daughter of the late Mrs Sarojini Naidu, Indian poet, and is inscribed by Gandhi: 'To Leilamani with love Bapu 11-10-40' . . . Other books that helped in the preparation of this chapter are: *Speeches and Writings of Mahatma Gandhi*; *Satyagraha in South Africa*; *Incidents in Gandhiji's Life*; 'Golden Number' of *Indian Opinion*; *Mahatma Gandhi's Ideas, including Selections from his Writings* by C. F. Andrews (London: George Allen & Unwin Ltd, 1930).

PART TWO

CHAPTER 1

The information on Sabarmati Ashram was gathered from a number of its residents. In the summer of 1948 I visited the settlement. Additional data are from a long and detailed article by P. R. Mehrotra in the Ambala (East Punjab) *Tribune* of 30 January, 1949, and *Mahatma Gandhi, Sketches in Pen, Pencil and Brush* by Kanu Desai, with an Essay by Verrier Elwin (London: The Golden Vista Press, 1932).

Speeches and Writings of Mahatma Gandhi furnishes the text of many of Gandhi's speeches of this period. The autobiography helps . . . Official facts on the Indian National Congress are found in a gigantic tome entitled *To the Gates of Liberty*, Foreword by Jawaharlal Nehru, Congress Commemoration Volume (Calcutta, 1947). The title of this Congress history is from a statement by Pearl S. Buck about Gandhi: 'He has brought his people to the gates of liberty. If they are not opened the people of India will open them' . . . Supplementary light on the early years of Congress can be gleaned from *Dadabhai Naoroji, the Grand Old Man of India* by R. P. Masani (London: George Allen & Unwin Ltd) and *India* by Sir Valentine Chirol (London: Ernest Benn, 1926).

The library on Rabindranath Tagore is rich and rewarding. The two lines of poetry cited in this chapter are from his *Gitanjali* (London: Macmillan & Co, 1914). Personal sidelights on his fascinating personality were given me by his literary secretary, Professor Amiya Chakravarty, Professor of English Literature at Howard University, Washington, DC, and by Humayun Kabir, an Indian writer whom I met in New Delhi. I interviewed Tagore in the Grand Hotel in Moscow, in 1933.

Knowledge of Gandhi's passion for chocolate-coated almonds and other facts about Gandhi's personal life come to me from Manilal Gandhi, with whom I spent much time in New York, in May 1949.

Hind Swaraj or Indian Home Rule by M. K. Gandhi, published by Navajivan Publishing House, Ahmedabad, India, has appeared

since 1909 in innumerable editions with new introductions by
Gandhi and Mahadev Desai. The facsimile of the original
manuscript as written by Gandhi ambidexterously in Gujarati has
also been published by Navajivan bound in greenish homespun. An
American edition (Chicago: Universal Publishing Co, 1924), with
an introduction by John Haynes Holmes and edited by Haridas T.
Muzumdar, appeared under the title, *Sermon on the Sea;* its
resemblance to the Sermon on the Mount is remote.

CHAPTER 2

There is no mention in Gandhi's autobiography of the speech at the
Benares University or of the episode. The full text of the speech, as
edited by Gandhi, is printed in *Speeches and Writings of Mahatma
Gandhi. To the Gates of Liberty* and Dadabhai Naoroji's biography
contained information on Mrs Annie Besant, as does a speech on Mrs
Besant by Sir C. P. Ramaswami Aiyar printed in his *Pen-Portraits,
Essays and Addresses* (Bombay: Hind Kitabs Ltd, 1948).

CHAPTER 3

Nehru's statement in the opening sentence of the chapter was made
to me at Gandhi's ashram in 1942 and is quoted from my *A Week with
Gandhi* (London: George Allen & Unwin Ltd). I have also used
Nehru's *The Discovery of India* (Calcutta: The Signet Press,
1946) . . . For the early history of India and for the description of
Mohenjodaro, I have leaned very heavily on and am heavily
indebted to Mrs Gertrude Emerson Sen's excellent, exciting, *The
Pageant of India's History* . . . other books used: *India,* by Sir Valentine
Chirol; *Mahatma Gandhi's Ideas, including Selections from his Writings* by
C. F. Andrews; *Selections from Gandhi* by Nirmal Kumar Bose;
Hinduism and Buddhism by Ananda K. Coomaraswamy; *Pen-Portraits,
Essays and Addresses* by Sir C. P. Ramaswami Aiyar; Gandhi's
autobiography; and *Gandhi and Stalin* by Louis Fischer (London:
Victor Gollancz Ltd, 1948). I also consulted the *Encyclopaedia
Britannica* articles on 'Caste', 'Untouchables', Sanskrit and
'Aryan' . . . On the intricate, delicate matter of caste, I have
questioned dozens of Hindus in India and the United States.

CHAPTER 4

Gandhi's conversation with me about Champaran is recorded in *A Week with Gandhi*. The autobiography supplies considerable information on the episode, but omits the very interesting Andrews episode which is covered by Rajendra Prasad in a chapter in *Incidents in Gandhiji's Life* by Fifty-four Contributors, edited by Chandrashanker Shulka (Bombay: Vora & Co, 1949) . . . Rajendra Prasad and the Reverend Dr J. Z. Hodge's chapter in the same *Incidents* volume, make intelligible the economic problem of the indigo sharecroppers, as Gandhi's autobiography does not. *Speeches and Writings of Mahatma Gandhi* also contains some material on the Champaran campaign.

When I finished writing this chapter it occured to me that Rajendra Prasad would have additional information on the Champaran episode. I put some question to him in a letter; his interesting reply is below:

My dear Mr Fischer, I have received your letter dated the 1 June and give you the information as far as I can from memory. The tenants used to grow other crops like paddy, maize, wheat, barley, etc., on the remaining $\frac{17}{20}$ of their holdings; $\frac{3}{20}$ being cultivated with indigo. I cannot give the number of peasants involved but it must have been in hundreds of thousands. There was hardly any peasant who was not under this obligation. The population of the district of Champaran was over 2,000,000 and most of the people are cultivators of land. The agreement which the planters got from the peasants for increase in their rent in lieu of Tinkathia (i.e. obligation to grow indigo on $\frac{3}{20}$ of their holdings) was obtained by force and coercion. Manufacture of indigo had ceased to be a profitable industry for the indigo planters, on account of the introduction of synthetic dyes early in the twentieth century, and they were anxious to avoid the subsequent loss which they apprehended. They took advantage of a provision in the land tenancy law which laid down that if a tenant was under obligation to grow a particular crop for the benefit of the landlord, the landlord could claim an unlimited enhancement in rent in lieu of giving the tenant freedom from the obligation to grow that particular crop notwithstanding another provision of the law which limited enhancement in rent to $12\frac{1}{2}$ per cent of the existing rent, and that only after a lapse of twenty years, and only when it was shown that there had been a general rise in the price of food grains. Under this limitation, landlords could not claim any enhancement at all if there was no general rise in the price of food grains calculated on the basis of the average of ten years' rent, and if they could claim any enhancement under this clause they could get it by private agreement with the tenants but subject to the maximum of $12\frac{1}{2}$ per cent. Both these limitations could be got over if the enhancement was agreed to in lieu of freedom from obligation to grow a particular crop. This particular section in the tenancy law had been introduced some fifty years earlier at the instance of the planters themselves and they took advantage of this at that time. The tenants knew that indigo manufacture had ceased to be a profitable business and they were shrewd enough to understand that sooner or later the planters would have to give up that business and they could never have agreed willingly to a permanent unlimited enhancement in their rents. They were coerced in various ways which I have described in great detail in a book which I have written. Shortly, they instituted false criminal prosecutions against them, had them beaten, their houses were looted, their cattle impounded, they were socially boycotted by withdrawing from them certain essential services like the services of carpenters and blacksmiths to repair their agricultural instruments, of barbers to shave them, of cobblers to supply them with leather goods which they required for their agricultural purposes, of midwives, forceful occupation of their lands, etc. They were cowed down and were unable even to lodge complaints against this tyranny and oppression in courts. The Government on the other hand helped the planters by appointing a number of special registrars to register the agreements. Under the law, these agreements were required to be registered before an official who is known as Registrar of Documents. The Government posted these additional registrars at the very places where the planters had their offices. As thousands and thousands of documents had to be registered, the ordinary staff could not deal with them, and therefore additional registrars were posted at each factory and they quickly registered the documents. This is how these agreements were executed and got. I cannot give the number of the peasants who signed these agreements but you can have an idea that the amount of additional income derived on account of the enhancement of rent by reason of these enhancement agreements was about 60 per cent of the existing rent. Some 30,710 enhancement agreements were executed between 1912 and 1914. The total enhancement of rent in rupees was anything between 200,000 to 300,000 annually. Where the planters did not get this permanent enhancement they realized cash compensation which they called Tawan and it was estimated at the time that the cash so realized was about Rs. 1,000,0001/-. All this was not paid in cash. Where the tenants were unable to pay in cash in one lump sum, they executed bonds which were realized later on by instalments in due course. The Tawan as the compensation was called was realized on an average of about Rs. 50/- to Rs. 60/- per acre on which the tenant was supposed to be under obligation to grow indigo.

There is no indigo grown there now or anywhere else so far as I know. The planters realized that on account of the legislation which the Government passed as a result of Mahatma Gandhi's movement abolishing compulsory growing of indigo under the Tinkatia system, they could not carry on in any other way and they were anxious somehow to get out of the difficulty which was thus created. The tenants on their side were anxious somehow or other to get rid of them. The planters found that with the loss of their prestige and with the advent of synthetic dyes they could no longer profitably grow indigo, and agriculture like the ordinary agriculturalists was equally unprofitable for them. They therefore began to sell their lands in small bits which the tenants were only too glad to purchase. So whatever land they possessed of their own they sold in this way and got good price for it and went away happy. A few of them converted their factories into sugar factories and their indigo plantations into sugar cane plantations and they are still there, but they do not have any of their old influence or prestige and are carrying on like any other owner of a sugar factory of which we have many in that district owned by Indians. I look upon this settlement of indigo trouble there as a very effective illustration of the working of Gandhiji's principle of non-violence. When he went there he declared that he had no enmity with the planters, but only wanted to stop their inequities. The planters were happy to get out of the situation which was becoming more and more difficult for them and the tenants were happy to get rid of their oppression. Both were pleased with the end of the system.

Mahatma Gandhi was in Champaran for a short period and busy with the inquiry and therefore the institutions which he established there towards the end of his stay did not flourish and leave any permanent effect in the way in which one would expect an institution to leave on the people who grow under its influence. But it was not only in Champaran but in the whole province of Bihar which was till then regarded as one of the most backward provinces in India that there was a great awakening amongst the masses at large, and this awakening has remained all through the movements which Mahatma Gandhi led in India during later years. From being one of the most backward provinces, Bihar came out as one of the most advanced provinces in Gandhiji's movement . . . Yours sincerely,

(Signed) *Rajendra Prasad*

CHAPTER 5

The chief sources used in this chapter are Gandhi's autobiography. *Teachings of Mahatma Gandhi*, edited by Jag Parvesh Chander, with a Foreword by Dr Rajendra Prasad (Lahore: The Indian Printing Works, 1947); and *History of Wage Adjustments in the Ahmedabad Industry*, vol IV, *Proceedings of the Arbitration Board and Awards of Arbitrators and the Umpire in the Wage Cut and Other Disputes (1936–37)* (Ahmedabad: Labour Office).

CHAPTER 6

Facts and quotations from the autobiography; *The Speeches and Writings of Mahatma Gandhi*; *A Sheaf of Gandhi Anecdotes* by G. Ramchandran; and *Gandhiji, his Life and Work*, published on his seventy-fifth birthday, 2 October, 1944 (Bombay: Karnatak Publishing House, 1944). This is a beautifully manufactured and beautifully illustrated volume of 501 large-size pages filled with invaluable matter. The suffix 'ji' is a mark of respect, Indians rarely speak of Gandhi except as 'Gandhiji'.

CHAPTER 7

My chief source for this chapter was *The Cambridge History of India*, vol V, *British India, 1497–1858*, edited by H. H. Dodwell (London: Cambridge University Press, 1929); and vol VI, *The Indian Empire, 1858–1918, with Chapters on the Development of Administration, 1818–1858*, edited by H. H. Dodwell (London: Cambridge University Press, 1932) . . . I had written of the pre-Portuguese invasions of India in *The Soviets in World Affairs*, 2 vols (London: Jonathan Cape Ltd, 1930). As part of the research for that book, I had access to the Czarist archives in Moscow where I copied

Napoleon's letters to the Russian emperors . . . Data on Indian ancient culture was found in *The Pageant of India's History* by Gertrude Emerson Sen . . . *India* by Sir Valentine Chirol, was also helpful. The secret report of Lord Lytton is quoted by Chirol who, incidentally, devotes considerable space to Tilak . . . *Subject India* by Henry Noel Brailsford (London: Victor Gollancz Ltd, 1943); *The Problem of India* by R. Palme Dutt (New York: International Publishers, 1943) and *The Autobiography of Jawaharlal Nehru* (London: John Lane, The Bodley Head, 1941) provided valuable material . . . Gandhi's autobiography, the big *Gandhiji* volume and *To the Gates of Liberty* supplied additional data on the development of the Indian nationalist movement . . . Light on Tilak came in written responses to questions I put by mail to Sir C. P. Ramaswami Aiyar, a former Tilakite and Prime Minister of Travancore and from Narhari Parikh, a close co-worker of Gandhi for many years; I also discussed Tilak with Sir C. P. in New York. The story of Tilak's bet with Gandhi is taken from B. Pattabhisitaramayya's contribution to *Mahatma Gandhi*, edited by S. Radhakrishnan. The statements of Lord Canning and Professor Rushbrook Williams on British policy towards the native Indian states are quoted from *Empire*, by Louis Fischer (New York: Duell, Sloan & Pearce, 1943). Canning's declaration will be found too in Brailsford's *Subject India* and many other studies of India.

CHAPTER 8

The story of the Amritsar massacre and all the quotations about it are taken from *East India . . . Report of the Committee Appointed by the Government of India to Investigate the Disturbances in the Punjab, etc.* (London: His Majesty's Stationery Office, 1920). Cmd 681. Most of the decisions of the Hunter Committee were unanimous, but the *Report* also contains a minority report by the three Indian members of the Commission who felt that the majority's strictures of General Dyer were too mild . . . General Dyer's own full account is printed in *Army, Disturbances in the Punjab*, Statement by Brigadier-General R. E. H. Dyer, CB, Presented to Parliament by Command of His Majesty (London: His Majesty's Stationery Office, 1920), Cmd 771.

The Congress party commission of inquiry also investigated the Amritsar shooting and published its detailed findings. I have preferred, however, to quote the British commission and, more particularly, General Dyer.

Other sources: Chirol's *India*, the *Gandhiji* volume and the autobiography. Biographical data on Dyer is to be found in the *Encyclopaedia Britannica*, vol VII (1947). This article says the Jallianwalla Bagh attack caused 'over 300 deaths'. The article on Amritsar in the same publication gives the figure as 'nearly 400 killed by gunfire'.

CHAPTER 9

The last meagre entry in Gandhi's autobiography deals with the Nagpur Congress session in December 1920. But rich raw material is available in the weekly issues of *Young India* which Gandhi edited. Many of his contributions during the 1919–22 period are collected in a book entitled *Young India 1919–22* by Mahatma Gandhi, with a Brief Sketch of the Non-Co-Operation Movement by Babu Rajendra Prasad, Secretary, Indian National Congress (New York: B. W. Huebsch, Inc, 1923). The book was lent to me by Morgan Harris, a Los Angeles college instructor. I bought the bound volumes of *Young India*, from December 1921 to 1931, in Bombay in the summer of 1948.

Invaluable for detail is a two-volume book by Gandhi's secretary Krishadas entitled *Seven Months with Mahatma Gandhi, Being an Inside View of the Non-Co-Operation Movement (1921–22)* (Behar: Rambinode Sinha, 1928). *To the Gates of Liberty*; the official Congress history; the *Gandhiji* birthday publication; and *Swaraj in One Year* by Mahatma Gandhi (Madras: Ganesh & Co, 1921), supply supplementary data.

Lord Reading's biography is entitled *Rufus Isaacs, First Marquess of Reading* by His Son, the Marquess of Reading, 1914–35 (London: Hutchinson & Co Ltd, 1945). This is the second volume of the biography. The first volume tells the romantic life story of the ship's messenger boy who became Viceroy of India and British Foreign Secretary. He was born on 10 October, 1860, and died 29 December, 1935.

The verbatim proceedings of Gandhi's 1922 trial are given in *Speeches and Writings of Mahatma Gandhi* and in *The Great Trial of Mahatma Gandhi and Mr Sankarlal Banker*, edited by K. P. Kesava Menon, Foreword by Mrs Sarojini Naidu (Madras: Ganesh & Co, 1922). The description of Gandhi's arrest is taken from an article by an eye-witness, P. R. Mehrota, in the Ambala *Tribune*, 30 January, 1939.

An illuminating interpretation of the politics of the Non-Co-operation period is to be found in *The Indian Struggle, 1920–34* by Subhas C. Bose (London: Wishart & Co Ltd, 1935). Also in Sir Valentine Chirol's *India*. Jawaharlal Nehru's *Autobiography* offers some personal background.

The official British explanation of Gandhi's popularity is from *East India (Progress and Conditions) Statement Exhibiting the Moral and Material Progress and Condition of India During the Year 1919* (London: His Majesty's Stationery Office, 1920), Cmd 950. It contains other interesting facts.

The authorities in London took official cognizance of Gandhi's jail sentence and disbarred him on 10 November, 1922.

CHAPTER 10

Gandhi's letter to his brother Laxmidas appears in the original Gujarati and translation in the big *Gandhiji* volume, published on his birthday.

Manilal Gandhi's statement of his relations with his father are printed in the 'Mahatma Gandhi Memorial Number' of *Indian Opinion*. He made oral statements on the same general subject to me. A number of Gandhi's closest collaborators have also talked and written to me about Gandhi as father and husband. The interpretations, however, are my own.

Horace Alexander's evidence, which supplements conversations I had with him in New Delhi in the summer of 1948, was given in a talk to the staff and students of Shantiniketan school on the eve of the immersion of Gandhi's ashes, 11 February, 1948. It was then published in the *Visva-Bharati Quarterly* (Calcutta: February–April 1948).

The tale of the pencil stump is told by Miss Slade in *Incidents of Gandhiji's Life*; the same volume is the source of Malavankar's story about the telegram which was mailed.

Mrdulla Sarabhai, Socialist daughter of the big Ahmedabad textile millionaire, told me of her attitude to the Mahatma. When I first met her at the Gandhi ashram in Sevagram in 1942, I christened her 'The Boss'. 'The Boss' is independent, modern and though she avers she is no 'Gandhian', she loved him deeply. She had done more Gandhian work than many of his loud followers.

Kasturbai's letter to her son Harilal is printed in full, in English and Gujarati, in the 'Kasturbai Gandhi Memorial Number' of *Indian Opinion* (Phoenix, Natal: 22 March, 1944). The English text is also printed in *Sati Kasturba, a Life-Sketch with Tributes in Memoriam*, edited by R. K. Prabhu.

CHAPTER 11

The story of the appendicectomy is told in *Young India* and the *Gandhiji* volume. The photograph is reproduced in *Speeches and Writings of Mahatma Gandhi*. The nurse who held the flashlight gave details of the operation to Dr Sushila Nayyar, who subsequently became Gandhi's doctor; Dr Nayyar wrote them to me. Mr Sastri tells of his visit to Gandhi on the evening of the operation in a chapter entitled 'At the Sassoon Hospital' in *Gandhiji As We Know Him* by Seventeen Contributors, edited by Chandrashanker Shulka (Bombay: Vora & Co, 1945).

The facts about Manu Gandhi's operation and the story of the penicillin were told me by Dr Bhargava. He also gave me two little snapshots of the operation.

Jawaharlal Nehru's autobiography, and Subhas Chandra Bose's less personal autobiography, *Indian Struggle, 1920–34*, as well as *Young India* and *To the Gates of Liberty*, throw light on the political situation that greeted Gandhi when he came out of prison.

Gandhi's letter to Charles Freer Andrews quoted in this chapter is one of fifty-two Gandhi letters to Andrews, copies of which were given to me by Pandit Benarsi Das Chaturvedi, a resident in the Mahatma's ashram. Excerpts from these letters will be used in other chapters. Andrews was closer to Gandhi than any other foreigner and than most Indians. Gandhi called him 'Charlie' and he called the Mahatma 'Mohan'. I therefore refer to the letters as the 'Charlie–Mohan Letters'. As far as I know, nobody else addressed Gandhi so familiarly.

Young India is practically a diary of the fast. Thanks for this achievement are due to Charles Freer Andrews and to Mahadev Desai, Gandhi's chief secretary, who had an eye to journalism and details. *Young India* appeared in eight pages, eight inches wide by thirteen inches long.

Gandhi's letters to Miss Slade in this and other chapters are quoted from *Bapu's Letters to Mira, 1924–48* (Ahmedabad: Navajivan Publishing House, 1949).

The first and last verses of Gandhi's favourite Christian hymn read:

> When I survey the wondrous Cross
> On which the Prince of Glory Died,
> My richest gain I count but loss
> And pour contempt on all my pride.
>
> Were the whole realm of nature mine
> That were an offering far too small.
> Love so amazing, so divine,
> Demands my life, my soul, my all.

CHAPTER 12

All quotations are from *Young India* magazine. Gandhi's statements on hand-spinning and hand-weaving from 1916 to 1940 are collected in a fat volume entitled *Economics of Khadi* by M. K. Gandhi (Ahmedabad: Navajivan Press, 1941). The book shows the development as well as the obstinacy of Gandhi's ideas on the subject.

For the attitude of the Swaraj party and other semi-co-operating and quarter-co-operating Indian organizations, reference was made to *The Indian Struggle, 1920–34*, by Subhas C. Bose.

CHAPTER 13

Sources: *Young India* and the 'Charlie–Mohan' letters . . . The minimum marriage age for girls in the ashram was stated by Gandhi in a letter to his granddaughter printed in *Harijan* of 19 June, 1949 . . . Romain Rolland's *Mahatma Gandhi* was published in 1924 (London: George Allen & Unwin Ltd).

CHAPTER 14

I discussed Gandhi's health and physiology with Dr B. C. Roy of Calcutta, Dr Manchershah Gilder of Bombay, Dr Dinshah Mehta, the head of the Nature-Cure Clinic in Poona and Dr Sushila Nayyar, who lived in Gandhi's ashram for many years.

The source materials on Gandhi's tours and meetings derives, in the main, from *Young India*. Descriptions of several meetings are to be found in *India and the Simon Report*, by C. F. Andrews (London: George Allen & Unwin Ltd, 1930).

Viscount Halifax, a Biography by Alan Campbell Johnson (London: Robert Hale Ltd, 1941) is invaluable for data on Lord Irwin's activities as Viceroy in India. While the biography is not official, the author did obtain aid and documents from his subject.

The official report of the Simon commission was published as *Report of the Indian Statutory Commission, volume I – Survey*. Presented by the Secretary of State for the Home Department to Parliament by Command of His Majesty, May 1930 (London: His Majesty's Stationery Office, 1930) Cmd 3568; and *Report of the Indian Statutory Commission, volume II – Recommendations*. Presented by the Secretary of State for the Home Department to Parliament by Command of His Majesty, May 1930 (London: His Majesty's Stationery Office, 1930), Cmd 3569.

CHAPTER 15

Vallabhbhai Patel's first impressions of Gandhi are recorded as he remembered them during an interview he gave me in New Delhi on 14 August, 1948, when an was Deputy Prime Minister of India.

Young India, a classic model of personal journalism, remains the chief source of material. Supplementary information comes from the biography of Halifax who was Irwin, the *Gandhiji* volume, the official Congress history: *To the Gates of Liberty*, Subhas Chandra Bose's memoirs, and Jawaharlal Nehru's autobiography.

The story of Bardoli is amply documented and admirably told in a 323-page book, with numerous appendices, entitled *The Story of Bardoli, Being a History of the Bardoli Satyagraha of 1928 and its Sequel*, by Mahadev Desai (Ahmedabad: Navajivan Press, 1919).

CHAPTER 16

The text of Gandhi's letter to Irwin announcing the Salt March was published in *Young India* for 12 March, 1930. The same issue contains the brief acknowledgement sent by the Viceroy's private secretary, G. Cunningham. Gandhi's hesitations and contemplations before arriving at the decision to march can be followed in *Young India* which also publishes the report of Tagore's visit to the ashram in January 1930.

The wise comments of Brailsford on events in 1930 are found in *Mahatma Gandhi* by H. S. L. Polak, H. N. Brailsford, Lord Pethick-Lawrence, with a Foreword and Appreciation by Her Excellency Sarojini Naidu, Governor of the United Provinces (London: Odhams Press Ltd, 1949).

The detailed account of the Salt March is pieced together from numerous small items in various issues of *Young India*. The staff Gandhi used on the march still stands in a corner of his room in Sabarmati Ashram where I measured it in 1948.

The aftermath of the Salt March is described from facts published in *Young India* and Bose's *The Indian Struggle, 1920-34*, as well as by Brailsford. Irwin's biographer is strangely silent on the historic march, but his testimony on the Viceroy's 'ruthlessness' in suppressing the unarmed insurrection is interesting.

The account of Gandhi's arrest is based on reports in *Young India*. A painting of the event by V. Masoji is reproduced in rich colour in the big *Gandhiji* birthday memorial volume. When Gandhi viewed the painting in an art gallery he was asked whether it represented the actual occurrence and he said, 'Yes, yes, exactly, exactly. They came like that.'

Webb Miller's eye-witness account is quoted from Chapter 16 of his book, *I Found No Peace, the Journal of a Foreign Correspondent* (London: Victor Gollancz Ltd, 1937).

Tagore's poetic interpretations of the psychological changes wrought by the Salt March and the events that flowed from it are published as appendices in *India and the Simon Report*, by C. F. Andrews (London: George Allen & Unwin Ltd.).

Gandhi's height and identification marks were printed in *Harijan*, of 26 June, 1949, after Kishorlal G. Mashruwala, Gandhi's successor as editor of that magazine, had obtained them at my request from the Bombay government's jail records. Mashruwala, of whom Gandhi said, 'He is one of the most thoughtful among the silent workers we have in India', and whom I met at Gandhi's ashram in 1942, has given me more assistance in the preparation of this book than any other Indian. Whenever I stopped for want of a fact, document, letter or book, whenever I did not understand an utterance or act of Gandhi's, I had merely to send an airmail letter to

Kishorlal Mashruwala at Wardha or Bombay, and back, by return airmail usually, would come a detailed, carefully considered reply. I had several dozen long letters from him about Gandhi; they were extremely helpful.

CHAPTER 17

The preliminaries of the Irwin–Gandhi talks were pieced together from items in Nehru's autobiography; *Gandhi Versus the Empire*, by Haridas T. Muzumdar, with a Foreword by Will Durant (New York: Universal Publishing Co, 1932); *Young India*; and Bose's *The Indian Struggle, 1920–34*.

The account of the talks themselves is based on the biography of Irwin: on *Young India: Naked Faquir* by Robert Bernays (London: Victor Gollancz Ltd, 1931); and H. N. Brailsford's section on the 'Middle Years (1915–1939)' in *Mahatma Gandhi* by H. S. L. Polak, H. B. Brailsford and Lord Pethick-Lawrence.

The full text of the Irwin–Gandhi Pact is published in *Speeches and Writings of Mahatma Gandhi*. Excerpts from it are contained in *Gandhi Versus the Empire*, and in an appendix of *The Nation's Voice*, a collection of Gandhi's speeches in England and Mahadev Desai's account of the sojourn (September to December 1931), edited by C. Rajagopalachari and J. C. Kumarappa (Ahmedabad: Navajivan Publishing House, 1932). Comments on the Pact are given by Irwin's biographer, Bose, Nehru, Brailsford and others.

Gandhi's activities in England are described in great detail in the above-mentioned *The Nation's Voice*, and amusingly in *The Tragedy of Gandhi* by Glorney Bolton (London: George Allen & Unwin Ltd, 1934). Some facts are added by Brailsford, and in the contributions of Horace G. Alexander, Muriel Lester, his hostess at Kingsley Hall, and Agatha Harrison to *Gandhi As We Know Him*. Among other things, Miss Harrison tells the tale of Gandhi's two Scotland Yard detectives.

Gandhi's CBS broadcast from London to America is recorded in Columbia Masterworks: 17523-D; WA 12082. The full text of the broadcast is published in *Gandhi Versus the Empire*.

The full text of Gandhi's address to the London Vegetarian Society on 20 November, 1931, is printed in *Harijan* (20 February, 1949). Dr Henry Salt, whom he had met while a law student at the Inner Temple, sat by his side. Gandhi limited his remarks to vegetarianism, arguing for its moral, not physical, justification.

The account of Gandhi's visit to Oxford, and especially the report on his discussion with the Oxford professors, is patchwork. The patches are from 'The Nation's Voice', a contribution by Edward Thompson in *Mahatma Gandhi, Essays and Reflections on his Life and Work*, and Lord Lindsay's 'Mr Gandhi at Oxford', in *Incidents in Gandhiji's Life*.

The official publication on the Round Table Conference is *Indian Round Table Conference, Second Session. 7th September, 1931–1st December, 1931, Proceedings* (London: His Majesty's Stationery Office, 1932), Cmd 3997. This is supplemented by *The Nation's Voice*, and *Speeches and Writings of Mahatma Gandhi*.

Some additional quotations on this period can be found in *A Searchlight on Gandhi*, by the [anonymous] Author of 'India on the Brink' (London: P. S. King & Son Ltd, 1931).

CHAPTER 18

Rolland's report of his talks with Gandhi were published years later in the Paris weekly *Figaro Littéraire*. My account has followed this report as well as a letter which Rolland wrote at the time to Lucien Price of the Boston *Globe*, who had it printed in the New York *Nation* of 10 February, 1932.

At first I merely recorded the cold fact that Rolland had played the Andante of Beethoven's Fifth and Gluck's *Les Champs Elysées*. But then it occurred to me that his choice must have had some significance. I consulted Nicolas Nabokov, a composer, and Richard Korn, a conductor. I have paraphrased their interpretations.

Rolland's book on Gandhi is entitled, significantly, *Mahatma Gandhi: the Man Who Became One with the Universal Being*. Gandhi never claimed that he had achieved Nirvana or perfect *Gita*-detachment . . .

Edmond Privat tells how he and his wife decided on the spur of the moment to go to India in 'With Gandhiji on Deck', a chapter in *Incidents in Gandhiji's Life* . . . In the same volume, Madeleine Rolland, the novelist's sister, recalls Gandhi's visit to Villeneuve.

The report of Gandhi's interview with Mussolini is based on a letter sent me by Kishoral G. Mashruwala . . . Gandhi's own account was given to a friend on 22 August, 1934, but not published until 24 October, 1948, in *Harijan*. Mussolini was killed on 28 April,

1945. The big *Gandhiji* volume records Gandhi's sentiments on art and the Sistine Chapel. A more ample statement of his views appears in *Young India* (5 November, 1924). I have quoted from it in this chapter.

The Tragedy of Gandhi by Glorney Bolton, tells the story of Gandhi's figs from a Queen.

My wife, Markoosha, did some research for me in Italy on Gandhi's Roman sojourn.

CHAPTER 19

Gandhi's two speeches in Bombay on 28 December, 1931, are published verbatim in *Speeches and Writings of Mahatma Gandhi*. The same volume contains the full text of the Gandhi-Willingdon correspondence quoted in the early part of this chapter as well as of the correspondence between Gandhi and Sir Samuel Hoare and Ramsay MacDonald about the separate electorate for untouchables.

The fullest account of the Government's actions against the nationalist movement in the last weeks of December 1931 and the first part of 1932 is to be found in *Condition of India, Being a Report of the Delegation sent to India by the India League, in 1932* (London: Essential News, 1933). This book, with a preface by Bertrand Russell, represents the findings of the India League of Great Britain's commission consisting of Monica Whately, Ellen Wilkinson, Leonard W. Matters and V. K. Krishna Menon. It gives the text of the Emergency Ordinances, their defence by British officials and their results in terms of police acts and arrests. The report also quotes excerpts from the Gandhi-Willingdon correspondence. Nehru's autobiography, Bose's memoirs, and Brailsford in *Mahatma Gandhi* likewise comment on that chapter of British rule.

K. Kalelkar, a disciple of Gandhi, tells the stories related in this chapter about Gandhi's relations with the prison authorities. Mahadev Desai's notes on the Gandhi-Patel-Desai conversations in jail are published in the first volume of his diary.

From Yeravda Mandir. Ashram Observances, by M. K. Gandhi, Translated from the Original Gujarati by Valji Govindji Desai (Ahmedabad: Navajivan Publishing House, 1945) - a reprint of the 1933 edition - is sixty-seven pages long; the pages measure four by six inches. The views expressed in it by Gandhi on God and morals are amplified in this chapter by Gandhi's writings in *Young India; The*

Mind of Mahatma Gandhi, compiled by R. K. Prabhu and U. R. Rao, with a Foreword by Sir Sarvepalli Radhakrishnan (London: Oxford University Press, March 1945); and *Selections from Gandhi*, by Nirmal Kumar Bose, Dr Jones is quoted from *Mahatma Gandhi, an Interpretation*, by E. Stanley Jones (New York: Abingdon-Cokesbury Press, 1948).

The complete, fully documented and detailed story of Gandhi's fast for the Harijans is told in *The Epic Fast* by Pyarelal (Nayyar) (Ahmedabad: Navajivan Publishing House, 1932). It has an introduction by Rajagopalachari, and contains the full text of the Gandhi-Hoare-MacDonald correspondence, of the Yeravda Pact, of many of the resolutions adopted in connection with the fast, and of the speeches by Tagore, Gandhi and the negotiators as well as the statements of Gandhi's physicians on his condition. It also lists the names of the temples opened to Harijans.

In his book, *What Congress and Gandhi Have Done to the Untouchables* (Bombay: Thacker & Co, 1945), B. R. Ambedkar prints the correspondence between Gandhi and MacDonald and Hoare, the text of the Poona Pact, and adds one page of his own comments.

Lord Willingdon in India by 'Victor Trench' (Bombay: Karnatak House, 1934) is a sympathetic account of the Viceroy which supplies some data on Gandhi's work during Willingdon's Viceroyalty.

R. N. Tagore, the great poet's son, who lives at Shantiniketan, has most graciously put at my disposal a thick file containing copies of all Gandhi's letters to Tagore and all Tagore's letters and telegrams to Gandhi. They are quoted in this and other chapters.

CHAPTER 20

This chapter and several earlier ones as well as chapters 46, 47 and 48, were read with care and a critical eye by Dr Sushila Nayyar, Gandhi's house physician during the period covered and until his death. She of course is not responsible for my views or facts. But her corrections and opinions are invaluable.

From 1933 to the end of Gandhi's life, *Harijan* magazine is the best source for statements by Gandhi. Many of these statements are conveniently collected in anthologies which include his sayings on a wide variety of subjects. I have used *Selections from Gandhi* by Nirmal Kumar Bose; *India of My Dreams* by M. K. Gandhi, compiled by R. K. Prabhu, with a Foreword by Dr Rajendra Prasad (Bombay: Hind

Kitabs Ltd., 1947); *Teachings of Mahatma Gandhi*, edited by Jag Parvesh Chander, with a Foreword by Babu Rajendra Prasad (Lahore: The Indian Printing Works, 1947); and *The Mind of Mahatma Gandhi*, compiled by R. K. Prabhu and U. R. Rao (London: Humphrey Milford, 1946).

In addition, there are Gandhi anthologies devoted to separate questions. One of these, *Christian Missions, Their Place in India*, by M. K. Gandhi (Ahmedabad: Navajivan Press, 1941), helped me in the preparation of this chapter. Gandhi's relationship to Christianity and Jesus is further elucidated in *Gandhi's Challenge to Christianity* by S. K. George, with Forewords by Professor S. Radhakrishnan and Mr Horace Alexander (London: George Allen & Unwin Ltd, 1939); *Mahatma Gandhi, his Life, Work and Influence*, by Jashwant Rao Chitambar (an Indian who was a Christian bishop), Foreword by John R. Mott; and *Mahatma Gandhi, an Interpretation*, by E. Stanley Jones (New York: Abingdon-Cokesbury Press, 1948).

Key to Health by M. K. Gandhi, Translated by Sushila Nayyar (Ahmedabad: Navajivan Publishing House, 1948), is one of the few books which Gandhi wrote; it is not an anthology. (The other books written by Gandhi are his autobiography, *Satyagraha in South Africa* and *Hind Swaraj.*) *Key to Health* summarizes Gandhi's knowledge on the nature of the human body, on food and drink, on continence and on air, water and sun cures. He wrote the little book in prison, in 1942. He says in a Preface: 'Anyone who observes the rules of health mentioned in this book will find that he has got in it a real key to unlock the gates leading him to health. He will not need to knock at the doors of doctors and vaidyas from day to day.'

Gandhi's view on economics, education, women's welfare, etc., are set forth in a 31-page pamphlet, *Constructive Programme, its Meaning and Place*, by M. K. Gandhi (Ahmedabad: Navajivan Publishing House, 1941) . . . An attempt to co-ordinate Gandhi's ideas into a rounded scheme has been undertaken in *Gandhian Constitution for Free India* by Shriman Narayan Agarwal, Foreword by Mahatma Gandhi (Kitabistan, Allahabad, 1946); *The Gandhian Plan of Economic Development of India* by Shriman Narayan Agarwal, Foreword by Mahatma Gandhi (Bombay: Padma Publications Ltd, 1944); and *Gandhian Plan Reaffirmed* by S. N. Agarwal, Foreword by Dr Rajendra Prasad (Bombay: Padma Publications Ltd, 1948). In his foreword to Agarwal's *Gandhian Constitution*, Gandhi warns the reader against the mistake of accepting the volume as 'being my view in every detail'. Though he 'endeavoured to read the Constitution twice, with as much attention as I was able to bestow on it during my

other engagements, I could not undertake to check every thought
and word of it. Nor would my sense of propriety and individual
freedom permit me to commit any such atrocity ... There is
nothing in it which has jarred on me as inconsistent with what I
would like to stand for.' How gentle the caveat! Gandhi's foreword
to *The Gandhian Plan* is equally affectionate and cautionary.

Minoo Masani gave me a photostat copy of Gandhi's letter to him
on Socialism. Masani's own analysis of Gandhi as a Socialist
constitutes a chapter in the big *Gandhiji* seventy-fifth anniversary
memorial volume. I have discussed the question with him, with
Jaiprakash Narayan and others.

Devadas Gandhi told me the story of his marriage.

Atulananda Chakrabarti gave me the original letters which
Gandhi wrote him. One day when I was in India in the summer of
1948 collecting material for this book, he simply stepped into my
hotel room and presented them to me and at the same time told the
story of his contacts with the Mahatma ... Amiya Chakravarty,
who taught at Howard University, Washington, DC, supplied me
with copies of several letters he had from Gandhi; he also wrote out
an account of Gandhi's kindness to him in Calcutta ... The general
information about Gandhi's correspondence was furnished by
Rajkumari Amrit Kaur, a Christian princess, for many years his
English secretary ... Except on very rare occasions, no copies were
ever made of the many letters which Gandhi wrote by hand. Some
are lost. Vallabhbhai Patel informs me that he received numerous
letters from the Mahatma but destroyed them after adequate study.
However, thousands of Gandhi's letters exist and a number of his
friends were generous enough to give me the originals or copies.

When Gandhi's autobiography was published in the United
States, in 1948, the late George Orwell reviewed it in *Partisan Review*.
I tore it out at the time and filed it. Orwell, author of the brilliant
Animal Farm, 1984, and other books, was born in India and was an
Anglo-Indian. His review, entitled, 'Reflections on Gandhi', is
perceptive, sensitive, rich in background and friendly to the subject.
He makes one comment that bears on the treatment in this chapter.
Discussing Gandhi as a non-attached saint, he says, 'But it is not
necessary here to argue whether the other-worldly or the humanistic
ideal is "higher". The point is that they are incompatible. One must
choose between God and Man, and all "radicals" and
"progressives", from the mildest Liberal to the most extreme
Anarchist, have in effect chosen Man.' I can see how the
autobiography, a very imperfect reflection of its author, might lead

one to imagine that Gandhi has chosen God. But I think Gandhi's greatness lay in his ability to choose both God and Man. His otherworldliness did not preclude worldliness; on the contrary, it compelled worldliness. Gandhi enlisted God in the service of Man.

Additional bibliography: *Economic Policy and Programme for Post-War India* by Nalini R. Sarker (Patna: Patna University, 1945); *The Story of India* by F. R. Moraes, an able Indian journalist, calls Gandhi 'A Great Humanist'.

Gandhi's statement on social revolution is quoted from *Harijan* (14 August, 1949).

The Reverend K. Mathew Simon is quoted from a letter he wrote me.

CHAPTER 21

All the Gandhi quotations are from *Harijan*. Gandhi's pronouncements on war, peace and non-violence between 1920 and 1940 are collected in *Non-Violence in Peace and War* by M. K. Gandhi (Ahmedabad: Navajivan Publishing House, 1942). The book contains 551 pages and is supplied with an introduction by Mahadev Desai.

The facts about the Congress are gleaned from the *Indian National Congress General Secretary's Reports* for (1) 1936-37; (2) January 1937-February 1938; (3) March 1938-February 1939 - all published by the Congress office at Allahabad.

India and Democracy by Sir George Schuster and Guy Wint (London: Macmillan & Co Ltd, 1941), presents a view of the Act of 1935 under which India was governed until independence was granted in 1947.

General Bradley is quoted from a press release of the National Military Establishment, Department of the Army, Washington, DC.

CHAPTER 22

Gandhi's writings of this period were published in *Harijan*. Some are collected in *Non-Violence in Peace and War* by M. K. Gandhi. Additional data on his differences with Congress are found in *Report of the General Secretary of the Indian National Congress. March, 1939 to February, 1940* (Allahabad), and *Indian National Congress, Report of the*

General Secretaries, March, 1940–October, 1946 (Allahabad) . . . Nehru's autobiography sheds further light on the Gandhi–Congress relationship.

Cripps, Advocate and Rebel, by Patricia Strauss (London: Victor Gollancz Ltd, 1943), and *Stafford Cripps, a Biography*, by Eric Estorick (London: William Heinemann Ltd, 1949) contain material on the Cripps Mission to India in 1942 . . . Another view of the Cripps Mission is given by Lord Pethick-Lawrence in his third of *Mahatma Gandhi*, by H. S. L. Polak, H. N. Brailsford and Lord Pethick-Lawrence.

When I returned to New York after my stay in India in 1942, I presented my version of the Cripps Mission in two articles entitled 'Why Cripps Failed', published in the New York *Nation* magazine of 19 September and 26 September, 1942. There followed 'A British Reply to Louis Fischer' in the *Nation* on 14 November, 1942, by Graham Spry, an official associate of Cripps in India. For a while I was tempted to include in this chapter a detailed story of the Cripps mission as told by available British and Congress documents and explained to me by Nehru, Azad, Rajagopalachari, Patel, the Viceroy, Wavell, Louis Johnson and others. But I refrained. The only part that is germane here is Gandhi's role. Nehru's comments on it are quoted from *The Discovery of India* by Jawaharlal Nehru (London: Meridian Books, 1946), and *Blood and Tears* by J. M. Deb (Bombay: Hind Kitabs, 1945). In a letter written to me from Delhi on 20 August, 1948, in response to a question, Pyarelal Nayyar, Gandhi's daily companion and close co-worker during the Cripps talks, states that the Mahatma attached little importance to the Cripps Draft Declaration 'and afterwards forgot all about it'.

Ambassador Winant, a lovable man, a sincere friend of freedom, told me of his conversations with Churchill on India.

The correspondence between Roosevelt and Chiang Kai-shek on India is printed in *The Great Challenge* by Louis Fischer.

References to Harry Hopkins are from *The White House Papers of Harry L. Hopkins* by Robert E. Sherwood (London: Eyre & Spottiswoode Ltd, 1948–49. Two volumes).

CHAPTER 23

The conversations recorded in this chapter were typed out almost immediately after they took place.

The statistical data are from the 1931 British census report on India, edited by J. H. Hutton, and from earlier and subsequent census reports.

Gandhi's description of his argument with Nehru was given in a letter to the Viceroy dated 14 August, 1942, and published in *Gandhi's Correspondence with the Government, 1942-44* (Ahmedabad: Navajivan Publishing House, 1945).

The full text of Mahatma Gandhi's letter to President Franklin D. Roosevelt follows:

> *Sevagram Via Wardha (India)*
> *July* 1, 1942

Dear Friend, I twice missed coming to your great country. I have the privilege of having numerous friends there both known and unknown to me. Many of my countrymen have received and are still receiving higher education in America. I know too that several have taken shelter there. I have profited greatly by the writings of Thoreau and Emerson. I say this to tell you how much I am connected with your country. Of Great Britain I need say nothing beyond mentioning that in spite of my intense dislike of British rule, I have numerous friends in England whom I love as dearly as my own people. I had my legal education there. I have therefore nothing but good wishes for your country and Great Britain. You will therefore accept my word that my present proposal, that the British should unreservedly and without reference to the wishes of the people of India immediately withdraw their rule, is prompted by the friendliest intention. I would like to turn into good will the ill will which, whatever may be said to the contrary, exists in India towards Great Britain and thus enable the millions of India to play their part in the present war.

My personal position is clear. I hate all war. If, therefore, I could persuade my countrymen, they would make a most effective and decisive contribution in favour of an honourable peace. But I know that all of us have not a living faith in non-violence. Under foreign rule, however, we can make no effective contribution of any kind in this war, except as helots.

The policy of the Indian National Congress, largely guided by me, has been one of non-embarrassment to Britain, consistently with the honourable working of the Congress, admittedly the largest political organization of the longest standing in India. The British policy as exposed by the Cripps mission and rejected by almost all parties has opened our eyes and has driven me to the proposal I have made. I hold that the full acceptance of my proposal and that only can put the Allied cause on an unassailable basis. I venture to think that the Allied declaration that the Allies are fighting to make the world safe for the freedom of the individual and for democracy sounds hollow, so long as India and for that matter Africa are exploited by Great Britain, and America has the Negro problem in her own home. But in order to avoid all complications, in my proposal I have confined myself only to India. If India becomes free the rest must follow,'if it does not happen simultaneously.

In order to make my proposal fool-proof I have suggested that if the Allies think it necessary they may keep their troops, at their own expense, in India, not for keeping internal order but for preventing Japanese aggression and defending China. So far as India is concerned, she must become free even as America and Great Britain are. The Allied troops will remain in India during the war under treaty with the free India govt. that may be formed by the people of India without any outside interference, direct, or indirect.

It is on behalf of this proposal that I write this to enlist your active sympathy.

I hope that it would commend itself to you.

Mr Louis Fischer is carrying this letter to you.

If there is any obscurity in my letter, you will have but to send me word and I shall try to clear it.

I hope finally that you will not resent this letter as an intrusion but take it as an approach from a friend and well wisher of the Allies. I remain yours sincerely   M. K. Gandhi

CHAPTER 24

The Working Committee's Resolution of 14 July, 1942, the AICC resolution of 8 August, 1942, the Gandhi–Linlithgow letters, the Gandhi–Wavell letters, and all other communications between Gandhi and the Government during this period are conveniently collected in *Gandhiji's Correspondence with the Government, 1942-44*. The same book contains excerpts from Gandhi's interviews with A. T. Steele and other foreign writers as well as quotations from his articles in *Harijan* on the subject of the war and the civil disobedience movement. The same material was printed by the British in *Correspondence with Mr Gandhi, August 1942-April 1944* (Published with Authority), Published by the Manager (New Delhi: Government of India Press, 1944). A selection of Gandhi declarations is also found in *What Does Gandhi Want?* by T. A. Raman (London: Oxford University Press, 1942).

The Viceroy's statement to me about the Gandhi interview was noted at the time in my diary.

Dr B. C. Roy and Dr Shushila Nayyar have told me about Gandhi's fast. Additional facts about the fast and about Kasturbai's illness and death and Gandhi's reaction to it are contained in *Kasturba, Wife of Gandhi*, by Sushila Nayyar. Dr Nayyar has also given me further details by letter.

Lord Pethick-Lawrence's third of *Mahatma Gandhi*, by H. S. L. Polak, H. N. Brailsford and Lord Pethick-Lawrence, reports the Famine Enquiry Commission's finding that 'no less than 1,500,000 people lost their lives either directly from starvation or from consequent disease' in the 1943 Bengal famine.

CHAPTER 25

I am indebted to Major C. B. Ormerod, chief of the British Information Services of New York, for facilitating my access to the files and bookshelves of the British Information Services Library in Rockefeller Centre in New York where, with the gracious and efficient aid of Miss M. Eleanor Herrington, the Librarian, and her assistants, I obtained most of the material used in this chapter. The Gandhi-Jinnah correspondence was in the form of bulletins issued at the time by the Government of India Information Services, Washington, DC. There was also a 'Note on the Gandhi-Jinnah Conversations', drafted by the British Embassy in Washington on 20 October, 1944, 'For the Information of British Officials', as well as the texts of Gandhi and Jinnah press interviews and clippings from Indian, British and American newspapers, and an article by Sir Frederick Puckle, entitled 'The Gandhi-Jinnah Conversations', in *Foreign Affairs* quarterly (January 1945).

Biographical data on Jinnah and comments on his personality were found in a number of magazine and newspaper articles and in *Tumult in Asia* by George E. Jones (New York: Dodd, Mead & Co, 1948).

The quotation from Herbert L. Matthews appears in *The*

Education of a Correspondent by Herbert L. Matthews (New York: Harcourt, Brace & Co, 1946).

The first forty-one chapters of this books were read critically in manuscript by Muriel Lester, Gandhi's hostess in London in 1931.

PART THREE

CHAPTER 1

My interview with Willkie was published in *Common Sense* (December 1944).

The contents of this chapter are based, in the main, on the texts of official announcements and on newspaper clippings made available to me by the British Information Services Library in New York.

The Congress view is given in *Indian Nation Congress, Report of the General Secretaries. March, 1940–October, 1946* (Allahabad).

CHAPTER 2

Harijan, the invaluable files of the British Information Services Library in New York and Pethick-Lawrence's chapters in *Mahatma Gandhi* by H. S. L. Polak, H. N. Brailsford and Lord Pethick-Lawrence, were indispensable to the preparation of this chapter. So was *The British Cabinet Mission in India, a Documentary Record (March–June, 1946)* (Delhi: Rajkamal Publications, 1946), which contains all the British, Congress and Moslem League statements of this crucial period. The full text of the Cabinet Mission's proposal of 16 May, 1946, is published in an appendix to Robert Aura Smith's interesting book, *Divided India*.

CHAPTER 3

This chapter is based on copious notes made after each interview. In Panchgani, however, my diary entries were inadequate and I therefore availed myself of the notes made by Pyarelal and Sushila Nayyar during the talks. I also availed myself of letters I had written from India to my wife and two sons and to friends. I re-read *Nehru on Gandhi, a Selection, Arranged in the Order of Events, from the Writings and Speeches of Jawaharlal Nehru* (New York: The John Day Co, 1948). I had lengthy talks about the Mahatma with Rajkumari Amrit Kaur, Prabhavati Narayan and other female, and male, disciples.

Mr Jinnah died in September 1948.

CHAPTER 4

The chief source of information on Gandhi's walking tour through Noakhali is *Harijan*, which printed his own daily reports with maps. Supplementary published material is found in *The Pilgrim of Noakhali, a Souvenir Album of Gandhiji's Peace Mission to Noakhali*, published by Photographer, Braja Kishore Sinha, with his own text (Calcutta, 1948). I also had long talks about the pilgrimage with two of its participants. Mrs Sucheta Kripalani and Dr Sushila Nayyar. Phillips Talbot's confidential report, posted to the Institute of Current Affairs in New York from New Delhi on 16 February, 1947, was invaluable for its sober appraisal of an outsider with a judicious mind.

The Pethick-Lawrence quotation is from *Mahatma Gandhi* by Polak, Brailsford and Pethick-Lawrence.

CHAPTER 5

Gandhi's travels in Bihar and his activities in New Delhi (including the text of his statements to the Asian Relations Conference) are covered in detail in the pages of *Harijan*. Official announcements and political news were found in the files of the British Information Services Library in New York. Lord Pethick-Lawrence's chapters in *Mahatma Gandhi* served as a general guide. Lord Mountbatten's speech is quoted from *United Empire*, Journal of the Royal Empire Society (London, November–December 1948). I also made good use of the 1 January, 1947, 8 February, 1947 and 26 March, 1947, issues of *Congress Bulletin*, issued by the Office of the All-India Congress Committee (Allahabad).

CHAPTER 6

Most of this chapter is based on *Harijan* and on extracts from Indian and foreign newspapers of the period as well as official announce-

ments by the British and Indian governments . . . Kurshed Naoroji
and Rajkumari Amrit Kaur were good enough to give me the Gandhi
letters from which I have quoted. Kurshed gave me the originals . . .
The story of St Francis is in the words of Dorothy Van Doren in the *New
York Herald Tribune* of 12 December, 1948 . . . Professor Kripalani's
speech and the facts about the Congress session at which he spoke are
taken from *Congress Bulletin*, 10 July, 1947 . . . The first forty-six
chapters were carefully read in manuscript by Harry Sigmund, my
brother-in-law, at whose house in Philadelphia I wrote part of the book.

CHAPTER 7

The story of the Bombay riot is from *The Bombay Government and its
Work: Official Report* (Congress in Office) (Bombay, 1938).

The account of Gandhi's activities in Calcutta and New Delhi
follows newspaper reports and *Harijan*. His speeches are recorded in
Harijan. I also used a book called *Delhi Diary (Prayer Speeches from
September 10, 1947, to January 30, 1948)*, by M. K. Gandhi
(Ahmedabad: Navajivan Publishing House, 1948).

Dr Zakir Hussain and others told me about the events in and
around the Okla school.

The facts about Gandhi's health were given me by Dr Sushila
Nayyar.

There are many descriptions of the Great Migration. But better than
any of these are the excellent photographs in *Halfway to Freedom, a Report
on the New India in the Words and Photographs of Margaret Bourke-White*.

CHAPTER 8

Professor Kripalani told me the reasons for his resignation when I
visited him in his New Delhi home in August, 1948. His speech of
resignation is printed in *Congress Bulletin*, 31 December, 1947.

Dr Rajendra Prasad gave me the details of his nomination and
election, and the exact words he and Gandhi used, in an interview at
his house in New Delhi on 4 September, 1948. His faithful description of the episode was confirmed from several other reliable sources.

The account of the Constructive Workers' Conference is based on
an eleven-page memorandum furnished me by Pyarelal, Gandhi's
secretary, who was present and took copious notes.

CHAPTER 9

Richard Symonds and Horace Alexander are authority for the experiences of the former with Gandhi. Mr Alexander told me of his talks with Gandhi on Kashmir.

Gandhi's speeches are recorded in *Harijan* and *Delhi Diary*. The fast was reported in Indian and foreign newspapers.

In addition to commenting in *Harijan* on Dr Holmes's letter to him, Gandhi replied to Dr Holmes in a personal letter dated 3 January, 1948.

Dr Sushila Nayyar gave me a day-to-day account of Gandhi's health during the fast. Several persons who saw Gandhi during the fast told me how he looked and felt.

Arthur Moore's statement is quoted from an Indian magazine called *Thought* in which he recounts his discussions with the Mahatma.

Nehru told me of his sympathy fast and of Gandhi's note.

CHAPTER 10

Gandhi is quoted from *Harijan* magazine and *Delhi Diary*.

The *New York Times* of 21 January, 1948, published an account of Madan Lal's attempt to kill Gandhi. The same newspaper of 8 November, 1948, quotes Godse's statement at his trial.

The trial of Nathuram Godse for the murder of Gandhi, Narain Apte for abetment of murder, and of seven others for participation in the conspiracy to murder, began on 26 May, 1948, when the indictment was given to the accused. Public hearings commenced on 22 June, 1948; the public examination of witnesses took eighty-four days to complete. The trial was concluded on 30 November, and sentence delivered on 10 February, 1949. Godse and Apte were condemned to death; notwithstanding the protests of many Gandhians in India and abroad, who felt that Gandhi would have shown mercy to those who killed him, they were hanged. Five other defendants, including Madan Lal, were sentenced to life imprisonment; V. D. Savarkar, the ideological leader of the Hindu Mahasabha, was acquitted; the ninth defendant, who turned state's witness, was discharged. The trial received full and objective coverage in the Indian press.

The facts about Gandhi's letter to Nehru were given to me by two persons who saw it.

The entire manuscript was read by Minoo Masani, Indian author, diplomat and parliamentarian.

Index